GASCOIGNE

THE LIFE OF A TUDOR POET

Ronald Binns

ZOILUS PRESS

A Zoilus Press paperback
First published in Great Britain by Zoilus Press in 2021

ISBN 9781999735944

© Ronald Binns, 2021
All rights reserved

The right of Ronald Binns to be identified as the author of this publication has been asserted by him in accordance with the Copyright, Design and Patents Act 1988

All unauthorised reproduction is hereby prohibited. This work is protected by law. It should not be duplicated or distributed, in whole or in part, by any means whatsoever, without the prior permission of the Publisher.

Typeset by Electrograd
Cover design by The Ever-Shifting Subject.
Cover photograph © Ronald Binns

ZOILUS PRESS
York, England

Contents

Preface	7

PART ONE: THE YOUNG GASCOIGNE

1: "Gascoigne"	13
2: Cardington Manor	29
3: Cambridge	43
4: "A lady once did ask…"	51
5: "Cyphered words" and Master F.J.	58

PART TWO: IN TUDOR LONDON

6: At Gray's Inn	73
7: The Lawless Law	82
8: Five Thousand Days	90
9: Under Mary	101
10: At the Court of the Virgin Queen	113

PART THREE: SCANDAL

11: "Elizabeth Brytayne"	135
12: A Great Fray in Red Cross Street	149
13: "My poore house at Waltamstow in the Forest"	165
14: Christmas Revels	180
15: "My muse is tied in chains"	209

PART FOUR: CONSPIRACY AND WAR

16: The Italian Connection	227
17: "A Spie, an Atheist and godlesse personne"	242
18: Minding Your P's and W's	256
19: Flushing Frays	264
20: Waterland	282

PART FIVE: THE RUNNING MAN

21: "offensive… and… scandalous"	305
22: The Fox and the Geese	325
23: Kenilworth	343
24: Authorship and a Hermit	365
25: *The Posies of George Gascoigne Esquire*	387

PART SIX: THE SUNDRY SHAPES OF DEATH

26: A Man with a Gun	405
27: Doomsday and Drunkards	419

28: The Spanish Fury	431
29: A Burial at Stamford	447
30: "When the Dirge is done"	470
Notes	483
Bibliography	508
List of Illustrations	523
Acknowledgements	525
Index	527

Preface

George Gascoigne once wrote a poem imagining that he would die far from home, of a broken heart.[1] Only the first part of that prediction came true. When he died on 7 October 1577, he was the leading writer of his day. But he was also a man at home with a gun and a sword, and rather more likely to be felled by a bullet or an attacker's blade than by the faithlessness of a woman. He was a friend and associate of some of the leading figures of the age but he was also a man with enemies. They called him a rogue, a spy, an atheist, a killer. Not all of their charges were false.

Only two unambiguously authoritative images of Gascoigne exist. In one he kneels before Elizabeth I, a book in one hand, a lance in the other and a sword at his side. In the second he is shown in breast armour with his books and writing materials on one side and his gun on the other. The first image, hand-drawn, invokes the values of chivalry and courtly romance. The second, a printed woodcut, promotes a writer who seeks both private patronage and a public readership. It expresses his role as a soldier-poet, serving his country and its religion with both gun and pen.

George Gascoigne was a cultured man who wrote poetry and fiction about love, passion and jealousy, but he also knew a lot about hunting, fighting and soldiering. Violence and death were everywhere in Tudor society but Gascoigne had more experience of them than most. He personally witnessed the greatest atrocity of his century, in which thousands of innocent civilians died. Afterwards he wrote a vivid and influential account of what he'd seen.

Gascoigne has rightly been described as having lived "a life that historical novels are made of".[2] He came from the backwaters of Bedfordshire but he ended up known to all the leading figures of the age – Elizabeth I, the Earl of Leicester, Lord Burghley, Sir Francis Walsingham, Walter Ralegh. His best known book, *A Hundreth Sundry Flowers*, scandalized conservative opinion and infuriated the censors. But the poet bounced back from his misfortunes to entertain the Queen at Kenilworth Castle. Once more in favour, he became an agent for Walsingham's intelligence service. Then, just as his fortunes were on the turn, he died, in obscure circumstances which have gone undiscussed for centuries.

As a writer, Gascoigne was astonishingly talented. He is remembered mainly as a poet but he was many other things as well – a translator, a dramatist, a pamphleteer, a satirist. He was involved in publishing the very first proposal to create an English colony in the New World. He wrote the first treatise on English prosody. He wrote a story which has been claimed as the first English novel – a book which any modern blurb writer would call a sizzling tale of sexual intrigue and betrayal. He wrote the first non-dramatic poem in blank verse, the first English prose comedy, one of the earliest sonnet sequences. It has been said that his achievement as a writer "really ought to be in the *Guinness Book of Records*".³

In both his life and his art Gascoigne was an instinctive rule breaker. As an innovator he was without parallel in his time. In Tudor England he was, temporarily, the fashionable writer that everyone wanted to imitate, but by the seventeenth century he was more or less forgotten, and it was another two centuries before his work began to circulate again. A two volume Victorian edition of Gascoigne's *Complete Poems* appeared in 1869-70 and *The Complete Works of George Gascoigne* were published by Cambridge University Press between 1907 and 1910. This last edition was the most substantial collection of Gascoigne's writing published for four centuries and supplied a foundation for the rapid acceleration of academic interest in the poet at the end of the twentieth century and on into the new millennium.

Today, books about the sixteenth century often briefly register Gascoigne's various achievements but demonstrate an unnerving imprecision about when he was born (estimated dates range from 1525 to 1544). There have been only two biographies, published as long ago as 1893 and 1942.

This book is a critical biography, which is to say it assesses everything Gascoigne wrote and offers a judgement on it. But in scrutinising Gascoigne's writing I have attempted to locate it in the context of the wider social issues it raises, such as censorship. Although not previously recognised as such, Shakespeare's famous line about "arte made tung-tide by authoritie" (Sonnet 66) is quite possibly a direct allusion to Gascoigne and his troubles. George Gascoigne was arguably the first professional English writer, promoting – quite literally – an image of himself, marketing his product, manufacturing favourable reviews, but forced back into patronage and self-censorship by the seizure and suppression of his books. His was a swashbuckling life, full of scandal and incident, but it was also one which challenged the very notion of what it was to be a writer in Elizabethan society.

For my brother, James Binns

PART ONE: THE YOUNG GASCOIGNE

1: "Gascoigne"

Cardington is, and always has been, something of a sleepy backwater, on a road leading nowhere special. South-east of Bedford and less than three miles from the town centre, it's separated from the town by the flood plain of the Great Ouse. Cardington is a classic English village with a church, a pub, and rows of old, weathered houses, grouped in a triangle around a broad village green. The population has barely fluctuated over the centuries. In 1671 there were 306 residents and 300 years later there were 324. The 2011 census recorded a population of 288.

In the sixteenth century the village was dominated by the Gascoigne family, but though traces remain of their existence, they are long forgotten. Nowadays Cardington is known, if at all, for its association with airships and the R101 airship disaster. This gigantic craft was developed and built at Cardington and a memorial to the 49 victims of the disaster marks their mass grave beside the road into the village. Nearby stands the church of St Mary's and beyond that the centre of the village. In Cardington the only place you will find the name Gascoigne is inside St Mary's – and even there you will have to make an effort to locate it.

George Gascoigne was born into a provincial and insular agricultural environment but some four decades later he was to publish a sophisticated literary book which was to make him not merely famous but also notorious among the cultural elite of Elizabethan England. Its title – *A Hundreth Sundrie Flowres* – was, by twenty-first century standards, innocuous, even a little quaint. All Gascoigne was really signalling (with a nod to the gardening craze that was taking hold among England's expanding middle class) was the variety of the book's contents. By the standards of the time it was a big volume. It was also very original in format. No one had ever published a book quite like it before, and no one else would again.

If the book appears odd to modern eyes that is in large part because after four centuries we have different conventions of what a book's form should take. No modern publisher would contemplate putting out a lengthy book by a previously unpublished writer which consisted of two plays, a novel and around 100 poems. A format like that would only be acceptable for a well-known writer commonly accepted as being of classic status. The best modern parallel to *A Hundreth Sundrie Flowres* which I can think of is *The Essential James Joyce* (1948), which includes Joyce's three act play *Exiles*, his poems, the whole of *Dubliners* and *A Portrait of the Artist as a Young Man* and extracts from *Ulysses* and *Finnegans Wake*.

But apart from possessing literary talent, George Gascoigne was also England's first professional writer. He committed himself to the medium of print at a time when gentlemen poets disdained anything as vulgar as reproducing their privately circulated manuscripts for a mass readership. Gascoigne believed in the book as product. Uniquely, when he had become widely read, he commissioned a portrait of himself for reproduction in what he hoped would be another popular book. It is the Tudor version of an author's publicity photograph. The contrast with the age's greatest writer is startling. Shakespeare, notoriously, had little interest in publishing his plays or in promoting himself as a writer or literary personality. The first and most famous image of Shakespeare to appear in a printed text – Martin Droeshout's copper engraving on the title page of the First Folio – did not appear until seven years after his death. When Gascoigne died, Shakespeare was still a schoolboy – yet Gascoigne had published all the plays he'd produced in his lifetime and almost everything he'd written.

George Gascoigne believed in promotion and one of the selling points of his first and best book was his surname: Gascoigne. His work had long circulated in manuscript and made him known to the literati of London. But his family name was also one of some distinction, which the poet was happy to exploit. The contents page of *A Hundreth Sundrie Flowres* was keen to emphasize the name Gascoigne, introducing it into the title of many of the poems listed: "Gascoyne his passion", "Gascoines libell of divorce", "Gascoines praise of his mistresse", "Gascoines Lullabie" – and on, and on, and on. The contents page manages to include his name, extravagantly, on seventeen separate occasions. George Gascoigne had a flamboyant streak in his make-up. *A Hundreth Sundrie Flowres* purported to be an anonymous anthology containing the work of various poets. But the book's true author couldn't quite resist shouting his achievement from the rooftops. It was *his* work. The work of a Gascoigne. Someone who was a member of a distinguished family: the Gascoignes. As whoever produced that contents page well knew, in the sixteenth century, "Gascoigne" was a name that rang a bell.

The Lord Chief Justice

In an early poem, probably written in his twenties, George Gascoigne boasted that he was "a lusty lad" descended "of ancient worthy race".[1] The Gascoigne lineage was certainly something worth promoting in an age obsessed with heredity and social status. One of the nicest things Gascoigne could think to say about a fallen comrade-in-arms in the Dutch war of independence was that he was such a fine man it was almost as if he was born into a good family: "He might for birth have boasted noble race".[2]

Gascoigne was the son of a knight and able, through heredity, to display a coat of arms. This entitled him to describe himself as George Gascoigne *Esquire*. The most striking feature of the paternal arms – "Argent, on a pale Sable, a demy Luce Or", in the jargon of heraldry – is a pike's head. The pike is a predator and the Gascoigne pike's head is a belligerent, sinister looking creature with a fierce, beady eye and two rows of sharp teeth. As a symbol, it hints at military prowess and ambition. This was apt. The Gascoignes were always loyal to the throne and prepared to fight on their sovereign's behalf when required. But they were also an ambitious family and George Gascoigne the poet was the third member to make his mark on the history of his time.

The most famous Gascoigne of early Tudor England appears in one of the best-known scenes of Shakespeare's drama. At the climax of *Henry IV, Part Two* Falstaff's affectionate, inappropriate familiarity is brusquely cut short by his former comrade-in-delinquency, the newly crowned King Henry V:

> I know thee not, old man. Fall to thy prayers.
> How ill white hairs becomes a fool and jester! (V.v.47-8)

The other central figure on stage with Falstaff at this moment is a Gascoigne and someone from whom Bedfordshire's George Gascoigne was directly descended. Shakespeare never names him: in the play he is simply identified as "the Lord Chief Justice" but everyone in the audience knew who he was.

Lord Chief Justice Gascoigne, or Sir William Gascoigne as the history books call him, was popularly supposed to have quarrelled with Henry, Prince of Wales. Henry struck Sir William, who had him arrested and imprisoned. In the pre-Shakespeare play *The Famous Victories of Henry V* Gascoigne is given "a boxe on the eare". The story is briefly alluded to in Shakespeare's *Henry IV, Part One* when the king tells the prince, "Thy place in Council thou hast rudely lost" (III.ii.32). At the start of *Henry IV, Part Two* the Chief Justice is merely a rather dull, sober figure of authority and an easy foil for the quick-witted and engaging rogue Falstaff. But at the end of the play the tables are well and truly turned. When the formerly disgraced Henry becomes king he confronts his old persecutor. The dramatic tension is sharp. Surely Justice Gascoigne is about to lose his job, be imprisoned, or suffer something worse? But the Lord Chief Justice is coolly unperturbed by the abrupt change in Henry's fortunes. Gascoigne makes a solemn speech about the impartiality of the law. No one is above it, he tells the new king. When the Prince hit him he was in reality lashing out at the king himself, whose authority the Lord Chief Justice embodied. His imprisonment was a just punishment. The repentant, transformed Henry accepts this slice of judicial wisdom and invites the judge to continue in his post. It is Falstaff, not Gascoigne, who is rejected.

In reality the story was apocryphal, even historically ludicrous. No sane person would have dared to lay a finger on the heir to the throne. But Shakespeare made good use of the story to promote the idea of the impartiality and objectivity of the law and Henry's exemplary moral transformation, giving a dramatic twist to what was really just Tudor propaganda.

Gascony

The name "Gascoigne" was originally a regional name for someone from the Gascogne (or Gascony) region of south-west France. Historically, that meant everything south and west of the River Garonne. Nowadays "Gascony" tends to be used more narrowly to refer to the Armagnac region, where there is no shortage of shops with names like "Maison Gascogne". George Gascoigne was very much aware of his family's French origins. In a letter written near the end of his life he playfully signed himself "G. le Gascoign".[3]

The name Gascony derives from the Basques, who once lived here and whom the Romans called "Vascones". In the Basque region of France "Rue Gascogne" remains a common street name. The ancient kingdom of Gascony was absorbed into the duchy of Aquitaine and in 1152 came under English rule when Eleanor of Aquitaine married Henry II. The English connection was comprehensively terminated in 1472 when Gascony was conquered by Louis XI and became part of France once again. Three centuries of trade and social interaction between Gascony and England resulted in "Gascoigne" becoming a reasonably common English surname, with one minor, less popular variation: "Gascoyne". These spellings, though not dominant in the sixteenth century, eventually outlasted or marginalized other variant forms such as Gascon, Gascone, Gasken, Gaskin and Gasking. In *Daniel Deronda*, which George Eliot seems to have first started making notes for in the autumn of 1872 (not long after the appearance of Hazlitt's major Victorian two-volume edition *The Complete Poems of George Gascoigne*), the opportunistic Captain Gaskin evidently finds some odium attached to that particular spelling, and deftly reinvents himself as "Mr Gascoigne".

Gascony was famous for two things. Gascon speakers were proverbial for their boastfulness, and even today "gascon" means someone who exaggerates or is a braggart, and a tall story is "une gasconnade". It's apt that Alexandre Dumas' *The Three Musketeers* is loosely based on a wildly colourful account of the supposedly true adventures of some Gascon *seigneurs*.

Outside France, Gascony is best known for its wine and brandy. The English have been importing Gascony's Armagnac brandy for centuries, regarded as second only to Cognac among the wine-based brandies. The link between Gascony and English literature goes back even to the time before George Gascoigne was born. In September 1529 the poet and courtier Sir Thomas Wyatt was given a licence by Henry VIII to import 1000 casks of Gascoigne wine. Even nowadays any British wine store or supermarket is likely to have a few bottles of the dry white wine *vins de pays des Côtes de Gascogne* on its shelves. It seems therefore a little ironic that among George Gascoigne's many achievements as a writer was his authorship of what has been called "one of the earliest temperance tracts in the language".[4] But that description is not entirely accurate and the pamphlet is suspiciously well-informed about sixteenth century alcoholic drinks.

Gascoign de Gauthorp

The Gascoignes of England first came to prominence in Yorkshire, under the new Tudor dynasty which followed the Wars of the Roses. Shakespeare's Gascoigne was Lord Chief Justice between 1400 and 1412 but the family tradition of service to the state continued. In the fifteenth century Gascoignes were twice made High Sheriffs for the county of York. The family's French origins are underlined by the appointment of "Will. Gascoign de Gauthorp" as High Sheriff in 1442, under Henry VI. In 1496, under Henry VII, another "William Gascoign" was made High Sheriff (the name was difficult to shake off: at least thirteen successive generations of male Yorkshire Gascoignes were named William). The Gascoignes "de Gauthorp" were the trunk from which other prominent branches of the Gascoignes grew, including one based at Parlington (now on the outskirts of Leeds), and the Bedfordshire branch to which the poet Gascoigne belonged. The northern origins of the Gascoignes are nowhere as evident as in the city of Leeds, which has a Gascoigne Avenue, a Gascoigne Court, two Gascoigne Roads and a Gascoigne View.

There has been considerable confusion about where "Gauthorp", or as it later became known "Gawthope", was located. The common assumption among writers on Gascoigne has always been that Gawthorpe Hall (also known as Gawthorpe Manor and Gawthorpe House) was found at the village of Gawthorpe in north Yorkshire. In fact "Gauthorp" was not there or at either of the two other hamlets named Gawthorpe but was situated in a valley west of the village of Harewood, north of Leeds. The estate came into the possession of the Gascoigne family when the Lord Chief Justice's grandfather, William Gascoigne "of Harwood", married Mansild, daughter and heir of "John de Gawkethorp". By the eighteenth century the Gascoigne line had long since died out and the estates had become split up, but in 1739 they were once again brought together under one owner. Gawthorpe Hall was demolished and replaced by Harewood House, which was completed in 1772. Today's 150-acre Harewood estate occupies the old Gascoigne lands and the tomb of Lord Chief Justice Gascoigne and his wife, together with other those of other prominent members of the Gawthorpe Gascoignes, can be found in the parish church tucked away at the edge of the woods just to the north of Harewood House.

The Bedfordshire Gascoignes

It is always said that George Gascoigne was born at Cardington but strictly speaking this is untrue. Cardington Manor, the poet's childhood home, was situated well outside the village. For generations Cardington Manor was the home of the main branch of the Bedfordshire Gascoignes, whose story began when the Lord Chief Justice's son James moved south and married a Bedfordshire heiress in the fifteenth century. The manor's impressive site was probably first constructed on behalf of the Picot family (also spelt Pycot, and later anglicized to Pigott) into which James Gascoigne married.

What remains of Cardington Manor today supplies the most tangible local link to George Gascoigne and his Bedfordshire childhood and adolescence. From Cardington village green a road leads southwards across a broad, open plain before eventually fragmenting into a labyrinth of narrow, twisting country lanes. It was once known as Manor Lane; today it is called Southill Road. Beside it, a mile and a half south of Cardington, a moat encloses an overgrown tract of land roughly the size and shape of a football pitch. The moat is about 10 metres wide by 2.5 metres deep and is one of the longest in Bedfordshire. In one corner there are possible traces of a drawbridge. The moat, probably excavated in the period 1350-1450, served no military purpose but was built as a decorative status symbol surrounding a prestigious residence. The land it surrounds, which is sub-rectangular, measures 185 metres by up to 115 metres and encloses an area of 1.8 hectares. At its centre is the site of the house where the poet George Gascoigne was born. He probably spent most of his childhood and adolescence here and did not finally leave until he was in his twenties. Documentary proof of the place and date of George Gascoigne's birth is lacking but there is no reason to doubt that he was born anywhere else but in the family home, here, at Cardington Manor.

Cardington Manor has over the years been known by other names, including Cotton End Manor Farmhouse, Manor Farm and Cardington Cotton End Manor Farm (which makes it easily confused with Cotton End Manor Farm in the adjacent parish of Eastcotts). As these names indicate, the land round here is farming country. Cardington appears in the Domesday Book of 1086 as "Chernetone" – a Saxon name which may mean "Caerda's Farm". Today the civil parishes of Eastcotts and Cardington form a single ecclesiastical parish of 5,339 acres. Eastcotts first appears in thirteenth-century records and derives from old English "cotum" or cottage, when apparently the area consisted of scattered cottages on the fringes of the wooded clay slopes to the south. The Domesday Book lists four holdings in Cardington and Eastcotts, from which developed three medieval manors: Cotton End, Fenlake Barns and Cardington. Cardington Cross, north of the village, may have originally marked the boundary with Fenlake Barns; the present-day cross was erected in 1837 to replace the medieval cross which once stood nearby.

The Picots were prominent in the county in the fourteenth and early fifteenth centuries. Sir John Picot "de kerdyngton" served as MP for Bedfordshire, as did his grandson Sir Baldwin Pigott, who in 1428 is recorded as holding the manorial rights in Cardington. Sir Baldwin's daughter and heir Dorothy married James Gascoigne, only son of the Chief Justice's second wife, and so by the late fifteenth century the manor had passed into Gascoigne hands. The couple had three sons but the two oldest were killed at the Battle of Barnet. The third,

George, married Elizabeth, daughter of Thomas Refford. Gascoigne the Elizabethan writer was undoubtedly christened George in honour of his great grandfather.

One of the earliest surviving Bedfordshire documents in English is a 1469 lease drawn up on behalf of George Gascoigne of Cardington. It leases his mills in Cardington "with water fro a place called the Washyngstole of the priory of Newenham unto the werkes of Castell mylles" to one Thomas Whytson. The Cardington watermill is mentioned in the Domesday Book. It was the main place where local farmers took their grain to be ground and it remained an important commercial asset for the lords of Cardington Manor. Demand was presumably great enough for it not to affect or be affected by the competition from the local windmill. In 1260 a windmill was recorded "in parochia de Kerdingt de novo constructi" – probably situated on the slight rise of the locality now known as Shortstown. The windmill, only a mile and a half from Cardington Manor, may well have formed part of the estate.

In 1361-2 John Pygot had a one-third share in the watermill, but when his widow died in 1374-5 Cardington Manor included two watermills under one roof, a fishery and a leet (or watercourse). At this period the word "mill" meant a set of mill-stones and in medieval mills each pair was driven by a separate water wheel. The implication is that by 1374 Cardington mills had doubled in capacity. The 1469 lease specifies that a new mill-house is to be built, sixty feet by sixteen. The landlord, George Gascoigne, promises to make the mills "able and sufficient to grynd all maner of Greynes" and to take responsibility for "water whelys, water Yates, mills stones, cogge wheles, trendels, cogges, rowngges, reyndes, spyndeles, hoopes, stone, grete tymber and small splentes, wyndyng roddes, strawe, and all maner of caryage to the reparacion of the said milles and howses". Cardington Mill was finally demolished in 1936 and its site by the river Great Ouse, north of the village (TL 078489), was probably the Domesday one.

Sir William Gascoigne

By 1485 it is known that the couple had a son, William (though he was probably born before this date). In material terms, William was the most successful of the Bedfordshire Gascoignes and he considerably expanded the family's land holdings. The estate of Sir Thomas Wake, who held land in "Kerdyntone, Bromham and elsewhere" was conveyed to William Gascoigne in 1506-7 and merged in the manor of Cardington. William Gascoigne married Elizabeth, the daughter and heir of John Vynter (or Winter) of Cardington. The marriage presumably substantially added to the Gascoigne estate. Elizabeth died, and Sir William (who was knighted in June 1520) remarried. His new bride, who had herself been twice widowed, was Elizabeth Pennington. William Gascoigne of Cardington may have been the William Gascoigne who appeared as an esquire at the funeral of Henry VII; if so it was his first recorded presence at court and he was probably sponsored by the Bedfordshire magnate Richard Grey, Earl of Kent. One advantage of owning the Cardington Manor lands was that it gave the title holder the right to serve as one of three almoners at a coronation, and William Gascoigne duly served in this role when Henry VIII became king in 1509, as well as in 1533 when Henry married Anne Boleyn. William Gascoigne held a number of minor offices during the early years of Henry VIII's reign.

In June 1520 Gascoigne was knighted in France, where the earl was attending the King at the Field of the Cloth of Gold. Two years later he was present at the reception of Charles V in England. In April 1523, shortly before the earl's death, he was recommended to Cardinal Wolsey by William Franklin, archdeacon and chancellor of Durham, and within six months was treasurer of the cardinal's household. He held this position until 1529, and was described as

> *A rough Gentleman*; preferring rather to *profit* then *please* his *Master*. And although the *pride* of that *Prelate* was far above his *covetousnesse*; yet his *wisedome*, well knowing *Thrift* to be the *fuell* of *Magnificence*, would usually digest advice from his *Servant*, when it plainly tended to his own *emolument*.[5]

This incorporates a stereotypical view of Wolsey but its portrait of Sir William Gascoigne may well be accurate. It is hard to believe matters could have been otherwise in such a ruthlessly acquisitive society as Tudor England. As a servant, albeit an important one, Sir William's presence as a member of Wolsey's household barely registers in the historical record. Another well-to-do Bedfordshire man, John Gostwick of Willington, was also in Wolsey's service; Sir William may have been responsible for this. Willington is near Cardington and the destinies of the two families would later become acrimoniously entangled in the life of Gascoigne the poet.

Sir William's association with Wolsey is best remembered for his contribution to that dramatic moment in the autumn of 1527 when the Cardinal left his Thames-side palace at York Place for the last time. Having been charged with being guilty of a *praemunire* (a form of lesser treason) Wolsey was stripped of the Great Seal and was in disgrace. On 22 October Wolsey pleaded guilty and was sentenced to be imprisoned during the King's pleasure and all his property to be forfeited to the King.

Word spread of the Cardinal's expulsion from York Place, and the Thames was packed with boats as hundreds watched to see him taken to the Tower. Wolsey's household and servants crowded to watch, and Sir William Gascoigne expressed his sympathies to his master that he should be taken to such a place of imprisonment.

This moment is only known because it was recorded in the first biography,

Thomas Wolsey late Cardinall, his lyffe and deathe, Written by George Cauendishe, his gentleman Vsshar. This autograph manuscript, written at some point between 1554 and 1558, remained unpublished for almost a century. As a gentleman-usher, Cavendish combined the functions of a personal assistant with the management of domestic matters for major occasions and travel. He was therefore standing alongside both men when he reported Gascoigne as saying

> Sir I ame sory for yor grace/ for I vnderstand ye shall goo strayt way to the tower// Ys this the good Comfort and councell q^d my lord/ that ye can geve yor m^r [master] in aduersitie/ yt hathe byn allwayes yor naturall Inclynacion to be very light of Credytt and myche more lighter in reportyng of falce newes/ I wold ye shold knowe sir w^m and all suche blasfemers that it is no thing more falce than that// ffor I neuer (thankes be to god) deserued by no wayes to come there/ vnder any arrest/ althoughe it hathe pleased the kyng to take my howse redy furnysshed for his pleasure at this tyme/[6]

Charles Ferguson argues that this episode indicates a certain feistiness on Wolsey's part: "Claims of innocence and independence were beginning to assert themselves".[7] After the Cardinal's rebuke to Gascoigne – described by one biographer as "half frosty, half submissive"[8] – Wolsey boarded his barge. To the amazement of the crowds of onlookers, instead of heading downriver to the Tower it went in the opposite direction: "And so went by water vnto Putney".[9] As Wolsey knew, Henry had ordered him to take up residence at Esher, at a house a few miles from Hampton Court.

Sir William was not personally affected by Wolsey's fall from power. Although also a good friend of Thomas Cromwell, Gascoigne was merely a servant and not directly involved in Henry's manipulation of state and church to effect his divorce from Katherine of Aragon. He retired to Cardington but soon found service again in the household of John Neville, Lord Latimer. By 1529 he was serving in Parliament as one of Bedfordshire's two county representatives. Eight years later he is recorded as living up to his reputation for shrewd acquisition:

> The dissolution of the monasteries, which was a precipitative factor in the outbreak of the Pilgrimage of Grace, caused the avaricious to contract Cromwell with a view to enhancing their financial status... In June 1537, Sir William Gascoygne implored Cromwell to plead for either Bridlington or Jervaulx Abbey. He stated that he had but a small living.[10]

John Gascoigne, Esq. and Lady Margaret Scargill

Sir William had two children. His heir was his son John (the poet's father), who was born to his first wife Elizabeth no later than 1510. He also had a daughter,

Joan. She later married a local landowner, Robert Bulkeley. In All Saints Church, Cople, one mile east of Cardington, there is a plate brass dated 1556 in memory of "Joan Gascoyne", her husband and their eight children. She is shown wearing a "dog-kennel" head-dress with what was by then the unfashionable early Tudor style of an over-gown with three-quarter length sleeves and a simple neck-line. Her children are similarly simply dressed. Evidently the growing fashion for ruffs was shunned in the Bulkeley household.

The early life of John Gascoigne is obscure but most of it was probably spent at Cardington Manor. He was presumably effectively the head of the household while his father was away working for Cardinal Wolsey or engaged on his other activities as a loyal servant of the crown. The date of John Gascoigne's marriage to Margaret Scargill of Thorpe Hall in Yorkshire is not known, but it had occurred by October 1531.[11] It was probably an arranged marriage, which served further to increase the wealth of Sir William Gascoigne's household.

The Scargills were a prominent landowning family whose connections with the Gascoignes of Gawthorpe went back to the fourteenth century, when Sir William Scargill married Margaret, daughter of Sir William Gascoigne. The Scargills had an estate not far from Gawthorpe, but their main residence was at Thorpe Hall. This has commonly been confused with the village of that name near Richmond but in fact there is no connection. The Scargill manor house, previously in the possession of the Stapleton family and then named Thorp Stapleton, was situated on the banks of the River Aire, two miles south-west of the village of Whitkirk. It lay in open countryside in the lush valley below Whitkirk Moor (south of today's Temple Newsam Park). A surviving sketch, made prior to the demolition of Thorpe Hall in the twentieth century, shows the ruins of a very substantial stone building. It was of at least two storeys and resembles the remains of a castle keep as much as manor house. Today the river follows a different course, and the environs of Thorpe Hall have been completely transformed by industrialisation. Whitkirk itself is no longer an outlying village east of Leeds but has become swallowed up by the vast urban sprawl of the city.

As the most important local family, the Scargills were closely involved with their local parish church, at Whitkirk. The name Whitkirk means "white church", and the church, prominently situated on a ridge above the valley of the Aire, must have always physically dominated the small settlement around it. The existing church assumed its present form over many centuries and there is an oblique reference to it in the Domesday Book of 1086. Though its origins are obscure, the first church built here seems to have been a wooden one or a "black" church (the wood darkened by exposure to the weather), subsequently replaced by a second one of stone (a "white" structure). The present church, now known as the parish church of St Mary at Whitkirk, is built in the perpendicular gothic style and underwent a general restoration in 1855-6, when the interior was much modernised.

In 1448 William Scargill Esquire endowed a chantry for two priests at the altar of the Holy Trinity on the south side of the choir. William Scargill's heir was his son John Scargill. Towards the end of his life George Gascoigne claimed that "M. Fourboisir" (i.e. Martin Frobisher) was "a kinsman of mine" on the grounds that John Scargill's daughter had married Frobisher's paternal great-grandfather. That link existed but it was a distinctly tenuous one: John Scargill's son William married Dorothy, daughter of Sir Thomas Conyers. Their son Robert Scargill and his wife Joan were the poet George Gascoigne's maternal grandfather and grandmother.

Of all the Scargills, Sir Robert and Lady Joan left the most tangible record in the form of an alabaster chest tomb in the church. The arch in which it stands was possibly cut in the second half of the fifteenth century, and may originally have been intended for the tomb of the William Scargill who founded the Chantry. If so, Scargill's wishes were ignored, and no memorial to him survives.

The tomb of Gascoigne's maternal grandparents displays two recumbent effigies with hands conventionally uplifted in prayer. Sir Robert Scargill is clad in armour, with a sword on his left side and a misericorde (or dagger) on the right. At his feet lies a stylized animal with a fierce face and immense claws. Beside him lies his wife, wearing a long gown with long hanging sleeves. On the west and north faces of the tomb are the Scargill arms. Round the edge of the slab is a partly obliterated Latin inscription identifying the pair.

Gascoigne never knew his grandfather, who died on 2 February 1531. Sir Robert and Lady Joan had two daughters, Mary and Margaret. In the Inquisition post mortem made some eight months after Sir Robert Scargill's death, Mary was described as being "aged 20 years and more" and her sister Margaret, the poet's mother, "17 years and more". These were probably precise figures, indicating that Margaret Scargill was born about 1513. Both sisters were also described as married, indicating that both girls were wed while still teenagers. Mary Scargill married Sir Marmaduke Tunstall, who was first cousin to Cuthbert Tunstall, Bishop of London, and later of Durham. Margaret Scargill was probably aged no more than 16 or 17 when she was wrenched from her idyllic home on the banks of the Aire and travelled south to become John Gascoigne's wife in Bedfordshire.

Whitkirk Church is undoubtedly the place where the poet's parents were married, probably in 1529 or 1530. The wedding of Lady Margaret Scargill to John Gascoigne, Esquire, would have been a spectacular affair, involving as it did a daughter of the most prominent family in the district and the son of Sir William Gascoigne of Cardington. Whitkirk Church is the location of the only image of George Gascoigne's mother that is known to exist. On the sides of the Scargill tomb chest are depicted five "weepers", representing the couple's daughters, Mary and Margaret. The figures shown may simply be stock images, just as the effigies themselves may not be intended to be realistic. The two identical weepers on the north side probably represent the older sister, Mary. The three identical weepers on the south side, which are smaller and bonnet-less, almost certainly depict Margaret Scargill, the poet's mother.

The birth of George Gascoigne

In a long poem about his life and his misfortunes, Gascoigne referred to his birth as

> The black hour of my constellation,
> Which framed me so luckless on the molde[12] [earth]

But to the vexation of his admirers in later centuries Gascoigne never said what that hour was – or what day, month, or year.

Well into the twentieth century the year of George Gascoigne's birth remained uncertain. In reference books and surveys of the period a variety of dates between the 1520s and 1540s are still commonly and somewhat arbitrarily given. However, in 1982 Mark Eccles discovered a deposition dated 15 February 1569 in which Gascoigne gave his age as 34.[13] It suggests that the poet was born between 16 February 1534 and 14 February 1535. This revelation needs to be tempered by recognition that in Tudor times a person's exact age was not regarded as socially important. As far as the state was concerned, only one moment in a life counted – when an individual became 21 and in law ceased to be a minor. A bureaucratic concern with social statistics was very slow in coming, and legislation requiring every parish to record baptisms and deaths was not introduced until 1536. However, the dating is consistent with other documents which indicate a year of birth in the 1530s.[14] In the absence of more compelling evidence the likeliest probability is that George Gascoigne was born at Cardington Manor in 1534.

Plate 1. The Gascoigne pike, displayed on a simplified coat of arms on the tower of Ross Wyld Hall in central Walthamstow.

Plate 2. The tomb of Lord Chief Justice Sir William Gascoigne and his wife Margaret Percy, All Saints Church, Harewood.

Plate 3. The tomb of Lord Chief Justice Sir William Gascoigne and his wife Margaret Percy.

Plate 4. The ruins of Thorpe Hall, childhood home of Gascoigne's mother, Margaret Scargill.

Plate 5. The tomb of Sir Robert and Lady Joan Scargill. The three "weepers" are representations of their daughter Margaret.

Plate 6. The two Scargill sisters, Mary and Margaret.

Plate 7. The poet's maternal grandparents, Sir Robert and Lady Joan Scargill.

2: Cardington Manor

Bedfordshire at this time was a rural backwater – an agricultural region of small estates. Its towns were small, its religious houses conservative and conformist. No figure of national importance was associated with the county. Printed books were only just beginning to circulate. The estate to which George Gascoigne was literally heir was a community centred on agriculture and which moved according to the slow, repetitive rhythm of the seasons.

A legal document dated 17 June 1562 provides an inventory of the manor of Cardington: "20 messuages, 16 cottages, a dovecot, a water-mill, 20 tofts, 20 gardens, 20 orchards, 1,000 acres of land, 600 acres meadow, 1000 acres pasture, 200 acres of wood". Agriculture and its related trades provided most of the employment in the parish, and the difference between town and country was negligible. Almost everyone had something to do with the land, and the subsidy lists classified taxpayers into a small number of esquires and gentry and a large number of yeomen and husbandmen. Lower down the social scale were cottagers, shepherds, warreners and woodwards. The local fields were sown with wheat, rye, barley, peas and oats. Servicing the community were craftsmen whose occupations were all centered on agriculture: carpenters, smiths, ploughwrights, whittawers (who made the collars for horses and oxen), wheelwrights, joiners and whipcord-makers. Other occupations involved trades concerned with food – miller, millwright, butcher, baker, poulterer, fisherman, oatmeal-maker, fowler, corn-dealer.

The exact boundaries of the Gascoigne estate are no longer known but it seems probable that its northern acres included two fields called "Further Bunyans" and "Bunyans", which were associated with a yeoman family whose fortunes had gone into a steep decline. By the time that the tinker's son John Bunyan was born in 1628 at a cottage somewhere east of Elstow the male line of the Bedfordshire Gascoignes had died out. It is an interesting coincidence of literary history that the Bedfordshire landscape which Bunyan imaginatively reconstructed for Christian's long, weary hike to salvation in *The Pilgrim's Progress* was also that of George Gascoigne's childhood. The "old monument, hard by the highway-side" which Bunyan's pilgrims encounter is believed to be based on the old Cardington Cross, which Gascoigne passed every time he went into Bedford.

But Bunyan's perspective was that of a poor and footsore man, who walked everywhere. His imagination was fuelled by a sense of himself (as he put it in *Grace Abounding to the Chief of Sinners*) "exposed to hunger, to cold, to perils, to nakedness, to enemies; and a thousand calamities; and at last, it may be, to die in a ditch, like a poor and desolate sheep".[1] The animal that George Gascoigne identified with was not the sheep but the horse – strong, handsome, fast, an essential accessory for any member of the ruling class. Gascoigne saw

Bedfordshire from a saddle, whereas Bunyan's Christian has a longing vision of "shoes that would not wear out". Gascoigne's point of view always involved that of a landowner, a rider and the privileged mobility accessed by class status and a ready supply of horses. But ironically both writers ended up in Bedford prison, and both men grew up with a keen sense that their birthright had been taken from them.

The county's chief town, Bedford, lay just north of Cardington. By the sixteenth century Bedford consisted of a small number of streets clustered around the Moot Hall and St Paul's Church. In the High Street there was a Saturday market, and close by were Pudding Lane, Butcher Row, Fish Row, Poultry Market and the inns – The Swan, The Falcon, The Cock, The George, The Crown, The Bell and The Christopher. Beyond lay open fields and meadow. Bedford was a trading centre and a place where you would find such craftsmen as glover, mercer, scrivener, tanner, chandler, draper, tiler, maltman and warrener.

The county may have seemed a sleepy, unchanging place but this period was far from tranquil in either European or English history. Shattering changes were about to take place in the English state. In Bedfordshire the first sign came in the winter of 1532-3, when Queen Catherine was brought for a few months to the castle at Ampthill. In May 1533, in the church of Dunstable Priory, the new Archbishop of Canterbury, Thomas Cranmer, opened a court to adjudicate on the validity of her marriage to the king. Soon afterwards the marriage was declared invalid. In July occurred the famous scene when Catherine objected to being addressed as "Princess Dowager" instead of Queen, and struck out those words from a report being prepared for the king.

To be born in 1534 was to be born at a significant and turbulent moment in English history. It was the year that the pace of the reformation suddenly quickened in the aftermath of the marriage of Henry VIII and Anne Boleyn. An Act of Parliament declared Henry VIII supreme head of the church in England. Another act began the process of divesting the religious orders of their power, property and wealth. It was the year of Sir Thomas More's arrest. In November the second, thoroughly revised edition of William Tyndale's translation of the New Testament into English was published in Antwerp. More regarded an English Bible as a revolutionary menace and Tyndale as a dangerous heretic, but the times were changing. The tide was flowing Tyndale's way, though he himself would not live to witness the triumph of English Protestantism. Probably one of More's last acts from his prison cell – he was at times a cruel and obsessive man – was to commission Tyndale's seizure in Antwerp and his burning.[2]

The Bedfordshire county representatives for the reformation Parliament, 1529-36, were George Acworth and Sir William Gascoigne. As always, the Gascoignes remained loyal to the throne. Sir William attended as an almoner at the coronation of Anne Boleyn on 1 June 1533. On 7 September the Queen gave birth to a daughter, who was named Elizabeth. The paths of the infant Tudor and the child born to John and Margaret Gascoigne the following year would one day cross, but not for several decades. The day would come when the poet would nearly kill her – though he would bounce back from that misfortune and climax his writing career with a presentation manuscript addressed to "the comeliest Queen that ever was".

*

In London, 1534 was a year of plague, and so again was 1535. George Gascoigne was far removed from such threats. The environment into which the newborn child was born was that of a large, affluent, many-roomed household full of people and activity. The baby would have been delivered by a midwife and her female assistants and breastfed by his mother. The convention was for baptism to take place, where possible, on the Sunday following the birth. It would have been a big social occasion involving family, relatives, friends and associates. The infant Gascoigne would have been carried into Cardington church on an expensive, finely embroidered ceremonial cushion. After baptism the priest wrapped the child in his white christening robe. Afterwards came the party, when the godparents and other guests gave such gifts as ceremonial cups and spoons, or teething rings and rattles fashioned out of silver or coral.

An Elizabethan baby spent its first months wearing a cap and buried under layers of clothes and bedding to protect it from the grave danger of fresh air and draughts. A privileged child like George Gascoigne would have had a fine wooden cradle fixed on rockers. One of his earliest experiences of life would have been of a woman – his mother, perhaps, or a servant – sitting beside him singing a lullaby. One of Gascoigne's finest lyric poems begins with just such a moment, before expanding into an old man's melancholy farewell to life:

> Sing lullaby, as women do,
> Wherewith they bring their babes to rest,
> And lullaby can I sing too
> As womanly as can the best.
> With lullaby they still the child,
> And if I be not much beguiled,
> Full many wanton babes have I
> Which must be stilled with lullaby.[3]

Infancy was short-lived, and once out of baby clothes both boys and girls wore the same clothes as adults. Gascoigne, like other children of his age, would have been expected to stand for his father and mother, and address them as "sir" and "madam". He would have been luckier than many children, in so far as his family would have been able to afford to buy him the very best toys – such things as toy soldiers and toy ships, hoops, balls, perhaps a drum. Outside the house in which he was born lay a massive private garden and the moat. It was a world where animals were everywhere – household mice, rats, cats and dogs; horses, sheep, cattle and goats; flocks of birds of numerous varieties. A child like Gascoigne would probably have had his own dog or dogs, and perhaps a tame bird.

Two other children were subsequently born to Sir John and Dame Margaret Gascoigne, whose birthdates are also uncertain – a son, John, and a daughter, Elizabeth. All three children probably spent most of their childhood and adolescence at Cardington Manor. It was a tranquil, privileged environment for these children to grow up in. George Gascoigne was doubly privileged, since in a patriarchal society like Tudor England the firstborn male was always regarded as being by far the most important child.

*

In comparison to other dwellings in the area, Cardington Manor was massive. At the time the two-storey house was demolished in the early 1960s it consisted of a section of the original Tudor nucleus with some Georgian and Victorian alterations. Its core may have been medieval. The manor house appears to have been substantially rebuilt in the sixteenth century and is likely to have been far more substantial than the building which survived into modern times. Prior to demolition traces of the old foundations of a larger building were visible. However, what remained into the twentieth century was impressive enough. The house consisted of two wings forming an L with a tiled roof and crow-stepped brick coped gables, with the angle filled in asymmetrically with two smaller extensions. Even without the later additions, it was something of an architectural curiosity. The house seems to have been partly timber-framed and partly built of hand-made red Tudor bricks. Its most striking feature, the moulded red brick spiral-fluted chimney shaft, is typical of the period 1530-1560 and compares with that at nearby Warden Abbey. The house was almost certainly either massively renovated or completely rebuilt for the poet's grandfather, Sir William Gascoigne, who was still living there with his son and daughter-in-law when George was born.

Inside, the house contained original Tudor features including a carved fireplace and a brick corbelled chimney. A large mantle in a first-floor room formed a segment of a large circle, decorated with a broad band of deeply cut sculpture. This design, showing interlaced vine branches, with leaves and bunches of grapes, also appears on the ceiling. It is also found on the cornices of canopied altar tombs in Cardington church.

The land north of the site was once known as Dovehouse Close, indicating that the Manor possessed a dovecote. A very large, impressive example of a Tudor dovecot survives in the nearby village of Willington.

To the south of the land enclosed by the moat was Kitchen Close. As its name suggests, the Manor would have been self-sufficient, with its own buttery and brewing facilities, and a ready supply of milk, game birds, beef, lamb and fish.

Although the surrounding district today gives the appearance of sleepy timelessness, it is not one which George Gascoigne would have recognised. In the sixteenth century the region was densely forested and he grew up in a landscape dominated by trees. In 1577 Cardington High Woods totalled 242 acres and there were many other local woods such as Lepen Quarter Wood, Cotton High Wood, Burnt Wood and Manor Wood. Much of this woodland was cleared away during the mid-nineteenth century and has now almost entirely vanished. Today's Manor Wood is no more than a fraction of its former size.

Gascoigne's Childhood

The garden of Cardington Manor had a feature shared by few other dwellings in England: the moat. This is probably the place where George Gascoigne learned a skill much rarer in Tudor times than in ours – how to swim. (The first treatise on swimming published in England, Everard Digby's *De arte natandi*, did not appear until ten years after Gascoigne's death.) Within the garden were also two large ponds, located close to the north-western arm of the moat. Only traces remain today. They were about 25 metres across and some 2 metres deep, and were probably fish ponds. The moat also contained fish, which were regarded as a significant property.[4]

These features of Gascoigne's childhood seem to permeate his writing. Swimming and bathing are frequently associated with pleasure and sensual enjoyment. When the young man in Gascoigne's novel *The Adventures of Master F.J.* enjoys "many dayes" of "more than speakable pleasures" in bed with a sexy married woman, he is described as "swimming now in delightes". Deepness and depth are recurring adjectives, possessed of special power. When the narrator cuts short his story at the end of Gascoigne's novel he explains that he could, if he wanted, "wade much further". Fish, fishing and bait are often used to describe the activities of men and women, especially in matters of love. Master F.J. sings a melancholy song with the line: "With sweet enticing bait, I fished for many a dame".

*

The first impact of the English reformation on life at Cardington Manor was felt in the autumn of 1536, when Gascoigne was two. The north of England rose up against the new reforms with a rebellion known as the Pilgrimage of Grace. Henry VIII hurriedly attempted to assemble an army and Sir William Gascoigne provided twenty men for the Duke of Suffolk's forces against the rebels. Some 2,000 prospective troops were mustered at nearby Ampthill. But in the end no large set-piece battle ever took place. The rebellion lacked a determined and united leadership and its impetus fizzled out in the face of vague promises and procrastination, followed by savage repression.

Curiously, there is fleeting evidence of the infant George Gascoigne spending some time in the north country in the 1530s, well beyond the region associated with the Yorkshire Scargills and Gascoignes. In one of his last pieces of writing Gascoigne referred to "suche English as I stale in westmerland".[5] But in what sense did he steal English in Westmoreland? No one has ever really understood what Gascoigne meant. The remark has even been taken to mean that he was born in Westmoreland, which seems very, very unlikely. Today Westmoreland (roughly speaking, an upland region encompassing parts of North Yorkshire, Cumbria, Durham and Northumberland) no longer exists under that name, having been abolished in the local government reforms of the early 1970s.

C. T. Prouty conjectured that the solution to the enigma lay in a family connection:

> A glance at the map shows how near to the borders of Westmoreland were the manors of Scargill, Thorpe, and Gawthorpe; so the clue to that enigmatic reference to English stolen in Westmoreland may well lie in a visit by young George Gascoigne to his relatives. There was, most probably, a tutor for Gascoigne's young cousins, and, if the young man joined them in his lessons, he would indeed be "stealing" his education.[6]

In fact Prouty had the wrong Thorpe and Gawthorpe, and Gascoigne's mother Margaret Scargill had no connection at all with the village of Scargill. That said, Prouty's theory remains the best that anyone has come up with to explain the poet's cryptic comment. It is remotely possible that Sir John or Dame Margaret did have relatives or friends in faraway Westmoreland. If Gascoigne was temporarily placed with another family at a young age it might even explain the coldness and hostility he felt towards his mother in later life. When Margaret Gascoigne died, aged about 62, neither of her sons attended her funeral. On the face of it, this indicates a striking lack of filial warmth or affection.

Some form of hurtful separation from the comforts of his home or his mother may lie behind the theme of a young boy's sufferings which is present in Gascoigne's long poem, *The Complaynte of Phylomene*. The poem re-told a popular story of sex, violence and retribution which Gascoigne, like other writers, found in Ovid's *Metamorphoses* and Chaucer's *Legend of Good Women*. But in Gascoigne's hands the poem, which took fourteen years to complete, was associated with two major moments of crisis in his life – his marriage and the ferocious attack on *A Hundreth Sundrie Flowres*. In its treatment of mother-child relations it may conceivably express even earlier anxieties. When Gascoigne completed this poem in April 1576 his mother had died some six months earlier. In the poem the Thracian king Tereus marries Progne but then meets her sister Philomene, rapes her and cuts out her tongue to prevent her speaking about her ordeal. Philomene, kept prisoner, produces a needlework account which reaches Progne, who frees her sister. Progne decides to take revenge on Tereus by slaughtering their son. It's a poem in which maternal feeling is ruthlessly suppressed:

>   tigerlike she took
> The little boy full boisterously
> Who now for terror quooke
>
> And (craving mother's help)
> She (mother) took a blade,
> And in her son's small tender heart
> And open wound she made.[7]

This is family life as nightmare. Gascoigne gives the sufferings of a child much greater emphasis than he found in his sources for the poem. He describes the piteous cry of Philomene transformed into a nightingale. Then, coming out of the world of classical myth into that of Tudor England, he says the cry is

> Much like the child at school
> With byrchen rods sore beaten, [birch]
> If when he go to bed at night
> His master chance to threaten,
>
> In every dream he starts,
> And *O good master* cries[8]

The interpolation is an odd one. Although many writers used the Philomene story in their work, no one but Gascoigne seems to have drawn an analogy between the suffering and cries of Philomene and those of a schoolboy. One senses something personal here but definition is elusive.

*

In 1540, when George Gascoigne was five or six years old, his grandfather died. It's likely to have been one of those first big events which impinge on a small child's consciousness. The funeral of Sir William Gascoigne would have been a major occasion for the district, with the funeral procession moving at a stately pace from Cardington Manor to the Church of St Mary the Virgin.

Today, the only part of the church which survives from Gascoigne's time is the early sixteenth-century chancel. It's here, on the north side, close to the altar, that the tomb of Sir William Gascoigne can still be found. On top of the tomb are fixed brasses of Sir William and his two wives. It shows the knight dressed in armour with sword and dagger, a sallet helmet and chain mail skirt. He is portrayed with his legs apart, standing over a dog. On each side a wife stares devotedly at him. They also have their dogs. The wives' robes are decorated with Sir William Gascoigne's armorial bearings. The heraldic devices shown include an ermined lion and a pike's head with an ermine spot.

Having lost one Gascoigne knight, Henry VIII evidently required another. John Gascoigne was knighted the year after his father's death. In the years that followed he continued the Bedfordshire Gascoigne tradition of expanding the family's property empire and acting, in a relatively minor capacity, as a loyal servant of the Tudor state. Henry VIII's break-up of the religious houses resulted in the Crown seizing control of a vast quantity of monastic property and lands. The rents of these properties now went to the king. Extensive ex-monastic property became available for purchase in Bedfordshire and the gentry scrambled to make a killing. Sir William Gascoigne's old associate John Gostwick put in a bid for the Franciscan friary at Bedford as a convenient second home, on the grounds that "if sickness should happen in his house, he has no other to resort to".[9] Bushmead Priory was also up for grabs, and Sir John St John insisted he had the first claim on it, asserting that it "lay so near his house that if he should be driven to remove he could find no place so meet". However, it was reported that "Mr Gascoigne labours for the same" – the Gascoigne undoubtedly being the poet's father.[10] Whoever won is not clear, but by 1562 Bushmead Priory and much of its estate had been sold to the Gerys family.

Sir John served as sheriff for Bedfordshire and Buckinghamshire (1542-3) and as MP for Bedfordshire (1542 and again in 1553 and 1558). In 1544 he purchased Eastcotts Manor. In 1546 he was Commissioner of the Musters and his twelve-year-old son may well have been with him at inspection time. In Gascoigne's novel *The Adventures of Master F.J.* the narrator half-apologises for the inadequacies of a poem by the hero, saying "yet have I seen much worse pass the musters, yea and where both the Lieutenant and Provost Marshall were men of ripe judgement". 1546 was also the year that Sir John Gascoigne became a Justice of the Peace, continuing as one until his death. He served as an almoner at the coronations of Edward VI and Mary.[11]

*

The education of a Tudor child was intensive and hard, and George Gascoigne was raised to be a gentleman in a society that put a high value on learning, languages and books. There was no conventional age for starting school (assuming that a child went to one at all) and continuous education between the ages of five and eighteen was unusual.

The first thing children learned was how to say their prayers. Next came the alphabet. The learning of the English language began with the Christ's Cross row – a cross-shaped piece of wood with the letters of the alphabet on. In his later career as a writer Gascoigne was to reveal an acute sensitivity to the charge that individual letters can carry. One of his finest poems is a brilliantly sustained exercise in playful puns on letters and the words that they might or might not suggest.[12] Similarly, in *The Adventures of Master F.J.*, the meaning of the letters "F.J.", as well as other initials, is teasingly withheld from the reader. The letters of the alphabet are associated with both concealment and revelation. From a rudimentary understanding of language the child moved on to spelling exercises, simple story books and the Bible.

For the sons of skilled artisans, shopkeepers and professionals, the next step would be attendance at a grammar school. Two years before his death Gascoigne remembered his own early education:

> My Schoolemaster which taught me Grammer, woulde always say that some schollers he woonne to studie by strypes, some other by fayre meanes, some by promises, some other by praises, some by vainglorie, and some by verie shame. But I never heard him repent him that ever he had persuaded any scholler to become studious, in what sort soever it were that hee woonne him.[13]

Though Gascoigne never names his teacher, the memory seems to be a fond one. It is not clear which method the young Gascoigne required – "strypes" and beating or "fayre meanes". Nor is it clear whether "Schoolemaster" means a classroom teacher. It is unlikely that the poet ever attended a grammar school. The probability is that he was educated at home, by private tutors. Interestingly, a document has survived which states: "For the upbringing of Sir John's s. John Gascoigne 20 marks are to be paid to Lewes Mordaunt & Peter Grey esqs. And Robt. Webb gent."[14] A lot hinges on what "upbringing" means. The probability is that it is used here in the secondary sense of "education", in which case it refers to three private tutors brought in to educate John Gascoigne, presumably at his home, Cardington Manor. But it is just possible that it indicates that John Gascoigne was sent away from home, to lodge and be educated at the home of a gentleman, probably with other boys of his age and social class.

Whatever arrangement was made for John was very probably also made for his older brother, George. Wherever the brothers were taught, the educational regime is likely to have been rigorous, involving a day that started at six or seven in the morning and went on until late afternoon. After mastering reading, the Tudor child was taught writing and arithmetic. Next came Latin, which began with vocabulary and grammar before moving on to composition and rhetoric. The ability to speak and to write Latin was essential for anyone who aspired to pursue a career in law, religion or state service. It was a language still widely used in its written form and was the common language of the European intelligentsia.

With a grounding in Latin the child then became acquainted with such writers as Virgil, Ovid, Cicero and Horace. Once fluent in Latin, a well educated child could expect to learn at least one continental language. In later life, George Gascoigne would demonstrate a more than adequate grasp of French and Italian. In C. T. Prouty's opinion, Italian was "Gascoigne's best [foreign language], both in its use of idiom and in fluency. However, [his] Latin and…French reveal a certain degree of skill, indicating that Gascoigne had a good knowledge of both."[15]

Gascoigne's education was not entirely formal. As a child (and future playwright) he was almost certainly taken to see popular theatre, as it then existed. One of his poems seems to express his memories of the old drama.[16] He talks of a stage being "staked out", indicating an outdoor performance, perhaps in a Bedford square or on the village green at Cardington or one of the other local villages such as Elstow.

> First Cayphas plays the priest, and Herod sits as king,
> Pilate the Judge, Judas the Juror verdict in doth bring.

The description is of the trial of Christ, from one of the old mystery plays. The memory then shifts to a morality play:

> Vain tattling plays the vice, well clad in rich array,
> And poor Tom Troth is laughed to scorn, with garments nothing gay;
> The woman wantonness, she comes with ticing train,
> Pride in her pocket plays bo-peep, and bawdry in her brain.
> Her handmaids be deceit, danger and dalliance,
> Riot and Revel follow her, they be of her alliance:
> Next these comes in Simme Swash, to see what stir they keep.

This is theatre as one-dimensional as a cartoon, with simplistic contrasts between good and bad, underlined by costume. "Simme Swash" is a braggart. This is the same imaginative world as Bunyan's. Fine clothing and wealth are associated with rottenness. The simple, honest poor are faced by temptation and corruption.

Finally, there seems to be a memory of travelling players from the earliest phase of Tudor commercial theatre. The image is of a botched musical performance following on from a comedy which has fallen flat:

> To pack the pageant up, comes Sorrow with a song;
> He says these jests can get no groats, all this gear go'th wrong:
> First pride without cause why, he sings the treble part,
> The mean he mumbles out of tune, for lack of life and heart:
> Cost lost, the counter tenor chanteth on apace,
> Thus all in discords stands the clef, and beggary sings the bass.
> The players loose their pains, where so few pence are stirring,
> Their garments wear for lack of gains and fret for lack of furring.

"Lack of furring" might simply signal the players' poverty. Equally it might indicate lack of patronage. To have a Lord as one's patron meant a livery and the chance to perform indoors, before a socially important audience. Such a patron brought respectability and protection.

As the son of an affluent knight with an extensive estate, Gascoigne was also educated in those other attributes of a gentleman – how to ride a horse, how to hunt on horseback, how to fight with a sword. He would have been taught how to use both a bow and cross-bow. Less typically, perhaps, he also seems to have learned how to use some of the rudimentary firearms of the period. He also learned the skills of a pursuit which was massively popular in the sixteenth century, but which is now remote from ordinary life, namely falconry. Gascoigne's writing is full of allusions to the sport, just as Shakespeare's is.

A part of Gascoigne always remained a country boy. When, many years later, the poet appealed to a hostile board of religious censors, he used farming metaphors to make the point that the good in his writing was far greater than the bad:

> I could aswell [*sic*] sowe good graine, as graynes or draffe. And I thought not meete (being intermingled as they were) to cast away a whole bushel of good seede, for two or three graynes of Darnell or Cockle.[17]

A bushel was a measure containing eight gallons (around 36 litres) and "graynes" were the husks or remains of malt after brewing or of any grain after distillation; "draffe" meant the lees or dregs, especially of malt after the liquor had been drawn off. Draffe was used to feed pigs and cows. "Darnell" is grass, "Cockle" a weed.

After the scandal of *A Hundreth Sundrie Flowres*, he attempted to rehabilitate his reputation by portraying himself in the image of a simple countryman: "I haue loytred (my lorde) I confesse, I haue lien streaking me (like a lubber) when the sunne did shine, and now I striue al in vaine to loade the carte when it raineth."[18] But Gascoigne's tone was not always so genial. In an early poem, probably written when he was associating with other literary sophisticates in the metropolis, he wrote contemptuously of

>country louts, which count none other praise
>But grease a sheep and learn to serve the swine.[19]

Plate 8. Cardington Manor in the early twentieth century, showing the Tudor wing and twist chimney.

Plate 9. The site of Cardington Manor today.

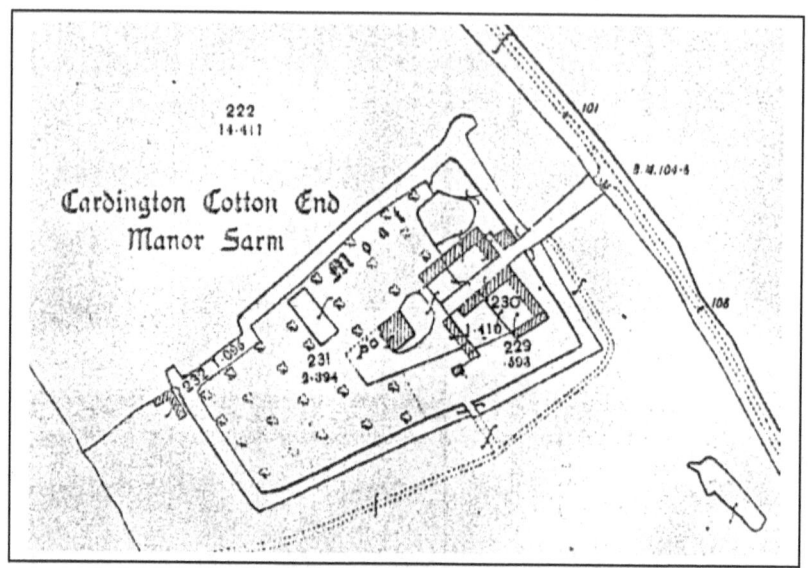

Plate 10. A nineteenth-century plan of Cardington Manor, showing the moat fish ponds and barns, with the Tudor manor house in the lower right-hand corner.

Plate 11. The weed-choked moat at the Cardington Manor site today.

3: Cambridge

The year 1547 was possibly the most important of Gascoigne's adolescence. Coincidentally, in January, in London, a seminal figure in the history of English poetry was put on trial for treason. This was Henry Howard, the Earl of Surrey. But it was not his writing which had got him into trouble but his ambition. Surrey was a member of the leading Catholic family in England and the heir of the Duke of Norfolk. One contemporary called him "the most foolish proud boy that is in England".[1] His most recent biographer notes that though he was "witty, urbane, innovative, generous, gracious and gentle" he was also "petulant, brutish, reactionary, vain, haughty and uncompromising".[2] When he displayed a coat of arms showing in the first quarter of the design the royal arms of Edward the Confessor he was almost exactly duplicating the arms of the Prince of Wales. The defence that silver labels distinguished Surrey's arms from those of the heir to the throne was unconvincing. By hinting at his own claim to the throne Surrey was playing with fire and Henry VIII, whose end was near, was in no mood to permit such provocative gestures. Surrey was found guilty of treason and beheaded on Tower Hill on 19 January 1547.

At the time of his death Surrey's writing was unknown outside a tiny aristocratic circle. Surrey was an astonishing innovator who wrote some of the finest early English sonnets in a clear straightforward diction which is still readily accessible today. He also invented the poetic metre which has come to be known as "blank verse". But though he would later be inspired by the Earl's writing, George Gascoigne, then aged about twelve, would have known little or nothing of Surrey and his execution.

The great national event was the death of the king, which was officially announced on 31 January 1547. Edward Seymour was nominated as Lord Protector of the new king, his nephew, who was just a boy. This impacted on the household of Cardington Manor because it meant that once again a Gascoigne was required to attend a royal coronation. Sir John duly made the journey to London and performed his role as almoner at the coronation of Edward VI. Although this can only be a matter of speculation, it seems plausible that Sir John would have taken his oldest son and heir with him to witness such an important occasion. On 19 February the long procession made its way from the Tower of London to Westminster – a scene captured in a much-reproduced painting in the National Portrait Gallery. The following day the coronation took place at Westminster Abbey.

*

George Gascoigne's father was not the only person to make a long journey from home that year. Gascoigne's grandmother Lady Joan Scargill died at Thorpe

Hall and his mother Margaret must have made the long journey north to Yorkshire to attend her funeral and burial in Whitkirk church. The death resulted in a bitter quarrel between the two sisters and co-heiresses, triggered by who was to take possession of a gold casting bottle. Margaret Gascoigne seems to have come out best from the complicated legal dispute which followed. Apart from getting the bottle she also inherited Thorpe Hall and substantial land in the area.³

Margaret Gascoigne may have taken her son George with her to Whitkirk. Alternatively, he may himself have been away at the time. At some point in his adolescence Gascoigne attended Cambridge University, and the likeliest time for this to have occurred is 1547-8. In writings from the end of his life, Gascoigne made two glancing references to having once been a student at Cambridge. In his introduction to "Hemetes the Heremyte" he apologised for his Latin (which was in fact perfectly fluent) with a self-deprecating reference to "such lattyn as I forgatt att Cantabridge". In his long satirical poem *The Steel Glass* (1576) he wrote

> Pray for the nources of our noble realm,   [nurses]
> I mean the worthy universities,
> (And Cantabridge, that have the dignity,
> Whereof I was, unworthy member once)
> That they bring up their babes in decent wise⁴

The grammar is ambiguous. Did Gascoigne mean "the worthy universities" have "the dignity" (meaning merit and estimation) or just Cantabridge (Cambridge University)? At this time there were only two universities, and Gascoigne doesn't mention the other one. To omit all mention of the word "Oxford" is, of course, just what one might expect from a Cambridge man. Even in the sixteenth century there was competition between the two institutions, as well as quite distinct differences in religious affiliation and educational method. Oxford tended to be Catholic, whereas Cambridge was more Protestant (though neither term would have been in use in quite this way in the 1540s). Cambridge was associated with the "new learning" and Gascoigne's time at Cambridge probably briefly overlapped with that of the famous Cambridge humanist, Roger Ascham, who left the university in 1548 to tutor the teenage Princess Elizabeth. Ascham gave public courses on mathematics, Greek and dialectic; in 1540 he became reader in Greek. Ascham's classic humanist text *The Scholemaster* appeared posthumously in 1570 and went through four more editions in the next two decades. Gascoigne may conceivably have known his earlier book on archery, *Toxophilus* (1545). The paths of the two men probably crossed on a number of occasions – at one point they were practically neighbours in Walthamstow – but there is no evidence of any friendship between them. Ascham was some twenty years older than Gascoigne and though both men wrote poetry they were temperamentally very different.

No record of Gascoigne having been at Cambridge exists but this in itself is neither unusual nor surprising. He never graduated and was there probably at most for only two years, perhaps less. Being sent to university was essentially a rite of passage for a young gentleman and there were many like Gascoigne who went there only briefly in their mid-teens and left without a degree. (Nicholas and Nathaniel Bacon, the sons of Sir Nicholas Bacon, Lord Keeper of the Great Seal of England, attended Trinity College, Cambridge, for less than a year, in 1561.)

A Bachelor's course of study took four years, and completing a Master's degree took a full seven years. Young gentlemen were only partly there to complete their education. They were also there to network. In a predominantly rural nation of fragmented and isolated towns and villages it was necessary for the sons of the ruling class to go to particular centres – Oxford, Cambridge, the London Inns of Court – in order to meet others like themselves and to establish the connections which might prove valuable in their later careers. By the period of Gascoigne's admission they were also there to have a good time, and complaints began to grow that poor hard-working students were increasingly being excluded in favour of the dissolute and idle sons of the gentry.

It's unlikely that the poet idled away his days at Cambridge. Gascoigne provided one important clue to his time as a student there. In his long poem *The fruites of Warre* he makes a glancing reference to "*Nevynsone* my master", remarking "by his help I learning first embraced".[5] Gascoigne evidently meant Stephen Nevynson, who was tutor at Christ's College from around 1544 to 1547, and at Trinity College, 1547-8. Gascoigne would have been too young to attend Christ's when Nevynson was there, but Trinity College is a much more credible possibility (indeed, Trinity today unhesitatingly claims Gascoigne as one of its alumni).

On the face of it, Cambridge was a surprising choice. Gascoigne's father's religious sympathies were very much with the unreformed church, and Oxford would have supplied a more congenial environment. Probably material factors influenced the choice. In 1537, just before the Dissolution, Newnham Priory leased Fenlake Barns and the "parsonage" or great tithes to Sir William Gascoigne. After the dissolution of the monasteries, Fenlake Barns, the great tithes and the advowson of Cardington church passed to Trinity College, Cambridge. This began a long association between the College and the parish, and, initially at least, between the College and the Gascoigne family. "Trinity House" in modern Cardington was once the vicarage and the name commemorates the connection. Trinity College was Henry VIII's foundation at Cambridge and the destruction of the religious houses resulted in it being showered with lands and property. In Bedfordshire it was given property at

Roxton and Stotfold, as well as several rectories and advowsons, such as Great Barford, Cardington, Eaton Bray, Keysoe and Felmersham. It's also an intriguing coincidence that after the dissolution the living of Whitkirk Church was also granted to Trinity College, Cambridge. Evidently there were strong associations between Trinity College, Sir John Gascoigne and Lady Margaret, making it a natural place to send their son and heir George.

If Gascoigne went to Trinity College in 1547 he was among its very first students. The royal college was only founded in December 1546. It incorporated a number of earlier and monastic foundations, including the very first Cambridge college, Michaelhouse, and King's Hall. The buildings of the Franciscans were demolished and several hostels extinguished. Trinity College is sometimes described as Henry VIII's best monument. There were then twelve other colleges. Trinity College is now Cambridge's largest college but in 1547 both the college and the town were very different from today. Nevile's Court and the Great Court and fountain at Trinity were all built later.

College life could be quite austere. In 1550 the preacher Thomas Lever described the bleak conditions of poor Cambridge scholars, who rose between 4 a.m. and 5 a.m., prayed until 6 a.m., studied or attended lectures 6 a.m. – 10 a.m., then dined on "a penny piece of beef amongst four, having a few porridge made of the broth of the same beef, with salt and oatmeal, and nothing else". They then taught or studied until 5 p.m., when they ate a supper little better than their earlier meal.

> Immediately after the which, they go either to reasoning in problems or unto some other study, until it be nine or ten of the clock, and those being without fire are fain to walk or run up and down half an hour, to get a heat on their feet when they go to bed.[6]

Gascoigne's existence is unlikely to have been as dispiriting as that. He probably lived well and may even have shared living quarters with his tutor, as many students did. Gascoigne's "master" Stephen Nevynson was born in the late 1520s and was a committed Protestant. Soon he was to become an important member of Archbishop Thomas Cranmer's household. With the accession of Edward VI these were exciting times for reformers. At the end of January 1548 candlemass candles, Ash Wednesday ashes and Palm Sunday palms were banned, and the following month the Privy Council ordered that all images be removed from churches. The old mass was replaced by Anglican "Holy Communion". These reforms climaxed in the 1549 prayer book.

Gascoigne once briefly alluded to his time at Cambridge as one in which he "shot…to hit Philosophy"[7] and in *The Steel Glass* (written some 30 years after his student years) he piously expressed the hope that the universities continued to teach in a responsible and proper way:

> That Philosophy smell no secret smoke,
> Which Magic makes, in wicked mysteries:
> That Logic leap not over every stile
> Before he come a furlong near the hedge,
> With curious *quids* to maintain argument.[8]

The critique of pedantry and what we would now call logic-chopping is clear enough, but what did Gascoigne mean by "philosophy"? Probably he was in part referring to the writings and ideas of Aristotle. In another poem Gascoigne explained that he had virtuously tried to lead his life "by Aristotle's rule".[9]

A flavour of the classical writers Gascoigne might have encountered at Cambridge is provided by the experience of Anthony and Francis Bacon at Trinity College three decades later. As well as Aristotle their studies included Plato and Cicero, Sallust's Roman History, Livy's History of Rome, Caesar's Commentaries, the Orations of Demosthenes and Homer's *Iliad*. Roger Ascham believed that Plato was the greatest philosopher of all and that almost all learning of value was written in Greek, with the major exception of Cicero. His favourite author, however, was Herodotus.

Apart from philosophy, the essential subjects which Gascoigne studied at Cambridge are likely to have been rhetoric and logic. *The Steel Glass* goes on to inventory other subjects on the syllabus.

Gascoigne prays

> That Sophistry do not deceive itself,
> That Cosmography keep his compass well,
> And such as be Historiographers
> Trust not too much in every tattling tongue,
> Nor blinded be by partiality;
> That Physick thrive not over fast by murder:
> The Numbring men, in all their evens and odds
> Do not forget that only Unity
> Unmeasurable, infinite, and one;
> That Geometry measure not so long
> Til all their measures out of measure be:
> That Music with his heavenly harmony
> Do not allure a heavenly mind from heaven,
> Nor set men's thoughts in worldly melody,
> Til heavenly Hierarchies be quite forgot;
> That Rhetoric learn not to over-reach:
> That Poetry presume not for to preach
> And bite men's faults with Satire's corrosives
> Yet pamper up her own with poultices:

> Or that she dote not upon Erato
> Which should invoke the good Caliope;
> That Astrology look not over high
> And light meanwhile in every puddled pit;
> That Grammar grudge not at our English tongue
> Because it stands by *monosyllaba*
> And cannot be declined as others are.
> Pray thus my priests for universities
> And if I have forgotten any Art
> Which hath been taught, or exercised there,
> Pray you to God the good be not abused
> With glorious show of overloading skill.

It seems unlikely that Gascoigne crammed all these subjects into his one or two years at Cambridge. This passage includes his current interests in 1576 – cosmography and a poetic style that treasured the use of monosyllables and a vigorous vernacular English. The pious note of caution he sounds in relation to the subversive possibilities of mathematics and geometry and the sensuous temptations of music is clearly pitched at the devout Protestant sensibilities of his current patron, Lord Grey of Wilton. When he wrote these lines Gascoigne was anxious to project himself as a repentant sinner, a pose which sometimes wears perilously thin. With cheerful inconsistency, he condemns didactic and satirical verse in a long poem which is both didactic and satirical.

Apart from improving his knowledge of Greek and Roman literature, Cambridge University probably had two important influences on Gascoigne as a writer. Firstly, the humanism associated with Cambridge figures like Roger Ascham, Sir John Cheke and Thomas Wilson promoted the ideal of clear, uncluttered English. It's evident from Gascoigne's essay on prosody, *Certayne notes of Instruction concerning the making of verse or ryme in English*, that this was something Gascoigne absorbed, practised and was himself keen to campaign for. Cheke wrote that he was "of this opinion, that our own tongue should be written clean and pure, unmixed and unmangled with borrowing of other tongues".[10] This echoed Ascham's assertion in the preface to *Toxophilus* that anyone who wanted to write well "must follow this counsel of Aristotle, to speak as the common people do… Many English writers have not done so, but using strange words, as Latin, French, and Italian, do make all things dark and hard."[11]

Secondly, there was the personal impact of Stephen Nevynson on Gascoigne's religious beliefs. Gascoigne's father, though a loyal servant of the Crown, was hostile to the reformation. He clung obstinately to the old faith and declined to adjust his beliefs to conform to those of the Church of England. Nevynson on the other hand was an ardent evangelical and reformer. He later became a valued member of the household of Thomas Cranmer and may have been responsible for publishing some of Cranmer's notebooks under the title *A Confutation of Unwritten Verities* (c. 1556). Nevynson is also the likely author of the anonymous "Life and death of Thomas Cranmer, late Archbishop of Canterbury". His dedication to the Protestant cause was well rewarded when Elizabeth I came to the throne; his appointments included Chancellor of the diocese of Norwich and various ecclesiastical offices in the Canterbury diocese.

If any one person can be held responsible for converting George Gascoigne to the reformed church it was surely Nevynson. Two poems in particular signify Gascoigne's Protestant sympathies (or to put it another way, his less than total commitment to the Catholic church). "Gascoigne's *De profundis*" is a loose, much-expanded translation of Psalm 130. In the closing lines of the final stanza Gascoigne writes:

> He will appease our discord and debate,
> He will soon save, though we repent us late.
> He will be ours if we continue His,
> He will bring bale to joy and perfect bliss.　　　　[transform evil]
> He will redeem the flock of his elect,
> From all that is
> Or was amiss
> Since Abraham's heirs did first his Laws reject.[12]

The explosive word in those lines is "elect". Verse eight of Psalm 130 simply reads (in the modern Bible): "And he shall redeem Israel from all his iniquities". Gascoigne's version retains that specific sense but expands it to include all humanity. But to say that the "elect" would be redeemed immediately contradicts that all-inclusiveness. The concept of the "elect" derived from the great reformation theologian Calvin (1509-64), whose power base was the city of Geneva. Calvin argued that Christ died on the cross not for all mankind but only for the elect. Some people were pre-destined to be saved; others to face a future of eternal damnation. The way of distinguishing the saved from the damned was faith in Christ, which was granted to the elect and refused to others. However, no one could really know if they were elect or not. Christian behaviour was no guarantee of election. All one could do was live in hope. In Owen Chadwick's words, "the moral and devotional power in the doctrine of election was mighty...For a hundred years [the Calvinists] were the most potent religious force in Protestantism."[13]

The Calvinist flavour of Gascoigne's verse would not have pleased his father. However, Sir John is unlikely ever to have seen the manuscript and the poem was not published until after his death. The same can be said for Gascoigne's poem of advice to his friend Bartholomew Withypoll, which cautions against three things beginning with the letter P: poison, pride and last of all that "double *P*" that "with a dash it spelleth Papistry, / A parlous *P*, and woorse than both the rest".[14] At the time this poem was written Gascoigne had strong reasons for wanting to flash his Protestant credentials, but there is no real reason to disbelieve that his own religious beliefs were closer to those of the reformed church than to Catholicism. The only obvious person in Gascoigne's life likely to have effected that radical shift in allegiance away from the religion of his upbringing is Stephen Nevynson.

The depth of Gascoigne's religious belief, however, is a very open question. The immediate impact of Nevynson may well have been intoxicating but probably wore off when the poet left Cambridge and came under other influences. A later poem, in which Gascoigne implicitly mocked Cranmer's martyrdom, would have shocked, angered and disappointed Nevynson, had he ever seen it.

Gascoigne's flexibility in religion was a pragmatic instinct in a nation where the official religion lurched from one extreme to the other. The impact of those revolutionary changes being imposed on the English church was reflected in widespread disorder across southern England in 1549. This was quite possibly the year that Gascoigne left Trinity College and returned to Cardington Manor to complete his upbringing as a country gentleman. On 14 October Somerset's Protectorship was revoked and he was committed to the Tower. He was later released but re-arrested on a charge of treason in 1551 and executed on 22 January 1552. During the remaining years of Edward's rule the reform programme continued, with revisions of canon law, changes to the prayer book and the formation of a statement of doctrine. All this came to a sudden end when Edward suddenly died on 6 July 1553 and Mary came to the throne. No one at that stage appreciated her depth of commitment to the papacy. Gascoigne, who would later serve in one of her Parliaments, was then about nineteen years old.

4: "A lady once did ask…"

In Gascoigne's lifetime everything to do with language and the book was in a state of flux. There was no consensus; no fixed rules. Dictionaries barely existed; spelling was phonetically based and very variable, including that of names. Punctuation was arbitrary, minimalist and often introduced by the printer, not the author. The modern paperback edition of Gascoigne's novel *The Adventures of Master F.J.* contains paragraphs but few of these exist in the original text, much of which consists of slabs of unbroken prose.

We do not know when Gascoigne first began writing verse but if it was as a teenager then Chaucer was the obvious model to admire and imitate. Gascoigne acknowledged two "masters". One was "Nevynson", the other "my master *Chaucer*".[1] Chaucer's influence, like Nevynson's, is likely to have been an early one. By the fifteenth century Chaucer was an established classic and many poets described him as their "master". William Caxton's edition of *The Canterbury Tales* was one of the very earliest works to be printed in England. In the sixteenth century Chaucer's status soared even higher. A canopied tomb was erected in Westminster Abbey, possibly as late as 1555. This may have been in response to a major cultural event: the publication in 1532 by William Thynne of *Geoffrey Chaucer: The Works*. It was the first complete edition of Chaucer's poetry and as Helen Cooper has observed, its title was provocative: "'works' was the English equivalent of the Latin *Opera*, and 'opera' was reserved for Classical authors – Aristotle or Virgil, for instance. To call a volume *Works* was making a great claim for it."[2] Its success was testified by the reprints of 1542 and 1561. Whoever was responsible for putting together an edition of Gascoigne's work after his death seems to have been keen to put him in the same elevated realms as the poet he so much admired, for in 1587 there appeared *The Whole woorkes of George Gascoigne Esquyre*. Edmund Spenser later unconvincingly claimed he was Chaucer's heir; Michael Schmidt argues that Spenser "read him somehow, perhaps inspired by Gascoigne's cogent enthusiasm".[3]

Chaucer provocatively made a point of writing in an unfashionable vernacular language, asserting at the start of *Anelida and Arcite* that he proposed "in Englyssh to endyte / This olde storie, in Latyn which I fynde, / Of queen Anelida and fals Arcite".[4] This was a radical act at a time when court culture was dominated by French, or at best Anglo-French. But Chaucer was also a poet of enormous ambition. His output was prodigious and he consciously aligned himself with the tradition of Virgil, Ovid, Homer and other classic writers.

Gascoigne probably knew all Chaucer except for his "Retraction". In his pioneering essay on prosody, *Certayne notes of Instruction concerning the making of verse or ryme in English,* Gascoigne was effusive in his praises of "my master *Chaucer*", "our father *Chaucer*" and "our Mayster and Father

Chaucer". He mentions "his Canterburie tales, and...divers other delectable and light enterprises". That word "delectable" occurs again in the preamble to one of Gascoigne's longest poems, in which he invites the reader to "receive the delectable historie of sundry adventures passed by Dan Bartholmew of Bathe". The title probably alludes to Chaucer's tale of the Wife of Bath. When Gascoigne recycled the tale of Antony and Cleopatra in "In praise of a gentlewoman who though she were not very fair, yet was as hard favoured as might be" his source was Chaucer's *Legend of Good Women*.[5] But though Chaucer's presence as an influence on Gascoigne's writing is not in doubt it was complicated by other, probably later influences.

Gascoigne's debt to Chaucer was a mixed blessing. Though the Tudor poet may not have entirely grasped it, much of Chaucer's language was rapidly becoming obsolete, both in grammar and vocabulary. The French-influenced placing of attributive adjectives after the nouns they qualified ("his shoures soote" [his showers sweet]) would, like numerous other features of Chaucer's grammar, soon come to seem wooden and archaic. At the moment of its greatest cultural supremacy Chaucer's writing was simultaneously imploding. *The Canterbury Tales* and the other texts would retain their status as classics of English literature but would henceforward be doomed to live on in a linguistic ghetto. Chaucer's stylish, everyday English was rapidly becoming obscure and unreadable and would eventually require an apparatus of scholarly annotation and a glossary to return it to comprehensibility. Today, the 744 pages of text in the standard modern Riverside edition of Chaucer's works require an additional 532 pages of notes. The language of *The Canterbury Tales* – Middle English – was being displaced by a different kind of English – Modern English – which was to endure for more than four and a half centuries and would allow Gascoigne and Shakespeare to remain readable in a way that Chaucer no longer is. As Park Honan has put it, by the time Shakespeare was a boy at school (which coincided with the end of Gascoigne's life) "the meandering, fuzzy, verbose English language [was] so unfixed and variable, so quickly changing that Chaucer was almost unintelligible after 200 years".[6]

Converting Tudor prose and verse into modern English is more or less inevitable if the writing is to remain accessible to today's readers but ideally one should always contrast the modern version with the original and be aware of what has been lost. The pronunciation of Elizabethan English was far more emphatic and accented than standard modern English, an aspect which is lost to us when a Tudor text is translated into modern English. This point has been eloquently made by Tom Paulin in a discussion of Shakespeare's sonnet 19, in particular line 4. In the original 1609 Quarto edition this line is printed as "And burne the long liu'd Phænix in her blood". In modern editions it appears as "And burn the long-lived phoenix in her blood". Paulin comments:

Reading the Quarto text with its furred type, I catch an accent which I once heard many years ago reproduced in a television documentary where John Barton coached members of the RSC in the "correct" pronunciation of Shakespearean English: the accent sounded like a mixture of the Ambridge, Birmingham and Ulster accents. In 19, we hear not "phoenix" but *Phaenix*, not "heinous" but *hainous*, not "old" but *ould*. Elsewhere there are other sounds still current in Ulster – *cowld* for "cold", *hower* for "hour" – and words such as *brave* for "fine, good, bold, nonchalant", or *miching* for "playing truant". Hearing that deep guttural accent – an accent made deeper by the collied print of the Quarto text – I register the fourth line like this: "And barn the lane-liv'd Phayinix in har bludd".

Reading the modernised equivalent beside it – "And burn the long-lived Phoenix in her blood" – is rather like emerging onto a trim lawn where tea and cucumber sandwiches are being served.[7]

Gascoigne's language is no different. On the night of its first performance, Gascoigne almost certainly himself spoke the prologue to his play *Supposes*. But when he reached the point where he described the role of substitution and mistaken identity in the play, including that of "the stranger for a well knowen friend", we lose the sense of that rich, rolling, drawn-out pronunciation if we modernise "knowen", shortening it to a monosyllabic "known". Yet that loss of the aural dimension of Tudor English is almost inevitable, as almost all editions of Shakespeare tacitly concede. Only a couple of modern editions of *Shakespeare's Sonnets* supply the luxury of the original text alongside its translation into modern English spelling and punctuation.

When Gascoigne writes "and taught him what to doo"[8] the instinct to modernize the spelling of the final word is irresistible. The Elizabethan spelling, which may indicate that the word was pronounced with a more emphatic drawl than its terser modern version, is too visually distracting. It looks wrong and in the end it seems better to translate the language as gently and delicately as possible into contemporary English so as to transmit as clearly as possible the sense of the original, rather than retain the lumpy, difficult original text in an attempt to evoke a lost and irretrievable mode of pronunciation. That said, each word, line and paragraph has to be judged on its own merits. Sometimes it is essential to retain the original spelling in order to capture the special sense or emphasis of the original.

Modern conventions of language, punctuation, spelling and pronunciation and even our accepted ideas of how authors should present their writing are inventions of a different world to Gascoigne's. *A Hundreth Sundrie Flowres* did not so much challenge an existing orthodoxy as put in a bid for how creative writing should appear in book format. From a modern perspective it resembles an anthology or a collected works more than a first book, and it has come to seem an oddity in the history of English creative writing. But that is not how it appeared to contemporaries and the disturbance which the book caused was not related to its form but its content. Subsequent writers established themselves as poets, or dramatists, or novelists, and very occasionally as poets and dramatists but rarely as all three. Convention usually required concentration on one genre only. Even when an author was skilled at poetry and drama it became the norm that his writing was published separately; even Shakespeare's plays have always been published detached from his poetry. In 1573 Gascoigne's publication of two plays, a novella and a collection of poems in a single volume was radically original rather than eccentric. It only came to seem eccentric in retrospect, when conventions about what a book should be developed into publishing and cultural orthodoxy.

Similarly the language in which men (and very rarely, women) wrote was bubbling and seething with possibility in a way which is not easy to recapture after almost five centuries. Shakespeare, famously, created new words – but like the format of *A Hundreth Sundrie Flowres* they did not always catch on. When Othello stoutly denies the possibility of him ever being jealous – "Exchange me for a goat / When I shall turn the business of my soul / To such exsufflicate and blown surmises / Matching thy inference" (III.iii.182-4) – no editor of the play really knows precisely what Shakespeare meant by "exsufflicate". This is the only time the word appears in the English language. Meaning is speculative ("swollen"? "puffed out"? "spat out"? "unsubstantial?" "contemptible"? "abominable"?), derived entirely from context and the imaginative possibilities of the word's sound to a modern ear.

Others, too, were reinventing English. Sir Thomas Elyot in *The Boke Named the Governour* (1531) coined several duds: "propice" (suitable), "illecebrous" (enticing), "demulced" (coaxed) and "adminiculation" (aid). Rather more illecebrous were Ralph Lever's strangely Orwellian coinages – "endsay" for "conclusion" and "saywhat" for "definition". But they, too, fizzled out. Not all did. Elyot decided "to usurp a Latin word" for identifying "an excellent virtue where unto we lack a name in English". That word was *maturity*. Other new words seemed ridiculuous to contemporaries but have endured into modern everyday use (Ben Jonson jeered at such self-evidently preposterous newfangled words as "spurious" and "strenuous"). But the person who had most impact on the English language as we know it today was surely William Tyndale. His revolutionary translations of the Bible into English were effectively plagiarised for the King James Bible. Modern analysis has shown that only 2.8 per of the King James version of the New Testament was original and that a staggering 83.7 per cent was taken straight from Tyndale.[9] Similarly, the King James versions of the books of the Old Testament that Tyndale translated are 75.7 per cent his work. Essentially, Tyndale was responsible for the wording of the single most influential book in English culture in the centuries that followed. So many phrases that we take for granted – "an eye for an eye, a tooth for a tooth", "the spirit is willing, but the flesh is weak", "blessed are the peacemakers", "not one jot or tittle" – are Tyndale's words. But language itself was highly politicised in the sixteenth century. Tyndale's punishment for tampering with the hegemony of the established church was to be burned at the stake. As Gascoigne himself was to learn, albeit from a very different perspective and without such terrible consequences, words were highly charged objects. It was a century when there was no one so easily provoked into intolerant rage by the printed word as a senior churchman.

A statistical sampling of words in use in 1600 has revealed that 39 per cent had entered the language after 1500.[10] This rapid shift away from the language of Chaucer is registered in Gascoigne's poem "A Riddle":[11]

> A lady once did ask of me
> This pretty thing in privetie:
> Good sir (quod she), fain would I crave
> One thing which you yourself not have,
> Nor never had yet in times past,
> Nor never shall while life doth last,
> And if you seek to find it out
> You loose your labour out of doubt:
> Yet if you love me as you say,
> Then give it me, for sure you may.

This is a poem in early modern English with two Middle English words lodged inside it. But it remains perfectly comprehensible today in spite of "privetie" and "quod", and despite three instances of a reversal of conventional word ordering ("fain would I crave", "which you your self not have", "Nor never had yet"). "Privetie" ("secret") remains close enough to "private" for the sense to be accurately guessed by a modern reader, and "quod" ("said") is reminiscent of its better-known later archaic variant "quoth", as well as its meaning being reasonably obvious from the context.

Once the riddle is solved the double entendre present in this poem becomes fairly straightforward. What the woman is asking for is the man's death – "death" in the common Elizabethan slang sense of detumescence. What she is asking for is sex: the last line's "give it me" means "fuck me". The man's "labour" alludes to copulation – the physical effort involved in sexual intercourse – and the "pretty thing" she asks for is his penis. What's more she wants "This pretty thing in privetie" – in other words "This penis in [her] cunt" (the modern phrase "private parts" retaining the Middle English meaning of "privetie" as "hidden part" or "genitals").

Elsewhere the Middle English heritage is more problematic and is what makes some aspects of Gascoigne's writing difficult for modern readers. Partly it is a simple matter of words changing their meaning. The word "dame" for "woman" enjoyed a brief revival in the hard-boiled detective fiction of the 1930s and 1940s associated with Dashiell Hammett and Raymond Chandler but nowadays is only used in Britain for comic figures in Christmas pantomimes or as a minor title in the government's annual honours list. Some Middle English words can perhaps just about be guessed at ("wot" for "know"). But others are simply incomprehensible without the aid of a glossary: "yfeere" ("together"), "ywis" ("surely"), "no boot" ("no use"), "trowe" ("believe").

This turbulent transition from the old and the new is perfectly captured in a single stanza of Gascoigne's, from the end of *The Adventures of Master F.J.*

And if I did, what then?
Are you aggrieved therefore?
The sea hath fish for every man,
And what would you have more?

Thus did my mistress once
Amaze my mind with doubt
And popt a question for the nonce
To beat my brains about.[12]

These are the first two stanzas of a six-stanza poem. With the exception of the seventh line the whole poem reads perfectly straightforwardly to the modern eye (even in the original Elizabethan English). But "popt a question for the nonce" now seems jarringly archaic. Partly this is because of the historic change in the meaning and associations of the verb "to pop". In the sixteenth century it meant "to put" or "to move suddenly" – a sense which lingers in the slang phrase associated with marriage proposals ("popped the question"). The other sense of an abrupt, explosive noise was only just entering the language and to modern ears is irredeemably associated with such trifles as balloons and popcorn. No modern poet or novelist describing a serious moment of high tension between two quarrelling lovers would ever write "and then she popped a question that amazed him".

The "hath" of line three is archaic but acceptably so, its use softened for twenty-first-century readers from cultural familiarity with the language of Shakespeare's plays. But "for the nonce" is an archaism which grates on the modern ear. In Middle English it had a multiplicity of meanings, any of which is appropriate to Gascoigne's usage: "then" or "at that time" or "for the occasion" or "indeed" or "purposefully". "For the nonce" occurs on seven occasions in Chaucer's works ("I kan a noble tale for the nones", boasts the drunken miller [*The Miller's Prologue*, 3126]). It is found twice in *Troilus and Criseyde* and the one closest in context to Gascoigne's use occurs in Book IV, 185.

If Gascoigne's source for his use of "for the nonce" was *Troilus and Criseyde* this would be apt as this, much more than *The Canterbury Tales*, was the key Chaucerian text for him. There are echoes of it in his novel *The Adventures of Master F.J.*, as well as allusions to it in his verse. In the introduction to *The Adventures of Master F.J.* the novel's mock-editor "G.T." salutes "that worthy and famous Knight *Sir Geffrey Chaucer*" (subscribing to the common but mistaken Elizabethan belief that Chaucer had been knighted). He also regrets that "amongst so many toward wits no one hath been hitherto encouraged to follow the trace" (i.e. follow in the footsteps of Chaucer). By implication, George Gascoigne remedies that deficiency.

5: "Cyphered words" and Master F. J.

Gascoigne's novel *The Adventures of Master F.J.* tells the story of a young man and his first, turbulent love affair. This protagonist is only ever identified by initials. "F.J." travels north to stay at a large country household. There he becomes involved in a triangular relationship with two women, Elinor and Frances. Elinor is a married woman and a serial adulterer. She and F.J. embark on a highly charged sexual relationship which ends in jealousy, rage and rape. When F.J. and Elinor separate, Frances makes clear her own sexual interest in the young man. But though she is "a virgin of rare chastity, singular capacity, notable modesty, and excellent beauty" F.J. spurns her and departs.

In spite of Gascoigne's admiration for Chaucer's *Troilus and Cressida* it did not provide a template for *The Adventures of Master F.J.*, even though the plots are broadly alike in following a trajectory of courtship, sex and betrayal. In the end the differences between Chaucer's poem and Gascoigne's novella are more striking than the similarities. Instead of Chaucer's five-part narrative structure of more than 8,000 lines in seven-line "rhyme royal" stanzas, Gascoigne choose the medium of prose.

The Adventures of Master F.J. is an extraordinary piece of fiction, quite unlike anything produced by any other sixteenth-century English writer. When it was first published it created a storm of controversy, intimidating Gascoigne into producing a bowdlerised edition prefaced by various statements of apology and explanation. This second edition, newly titled *The pleasant Fable of Ferdinando Jeronomi and Leonora de Valasco*, purported to be simply a translation from an original piece of Italian fiction – one of the "riding tales of Bartello" (an author who existed nowhere but in Gascoigne's imagination). Both versions of the novel were then largely forgotten for some three and a half centuries.

The use of the word "adventures" in the title of Gascoigne's novella is misleading in so far as it suggests a conventional picaresque tale full of dramatic incidents. But F.J.'s "adventures" derive not from a travel itinerary but from remaining within a restricted domestic location. There is really only one "adventure" – his affair with a married woman. The exotic location is simply a grand Tudor house or castle and the "adventures" are the risks and hazards, including emotional ones, involved in an adulterous liaison.

In 1930 Leicester Bradner suggested that "the real significance of Master F.J.'s adventures" probably lay in Gascoigne's own experiences, but that in the absence of biographical fact such matters could only be speculative. For a modern reader the importance of *The Adventures of Master F.J.* lay in the fact that it was, quite simply, "The first English novel":

> Gascoigne...recognized that a novel must first of all be a story and not a series of elegant essays on love and friendship. His novel has an excellent

plot, fully developed and adequately motivated, embellished with a diversity of scenes and incidents, yet all restricted to a four-months' visit at a country estate. His conversation is life-like and witty, and its tone has a convincing reality. Finally, the characters, because drawn from the life, are intensely real. The tale is an unrivalled picture of the daily activities and amusements of an Elizabethan noble's household. In this respect it is almost unique in its period.

It is just this adherence to realism which shows Gascoigne's originality and independence of his models. His work is modern in its presentation of the complete *mise-en-scène* in which the characters are placed. We walk with them in the park, we listen to their conversation at dinner, we are present at their dances and evening amusements. The method is that of Jane Austen – a few characters are set in a restricted scene and slowly turned about until all sides of their nature are shown. The action rises slowly and logically to an inevitable conclusion.[1]

Writing in 1942, C. T. Prouty agreed with Bradner's assessment, hailing *The Adventures of Master F.J.* as "Gascoigne's most important work, the first original prose narrative of the English Renaissance":

he created a verisimilitude which today gives us a story with the full flavour of Elizabethan country life and which has the added distinction of being not only the first novel, but indeed the first psychological novel.[2]

He was in no doubt that the novel was autobiographical, surmising that it was based on a love affair Gascoigne had as a young man. Prouty believed that the letters and poems were authentic documents: "He remembered his summer in the North; he had preserved the letters and poems, as does every young lover..."[3]

In recent years *The Adventures of Master F.J.* has attracted more attention than anything else Gascoigne wrote, with scores of scholarly articles appearing in academic journals. It has also become Gascoigne's most accessible piece of writing since appearing in Oxford University Press's World's Classics paperback *Anthology of Elizabethan Prose Fiction*. But modern critical attention has focused on the complex narrative structure of the novel and generally disregarded Prouty's claim that it involves raw autobiography. Certainly Prouty's argument that the book is about Gascoigne's own experiences is often far from convincing. His claim that G.T.'s account of how Elinor pressed her body against F.J. and bit his lips with her teeth must be autobiographical because "no one would relate to another the details of this passage"[4] now seems priggishly quaint. But at the other extreme, to deny that *The Adventures of Master F.J.* can possibly have anything to do with Gascoigne's own life is to be equally single-minded.

The first thing to be said about *The Adventures of Master F.J.* is that Gascoigne invites the reader to view it as a narrative about real people. In appearance it is what we would nowadays call a *roman à clef*. The novel begins in a sober documentary tone of voice with an address by "H.W. to the Reader", in which H.W., writing from his London lodging on 20 January 1572, explains the background to what follows. In August 1571 his friend Master G.T. passed him in confidence a manuscript collection of "divers discourses and verses, invented upon sundrie occasions, by sundrie gentlemen". H.W. found the contents so good that he urged his friend A.B. to print it. With additional help from G.T., set out in a letter dated 10 August 1572, this was duly accomplished. G.T. then takes over as narrator and goes on to tell the story of F.J.'s adventures "in the north parts of this Realm", incorporating verbatim the poems and letters which passed between F.J. and Dame Elinor. Elinor's previous lovers include "H.D." and "H.K." The poems and letters are linked by G.T.'s commentary, which narrates what F.J. has told him about the affair.

This blizzard of initials immediately invites the question: what do they stand for? Who are these four men, three of whom have become central to the publication of the amorous intrigues of the fourth? And who are the two men who have previously bedded Elinor? The concealment of the hero's identity inside the initials "F.J." invited guesses as to who he *really* was, especially since an address "From the printer to the reader" explains the initials as signifying "Freeman Jones" – the sixteenth-century parallel of John Doe, or any Tom, Dick or Harry. The circumstances in which the narrative is produced for the reader – confidentiality and discretion – mirrors the secrecy and duplicity involved in the scandal which is about to be unfolded. A gentlemanly hesitation in permitting very personal material about a sex scandal to reach a larger audience through the vulgar medium of the printed page is broached – but the sheer quality of the material demands that it be shared with a wider readership. This is the fiction which precedes the fiction.

In fact none of these four half-identified figures existed. Nor were there "sundrie gentlemen" whose writings had been assembled by others to make up the contents of the volume. There was only one individual involved in all this: George Gascoigne, orchestrating the reception of his work. *A Hundreth Sundrie Flowres* was not an anthology but a one-man production. But the readers of his book were not to know this. Even today some readers are fooled by fiction pretending to be extraneous commentary, perhaps the best known example being the Foreword to *Lolita* by John Ray, Jr., Ph.D. The Victorian editor William Hazlitt fell for Gascoigne's spoof completely, and was convinced that "G.T." was George Turberville and that "H.W." was Henry Wotton, author of the novel *A Courtlie Controversie of Cupids Cautels*.[5] One twentieth-century Gascoigne editor even scented a conspiracy, arguing that the leading figure behind *A Hundreth Sundrie Flowres* was really Edward de Vere, Earl of Oxford, who, without permission, maliciously included unpublished verse by Sir Christopher Hatton in order to damage his standing with Elizabeth I.⁶

Gascoigne's tricks almost certainly influenced others. The enigmatic "E.K." who introduced and edited Edmund Spenser's *The Shepheardes Calender* (1579) has never been identified, quite possibly because he never existed and was none other than Spenser himself. If so, "E.K."'s praise of Gascoigne as "a wittie gentleman", was wonderfully apt. The impact of *The Adventures of Master F.J.* is evident on a later, even more celebrated publication. Thomas Thorpe's dedication page to *Shakespeare's Sonnets* (1609) is notoriously addressed "To The Onlie Begetter Of These Ensuing Sonnets Mr. W.H.", generating an enormous commentary as to who this elusive figure might be. In fact he may well simply be Gascoigne's "H.W." reversed – a mere typographical tease. Like *The Adventures of Master F.J.*, Shakespeare's *Sonnets* describe a triangular relationship involving three mysterious figures. One, the poet or narrator, is that phantom we call "Shakespeare". But who is the socially superior youth to whom the bulk of the sonnets are addressed and who is the promiscuous woman who appears to be the focus of sonnets 127-154? At what period or periods in Shakespeare's life were the poems written and are their expressions of personal emotion deeply felt or just rhetorical exercises? If the former, was Shakespeare bisexual? What are the "pyramids, built up with newer might" (sonnet 123)? Should the "mortal moon" in sonnet 107 be read as a reference to the crescent-shaped Spanish Armada, the 1595 eclipse or the death of Elizabeth I?

The sonnets teasingly withhold the keys which might unlock such mysteries. They are packed with all kinds of unexplained allusions and references and there has never been any shortage of interpreters keenly prepared to offer solutions, ranging from lunatic fringe amateurs who are convinced the poems embody coded messages from Francis Bacon in his capacity as the secret bastard of Elizabeth I, to the soberest of professors, who cannot quite resist lobbying for William Herbert, Earl of Pembroke.

Thorpe, by titillating the reader with a pair of enigmatic initials, was peddling his wares in the market-place. "T.T." in other words – or initials – was kin to Gascoigne's mock-editor "G.T." Shakespeare's collection was, by implication, coterie literature – a private collection of verses at last being made available to a general readership (indeed, its first appearance in literary history was as "his sugred Sonnets among his private friends"). It involved "W.H." – someone whose name could only be whispered, just outside the range of the audience's hearing. By setting up a little mystery the publisher was responding to his author. Most critics see Shakespeare's sonnets as sensationally and scandalously autobiographical. Only a minority views them as fictional exercises in what was by 1609 a tired and dying literary form: the sonnet sequence. As Park Honan has sceptically noted, "Shakespeare writes with a sense that sonnets are indeed toys, little games in which a mystifying poet (aided, if possible, by a publisher's mystifications) pretends to unlock autobiographical secrets".[7] At the heart of the volume lies an absence – literally so in the case of the two empty lines enclosed by brackets at the end of sonnet 126. Filling them in is both an irresistible temptation and a trap.

Such games began with Gascoigne and his teasingly scandalous novel. The games-playing involving questions of identity and meaning was perhaps never so well expressed as by Master F.J. himself who, after an exchange of coded poems and letters with the woman he lusts after, acknowledges "a confusion to my dull understanding, which so rashly presumed to wander in this endless Labyrinth".[8] What he does not initially realise (pun deliberate) is that Elinor's first letters to him are not written by her but penned by a man who is her lover. The games-playing narrative mirrors the games played by its duplicitous and teasing characters.

It is open to question whether or not *A Discourse of the Adventures Passed by Master F.J.* (to give the novel its full and now rarely used title) was perceived as fiction by Elizabethan readers. It purports to be a true and confidential account written to H.W. by G.T., who acknowledges the scandalously erotic nature of what he describes: "Were it not that I know to whom I write, I would the more beware what I write". The commentary by G.T. (which was deleted from the second, bowdlerised edition) underscores the idea that this is a reliable account of real people. But every revelation is tempered by the deliberate withholding of information. Elinor is named but her lover F.J. is only identified by his initials. Her husband is referred to as "the married Knight". Her existing lover is not named but is slightly identified as her "secretary". He is not, as most critics assume, a servant but another guest, so called because he wields his pen in the service of the lady – both literally and in a sexual sense.

Frances is named but "the Lord of the Castle" is not. The castle or country house is somewhere in the north of England but no more precise location is given. There are other guests but they are not named. One in particular is described: "A gentlewoman of the company whom I have not hitherto named, and that for good respects, lest her name might altogether disclose the rest…" A few lines later the narrator makes a point of describing her character while still withholding her identity: "This dame had stuff in her, an old courtier, and a wily wench, whom for this discourse I will name *Pergo*…" G.T. insists on the necessity of a pseudonym: if he gave the name of this "old courtier" it would, by implication, inevitably reveal the identity of the household and its occupants. He also hints of something shocking in Pergo's past.

The entire narrative is a true account of a scandal involving real people. That, at least, is what G.T. suggests. Because of this he cannot "tell all" but only a coded, partial version, to protect the identities of everyone involved in these scandalous goings-on.

Unfortunately for Gascoigne when his book was published that is precisely how *A Discourse of the Adventures Passed by Master F.J.* was read. Worse, it seemed that there was no shortage of real-life candidates for the roles of ardently promiscuous Lady, her young lover and the cuckolded Knight. In the second edition Gascoigne was obliged to acknowledge that his novella had greatly upset some people: "I understande that sundrie well disposed mindes have taken offence at certaine wanton wordes and sentences passed in...The adventures of master F.J. And that also therwith some busie conjectures have presumed to thinke that the same was indeed written to the scandalizing of some worthie personages, whom they woulde seeme therby to know."[9]

Guessing who the characters of the novel were based on was an impulse which did not end in the sixteenth century. Elinor Manners, wife of John Bourchier, Earl of Bath, has been proposed as the original of Gascoigne's promiscuous heroine.[10] Eric Brooks thought that "F.J." was Sir Christopher Hatton and that Gascoigne's novel was about his brief affair with Elizabeth Cavendish at Sheffield Castle in 1572.[11] C. T. Prouty found the similarity between the events of the novel and the Earl of Leicester's affair with Douglas Sheffield at Belvoir Castle in 1568 "striking", though he wondered if the setting might not be Barnard Castle.[12] But none of these suggestions is remotely plausible. Gascoigne hints on four occasions that "F.J." is no one but himself. Friends who read the novel in manuscript would have guessed that "F.J." stood for Filius Johannis – "the son of John", which is literally what the author was. Secondly, F.J. is described as his "father's eldest son". Thirdly, he is described as "a tall Gentleman", which Gascoigne seems to have been. Lastly, F.J. "apparelled him selfe in greene" – a description which links him with Gascoigne's later alter ego, "the green Knight".

If F.J. is based on George Gascoigne, in what sense is the novel autobiographical? The young man goes north and stays several months at a residence which is at different times referred to as a "house" or a "castle". One of the women who lives there, Mistress Frances, is identified as his kinswoman. Only two grand homes in the north of England had such a connection for Gascoigne. The first was Thorpe Hall, which after 1547 seems to have come under the control of his mother. But F.J. is described as a stranger in the household, which makes Thorpe Hall an unlikely candidate. It also seems unlikely to have been quite as grand as the setting of the residence in Gascoigne's novel.

The household where F.J. stays is clearly a very substantial one. The "knight of the castle" rules over a house or castle which contains his daughter Frances, his other "daughter" Elinor (whose father in fact seems to be dead; she may be a step-daughter, although in the revised edition she is identified as his daughter-in-law), Elinor's husband (who is also a knight), Elinor's existing lover, an old female courtier, Master F.J., "diverse other gentlemen and gentlewomen", as well as maids and manservants. Mornings are spent in walks in the garden, the park or in visits to guests' or residents' rooms. But the inhabitants are also "called away unto prayers" in the late morning, implying the presence of a chapel or nearby church. After prayers there is dinner.

There are so many people in residence that F.J. pretends not even to know Elinor's name, even after staying there some time. At one point the assembly is referred to as "the court", as if this place was a microcosm of the royal household. In this large establishment the guests eat dinners, talk, and play games. The household also employs a band of musicians – there are references to "the Instruments", "the violands" and "the viols". The residents listen to music and dance the slow and stately pavan, the French brawl (involving everyone holding hands, sometimes in a circle) and a lively, merry galliard. F.J. urges Frances "to dance a Bargynet", which has been identified as "a rustic dance accompanied with a song".[13] He asks the musicians "to sound the Tyntarnell" – an unidentified dance measure – and clearing his voice sings "*Alla Napolitana*" (in the Neapolitan style) a song of longing and love requited.

The building includes a "great chamber", a gallery and a large base court (i.e. an outer or lower courtyard) with stairs leading off it to the chambers of some of the residents. At one point Elinor is described as "Walking in a garden among divers other gentlemen and gentlewomen" and F.J. leaves the garden and goes "walking into a park near adjoining". There are other references to "the castle gate", "the park near adjoining to the castle wall" and "a thicket". In one episode there is a deer hunt.

If this fictional country house ever really existed then by far the likeliest location for the building and its environs is Gawthorpe Hall, home of the original trunk of the Gascoigne family. This was a substantial building, and was surrounded by an extensive park. A surviving engraving (probably made in the seventeenth century) shows a very large country residence with the features described in *The Adventures of Master F.J.* On the south side is a large base court, on the west a great chamber with a massive east-facing window. The house is surrounded by a tall stone wall and has substantial stables set in the north-west corner of the grounds. Surrounding it is a massive estate of formal gardens, parkland, woods and a dammed lake with a mill.

Gawthorpe's modern incarnation is the magnificent Harewood House. The spectacular grounds remain but Harewood, partly built from the stone of Gawthorpe, was relocated to the ridge overlooking the Gawthorpe site (the location from which Gawthorpe is seen in the engraving). Gawthorpe makes sense as the location of *The Adventures of Master F.J.* in other ways. It was the home of a "Lord of the castle" or "knight of the castle" and George Gascoigne would have been both a stranger there but also kin to some of its residents in the sense that he, too, was a Gascoigne, albeit of the Bedfordshire branch.

Did Gascoigne travel north as a young man and have a serious sexual relationship at Gawthorpe with a promiscuous married woman? The strong probability is that he did. It may be what he had in mind when he wrote that "A yong man well borne, tenderly fostered, and delicately accompanied, shall hardly passe over his youth without falling into some snares of the Divell, and temptations of the flesh."[14] The experience was memorable because it was in this country house that (as G.T. notes of F.J.) "his manhood in this kind of combat was first tried". Like Elinor, "Mistress Frances" was probably also rooted in the poet's personal experience; as David R. Shore has remarked, she is "a fascinating figure whose ambiguities belong to life rather than the art of Elizabethan fiction".[15] It is equally likely that the poems in *The Adventures of Master F.J.* were, as G.T. asserts, the very first ones that F.J./Gascoigne ever wrote and that they were occasioned by the affair. I think Shore is right to suggest that "*Master F.J.* began in all probability, as a collection of occasional poetry which contained from the beginning in embryonic form the prose commentary which would later be substantially expanded."

But that expansion probably took place over a period of 20 years, complicating the tale's autobiographical base. There is no reason to suppose that the letters are authentic letters or that the affair followed the pattern mapped out in the narrative. Nor should it be assumed that Gascoigne raped his lover. He would not be the first writer to project fantasy punishments or fates on to a character based on someone he knew.[16] In the end we have no way of knowing what actually happened and what was imaginary. In the first version of the novel much is left unexplained. What is F.J. *doing* at the castle? How long is he there? In the revised version Ferdinando Jeronimo is "of a very good parentage" and is invited to stay at the Castle of Valasco by its Lord, who hopes that the young man will marry his daughter Francischina. He stays for four months.

If there really was an affair between Gascoigne and a married woman it seems to have been emotionally damaging and to have left a residue of bitterness and cynicism. The poem "And if I did, what then?" has the ring of truth to it and if it was based on lived experience may have been what provoked in Gascoigne his equivocal attitude to love and women. The ending of *The Adventures of Master F.J.* is bleak. Elinor reverts to her life of casual sex with whatever attractive man is available and F.J. spurns the love of the virtuous Frances and departs. He bitterly concludes that the "tides of turning time" throw all lovers "on the shelf" so that "they stick on sands". It is probably significant that H.W. introduces the story to the reader from his "lodging nere the Strande". He is referring to the famous London street, but "strand" also means foreshore. In that sense H.W. is, like G.T., another version of F.J. in later life, older, wiser, and still suffering from the wound of that first, unforgettable love affair.

G.T. brings the narrative to an abrupt conclusion, explaining that he "could wade much further, as to declare his departure, what thanks he gave to his *Hope* and etc., yet I will cease…" In short, "It is time now to make an end of this thriftless history". In the revised version of the tale the ending is even more despairing. Elinor "lived long in the continuance of her accustomed change" (i.e. continued to thrive in her life of promiscuity), Frances sinks into depression and dies three years later of "a miserable consumption" and F.J. returns home "spending there the rest of his days in a dissolute kind of life".

If there was an affair it probably took place some time between 1552 (when he was 18-19) and 1555 (when he was 20-21). In the record of Gascoigne's life these are the "missing years". He was probably at Trinity College during 1547-48, and he was admitted to Gray's Inn in 1555, but between those dates his life was a blank. The probability is that much of that time he was at Cardington Manor, continuing his education with private tutors on the family estate. Such a scenario would fit with F.J.'s laconic remark to Frances that she is talking in Greek, "the which I have now forgotten, and mine instructors are too far from me at this present to expound your words". In the revised mock-Italian version of the novel this is made plain: Ferdinando Jeronimi "delighting more in hawking, hunting, and such other pastimes than he did in study, had left his own house...and was come into Lombardy to take the pleasures of the country".

The affair may also have inspired at least two of the poems in "The Devises of Sundrie Gentlemen" which follow *The Adventures of Master F.J.* One early poem is entitled "The lover being disdaynfully abjected by a dame of high calling, who had chosen (in his place) a playe fellowe of baser condicion: doth therfore determine to step a side, and before his departure giveth hir this farewell in verse". It mirrors the situation in the novel in so far as the woman is of "high estate", the lover is concerned to preserve her reputation, and he is displaced by another man, "A wandring guest" – "guest" meaning "visitor" or "stranger".[17] The woman's new lover, who is of lower social status, inspires some angry lines which resemble the outburst against the "apishly witted, knavishly mannered, and crabbedly favoured" rival lover of Elinor in *The Adventures of Master F.J.*:

> For thou has caught a proper paragon,
> A thief, a coward, and a peacock fool:
> An ass, a milksop, and a minion...

Elinor's "secretary" – "This manling, this minion, this slave..." – is twice described as a "minion" (meaning both "spoiled darling" and "impudent person"). The poem, like the novel, uses jeeringly coarse innuendo: "thou knowest his saddle best" the lover tells his mistress, alluding to how his rival "rides" her by mounting her sexually. There is nothing for the wounded lover to do but depart and snarl his farewells "in this my parting verse":

> And far from thee now must I take my flight,
> Where tongues may tell (and I not see) thy fall

But in the last line the lover's fury and bitterness is muted by a kind of compassion:

Wishing thee better than thou doest deserve.

In a later sonnet "An uncourteous farewell to an unconstant dame" Gascoigne compares himself to Troilus and his lover to the faithless Cressida. This poem is more clotted, abstract and bitter, and concludes with the searing assertion that the price of the affair has been too much:

The price is great, that nothing gives for nought.[18]

If, as seems likely, a real-life affair inspired *The Adventures of Master F.J.*, it almost certainly occurred two decades before the publication of the novel. Gascoigne must indeed have been bemused and aghast to find the plot of his story being read as a true account of the amours of other people in the early 1570s.

When he insisted in 1575 that "there is no living creature touched or to be noted therby"[19] in his tale he might have been telling the truth, Elizabethan mortality rates being what they were. The originals of Elinor and Frances may well have been dead by that time. In any case, it is unlikely that the residents of Gawthorpe Hall in 1573 would have known anything about a scandalous novel published in the capital for the delectation of a sophisticated metropolitan elite or would have connected its plot with a young man's sexual indiscretions there some twenty years earlier.

Plate 12. Gawthorpe Hall.

Plate 13. The lake at the Gawthorpe site.

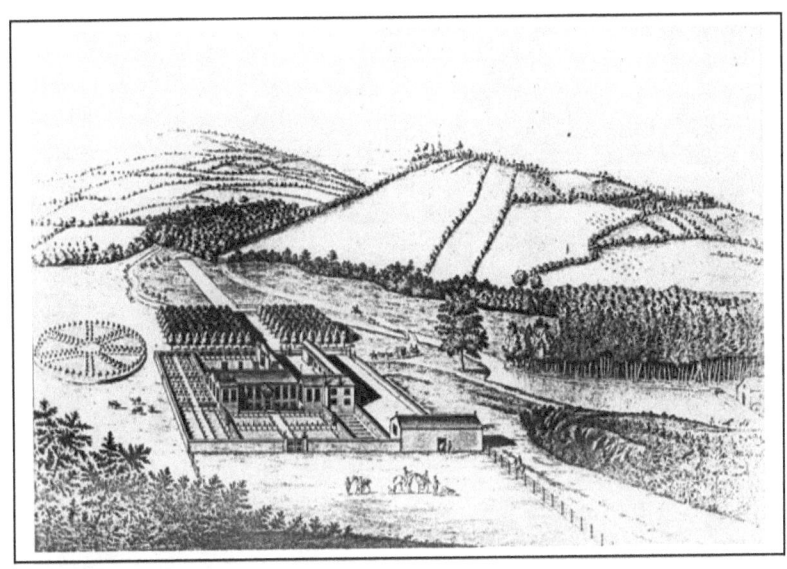

Plate 14. Gawthorpe Hall and its estate.

Plate 15. The artifical lake at Gawthorpe.

PART TWO: IN TUDOR LONDON

6: At Gray's Inn

In 1555 George Gascoigne, who had probably spent most of his first 21 years at Cardington Manor, was admitted to Gray's Inn. He was there ostensibly to study law. Gray's Inn was one of the most eminent of London's legal inns, which first developed their identity as law colleges in the fifteenth century, sited around Holborn, Fleet Street and Chancery Lane. As the name indicates, these were self-contained institutions which provided board and lodgings as well as instruction.

England's two universities taught Roman law but though still used in the ecclesiastical courts this was of little relevance to the civil courts of Tudor England. The inns were concerned with English law as it had developed over centuries. Legal authority lay not in the Latin classics of imperial Rome but in court proceedings transcribed in Year Books, in statute law from the Parliament rolls, in case reports, and in the treatises of former judges. The top four inns were the Inns of Court – Gray's Inn, the Inner Temple, Lincoln's Inn and the Middle Temple. There were also ten lesser Inns of Chancery, which took around 100 students. Apart from servants, these were all exclusively male institutions.

Gray's Inn had around 250 members present at any one time and was bigger than most Cambridge colleges. It lay at the very edge of the north-western sprawl of early Elizabethan London, well beyond the city walls and outside the City's jurisdiction. It was the best situated of the four major inns, free of the seedy, congested, densely packed alleys which pressed in on Lincoln's Inn and the Temple. On three sides it was surrounded by open fields. Rabbits could be caught in a nearby coney garth. The fourth faced on to "Greys Ynne Lane" (today's Grays Inn Road). This lane was built-up as far as Gray's Inn. Beyond that it led north into open countryside and distant Highgate village.

Attendance at one of the Inns of Court was a rite of passage for the sons of the aristocracy and gentry. Membership, which was for life (but only if you paid your bills), did not in itself signify any serious intention to study law. There were those who took their studies very seriously – men like Thomas More and Nicholas Bacon, who later rose to some of the highest positions in the Tudor state. One of the young men who was diligently working at his law studies when Gascoigne arrived in London was William Danby, who forty years later would be Coroner to the Royal Household and the man who presided over an inquest into the stabbing to death of one Christopher Marlowe. But there were others, like Sir Nicholas Bacon's two older sons, who simply treated their Inn as just that: a pleasant place to stay, with agreeable company, conveniently situated half-way between the City of London and Westminster.

To become a lawyer was profitable but it required years of study and practice. The profession had its own mystique. English common law involved a complex system of precedents and procedures which required any litigant to seek professional help. Writs and statutes were generally in Latin, pleadings in "law French" and general court arguments in English. Common lawyers acted as accountants, brokers, financiers and land agents, besides dealing in litigation. Families such as the Littletons and the Yelvertons founded great legal dynasties which supplied lawyers over many generations.

The inns were far more exclusive in their intake than Oxford and Cambridge, and more like residential clubs than universities. Only the affluent and privileged went there. Entry was not based on merit, qualifications or aptitude. There were no scholarships for poorer students and no opportunities for students to pay their way while studying. The Inns of Court depended financially on a range of fees charged to members. Apart from these, a student needed money for the mandatory sleeveless black gown with a flap collar and round black cloth cap, as well as a fashionable wardrobe for wearing outside his Inn. Other conventional expenses included gaming, drinking and dining out in the City and the cost of dancing and fencing lessons. Many members also kept a personal servant.

The usual age of admission to an Inn was around 16 to 20 years. In 1555 there were 40 admissions to Gray's Inn, including George Gascoigne. Admission often depended on family and regional ties and status. None of Gascoigne's family had been there before him, so clearly some form of influence was being exerted somewhere to get him into what was arguably the elite Inn of Court. Gray's Inn was popular with the aristocracy and some of its members were well-connected in court and government circles. Its alumni included Sir Nicholas Bacon, Sir William Cecil (later Lord Burghley), and Francis Walsingham (later Secretary of State).

Gray's Inn was enclosed by a high wall and consisted of a number of substantial buildings two or three storeys high, including chapels, halls, a library and a great hall, all grouped around three sides of a large courtyard. Between 1555 and 1560 the hall was rebuilt with a gallery, a hammer-beam roof and stepped gables in the Flemish style. The grounds included a very large ornamental garden, entry to which was forbidden to persons of mean quality (a category presumably determined by personal appearance and a dress code). The garden was laid out symmetrically in a pattern of slender parallel rectangles, with long pathways running between the flowerbeds. This was the fashion of the time: a "fair walk under the trees" had been constructed at the back of Lincoln's Inn in 1553.

A short walk away to the south was Holborn and a cluster of other law inns. The quickest route to the river was down Chancery Lane and Middle Temple Lane to Temple Stairs. To get to the City you turned left at the bottom of Grays Inn Lane and headed for Holburne Bridge over the Fleet River. Beyond lay Newgate and St Paul's. For Westminster and the law courts the quickest route on foot or by horse was across Lincoln's Inn Fields to Little Drury Lane, along the Strand to Charing Cross and down "Kinges Streate" and through its towering, impressive gates. Here, in the courts of Westminster Hall, a barrister would stand on a floor covered with sweet-smelling rushes, at the bar before the judges, or beside a table covered with legal papers.

Getting rooms at Gray's Inn wasn't always easy. People came and went all the time and student numbers were swelled by their servants, domestic staff, lawyer's clerks and those seeking to avoid their creditors. Sometimes students were accommodated in neighbouring lodgings and tenements. Authorised annexes included Fulwood's and Bentley's Rents near Gray's Inn. Some families (such as the Finches and the Yelvertons) had long-running associations with Gray's Inn and had the privilege of their own family chambers. The Bacon family chambers were opposite the gateway, next to the library. There were private family lodgings at Gray's Inn including "Kyndelmarshes Buyldinges", built by the Kinwelmershe family. Gascoigne would later become close to Francis Kinwelmershe, who was admitted in 1557, and his brother Anthony, admitted in 1561.[1] A number of legal documents identify Gascoigne's London residence as being "of Gray's Inn", so perhaps he was lucky enough to get chambers on site.

The student year consisted of four terms: Michaelmas (of about 7 weeks duration), Hilary, Easter and Trinity (about 3 weeks each), plus the Lent and August learning vacations. Collectively, that amounted to less than 6 months of the year. But absences were tolerated and there was a high turnover of members who came and went as they pleased. There was no supervision of the student body, no sanctions for failing to do work and no tutorials. It was entirely the individual's responsibility what he chose to do. Students could take as long as they wanted to qualify, if they ever did. Many members were of mature age and were at Gray's Inn as much for its social life as to learn about law. After about a decade of nominal or actual residence a member would receive the honorary title of "Ancient".

What was taken very seriously was the strict hierarchy of seniority, as expressed in dress and position in the dining hall. Meals were served according to rank and reserved table. Lowliest of all were the apprentices and student "inner barristers". Next came the Ancients, followed by the "utter [outer] barristers". Utter barristers wore a black robe with two velvet tufts on long hanging sleeves. They had qualified and been called "to the Bar" instead of sitting "under the Bar" with the inner barristers. At the high table sat the benchers in gowns tufted with silk and velvet. They ruled over Gray's Inn. Only they and knights of the realm were permitted to wear velvet caps or light coloured clothing. Other rules included a ban on the carrying of swords or rapiers in the inn and on the wearing of study gowns outside it. The early years of Elizabeth's reign witnessed a fashion for beards but benchers were not permitted to have beards of more than three weeks' growth.

Even in the twenty-first century many people remain faithful in middle age to the hair styles of their twenties, and perhaps in Gascoigne's day it was no different. The portrait reproduced in *The Steel Glass* shows the poet some twenty-one years after he was first admitted to Gray's Inn but his beard is trim and neat and would attract no attention in a modern street.

Other institutions were more inflexible than Gray's Inn. 1555 was the year that some students withdrew from Lincoln's Inn in protest at a ban on beards, and said they'd set up a new inn. But even at Gray's Inn the benchers in later years sought to suppress such dangerously radical trends as ruffs, white doublets and hose, unauthorized velvetings on gowns, and lawn caps.

Gray's Inn was where the sons of the ruling class went to bond, to network and to share a comradeship of ideas and literature. In 1555 there were 40 young men admitted to Gray's Inn and for George Gascoigne perhaps the most important of them was Paul Withypoll. Withypoll was named after his grandfather (1480-1547), a former head of the Merchant Taylors' Company, Alderman of the City of London, city representative in Parliament and magistrate. The family owned land in Walthamstow and Leyton but since 1546 his father Edmund and mother Elizabeth had been based at Ipswich in the town's most impressive residence, Christchurch. This massive new brick mansion was built on confiscated monastic land to the north of the town, alongside the Church of St Margaret. The mansion and its grounds still exist today, as a museum and public park; close by is Withipoll Street.

Paul Withypoll, who was then aged about nineteen, came from a very large family (altogether, Edmund Withypoll fathered eleven sons and eight daughters, though not all survived childhood). At some point in his life Gascoigne became a very good friend of two of Paul's brothers, Daniel (born c. 1541) and Bartholomew (who was born c. 1539). One of his most impressive poems is "*Gascoignes councell* [advice] *given to master* Bartholmew Withipoll". The poet's close friendship with Bartholmew and Daniel surely came later, when they were older. But it seems very probable that a friendship with fellow law-student Paul resulted in him first meeting Withypoll's two younger brothers.

The problem for all young men at the Inns of Court was the proximity of the city and its temptations. London was the commercial and political centre of England. Its population in 1550 was around 75,000; by the end of the century it had grown to 200,000. It was a noisy, congested city of brothels and churches, ale-houses and bowling alleys, public executions, bear baitings and carnival processions. Its focal points were the Tower, the great cathedral of St Paul's (much bigger than today's Wren cathedral), the River Thames and London Bridge. There was so much for a young gentleman to do apart from study law – including the development of one's dancing, musical and fencing skills at a specialist academy or with a private tutor. But in 1555 it was also a city which bore the shattering impression of the reformation – a place of desolate, ruined monasteries and churches which had been closed down and defaced. But now all that was over and a monarch committed to the old, unreformed faith was on the throne again.

It is very unlikely that Gascoigne's arrival at Gray's Inn marked his first encounter with London. He had probably first been taken by his father to see the capital years earlier. More recently, Sir John Gascoigne and his heir were likely to have attended the funeral of the Earl of Bedford, who died at his grand house in London on 20 March 1555. In view of the Earl's local connections and influence in the town after which his earldom was named, it would have been politic to be among the 300 riders who took part in the massive and extravagant funeral procession. Whether or not he had come to know the city prior to his arrival at Gray's Inn, George Gascoigne now found his life focused on it. London was important to George Gascoigne. It was where a young man from sluggish rural Bedfordshire became a sophisticated metropolitan writer. It was somewhere where Gascoigne fell in love; a place of romantic assignations; the city in which the poet would one day get married.

Walter Benjamin famously remarked that "There is no document of civilization which is not at the same time a document of barbarism".[2] This is as true of Gascoigne's writing as of any other Tudor writer. He was born into a society with a ferocious criminal justice system, but it was one from which he was shielded by the fact of being male, affluent, educated and well-born. Some idea of the London of 1555 can be gleaned from the chronicle kept by Henry Machyn.[3] Beneath Machyn's dry, deadpan prose, it's clear that London that year was a city of ferocious repression and searing religious divisions.

The chronicle reads oddly to modern eyes because of the complete absence of emotion or opinion. Machyn, who was no Pepys, is almost invisible and his diary provides a largely colourless list of events and facts. He was clerk of the small parish of Holy Trinity-the-Less, in which capacity he attended and sang at funerals. His interest in funerals was reinforced by his role as supplier of hearse cloths and escutcheons. The focus of his so-called "diary" is a little like that of a modern tabloid newspaper – celebrity weddings and funerals, crime and punishment, the activities of royalty and grand public occasions. It is news without a history, a context or an explanation – one event suceeding another. As Machyn shows, public burnings for heresy were frequent that year but Protestant dissent was everywhere. On 14 June 1555 there was a public proclamation that all books by Luther, Tyndale, Coverdale and Cranmer, and all other heretical books, be surrendered within 15 days or their owners would go to prison. Protestants retaliated with midnight raids on saints' images, which were smashed up. A reward of 100 crowns of gold was offered for the apprehension of image-breakers. Protestants held an illicit service in Bow churchyard at night but were caught. A "frantyke man" – either a religious dissident or someone mentally disturbed – ran up to a priest and mockingly hung two puddings round his neck. A monk had his hand amputated as a punishment for assaulting a priest. This was followed by his burning to death outside the churchyard of St Margaret's. There were arraignments for heresy, with heretics ordered to be burnt at various locations. In London, Smithfield was the favoured location for incinerating religious dissidents.

Public burnings for heresy were happening across the land. The most famous martyrs of 1555 were Ridley and Latimer in Oxford. In London the victims were usually much humbler, such as the weaver from Shoreditch, whose name was Tomkins. The London burnings that year climaxed with another burning at Smithfield, that of the former archdeacon of Winchester on 18 December.

Tudor London was a city seething with street drama and spectacle. Violent crime and violent punishments were very visible. Three men were transported in a cart from the Marshalsea prison to the gallows at Charing Cross for robbery. Machyn noted that one of the men was hanged in a gown of tawny fryse, a doublet of tawny taffeta and a pair of fine hose lined with sarsenet, and died shouting abuse against the Pope and the mass. The felon was left to hang there for four days before being cut down and buried by the gallows. A fortnight later the corpse was exhumed and burned beside the gallows.

In May three prisoners were exhibited for unclean living and whoring. They were taken throughout the city on a cart, from Guildhall to Cheapside, through Newgate and Smithfield, and back to the Standard in Cheap. They were a gentleman pimp named Manwaring and two women, one named Warren living at the Hare in Cheap and the other a goldsmith's wife. A lad was whipped at a post in Chepe for loitering and running about masterless as a vagabond. Another young man was attached to a post by an iron collar and whipped; the post was known as "the post of reformation". A man and a woman were taken through the streets on "a care-arse" (cart's tail) "for baudry". In October a man was put in the pillory "for spykyng of sedyssyous wordes". Important prisoners were marched through the streets escorted by a great company of the guard. Sir Anthony Kingston was briefly imprisoned in the Tower and then the Fleet prison for disorderly conduct in Parliament. When a high-ranking prisoner was taken to the Tower his imprisonment was followed by a great shooting of cannon.

Men and women were constantly being taken out of "Nugatt" (Newgate prison) and sent to be hanged at Tyburn. On 4 July 1555 four men were taken to Tyburn to be hanged "for qwynnyng [coining] of money". On 28 October 1555 in the morning was set up in Fleet Street, beside St Bride's well, a pair of gallows, upon which two men were hanged for robbing a Spaniard; they were executed in the morning and their bodies hung all day in the rain.

Apart from the scenes of state punishment, there were many other occasions for the public to observe. There were regular sermons at Paul's Cross. One day there was a general procession of all London schoolchildren. Machyn was a keen recorder of lavish funeral processions such as the grand funeral of the

Duchess of Northumberland at Chelsea. There were religious processions, with 160 priests and clerks singing *Salve festa dies* ("Hail, oh festive day"). There was tilting at Westminster. There was the spectacle of the royal barge as it took the Queen along the Thames from one palace to another. On the last day of April 1555 came tidings that the Queen was delivered of a prince. There followed a great ringing of bells and a *Te Deum laudamus* was sung in many churches. But the story turned out to be false. There were other forms of hysteria. Machyn recorded how on one occasion a poor man with two crutches was watching the Queen when, miraculously healed by her royal presence, he threw his crutches away and ran after her. Flattered by this clear proof of her divine powers, Mary commanded that the man be given a reward.

In August there came from Rome the Bishop of Ely, the Bishop of Bangor and "the lord Montycutt vycontt". Later that month the King and Queen landed at Greenwich and there received the Lord Chancellor, the Bishop of Ely, "and my lord vycont Montyguw". As yet George Gascoigne had not met the Catholic grandee Anthony Browne, first Viscount Montagu, but some 17 years later the destinies of the two men would become intertwined and would lay Gascoigne open to the charge of subversion.

There were entertainments, such as the May games at St Martin's in the Field, with hobbyhorses, a giant and a morris dance. The day that Latimer and Ridley were burnt in Oxford was the day of the Sergeants' of the Law feast, with a great dinner at the Inns of Court. Later that month, on 29 October 1555, two pinnaces decorated with flags and streamers escorted the new lord mayor as he made a ceremonial passage to Westminster in a barge, accompanied by the city's sheriffs and aldermen. The pinnaces fired their cannon and the Thames was full of vessels gaily decorated with streamers. Afterwards the mayor returned to Paul's wharf, where there was more gunfire and music. In Paul's churchyard trumpets played and the party met the bachelors of law and watched a pageant. This included a devil figure and 66 men in blue gowns, with targets and javelins. Gascoigne might just have participated in this festivity, since it featured "iiij talle men lyke wodys alle in gren". If he was simply a spectator it was something he remembered. Twenty years later Gascoigne would masquerade as just such a wild man of the woods and appear before Queen Elizabeth, dressed in leaves and moss.

Lastly, there was also one other aspect of London life that Gascoigne would have to learn to get used to: the weather. The day of 29 September 1555 "was the grettest rayn and fludes that ever was sene in England". The surrounding countryside was deluged. Men and cattle were drowned. Marshes turned into lakes. London's cellars were flooded, ruining beer, ale and other merchandise.

Poplar walls

London is the setting for one of Gascoigne's most haunting and intriguing love sonnets.[4] It describes an anguished separation from a beautiful woman. The poet is forced to leave her for reasons of "steadfast friendship (bound by holy oath)". In dreams he recalls (lines 5-12) how the woman was troubled and loath to part from him.

> When Poplar walls enclosed thy pensive mind,
> My painted shadow did thy woes revive:
> Thine evening walks by Thames in open wind
> Did long to see my sailing boat arrive.
> But when the dismold day did seek to part
> From London walls thy longing mind for me,
> The sugared kisses (sent to thy dear heart)
> With secret smart in broken sleeps I see.

The template for this poem was a sonnet by the Earl of Surrey, "When Windsor walls sustained my wearied arm". Surrey's poem provides a melancholy account of his confinement at Windsor Castle in 1537. Separated from the vibrant life at Henry's court he broods mournfully on what he's missing. The Earl sighs, and his "vapored eyes" distill "drery teares". Gascoigne creatively rewrites Surrey's melancholy in the guise of a Petrarchan love lyric.

By "painted shadow" Gascoigne means a painted miniature of himself, which he has given his lover. Although "Poplar" walls might refer to rows of poplar trees Gascoigne probably means Poplar the place, then a village a few miles out of London, on the banks of the Thames. The "walls" are either the walls of a house there or, more likely, a reference to the high banked walls along the river (which gave their name to the nearby villages of Millwall and Blackwall). The episodes which the poet sees "In dreams" are a mixture of memory and imagination. The woman's misery at parting is real but the scenes of her grieving over his picture and walking along the riverside, hoping to see him sailing towards her, are imaginary. Lines 9-10 are ambiguous. At first glance they might seem to indicate that it is the woman who is in London (in which case she cannot be in Poplar). But Gascoigne may mean "But when the dismal day sought to remove for me, here by these London walls, the image of you by the river in Poplar longing for my return…" In this reading the poet is locked inside "London walls" – both those of his bedroom and, probably, the old Roman walls. There, the dismal day threatens to blot out the memory of her desire for him there. Restless and half-awake he remembers "sugared kisses" he has sent her in the past.

The key word in the sonnet is "secret". Gascoigne is uncharacteristically tight-lipped about the situation he's describing. Most of his poems have explanatory titles and sometimes expansive introductions. Not this one. Its full title is *"This Sonet of his shall passe (for me) without any preface"*. Even with the available fiction that the poem was written by and about someone else Gascoigne chose silence. Who, we might wonder, is the person responsible for separating Gascoigne from his lover? Was it a man or a woman? What was so important that he had to go?

Gascoigne doesn't tell us whether the person who draws him away from his lover is male or female. What is this "holy oath" which is involved in his departure? Is the woman troubled simply by the prospect of his absence, or is there something more involved? Is the relationship, like the day, dying? Does "dismold" simply mean "dismal" or does it also carry that other sixteenth-century sense of something ominous about to happen? Were the sugared kisses originally *sent* in painful secrecy – implying some kind of illicit relationship – or are they simply *remembered* in private grief?

The syntax cannot help us to resolve these ambiguities. Clearly the poem's first interpreter was the printer, who supplied at times very questionable punctuation, including the brackets in line eleven. This sonnet is an early ancestor of John Berryman's "Dream Songs". It gives us a flickering, jerky movie show of images, rooted in something deeply personal. Scenes flash up, then melt away. It is all viewed through a screen of misery and tears and restlessness. This is a love affair seen only "in broken sleepes". And where we might hope for some kind of resolution, there is only hyperbole:

Wherefore in tears I drench a thousand fold,
Till these moist eyes thy beauty may behold.

This sub-Petrarchan banality supplies an unsatisfactory closure. The sonnet is not so much concluded as walked away from.

The mysteries of this sonnet are compounded by its disappearance from the second edition of Gascoigne's poems. *The Posies of George Gascoigne Esquire* omitted three poems from *A Hundreth Sundrie Flowres*.[5] The first – *"A translation of Ariosto allegorized"* – was probably discarded for reasons of style. The other two – this "dream" sonnet and a playful poem about a love rival – were probably dropped because they touched on something dangerously personal and perhaps offensive to those closest to the poet. The identity of the woman in the third poem is known and within six years of Gascoigne being admitted to Gray's Inn she would turn his life upside down.[6] The identity of the woman in the Poplar sonnet is not known. It is possible, of course, that she was the same woman.

7: The Lawless Law

Gascoigne wrote of his law studies at Gray's Inn in a much-anthologised poem which is usually printed under the title "Gascoigne's Woodmanship":

> he shot to be a man of law
> And spent some time with learned Littleton

He also mentions "Fitzharbert" and describes how

> Old Parkins, Rastall, and Dan Bracten's books,
> Did lend me somewhat of the lawless Law.[1]

These were names which would have rung bells with anyone who'd studied at an Inn of Court. Sir Thomas Littleton's *Tenures* was one of the basic text books of common law as were Anthony Fitzherbert's *La graunde abbregement* or *Abridgement*, John Perkins's *Perutilis tractatus* or *Profitable Book* and Henry de Bracton's *De legibus et consuetudinibus Angliae*. John Rastell (who was the brother-in-law of Sir Thomas More) published the first two books as well as his own law dictionary.

Some students keenly pursued their interest in law. Others made no effort whatsoever. Probably most were like George Gascoigne. They attended to their law studies and learned something of common law, but lacked the temperament to plough on, year after year, until they had finally qualified. After a minimum of eight years a student might hope to qualify as a barrister and be called to the bar. It required another eight years to become a senior member of the profession and be named a serjeant-at-law.

Law at this time was dominated by the practice of the civil rather than criminal law. Knowledge of law and procedure was only acquired through years of reading, learning exercises and court observation. The would-be lawyer had to learn how to plead, the rules of confirmation and confutation and how to engage in disputation and make elaborate legal arguments. Apart from procedure, law study required an encyclopaedic knowledge of statutes, writs and commonplace cases. From his description of his abortive legal career, Gascoigne evidently studied land and testamentary law. This was an orthodox approach, since disputes about land inheritance and tenure were the main concern of common lawyers. Land holding could involve a complex variety of tenures and terms and controversies over the possession of land were commonplace.

By his sardonic comments about law being "lawless" and "dark" it's clear Gascoigne had little appetite for protracted legal study:

> Next that, he shot to be a man of law

And spent some time with learned Littleton,
Yet in the end he proved but a daw,
For law was dark and he had quickly done.
Then could he wish Fitzherbert such a brain,
As Tully had, to write the law by art,
So that with pleasure, or with little pain,
He might perhaps have caught a truant's part.
But all too late he most misliked the thing
Which most might help to guide his arrow straight:
He winked wrong, and so let slip the string,
Which cast him wide, for all his quaint conceit.

The metaphor is that of a bungler with a crossbow. He aimed at a target but the target was dark and obscure. He closed his eyes, fell asleep, let slip the string – and missed. He is not merely a bungler but "a daw" or jackdaw – to the Elizabethans, a proverbially stupid bird. Gascoigne's "quaint conceit" is simultaneously the figurative language used and his vanity in foolishly aspiring to be "a man of law".

But though Gascoigne presents himself as both inadequate and comically inept his criticisms of the contemporary legal training system were perfectly reasonable. English common law was a nightmarish accretion of fragments which had never been organised into any kind of system or order. Although Littleton's *Tenures* was one of the most basic legal texts it was a clotted, meandering, unstructured book. Later in the century Henry Spelman was admitted to Lincoln's Inn and recalled encountering "a foreign language, a barbarous dialect, an uncouth method, a mass which was not only large, but which was to be continually born on the shoulders; and I confess that my heart sank within me". When Gascoigne wrote that "he [could] wish Fitzherbert such a brain, / As Tully had, to write the law by art" he was contrasting the lucidity and organisation of Roman law as expressed in the writing of "Tully" (i.e. Cicero) with the muddle and confusion of Fitzherbert's huge digest.

If Gascoigne's English texts had matched the exemplary form of the Latin jurists then he might "perhaps have caught a truant's part" (i.e. dodged lessons without his studies suffering). The conflict between the conservatives and the reformists was fundamental. Francis Bacon had studied Roman law and his criticisms, made later in the century, echoed Gascoigne's. In the words of one of Bacon's biographers, the eminent jurist Edward Coke "could not have enough of Plowden's *Reports*, of the archaism of Littleton's *Tenures*, of the old charters and *Year Books*... To Edward Coke, the common law was the perfection of reason; [Francis] Bacon saw it as limited by medieval technicalities and accretions, rigid and slow, urgently needing the relief of equity."[2]

There was one later, unpredictable spin-off to the rueful tale unfolded in

"Gascoigne's Woodmanship". When Shakespeare wanted to get inside the minds of characters who'd studied law but who wished to make excuses and avoid expressing an opinion on a constitutional point, he turned to Gascoigne's lines about Gray's Inn. In the scene in the Temple garden in *Henry VI, Part One* Suffolk says, "I have been truant in the law" (II.iv.7) and Warwick: "But in these nice quillets of the law, Good faith, I am no wiser than a daw" (17-18).

*

In 1565 Gascoigne was made an Ancient. Throughout this decade-long association with Gray's Inn he is likely to have spent much time elsewhere. Even the most devoted career lawyer was only required to be there six months of the year. Like most members, he came and went as he pleased. As he wrote in "Gascoigne's Woodmanship" the "law was dark and he had quickly done". This suggests the period devoted to his law studies was of short duration. But though Gascoigne had no enthusiasm for learning about case law or statutes, he clearly picked up a basic knowledge of the judicial system. The language and imagery of the law permeates his writing.

As a writer, what Gascoigne perhaps learned most from Gray's Inn came from the practice of disputation. Students participated in mock trials and made pleadings for and against a hypothetical case. Counsel for the plaintiff dealt with the legal issues at stake, citing authorities and precedents. This was followed by a speech on behalf of the defendant. Points were disputed, cases from the Year Books cited. What this taught Gascoigne the writer was perspective. One proposal was followed by an amendment or its very opposite. This is an essential feature of Gascoigne's *oeuvre*: a multiplicity of points of view, ranging from the Chinese-box structure of *The Adventures of Master F.J.* to the male-female dialogues of "The Devises of Sundrie Gentlemen".

The poet's law training may also have informed that other striking aspect of his writing: the bold, confident, assertive voice that gives us the character "Gascoigne" in all his complex and colourful endeavours. Possibly he absorbed something from the Gray's Inn readings, in which a statute was explained in all its complexity. Though the reader would be a senior member of the profession it was the tradition that he began his exposition with a speech in English in which he disparaged himself. This is a posture found time and time again in Gascoigne's verse. "Gascoigne's Woodmanship" is about his clumsy incompetence and failure while being simultaneously one of his most accomplished poems.

Gascoigne's law studies animate two poems which are wittily cast in the form of legal cases – "Gascoigne's Libel of Divorce" and "Gascoigne's Arraignment". In the first Gascoigne is the plaintiff, in the second the defendant. By "libel" Gascoigne did not mean "defame" but the secondary legal sense of "a declaration in writing exhibited in court" or "to proceed against by a written complaint". The first of these two poems is a request for a divorce, not an attack on the legal dissolution of marriage. But the judge in the case is Death, and what Gascoigne requests is a divorce from two women – his "wife" (who is the personification of both life and old age) and his "concubine" or kept mistress (who personifies both love and youth). In short, Gascoigne asks to be put out of his misery by Death:

> cast thy piercing dart, into my panting breast,
> That I may leave both love and life, and thereby purchase rest.[3]

The poem is a gigantic spoof, and not remotely serious. According to Gascoigne it was set to music, and clearly it was designed, whether sung or read aloud, as a performance to be staged before an audience of fellow law students. The solemn language of the law is applied to something essentially comic and absurd: a mock request for a death sentence to release the plaintiff from the troubles of love and old age.

What follows captures an essential aspect of the reality of any court case: its theatricality and the exaggeration involved in seeking to persuade a judge or a jury. Gascoigne plays on the two meanings of "plaint" (a complaint setting out the reasons for a legal action or a sad song). Gascoigne's plaint is both an inventory of his troubles – cast-off and held in disdain by love – and a lamentation. But "libel" can also mean "lampoon" and the lamentation is played strictly for laughs. It would be naïve in the extreme to read this as autobiographical. Gascoigne was not melancholy but hooting with laughter as he sang or spoke of his decrepitude:

> My wrinkled cheeks bewray, that pride of heat is past,   [discover]
> My staggring steps eke tell the truth, that nature fadeth fast,
> My quaking crooked joints are combred with the cramp   [burdened]
> The box of oil is wasted well, which once did feed my lamp.
> The green-ness of my years doth wither now so sore
> That lusty love leaps quite away, and liketh me no more.

This is a comic posture, not a statement of fact. There is no reason to believe that Gascoigne was old and doddery when he wrote these lines. He may well have been only in his twenties. When he performed these lines in front of his friends and associates he was clowning around, not opening a window into his soul. But when the poem appeared in print, probably many years after it was first written, some solitary readers evidently took it literally. Some people thought Gascoigne really *was* in deep despair and begging for death to release him from the troubles of his earthly existence. In fact both his law poems were comic, as he wearily explained when his book was republished in 1575: "I will not say how much the areignment and divorce of a Lover (being written in jeast) have bene mistaken in sad earnest."[4]

The speaker in the poem – "Gascoigne" the comic persona, not Gascoigne the man – appeals to Death to find in his favour:

> Be judge then gentle death, and take my cause in hand,
> Consider every circumstance, mark how the case doth stand.
> Percase thou wilt allege that cause thou canst none see,
> But that I like not of that one, that other likes not me.

This echoes a courtroom strategy which all law students must have been very familiar with: special pleading. The plaintiff tacitly acknowledges how threadbare is his case; how, in fact, the whole case is founded on a trivial falling-out between former friends (or lovers). The plaintiff goes on to promise proof but instead of supplying it simply asks for a speedy and favourable judgement. "But cast thy piercing dart, into my panting breast!" cries Gascoigne – no doubt then falling to the floor before his laughing and cheering audience.

But the poem does not simply satirise the solemn yet often bogus rituals of courtroom justice. It also mocks love and women. Here there may well have been an autobiographical element. Love is identified as a young woman who has cast Gascoigne off "long since" and is now "incontinent, a common whore". Life is "loathsome", a "crooked crone", "her comfort is but cold". But life is also a wife:

> No day can pass but she begins to brall,   [quarrel]
> No merry thoughts conceived so fast, but she confounds them all.
> When I pretend to please, she overthwarts me still,
> When I would faynest part with her, she oversways my will.

Was Gascoigne married when he wrote these lines? It is perfectly possible that he was, and that some of the charge carried by the poem relied on knowledge of Gascoigne's own love life. But it may simply have been a young bachelor's easy joke about a man broken by matrimony. In any case the "wife" is a personification of life, not a real woman. That, at least, is what the poem proposes in its argument. But the case it sets out is perhaps as flawed as the plaintiff's legal action which the poem dramatises. To personify life and old age as a "wife" is as odd as it is to seek a divorce from a mistress, who under Tudor law had no rights whatsoever. The poem's controlling metaphor, though witty, is desperately shaky. There is a sense that the poem is straying into dangerously personal territory. If so, it is hastily and comically terminated by the hurried request for a favourable judgement.

By far the most successful of the law poems is "Gascoigne's Arraignment". Here Gascoigne dramatizes himself as a luckless defendant. To be arraigned is to be called to account, or in judicial terms, to stand as a prisoner at the bar of a court, to answer an indictment. But the bar of this court is "Beauty's bar" and Gascoigne has been brought there accused by her baseless suspicions:

> George (quod the judge) hold up thy hand,
> Thou art arraigned of flattery

This court is oddly informal. Not only does the judge familiarly address the defendant by his first name, he even invites him to choose how he will be tried and whose judgement he'll accept.

> My lord (quod I) this lady here,
> Whom I esteem above the rest,
> Doth know my guilt if any were:
> Wherefore her doom shall please me best.
> Let her be judge and juror both
> To try me, guiltless by mine oath.

Gascoigne's accuser declines the offer, and for the first time it becomes clear that it is Beauty herself. She is not just any woman, however, but "A Prince" (in the ungendered sixteenth-century sense of a sovereign ruler). Gascoigne may have intended an allusion to Elizabeth I, another Prince who presided over a court and whose supposed beauty was constantly praised by sycophants. Beauty puts the matter back in the hands of the court:

> If you will guiltless seem to go,
> God and your country quit you so.   [acquit]

The fourth stanza gives a glimpse of the realities of a contemporary court:

> Then craft the cryer called a quest,   [jury]
> Of whom was falsehood foremost feere,   [companion]
> A pack of pickethankes were the rest,   [tale-bearers]
> Which came false witness for to bear.
> The jury such, the judge unjust,
> Sentence was said I should be trussed.

This is a cynic's view of the Tudor judicial system as corrupt and partial. The Inns of Court crowd doubtless hooted and laughed at this mockery of the system, which was not entirely inaccurate. For example, Edward de Vere, seventeenth

Earl of Oxford, killed a servant, "escaping a charge of capital murder on the plea that the undercook committed suicide by deliberately running himself upon the young earl's rapier".[5] Trials were often of very brief duration and jurors often knew the defendant or the accuser. That law and justice were two quite separate matters was illustrated the year before Gascoigne's admission to Gray's Inn, when a Guildhall jury found Sir Nicholas Throckmorton not guilty of treason. The jurors were thrown in prison. The foreman, Robert Whetstone, spent seven months in the Tower of London and was finally only released after paying a fine of £220. In a curious twist of literary fate his son George many years later became a witness to the death of George Gascoigne.

Next "Jealous the jailer bound me fast / To hear the verdite of the bill". This keeps the poem fixed in the real world of existing legal terminology ("the verdict of the bill", i.e. the written judgement of the court) but also shifts it back into the less dangerous world of metaphor and poetic fancy. The jailer's name is Jealous(y), and he personifies those who resent Gascoigne's relations with Beauty. This, too, no doubt brought laughter and applause from those listening to the poet recite these lines. As in the case of "Gascoigne's Libel of Divorce" there may well have been a personal story behind the poem but it is not one which we can now ever recover. All we can do is recognise that the circumstances of literary production – the circulation of a written manuscript or the singing or spoken performance of a lyric to a coterie audience, with publication in print not occurring until many years later, or even posthumously – was very different to today. "Gascoigne's Arraignment" stars "George" – a figure of fun who is simultaneously George the trainee lawyer entertaining his friends and Gascoigne the fictional persona. The poem is like a mini-play with three speaking parts.

"George," says the judge, "now thou art cast". This means "convicted" (with a secondary sense of "dismissed"). "Thou must go hence to heavy hill / And there be hanged, all but the head." The term "heavy hill" is obscure but presumably means the scaffold (a small hill?) with "heavy" used in the sixteenth-century sense of "grievous" or "gloomy". Similarly, though it reads oddly to a modern reader, the judgement that a prisoner "be hanged all but the head" was a conventional judicial formulation for a death sentence by hanging.

The prisoner then throws himself to the ground and prostrates himself before Beauty, begging for her pardon:

You know if I have been untrue
It was in too much praising you.

Beauty, contradicting her previous refusal to get involved in the case, asks if he is willing to be bound over to keep the peace "And be true prisoner all thy life?" He is – and is pardoned. Gascoigne escapes his fate, and wittily reverses the logic of the poem. Charged with flattering Beauty he is found guilty, flatters Beauty to be pardoned, and is freed to flatter Beauty in the future.[6]

It's a poem written from a safe, privileged perspective. Gascoigne treats his death sentence in jest but hanging formed a large and ugly part of Elizabethan justice. Tudor hangings involved a slow death from strangulation (unlike twentieth-century British hangings, where the prisoner dropped into a pit and died instantly from dislocation of the neck vertebrae). The penal code was harsh and offences which merited a possible death sentence included the theft of goods worth more than the very minor sum of one shilling. Each year some 800 people were hanged in Elizabethan England. Figures from Essex for the years 1570-71 show 49 hangings, including sixteen for burglary, twelve for the theft of livestock and six for witchcraft.[7] But to Gascoigne such matters were just a part of the natural order of things. His poem treats both the judicial system and hanging as material for laughter. His attitude here, as elsewhere, is disrespectfully mocking. But the comedy is not that of the satirist. There is no anger here, or desire for an alternative. The stance is rather that of a weary, sardonic acceptance of the state of things. Gascoigne is simply being wittily facetious.

This poem seems to have been much admired. It appears in a Tudor verse miscellany owned in 1642 by Gabriell Penne. It was imitated by Thomas Howell in his poem "Truth feareth no tryall" (1581). It may have been printed as a ballad after Gascoigne's death if, as seems likely, "Beauties Barre where th[e] auctor stoode" is the same poem. After Gascoigne, the figurative use of a courtroom as the location for resolving matters of love remained popular. It is found in Shakespeare's Sonnet 46 (cast in the form of a legal dispute over the youth's attractiveness, with the heart as prosecutor, the eye as the defence). It has continued to the present day.

8: Five Thousand Days

When did Gascoigne first begin his career as a writer? In the second Prefatory Letter to *The Posies of George Gascoigne Esquire*, he made a cryptic reference to "at the least five thousande dayes verie vainly spent".[1] At the time he was defending himself against the charge of having written frivolous and offensive material. The tone is deferential and acknowledges the vanity of creative endeavour but it is unlikely to have been sincere.

If, as seems likely, Gascoigne's 5,000 days refers to the time he "wasted" producing the contents of *A Hundreth Sundrie Flowres*, then, since the letter is dated 2 January 1575 (most probably modern style), it would signify 1561 as the year he first began writing. Alternatively, if the 5,000 days date back from the publication of the book, that would signify 1559. However, the phrasing is vague and Gascoigne's efforts at versifying are much more likely to have begun around the early to mid-1550s than in the later decade. But like most writers he probably preferred to forget about his juvenilia and apprentice work and date his writing from the time he began to produce material which he could look back on without embarrassment.

The years 1555-1560 were probably key years in the development of Gascoigne's taste in poetry and fiction and his growing sense of himself as a writer. As a resident of Gray's Inn he was ideally situated. Here he came into daily contact with cultured young men who valued learning and books, and who made translations from the classics and modern languages. Some of them wrote verses and circulated them in manuscript.

If we accept that Gascoigne's novella is autobiographical in its origins and that his affair with a married woman occurred before his arrival at Gray's Inn, then it is reasonable to accept G.T.'s claim that the verses written for "Elinor" were "the first beginnings of his writings, as then he was no writer of any long continuaunce".[2] But if neither premise is true and if Gascoigne hadn't already conceived of himself as a writer and started writing the wooden verses which later formed the foundation of *The Adventures of Master F.J.*, then it was surely now that he first began to pen his earliest lines.

Whenever it was that his literary career began, his earliest conception of himself would have been as a poet. Verse was the chosen literary form of England's great vernacular writer Geoffrey Chaucer, and its cultural dominance was reinforced by a major event which occurred two years after Gascoigne arrived at Gray's Inn.

Songes and Sonettes

On 5 June 1557 the law publisher Richard Tottel put out a book entitled *Songes and Sonettes by Henry Howard, Earl of Surrey, Sir Thomas Wyatt, the Elder, Nicholas Grimald, and Uncertain Authors*. It comprised 40 poems by Surrey, 96 poems by Wyatt, 40 poems by Nicholas Grimald, and a bundle of 95 poems by "Uncertain Authors", collectively attributed to Thomas Churchyard, Thomas Lord Vaux, Edward Somerset, John Heywood and Sir Francis Bryan and others.

It turned out to be one of the most popular and influential books of poetry in sixteenth-century England, taking coterie material which had previously only been circulated in private among members of the ruling class, and releasing it to the world. The collection was headed by a celebrity author, the Earl of Surrey – disgraced and executed in the reign of Henry VIII but, as one of England most prominent Catholics, culturally rehabilitated under Mary. Surrey also came first because Tottel listed his authors in order of social rank and an earl came before a knight.

The volume marked the emergence of verse from a private handwritten craft conducted by gentlemen for a very restricted courtly readership into a printed commodity sold in the public market-place. In their lifetime Surrey and Wyatt did not contemplate anything as vulgar as publishing collections of their poetry; only after death was publication possible. Part of Tottel's difficulty lay in the fact that poems which circulated in manuscript among family and friends often did not even include the name of the author and were difficult to attribute. The problem continued to the end of the century: courtly writers like Edward Dyer and Walter Ralegh shunned the publication of collections of their verse.

Court poets like Surrey and Wyatt, indifferent to publication, did not even give their poems titles. Tottel dealt with this deficiency by supplying titles of his own, which usually offered a snappy précis of a poem's contents ("Complaint that his lady after she knew of his love kept her face always hidden from him"; "Of Love, Fortune, and the lover's mind", etc.).

The book was a huge success and sold out. Tottel rushed out a new edition just weeks later – a phenomenon quite extraordinary for the time. The second edition of 31 July 1557 was enlarged with "Thirty-nine additional poems by uncertain authors". The success of the book perhaps partly derived from the *frisson* of reading intimate personal verse by a tragic figure like Surrey. It also introduced the Petrarchan lyric to England in an anglicized form and offered a template for young men to address solemn verses of undying love addressed to a desirable but remote mistress. Half a century later Shakespeare guaranteed a roar of laughter from the audience when the lecherous Slender contemplates making advances to Mistress Anne Page and wails "I had rather than forty shillings I had my Book of Songs and Sonnets here" (*The Merry Wives of Windsor*, I.i.183-4).

The joke was double-edged. The new poetry might have a utilitarian function – persuading a woman to have sex – but all writing in this era was beginning to assume a utilitarian function. Wyatt and Surrey may have written for personal pleasure but now their work had become a marketable commodity. In later years Shakespeare attempted a career as a poet who hoped for patronage but moved on to the more profitable world of commercial theatre. Gascoigne, too, used writing as a means of getting something in return. He sought patronage and, like other writers, dedicated writings to wealthy, influential men. But he was to become the first modern writer to be aware of books as a marketable commodity depending on publicity, good reviews and the promotion of the author as a celebrity.

The poetic model which Tottel put before an avid readership was that of the short lyric – usually on the subject of love, ostensibly autobiographical, and usually addressed from a man to a woman. Tottel also introduced the young men of the Inns of Court to a style of writing utterly unlike that of Chaucer. Wyatt and Surrey wrote a new kind of vernacular – what we would now call early modern English rather than Chaucerian middle English. Their preferred form – the sonnet – also offered a model which was concentrated, stylish, punchy and stunningly different to Chaucer's long, chatty, expansive verse narratives. It was like the difference between a three-minute pop song and a musical. Surrey also had the distinction of inventing a new metre which gave the flexibility of prose to the concentrated language of poetry. After his death it became known as blank verse.

Tottel's impact on Gascoigne was enormous. Hazlitt shrewdly described *Songes and Sonettes* as "an inspiring and stimulating influence".[3] When, two decades later, Gascoigne published his first book it was modelled on Tottel in so far as it purported to be an anthology. "The Devises of Sundrie Gentlemen" was Gascoigne's mock equivalent of Tottel's "Uncertain Authors". Just as Tottel invented snappy titles for Wyatt's and Surrey's untitled verse, so Gascoigne provided similarly explicatory titles (*"The careful lover combred* [burdened] *with pleasure, thus complayneth"*).[4] But Gascoigne went one better, sometimes prefacing his verse with a prose preamble which supplied a dramatic context for its composition. While composing one poem (*"He began to write by a gentlewoman who passed by him with hir armes set bragging* [swaggering] *by hir sides, and left it unfinished as followeth"*) he claimed to be interrupted by the woman's appearance in the street outside his lodgings. He therefore abandoned it and wrote a sequel because she *"cast a longe looke towards him, whereby he left his former invention and wrote thus:"*.[5] This, once again, is text masquerading as paratext and as a literary device it is rare in the subsequent history of English poetry. Most later poetry just has a title, and it is left to literary critics and biographers to supply a context for the original act of composition.

Gascoigne seems to have had a shrewd notion of what the market required, since his own bogus but popular anthology was followed by other, genuine anthologies. In 1576 Richard Edwards, master of the children of the chapel, brought out *The Paradyse of Daynty Devises* (echoing Gascoigne's use of "Devises"). As editors of contemporary poetry anthologies sometimes do, Edwards regarded himself as a major talent and the largest contributor to the volume was himself. Unlike "The Devises of Sundrie Gentlemen" the other contributors were, however, genuinely other writers. Edwards's anthology went through eight editions in the next 24 years. Other miscellanies followed thick and fast, including *A Gorgeous Gallery of Gallant Inventions* (1578), *A Handefull of Plesant Delites* (1584), *A Banquet of Daintie Conceyts* (1588) and *England's Helicon* (1600). The verse in such anthologies was almost entirely lyrical.

Gascoigne's title, *A Hundreth Sundrie Flowres*, offered a distant horticultural echo of Tottel's exhortation to "the unlearned, by reding to learne to be more skilfull, and to purge that swinelike grosenesse, that maketh the swete majerome not to smell to their delight".[6] As G. W. Pigman points out, the word "anthology" derives "from the Greek *anthologia*, 'flower-gathering'".[7] Gascoigne's title page offers contents "bothe pleasaunt and profitable to the well smellying noses of learned Readers". Today, such metaphors have lost their pungency but at the time they were rooted in the everyday realities of a society without running water, with very primitive sanitation and where personal hygiene was poor. The stench of everyday life was never eliminated but merely held at bay by such devices as casting bottles containing perfume and *pot pourris* of herbs.

"The Printer to the Reader" which prefaces *A Hundreth Sundrie Flowres* – undoubtedly written not by the printer Richard Smith but, like everything else, by George Gascoigne – echoes Tottel's own "Printer to the Reader" and continues the metaphor of good and bad smells. Tottel was confident of the "profit and pleasure" an anthology afforded which contained works by poets such as "the noble earl of Surrey, and…the depewitted sir Thomas Wyat". Gascoigne, however, was nervously aware that not all his poems might smell quite so sweetly in the noses of some readers. "But you may take any one flower by itselfe, and if that smell not so pleasantly as you wold wish, I doubt not yet but you may find some other which may supplie the defects thereof", he pleaded. Unfortunately for Gascoigne, the idea of a sweet smell cancelling out a bad one was not one that appealed to the ecclesiastical censors. When he revised the book and re-arranged its contents he thought once more of Tottel, and echoed his title in a reference to his own collection as "so many sundrie Songs or Sonets".[8]

Petrarch

After Chaucer, the second great influence on Gascoigne's early writing – possibly by way of Tottel – was the *Canzoniere*, the volume of Italian vernacular lyrics by Francesco Petrarca, better known as Petrarch (1304-74). Gascoigne owned an Italian copy of Petrarch's writings and may have encountered the poet before Tottel's anthology was published. Alternatively, Tottel may have served as an introduction to the Italian and whetted Gascoigne's appetite for more.

In his lifetime Petrarch was a European celebrity intellectual and writer. He was admired by Chaucer as a man "whos rethorike sweete / Enlumyned al Ytaille of poetrie" (*The Clerk's Prologue*, 32-3). But this fame rested on Petrarch's work in Latin, which was then the language in which the European intelligentsia wrote and communicated. After Petrarch's death interest in the writings that had made his name ebbed, and attention switched to a collection of poems in Italian which he'd spent his life restlessly reworking and expanding.

The story behind the *Canzoniere* is well-known. When he was twenty-two, Petrarch saw and fell in love with a girl named Laura. She became his muse, inspiring what eventually became a volume of 366 poems, many in sonnet form and many on the theme of unrequited love. The *Canzoniere* became hugely popular across sixteenth-century Europe and the Petrarch/Laura romance template endured in English cultural circles throughout Elizabeth's reign. Towards the end of his life Gascoigne presented Elizabeth I with a gorgeous illustrated manuscript, inscribing it with the message "Yf god wolde deigne to make, a *Petrarks* heire of me the coomlyest Queene that ever was, my *Lawra* neds must be." The analogy was fatuous for two people who were by then middle-aged but it was well calculated for a Queen who was both learned and adored flattery.

Surprisingly, in sixteenth-century England no edition or translation of the *Canzoniere* ever appeared. This was probably because Petrarch used a clear, straightforward diction that made his Italian easily accessible to educated English readers. (To be an educated gentleman in sixteenth-century England was by definition to be bi- or multi-lingual.)

The only book from George Gascoigne's library which is known to exist today is his copy of *Il Petrarcha, con la spositione di M. Giovanni Andrea Gesualdo al Magnif. M. Bernardo Priuli, fu del Magnifico M. Giacomo*, published in Venice in 1553, which is now held at the Cudahy Library, Loyola University, Chicago. Gascoigne's signature, with accompanying flourishes, is on the title page.[9] Whether this was his only copy of Petrarch, or how important the book was to him, is not known. It contains no markings or marginalia, and an archivist reports that she "does not think the book has been much used at all; a number of the pages are still quite white".[10]

The biggest impact which Petrarch made upon Gascoigne and other English poets may have been through the translations and imaginative adaptations of individual sonnets from the *Canzoniere* done by Surrey and Wyatt, as published in Tottel. This anthology contained over 30 poems which derived from Petrarch – nine by Surrey and twenty-two by Wyatt.

Petrarch's influence took various forms. One was to popularise the Italian sonnet form and make it fashionable to repeat variations on a theme. Virtually all of Surrey's and Wyatt's translations/adaptations were sonnets. "Soon after," writes Don Paterson, "the sonnet craze broke out through the Elizabethan court like the yo-yo or the hula-hoop".[11]

The idea of grouping sonnets together took root in English writing in the 1560s, albeit in a fairly rudimentary way. Gascoigne's *Hundreth Sundrie Flowres* (1573) incorporates a trio of sonnets in *The Adventures of Master F.J.*, "Three Sonets in sequence" and "seven Sonets in sequence" written for a friend at Gray's Inn.[12] In England the tradition is generally agreed to have reached fruition with the full-blown extended sonnet sequences of Sir Philip Sidney's *Astrophil and Stella* (written 1582, published 1591), Edmund Spenser's *Amoretti* (1595) and *Shakespeare's Sonnets* (1609).

The central theme made popular by Petrarch was that of the anguish of love, often expressed by the juxtaposition or elision of opposites – the so-called "Petrarchan conceit", using devices such as antithesis, oxymoron and paradox. The most influential English example is Wyatt's version of *Canzoniere* 134, which begins

> I find no peace, and all my war is done.
> I fear and hope, I burn and freeze like ice.
> I fly above the wind yet can I not arise.
> And naught I have and all the world I seize on.

Notoriously, the over-use of these devices soon solidified into cliché. Gascoigne himself wrote two Petrarchan poems which illustrate the worst excesses of this fashion – not direct translations or adaptations so much as imitations. "Amid my bale I bath in bliss, / I swim in heaven, I sink in hell", one begins, before going on to develop a series of wooden Petrarchan clichés ("I live and lack, I lack and have: / I have and miss the thing I crave"). "Gascoigne's Passion" is no better, piling up contraries in a mechanical and unpersuasive way ("I dwell in dole, yet sojourn with delight, / Reposed in rest, yet wearied with debate").[13] At the very end of his life, Gascoigne presented Elizabeth with a long poem with the very Petrarchan title *The Grief of Joy*. Fortunately, in spite of maintaining that he was "*Petrarks* jorneyman" (517), the Petrarchan influence was limited.

Petrarchan conceits flicker into life intermittently and without distinction throughout Gascoigne's writing, but his best poetry evades that particular Italian fashion. His most successful response to Petrarchan orthodoxy, in fact, was to mock it. "Gascoigne's Anatomy" is a comic description of the abject Petrarchan lover, physically fading away for want of his remote mistress. The title is double-edged: anatomy partly means "an account of the body", referring to the poem's inventory of the lover's bodily parts – hair, eyes, teeth, tongue, cheeks, shoulders, arms, heart, lung, thighs, knees, legs and feet. But it also puns on the sixteenth-century sense of "anatomy" as meaning "skeleton". The lover in Gascoigne's poem is the "pattern of a ghost", a pitiful wretch who is little more than skin and bones:

> I pray you say, lo this was he, whom love had worn to naught.[14]

The poem's comedy chiefly relies on hyperbole. Gascoigne takes every aspect of the Petrarchan lover's wan despair and magnifies it preposterously. This is another poem written to be recited before an audience of cynical young men, with Gascoigne no doubt putting on a one-man theatrical performance as he described

> These locks that hang unkempt, these hollow dazzled eyes,
> These chattering teeth, this trembling tongue, well tewed with care full cries.
> These wan and wrinkled cheeks, well washed with waves of woe

The biggest joke of all is to point to a part of the Petrarchan lover's anatomy usually never mentioned:

> My secret parts are so with secret sorrow soken,
> As for the secret shame thereof, deserves not to be spoken.

In other words, the lover has pissed himself with sorrow. As a parody of rarefied Petrarchan verse – a piss-take, you might say – "Gascoigne's Anatomy" deserves to be much better known than it is. Its vein of humour is perhaps only matched by Alexander Pope's squib "On a Lady Who Pissed at the Opera", which notes that while others weep with emotion,

> She shows her grief in a sincerer place.

But though Gascoigne's comic instincts were to mock Petrarchan cliché, the example of the *Canzoniere* was nevertheless arguably very important for him. Petrarch's book was written over a forty-year period and conceived as a whole, rather than merely a random series of poems. *A Hundreth Sundrie Flowres* likewise organises a lifetime's work into a single entity. Tottel's *Songes and Sonettes* supplied unauthorized, explicatory titles to the untitled verse of Surrey, Wyatt and other contributors, and Gascoigne imitated this idea. But he also took it further by often providing prose introductions to individual poems, explaining their background or intended meaning. This textual innovation (which never caught on in English poetry, unlike titles) may have been inspired by contemporary editions of Petrarch, which linked the poems with prose passages.

Fontainebleau

At some point in his early adulthood, Gascoigne went abroad. That, at least, is what two of his poems suggest.[15] He visited the main palace of the French court at the magnificent Chateau of Fontainebleau, south-east of Paris, and wrote a rather wooden, undistinguished sonnet "in commendation" of it. The palace, which could hold 5,000 people, was built around an old hunting lodge close to the Seine, amid a vast pine forest. Apart from its beautiful setting, Fontainebleau was famous for its gardens, its fabulous art collection and its imitation Roman bath with sweat-rooms and frescos. Among the paintings hung on the walls of the vestibule leading to the baths were Leonardo da Vinci's "Mona Lisa", "Leda and the Swan" and "Virgin of the Rocks".

Most of Gascoigne's sonnet is devoted to describing great civilisations which shrink by comparison to "the said house of Fountaine bel'eaü". Although it's a tourist's poem it is not clear how much of the palace Gascoigne managed to see, and the garden seems to have excited him as much as the building. Today, only traces of the sixteenth-century structure remain and the palace is very different from the one Gascoigne encountered.

The sonnet written "unto a Skotish Dame whom he chose for his Mistresse in the French Court" presumably derived from the same visit to France. It's a banal sonnet addressed to a woman with "heavenly eyes" which recycles a stale Petrarchan conceit ("Let be this verse true token of my flames / And do not drench your own in deep despair"). Gascoigne's acknowledgement of his "ragged verse" and "rude ill scribbled lines" is less wittily modest than flatly accurate. The fact that the object of Gascoigne's affection was Scottish suggests that his trip to France probably occurred between April 1558, when Mary Stuart (Mary Queen of Scots) married the French dauphin, and the dauphin's death in December 1560.

Travel in Europe was as much of a rite of passage for a privileged and affluent young man as admission to Oxford or Cambridge and the Inns of Court. It helped to improve language skills and brought direct contact with other cultures. But Gascoigne would not have travelled alone on such a venture. He may have gone with a friend or friends from Gray's Inn. At the very least he would have had a servant with him. But the key European literary influences upon him came not from France but Italy.

Ariosto

Apart fom Petrarch, there was one other Italian author whose work Gascoigne would have encountered among the literati of Gray's Inn, if not earlier. This was the rather more scandalous Ludovico Ariosto (1474-1533), a lyric and epic poet and dramatist. Ariosto spent much of his life at Ferrara, where he studied law from 1489 to 1494. He was one of the first dramatists to produce comedies in the vernacular, and wrote seven satires and five comedies. Nowadays he is remembered primarily for *Orlando Furioso*, a long narrative poem in ottava rima first published in 1516 and in a final, expanded version of 46 cantos in 1532. Voltaire called it "the *Iliad* and the *Odyssey* and *Don Quixote* all rolled into one" and it was hugely popular in the sixteenth century.[16] Spenser's *The*

Faerie Queene was a conscious attempt to produce something on an equally epic scale. The first English translation of *Orlando Furioso*, by Sir John Harington, did not appear until 1591; Gascoigne may first have read the book in a French translation before he tackled the original Italian. The poem's success is not hard to understand. Ostensibly it tells the story of how its main character, Orlando, goes mad ("furioso") because his love for the beautiful Angelica is not returned. In actuality a supporting love story involving the heroine Bradamante and the infidel Ruggerio takes centre-stage, dominating a picaresque story that ranges across a vast imaginative terrain that extends as far as the legendary realm of Prester John, India, China and even the mountains of the moon. The characters pursue each other frantically around an imaginative labyrinth peopled with giants, magicians, enchantresses and monsters. Everything is wacky and faintly surreal. At one point Ruggerio mounts a fantastic winged beast named a hyppogryph, which flies him past China, over the land of the Scythians, towards the Hyrcanian sea – arriving one morning at London. Epic wars rage between the Christians and the Saracens and knights in armour clash in dark, mysterious forests. But a strong vein of realism runs through the tale. The descriptions of warfare and sieges are brutally accurate and the characters are not ciphers but persuasively lifelike with human feelings. The poem is also, by the standards of a romance, daringly explicit about sex. Its laconic tone also held a natural appeal for the briskly cynical young men of the Inns of Court: "the poem as a whole remains light-hearted, at times almost flippant, and nonsense, magical nonsense, keeps breaking in".[17]

Gascoigne would have had his own special reasons for liking *Orlando Furioso*, not least the presence of "the land of the Gascons" among its richly imaginative landscapes (Gascony appears in Cantos 8, 9, 12, 14 and 27). Ariosto's interest in advances in military technology probably also interested the poet. Canons and guns rip through the fairy-tale world of chivalrous knights in armour, and Gascoigne, who may already have encountered the arquebus at Cardington Manor, was later to display an interest and pride in weaponry. Better still, as a former law student, Ariosto held a cynical view of the profession. In Canto 14 the hideous figure of Discord is loaded down with legal papers and surrounded by a crowd of notaries, attorneys and barristers.

The very first poem in "The Devises of Sundrie Gentlemen" is entitled "A translation of Ariosto allegorized" and consists of a version of stanzas 62-4 from Canto 33 of *Orlando Furioso*. The context of this passage is significant. In the previous Canto Bradamant encounters "a Gascon knight" who tells her how Ruggiero has defeated in single combat Mandricard, one of the great Saracen warriors. This news is tempered by the revelation that Ruggerio has fallen in love with a female warrior named Marfisa and their wedding is expected soon. Bradamant gallops off in a rage and later spends the night at a castle, where she dreams of Ruggerio, who tells her to trust him and not fret herself over something that is untrue. Bradamant then wakes, denounces her deceitful dream and yearns for the rest that death brings. The twist in the story, which Bradamant is as yet unaware of, is that Marfisa is in fact not Ruggerio's lover but his sister. The passage translated by Gascoigne is thus about the frenzy brought about by an unjustified jealousy.

Gascoigne ignored Ariosto's verse form, stanzas and rhyme scheme and expanded the original Italian lines into a single block of 32 lines in Poulter's Measure. To this he added an "envoy" of six lines of his own, climaxing with a motto or "posy":

Lo Lady, if you had but half like care for me
That worthy Bradamant had then her own Ruggier to see:
My ready will should be so pressed to come at call,
You should have no such sight or dream to trouble you withal.
Then when you list command, and I will come in haste,
There is no hap shall hold me back, good will shall roon so fast.

Si fortunatus infoelix [If I am fortunate, I am unhappy][18]

Gascoigne presumably relished the fact that Bradamant has been reduced to despair by a tale told by a Gascon knight and converted the passage to his own use as the prelude to an appeal to an indifferent mistress. However successful this may have been as a courtship strategy, the poem fails. Gascoigne's translation is awkward and cumbersome and entirely lacks the grace and music of the original. And, as G. W. Pigman has demonstrated, Gascoigne is an unreliable translator.[19] There are moments when he clearly misunderstood Ariosto (mistaking "animai" [animals] for "anime" [souls], and then bluffing his way out of his difficulties). Gascoigne's enthusiasm for *Orlando Furioso* surfaces in *The Adventures of Master F.J.* and in two later poems in "The Devises of Sundrie Gentlemen".[20] In "The lover disdainfully rejected contrary to his former promise, thus complaineth" – a title which might have come straight out of Tottel – the lover compares his faithless mistress to Angelica and himself to Orlando. The allusion is to Canto 23, in which Orlando encounters inscriptions on trees in Angelica's handwriting, her name united in love-knots with Medor, and a verse by Medor which celebrates how Angelica often lay naked in his arms. This is the turning point of Ariosto's poem, in which Orlando is stunned to discover that Angelica has chosen to become the wife of a simple soldier. It is this shattering revelation which makes Orlando mad with rage and despair and gives the poem its title.

In "Gascoigne's Recantation" the poet laconically notes that there is no woman who isn't faithless, and that any man who trusts in womankind must be "madde":

> *I spare not wedlock I, who list that state advance,*
> *Ask Astolfe king of Lumbardie, how trim his dwarf could dance.*[21]

The reference is to Canto 28 and Ariosto's story about Jocondo and Astolfo, King of the Lombards. Jocondo is plunged into melancholy when he unexpectedly discovers his wife in bed with a young man but cheers up when he discovers that even Astolfo's queen is cuckolding her husband with a dwarf. He arranges for the king to see the evidence for his own eyes: "he revealed the grotesque little dwarf: he was mounted on another's filly, spurring her as his back jerked up and down".[22] Disillusioned by their wives' infidelity the two set out on a successful mission to sleep with as many married women as possible. Ariosto's story perfectly matches the brittle cynicism of Gascoigne's poem.

Gascoigne referred again to Canto 28 in his commendatory poem to the *Posies*, defending the possible "stain" caused to the "fellow flowers" by "any weed" on the grounds that his book was no worse than some of the writings of Virgil, Ovid, Ariosto or Clément Marot:

> Read Faustoes filthy tale, in Ariostoes ryme[23]

Fausto Latini is one of Astolfo's courtiers. He is instrumental in bringing his brother Jocondo to the king and unintentionally setting in motion the exposure of the two unfaithful wives.

But although Gascoigne continued to use examples from their work, in many ways Ariosto, Chaucer and Petrarch were influences that he had to get out of his system before he reinvented himself as "Gascoigne" the mature poet, novelist and satirist.

9: Under Mary

One of the smells of London during Gascoigne's early years at Gray's Inn was that of burning human flesh. The second half of the 1550s was a time of some of the most frequent and best-remembered killing of ordinary people for their religious beliefs in English history.

In 1539 Henry VIII had attempted to quell religious dissent by bullying the House of Commons into passing legislation entitled, with wild optimism, "An act abolishing diversity in opinions". Under Henry and his son Edward VI the reformation of the English church had proceeded in fits and starts, a mixture of revolutionary change, retreat and cautious advance. The solidity of these massive reforms was now threatened by the accession of a zealous upholder of the old faith to the throne.

Portraits of Mary very aptly show a hard, sour-faced, miserable-looking woman. Under Mary the struggle between the old and the new religion took a sharper form and two new words entered the language as the conscious expression of an ideological belief and group affiliation: "Catholic" and "Protestant". In the year that Gascoigne first went to Gray's Inn, Queen Mary's urge to restore the Catholic religion and turn back the reformation clock took an ugly new form. The burning of heretics began in February 1555. Her enthusiasm for putting Protestants to death was to earn her the soubriquet "Bloody Mary". What was particularly shocking was that the majority of her victims were ordinary people, subjected to a barbaric death simply for a devout commitment to their personal faith.

But no one had to die. Those charged with heresy were invited to recant. To recant, in the words of the dictionary, is to retract a formerly held opinion, belief or statement as erroneous and false. Those who did were welcomed back into the one true church. But of course no devout believer with an iron will was ever going to recant, especially in an age when the thought of eternal damnation held a powerful grip on the human imagination. Those who recanted were those whose strength of will crumbled when faced by the prospect of a horrifying death.

A total of 288 Protestants were burned at the stake during her reign. In the year Gascoigne joined Gray's Inn, seventy-one died. In 1556 eighty-nine were burned, in 1557 eighty-eight and, in the final year of Mary's reign, forty. When people were burned alive at Smithfield the smoke drifted to nearby Gray's Inn.[1] Heretics were burned at the stake under all the Tudor kings and queens but never in such numbers and never driven by such zealous enthusiasm on the part of the monarch. The last burning of a heretic in England took place under James I, in 1612, around the time of *The Tempest*, just four years before Shakespeare's death.

Shakespeare was silent about such burnings, as was almost every other writer of the era. George Gascoigne, however, published "Gascoigne's Recantation", which adverts quite specifically to the burnings of the 1550s and carries echoes of one in particular: that of the former Archbishop Cranmer.

The most prominent victims of Mary's wrath were the three senior ecclesiastics most closely associated with the reformation of the English church: Cranmer, Ridley and Latimer. In March 1554 they were taken to Oxford and the following year they were put on trial for heresy. The trial caused a sensation, as did its consequences. On 16 October 1555 Ridley and Latimer were burnt to death outside the city gate, in Broad Street, in front of Balliol College. Cranmer was taken to a tower of the gatehouse to watch. Latimer put a brave face on the fate which awaited him, famously remarking, "Be of good comfort, Master Ridley, and play the man. We shall this day light such a candle, by God's grace, in England, as I trust shall never be put out." But Latimer died quickly, unlike Ridley. Cranmer was visibly horrified by the sight of Ridley's agony. He tore off his cap, dropped to his knees and cried out in terror.

This crude mental softening-up worked. Unlike Ridley and Latimer, Cranmer recanted. He recognised the supreme authority of "the Catholic Church of Christ, and...the Pope". Publicly humiliated, he was obliged to appear in Christ Church Cathedral, where he took part in liturgical processions and celebrated mass. On 14 February 1556 the man who was the leading ecclesiastical symbol of reform and who had been responsible for annihilating thousands of images and roods was made to stand in the rood-loft of Christ Church beside the figure of the rood.

The word "recantation" carries a subsidiary sense of making a public confession of error. Cranmer's public humiliation in Oxford was complete but now it was necessary for him to retract his heretical beliefs in a written statement suitable for publication and widespread distribution. On 26 February 1556 Cranmer made his first full recantation, acknowledging the Pope's supreme authority and accepting the doctrines of transubstantiation and of purgatory. Having comprehensively recanted his reforming Protestant beliefs, Cranmer suffered a nervous breakdown. He begged for sacramental absolution, repeatedly broke down in tears, sobbed over his disobedience to the Pope and expressed his joy at returning to the Catholic faith.

Thrilled that the most important English religious representative of the reformation had recanted and was asking all those seduced by his false teachings to return to the Catholic faith, the local friars hurried to circulate Cranmer's sensational statement. It was published in London by William Ryddall and William Copland. But almost at once it was suppressed by the Privy Council. In London that spring there was unrest over Mary's assault on Protestantism. A rumour that Edward VI was still alive was circulated; those responsible for publicising it were hanged in February. In March a comet became visible over southern England; twelve men were arrested for proclaiming that the Day of

Judgement was at hand. Cranmer's recantation caused uproar in the capital because it carried the signatures of two Spaniards, de Soto and Villagarcia. Anti-Spanish feeling among Londoners made a new version of the recantation essential.

His recantation was as comprehensive as could possibly have been desired. New and longer versions kept being drawn up, all of which Cranmer agreed to. On 18 March he put his signature to the sixth and longest text of his recantation, confessing his numerous offences and crimes, including his published writings. According to canon law Cranmer should now have been spared from execution. But Mary was determined he should die. Dubious theological and legal grounds were duly discovered for burning to death a repenant sinner. On the morning of 21 March 1556 Cranmer signed fourteen additional copies of his recantation. It was the day for him to die and he was led away to church to make a final public recantation of his reforming Protestant beliefs.

Cranmer was in many ways an unattractive man. Expediency was central to his character. He himself had been complicit in the burning to death of people regarded as heretics. His recantation was clearly the abject act of a broken man willing to do anything to avoid a similar fate. But when it became brutally obvious that he was to be burned, Cranmer did an astonishing thing: he recanted his recantation. In church that morning Cranmer ignored the agreed text of his final public statement and spoke instead of "the great thing, which so much troubleth my conscience". He denounced "all such bills and papers which I have written or signed with my hand since my degradation", shouting that they were "contrary to the truth which I thought in my heart, and written for fear of death". Pandemonium broke out as the Protestants cheered and Catholic officials rushed to the pulpit. "As for the Pope," Cranmer cried, "I refuse him as Christ's enemy and Antichrist with all his false doctrine...and as for the sacrament, I believe as I have taught in my book against the Bishop of Winchester!"

Cranmer was seized and pulled from the pulpit. Amid chaotic scenes he was dragged out of church and through the streets of Oxford to the place where Latimer and Ridley had burned. As the stake was lit Cranmer plunged his hand into the flames, calling out "for as much as my hand offended, writing contrary to my heart, my hand shall first be punished therefore".

Cranmer's last day was a public relations disaster for Mary. Her vindictive desire to see him die transformed Cranmer from a demoralized and demoralizing abjurer of reforming Protestantism into a last-minute martyr for his faith. Ironically, he became the best-known martyr of her reign. Mary's government rushed out a pamphlet containing all Cranmer's recantations and the text of his agreed final speech – the one he hadn't made. But the truth of what had occurred that day in Oxford was soon widely known.

In 1559 a book was published in Basel entitled *Rerum in ecclesia gestarum commentarii*. Written in Latin, the book made a much greater impact when the first English edition appeared in 1563 under the title *Acts and Monuments*. It subsequently became one of the great propaganda successes of the reformed English church under its popular title *Foxe's Book of Martyrs*. One of its many powerful illustrations pictured the moment when Cranmer was dragged from the pulpit and silenced.

"Gascoigne's Recantation" is a poem with a highly charged title. It begins with a solemn line which echoes Cranmer's double retraction of his religious affiliation:

Now must I needs recant the words which once I spoke[2]

The implication is that the speaker is just that: a preacher. But the second line introduces two very ambiguous words – "fond" and "fancy":

Fond fancy fumes so nigh my nose, I needs must smell the smoke:

"Fond" is a word with at least five different meanings in the sixteenth century and "fancy" half a dozen. A reader expecting a solemn poem on a religious theme could interpret this line as meaning "foolishly imagining the fire I can almost smell the smoke". The next two lines are equally ambiguous:

And better were to bear a faggot from the fire,
Than wilfully to burn and blaze in flames of vain desire.

Again, a solemn religious reading might conclude that "vain desire" means "spiritual pride". The poem continues:

You Judges then give ear, you people mark me well
I say, both heaven and hell record the tale which I shall tell,
And know that dread of death, nor hope of better hap,
Have forced or persuaded me to take my turning cap,
But even that mighty Jove of his great clemency
Hath given me grace at last to judge the truth from heresy.

What Gascoigne would have called the "invention" of the poem is clear. The speaker is standing before the stake surrounded by heaped wood which heretics were traditionally tied to and burned. But at the very last moment, with the twigs already ignited and smoke rising upward (or possibly with the imagined smell of smoke up his nose) the heretic dramatically tells his trial judges and the assembled crowd of onlookers that he has recanted. Instead of dying at the stake he repents his past errors and opts instead "to bear a faggot from the fire" – i.e. penitentially to bear a bundle of sticks as a symbol of recantation. Gascoigne probably witnessed such a scene at one or more of the public burnings staged under Mary. If he didn't he could have read about it in Foxe's *Book of Martyrs*.

The first ten lines of the poem set the scene. The remaining 26 lines supply the text of the recantation. Having stoutly asserted that his recantation is motivated not by fear of death but by God's generous intervention, enabling him at last to distinguish truth from heresy, the speaker solemnly begins:

I say then and profess, with free and faithful heart,

What follows is wholly unexpected. It comes close to blasphemy and abruptly tips the poem into comic absurdity:

That women's vows are nothing else but snares of secret smart:
Their beauty's blaze are baits which seem of pleasant taste,
But who devours the hidden hook, eats poison for repast:
Their smiling is deceit, their fair words traynes of treason,   [traps]
Their wit always so full of wiles, it scorneth rules of reason.

This is the message that God's clemency has vouchsafed to Gascoigne and it's an astonishingly facetious one. The great theological battles between Catholics and Protestants concerned such matters as the text of the Bible, the Prayer Book, the Eucharist, church services, church furnishings and who held supreme human authority over the church. By a comic sleight of hand Gascoigne mockingly transfers the concept of heresy to love and the relations between men and women. It suddenly becomes clear that "vain desire" in the fourth line refers to sexual desire, not spiritual pride. "Fancy" signifies both love and lust. It emits smoke, then bursts into flame. The imagery invokes a central Petrarchan conceit – love as something hot and fiery – but conflates it with the historical reality of Protestant martyrs burned for heresy. This was extraordinarily daring, original and witty – and also brutally insensitive to the feelings of anyone of a devout temperament. The poem displays an impudent disregard for solemn, serious theological disputation and the concept of heresy. Shockingly, Gascoigne turns the idea of recantation into an occasion for mockery and laughter.

Like Cranmer, Gascoigne disavows his heretical writings:

Percase some present here have heard myself of yore
Both teach and preach the contrary, my fault was then the more:
I grant my works were these: first, one *Anatomy*,
Wherein I painted every pang of love's perplexity,
Next that I was *arraigned*, with *George, hold up thy hand*,
Wherein I yielded Beauty's thrall, at her command to stand.
Mine eyes so blinded were (good people mark my tale)
That once I sang *I bathe in bliss, amid my weary bale,*

And many a frantic verse then from my pen did pass,
In waves of wicked heresy so deep I drowned was,
All which I now recant, and here before you burn
Those trifling books, from whose lewd lore my tippet here I turn,
And henceforth will I write how mad is that man's mind
Which is enticed by any trayne to trust in womankind.

The heretical works alluded to are "Gascoigne's Anatomy", "Gascoigne's Arraignment" and – misquoting the first line – "A strange passion of another author".[3] The latter poem is a wooden, conventional Petrarchan account of the miseries of a lover, the first is a parody of that kind of Petrarchan posturing and the other poem is a witty account of the worship of beauty. But this is comedy, not soul-searching. Gascoigne claimed that the poem was written as a song for a musical accompaniment and it certainly reads as a kind of comic mini-drama. "Gascoigne's Recantation" requires *performance* to achieve its fullest impact. It is the sixteenth-century analogue of stand-up comedy.

His audience, once again, would have been cynical young men of the Inns of Court or, possibly, courtiers. Though the dramatic setting of the poem is the burnings of 1555-58 it may well have been written at a later date. It assumes an audience which would have been detached from earnest religious debate and would not have been particularly upset by a comic treatment of the topics of heresy, recantation and martyrdom. Though Gascoigne's attitude to the burning of martyrs was facetious and would have been deeply offensive to devout Protestants, his poem is not one that would give any comfort to Catholics either. He regards all theological disputation as a matter for jest.

The poem also has a twist at the end:

I spare not wedlock I, who list that state advance;
Ask Astolf, king of Lombardy, how trim his dwarf could dance.
Wherefore fair ladies you, that hear me what I say,
If you hereafter see me slip, or seem to go astray,
Or if my tongue revolt from that which now it sayth,
Then plague me thus, *believe it not*, for this is now my faith.

A lot hinges on when the poem was written and how the phrase "who list that state advance" is interpreted. If the poem was written after 1561 then it seems quite insulting to Gascoigne's wife Elizabeth, insinuating either that she has been unfaithful or, like women in Ariosto's tale and women in general, she will be in the future. The Latin posy or motto after the poem – "Haud ictus sapio" (roughly meaning "I have not learned from experience") – repeats the one used at the end of "Gascoigne's Libel of Divorce". That poem also attacks the figure of a wife and was likewise a dramatic performance set to music.

As a recantation, the comedy continues to the very end. The speaker anticipates reverting to his original heresy and once more believing in women's vows, wit and beauty. This mockingly alludes to Cranmer's slippery principles and to his ultimate recantation of his recantation. The speaker in Gascoigne's poem does not go quite that far. He simply suggests he will probably slip back into his old ways. When he does, he warns women not to believe him. In other words, he is having his cake and eating it. He recants his former faith in women but knows he will fall in love again. When he does it will be the woman's responsibility to know he doesn't really mean it.

The "posy" after the poem – *Haud ictus sapio* (literally "struck, I am not wise") – hints at another level of meaning in the poem. The lines "And better were to bear a faggot from the fire, / Than wilfully to burn and blaze in flames of vain desire" may involve a pun on "faggot". In 1600 the word was a pejorative term applied to a woman; in the nineteenth century "to faggot" meant "to fuck" or "to frequent whores". If one or some of these senses existed in the mid-sixteenth century then these lines may mean "it is better to have sex with a woman than languish in a state of Petrarchan longing" – or even "it is better to have sex with a whore and risk a disease than be sexually frustrated". The entire poem in fact may toy with the idea that sex with a woman is risky and that "the hidden hook" and "poison" are metaphors for disease. A woman may perhaps "plague" him in more ways than one. If he has been "struck" before it may have been by more than the darts of Cupid. Religious belief, in short, is not the only thing that can force a man to burn.

If religion makes Gascoigne think of sex, the reverse is equally true. When Eleanor returns to the sexual comfort of her "secretary" in *The Adventures of Master F.J.* she is partly motivated by "a scruple which lay in her conscience touching the eleventh article of her belief". This laconically alludes to the much-contested 39 articles of the Church of England, one of the central achievements of reforming Protestantism. The eleventh article insists that righteousness before God derives only from "the merit of our Lord and Saviour Jesus Christ by faith, and not for our own works or deservings". Gascoigne comes close to blasphemy as he comically suggests that Eleanor's faith in her previous lover has been mildly shaken by her bedroom antics with Master F.J. Her speedy return to the embraces of her old lover is described as "the reformation of her religion". We might say that Eleanor's moral principles are as flexible as Cranmer's and adjust themselves to the realities of any situation just as easily.

Gascoigne's cynicism about the great religious divisions of his time indicates a man whose own religious beliefs were neither rigid nor deep. His flippancy was daring for its time and it would make him enemies. In later years it would lead to one of the worst charges that could be made against anyone in that dangerous, theologically disputatious century.

Bedfordshire 1556-9

Gray's Inn required some sixth months' residence for serious-minded law students. The rest of the year could be spent wherever the student wished, either in London, returning to his parent's home, or elsewhere. It is reasonable to assume that Gascoigne spent the years from 1555 to 1559 commuting between London and Cardington.

Returning home, Gascoigne would not have been going back to a happy household. The relationship between his parents had long since broken down. The marriage was a quarter of a century old and Sir John Gascoigne had a mistress. Worse, she was a servant – a member of the Cardington Manor household.

In 1556 Sir John was obliged to appear before an ecclesiastical court presided over by Cardinal Pole, Archbishop of Canterbury, charged with adultery. The court record – *Anna Drewrie, adulterium* – reads as follows:

> Anna Drewrie parochie de Noviell vivit in amplexibus adulterinis cum Dno. Johanne Gascoine, milite. Super quo citamus utrumque. Dictus Johannes comparuit, et submisit se. Cui injunctum est, ne dictam Annam in suum consortium amplius admitteret; sed suam uxorem ultiman ad se reciperet. Quod promisit se facturum. Sed promisso non setit.
>
> Eadem Anna non comparuit. Quare stat excomunicata. Quare decrevimus scribendum regie majestati pro brevi *De excomunicata capiendo*.

> Anna Drewrie of the parish of Noviell lives in an adulterous relationship with Sir John Gascoigne, knight. And for this reason we summon both parties. The said John has appeared, and submitted himself to the judgement. And it was enjoined upon him that he no longer allow the said Anna to consort with him, but should receive again his last wife. And he promised that he would do this. But he did not stand by his promise.
>
> The Anna in question did not appear. And so she stands excommunicate. And so we have decreed that we should write to the sovereign for a writ about arresting an excommunicate.[4]

The spectral figure of Anna Drewrie reappears in Sir John Gascoigne's will, written 12 years later. Here she is described by Sir John as "sometime my servant". What happened to Anna Drewrie after the court judgement is not known (quite possibly nothing at all). She was presumably a young woman from a nearby village, employed as a servant in the Gascoigne household. No parish of "Noviell" appears to have existed; the name is presumably a mistranscription of "Northill", a village some four miles east of Cardington Manor.

Although a man who stubbornly clung to the old faith, Sir John did not allow his strong religious feelings to interfere with his affair. The situation was not unique. The poet Earl of Surrey's father, the Duke of Norfolk, installed a young mistress in his home, which his humiliated wife simply had to accept. Dame Margaret's position must have been even more uncomfortable, bearing in mind that Cardington Manor was hardly on the scale of the Norfolk household.

Perhaps Sir John made Anna Drewrie pregnant – or perhaps she just made him very, very happy. For whatever reason, Sir John made a generous financial settlement on the young woman. However, by 1564 or 1565 the relationship had evidently broken down and Sir John had failed to pay money he'd promised Anna. She therefore sued him for what was lawfully hers. When the case was due to be heard, Sir John ignored his summons to court. But not even a knight of the realm could lightly spurn the judicial process in this way. He was "outlawed" – an offence which required the Queen's pardon to be rectified. Sir John had dug himself into a hole from which he was only freed by paying 68 shillings in damages and £200 to Anna Drewrie. He was duly pardoned.

Sir John did not forget his obligation to Anna Drewrie in his will, which stated that she was in receipt of an annuity of £20. He ordered "That my said son George within one year after my decease shall procure the same to be paid or compounded within such sort that the same may be discharged".[5] He also gave instructions for the executors to take punitive sanctions against his son if he failed to meet this obligation. Sir John's will was drawn up two days before his death, so perhaps the dying man felt an urgent desire to make full restitution to Anne before he had to meet his heavenly maker and account for his sins. In the long run Anna Drewrie looked to do almost as well as Dame Margaret, who was bequeathed "household stuff" to the value of 300 marks. But George Gascoigne did not obey his father's instructions, the processing of the will became a long-drawn out affair, and it is an open question whether or not Anna Drewrie ever received her bequest.

It is hardly surprising in such circumstances that Dame Margaret chose not to be buried with her husband but instructed that her corpse be transported north and interred in the church of her Yorkshire childhood. In life she was stuck with Sir John; in death she wanted to get as far away from him as possible.

A year after his appearance before Cardinal Pole there was another local difficulty which may have brought Sir John before the courts. A gentleman named Edmond Conquest protested that on Easter Monday 1557 Sir John had launched an unprovoked assault on him and beaten him so badly with a long staff that it was touch and go whether he lived or died. Conquest's story was that he had been with a group of gentlemen who were hunting a great stag with Sir William Dormer. Dormer was Master of the Game for the Queen Majesty's Honour of Ampthill in the county of Bedford. The stag had been "stirred" in Bickering Park, the western part of the honour ("honour" meaning a group of manors). It had then fled into Cardington Wood, from where it had been chased back into Bickering Park and killed.

On his way out of Cardington Wood, Conquest encountered Sir John Gascoigne, his son George, and their men. According to Conquest, he acted like a complete gentleman. Upon seeing Sir John he dismounted from his horse, took off his cap and saluted his dear friend. Sir John "with gentle countenance" saluted him back – then treacherously and without warning launched his ferocious assault. Conquest petitioned Queen Mary, seeking a writ of subpoena to bring Sir John and George Gascoigne into the Star Chamber. This was a court made up of privy councillors and senior judges which adjudicated on cases involving accusations of public disorder or the perversion of justice.

Prouty, who began his biography with this incident, remarked "such events seem to have been usual in the lives of father and son".[6] But Prouty naïvely accepted Conquest's account as the unvarnished truth. His portrait of Sir John and son George as swaggering, belligerent rogues is a gross caricature. In fact the fracas in Cardington Wood was typical of the age, not of the participants. In the absence of a national police force, men frequently resorted to force to resolve disputes. It was not rare for members of the gentry supported by armed groups to clash over land or property.

Conquest's account of what happened is very questionable. Can we really be sure that the stag was chased into Cardington Wood, the property of the Gascoigne family? Was it, perhaps, never in Bickering Park in the first place? And was the stag really chased into Bickering Park and killed there, or was it, perhaps, killed in Cardington Wood, and the carcase quickly hurried off the Gascoigne land?

From Sir John Gascoigne's point of view the situation was certainly provocative. A group of men had invaded his property without his permission. They had hunted a stag in Cardington Wood and killed it. When news of this outrageous action reached his ears, Sir John went out in search of the trespassers. He took with him twenty men, including his son George, some local yeomen and some of the household retainers, armed with mainly agricultural weaponry – staves, bills, swords, bucklers, pitchforks and partisans. Somewhere in Cardington Wood they came across a straggler from the hunt, Edmond Conquest.

Conquest had every reason to be frightened, having been caught without authority on the Gascoigne lands. He had evidently become separated from his associates. It is perfectly plausible that he sprang from his horse, doffed his cap and tried to put a brave face on the situation. He was after all faced by an angry landowner and some twenty of his men. But it is most unlikely, as Conquest alleged, that Sir John was in a sweet, gentle mood. Rather, he would have been in a towering rage. And now he had caught one of the trespassers red-handed. That Sir John began to beat Conquest with a staff and had to be dragged away before he killed him is quite likely. But by the rough justice of the time Conquest was only getting what he deserved. Sir John gave Conquest a brisk thrashing, then galloped off in search of the other huntsmen. Any other Tudor landowner in this situation would have done the same.

Conquest's account of being conveyed home, "swooning" frequently, and lying in bed for a week, hovering between life and death, sounds like colourful exaggeration. Whether or not his writ was granted is not known. It may well not have been. Justice was often determined by a man's standing in the social scale, and Sir John Gascoigne was a much more important local figure than Edmond Conquest, gent. In any case, the sympathies of those who sat in judgement in such cases were more likely to have been with the landowner whose rights had been violated than that of a trespasser of lower social status.

*

The importance of Sir John and his heir on the Bedfordshire scene was underlined by their entry into Parliament as Bedford MPs on 20 January 1558. It was the last Parliament of Mary's reign. Then as now it consisted of two chambers, the House of Lords and the House of Commons. The Lords was made up of the Lords Temporal (i.e. the nobility) and the Lords Spiritual (i.e. the leading churchmen). Members of Parliament in the lower chamber were either Knights of the Shires (two representing each English county) or Burgesses (representing enfranchised urban boroughs). During George Gascoigne's brief period as an MP the House of Commons had around 400 members.

Parliament in the sixteenth century had very limited power. It could only be summoned by royal writ. Under Elizabeth I Parliament was in session for less than three years of her 45-year reign. Political power lay primarily with the sovereign, followed by the Privy Council. The monarch determined when a Parliament should be dissolved or adjourned, and the monarch chose the Speaker, who directed Commons business. Ministers appointed by the crown sat in both Houses, helping to control the agenda.

Parliament had three functions. Perhaps its most important from the point of view of the sovereign was financial. When Tudor kings or queens wanted to go to war their own income was insufficient and they were obliged to summon Parliament to vote for a new tax on goods and land. Parliament's other major role was to pass legislation which thereby acquired the status of statute law. Legislation needed the consent of the monarch and both houses. Lastly, Parliament passed private bills, usually dealing with parochial matters. To be an MP carried one valuable perk which was unlikely to have been of any great significance to George Gascoigne in 1558 but which was to prove attractive at a later date. When Parliament was in session an MP enjoyed freedom from arrest. It was an immunity unlikely to encourage any member promptly to pay off his debts.

When Sir John Gascoigne sat in Parliament he did so as the Member for

Bedford County; his son George sat as Burgess for Bedford Borough. They were not in any meaningful sense elected but were rather chosen as appropriate representatives of the nobility and gentry who ruled Bedfordshire and its chief town. The dominant figure in this clique was the Earl of Bedford, whose influence went far beyond that provincial town. The Earl's patronage extended to Parliamentary seats in other parts of the country, and the task of his MPs was to promote his legislative and political interests. Gascoigne was not there to think for himself or to make original speeches, merely to vote in the manner required of him by his social superiors.

George Gascoigne's experience as an MP was of very brief duration. In his later autobiographical writings he never mentions it. Parliament was adjourned in March and did not resume its session until November. By this time Mary's reign was rapidly approaching its end. Gascoigne and his father were in attendance at the house on the morning of 17 November 1558 when a messenger brought news of the Queen's death to the Lords. All MPs were called into the Lords to listen to an announcement from the Chancellor, Archbishop Heath. He broke the "most heavie and grievous" news to them but thanked "almightie God; for that he hath left unto us a true, lawfull and right inheritrice to the crowne of this realme, which is the ladie Elisabeth":

> Wherefore the lords of this house have determined with your assents and consents, to passe from hence into the palace, and there to proclame the said ladie Elisabeth queene of this realme, without further tract of time.

The response of the MPs was unanimous. With "evident appearance of joy" they cried out, "God save Queen Elizabeth!" "Long may Queen Elizabeth reign over us!"

Catholic England was finished. For that reason, Sir John Gascoigne's delight at the new monarch was probably diplomatic rather than wholehearted. The enthusiasm of George Gascoigne MP, however, is likely to have been lustier and more vigorous. His commitment to the old religion was very much weaker than his father's. He was about twenty-four years old, almost the same age as the new Queen. Though no one knew it at the time, a legendary era in English history was about to begin. It was one on which George Gascoigne would make his mark for all time.

10: At the Court of the Virgin Queen

At about 2 p.m. on the afternoon of Saturday 14 January 1559, George Gascoigne, like thousands of other Londoners, heard the guns of the Tower of London firing a noisy salute to the new monarch. Gascoigne was not there to watch the Queen but to participate in her coronation. Two days earlier she had taken formal possession of the Tower. Now she left it, moving through the cheering crowds of the city towards Westminster.

George Gascoigne was one of three almoners in this great, sumptuous, slow-moving Recognition Procession. Its purpose was to give Londoners a sight of their new Queen and to dazzle them with the splendour of the Tudor dynasty and the establishment that buttressed it. The streets had been gravelled and were decorated with streamers and banners. Brightly coloured silk hung from the buildings on the route. Hundreds escorted the young red-haired Queen, including members of her household, officials from the city, churchmen, judges, the nobility, officers of the government and a host of minor functionaries like Gascoigne. The procession threaded its way to the city boundary at Temple Bar, pausing for presentations, speeches and tableaux.

The role of an almoner was to distribute money to the needy, so presumably at certain points along the route Gascoigne and his associates were involved in formal presentations of gifts to the poor. It should have been Sir John Gascoigne who was present but he was sick and unable to leave Cardington. That was his excuse, and it may have been true. But perhaps he did not wish personally to celebrate the accession of a Protestant to the English throne, and was happy to promote the interests of his heir instead. A second traditional almoner was also absent. Lord Latimer was unavoidably detained by virtue of being incarcerated in the Fleet prison. He sent Henry Darcy in his place. Only the third incumbent, Sir Edward Bray, turned up.

By the time the great, slow-moving procession reached Westminster night was coming on and the procession concluded by torchlight. Coronation Day involved another spectacular, if shorter, procession, followed by a grand banquet at Westminster Hall.

Gascoigne's involvement in the coronation was important because it gave him access to the very centre of power in Tudor England. He had spent the past four years in London, networking among the other sons of the ruling class at the Inns of Court. Now his world expanded to include that of the royal court and it was there that he re-invented himself as a courtier and a courtier poet. These terms are often used loosely, however. The royal household was a relatively compact and closed society. The Queen's regular personal attendants consisted of about one-hundred people – gentlemen of the Privy Chamber, grooms, ushers and waiters. The ladies attendant upon the Queen were made up of her cousins, the ladies Knollys, Ashley and Cary, and the wives and daughters of the leading new courtiers such as Cecil, Throckmorton, Warner, Benger and Cheke.

Gascoigne was never a courtier in the strict definition of someone employed or patronised by the Queen. Rather he was one of the crowd of affluent, immaculately-dressed hangers-on, who lingered at court in the hope of attracting the Queen's attention and the benefits which might flow from her favour. They were courtiers in the sense that their days were spent at court and Gascoigne can reasonably be described as a courtier poet in so far as his verse expresses and describes the leisured interests of this narrow world. Among the figures praised by his verse are an unidentified countess and Catherine Brydges, who was the daughter of the 2nd Baron Chandos of Sudeley, and later the wife of William, Lord Sandys.[1] Gascoigne was never a member of the inner circle at court but what connections he did have among the ruling elite he exploited for all they were worth. In this he was entirely a man of his time.

Loitering at court in hope of preferment was an accepted occupation among the leisured children of the aristocracy and gentry. It was not in itself a foolish hope and the rewards could be stupendous. Much later in the reign a relatively minor, obscure figure named Walter Ralegh became a leading figure in the land, entirely as a result of Elizabeth's favour. But in the early years, competition for Elizabeth's attention was more difficult. The young Queen was surrounded by ardent young men. But Gascoigne belonged to the gentry, not the nobility. He had no sponsor at court. He was just another face in the crowd and his access to Elizabeth was strictly limited.

At first, Gascoigne was stunned and dazzled by what he saw:

>   when first my wandering mind
> Beheld the glistering court with gazing eye
> Such deep delights I seemed therein to find
> As might beguile a graver guest than I.
> The stately pomp of princes and their peers
> Did seem to swim in floods of beaten gold,
> The wanton world of young delightful years
> Was not unlike a heaven for to behold,
> Wherein did swarm for every saint a dame
> So fair of hue, so fresh of their attire,
> As might excel dame *Cynthia* for fame,
> Or conquer *Cupid* with his own desire.
> These and such like were baits that blazed still
> Before mine eye to feed my greedy will.[2]

In no time at all Gascoigne was part of the court set, "A gladsome guest embraced of all and some".[3] But the court was also a place of sycophancy, naked ambition and intrigue. Even Gascoigne's participation as an almoner exposed the ruthless and often petty self-interest at work among members of the ruling elite. According to Sir John Gascoigne, the three almoners were supposed to share a tun of wine (a large cask containing 252 wine gallons) and a lump sum. Sir Edward Bray simply kept both. When the matter went before the courts, Bray's defence was that no payment was owing to Gascoigne, who was not a full almoner but merely "an Aider". It sounds very much as if Bray exploited his seniority to cheat the young George Gascoigne out of his fair share, although we can't be certain as no papers have surfaced giving a final judgement in the case.

The impact of power and influence at a personal level is registered in Gascoigne's bitter poem about a former lover who disdained his company once she was lodged at court:

A Lady have I served, a Lady have I loved,
A Lady's good will once I had, her ill will late I proved.
In country first I knew her, in country first I caught her,
And out of country now in court, to my cost have I sought her.
In Court where Princes reign, her place is now assigned,
And well were worthy for the room, if she were not unkind.
There I (in wonted wise) did show myself of late,
And found that as the soil was changed, so love was turned to hate.[4]

In Bedfordshire, Gascoigne was a figure of some importance. He was the heir to Sir John Gascoigne and the Cardington estate. He had served as Bedford's MP. To any daughter of a local gentry family, George Gascoigne was quite a catch. But at the court of Elizabeth he was a nobody, a mere hanger-on. We will never know the identity of this woman from a rural gentry family who evidently found some kind of position in the royal household. But that she dumped Gascoigne in favour of a richer suitor, higher up the social scale, is an entirely plausible scenario.

The poem is not just about rejection. It is also about the physical obstruction which Gascoigne (and others like him) faced at court. Its bitterest line describes how "porters put me from my wonted place". The "danger" which "keeps the door of lady beauty's bower" evidently consists of palace footmen, refusing Gascoigne entry. In a rage of insulted pride he announces that he has had enough of all this and

Will home again to cart, as fitter were for me,
Than thus in court to serve and starve, where such proud porters be.

But these are just words. We can be certain that Gascoigne did not in fact return to Bedfordshire and melodramatically take up a life of honest toil like a labourer or a husbandman with a two-wheeled cart. The verb "to cart" perhaps springs from Gascoigne's sense of hurt pride and expresses a subconscious association with a common London sight: the public mockery of prisoners who were paraded around the city in a cart with signs displaying their offences, usually sexual. To Gascoigne, being turned away by a palace footman would have seemed an equal public humiliation.

*

In his autobiographical poem "The Green Knight's Farewell to Fancy" Gascoigne wrote:

> The gloss of gorgeous courts by thee did please mine eye[5]

In other words, "fancy" – his imagination – magnified the "gloss" of courtly life. He loved it. The court was the nation's epicentre of power and style. Anyone and everyone who mattered were there. But "gloss" is a double-edged word, signifying both surface lustre and specious appearance. It signals Gascoigne's ambivalence. He loved being at court. But his excitement and enthusiasm waned. In time, as this poem indicates, he became bitter and satirical.

> A stately sight me thought it was, to see the brave go by:
> To see there feathers flaunt, to mark their strange devise,
> To lie along in Ladies' laps, to lisp and make it nice:
> To fawn and flatter both, I liked sometimes well,
> But since I see how vain it is, *Fancy* (quoth he) *farewell*.

This is a late poem, published when Gascoigne was disillusioned by the glittering world of the court but still drawn to it. But which "gorgeous courts" did he mean? He may have seen something of the French court and perhaps briefly experienced Queen Mary's. But the court that mattered most in his life was always Elizabeth's and a central aspect of courtly life was mobility. The plural in "gorgeous courts" may simply acknowledge the fact that the court did not exist at a fixed location but was always on the move. There were royal palaces at Greenwich, Whitehall, Nonsuch, Hampton Court and Richmond, as well as Windsor Castle and what were effectively hunting lodges like Eltham Palace and Oatlands in Surrey.

In the summer the royal household often left London and went on a "progress" to visit different parts of the realm. In 1560 Elizabeth visited Hampshire and the following year she ventured into Suffolk. It is unlikely that Gascoigne went on these progresses. They were grand formal occasions and the opportunities for attracting the Queen's attention were restricted to those on the royal route, who supplied her with hospitality and greeted her with speeches, entertainments and gifts.

The next line in "The Green Knight's Farewell to Fancy" reads:

When court had cast me off, I toyled at the plowe

Since by 1563 Gascoigne was back in Bedfordshire, trying his luck as a farmer, he was evidently "cast off" before then. In November 1561 an important event in his life was to terminate, at least initially, his life as a footloose man about town. The indications are, then, that the key first period of his association with the royal court was between the spring of 1559 and autumn 1561. This was the period which surely inspired many of the witty, erotic, sophisticated love poems published in his first collection.

*

The years of Gascoigne's initial association with the Elizabethan court were momentous ones for the new regime. Mary's war with France had been a disaster and the treasury was empty. Three great intertwined matters needed to be determined. The first was to reinforce and clarify the nation's return to a reformed state religion. The second was diplomatic: to sort out the potential threat from Scotland and to avoid isolation in foreign affairs by negotiating with the great powers of mainland Europe. The third was to ensure a Protestant succession through the sovereign's marriage.

Gascoigne would have known or cared little about the first two matters. He was not a man driven by strong political or religious beliefs and only a tiny fraction of his verse employs religious themes. But the question of Elizabeth's marriage interested, vexed, and sometimes obsessed everyone, from the Privy Councillors and the court to the nation at large.

Who was the legitimate successor if the Queen were to die? In 1559 the answer was far from clear and, until Elizabeth married, the possibility of unrest or even civil war in the event of her death seemed a real one. The problem was given new urgency in October 1562 when Elizabeth contracted smallpox and appeared to be on the brink of death. According to the Spanish ambassador the scene at court was one of total confusion. Some Protestant Councillors believed Elizabeth's cousin Catherine Grey was the true heir to the throne. Others backed the Protestant Earl of Huntingdon. Catholics believed Mary Stuart should be proclaimed queen. But Elizabeth did not die and when she returned to consciousness she expressed her preference for Lord Robert Dudley, in the role of protector of the realm. At the very beginning of her reign the question of the succession was given an added twist by the Queen's intimate friendship with Dudley. In 1560 matters reached boiling point, with a new added ingredient: tantalising rumours of celebrity sex and violence.

Dudley, probably born in 1532, first met Elizabeth when he was a child and subsequently claimed that he knew her better than anyone else since she was eight years old. He was a characteristic Renaissance man of his time: highly educated and learned, and before long a patron of the arts, and an expert horseman. 1560 was a year of feverish agitation at court. Robert Dudley's wife was ill. If she died he was free to marry the Queen. Elizabeth, aged 26, was clearly in love with her handsome Master of Horse. In August Cecil contemplated – or at any rate threatened – resignation over the Queen's relationship with Dudley. Elizabeth was in danger of alienating and fragmenting the Privy Council over her infatuation. Then, on 8 September 1560, Dudley's wife Amy Robsart died in mysterious and sensational circumstances. She was found with a broken neck, at the foot of a flight of stairs. To Dudley's enemies the truth was self-evident. He had arranged her murder to make himself free to marry Elizabeth. The matter was never conclusively cleared up and the most recent study of the affair concludes that there were reasonable grounds for suspecting that Amy's death may not have been an accident.[6] To make matters worse, malicious tongues hinted that the Queen was pregnant. In November the Spanish ambassador, Álvaro de la Quadra, reported the rumour that Dudley and Elizabeth had been secretly married. Sir Henry Killigrew leeringly reported that "Lord Robert shall run away with the hare and have the Queen". But according to Sir Nicholas Throckmorton's secretary the Queen had cut into pieces the patents drawn up for Dudley's creation as a peer.

It seems likely that Elizabeth would have married Dudley if the marriage had had strong backing at court and in the Privy Council. But the mood among the majority was at best one of surly detachment. By the end of the year the matter was still unresolved. Throckmorton warned Cecil of the disastrous consequences of a marriage to Dudley: "if Her Majesty do so foully forget herself in her marriage as the bruit runneth here, never think to bring anything to pass, either here or elsewhere".[7] At this point the pair looked elsewhere for support. In January 1561 Dudley saw the Spanish ambassador and said that if King Philip could be persuaded to back his marriage to the Queen the couple would undertake the re-establishment of Catholicism by means of a General Council. This was an astonishing suggestion. But the scheme came to nothing. The prospect of marriage between the two ebbed but it became clear that Dudley continued to enjoy the Queen's special favour and protection. In 1564 she created him Earl of Leicester. The couple's intense, tormented friendship was to endure until the end of their lives. Some fifteen years later Dudley was to involve Gascoigne in his final marriage proposal to Elizabeth, an episode which exploded into angry emotion and high drama. But that episode was far in the future. In 1560 it is unlikely that Gascoigne knew Dudley, other than by sight.

*

Until the decade of Gascoigne's birth, Tudor court culture was still based on the chivalric ideal, with tournaments involving mounted knights in full armour, each bearing a massive lance, charging towards each other in the "lists". Elements of that culture remained but it was in sharp decline in Gascoigne's lifetime. When Gascoigne later described himself as "the green knight" he did so ironically. The traditional livery of the Tudors was, coincidentally, green and white, but Gascoigne used green as the colour of innocence and naïvety. Modern warfare was becoming mechanized. Though Gascoigne posed for a picture in his armour his prized weapon was not a sword but a gun.

The times were changing. Elizabeth altered the livery of her men to scarlet or fine red guarded with black velvet. But in other ways they stayed much the same. While behind the scenes the destiny of the nation was being shaped by Elizabeth and her Privy Council, in public life at court was one long holiday. Day after day was passed in playing cards, fencing, dancing, singing and playing or listening to music. The specialized vocabulary of these activities passed into the language of contemporary literature.

But the court was also a place of romance and sexual intrigue. When critics describe Gascoigne as a courtier poet they have in mind his love poetry. There are some forty love poems – numbered 8 to 47 in the modern edition of *A Hundreth Sundrie Flowres* – which probably belong to the three years Gascoigne spent loitering on the fringes of Elizabeth's court. Many are addressed to unidentified gentlewomen, "Dames" and mistresses. Some, probably influenced by the example of the Earl of Surrey's courtly verse, express a woman's point of view. The social location of the verse is vague – but this is true of most lyric poetry. Only one poem is specifically written about "a Gentlewoman in court".[8] But this is the implicit setting for most if not all of these poems about "pampered beauty".[9]

The poems in *A Hundreth Sundrie Flowres* seem to be arranged in roughly chronological order of composition and by number 61 Gascoigne's time as a courtier is evidently long past:

> I left the Court at large,
> For why? The gains doth seldom quit the charge.

Unpoetically, he ran out of money. The preferment he'd hoped for failed to materialize. And once he'd plunged into debt, his fair-weather friends deserted him. That, it seems, is what happened, and it's a convincing tale. But before the court "cast [him] off" Gascoigne clearly had a good time there. He was tall, handsome and talented and his verses would no doubt have circulated in manuscript, adding to his attraction.

The poems which poured from his pen at this time are of very variable quality and include both some of his best and some of his worst. There are mediocre outpourings like the poem of rejection addressed to a "gentlewoman", full of clanking alliteration, chivalric imagery and tired Chaucerian phraseology.[10] The poem was unfinished but Gascoigne still included it in *A Hundreth Sundrie Flowres* perhaps to help bulk it out or possibly because it memorialized a love affair he didn't want to forget. In a preamble to the next poem he explains why the poem was incomplete – the woman walked past as he was writing it, inspiring him to break off and begin a new poem. When that was finished he went straight on to write a sonnet "uppon the same occasion".[11] It was an undistinguished piece, melodramatically envisaging his cruel mistress with her hands stained by true love's blood. "Enough of this Dame", exclaims Gascoigne with an exasperation it is easy to share. He then invites the reader to "peruse his other doings which have come to my hands, in such disordred order".[12] But this is Gascoigne in his role as pretend editor commenting on the writings of an unidentified third party. In fact the "doings" are Gascoigne's own and the "disordred order" is a fraud. The collection is shaped according to his wishes; the order is one consciously imposed by choice.[13]

*

Gascoigne's court verses are lyrics and a lyric, in its literal sense, means a song sung to the accompaniment of a lyre. It's clear from his writing that Gascoigne himself was an accomplished musician, singer and dancer. The court was a place of extravagant display and show, and performance was something dear to Gascoigne's heart. His primary instrument was probably the lute – the Tudor guitar.

Masquerading as the anonymous editor of his own poems, the poet explained that "Gascoigne's Good Morrow", "Gascoigne's Good Night", "Gascoigne's Passion", "Gascoigne's Libel of Divorce", "Gascoigne's Lullaby", "Gascoigne's Recantation", "Gascoigne's *De profundis*" and "His Farewell" (part 11 of the long narrative poem "Don Bartholmew of Bathe") had all had "very sweet notes adapted unto them". So, too, had "dyvers other Ditties" in *A Hundreth Sundrie Flowres*. This music, which Gascoigne was keen the reader should hear ("For I know you will delight to hear [it]") has not survived. The long lines, rhyme and use of repeated words or phrases at the beginnings of lines often seem to indicate that these lyrics were composed with music in mind.

Gascoigne wrote many conventional lyrics addressed to well-bred "Dames". One poem inside that courtly love tradition is "Gascoigne's Passion",[14] which seems to have caught Shakespeare's eye when he was working on his sonnets. Gascoigne's poem is a response to Wyatt's classic Petrarchan sonnet beginning "I find no peace and all my war is done". By way of retort, Gascoigne writes "Some say they find nor peace, nor power to fight", asserting that his condition is "stranger". In fact it is identical to Wyatt's – torments of hot passion and cold despair. What's different is that Gascoigne enlarges the standard Petrarchan metaphor of burning/freezing by making it into a fever, with concrete physical symptoms.

From a biographical point of view the poem is of interest as a marriage proposal. It is addressed to an un-named woman, who has the power to "cure" the poet's "disease" of passion by marrying him. In return her "greatest gain" will be "A noble name". But the offer seems both perfunctory and a little too self-regarding. It sounds suspiciously like something addressed to an heiress who crossed Gascoigne's tracks at a moment of fiscal anguish. The poem comes across more as a literary five-finger exercise than as a very plausible expression of intense emotion. Gascoigne's repetitions

> What fits I feel? What distance? What delays?
> What grief? What ease? What like I best? What worst?

possibly find an echo in Shakespeare's Sonnet 97:

> What freezings have I felt, what dark days seen,
> What old December's bareness everywhere!

Sonnet 147 ("My love is as a fever, longing still") also seems to derive some of its features from Gascoigne's model. Shakespeare's fever feeds "on that which doth preserve the ill", replicating Gascoigne's "And feverlike I feed my fancy still, / With such repast, as most impairs my health". But just as the suffering lover Gascoigne is keen to establish his anguish as greater than Wyatt's, so Shakespeare outdoes Gascoigne. Gascoigne can envisage a cure for his passion from his beloved, who, as a wife, would possess "drams for my disease". But Shakespeare is "Past cure". Katharine Duncan-Jones is surely right to criticise "a post-Romantic determination to conventionalize and familiarize *Shakespeare's Sonnets*, to attach the poems to that very courtly love tradition which… Shakespeare was explicitly rejecting and debunking".[15] Shakespeare in fact seems to have gone back to Gascoigne's poetry time and time again for inspiration, particularly when he was portraying scenes at court. These borrowings have never been acknowledged, largely because Gascoigne has been little read by Shakespeare specialists. For example, Gascoigne's idiosyncratic fondness for the phrase "haste post haste" (meaning "mad rush" or "passionate urgency"), which he used to describe his breathless response to the excitements at court – "In haste post haste… in haste, (yea post post haste)" – is echoed in *Othello* ("requires your haste post haste appearance" [I.ii.37]; "Write from us to him / Post post haste dispatch" [I.iii.45-6]).[16]

Like Shakespeare's, Gascoigne's own best verse mocks the court and the timid orthodoxies of the Petrarchan lyric. The sonnet written "for the love of

Mistress E.P." is one such poem.[17] Mistress E.P., whoever she was, was clearly not someone at court. She had "A lovely nutbrown face", indicating a woman well down the social scale. A sun tan represented long hours out of doors, under the sun – something every "pampered beauty" shunned. A nutbrown face suggests a Bedfordshire countryside beauty – not the artificial urban beauty of fashionable London. The court is the place of "The painted pale, the (too much) red made white". Cosmetics are used to make complexions paler; red, flushed faces are whitened with paste. This is an anti-court poem, in which Gascoigne expresses his revulsion for

>   The garments gay, the glittring golden gite,   [gown]
>   The tysing talk which floweth from *Pallas* pools:

The talk at court is "tysing" (enticing). What "*Pallas* pools" are is not clear. The italicization of "*Pallas*" indicates a proper name and suggests Pallas Athene, goddess of war or wisdom. "*Pallas* pools" could be read as "liquid eyes like those of the goddess Pallas" – with a pun on "palace", signifying "the eyes of goddesses at court".

At court, appearance was everything. A major part of Gascoigne's expenditure would have been on fashionable clothes. In a pre-industrial era these were hand-made, individually crafted and often staggeringly expensive. As the Mistress E.P. sonnet suggests, a central aspect of court life was fashion, clothes, appearance and *looking*. The expensively dressed courtiers chattered among themselves, looking out for that exciting moment when the Queen put in her daily appearance. They examined the spectacle of her presence and her gorgeous clothes. They enviously eyed Elizabeth's closest associates, her favourites and her chief advisers. And most of all, as the minutes and hours passed, they scrutinised each other.

Talking Dirty: The Sex Poems

In this hot-house atmosphere at court, the act of looking, watching, eyeing – of perpetual surveillance – quickly became imbued with sexuality. The first of Gascoigne's verses about looking is addressed "*to a Gentlewoman whom he liked very well, and yet never had any opportunity to discover his affection, being always bridled by jealous looks, which attended them both, and therefore guessing her looks that she partly also liked him, he wrote in a book of hers as followeth*".[18] The implication of these "jealous looks" is that Gascoigne had a partner at court who objected to him eyeing other women, and likewise the gentlewoman had a male companion who resented Gascoigne's attentions. The woman's "book" was presumably a personal anthology of the type which circulated at court and which seems to have been especially popular with women. They were known as commonplace books. Such collections featured copies of verses which circulated in manuscript at court, often with variants on the originals as they were "improved" by other hands, or distorted by failures of memory.

In writing one of his own verses in the woman's book Gascoigne obviously cannily retained the original. Though Gascoigne claimed that he wrote fast there is more calculation than spontaneity involved in these sexual overtures at court. The poem unfolds a pretty conceit: the woman's *looks* make Gascoigne want to *look* at her. In what is a short poem, the word "look" (or slight variants) occurs sixteen times. But perhaps he wants more than just to look. He is in thrall to her beauty, even though his "death draws on apace" and looking at her will cause him "for to die".

It sounds innocent enough, but poets were fond of using death as a metaphor for detumescence after orgasm. There is also something suggestive about his desire to yield "all / Into thy hands". *All?* What does he mean by "all"? The poet resigns all *things* to his beloved. He asks for liberty to gaze upon "thyne eyen",

Which when I do, then think it were thy part,
To look again, and link with me in heart.

It sounds bland and harmless, but some of these words were highly charged. To yield could mean "to sexually submit". To resign "all things" could mean "to give up other women's cunts". Freedom "to gaze upon thyne eyen" could mean "freedom to gaze at your cunt" (Tudor poets sometimes enjoying drawing an analogy between the eye and a woman's vulva on the grounds of shape, moistness and being surrounded by hair). Gascoigne even underlines the erotic analogy, saying that when he gazes upon her "eyen", "then think it were thy part" (i.e. her private part).

This is classic double entendre. The poem can be read in two entirely separate ways. At first glance, on the printed page, it reads like courtly love poetry of a fairly banal and humdrum kind. But beneath the Petrarchan clichés an altogether different kind of meaning emerges. By the last line it is clear that when the poet invites the woman to "link" with him he means to connect sexually as much as romantically.

A dimension which is missing from the poem in its printed form is that of its performance. These lines are surely ones which Gascoigne either sang, perhaps accompanying himself on a lute, or spoke aloud. Read in a monotone the poem is harmless enough; everything depends on the emphasis given to certain words – the pregnant pause, the innuendo breaking to the surface with a push from the performer. It cries out for an audience of sophisticated young men (and perhaps young women) able to decode Gascoigne's risqué message.

If Gascoigne is to be believed the woman, it seems, was every bit as game for this kind of innuendo as the poet: "*With these verses you shall judge the quick capacity of the Lady: for she wrot therunder this short answer:* Look as long as you list, but surely if I take you looking, I will look with you." This could just innocently mean "if I see you looking at me then I'll look back at you". But "take" can also be read as "take sexually" or "sexually devour" (as in Shakespeare's *Venus and Adonis*: "He now obeys, and now no more resisteth, / While she takes all she can" (563-4)). This exchange is the sixteenth-century equivalent of a couple exchanging erotic emails.

In the preamble to the next poem the masks slip a little. The composer of the verses (but not the linking editorial commentary) is identified as one "G.G." – which is a bit of a giveaway. Too much so, perhaps; in the second edition Gascoigne half-heartedly muted it by changing it to "the Aucthour". The object of Gascoigne's affection is revealed as a married woman and the scene is set for the next teasing poem.

Gascoigne describes how he was at supper with this woman, her husband, her brother "and an old lover of hers by whom she had long been suspected". Everyone at the supper table was watching everyone else, from motives which ranged from jealousy and lust to brotherly concern. After supper they contrived a game of riddle verses and Gascoigne came up with one about ten eyes. The message from every eye that desired the lady was "I would that eye were mine". Again, "eye" equals "cunt" but Gascoigne – no doubt drawing sniggers from his listeners – explains that "In all this lovely company was none that could and would expound the meaning hereof" – none, that is, except the lady. She dryly remarks that his "dark speech is much too curious for this simple company" and invites him to decipher her own riddle:

> What thing is that which swims in bliss,
> And yet consumes in burning grief:
> Which being placed where pleasure is
> Can yet recover no relief.
> Which sees to sigh, and sighs to see,
> All this is one, what may it be?[19]

The answer is a penis. This is a well-bred Tudor woman talking dirty. To swim in bliss is to fuck. To consume in burning grief is to ejaculate and go limp. Lines three and four repeat the message that detumescence is the consequence of orgasm. Line five is more obscure. It might refer back to the two previous poems, which pun on seeing the woman's "eye" or vulva. "Sigh" perhaps refers to "burning grief" and hence ejaculation. Alternatively, "sees to sigh, and sighs to see" might allude to the orifice of the urethra opening to emit semen. Finally, "All this is one" means the digit one, the visual symbol of an erect penis.

The underlying message of the woman's riddle poem is: *fuck me*. Which, if the poem is autobiographical, Gascoigne evidently did. This exchange of titillating verses left him, he confesses, "contented". Afterwards they were, he says with a wink, "better acquainted". Aptly, both "content" and "acquaint" were recognized in Elizabethan times as punning on "cunt" – or "quaint" as the slang for the female sex organ was then sometimes spelled. The joke was still going strong in the seventeenth century and crops up in Andrew Marvell's "To His Coy Mistress": "... then worms shall try / That long-preserved virginity: And your quaint honour turn to dust".

But the woman was evidently promiscuous and soon Gascoigne was as jealous of her wandering eye – in every sense – as her husband. In a further exchange of verse[20] Gascoigne protests he found papers and letters in her pocket which he "liked not". The woman spiritedly replies that she will do as she likes, and he should do the same. At this point the relationship evidently ended.

What we don't know, of course, is who the woman was or if the verses attributed to her were really by her or by Gascoigne. The sequence is dramatic, constructed for performance; almost like a mini-play. These events may, of course, only have existed in the poet's imagination. Gascoigne was unequivocally playing games when he advertised his poems as the "Devises of sundrie gentlemen". Perhaps the woman's poems were part of the same subterfuge; what a Tudor woman *should* have written, rather than did. Perhaps they weren't really a woman talking dirty but a male author *fantasising* about a woman talking dirty. The sequel to the riddle of "Her Question" is "A Riddle", in which a woman – perhaps the same woman – puns on death (orgasm) and "labour" (fucking), and begs "Then give it me, for sure you may."

Whether or not this feisty, sexually liberated woman really wrote those replies, Gascoigne himself hadn't finished with the bawdy vein. His much-anthologised poem "Gascoigne's Lullaby" explicitly addresses the topic of his penis.[21] Its capacity for causing offence was indicated by the form in which it appeared in the *Oxford Book of English Verse 1250-1900*, edited by Arthur Quiller-Couch (1900), which, without any indication, missed out the fifth stanza.

It is one of Gascoigne's finest poems but like so much of his courtly writing it is double-edged. It calls itself a lullaby, and as a lullaby should be it is softly repetitive and soothing. But the singer of the lullaby reveals himself as a man, not a woman. He has many "wanton babes" that "must be stilled by lullaby". These babes turn out to be his youth, his lustful "gazing eyes", his "wanton will", his "little Robyn" (or penis), "My will, my ware, and all that was". "Ware" is an obsolete word for the genitals of either sex.

The governing conceit of the poem is that of an old man bidding farewell to the pleasures of the flesh. "It is," he says, "now time to go to bed". But whereas going to bed once meant sex and pleasure, now it signifies fuddled old age, pain and beguiling the mind with empty dreams. In the lines which Quiller-Couch found unfit for his Oxford anthology, the speaker bids a wistful farewell to his penis:

> Eke Lullaby my loving boy,
> My little Robin take thy rest,
> Since age is cold and nothing coy,
> Keep close thy coin, for so is best:
> With Lullaby be thou content,
> With Lullaby thy lusts relent,
> Let others pay which have mo pence,
> Thou art too poor for such expense.

It is a melancholy poem and an oddly moving one. Colin Burrow has called it "as good a set of octosyllabic lines as you will find in the 16th century".[22] But though the poem can be read as a mournful farewell to a man's younger days, it can equally be interpreted as a raucous mockery of its ostensible subject matter.

In *A Hundreth Sundrie Flowres* the poem is juxtaposed with the explicitly comic and irreverent "Gascoigne's Recantation". "Gascoigne's Lullaby" is not overtly humorous but neither is it free from punning. "Keep close thy coin, for so is best" puns on the resemblance between "coyne" (as it is spelt in the original) and Gascoigne (or Gascoyne). There is a further pun on the verb "to coin" – a coiner was someone who counterfeited money, illicitly reproducing it.

It could be read as a command to his penis ("Stay close to Gascoigne and don't go inside a woman, for so is best"). But "coin" in this context signifies semen, and the line also means "do not ejaculate but retain your semen". Gascoigne mockingly alludes to the theory that sex in old age shortens a man's life – or as Gabriel Harvey ominously put it, "After fifty all coitus is pernicious".[23] "Let others pay which have mo[re] pence" develops the metaphor. The final two lines of the stanza mean "let others fuck who have a richer quantity of semen in them, your semen is too thin and weak for sex". But the metaphor also carries a hint of paying for sex.

If Gascoigne read the poem out aloud to an audience then the strong probability is that it was played for laughs. The speaker purports to be an old man, brought low by "crooked age and hoary hairs". But Gascoigne was at most in his late thirties when the poem was written, and may only have been in his twenties. It is not hard to imagine Gascoigne performing it to the accompaniment of suggestive hand movements, underlining the erotic possibilities of otherwise innocent-seeming lines. Indeed, the poem ends with a sly wink. "And when you rise with waking eye / Remember Gascoigne's Lullaby" could mean "When you get an erection, remember the vision of old age contained in this poem."

Gascoigne's finest sex poem has the dull-sounding title "*He wrote (at his friends request) in prayse of a Gentlewoman, whose name was Phillip, as followeth*".[24] Usually referred to as "Phillip Sparrow", it begins:

> Of all the birds that I do know,
> Phillip my sparrow hath no peer:
> For sit she high or lie she low,
> Be she far off, or be she near,
> There is no bird so fair, so fine,
> Nor yet so fresh as this of mine.

It seems straightforward enough. The woman the poet admires is affectionately compared to a sparrow – fair, fine and fresh. It is "heaven" to hear her "chirp with cherry lip". She can sing and dance; she is "tender, sweet and soft".

> Let others praise what bird they will,
> Sweet Phillip shall be my bird still.

An adaptation of the poem set to music for four accompanied singers appeared in John Bartlet's *A Book of Ayres* (1606). It cut 20 of the poem's 54 lines. This may indicate an early anxiety about the sexual connotations of certain sections. In the twentieth century C. T. Prouty praised Gascoigne's double entendre in "Phillip Sparrow" and regretted that the poem had been omitted from anthologies. However, he found himself unable to discuss the poem at all, complaining that it amounted to "a form of jesting, hardly in the best of taste".[25]

In the sixteenth century the sparrow was commonly regarded as lecherous and promiscuous and a famous poem by Catullus to Lesbia's sparrow invited an erotic reading. This provides the context for Gascoigne's representation of the woman in his poem. She is sexually insatiable. In the mornings she has "been lately fed". At bedtime it is heaven to hear her "chirp" (i.e. cry out in orgasm). Her orgasms are spectacular:

> She chants, she chirps, she makes such cheer
> That I believe she hath no peer.

A description of the woman's throes of sexual pleasure is repeated four stanzas later:

> For when she once hath felt a fit,
> Phillip will cry still, yit, yit, yit.

She likes "good sport" – meaning sexual sport.

> With newfound toys of sundry sort
> My Phillip can both prick and prance:
> As if you say but fend cut Phipp,
> Lord how the peat will turn and skip.

In other words, the woman likes every kind of penis ("toys") with which to "prick and prance". What the next two lines signify is more ambiguous. The implication is that they are an illustration of Phillip's ability to "both prick and prance". "Fend" is a fencing term, meaning to parry a stroke. "Cut" is yet another pun on "cunt". The "peat" (meaning "spoiled girl") is Phillip herself. In other words, if Phillip ("Phipp") is told to defend her cunt, the result is that she "will turn and skip". But what does "turn and skip" *mean?* There seem to be at least three possibilities. One is that if Phillip is told to abstain from sex she'll "turn and skip" (i.e. dance with frustration). The second is that Phillip turns and skips away if ordered by her master to decline intercourse with another. This suggests that the relationship between the master and his pet resembles that between a pimp and his whore. Or perhaps thirdly, if told to defend her cunt the woman turns over, making herself available for anal sex instead. When, in the second prefatory letter to his *Posies*, Gascoigne spoke of "the doubtfulnesse of some darke places" in his verse and how "they have also seemed (heretofore) daungerous",[26] he surely had in mind such highly charged lines as these. How "daungerous" such material could be is underlined by the reluctance of printers and editors to allow Mercutio's description of Rosaline as "An open-arse": "When *Romeo and Juliet* first appeared in print, in the corrupt text of 1597, the passage substituted a euphemism, 'open Et caetera', in an early example of censorship." The accurate words did not appear in any edition until 1957.[27]

Of course one very obvious joke in Gascoigne's poem is that Phillip is much better known for being a man's name than a woman's. "Philippa" is the common female counterpart and even in the sixteenth century "Phillip" seems to have been very rare as a woman's name. At one level the poem could therefore be interpreted as being about what we would now call bisexuality. If Phillip "can both prick and prance" this is perhaps because he is not "a Gentlewoman" at all but a bisexual man who can both fuck and be fucked.

Whatever meaning Gascoigne had in mind – and he seems to have wanted to encourage a multiplicity of readings – he was coming dangerously close to obscenity with lines like "She lacks none oyle, I warrant you" – meaning: she gets all the semen she needs to satisfy her ravenous sexual appetite. More provocative still is the suggestive line that follows:

She lacks none oyle, I warrant you:
To trimme hir tayle both tryck and gay.

"Tayle" or tail is one of those words open to a variety of meanings in the sixteenth century. It can mean anus, buttocks, vagina or penis. Again, Gascoigne could mean any number of sex acts ranging from straight heterosexual intercourse to buggery between two men. "Trimme" means "to smarten" or "to make attractive"; "tryck" means "neat" or "handsome". "Gay" does not carry its modern meaning but simply means "excellent" or "estimable". Whatever the sex organ – whether vagina, penis or anus – Gascoigne leeringly insists it is attractive, admirable and well lubricated.

The central argument of the poem is that the woman has an insatiable sexual appetite which the speaker – Gascoigne – is well able to satisfy. It is a swaggering, boastful poem about possession (in every sense) of a nymphomaniac. The woman is

> well fed and feedeth oft:
> For if my Phipp have lust to eat,
> I warrant you Phipp lacks no meat.
>
> And then if that her meat be good,
> And such as like do love always:
> She will lay lips theron by the rood,
> And see that none be cast away

Those last two lines indicate another sexual practice which the poem daringly alludes to: fellatio, or oral sex from a woman to a man. There is repeated emphasis on the woman's mouth. Her "cherry lip" is a banal cliché; not so the lines

> If I command she layes on lode,
> With lips, with teeth, with tongue and all.

The term "layes on lode" means "sings for all she is worth". Her mouth, we are told, is of generous proportions:

> And though her mouth be somewhat wide,
> Her tongue is sweet and short beside.

It is a mouth built for singing, eating and making "cheere". She likes her "meat" and "will lay lips theron by the rood, / And see that none be cast away". She puts her lips to her "meat" – in other words, puts her mouth to the man's penis. The phrase "by the rood" is double-edged. Superficially, it is a harmless oath ("by the holy cross"). But to "lay lips thereon by the rood" can also be read as meaning "puts her mouth by the cross" – the cross symbolizing an erect penis. This blasphemous merging of Christian iconography and eroticism is the most provocative moment in Gascoigne's entire *oeuvre* and he was fortunate that the state censors were so distracted by *The Adventures of Master F.J.* that they did not scrutinise his verse with the same peevish intensity.

The woman's desire, with her lips touching her meat/holy cross/penis, that "none be cast away" could mean either (i) she was determined to prevent detumescence, or (ii) she wanted to swallow all the semen he ejaculated. "Phillip Sparrow" yields other double entendres. In Latin the word sparrow is a synonym for penis, and the poem can equally well be read as a celebration of Gascoigne's penis and its sexual triumphs. His sparrow sits "high" (erect) or lies "low" (detumescent). "There is no bird so fair, so fine, / Nor yet so fresh as this of mine" sang or spoke Gascoigne, no doubt making appropriate gestures towards his crotch for the amusement of his audience. His "bird" is quite literally "at hand".

> My Phillip can both sing and dance:
> With newfound toys of sundry sort,
> My Phillip can both prycke and prance:
> As if you say but fend cut Phippe,
> Lord how the peat will turn and skip.

On this reading, these lines mean something like: "My penis can entertain many different cunts. It can both penetrate and become tumescent ("prance") again, after sex. If you tell it to fend off all this cunt, Lord how agitated the women will be!" Gascoigne boasts that his penis is in great demand. It "never lacketh dainty fare". It "is well fed and feedeth oft". In this reading, when the bird "hath felt a fit, / Phillip will cry still, yit, yit, yit" Gascoigne is describing the male orgasm and ejaculation.

Any man would be to blame, Gascoigne half-mockingly, confesses:

> Which had so fine a bird as she,
> To make him all this goodly game,
> Without suspect or jealousy:
> He were a churl and knew no good,
> Would see her faint for lack of food.

Or to put it another way: "Anyone who had such a fine penis as this couldn't help having sex with all these available lovers without arousing suspicion or jealousy [by virtue of his limitless virility?]; he would be ill-bred and ignorant to leave his penis lying limp for lack of sex."

The final stanza of this song of praise is boisterously triumphant and an unashamed celebration of virile masculinity:

> Wherefore I sing and ever shall,
> To praise as I have often prov'd,
> There is no bird amongst them all
> So worthy for to be belov'd.
> Let others praise what bird they will,
> Sweet Phillip shall be my bird still.

If Gascoigne or his lovers had a pet name for his penis, this poem surely unequivocally supplies what it was. Perhaps this was part of the poem's impact when Gascoigne recited or sang it to a knowing clique at court. That young men enjoyed this kind of risqué game-playing is not in doubt. If well-bred young women joined in the fun too is not known. On the surface, the court was a place of great respectability. On 2 April 1560, William Alley, bishop elect of Exeter, preached at court "aganst blasphemy, dysse [dice], and women, and drunkenes". His solemn warning was no doubt dutifully received. But perhaps the Elizabethan court was a much raunchier and more decadent place than we have traditionally been led to believe.

The success of Gascoigne's Phillip Sparrow poem depends on its witty multi-dimensionality. Its technique is reminiscent of those surrealist paintings where objects turn into something else altogether. Magritte's "Le viol" (1934) shows a woman's face but it is one where her eyes are nipples and her mouth is formed of pubic hair. In "La lampe philosophique" (1936) the candle is a candle, a snake and a penis; the man's nose is a nose, a flaccid penis and an elephant's trunk. The effect, as in Gascoigne's poem, is unnerving, comic, erotic, bizarre. Gascoigne's sparrow is a bird, a sexually voracious woman, a bisexual man, a lusty penis. It is all of those things and none of those things. And just as surrealist art sometimes feeds on classical art in order to subvert it, so too is Gascoigne's poem a mocking response to an older poem, namely John Skelton's "Phyllyp Sparowe". Skelton's long poem, an elegy for a girl's pet bird, was at the time regarded as shockingly irreverent for giving such a trivial subject a mock-solemn treatment which included using the Latin Mass for the Dead. Gascoigne literally rewrites such lines of Skelton's as:

And when I said Phip Phip,
Then he would leap and skip,
And take me by the lip.[28]

Gascoigne seems to relish converting Skelton's innocent whimsy into something obscene. His motivation was probably deeply personal. Skelton was, notoriously, a bitter enemy and satirical critic of Cardinal Thomas Wolsey. But Wolsey had been a good friend to the Bedfordshire Gascoignes and a valued patron of the poet's grandfather, Sir William Gascoigne. In putting the boot into Skelton, George Gascoigne was settling an old family score.

PART THREE: SCANDAL

11: "Elizabeth Brytayne"

In 1561 George Gascoigne made a fateful decision. It occurred with unintended aptness at the end of a sequence of strangely ominous events for Londoners. In June lightning struck St Martin's by Ludgate, dislodging seven great stones from the battlements around the steeple. They came crashing down, breaking the leads and boards and splitting a great chest in two. Later that day lightning hit the steeple of St Paul's some two yards below the ball. The steeple caught fire, the bells collapsed on to the great organ, and the wood and lead of the great arches were consumed by fire.

That summer London was battered by heavy rain and giant hailstones. There was a storm of such intensity that the diarist Henry Machyn and his family believed that the world was coming to an end and the Day of Wrath was close at hand. These apocalyptic thoughts seemed confirmed by the exotic rumour that nine tribes which had been driven out of Egypt were about to launch an attack on the Great Turk with mighty armies. Then three houses by Smithfield pond were consumed in a conflagration. Fire also broke out at the Tower of London.

As autumn came on and another bleak winter in Tudor London drew near, a momentous event occurred in Gascoigne's life. Its ramifications were to be complex, violent and bring about the intervention of one of the most powerful figures in the land.

George Gascoigne got married.

*

On Wednesday 23 November 1561, at Christ Church Newgate, were wed "George Gascoyne and Elizabeth Brytayne". It was Gascoigne's seventh year in London since first arriving at Gray's Inn. He was around 27 years old. Unfortunately there was one major impediment to this union.

"Elizabeth Brytayne" already had a husband.

It was bigamy. The marriage was unlawful.

*

Who was "Elizabeth Brytayne"? In representing this as her name, Elizabeth was being less than honest. "Brytayne" – more commonly spelt "Britten", "Bretton" or "Breton" – was her first husband's name. But before her marriage to George Gascoigne, and following the death of Mr Breton, she'd married again. And in 1561 this second husband was still very much alive. Her lawful name, though she sought to conceal it, was Elizabeth Boyes.

Elizabeth was one of four children born to John Bacon and his wife, of Bury St Edmunds in Suffolk. No picture of her exists, as either a child or an adult. This is not unusual for the time: only the super-rich spent money commissioning portraits of themselves. Tudor women were only very rarely regarded as deserving a painted record of their existence. In his will, Elizabeth's father John Bacon is described as a "gentilman".[1] The Bacons, originally from the nearby village of Hesset, were a yeoman family with long connections to the area. The youngest child was Dorothy, who in 1559 was not yet sixteen, and there was a brother, George, who was then not yet twenty-one. The two other sisters were by this time married (in Elizabeth's case, for the second time). Elizabeth's date of birth is not known but she may well have been the oldest of the four. At any rate in 1545 – when George Gascoigne would have been about eleven years old – she married William Breton (pronounced "Briton").[2]

Breton was most probably a younger son of a gentry family from Layer Breton in Essex. He certainly came from an Essex family with strong local connections. Records of the Breton family (variant spellings include Bretounn, Britton and de Bretton) date back to the fourteenth century in the Colchester area. William Breton's father was a Colchester man who in his will asked to be interred in the local monastery of St John "near the pillar where the body of my father lieth buried".[3] The family may well have been descended from the Earl of Bretagne, who commanded the rear of William's army at the Battle of Hastings. At least one member achieved local prominence: Sir John Le Bretoune was a knight banneret in Essex in the time of King Edward I.

William Breton was a property speculator and landowner, and his marriage to Elizabeth Bacon sounds very much like an arranged one, a young girl being paired off with a wealthy older man. If Elizabeth was somewhere between fifteen and eighteen when she married, then her year of birth lay probably somewhere in the period 1526-30. If true, that would make her as little as three to four years older than Gascoigne, or at most his senior by no more than eight years. But she was possibly older, in which case her attraction for Gascoigne may have been as much to do with her considerable wealth as her beauty. His poems suggest that his marriage coincided with the draining away of his fortune after years of extravagant living in the capital. Gascoigne's attraction for Elizabeth was perhaps less ambiguous: he was tall, probably handsome, fashionably dressed, an Inns of Court wit and a courtier of sorts. In a status-obsessed age Gascoigne's credentials as a knight's son and a member of the distinguished Gascoigne family were also impressive.

Elizabeth's first husband William Breton owned extensive property in London and it seems likely that after their marriage that is where he went to live with his new and probably very young wife. During the fourteen years of their marriage, Elizabeth gave birth to two sons – Richard (born 25 November 1550) and Nicholas (born c.1555) – and three daughters: Thamar, Anne and Mary. On 12 January 1559 William Breton died. Within weeks Elizabeth had re-married. Her second husband was Edward Boyes, a gentleman from Nonnington (nowadays spelt Nonington) in Kent.[4] For Boyes, it was his third marriage. His first marriage had also been to a widow, one Jean Ashenden. She must have died, for he then married Clara Wentworth. Boyes's mother was the sister and heir of Sir Edward Ringeley, Marshall of Calais. The French connection was presumably how he came to marry Clara, for her father was Knight Porter of Calais. The value of these grand titles crumbled to dust when the French recaptured the city in 1558.

Boyes seems to have been, like Elizabeth, newly widowed, and had an infant son who'd been born the previous year. Perhaps his wife, Clara, had died in childbirth. In the Tudor era, younger widows and widowers had a briskly pragmatic attitude to death. Remarriage with what would now seem indecent haste after the death of a spouse was then not unusual. Hamlet may have been disgusted by the idea but the courtiers of Elsinore were not, and nor were most Elizabethans. In the seventeenth century Francis Bacon's widow waited just eleven days before marrying her late husband's gentleman usher. Elizabeth Breton may have acted with similar speed. She was a married woman when, in the second week of February 1559 she and Edward Boyes and "divers other as well women as men" were involved in a violent property dispute. Together, they seized the parsonage of Ealing, a village in the countryside west of London, in the county of Middlesex. That, at least, was what a local magistrate named Christopher Rythe claimed, who said the property belonged to him.[5]

Edward Boyes was born about 1528, which meant he was probably around the same age as Elizabeth. He came from a respectable and evidently reasonably affluent background, and was a landowner. What could more natural than that the widower of thirty-one with an infant son should marry a wealthy widow, also in her thirties, with five children of her own? A gentleman, after all, could hardly be expected to bring up a child himself.

By the sound of it, Elizabeth was no delicate and pampered creature of the court but a woman prepared to roll up her sleeves and stand by her man. In the Ealing parsonage affair, Elizabeth was named alongside Boyes as being responsible for forcibly entering the parsonage and taking control of it. Christopher Rythe petitioned the Queen requesting a subpoena to bring Boyes, Elizabeth and their associates into the Star Chamber. He asserted that he owned the lease of the parsonage. Witness statements described how the occupants of the parsonage had used pikes and other weapons to prevent Rythe and the constable gaining access. Whether or not Rythe was successful in his action is not known. Boyes may have been an opportunist and a rogue or he may simply have been forcefully acting to take control of what was lawfully his. Ownership of land and property was often a vexed issue under the anarchic conditions of civil law and land-leasing.

The brief glimpse that we get of Elizabeth during this episode seems to fit Gascoigne's own image of her. One of his poems invites visitors to enjoy his hospitality – but only on the condition that they return it. Its chorus runs:

> For some and some is honest play,
> And so my wife taught me to say.⁶

The poem insinuates that Gascoigne was an easy-going, generous kind of fellow – a bit of a soft touch, really. But thanks to Elizabeth's influence he now takes a much tougher line when people enjoy his favour. She is a hard-headed woman with her feet on the ground. There's no nonsense about it being better to give than to receive when she's around.

At a later date it seems to have suited Elizabeth to pretend that she had somehow been tricked into a mock marriage by Boyes. The arrangement was described as having been "solemnised" but the term is a slippery one. Probably there had been no church wedding – particularly since they had both been married before and both had children. In Tudor times an exchange of rings and vows was in law a perfectly acceptable and lawful form of marriage, though its private nature could later lead to difficulties. Lady Sheffield said she had married Robert Dudley, Earl of Leicester, in a secret ceremony, and later gave birth to his child. Dudley acknowledged an affair but denied the marriage.

That the Breton-Boyes marriage *was* lawful and above-board is indicated by Elizabeth's father's will, dated 7 April 1559. In this document John Bacon refers to his "daughter Boyes" and "Mr. Boyes my son-in-law".⁷ In addition, Rythe's petition for a writ of subpoena refers to Edward Boyes *and his wife Elizabeth*. A later legal document refers to "the jointure which the said Elizabeth might claim out of the lands of the said Edward Boys", which underlines the legality of the marriage. It meant that in the event of Boyes pre-deceasing his wife she was entitled to profits and rents from his land holdings.

The question then arises of how, having married Edward Boyes in the spring of 1559, Elizabeth Boyes came to walk up the aisle of Christ Church some two-and-a-half years later and go through a bogus marriage ceremony with George Gascoigne.

The Boyes-Breton-Gascoigne Triangle

We do not know how or where George Gascoigne first met Elizabeth. It might have been at court, though this seems unlikely. It might have been at Walthamstow in Essex – a village with which William Breton and (possibly) Gascoigne had connections, and where Gascoigne later went to live. It might have been, as C. T. Prouty suggests, through the links between Gascoigne's Cambridge tutor Stephen Nevynson and the Kent town from which Edward Boyes came.⁹ Or it might simply have been through socialising on the London scene. However they met Gascoigne would surely have noted that their surnames were alike in being of French origin: Gascon, Breton. Etymologically, they were destined for each other.

One poem – "Either a needless or a bootless comparison between two letters" – makes it crystal clear that Gascoigne knew of Elizabeth's involvement with Edward Boyes.[8] Other poems may be about Elizabeth and Gascoigne's love for her but if so they deliberately conceal her identity. The big question is when he learned of her other relationship. Was it before his bigamous marriage or wasn't it until afterwards?

The eighth poem in "The Devises of Sundrie Gentlemen" may shed some light on this murky episode in Gascoigne's life. It is addressed to "a gentlewoman" who spurned the poet's marriage proposal and chose instead a husband of inferior education, social status and character. The preamble to the poem describes how the poet's rival won her "with sweet gloves and broken rings" (alluding to the fashion for lovers to exchange perfumed gloves and the halves of a broken ring). Gascoigne also claims that it contains "both their names in clouds" – meaning that their identities are playfully concealed somewhere in the poem.

It is possible that this is a poem about the Boyes-Breton-Gascoigne triangle. The woman in the poem is someone two men are competing for. Or, rather, Gascoigne is pursuing a woman who has already settled on another man and slept with him. The bitter line, "Too late I found that gorged hawks do not esteem the lure" – i.e. hawks that have already eaten ignore tempting bait – uses the verb "to feed" in a sexual sense.[10]

The poet professes his friendship for the woman in spite of the misery she has caused him but forecasts that her other lover will one day leave her for another woman. The names of both the woman and the rival are visible within the poem. The "ancient worthy race" could mean Britons, punning on "Britayne" or "Breton". And as Prouty notes, the rival lover "Of stature small and therewithal, unequal for thine age" describes a boy (punning on Boyes). Prouty believes Gascoigne's name is also present, arguing that "His thewes unlike the first" both attacks the rival's slim, unmanly thighs, with an associated pun on "gaskins", meaning a horse's thighs (or the thick, manly thighs of a Gascoigne).[11]

G. W. Pigman believes such speculations are implausible.[12] He may well be right, though the poem's closing description of the woman's "careless childish love" sounds like another pun on Boyes/boy. If this poem *is* about Elizabeth Breton and Edward Boyes it suggests that Gascoigne first knew her in the winter of 1558-59, around the time of William Breton's death and in the weeks or months leading up to her hasty re-marriage to Edward Boyes. The main difficulty for this theory is that the poem is unequivocally about a woman preferring another man to Gascoigne for her husband. But if Gascoigne knew Elizabeth was married to Edward Boyes, why did he attempt to marry her two years later? The couple had not been divorced. It was exceptionally difficult for a woman to divorce a man, and even for a man divorce in the sixteenth century was, as Henry VIII discovered, very rare and fraught with difficulties.

It is difficult to believe that Gascoigne would have lightly contemplated a church marriage in the full knowledge that he was committing bigamy. If the poem *is* about Elizabeth and Boyes one can only conclude that Gascoigne broke up with her before her marriage to Boyes, lost contact, and upon renewing their friendship in 1561, was persuaded that her marriage had either never occurred or was in some way invalid.

One of Gascoigne's finest poems puts forward a series of comic variations on two letters of the alphabet, showing why "G" is better than "B". It is a courtship poem addressed to Elizabeth and it makes it very clear that Gascoigne knew all about her and Edward Boyes. Unfortunately there is no indication when "Either a needless or a bootless comparison between two letters" (titles were not always Gascoigne's strongest point) was written. It may have been written to Elizabeth *before* she married Edward Boyes, some time between mid-January and early April 1559, or it may have been addressed to her at a later date. The final two stanzas seem to allude to the scandal of her bigamous third marriage, so Pigman is probably right in concluding that it was written in the period between October 1562 and March 1563.[13]

The wedding day and after

"I require and charge you both, as ye will answer at the dreadful day of judgement, when the secrets of all hearts shall be disclosed, that if either of you know any impediment, why ye may not be lawfully joined together in Matrimony, ye do now confess it."

Such are the words of the priest to the persons to be married in the Church of England marriage service. It was the fourth year of the reign of Elizabeth. 23 November was St Clement's Day, to those of the old faith who still remembered their saints' days. Elizabeth chose to be married not in her local church – St Giles, Cripplegate – but in the rather grander surroundings of Christ Church Newgate. Conceivably the choice of Christ Church was another attempt to conceal her unlawful act from her neighbours (although the marriage ought to have required a reading of the banns three times in her local church). Elizabeth may, of course, simply to have wanted to avoid remarrying in the church where the father of her five children probably lay buried, especially if they were in attendance. But quite possibly it simply expressed a wish on her part or Gascoigne's for a more ostentatious venue than St Giles.

Christ Church was one of the biggest city churches, situated just north of Newgate market, not far from Butchers' Hall and the Shambles. It was originally known as Grey Friars Church, but the name was changed after the dissolution of the monasteries. It was a magnificent fourteenth-century church, 300 feet by 89 feet and 64 feet high, originally built for Queen Margaret, wife of Edward I. It was entirely paved with marble and until the reformation contained at least eleven altars. In 1547, after nine years of disuse, it became the parish church for

St Nicholas Shambles and St Ewin. Its site remains today, on the corner of Newgate Street and King Edward Street. However, this represents only the shell of the Wren church which replaced the Elizabethan church, destroyed in the Great Fire of London, 1666. The interior of the Wren church was destroyed by bombing in December 1940 and only the tower and two walls survived. The site is now known as Christ Church Greyfriars and a public rose garden copies the floor plan of the Wren church. This location has associations with another English poet, for it was here that Coleridge worshipped when he was a schoolboy at Christ's Hospital.

When Gascoigne stood before the altar of Christ Church on his wedding day it is possible that he did not know that Edward Boyes existed. But even if he knew about Elizabeth and Boyes, he was surely either ignorant of their marriage or had been persuaded that it was invalid. Elizabeth herself had evidently convinced herself she was Elizabeth Breton, not Elizabeth Boyes. From what little we can glean of Elizabeth's character from Gascoigne's poem and from the fact of her second and third marriages, she seems to have been impulsive, indecisive and easily influenced. In her defence, we can say that Tudor women were not encouraged to think for themselves.

By a curious quirk of fate, on the very same day that Gascoigne and Elizabeth were married at Christ Church Newgate, just a short distance away the chronicler "Henry de Machyn" was being publicly humiliated in the churchyard of St Paul's. Machyn was made to sit in the place of penance by the great cross of timber, mounted on stone steps and covered with lead, known as Paul's Cross. It formed an outdoor pulpit for sermons preached by leading churchmen. Since it was in sight of Christ Church it is even possible that the newlyweds witnessed Machyn's humiliation as they passed by.

That day's preacher was John Reniger, and Machyn was obliged to listen to what he had to say, while the congregation stared at the wrongdoer. Machyn's punishment was for passing on a story that the preacher John Veron "was taken with a wenche". Veron was a French preacher who Machyn had a particular animus towards, for reasons not disclosed in his diary. After Reniger's sermon Machyn was obliged to kneel down before Veron and the bishop and apologise. In a display of unchristian stony-heartedness neither man was prepared to forgive him, in spite of pleas made by Machyn's devout friends. Whether or not Machyn had to endure further and more severe punishment is unclear, though it may be significant that his diary falls silent until 13 December 1561, when it resumes its inventory of crimes, funerals and formal events.

Meanwhile the young poet and his older wife went to live in her home on Red Cross Street, in the parish of St Giles, just outside the city walls. The parish had a population of some 4,000 adults. Today Red Cross Street no longer exists. The area was heavily bombed during the Second World War and then levelled to make way for the Barbican development. Red Cross Street followed a route from what is now the entrance to the Barbican underground car park to the church of St Giles, which still exists, albeit in a much restored form.

In Gascoigne's day Red Cross Street was a street of substantial three-storey houses of the kind owned by wealthy city merchants. Just a few weeks earlier Lady Walgrave, wife of the political prisoner Sir Edmund Walgrave, had been released from the Tower following the death of her husband and went to live there. In his *Survey of London* John Stow described how between St Giles Church and the cross that gave the street its name were "divers fair houses" on the east side, and on the opposite side "many fair houses built outward, with divers alleys". Here the alleys led to a large plot of ground called the Jews' Garden – once a Jewish cemetery, "now turned into fair garden plots and summer-houses for pleasure". Round the corner, on Beech Lane, were "beautiful houses of stone, brick and timber". But north of Red Cross Street the affluence came to a sudden end on Golding Lane, which "on both the sides is replenished with many tenements of poor people".

Here Gascoigne and Elizabeth settled down to family life, with her five children from her first marriage. The household had at least seven servants, including the gardener and his wife. The house was clearly a very substantial property indeed. In his will William Breton described it as "my chieff capitall mansion house in Redcrostrete", and he bequeathed it to Elizabeth together with "the gardeyn Teñtes [tenements]". Elizabeth had probably lived there for at least seven years with her first husband, sleeping in a gilt bed with a "Tester and curteyns of blewe and yellowe sarcenett".[14] Breton's will makes clear the staggering wealth that Elizabeth took possession of. It included other property in Red Cross Street and the adjacent "Barbycan" (today's Beech Street) as well as "dyse Key" (Dice Quay), near Billingsgate. There were other properties in Eastcheap, Tower Street, New Fish Street, Finch Lane and scattered across four London parishes, as well as residential accommodation, a brewery and an inn called The George, in Aldersgate Street. There was other property and land in Essex and in Lincolnshire at Burgh le Marsh. William Breton bequeathed £100 cash for Elizabeth, £60 cash for Richard Breton, £40 cash for Nicholas Breton, and 200 marks for each daughter, as well as other property including plate, expensive clothes and a variety of household goods. But to many of these bequests William Breton had attached a condition, namely "that my saied wif kepe her self sole and do not marye after my decease".[15] If she remarried, the children's property was to be held in trust by her father John Bacon and Lawrence Eresbye. This may simply have been the caution of a man with a very much younger wife, or it may indicate that Breton had doubts about his wife's faithfulness both to his memory and to their children's best interests. If so, these doubts were more than justified. The processing of the will was delayed for more than eight years and one wonders if the poor scholars of Cambridge ever received the £5 allocated to them or "Lame Joan" got her 40 shillings.

As Gascoigne moved into Breton's splendid London house with his "wife" the great enigma is: where was Edward Boyes? How did Elizabeth think she could get away with bigamously marrying a third husband and moving him into the family home? Was Boyes in prison? Abroad? Had he gone back to live in Kent? Was he indeed a predatory adventurer who had only married Elizabeth for her wealth, then dumped her for another woman? One assumes that his second wife, Clara Wentworth, really *had* died in 1558 and that it was not all along Boyes who was the bigamist. An action later brought against Boyes by the Breton children refers to "a pretended marriage solemnised between the said Edward and the said Elizabeth" but the nature of that pretence is obscure. The action was in any case brought in their name only; the driving forces behind it were Elizabeth and Gascoigne, who had their own reasons for wishing to discredit Boyes.

One can only assume that Elizabeth's marriage to Boyes had in some way broken down and that he had left her, perhaps returning to Kent. He had presumably taken his only son and heir, Edward, then aged about three, with him. It also seems to be the case that he had made off with a substantial amount of cash and property from the house on Red Cross Street which, since the will had never been processed, was not legally his. In these circumstances Elizabeth presumably felt it was acceptable for her to marry again. Perhaps she was unable to get in touch with him, or he did not answer her letters. One can only speculate, fruitlessly. But somehow she had persuaded herself that her lawful name was Breton and that her marriage to Boyes was invalid.

She also seems to have persuaded others that this was the situation. On 14 May 1562 Elizabeth's uncle, Francis Bacon, signed an agreement with Sir John Gascoigne which gave him title to most if not all of Sir John's Bedfordshire estate "for a jointure to be assured to and for Elizabeth then and now wife of George Gascoigne".[16] But control would only pass to Bacon after the death of Sir John, his son and Elizabeth. In return Bacon presumably passed over a large sum of money. It was in effect a generous dowry, but with strings attached. It protected Elizabeth's interests in the event of her husband dying. But it also ensured that Bacon would get something back in the event that Sir John, his son and Elizabeth were suddenly snuffed out by illness.

Whatever had happened to Edward Boyes, it seems on the face of it unlikely that Elizabeth would have installed Gascoigne in the family home as her new husband if she had ever thought that Edward Boyes might one day return to her. But that is exactly what did happen. Boyes was out there, somewhere. And somehow word seems to have reached him of what his wife had done.

Boyes began legal proceedings to reclaim his wife and London home. Was it a great shock to Gascoigne to discover that his wife already had a husband? This possibility cannot be ruled out. It seems more than a coincidence that in April 1562 Gascoigne began writing *The Complaynte of Phylomene*. In its earliest incarnation the poem may have expressed Gascoigne's sense of being a victim, perhaps conveying his disgust with Elizabeth at the fraud she had perpetrated upon him. He was used to writing witty poems about his sexual desire for attractive women at court and around town. Now the lust of an older woman had enmeshed *him* in a legal quagmire. That, at any rate, is one way of reading these explosive lines:

Could not my sister's love
Once quench thy filthy lust?
Thou foilst us all, and eke thy self,
We grieved, and thou unjust.

By thee I have defiled
My dearest sister's bed,
By thee I count the life but lost
Which too too long I led.

By thee (thou Bigamus*)*
Our father's grief must grow,
Who daughters twain, (and two too much)
Upon thee did bestow.[17]

These lines are nominally addressed to Tereus by Philomene, after his sudden, brutal assault on her. But in no version of the legend but Gascoigne's is the king accused of being a bigamist. In context, the insult is a bizarre one. Bigamy involves going through a fraudulent marriage ceremony. It is a legal sleight-of-hand or confidence trick. It is a social crime, performed in a public place. It is an odd accusation to level against a rapist. Tereus's deed is done in secret. It is a furtive act of violence, known only to the rapist and his victim. But Gascoigne gives special typographical emphasis to the insult. All the other words but that one are italicised to show that this is dialogue by Philomene.

As the dramatic expression of a tormented sexual triangle it is easy enough to interpret these lines as a displaced version of Gascoigne's feelings about the mess he now found himself in. Tereus is Elizabeth, impulsively attaching herself to a desirable younger man. She foiled (and fooled) everyone around her – Gascoigne, her real husband Boyes, Gascoigne's family, perhaps her own. She is "unjust". The "life" which Philomene has "too too long" led and now "lost" is Gascoigne's carefree life at court. Elizabeth is a woman who, not content with one husband, now has "two too much". She is – Gascoigne practically spits the word out – a "Bigamus".

If this interpretation is correct, the poem was obliquely expressing Gascoigne's sense of impotent fury and self pity. True or not, he abandoned the poem and only returned to complete it over a decade later, when another crisis engulfed him. Years afterwards Gascoigne published a number of accounts of how he came to abandon the poem. In the poem's dedication he described how some "twelve or thirteen years past" he was riding back to London writing *The Complaynte of Phiyomene* when a sudden shower of rain hit him. He then "changed [his] copy, and stroke over into the *Deprofundis*" (*sic*).[18]

The reference is to Gascoigne's translation of Psalm 129 in the Latin Bible (Psalm 130 in the Authorised Version, which translates verse one's "De profundis clamavi ad te Domine" as "Out of the depths have I cried unto thee O Lord"). If this is to be believed, Gascoigne was a man who literally wrote on the hoof. In an afterword, he identified the time of the poem's initial composition very precisely: April 1562.

The anecdote is a revealing one. Perhaps it's true and it really did rain like that. Even so, it's hard not to see it as yet another symbolic expression of a force outside his control, striking without warning. This is expressed more emphatically in the preamble to "Gascoigne's *De profundis*":

> riding alone between Chelmisforde and London, his minde mused upon the dayes past, and therewithal he gan accuse his owne conscience of muche time misspent, when a great shoure of rayne did overtake him, and he beeing unprepared for the same, as in a Jerken without a cloake, the wether beeing very faire and unlikely to have changed so: he began to accuse him selfe of his carelesnesse, and thereupon in his good disposition compiled firste this sonnet, and afterwards, the translated Psalme of Deprofundis[19]

This is Gascoigne as Lear: a poor creature exposed to a great shower of rain bursting out of a clear sky. He is, in the words of the sonnet which prefaces his translation of the psalm, a "wretch", lashed by the wrath of God. It is a titanic moment of crisis. Under a louring, scowling sky, "bright *Titan*" (the sun) "shroudes / His hed abacke". The sonnet reiterates Gascoigne's solitude and his "Clokeless, unclad" state. The former courtier who once paraded in gorgeous silks now finds himself exposed and vulnerable, dressed in a mere jerkin or common short coat. He broods over the days past and accuses himself of wasted time. He condemns himself for carelessness in not being better prepared for adverse weather. But does getting wet on a rainy day send a man plunging into rewriting a sombre penitential psalm? Not usually. In this passage Gascoigne is once again projecting himself as a victim and it's plausible to read the scene as the symbolic expression of his injured status as the husband of a bigamist. His "carelessness" was in marrying Elizabeth without finding out more about her.

One wonders what the poet was doing on the road from Chelmsford in Essex. A possibility is that he'd been up to Ipswich to Christchurch Mansion for a heart to heart with his friend Bartholomew Withipoll (from Christ Church Newgate, to Christchurch, Ipswich, you might say). Chelmsford lay on the route back.

That Gascoigne's marital difficulties fuelled his version of the biblical psalm is credible enough, given that his poem "Gascoigne's *De profundis*" belongs to the year 1562. As if matters were not bad enough, a Chancery Order dated 25 April 1562 indicates that Gascoigne was now being sued by Sir Ambrose Jermyn. Jermyn was the executor of the will of a Suffolk man named Robert Ashefeilde and Jermyn sought compensation for the man's children in a dispute over land.[20]

Ironically, the matter had nothing at all to do with anything Gascoigne had done. He was being sued in his capacity as Elizabeth's new husband. The dispute concerned an old land transaction of her first husband, William Breton. Years earlier, Robert Ashefeilde and his brother Henry bought confiscated church land but to save money had allowed it to be included in letters patent obtained by William Breton to confirm his acquisition of quite separate land. Breton had then deviously used the letters patent to keep control of the land. Sir Ambrose Jermyn wanted compensation for this injustice, which denied the Ashefeilde children land that was rightfully theirs.

Gascoigne was now under attack from all sides. Boyes had taken him to court on the grounds that he was *not* Elizabeth's lawful husband. And Jermyn had taken him to court on the grounds that he *was*. Almost overnight George Gascoigne been transformed from a happy-go-lucky young man about town to the husband of a bigamous woman, mired in crisis and uncertainty. It was against this background that he poured out his heart in "Gascoigne's *De profundis*".

This particular psalm was one of a group of seven known as the Penitential Psalms, which traditionally had often been printed together and were sometimes used to prepare people for death. The best known sixteenth-century English verse translation was Sir Thomas Wyatt's, with which Gascoigne is likely to have been familiar. This used a narrative frame involving King David, his adultery with Bathsheba and the fate of her husband, Urias (another tormented triangle). The original psalm consists of eight short verses – little more than single lines. From the depths of despair, the singer cries out to the Lord to be heard. He begs the Lord to pay attention to his supplications. His soul looks for the Lord more than watchmen look for the morning. He hopes for mercy and redemption from all his iniquities.

Gascoigne's translation pumps up this short psalm into a substantial poem of 88 lines. Even Wyatt's expanded version was only 31 lines. But then Gascoigne had a lot to say, and his poem is as much an imaginative rewriting of the original as a literal translation. "De profundis clamavi ad te Domine" ["Out of the depths have I cried unto thee O Lord"] becomes

> From depth of doole wherein my soul doth dwell,   [misery]
> From heavy heart which harbours in my breast,
> From troubled sprite which seldom taketh rest,   [spirit]

> From hope of heaven, from dread of darksome hell,
> O gracious God, to thee I cry and yell.

The key word here is "yell". Timidity was not Gascoigne's style. This is the poem of a muscular Englishman, railing against his fate. Gascoigne doesn't whisper in God's ear – he screams for attention. This is not someone undergoing a private religious crisis but a man overwhelmed by earthly problems and difficulties:

> O mark in mind the burdens that I bear:
> See how I sink in sorrows everywhere.
> Behold and see what dolors I endure,
> Give ear and mark what plaints I put in ure. [practise]

This is the defendant speaking from the witness box. But it is also the prosecuting counsel asking for the court's attention as he states his case. The word "plaints" is double-edged. It can mean "lamentations" or "complaints". But it is also a legal term for an accusation or charge. God is told to listen to the charges that Gascoigne wants to lay. But these are never articulated in the poem. Instead, the poet heaps praises on his Lord. Repetition hammers home the thought that God is all merciful. The speaker visibly cheers up in the course of this rhythmical, incantatory poem.

Gascoigne claimed that it was set to music but it sounds more like Tudor rap than something to be sweetly accompanied by a lute. It is more likely to have been chanted than sung, and the most suitable accompaniment seems to be a drum rather than a stringed instrument. The poem is also, as Roy T. Eriksen has noted, "an early Elizabethan example of typologically structured poetry" – a predecessor of the psalms of Sir Philip Sidney and the better known examples by George Herbert.[21]

Having had his loud, hearty one-to-one with the almighty, Gascoigne finishes on a note of thunderous optimism:

> He will redeem our deadly drowping state,
> He will bring home the sheep that go astray,
> He will help them that hope in him always,
> He will appease our discord and debate,
> He will soon save, though we repent us late,
> He will be ours if we continue his,
> He will bring bale to joy and perfect bliss,
> He will redeem the flock of his elect
> From all that is,
> Or was amiss
> Since Abraham's heirs did first his laws reject.

The nervy, febrile mental agonies of the Victorian religious poet Gerard Manley Hopkins would have been incomprehensible to Gascoigne. The Tudor poet expresses no anxiety or doubt about the possibility of God's interest in him and his problems. He *knows* God is listening. Gascoigne yells at God to lend an ear, puts his case before the divine court, throws in some flattery, then sits down with a smile on his face, utterly confident of the heavenly verdict. God *will* sort everything out – no question.

Some of the biblical allusions seem pointed. The poem's thunderous conclusion is that humanity's fallen state is all the fault of those who rejected *laws* – surely paralleling the misfortunes of a man whose bigamous wife has flouted earthly law. The "household of the Lord" containing "*Abrahams Brattes*" perhaps bears some resemblance to that other household on Red Cross Street, where Gascoigne lived with his five stepchildren.

Gascoigne's theology is strikingly orthodox. Although brought up in the old faith, the poet evidently discarded it along the way and had no problem aligning himself with the moderate Protestantism of the new Elizabethan regime. Gascoigne's religion seems to have been of the comfortable, easy-going, flexible kind. Before the divine judge, Gascoigne felt himself on familiar ground. The heavenly court he had in mind was not really any different to the kind he'd trained in as a law student. He felt confident there. He knew how to plea bargain and how to win over the judge. It was all a question of tactics and knowing the system.

"Gascoigne's *De profundis*" has a proprietorial title, as if he'd staked his own claim to a portion of the Bible. At the same time it indicated he was a man of religion, capable of engaging with the most profound issues of human existence. When he later came to put together a collection of his poems, his religious verse must have seemed like a useful insurance policy against any charges which might be laid against some of his riskier love poems. With luck, no one idly glancing at the book would ever realise that the dignified poet of the penitential psalm was also a man who wrote about penises, vaginas and orgasms.

12: A Great Fray in Red Cross Street

Apart from expressing his feelings in verse, Gascoigne was preparing to leave London. On 14 May 1562 Elizabeth's uncle, Francis Bacon of White Friars, entered into an indenture with Sir John Gascoigne to provide a home for the newlyweds at Eastcottes Manor, which lay just across the fields from Cardington Manor.[1] But the arrangement fell through and six days later George Gascoigne signed an agreement to rent the manor of Willington, east of Bedford.[2] However, there are no signs that he and Elizabeth moved there on a full-time basis. Perhaps Gascoigne took her down there for the summer to meet her new in-laws but by the autumn they were back at the big house on Red Cross Street. The subsidy roll in 1562-3 for the parish of St Giles without Cripplegate assesses George Gascoigne as worth 100 marks a year.[3]

Back in London Boyes's legal action continued. Matters relating to marriage fell under ecclesiastical jurisdiction and three commissioners were therefore appointed out of Chancery to constitute a Court of the Arches and judge the curious case of the woman with two husbands. The commissioners – Mr D. Yale, William Cordell (Master of the Rolls) and the Recorder of London – evidently decided in favour of Edward Boyes. George Gascoigne and Elizabeth promptly appealed against the decision to the Queen's Majesty's Court of Delegates. The case ground slowly on, evidently at a pace too slow for Edward Boyes. His patience seems to have snapped – with violent consequences.

At first, Wednesday 30 September 1562 seemed a day like any other. Gascoigne and Elizabeth had now been "married" for ten months. Tudor London went about its ordinary business. On that day William Allen, leather merchant, and alderman Richard Chamberlain, two newly appointed sheriffs of London, boarded their ceremonial barges and went to Westminster hall to be formally sworn in. Back in the city, just outside the old walls, the Church of St Giles without Cripplegate, was hung with black. It was the day of the burial of the knight Sir Henry Grey of Wrest, who lived in the parish. The church was just a couple of minutes away from where Gascoigne and Elizabeth were living, and as affluent members of the local community they may well have been there, among the mourners in black filing into the church for the lavish funeral. The corpse lay covered with a black velvet pall with a white cross of satin and Sir Henry's coat of arms upon it. Two heralds of arms were in attendance and the sermon was preached by the Dean of St Paul's. Afterwards a dinner was held until 4 p.m. Henry Machyn may have been present at the funeral, in some professional capacity. At any rate, he was very well informed about the details. Machyn's obsessive interest in funerals, which focused his attention that day upon the parish of St Giles, is something for which we must be grateful, for he supplied the only record of what happened there later that day. Perhaps he lingered after the funeral dinner and saw for himself what happened, or perhaps the information was supplied by an associate in the funerals business. Either way, the diary entry undoubtedly represents the unvarnished facts as seen by an eye-witness:

> "The sam day at nyght be-twyn viij and ix was a grett fray in Redcrosse stret between ij gentyllmen and ther men, for they dyd mare one woman, and dyvers wher hurt; thes wher ther names, master Boysse and master Gaskyn gentyllmen.[4]

This is a characteristic of the dryly factual tone of Machyn's diary. Facts are what he likes – times, numbers, names. Nothing more. Machyn was a commoner, with no access to privileged information from inside the ruling circles. He notes the details of what happened on Red Cross Street between 8 p.m. and 9 p.m. and no more than that. In the days and weeks that follow the diary has nothing to say about the consequences of this "grett fray" (great disturbance) or what happened to "master Boysse" (Edward Boyes) and "master Gaskyn" (George Gascoigne). Machyn knew no more than what he'd recorded.

But what he did record was sensational enough. It reveals that Edward Boyes returned to reclaim his marital home (and perhaps his estranged wife), by force. Gascoigne repelled the invader. It was a re-run of the battle for Ealing parsonage three years earlier, but this seems to have been far more violent than the earlier episode, which was evidently more of an Ealing comedy. This time no women seem to have been involved. There was a pitched battle in Red Cross Street between the two gentlemen and their men. However many fought – ten men? twenty men? fifty? – "dyvers wher hurt". It was a savage, brutal street battle. Many were injured.

It is a puzzle why it took some ten months for this to happen and why it happened when it did. One wonders if the funeral of Sir Henry Grey had something to do with it. Did Edward Boyes feel obliged to return to the parish to attend the funeral of an old neighbour and friend, only to be enraged by the sight of Elizabeth with her new "husband"? It's an intriguing possibility but no more than that (and it may be a complete red herring: another account gives Grey's death as occurring on 16 September and his funeral six days later).

Machyn's description of the "grett fray" occurring "at nyght be-twyn viij and ix" is ambiguous. It might simply mean it occurred between 8 p.m. and 9 p.m. and he doesn't know the exact time. Or it could mean the battle lasted for a full hour. At that time, in late September, the street would have been in darkness. This was a battle fought out by torchlight – a confused, bloody affair.

Gascoigne never wrote about the incident. We do not know who won. Perhaps no one did. Street battles in London between gentlemen and their servants were not uncommon. They were usually ended by the arrival of someone in authority supported by armed men – the mayor, or city sheriffs.

Gentlemen were usually treated relatively leniently – provided there was no repetition of the offence. But the great fray in Red Cross Street was sensational, even by the rough standards of the Tudor streets. Men sometimes fought but not normally because "they dyd mare [marry] one woman". This was an explosive situation which now drew in one of the leading figures of the Queen's administration.

*

Sir Nicholas Bacon, Lord Keeper of the Great Seal of England, is remembered for two things. He was the father of the writer, philosopher, lawyer and statesman Francis Bacon (1561-1626). And for twenty years he was a leading member of Elizabeth I's administration. Nicholas Bacon was a sturdy, reliable figure – neither as flamboyant and erratic as the Earl of Leicester nor as omnipresent as the all-powerful Lord Burghley. But he was almost as important as either of these much better known statesmen.

The most familiar image of Bacon is the much reproduced painting in London's National Portrait Gallery. It shows a vast, frog-faced, genial man, his chubby face resting on several layers of enormous chin. Much less well known is the bust of Bacon at New Gorhambury House outside St Albans. It shows a younger, much tougher, leaner, ambitious-looking man.

Bacon's involvement in the Boyes-Gascoigne scandal was not the action of an impartial, neutral servant of the law. There was a personal aspect to his intervention which was never mentioned in the legal papers which piled up around the case. Firstly, he was distantly related to the bigamist Elizabeth. They both came from Suffolk families with strong local connections. Secondly, Bacon was a former business partner of Elizabeth's first husband, William Breton. Breton had been a property speculator who benefited enormously from the dissolution of the monasteries. He was involved in the acquisition of literally hundreds of pieces of real estate in every part of England, including valuable lands and properties in London.[5]

Some of his land deals involved partnership with three key officers of the Court of Augmentations. These were Richard Sackville, Chancellor of Augmentations, Richard Goodricke, Attorney of the Augmentations, and Nicholas Bacon, Solicitor of Augmentations. Nowadays we would call this corruption but in Tudor society the ruthless acquisition of land and wealth through favouritism, personal influence and a division of the spoils was regarded as the acceptable norm, not the criminal exception. Effectively, Nicholas Bacon was one of those who saw to it that William Breton was granted the right to buy confiscated church property at a dirt-cheap price. Breton then promptly sold it on, making a fat profit which he shared with Bacon and others who'd helped to set up the transaction.

As an old friend and business associate of William Breton, Bacon undoubtedly knew his wife Elizabeth. It meant she had a direct line to a man who was now one of the most powerful legal figures in the land. It helps to explain why she was never prosecuted for bigamy and how the crisis of her marital affairs was eventually resolved in a way that suited her and not the husband she chose to discard.

*

The direct intervention of Lord Keeper Bacon brought about an emergency sitting of the three senior law officers who'd formed the original Court of the Arches which had judged the case. George Gascoigne, plaintiff, and Edward Boyes, defendant – on this occasion, one suspects, bruised, bloodied and bandaged – once again appeared for a hearing into the vexed issue of "Elizabeth Brytaine alias Gascoyne alias Boys" and her marital status and property. A Chancery Decree dated 1 October 1562 was issued, in which Bacon ordered, with the consent of both parties, that Gascoigne and Elizabeth drop their ongoing appeal to the Court of Delegates. A new case would be heard "between this and the feast of all Saints next" (i.e. in the next four weeks, and no later than 1 November) by Mr D. Weston with the assistance of Mr D. Lewis and Mr D. Yale. Furthermore, the three central figures in this lurid marital drama agreed to accept whatever judgement the court came to, without any further appeal.[6]

In the meantime Bacon ordered that the house in Red Cross Street and its contents remain with Elizabeth. She was forbidden to contact either Gascoigne or Boyes. Both men were ordered to stay away from her, and a bond for £500 was drawn up between the two to secure the agreement. Certain "household stuff and goods" the ownership of which was hotly disputed – evidently items of great value rather than mere pots and pans – would remain in the possession of either Elizabeth or a neutral third party. The rents and profits of land owned by Elizabeth was to be paid into the court, which would allocate an appropriate sum for the upkeep of her and her children and retain the rest until it delivered its verdict.

Boyes and Gascoigne were ordered to return to each other "such goods and chattels" as belonged to the other man. If the court judged that Boyes was not Elizabeth's lawful husband, then Elizabeth forfeited her rights as his heir and likewise Boyes was freed from his obligation to make certain payments under the terms of William Breton's will. It was, in short, winner takes all. The lucky husband got the wife, the house, the valuable property – everything. The loser got nothing. After the spectacular disturbance on Red Cross Street, the matter needed resolving as quickly as possible.

Perhaps it was at this point that Gascoigne sat down and wrote "Either a needless or a bootless comparison between two letters".[7] Separated from

Elizabeth during the whole of October 1562, he probably returned to his rooms at Gray's Inn. Maybe, having impulsively opted for Gascoigne, she was now wavering. The poem certainly suggests a woman who cannot quite make up her mind between the two men. Lord Keeper Bacon's instruction required Gascoigne to stay away from Elizabeth but it did not order him not to communicate with her, either by letter or in verse. The poem begins by anxiously acknowledging Elizabeth's liking for Boyes:

> Of all the letters in the christ's cross row
> I fear (my sweet) thou lovest *B* the best,
> And though there may be good letters many mo,
> As *A.O.G.N.C.S.* and the rest,
>   Yet such a liking bearest thou to *B*
>   That few or none thou thinkest like it to be.

The christ's cross row was the simple wooden cross-shaped alphabet board upon which all small children first encountered the letters of the alphabet. "B" represents Boyes (and Gascoigne's image of the alphabet board suggests he was probably unconsciously associating his hated rival with small boys and their education). The "good" letters "A.O.G.N.C.S." can be re-assembled to spell GASCON – a variant spelling of Gascoigne.

The poem continues:

> And much I muse what madness should thee move
> To set the cart before the comely horse:
> Must *A* give place to *B* for his behove?   [advantage]
> Are letters now so changed from their course?
> Then must I learn (though much unto my pain)
> To read anew my christ cross row again.

> When first I learned, *A* was in high degree,
> A captain letter, and a vowel too:
> Such one as was always a help to *B*,
> And lent him sound and taught him what to do,
> For take away the vowels from their place
> And how can then the consonants have grace?

Why, the poet asks, does Elizabeth prize "B" – Boyes – above everything else? The first witty conceit of the poem is that her preference for "B" violates the natural order of things, in learning, society and the cosmos at large. To prefer "B" disturbs normal alphabetical precedence. "A" – the first "good letter" in the list of highly selective other "good" letters which spell "GASCON" – is a much better letter than "B". "A" is a captain, as opposed to a mere foot soldier. To put "B" before "A" is as perverse as putting a cart in front of a horse. In this equation Boyes equals a cart – something common and of little value – and Gascoigne equals something much more valuable, graceful and admirable. The phrase "comely horse" brings to mind the "gaskins" pun in the earlier poem. If that poem is to be believed, Edward Boyes was skinny and small whereas Gascoigne was full-bodied, manly, with big, firm thighs.

Elizabeth's fondness for Boyes/boys makes Gascoigne feel he has to return to his own boyhood and painfully re-learn his alphabet. Her unnatural prioritising of "B" is cosmic in its implications – the very letters of the alphabet are, like heavenly objects, "changed from their course". "B" on its own is graceless: it requires the assistance of a vowel such as "A".

In the face of this dazzling display of wit, did Elizabeth remember that Edward Boyes also had the letter "A" in his name? Probably not. Gascoigne is not interested in truth but in persuasion. He is, in short, back in his old role as lawyer – but this time in the court of love he is not the defendant. He is prosecuting counsel, ruthlessly determined to break the case for Edward Boyes in every way he possibly can.

In the fourth stanza Gascoigne abruptly changes his argument. Having rubbished "B" as a graceless consonant, he then puts forward the case for... a consonant.

> Yet if thou like a consonant so well,
> Why should not *G* seem better far than *B*?
> *G* spelleth God, that high in heaven doth dwell,
> So spell we Gold and all good things with *G*.
> *B* serves to spell bold, bawdy, brainsick, bold,
> Black, brown and bad, yea worse than may be told.

The poet is careful not to do anything so crass as to identify what G stands for above all else – i.e. his own surname – just as he avoids ever directly mentioning his rival's name. But there is something recklessly impudent about the implicit parallel between "Gascoigne" and God, gold and "all good things". Elizabeth was not, on the face of it, someone devout or easily offended.

The repetition of "bold" in line 23 – "*B* serves to spell bold, bawdy, brainsick, bold" – is problematic. Prouty changed the first one to "bald", in the belief it was a printer's error.[8] This is possible: the typesetter's eye may have been caught by "Gold" and "good" in the line above and carelessly made "o" the second letter. Or he may simply have misread the manuscript. As the poem was not republished in *The Posies of George Gascoigne Esquire* there are no clues as to what Gascoigne intended. It could have been a Freudian slip on Gascoigne's part. He meant to write "bald" but what he hated more than anything about

Boyes was his insolent pushiness, so it came out "bold". The repetition is unlikely to have been intentional but whether the mistake was Gascoigne's or the typesetter's is impossible to resolve. Consistency was not always Gascoigne's strong point, of course. He lists "brown" among the "bad" words, cheerfully ignoring his conclusion elsewhere[9] that "A lovely nutbrown face is best of all".

The list of bad things beginning with "b" is comically insulting to Boyes, who by implication is himself bad, brainsick (meaning mad), bold (meaning impudent rather than courageous) and bawdy. The word beginning with "b" that spells something "worse than may be told" is probably "bugger" (or "bowger" as Gascoigne spells it elsewhere,[10] punning on its phonetic similarity to "burgher"). Another contradiction, of course: it is Gascoigne, not Boyes, who is indulging in sexual innuendo.

In the fifth stanza Gascoigne works another variation on his argument. This time he focuses on music to prove that G is superior to B:

> In song, the *G* clef keeps the highest place,
> Where *B* sounds always (or too sharp or) flat:
> In *G sol, re, ut*: trebles have trim grace,
> *B* serves the base and is content with that.
> Believe me (sweet), *G* giveth sound full sweet,
> When *B* cries buzze, as is for bases meet.

Some of these musical allusions are clever, complex and archaic and refer to the solmization system of the medieval monk Guido Aretinus (also known as Guido d'Arezzo) – a superior musical intellect whose name also began with a G. But Gascoigne's point is simple enough. The note G is higher and sweeter than B. B is always flat – or it is always too sharp. In Guido's system *sol, re, ut* represent the notes G-D-C, which make a more graceful sound than music involving the note B. B, Gascoigne asserts, is a musically unsatisfactory note. It is a bass note – entirely fitting for a man as *base* as Boyes. B makes a common and contemptible sound: "buzze". But "buzze" is phonetically almost synonymous with the name "Boyes". Metaphorically, Boyes is a mere insect: something that bothers people – a fly, a slow-moving droning bee, perhaps, or an annoying, persistent wasp. Gascoigne's contempt for Boyes is matched by that of Hamlet for Polonius. When the pompous old man tells the prince something he knows already – "The Actors are come hither my Lord" – he jeeringly retorts: "Buzze, buzze" (I.ii.372-3; First Folio spelling).

In the penultimate stanza, the poem begins to wind down to its conclusion:

> But now percase thou wilt one *G* permit,
> And with that *G* thou meanest *B* to join:

> Alas, alas, me thinks it were not fit
> (To cloak thy fault) such fine excuse to coin.
> Take dooble *G* for thy most loving letter,
> And cast off *B*, for it deserves no better.

The meaning of the first four lines is oblique. The poet can envisage Elizabeth accepting one "G" but only for the purpose of joining "B" to it. But what does "GB" (or "BG") represent? Is this a reference to their bigamous marriage, which made her, unlawfully, Elizabeth Boyes Gascoigne? In assaulting the letter "B" and words it stands for Gascoigne relies on Elizabeth overlooking the fact that her own surname began with a "B", in all its incarnations (Bacon, Breton, Boyes). But the poet is clearly not thinking of the first two, because the consequences of joining B and G provoke dismay on Gascoigne's part. Their linkage somehow involves the invention of an excuse which is not appropriate as a means of concealing Elizabeth's fault. But what exactly is her "fault" or her "fine excuse"? One possible reading of these lines is: *Your excuse for committing bigamy was that you didn't think it mattered if you became Boyes Gascoigne but that was not an appropriate explanation for your fault. In law, B and G don't go together at all.*

The verb "to coin" means both "to invent" and "to counterfeit". And that is what Gascoigne's and Elizabeth's marriage was: a counterfeit. "To coin" (spelt "coyne" in the original) also half-puns on "Gascoyne", signifying that Elizabeth Boyes Gascoigne is herself a fake. Her identity is fraudulent and unlawful. Her "fault" was to enter knowingly upon a deliberately bigamous marriage, from which she cannot free herself until she has "cast off *B*[oyes]", divorced him, and taken "dooble *G*" [George *G*ascoigne] as her lawful wedded husband.

This hard-headed recognition of the situation they are in leads to the final, sombre stanza:

> Thus have I played a little with thy *B*
> Whereof the brand is thine, and mine the blame.
> The wight which wounds thy wandring will is he,
> And I the man that seek to salve thy name:
> The which to think, doth make me sigh sometime,
> Though thus I strive to jest it out in rhyme.

That first line summarises the entire poem. It is a playful account of a painful, lawless and scandalous situation. These last two stanzas surely indicate that the poem was written after Gascoigne's marriage, when he had become aware that it was bigamous. But even in these dire straits Gascoigne couldn't quite resist double entendre. To have "played a little with thy *B*" primarily means Boyes but is open to a secondary, bawdy reading. If Gascoigne read it aloud to male associates and paused meaningfully after "*B*", then laughter and sniggers would surely have been the response – for "b" could signify breasts, buttocks or bum.

The joke ends abruptly. The next line asserts that the "brand" is Elizabeth's – meaning the stigma or mark of shame. The metaphor comes from the common Elizabethan practice of stamping the skin of criminals with red-hot iron – usually on the face. Elizabeth's brand is both her lawful name – Boyes – and the shame which attaches to the public exposure of her bigamy. But Gascoigne's is "the blame". In what sense, we might ask? Does he mean that he himself was aware *in advance* that their marriage was bigamous or does he mean that people in general blame *him* for this scandalous episode, not her? The second seems to be the likelier of the two possibilities. Underneath the wit and humour, Gascoigne sounds vexed with Elizabeth. She has cloaked a fault in an unfit way by fabricating a fine excuse. Now, stingingly, he refers to her "wandring will". She is, in other words, inconstant, indecisive – by implication, unreliable.

The whole poem is an expression of Gascoigne's frustration with her mercurial temperament. After the death of her first husband she married Edward Boyes in haste. Then, impulsively, she married George Gascoigne, careless of the consequences of her bigamous act. Now, exposed as a bigamist, she can't quite decide which of her two husbands she prefers. The whole poem is an attempt to persuade her not to go back to Boyes.

> The wight which wounds thy wandring will is he,
> And I the man that seek to salve thy name

In other words, "The person who is injuring your indecisive character is Boyes and I am the man who is seeking to repair your wounded name". Only the healing ointment of "Gascoigne" can cure the raw wound of "Boyes". The verbal fireworks of the poem fizzle out and leave us with Gascoigne effectively on his knees, melancholy and pleading with Elizabeth to divorce Boyes and marry him again, lawfully this time.

*

A curious echo of the Gascoigne-Boyes dispute surfaces briefly in one of Shakespeare's most popular plays, *Richard III*. Gascoigne's playful poem about "the letters in the christ's cross row" evidently lingered in Shakespeare's mind, for when the scheming Richard, Duke of Gloucester, ingenuously asks his brother why the king has incarcerated him in the Tower of London, the Duke of Clarence replies, perplexed:

> He harkens after prophecies and dreams,
> And from the crossrow plucks the letter *G*,

And says a wizard told him that by *G*
His issue disinherited should be;
And, for my name of George begins with *G*,
It follows in his thought that I am he. (I.i.54-59)

Clarence is baffled by this alphabetical whimsy. But as both Gascoigne and Shakespeare understood, a single letter can be charged with entire worlds of meaning and consequence.

*

By the end of October 1562 the court had failed to reach a verdict. Bacon's command that the matter be settled no later than All Saints Day was coolly disregarded. Gascoigne blamed "the delays and means of [Boyes's] Counsel".[11] Since the Lord Keeper's instruction had been flouted, Gascoigne felt justified in returning to see Elizabeth on Red Cross Street. However, he did not move back in with her. Three close roll entries between 7 November and 11 December 1562 identify him as "George Gascoigne of Willington";[12] two more in December describe him as being "of Gray's Inn".[13] On 18 December 1562 Gascoigne signed a bond promising to pay £100 at Christmas to "Thomas Wood of London, gent." In it he identified his residence as being "of Gray's Inn". The debt was paid on time.[14] When Gascoigne renewed his association with Gray's Inn it seems highly unlikely that it was in order to return to his law studies. Probably he simply moved back into his old rooms there as a convenient place to wait for the dispute with Boyes to be sorted out. Elizabeth wasn't too far away if he wanted to visit her, or meet her somewhere in the city. There would also have been the attraction of the mid-winter revels.

Three legal documents from the period November 1562 to January 1563 indicate an association between Gascoigne and a young man in his early twenties named Arthur Hall.[15] As a well connected, educated gentleman, from an affluent background but sometimes in need of a serious loan, Hall was a typical Gray's Inn student. He'd been admitted a year after Gascoigne, in 1556. Before that he was probably a student at St John's, Cambridge. Like George Gascoigne, he had literary interests.[16]

Hall, born in 1539, had been brought up in Calais, where his father was the fortified city's Deputy Surveyor or "Comptroller". The Calais connection is intriguing because it suggests a possible link to Edward Boyes's mother and the family of his second wife. However, if there was one it is unlikely to have been of any significance, for after the death of his father in 1552, Hall, then aged 12 or 13, was brought back to England. There he was taken under the wing of Sir William Cecil and made his ward.

Cecil's motives were not entirely philanthropic as the Hall family lands supplied him with a lucrative source of income while the boy was a minor. However, in spring 1558 Calais surrendered to the French and Hall lost all his lands in France. The family's main estate at Grantham was agreeably close to Cecil's own estate at Stamford, and perhaps held the promise of being absorbed into his own burgeoning property empire. Cecil at this time had some 36 followers who lived in his household and wore his badge and livery. Their duties included appearing with their lord in public and carrying messages for him. Arthur Hall occupied a more privileged position than most as he was about the same age as Cecil's oldest son, Thomas and became his close companion.

It was while he was a member of Cecil's household that Hall began work on the first English translation of Homer's *Iliad*. He started it when he was about seventeen and seems to have still been working on it some six or seven years later. Roger Ascham, who was distantly related to Hall and who would have met him often as a favoured member of Cecil's household, urged him not to give up.

It was not such a weighty project as it seemed. Hall knew no Greek, and was simply producing a translation of a French version by Hugues Salel, which was itself merely, in the words of one critic, "a faithful and mediocre reproduction made by a worthy plodder".[17] Gascoigne, who before too long would be attempting his own translation of a Greek classic, was surely interested in this project and is likely to have seen the manuscript. How close the friendship was it is hard to say. Gascoigne seems to have been happy enough to guarantee Hall very substantial sums of money but his generosity may have been strengthened by a shrewd awareness of Hall's closeness both to Cecil and his son Thomas.

Arthur Hall's friendship with Gascoigne may have been one of those which flares up, burns brightly, then quickly dies away. In later years Hall developed a reputation for being quick-tempered, belligerent, outspoken, difficult and arrogant.[18] No archival material links the two men after the winter of 1562-3, though that in itself proves little. More eloquent is the absence of any reference to Hall's involvement in the collaborative project which was to occupy Gascoigne at Gray's Inn three years later. Hall's disdain for *Orlando Furioso* and other "such trifling Fables" is unlikely to have endeared him to such an admirer of Ariosto as Gascoigne.

In later years he identified himself as "Arthur Hall, Esquire" and referred to "M. George Gascoigne", which, had he still been alive, would have infuriated the status-conscious knight's son from Bedfordshire (who was never "Mr Gascoigne" but always George Gascoigne *Esquire*). However, though Hall was a great quarreller he never seems to have fallen out with the easy-going George Gascoigne. Four years after Gascoigne's death he paid tribute to his skills as a translator and his "pretie and pythie conceites".

*

When the poet entered into another financial transaction on 28 January 1563 he described himself as "George Gascoigne of Willington, Beds., esq." But another legal document shows that on 3 April he was back at Gray's Inn.[19] By now Boyes had found out that Gascoigne was seeing Elizabeth. He brought an action for debt against him, on the grounds that he'd broken the terms of the agreement reached the previous October and thereby owed him £500. Gascoigne retaliated with a Chancery Petition to the Lord Keeper. In it he protested about the delay in settling the dispute according to the terms of the Decree. He also requested a writ of injunction against Boyes over the £500. The writ was granted on 24 May 1563.

Now, suddenly, things give the appearance of speeding up. Quite possibly Lord Keeper Bacon was exasperated and furious to discover that his firm ruling of the previous October had been ignored by the court. Probably a second intervention was decisive, for at some point the second Court of the Arches now ruled against Edward Boyes. It seems, on the face of it, to have been a perverse verdict. Such evidence as there is in the case suggests that he was the wronged party. But perhaps by then Elizabeth had made up her mind and Bacon applied pressure behind the scenes on her behalf. Boyes appealed against the decision, but got nowhere. Elizabeth was duly divorced from her second husband and granted a licence to remarry. When and where her second and lawful marriage to George Gascoigne took place is not known but probably it occurred some time in the summer of 1563. Putting the last turbulent year behind them, the couple left London. It was a good time to get out of the city. That year there was a massive epidemic of bubonic plague, which killed thousands upon thousands – somewhere between a fifth and a third of the population. Among the victims seems to have been Henry Machyn, whose diary comes to a sudden stop. George and Elizabeth Gascoigne, meanwhile, had retired to their new home in Bedfordshire.

Willington

"When court had cast me off, I toyled at the plowe", Gascoigne wrote, looking back at those events some twelve years afterwards.[20] But the ostensible switch from a life of leisured hedonism to one of simple, manly toil was neither as sudden nor as straightforward as the poet pretended. Gascoigne's bigamous marriage came between those two events but whether or not it was connected to the first is not clear. The scandal of his marriage may have left him *persona non grata* at court. Alternatively he may have already departed penniless from court before he ever got involved with Elizabeth Boyes.

If Gascoigne is to be believed, his marriage had nothing to do with his being "cast...off" by the court. In this situation perhaps the attractions of settling down with a widowed older woman with five children were as much to do with her wealth as her looks. Gascoigne, like all autobiographers, conflated, suppressed and re-ordered certain episodes in his past when it suited him. All we can be certain of is that he spent some time at court, that he married, and that in the second year of his marriage he moved to Willington with his new wife.

Leaving the house on Red Cross Street, the couple went to live at Willington Manor, an estate three miles due east of Bedford and only two miles from the poet's family home of Cardington Manor, where his parents still lived. Sir John Gascoigne seems to have been on good terms with his eldest son at this time. By an indenture of 15 June 1563 he gave George a property known as Haynes Park, south of Cotton End, on the edge of the Gascoigne estate. Whether this was a wedding gift now that Elizabeth's marital status had been finally clarified in law or was another convoluted transaction involving an exchange of cash is unclear. Gascoigne for his part seemed happy to continue as a tenant at Willington Manor and does not seem ever to have lived at Haynes Park.

Willington Manor had been bought in 1529 by Sir John Gostwick, an associate of Sir William Gascoigne and, like him, a member of the household of Cardinal Wolsey. Parts of the Tudor estate still remain in existence at Willington today, most notably the strikingly large and impressive dovecot, probably built in the 1530s, which is now owned by the National Trust. Near it is a derelict and partly bricked-up stone building known as "the stable", after its nineteenth-century function. This in fact is probably the manor house which Gascoigne moved into with Elizabeth and her children. Though the chimney stack has been removed externally, the building has been only been lightly tampered with over the centuries. It is a good, solid Tudor construction with windows of finely moulded stone glazed with leaded lights. Upstairs is the main private room with a fireplace beside which George Gascoigne and his new family would have sat for warmth as the winter of 1563 drew on.

Gascoigne was now a respectably married man and a tenant farmer. How much toiling at the plough he personally did is very questionable – gentlemen (particularly, perhaps, those who enjoyed whiling away the time reading Ariosto or writing sonnets) employed labourers for manual work like that. But Gascoigne was keen to picture himself as a modest, hard-working man engaged in frenetic agricultural activity:

My fancy stood in strange conceits, to thrive I wot not how:
By mills, by making malt, by sheep and eke by swine,
By duck and drake, by pig and goose, by calves and keeping kine: [cattle]
By feeding bullocks fat, when price at markets fell,
But since my swains eat up my gains, *Fancy* (quoth he) *farewell*.[21]

Here, "swains" might mean Gascoigne's rustic employees, or it could be an acid reference to the six extra mouths he now was responsible for feeding.

The arrangement at Willington Manor did not last long. Perhaps it was never meant to. The following year the Gascoignes moved to a new home outside London. Their tenancy of the manor may just have been a stopgap measure – a temporary escape from the plague-ridden capital and a convenient way for Gascoigne to show off his new wife and family to his relatives and friends in the Bedford area. But Willington Manor was never a very satisfactory home. For a start, the Gascoignes had the uncomfortable experience of having to share it with the owner, John Gostwick and his wife (another Elizabeth). Gascoigne grumbled that he had to pay "a great yearly rent" because it was a furnished property. Also housed at the manor were four servants, two maids and six horses, which amounted to "a great charge and expense". Worse still, Elizabeth Gostwick secretly removed furniture, plate and other household goods from the manor and sold them in order to sustain "her disordered life".[22]

That, at least, was Gascoigne's story when it all collapsed into acrimony and a law suit. But Gascoigne perhaps protested too much. His tenancy seems to have lasted until 1565 or 1566 – rather a long time if the conditions were really so intolerable. As a tenant farmer the poet seems to have been a dilettante, who soon became an absentee. It is all far removed from the image of the simple, dignified country worker trying his hand at everything and struggling bravely to make a living.

Plate 16. The tomb of Sir William Gascoigne and his two wives in Cardington Church.

Plate 17. The local connections of Gascoigne's close friend Bartholomew Withypoll are commemorated by this street, close to the family home in Ipswich.

Plate 18. The modern site of Christ Church Greyfriars (formerly Christ Church Newgate), where Gascoigne was bigamously married to Elizabeth Breton. The church was destroyed in the Great Fire and its Wren replacement gutted by bombs in 1940.

13: "My poore house at Waltamstow in the Forest"

In March 1564 the poet identified himself as "George Gascoigne of Gray's Inn".[1] Perhaps in the spring of that year Elizabeth and the children were still stuck with the Gostwicks at Willington, while Gascoigne enjoyed himself among the literati of the Inns of Court. If so, liberation was near at hand. By November he'd become "George Gascoigne of Walthamstowe, Essex, esq."[2]

It was by then exactly three years since his first, bigamous, marriage to Elizabeth Boyes, and the wealth which she brought him now appears to have taken material form in the shape of a substantial new home in the small Essex settlement of Walthamstow. The house on Red Cross Street seems to have been sold off; there is no further record of them at this location. Gascoigne's to-ing and fro-ing between various addresses during 1563 and 1564 may partly have been connected to the design and construction of this new house. It was to remain his and Elizabeth's home for the rest of their lives. It was also probably the place where the bulk of Gascoigne's writing was completed.

Today, Walthamstow is no longer part of the County of Essex but has become swallowed up by Greater London.[3] Situated 6½ miles north-east of the City of London, it's a densely populated suburb at the edge of the capital, sandwiched between Chingford and Leyton in the London Borough of Waltham Forest. Though traces of a pre-industrial past remain, it requires a massive leap of imagination to recognise it as a location which was, until the mid-nineteenth century, a tranquil village of fields, farms and woodland.

"Walthamstow" in Gascoigne's lifetime referred not to a single village but was the collective name given to a parish which comprised five separate hamlets. The first documented reference to "Wilcumestouue" is in a charter of 1067. Situated alongside the flood plain of the River Lea, Walthamstow was originally an isolated parish, far from any important travel route. It developed out of a group of settlements located on the fringes of the vast royal forest of Waltham (now much reduced and known as Epping Forest) which formerly stretched south from Epping to Chingford, Woodford and Wanstead, down to the marshland of the valley of the River Lea.

The ancient parish of Walthamstow comprised 4,472 acres and was 2½ miles long from north to south. To the north the River Ching ran westward from Chingford Hatch to the Lea, where the marshes formed Walthamstow's western boundary, beyond which lay Tottenham and Hackney. To the south was Leyton, to the east Woodford and Wanstead. By the sixteenth century Walthamstow still retained its fragmentary identity as a collection of scattered hamlets separated by commons, fields and farmland. In the north of the parish were four areas of settlement: Higham Hill, a hamlet close to Higham Bensted manor house; Chapel End, close to St Edward's Chapel and Salisbury Hall; and Hale End and Wood End, by the forest. Further south, and closest to the geographical centre of the parish, was Church End, dominated by St Mary's Church, crowning a hill some 125 feet above the Lea. Facing St Mary's was a substantial hall, dating from the fifteenth century and probably sited on the former Manor House of Walthamstow.

Why did Gascoigne choose to live in Walthamstow? Felix E. Schelling wrote that Gascoigne's wife Elizabeth inherited from her first husband, "numerous monies and properties of a considerable value both in London, at Walthamstow in Essex and elsewhere".[4] C. T. Prouty went further, claiming that Gascoigne retired "to a cottage in Walthamstow, owned by Elizabeth" and that "The property is listed in the will of William Bretton".[5] These claims are simply not true. The only property Breton owned in Walthamstow was "Tenne Kyen" (ten cows).[6] However, he did leave a shilling each to twenty of the poorest of Walthamstow, which in the view of Jean Robertson "indicates a firm connection with the place".[7] If such a connection existed, then it might have been Elizabeth who knew Walthamstow and wanted to live there, rather than her third husband. Another possible link is through Arthur Hall and his connection with Roger Ascham. Ascham rented a very substantial property in Walthamstow in 1556 and in theory Gascoigne and his new friend Hall might have ridden over to Essex to show Ascham the latest instalment of the ongoing *Iliad* translation.

But all these hypothetical associations may be spurious. Walthamstow was a popular place for the well-off to settle – away from the congestion and crime of the city but within riding distance of the Inns of Court, Whitehall and the House of Commons. It was also conveniently situated the right side of London if Elizabeth Gascoigne wanted to make trips back to Bury St Edmunds to visit her old friends and relatives.

Tudor Walthamstow had a relatively small population. In 1523-4 just 99 persons were assessed to the subsidy (i.e. were liable for taxation). By the end of the century the combined population of the five villages of Higham Hill, Chapel End, Hale End, Wood End and Church End amounted to some 500. Walthamstow's proximity to London made it an attractive choice for wealthy men looking for a country residence in quiet and attractive surroundings. In 1507 the merchant George Monoux (d. 1544) settled at a substantial moated house on a site subsequently known as Moons. He became Lord Mayor of London in 1514-15. Another merchant, Paul Withypoll, first arrived in 1527 and became good friends with the Monoux family. In 1533 George Monoux acquired the lease of the Rectory Manor and the following year Paul Withypoll's brother, Richard, became Vicar of Walthamstow. The two families were the driving force behind a very substantial refurbishment and rebuilding of the Church of St Mary in the years that followed.

If the location selected for a new home was Gascoigne's choice then it is feasible that he first became acquainted with Walthamstow through his friendship with Bartholomew and Daniel Withypoll. In 1544 their father

Edmund and their grandfather, the merchant Paul Withypoll, were granted the manor of Mark in Leyton and Walthamstow, which lay on both sides of the parish boundary ("mearc") between the common marsh and Hoe Street. Daniel Withypoll (born c.1541) registered his county of birth as Essex, possibly indicating that he was born in Walthamstow. In 1545 Edmund was involved in a murky incident in which he killed a local man who had two identities. He was pardoned by the Queen on 16 December for slaying "Williame Mathewe, late of Walchamstowe, yeoman, alias Guellyan Frenchman, of Lowhall in Walchamstowe, serving man". After this violent episode the main branch of the family moved to Ipswich. At this stage Edmund had seven sons and four daughters; some of these may have stayed behind. According to one local historian, "The Withypolls flourished in Walthamstow until the end of the [sixteenth] century", and when Edmund Withypoll made his will in 1568 he left his wife "all my lande in Walthamstow and Leight[on]".[8] If Gascoigne visited Walthamstow in the 1550s then he might even, in theory, have first met Elizabeth Breton there.

A typical contemporary of Gascoigne's during the time the poet was living there was the merchant and alderman Sir Thomas Rowe, Mayor of London in 1568, who owned the manor of Higham Benstead. The poet may well have known him personally. In his long poem *The fruites of Warre* Gascoigne grumbled that most merchants were devious "Hard hearted men" but among the rare exceptions was "gentle *Rowe*".[9] A memorial brass to his son William Rowe, mentioning the father, survives on the east wall of the north aisle of the church of St Mary, Walthamstow.

The most distinguished resident of Walthamstow while Gascoigne lived there was Roger Ascham, who occupied Salisbury Hall from 1556 until his death in 1568. The manor was in the possession of the Crown and it was leased to Ascham by a grant of 1557. The Withypolls left no traces but several of those other prominent sixteenth-century residents are still remembered today at sites not related to their residence – Ascham End E17, Monoux Grove E17 and Gascoigne Gardens, Woodford Green.

Thorpe Hall

Where in Walthamstow did George Gascoigne live? No one seems to have asked this question until the twentieth century, when it was addressed by Walthamstow Antiquarian Society. The Society's conclusion was that Gascoigne probably lived at the house known as Thorpe Hall (or Thorpehall and, later, Thorps Hall), situated to the west of what is now Hale End Road, Walthamstow. This was because "On his mother's side he was descended from the Scargills of Thorp Hall (Yorks) and this place was probably so called for sentimental reasons."[10] But sentimentality is not a quality one readily associates with either Gascoigne or his mother, who by the end of the decade were not on speaking terms. Gascoigne seems to have had no special fondness for the

Scargills, that we know of. If he did name Thorpe Hall in his mother's honour he is likely to have had hard-edged, probably financial reasons for wanting to humour her in this way. But it is just as feasible that Gascoigne did it to mock and insult her. Gascoigne was, after all, very aware of the force of words. He was, quite literally, putting another Thorpe Hall on the map. He was rewriting family history by flamboyantly occupying a new Thorpe Hall with a twice-divorced woman of lower social status and her five stepchildren.

Whether Gascoigne's motives were benign or otherwise, there is no real reason to doubt the Antiquarian Society's conclusion that Thorpe Hall was the site of his new home in Walthamstow. The historic place-names of Walthamstow mostly consist of common descriptive topographical terms, and "Thorpe" had no such significance and existed nowhere else locally. The name undoubtedly replicates that of his mother's childhood home, even though we cannot be sure why Gascoigne chose to do this.

Other factors also strengthen the case for Thorpe Hall being the poet's home. A Close Roll entry of 28 May 1569 refers to "George Gascoigne of Walthamstow Tony, Essex".[11] This refers to the Manor of Walthamstow Tony (named after the Toni family), which included the land on which Thorpe Hall was situated. And when Gascoigne referred to his house "at Waltamstow [sic] in the Forest"[12] he did not mean "Walthamstow which is in the forest" but "*that part* of Walthamstow which is in the forest". Of the five hamlets which made up Walthamstow, probably only one – the revealingly named Wood End – was surrounded by forest. "Walthamstow in the Forest" may even be a lost local name for Wood End. This is the area in which Thorpe Hall was situated. Indeed, the existing Wood End Road, Walthamstow, may quite possibly have once formed part of the Thorpe Hall estate.

What kind of home was Thorpe Hall? Prouty erroneously described "a cottage in Walthamstow".[13] Nowadays "cottage" is a largely meaningless term, sometimes used for substantial country properties. Traditionally, a cottage was a small, humble, very basic dwelling of a labourer. Prouty may have been misled by Gascoigne's self-deprecating reference to his "poore house"[14] into thinking that the poet's Walthamstow home was exceptionally modest. In reality the phrase tells us nothing. When Cardinal Wolsey invited Henry VIII to stay at his sumptuous residence at York Place he described it as his "poor house".[15] The phrase was simply a convention, as empty and insincere as the words "yours sincerely" in a modern letter. It should also be remembered that Gascoigne described the fabulous palace of Fontainebleau as a "house".[16]

Thorpe Hall was demolished at the end of the nineteenth century. No map of Tudor Walthamstow exists and surviving archival material from the sixteenth century is very sparse. No drawings or photographs of the house survive. The earliest known written reference to Thorpe Hall is in a deed of 12 August 1698. This refers to "all that messuage, tenement or farmhouse with barns etc., belonging called Thorpehall, and all those closes, arable meadows and pastures to same belonging". The description is a vague one and fails to specify either the nature of the structure or the full extent of the estate. "Tenement" in this context means a house and "messuage" means a house with out-buildings and garden. Thorpe Hall is marked on Chapman and André's 1777 plan of the area, showing that even 200 years after Gascoigne's death it remained one of a handful of very substantial properties in Walthamstow, along with the manor houses of Salisbury Hall, High Hall and Higham Hill, as well as Low Hall, Mark House and Moon's Farm. In its original form Thorpe Hall is unlikely to have been a farmhouse but it was a common fate of Tudor manor houses to be converted at a later date to farms. Gascoigne's childhood home at Cardington ended this way. So did Roger Ascham's Walthamstow home at Salisbury Hall. Likewise Moon's Farm was named after George Monoux; once a large moated building it was subsequently rebuilt on a smaller scale in the seventeenth century as a timber-framed farmhouse.

Thorpe Hall was located just west of what is now called Hale End Road E17. Thorpe Hall School now occupies its approximate site. The Chapman and André map shows a nucleus of three buildings – a substantial building, rectangular in shape, facing (and linked to it by a short drive) what in the sixteenth century was probably called Inks Green Lane. This rectangular building was undoubtedly the hall and its dimensions were probably similar to those of nearby Salisbury Hall and the one which faced St Mary's. Two smaller square-shaped structures adjacent to the main building on the north side may have been the barns mentioned in the 1698 lease, in which case they were probably built after Gascoigne's lifetime. If they were original features they probably included stables as well as being used for all those other activities associated with a big house such as brewing, baking and a dairy. There may be a glimpse of the poet's life here in his lines

> To drink a draught of sower Ale (some season)
> To eate browne bread with homely handes in Hall
> Doth much encrease mens appetites by reason[17]

Aside from the pleasures of home-brewing and home-baking there were problems which no Tudor house was free from, vividly expressed in the simile of the destructive power of desire over a man:

> And though (with paine) thou put him from thy house,
> Yet lurkes hee styll in corners lyke a Mouse.
>
> At every hole he creepeth in by stelth,
> And privilye he feedeth on thy crommes, [secretly / crumbs]

With spoiles unseene he wasteth all thy welth,
He plays boe peepe when any body commes[18]

Gascoigne is unlikely to have re-named an existing building; the implication of the name "Thorpe Hall" is that it was the new name for a new building. If the hall was constructed in 1563-4 it probably included that radical, fashionable new architectural feature of a first floor and rooms upstairs. However, the site has never been excavated. If at some point in the future archaeologists have the opportunity to investigate the site currently occupied by the school and its grounds it may be possible to get answers to some of the unanswered questions about the structure and history of Thorpe Hall.

In his address "To al yong Gentlemen, and generally to the youth of England" written "From my poore house at Waltamstow in the Forest the second of Januarie. 1575." Gascoigne perhaps gave us a fleeting glimpse of life at Thorpe Hall in his reflection that "in a house where many yong children are, it hath bene thought better pollicie quite to quench out the fire, than to leave any loose cole in the imbers, wherewith Babes may play and put the whole edifice in daunger".[19] At some time between October 1562 and 1565 Elizabeth bore him a son, William, and Gascoigne's image suggests an anxiety both about his own young child and his expensive new property.

All the evidence suggests that Gascoigne's "poore house" off Inks Green Lane was one of the finest in Walthamstow. The household must have been a substantial one. Apart from Gascoigne, Elizabeth and their six children there would have been Gascoigne's manservant or servants, as well as Elizabeth's. They would have needed a cook, maids, gardeners, a stable boy; tutors for the children, perhaps. History from this era virtually never records the lives of servants, but all in all, a small army of attendants must have been there to service the family's needs.

The reference to "closes, arable meadows and pastures" in the seventeenth-century lease indicates that the size of the hall's estate was probably very substantial, with the current school grounds only occupying a fraction of the original site. By the nineteenth century the site was known as "Thorpe Hall Farm" and John Coe's 1822 map of Walthamstow shows a much developed site with a pond and a cluster of new outbuildings grouped around the original house. By this time the original building may have either been demolished and rebuilt or substantially renovated; the structure demolished in the late nineteenth century has been described as "a fairly large eighteenth-century building". It seems unlikely that Gascoigne himself ever put the estate to agricultural use. His farming ventures had formerly been unsuccessful and he wasn't at Walthamstow very long before he returned to the capital to renew his association with Gray's Inn and the exclusive society of law students.

Tudor Walthamstow

Walthamstow was an agricultural parish in the sixteenth century and continued to be so until the mid-nineteenth century. A mill existed in Walthamstow Manor in 1066; by 1611 there were four. The scenes which unfolded before Gascoigne's eyes as he rode through Walthamstow would have been little different to those surrounding his childhood home in Bedfordshire. There were osier grounds in Walthamstow Toni. Flocks of sheep and beef cattle were grazed in local fields. There are records of hopfields by Moon's and elsewhere in the parish. Salisbury Hall held a fishery on the Lea.

The dominant feature of the landscape immediately surrounding Gascoigne's new home would have been trees. On the east side of the parish a belt of open forest stretched from Phipps Cross to Chingford Hatch, with some 442 acres in Walthamstow Toni manor as late as the seventeenth century. Even in the nineteenth century fragments of Epping Forest survived west of Hale End Road. Thorpe Hall itself may have been quite literally "in the Forest". Today the fringes of the forest survive on the ridge which slopes down to the old site of the house. But though his new home was as isolated as that of the manor in which he had spent his childhood, he was not too far from the crowded, raucous world of London. Walthamstow had good communication links with the capital and elsewhere. Inks Green Lane was the third and most easterly of the three north-south routes through the parish. It led from Chingford, past Thorpe Hall and on to Wood Street and Phipps Cross (now known as Whipps Cross). The chief east-west route through Walthamstow came from Epping, emerging from the forest as Hangerstrete, not far from Thorpe Hall. It led on to Clay Street, Mill Lane, a bridge over the Fleet River and Mill Bridge, the most important of the crossings of the Lea. Beyond that lay Tottenham. Further south, Lockbridge in Leyton provided a crossing to Clapton; from here it was not much more than 3 miles to Shoreditch Church.

Almost all these routes still exist today, albeit often under different names and as two-lane highways crammed with motor traffic. Many of the other streets of Tudor Walthamstow survive, including the main north-south road which ran from Salisbury Hall and the bridge over the River Ching (today little more than a stream), through Chapel End to Hoe Street, on to Leyton.

Gascoigne is unlikely to have had much contact with the local community, other than in his role as householder and employer. There is no reason to believe he ever went to visit Roger Ascham at nearby Salisbury Hall. Ascham was a paid member of the royal household and would have been away at court much of the time. The two men were, in any case, temperamentally very different and, though their paths may have crossed, were most unlikely to have been friends. It is marginally more likely that he socialised with Sir Thomas Rowe's son, William (b. 1545), who after 1570 became lord of the manor of Higham Benstead. Rowe won a European reputation as a Cambridge scholar, divine and good friend of Théodore Beza. Alan Stewart has described Beza as "the living cornerstone of reformed Genevan morality, the acknowledged successor to Calvin, who died in his arms".[20] In his younger days Beza had published a volume of poetry which contained outspoken erotic subject matter, all deleted when he republished the volume two decades later. Gascoigne was keen to draw parallels with his own experience, blandly (and inaccurately) claiming to have solemnly purged his writing of offence. William Rowe, like Ascham and Gascoigne, is today memorialised on the exterior wall of Wood Street library in Walthamstow.

The only part of Walthamstow in which Gascoigne was obliged to show some interest was St Mary's Church, where weekly attendance was compulsory. The existing church is much renovated, though it incorporates sixteenth-century features such as the West Tower, built substantially of Tudor brick, with an early sixteenth-century tower arch. Today the charm of the church is muted by a hideous nineteenth-century cement rendering but in Gascoigne's day it would have been of a striking deep red colour. It was also asymmetrical. At the east end stood the immense Monoux Chapel (which was out of alignment with the rest of the church) and the Chancel, with gables; Thorne's Chapel, on the south side, had none. The Monoux Chapel was possibly constructed out of an earlier Lady Chapel, which in pre-reformation times may have contained a statue of St Mary. These Chapels celebrated a leading local Tudor dignitary, Sir George Monoux (whose career included being Mayor of Bristol, Mayor of London and six times Master of the Drapers' Company) and Robert Thorne, a west country trader who left money to various Bristol and London churches. Monoux died in 1543 and Gascoigne would have been familiar with his marble and stone table tomb, which had at its head the brass figures of Sir George and his wife, the arms of the City of London, the arms of the Drapers' Company, and of Sir George and the town of Ipswich. The tomb has long since vanished but the brass plates survive, fixed to a wall.

St Mary's was a troubled church. Henry Siddall (or Sydall), vicar from 1557-63, was only appointed as a punishment for getting married, for which he'd been stripped of his previous living at nearby Woodford. Siddall was then forcibly evicted from the vicarage and glebe lands by the patron, who refused to recognise him. His successor, Richard Pattenson (vicar 1563-5), prosecuted a number of parishioners for withholding tithes, and seems to have simply abandoned the living. The report of the Archdeacon's Visitation on 4 June 1565 noted that the vicar "ys not resydente upon his benefice nor hath bin this halfe yere at the leaste" and that the vicarage was badly in need of repair. George Johnson, vicar of Leyton, became vicar of Walthamstow in 1567. He was 27 years old and held the post for almost a decade, dying in 1576. These troubles dragged on for decades. John Reynolds (vicar 1583-1611) appeared in the list of "insufficient or negligent" ministers.

Gascoigne's gardenings

Gascoigne's main reasons for living in Walthamstow are likely to have been to write in a quiet environment and to relax in agreeable surroundings with his new family. The chief form of relaxation at this time would have been the enjoyment of a substantial and imaginatively laid out garden. No plan of any garden at Thorpe Hall survives. The only known description of the house and its immediate surroundings dates from 1840, when an American, the Reverend John Clark, enthusiastically described Thorpe Hall as

> situated in a most romantic spot, environed with ten thousand rural beauties. On one side is the extended forest, and on the other a smooth and closely-shorn lawn of the most exquisite green; gardens and fields, shrubbery and trees, and all the varied groupings of rural scenery are spread in delightful prospect around this dwelling.

Three centuries after Gascoigne, the future poet and novelist William Morris lived in Walthamstow in similarly leisured circumstances, in a big house with a big garden on a tranche of land less than two miles south-west of Thorpe Hall. Morris's home and its garden survives today, including the private moated island where he played as a child, and which today is a public park. Walthamstow's identity over four centuries as an exclusive place of big houses, gardens and lush rural surroundings began to fade with the arrival of the railway in 1870 and with the advent of the car soon vanished. A photograph of Wadham Road, shortly before the construction of the first North Circular Road, shows how heavily wooded the area by the site of Thorpe Hall still was, even as late as the mid-1920s. The view is of a mass of billowing foliage, in the foreground a section of someone's spacious garden, with a rose arch, stone bird table, small fruit trees and bushes.[21]

The craze for gardening, horticulture and patterned gardens first began with the reign of Elizabeth I. It arose from the relative social stability associated with the new monarch and the rapid extension of the middle class. Homes were no longer built like fortresses and gardens began to be places of style, pattern and ornament. In the words of Richard Mabey, "An increasing number of families had the money and leisure to indulge in 'pleasure grounds', and to some extent gardens became status symbols, fashionable insignia of wealth and taste. Yet there is no doubt that they were also sincerely viewed as perfect expressions of the era's devotion to art, romance and learning."[22]

William Turner's *Herball* (1551) was the first significant book on plants to be published in the English language, with advice on the use of herbs in medicine and cooking, but the first gardening book in English did not appear until 1563, by Thomas Hill. His treatise appeared in an expanded and rewritten form as *The Profitable Arte of Gardening* (1568) and went through three more editions before the end of the century. Cashing in on the growing craze, Hill published a fuller edition under a pseudonym as *The Gardener's Labyrinth* (1577). Hill was fond of scented plants and recommended their use in edging and overhanging geometrically patterned walks which were used to divide flowerbeds. John Lyly's *Euphues: The Anatomy of Wit* (1578) alludes to the craze in his reference to "good gardeners who in their curious knots mix hyssop with thyme, as aiders the one to the growth of the other, the one being dry, the other moist". The "curious knots" refers to flowerbeds laid out in fanciful patterns.

Between 1572 and 1596 there were at least six editions of a book on grafting by L. Mascall. The craze for experiment and grafting seems to have gripped Gascoigne as much as anyone, judging by a rueful stanza in "The Green Knight's Farewell to Fancy":

> To plant strange country fruits, to sow such seeds likewise,
> To dig and delve for newfound roots, where old might well suffice:
> To prune the water boughs, to pick the mossy trees,
> (Oh how it pleased my fancy once) to kneel upon my knees,
> To griffe a pippin stock, when sap begins to swell: [graft]
> But since the gains scarce quit the cost, *Fancy* (quoth he) *farewell*.[23]

The garden at Thorpe Hall is likely to have originated with Gascoigne and four of the "Devises" in *A Hundreth Sundrie Flowres* almost certainly describe aspects of it.[24] Its presence, and that of the growing gardening craze, is embedded in the title of Gascoigne's masterpiece, *A Hundreth Sundrie Flowres bounde up in one small Poesie* where the primary meaning of "Poesie" is a posy or bunch of flowers. The horticultural imagery ramifies in the subtitle: these flowers are "Gathered partely...in ...fyne outlandish Gardins...and partly by invention, out of our owne fruitefull Orchardes in Englande: Yelding sundrie sweet savours...to the well smellyng noses of learned Readers".

By a curious and striking coincidence, at about the same time was published a collection of verse by the pioneering woman poet Isabella Whitney, *A Sweet Nosegay or Pleasant Posy, Containing a Hundred and Ten Philosophical Flowers*. It is prefaced by a dedicatory letter dated 20 October 1573 and was presumably published soon afterwards. On the face of it, neither Whitney nor Gascoigne influenced each other; their titles were simply symptomatic of a trend. When *A Hundreth Sundrie Flowres* was republished it was as *The Posies of George Gascoigne Esquire*. This second edition was revised according to the categories Flowers, Herbs and Weeds. Flowers were "pleasant" with "some rare invention and Methode" but essentially superficial. Herbs were "morall discourses" and "more profitable than pleasant". Weeds might be "neither pleasant nor yet profitable...But as many weedes are right medicinable, so may you find in this none so vile or stinking, but that it hath in it some virtue if it be rightly handled."[25]

Also part of this trend was a volume published in 1575 entitled *A Smale handful of fragrant Flowers, selected and gathered out of the louely garden of sacred scriptures, fit for any Honorable or woorshipfull Gentlewoman to smell vnto*. It was written by a fellow-resident of Thorpe Hall, namely the poet's stepson Nicholas. When the boy first moved to Walthamstow with the rest of the family he was probably aged about nine or ten. As he grew older he evidently decided he wanted to become a writer, just like his new stepfather. If Prouty is correct that the poems in *A Hundreth Sundrie Flowres* were published in chronological order of composition, then these three garden poems and the associated garden "poesie" or motto were written between the winter of 1572 and 19 March 1573, some eight and a half years after Gascoigne moved his family into Thorpe Hall. By this time the garden would have been planned, laid out and sufficiently grown to be enjoyed. These four pieces of writing tell us something of its contents. The garden was "a pleasant place" of flowers. It contained at least one "chayre" as well as "a close walke", i.e. an enclosed walkway (the fashion was for gravel walks hedged by trellis or shrubs). Herbs "that serve the pot" were grown. There are references to manure, weeding and sticks to support plants. Upon a stone in the wall of the garden was "written" (presumably engraved)

> The yeare wherein he did the coste of these devises, and therwithall this poesie in Latine.
>
> *Quoniam etiam humiliatos, amoena delectant.*[26]

"Coste" here means not "expense" but "ornament" and "devises" refers to three previously mentioned aspects of the garden – the two ends of the "close walke" and the chair. It becomes clear that these poems were "written" not in the sense of being composed there (though they may have been) but in being put on display at these locations in the garden.

The Latin motto means "For pleasant things delight even those who have been humbled". It is an original motto, not a quotation. That "yeare wherein he did the coste" is not identified but by "humbled" Gascoigne was probably referring to at least one of two unpleasant episodes in the period 1570-72, when his fortunes were at their lowest. A note of weariness and disillusion is present in the poem displayed by the garden chair. There's a sense of how easily the "flowers" of life vanish, and how even the enjoyment of a garden is tempered by the shadow of death. "If thou sit here…" gloomily insists on presenting itself as a *memento mori* amid the blossom:

If thou sit here to view this pleasant garden place,
Think thus: at last will come a frost, and all these flowers deface.
But if thou sit at ease to rest thy weary bones,
Remember death brings final rest to all our grievous groans.
So whether for delight, or here thou sit for ease,
Think still upon the latter day, so shalt thou God best please.[27]

Thomas Hill recommended the benefits of creating walks and alleyways in an ornamental garden:

> The commodities of these Allis and walks, serve to good purposes, the one is, that the owner may diligently view the prosperity of his herbs and flowers, the other for the delight and comfort of the wearied mind, which he may by himself or fellowship of his friends conceive, in the delectable sights and fragrant smels of the flowers, by walking up and down, and about the Garden in them, which for the pleasant sights and refreshing of the dul spirits, with the sharpening of memory, many shadowed over with vauting or Arch-herbs, having windowes properly made toward the Garden, whereby they might the more fully view, and have delight of the whole beauty of the Garden. But the straight walks the wealthy make like Galleries, being all open towards the Garden, and covered with the vine spreading all over…[28]

A visitor to Thorpe Hall, strolling along the close walk, would have come to two rather more substantial messages from the garden's proprietor than that by the chair. The first, a 42-line "discourse", offered a sententious comparison between "garden plots", human society and the lives of men:

> thus the restless life which men here lead
> May be resembled to the tender plant.
> In spring it sprouts, as babes in cradle breed,
> Flourish in May, like youths that wisdom want,
> In autumn ripes and roots, lest store wax scant,
> In winter shrinks and shrouds from every blast,
> Like crooked age when lusty age is past.[29]

These were sentiments which no one could disagree with. One could nod one's head wisely at the thought of men being "Subject, like bloom, to blast of every wind" and the need for "A well grown root" in life.

In one of his last pieces of prose, Gascoigne gives us a bucolic glimpse of "the good Gardener [who] doth cover his tender herbes in winter, and cherishe them also in summer" and of a "good huswife" (perhaps his wife, Elizabeth) who "is no less curious to decke her bees hive, to rub and perfume it with sweete herbes, to cover and defend it from raine with clay and boordes, and to place it in the warme Sunshine safe from the Northerly blastes". But, if you strolled to the far end of the close walk, a rather more acerbic message presented itself, in the guise of "toyes in ryme":

> If any flower that here is grown,
> Or any herb may ease your pain,
> Take and account it as your own,
> But recompense the like again.[30]

This is not exactly Christian charity. *Help yourself to anything in my delightful garden and DO stay for supper*, is the poem's message – *but make sure you supply me with something equal in exchange and also invite me back for a meal at your home.* Worse still is the innuendo in the next two lines, a couplet which gets repeated twice:

> For some and some is honest play,
> And so my wife taught me to say.

Here Gascoigne presents himself as an easy-going and perhaps over-gullible man whose naturally generous impulses have been sensibly curbed by his wife's sober shrewdness. It's an odd poem to put on display for visitors. Perhaps it was there to provoke an easy laugh among Gascoigne's swashbuckling male friends. Demanding recompense for the gift of a handful of flowers or herbs seems somehow oddly trivial and unfitting in a garden containing a plaque which solemnly requires due consideration of the Day of Judgement.

Ironically, it's by far the best of the three garden poems. This is largely because it avoids the tired metaphors and conventional sentiments of the other two. "If any flower that here is grown" is simple, punchy and straight to the point. It is also a bravely honest and original poem. It captures the mercenary spirit of the age, as well as expressing something more enduring. Probably most of us, when we provide hospitality, don't, if we are honest, do it entirely out of the goodness of our hearts. Friends who accept hospitality but never return it are unlikely to remain on the guest list for long. Gascoigne was acknowledging a truth, and perhaps also one about his marriage. Though his wife Elizabeth may have influenced Gascoigne's decision to cut at least one of the poems in the revised version of *A Hundreth Sundrie Flowres* she seems to have had no difficulty with this one. One can only conclude that if visitors laughed at this "devise" displayed in the garden, she laughed too.

Plate 19. This building in Willington is probably the manor house where Gascoigne lived with his new wife, Elizabeth.

Plate 20. The adjacent Tudor dovecot at Willington.

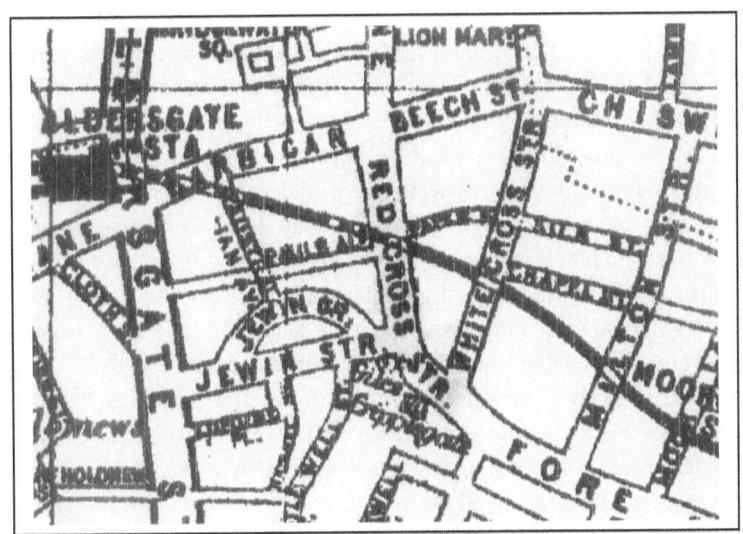

Plate 21. Red Cross Street. Much of the local Tudor street network, including Red Cross Street, survived into the twentieth century, as shown here, but was later damaged by bombing during the 1939-45 war, and was then erased by the 40-acre Barbican development of the 1960s.

Plate 22. Thorpe Hall School on Hale End Road occupies the site of Gascoigne's Walthamstow home.

14: Christmas Revels

The garden poems suggest domestic contentment on Gascoigne's part. But by the spring of 1566 the idyll of married life in Walthamstow, if it ever existed, may have been over for Gascoigne. He was in his early thirties by now. Elizabeth was probably at least forty years old, possibly even older. By the standards of the time she was well into middle age. After giving birth to six children any physical attractiveness she may have once possessed for her younger husband had possibly begun to wane. Whether or not these speculations are justified and they indeed had grown apart cannot ever be known. But all the evidence points to Gascoigne spending more and more time away from his wife from now on. Even when he died, he was far from home.

For the next two years the centre of his life was not his family in Walthamstow but Gray's Inn. A flurry of Close Roll entries list Gray's Inn as his residence between 29 March 1566 and 10 May 1568.[1] In his own words, posing as the anonymous editor of "The Devises of Sundrie Gentlemen", "[Master Gascoigne] had (in middest of his youth) determined to abandone all vaine delights and to retourne unto Greyes Inne, there to undertake againe the study of the common lawes."[2]

But this sober, penitent perspective puts a very flattering spin on the realities of the situation. Gascoigne was by this time hardly a callow youth. He was a married man in his early thirties. It was not "vaine delights" which he was abandoning but a wife and five stepchildren, as well as his own small son, William.

One possibility is that Gascoigne was bored and restless and felt that his life had reached a dead end. Family life may have begun to grate; a small, howling baby is not necessarily conducive to the writing of lyric verse. Biographies of modern novelists (the case of Saul Bellow springs to mind) often expose a cold egocentricity when it comes to balancing a commitment to writing and the responsibilities of parenthood.

A return to his legal studies allowed Gascoigne to pursue once again the prospect of a respectable legal career and the financial security it would bring. But perhaps more to the point, at Gray's Inn he was once more back inside a privileged, affluent male world of learning and culture. It was a world where a wit could amuse other young bloods by circulating droll verses which mocked marriage and wives:

> If so thy wife be too fair of face
> It draws one guest too many to thine inn;
> If she be foul, and soiled with disgrace,
> In other pillows prickst thou many a pin:
> So foul prove fools, and fairer fall to sin.[3]

One can almost hear the easy male laughter of Gascoigne's Gray's Inn cronies as they listened to the poet recite these lines in a tavern, or passed the manuscript from hand to hand. And if "Gascoigne's Libel of Divorce" was written at this time, then the personal element was even more searing:

> In my wife I find such discord and debate
> As no man living can endure the torments of my state.[4]

Gascoigne was both having his cake and eating it. If he required the sexual and other comforts of married life, then Elizabeth was a relatively short horse ride away. As he once rather crudely put it, "I have man's meat enough at home".[5] But if he preferred the company of intellectuals and poets of his own generation then he could stay at lodgings in the capital and pursue his legal studies and his writing. It was an arrangement that Elizabeth Breton was in no position to object to; as a sixteenth-century wife, she was entirely subordinate to her husband.

A fellowship of gentlemen

Back once more at Gray's Inn,[6] Gascoigne was invited to join a "fellowship" of "five sundrie gentlemen".[7] These new friends were John Vaughan (admitted to Gray's Inn 1562-3), Richard Courtop (admitted in 1559), Anthony Kinwelmershe (admitted 1561), Francis Kinwelmershe (admitted 1557) and Alexander Neville. The admission dates suggest that the first four of these five soulmates were between four and eight years younger than Gascoigne – a supposition reinforced by the fact that Francis Kinwelmershe is known to have been born in 1538. Anthony Kinwelmershe was evidently his younger brother. A third brother, Robert Kinwelmershe, was admitted to Gray's Inn 1563. The family seems to have had long-running associations with Gray's Inn, as there were lodgings there known as "Kyndelmarshes Buyldinges".

Neville may simply have been an affluent gentleman hanger-on, as his name nowhere appears in any Inns of Court register. He was born in 1544 and was already making a name for himself. In 1563 he published a translation of Seneca's *Oedipus*. A handful of his poems appeared that same year in his cousin Barnabe Googe's collection *Eglogs, Epytaphes, and Sonettes*. The concept of a professional career as a writer did not at that time exist, but in retrospect it would have seemed at that moment that if anyone had a future as a writer it was surely Neville, not the knight's son from Bedfordshire.

Before being admitted to this group of friends, Gascoigne had to pass a test. He was required "to wrighte in verse somewhat worthy to be remembered…five sundry sortes of metre upon five sundry theames whiche they delivered unto him".[8] It was the literary equivalent of a law disputation. The "themes" were proverbs or wise sayings, mostly drawn from the Latin classics. The results of this challenge ranged from the banal to the outstandingly good. Francis

Kinwelmershe proposed a poem on the theme *Audaces fortuna iuvat* ("Fortune favours the bold" – a tag adapted from Terence, *Phormio*, line 203). Gascoigne responded with a stodgy sonnet setting out examples from ancient Rome and Greece. He used the rhyme scheme and metre associated with the Earl of Surrey and popularised by the contents of Tottel's *Miscellany*.

Anthony Kinwelmershe suggested the theme *Satis sufficit* ("Enough is enough" – a popular proverb) and Gascoigne produced in rhyme royal a series of uninspired contrasts between the perils of extreme wealth and poverty.[9] Not until John Vaughan's *Magnum vectigal parsimonia* ("frugality is a great income" – a quote from Cicero's *Paradoxes of the Stoics*, vi, 49) does Gascoigne's imagination catch fire.

The theme of resisting the impulse to spend wildly and instead to hold on to one's money was one very close to the heart of Gascoigne, who developed the persona of a penitent spendthrift. The poem begins with a defiant, scornful challenge to the popular sixteenth-century saying "spend and God will send":

The common speech is: spend and God will send,
But what sends he? A bottle and a bag,
A staff, a wallet and a woeful end[10]

The bottle, bag, staff and wallet were what beggars carried around with them. Gascoigne does not define what their "woeful end" might be but the first volume of Marx's *Capital* lists some contemporary punishments: "For the second arrest for vagabondage the whipping is to be repeated and half the ear sliced off; but for the third relapse the offender is to be executed as a hardened criminal and enemy of the common weal".[11] For Marx, the prevalence of beggars and vagabonds in sixteenth-century society was the consequence of land enclosure and the collapse of feudalism. Gascoigne, of course, saw it differently. The implied reader of his poem is a gentleman, and its advice is that wealth or poverty is a matter of individual responsibility, of thrift and self-discipline versus extravagance and self-indulgence.

This poem is written in a slightly modified virelays form (ababa ending with a rhyming couplet). But what is striking about the poem is not its barely noticeable rhyme scheme but its vigorous, dramatic tone. It might almost be a monologue from a Shakespeare play. After the previous two contributions, one woodenly reiterating well known classical anecdotes, the other full of empty generalisations, this poem is animated and lively. It is a moralizing poem but one which transcends its platitudinous message. What drives it is not piety but anxiety. This is a poem rooted in the material basis of Tudor life. It is about food, drink and clothes but above all it is about money. Gascoigne's focus on the need to have "coin enough to spend" is not abstract. The fine life of the Tudor gentleman, with his Malmesey wine, fine food, silk suits and brooch-studded hat is haunted by spectres of poverty – beggars, "Hick, Hobbe and Dick, with clouts upon their knee" and the personification of bankruptcy:

> So oft thy neighbours banquet in thy hall,
> Till Davie Debet in thy parlour stand,
> And bids thee welcome to thine own decay.

Between these extremes the poem frets about finance and money, purses, spending, budgeting, gold, silver, pounds, groats, crowns, and the gold coins known as "angels", which showed the archangel Michael spearing a dragon. It contrasts the "goodly rent" of thrift with the folly of those who, as perhaps Gascoigne himself had done, "let their lease and took their rent before", i.e. sold a lease for cash and took their payment for rent in advance. In this vicious society of flatterers and sharp practice, where men are like hawks, a gentleman is advised to be as equally cold-hearted, ruthless and predatory:

> Catch, snatch, and scratch for scrapings and for crumbs
> Before thou deck thy hat on high with brooches.

This is a view of Tudor gentlemen as animals, clawing for even the most minute advantage. In the end, Gascoigne's dark, cynical vision of Tudor England is perhaps not really all that different from that of Marx.

*

Alexander Neville proposed a poem on the theme *Sat cito, si sat bene* ("If well done, that's soon enough" – from Cato's *Dicta memorabilia* ["Memorable sayings"], no. 80). Gascoigne responded with "seven Sonets in sequence", sometimes claimed as the first sonnet sequence in English. This is not quite accurate – a number of rudimentary and unmemorable sets of sonnets were published in the 1560s, although the first extended sonnet sequence in English is generally recognised to be Thomas Watson's *Hekatompathia* (1582). But Gascoigne's conscious use of the phrase "Sonets in sequence" was a pioneering one, unmatched by any other sixteenth-century English poet. The sequence itself, unfortunately, is slack and undistinguished. Although autobiographical in thrust the sonnets offer little more than a series of unfocused generalisations about youthful folly and extravagance.

The poem for Richard Courtop continues this generalising vein. Courtop supplied the theme *Durum aeneum et miserabile aeuum* ("A hard, bronze and miserable age" – referring to the Roman notion of the four ages of man: gold, silver, bronze and iron). This poem, 46 lines in the metre known as Poulter's Measure, lists the evils of the age – flattery, perjury, presumption, rebellion etc. – to make the point that

now the times are turned, it is not as it was,
The gold is gone, the silver sunk, and nothing left but brass.[12]

The poem reads like a sketch for Gascoigne's later, more substantial satire *The Steel Glass*. So does the next poem in *A Hundreth Sundrie Flowres*, "Gascoigne's gloss upon this text, *Dominus his opus habet*", which seems like a sequel to the one written for Courtop. Its Biblical theme ("The Lord hath need of them" – an allusion to Matthew, 21, 3) supplied Gascoigne with another "text to try the truth"[13] and map the sinful condition of England. If, as seems probable, it was written at the same time as the Gray's Inn themed verses, Gascoigne seems to have forgotten his posture as someone "in middest of his youth", for he now bemoaned his "sight...now so dim" and announced that his "green youth and pride be past". The truth is that he was probably neither as doddery as he pretended, nor as rashly youthful. He was in his maturity, with a choice of a comfortable home in Walthamstow or the agreeable companionship of cultured, affluent, like-minded young gentlemen at Gray's Inn and elsewhere.

Each of the five poems ends with the tag *Sic tuli* – "this is how I have rendered it". The assertion perhaps has a slightly self-satisfied edge. Once again adopting the persona of impartial third-person editor of his own writings, Gascoigne reminds the reader that, as required, "as the theames were sundrie and altogether divers, so Master Gascoigne did accomplishe them in five sundrie sortes of metre".[14] He also boasted that, though it "seemeth most strange" he devised these five poems "riding by the way, writing none of them until he came at the end of his Journey, the which was no longer than one day in riding, one day in tarrying with his friend, and the third in returning to Greys Inne: a small time for suche a taske, neyther wolde I willingly undertake the like".

This claim should perhaps be taken with several pinches of salt. It is Gascoigne the publicist speaking, anxious to establish himself and his writing as an interesting and marketable commodity. That Gascoigne composed every word of these five poems in his head while riding a horse seems improbable. But it is quite possibly true that long dreary hours in the saddle gave him the impetus to plan out the verses in some detail. It's probably also the case that he was able to commit verse to memory in a way which would be beyond the capacity or desire of any modern poet. Gascoigne's education and his law studies involved rote learning and training in remembering to a degree inconceivable in the modern world. There was also the reality that life moved much more slowly in the sixteenth century than today. There was a lot of empty time to kill.[15]

*

The dreariness of Tudor life was punctuated by feasts, festivities and great social occasions. It was about this time that Gascoigne was an honoured guest at a very grand occasion indeed – a wedding celebration at Montague House in Southwark. The Montagues were one of the great Catholic families of England, and Viscount Montague was perhaps second only to the Duke of Norfolk in importance. Since his father was a staunch Catholic and hostile to the moderate Protestantism of Elizabeth, the poet was probably invited in his role as Sir John Gascoigne's son and heir. Whose wedding it was is not known; Pigman suggests the marriage of Mary Browne to Henry Wriothesley, 2nd Earl of Southampton, which took place on 19 February 1566.[16] If true, Gascoigne was present at the nuptials of the couple to whose son Shakespeare would many years later dedicate *Venus and Adonis* and *The Rape of Lucrece*.

Another wedding which Gascoigne and Elizabeth would surely have attended in the early years of their married life would have been that of Paul Withypoll. Some time around 1563 he married Dorothy, daughter of Thomas, Lord Wentworth, of Nettlestead, a village in Suffolk just outside Ipswich. It sounds very much like an arranged wedding between the children of two powerful East Anglian families. There Gascoigne would have had the opportunity to renew his acquaintance with Paul's brothers Bartholomew and Daniel.

By this time Bartholomew was spending a lot of time abroad, some of it on government business. In 1562 he was in Spain. On 30 April 1562 his father Edmund wrote to Sir Thomas Chaloner, the English envoy at Madrid, thanking him for the kindness he'd shown to Bartholomew. In July Chaloner used Withypoll to send a letter to Robert Cecil. Another letter sent by Chaloner to Elizabeth I is endorsed "3 August sent by Withipol by Bilboa". On 5 August the envoy wrote to Edmund Withypoll congratulating him on Bartholomew's aptitude for languages. In the few months he'd been there he'd acquired more of the Spanish tongue than either Chaloner or any of his staff in such a short time. Bartholomew does not seem to have returned to Spain. On 23 January 1563 he gave a £30 bond to his friend Alexander Culpeper Esq of Kent, who was planning to visit Jerusalem.

Meanwhile Daniel Withypoll was carving out a career for himself as a Cambridge academic. He matriculated as a pensioner of Gonville Hall "impubes" in Easter Term 1554, graduated B.A. in 1559-60 and M.A. in 1563, having been admitted as a Fellow of St John's on 6 April 1560. It was almost certainly through Daniel that Gascoigne became friendly with Gabriel Harvey. Harvey was a prolific poet and man of letters, who at the end of the century became involved in a famously acrimonious exchange of pamphlets with Thomas Nashe. Harvey graduated B.A. 1569-70 from Christ's College, and M.A. in 1573 from Pembroke Hall. He has been described as having "an arrogant egotism that at times comes near to megalomania"[17] and Edmund Spenser described him as someone

> That, sitting like a looker-on
> Of this world's stage, dost note, with a critique pen,
> The sharp dislike of each condition.

But though prickly and hyper-critical, Harvey never fell out with Gascoigne, though he disapproved of the poet's "vanity" and "levity".[18] It says a good deal for Gascoigne's genial, easy-going nature that he tolerated and evidently got on well with Harvey. Years later, after Bartholomew, Daniel and Gascoigne were all dead, Harvey pictured the three of them meeting up again in paradise. If his published writing is anything to go by, Gascoigne himself was closest to Bartholomew. But his poem about "Mine owne good *Bat*"[19] belongs to the year 1572. At this point in his life Gascoigne probably knew the Withypolls reasonably well. Over the years his friendship with Daniel and especially Bartholomew seems to have deepened.

The early English theatre

The poem for Richard Courtop supplied an unintended preface to the next spectacular development in Gascoigne's career as a writer – his metamorphosis into a theatrical producer and dramatist.

The poem splits sharply into two.[20] The first half describes how the institutions of the Tudor state are rotten – the Court, the House of Commons, the law courts, the priesthood, the nobility. It is an age which has lost its gold and silver glory, with "nothing left but brass". Treachery and "vain ambition" are everywhere. The moralising is general and somewhat conventional, although it may express the rancour of a disappointed man. The poem looks back nostalgically to an age when "right rewards were given, by sway of due desert".

Having listed the evils of the age, Gascoigne enters the poem to announce:

> Thus is the stage staked out, where all these parts be played,
> And I the prologue should pronounce, but that I am afraid.

The metaphor is that of the popular drama of his childhood, where the stage was literally "staked out" on a temporary basis in a town square or a village green. Sometimes mystery plays, miracle plays and moralities included a Prologue in which a confiding angel or some other spokesman for the dramatist pointed out the meaning of the play and the appropriate conclusions to be drawn from it. But why should Gascoigne be "afraid" and fall silent?

One reason might be the perils of attempting satire in a Tudor state which employed censorship and could punish dissenting opinions with bans, book burning, imprisonment, amputation or even execution. It is perfectly possible that Gascoigne was at court for the Christmas entertainments in December 1559 when a play was put on for Elizabeth which enraged her. What the "matter" was which upset the Queen we don't know, though probably it touched on either religion or her unmarried status. The players were sharply commanded to stop, the play was abandoned and masquers rushed on to the stage and began a dance.[21] Gascoigne himself was to discover just what offence he was capable of causing when *A Hundreth Sundrie Flowres* was published during the following decade.

But in this particular poem the satire is diffuse and unfocused, not really threatening or upsetting to the status quo. The fear of which Gascoigne speaks seems to be a rhetorical device to introduce the theatrical metaphor which controls the second half of the poem. Gascoigne is frightened – or purports to be frightened – because the modern world has become like a play:

First Cayphas plays the priest, and Herod sits as king,
Pilate the Judge, Judas the Juror verdict in doth bring.

This is a scene from an old mystery play, the trial of Christ – but it is also by implication the condition of corrupt contemporary justice. Tudor society, in its immorality, has become identical to the world of the old moralities, with its stock figures like Pride, Wantonness, Riot and Revel. In the face of this monstrous alliance even "Climme of the Clough then takes his heels, tis time for him to creep". Clym of the Clough was akin to one of Robin Hood's merry men, a stout-hearted yeoman outlaw from a medieval ballad, *Adam Bell*, which enjoyed a great vogue in sixteenth-century England. The hideous "pageant" of Tudor society is terminated by "Sorrow with a song". But this song is a cacophony: "all in discords stands the clef, and beggary sings the base". A weary disgust saturates the poem's throwaway conclusion:

When all is done and past, was no part played but one,
For every player played the fool, till all be spent and gone.
And thus this foolish jest I put in doggerel rhyme,
Because a crozier staff is best, for such a crooked time.

The last line, referring to the hooked staff which is a bishop's symbol of authority, puns both on the sixteenth-century word "staff" meaning stanza and the five lines of the musical staff.

Although Gascoigne's regrets for his squandered youth and fortune were no doubt genuine the poem should probably be seen more as an exercise in rhetoric than taken too seriously as an expression of his fixed views about the age. His indignation about dissolute womankind with "bawdrie in her brain" is scarcely consistent with those other verses in *A Hundreth Sundrie Flowres* which celebrate sexy, merry-eyed women who seem to enjoy double entendres about fucking just as much as the poet. Once again Gascoigne is adopting a persona and putting on a performance, as is apt for a poem which draws on the imagery of drama.

The poem for Courtop indicates that Gascoigne had theatre on his mind as his five "fellowship" poems drew to a close. But the Mystery plays rooted in the Bible, which dramatized such matters as the Nativity, the Passion and the Resurrection, and the Miracle plays, rooted in the lives of the Saints, were dying out. The reformed Church of England had no need of them and they were gradually being suppressed. At the same time the popular shows put on in halls or town squares by travelling players as yet lacked the sophistication and resources which would develop out of the first purpose-built commercial theatres in London from the late 1570s. It was only natural that when George Gascoigne turned his own hand to play-writing he wrote in that third contemporary English theatrical tradition which had developed inside the universities and the Inns of Court. It consisted of gentlemen amateurs putting on plays for their peers in the great halls of those institutions. The association between the Inns and drama is not perhaps surprising since law was (and is) an immensely theatrical enterprise. Barristers argued for and against the defendant but, though on one level deadly serious, on another it was all just a game. Even in real court cases the barristers were like actors. They might privately believe a defendant was guilty but they would nevertheless passionately plead his innocence.

Whether at the universities or the inns, plays were usually full-length five-act productions, often drawn from Roman, Greek or Italian theatre. At Oxford and Cambridge plays were as likely to be performed in Latin as in English. But at the London law schools there was more enthusiasm for drama in the vernacular. And for anyone contemplating putting on a play there in the mid-1560s there was a recent and impressive example of what drama could achieve.

Jocasta

For the legal community at Gray's Inn the long, grey, cold dreary heart of a winter in Elizabethan London was briefly enlivened by the music and spectacle of the Christmas revels. "Revels" formed a central aspect of Inn life and the term encompassed everything from grand formal banquets given by Readers at their installation to music and dancing and spectacular masques and plays. Each Inn had its Master of Revels, who organised entertainments from a period which began shortly before Christmas and continued until Candlemas Night (2 February) and sometimes later.

In 1566 or 1567 – the exact year is uncertain – these midwinter revels were dominated by one man: George Gascoigne. He worked with other law students to put on two plays, one a solemn tragedy, the other a slapstick comedy. But though these entertainments were collaborations which drew in scores of Gray's Inn members, the dominant and controlling figure was Gascoigne.

The tragedy was *Jocasta*, which Gascoigne described as "A tragedie written in Greke by *Euripedes*, translated and digested into Acte by George Gascoigne, and Francis Kinwelmershe".[22] In fact Euripides wrote no play with that title. Gascoigne's *Jocasta* is a version of Euripides' *Phoenissae*, otherwise known as *The Phoenicean Women*. By "digested into Acte" Gascoigne acknowledged that the original free-flowing eight-scene drama had been recast into five acts, to conform to orthodox Renaissance dramatic theory.

Of the five other members of the "fellowship" Francis Kinwelmershe was probably the oldest and the one closest to Gascoigne. Unlike the others, he may even have known Gascoigne back in the 1550s, during the poet's first stint as a student of law. He was himself a poet, contributing several verses to the anthology *The Paradyse of Daynty Devyses* (1576). He was elected MP for Droitwich, Worcestershire, in 1571 and Bossiney, Cornwall, in 1572, probably through the patronage of the second Earl of Bedford. The Bedford connection suggests that his association with Gascoigne continued long after both men had left Gray's Inn.

Francis Kinwelmershe, like Gascoigne, had his limitations as a scholar. Gascoigne was characteristically ingenuous in suggesting that he and Kinwelmershe had translated the play from the original Greek. This was a cheeky bluff. What they had actually done was to translate the play from an Italian adaptation, *Giocasta*, by Lodovico Dolce, published in Venice in 1549. It seems likely that Dolce himself translated the play into Italian not from the original Greek but from an existing Latin translation. The Gascoigne/Kinwelmershe *Jocasta* is not, therefore, an exact translation of the Euripides play but rather a distorted, imaginative adaptation subject to such variables as Dolce's own unreliable text and Gascoigne and Kinwelmershe's sometimes shaky grasp both of Italian and aspects of the original play.[23] "Go to the land of Thesbrotia", commands Queen Jocasta's brother, Creon, to which his son Meneceus replies, "Where Dodona doth sit in sacred chair?" "Even there my child," Creon solemnly replies. Sadly for George bluff-your-way-in-Greek Gascoigne, Dodona was not a person but a place – the location of a legendary oracle rather than its priestess.

The biggest clue that *Jocasta* is not a very accurate *Phoenissae* lies in the rather stark fact that the chorus of Phoenicean women who supplied Euripides with his title are changed to four Theban women. The casting of the drama into blank verse further distanced it from the original. It is also safe to assume that the actors were not masked, as they would have been when the play was performed in ancient Greece. However, there is no reason to suppose that anyone at Gray's Inn noticed or cared that *Jocasta* was an inexact version of Euripides' play. Even a prickly, pedantic academic like Gabriel Harvey thought *Jocasta* was wonderful and one of Gascoigne's finest works.

The *Phoenissae* was itself a variation on an original narrative. Probably first staged in 409 BC, the play offers a different account of the story of Oedipus to that already familiar to contemporary Greek audiences from Aeschylus' *Seven Against Thebes* and Sophocles' *Antigone* and *Oedipus the King*. It has been described as "less an alternative view of the myth than a positive riposte to the work of the previous dramatists".[24] At the start of the *Phoenissae* Oedipus is not banished from Thebes (as at the end of *Oedipus the King*) but lives as a prisoner in the royal palace. Nor, as in Sophocles, has his wife/mother Jocasta committed suicide. On the contrary, she is very much alive. The play has often been criticised for its episodic and rather haphazard structure. It hinges on the struggle for the throne between the brothers Eteocles and Polynices, the sacrifice of Creon's son Meneceus in order to save Thebes, and the despairing death of Queen Jocasta. Oedipus does not appear on stage until after these four are dead. Creon becomes King and demands that Antigone marry his son Haemon but relents and allows her to go into exile with Oedipus.

Francis Kinwelmershe translated Acts I and IV (almost exactly one-third of the text). Gascoigne gave himself the best acts, including Act II, the longest and most dramatic, which features the the clash between Eteocles and Polynices, and Act V, when Oedipus appears. These divisions may not have been watertight. Gascoigne probably involved himself in Kinwelmershe's contributions, some sections of which exhibit a style very characteristic of Gascoigne. A third collaborator, Christopher Yelverton, was brought in to supply a forty-line epilogue (not found in Dolce or Euripedes). Yelverton, of a distinguished law family, was admitted to Gray's Inn in 1552 and possibly knew Gascoigne from the poet's first period as a law student. His undistinguished contribution to *Jocasta* was probably more a case of Gascoigne cannily both doing a favour to an old friend and giving the production credibility by involving one of the more sober and respectable members of Gray's Inn. Yelverton later became a Lent reader and treasurer of Gray's Inn, served on the bench and became Speaker of the House of Commons in 1597. Seven or eight years after *Jocasta* was performed, in the long narrative poem "The Fruits of War", Gascoigne remembered his companions "Of good Gray's Inn", including "honest Yelverton":

> When amity first in our breasts begun
> Which shall endure as long as any sun
> May shine on water, or water swim in seas[25]

*

What was the attraction of the *Phoenissae* to Gascoigne? One explanation is that its plot had an acute contemporary significance in London in 1566-7. This was a time when the Protestant ruling elite was deeply anxious about Queen

Elizabeth's single status and her brush with death from smallpox in 1562. Her failure to marry and produce a male heir left the succession wide open to the return of a Catholic monarch, through the claims of Mary Queen of Scots. In 1565 Mary had married Lord Darnley, strengthening her claim to Elizabeth's crown. The issue of the succession dominated Parliamentary proceedings between September 1566 and January 1567, with Elizabeth pledging to marry when a suitable person could be found but expressing her anger at public discussion of the subject. If Gascoigne was hoping to benefit from this Parliamentary storm – and it would have been entirely in character for him to want to do so – then *Jocasta* was probably composed in the autumn of 1566 and performed early in 1567.

Topicality was not permitted in drama, in so far as plays about contemporary politics and the state were banned. A proclamation of 16 May 1559 forbade drama which touched on "governaunce of the estate of the common weale". But *Jocasta* belonged to antiquity. It was topical, but only in general terms. Its theme of a disputed succession spreading a vast circle of disaster was an idea very acceptable to the ruling Elizabethan elite and to its sons at Gray's Inn. Gascoigne himself probably did not share those anxieties about the succession but he would have certainly wanted to please his audience. The nature of that Gray's Inn audience is identified in the closing sentence of Gascoigne's second winter revels play, which is addressed to "Nobles and gentlemen".[26] (Presumably women were not in the audience or if so in very small numbers, their presence not felt to be worth recognising in the text.)

Gascoigne was driven not by ideology but by creative ambition. Just as *A Hundreth Sundrie Flowres* was intended to be a bestseller in imitation of that very successful anthology *Songes and Sonettes*, so *Jocasta* was written very much with one eye on the great theatrical hit of the decade – Thomas Norton and Thomas Sackville's *Gorboduc*. This, too, addressed the theme of a disputed succession, but it had been staged in 1562, before the issue had reached boiling point. It was even performed before Elizabeth, indicating that it was essentially inoffensive in its thrust. More to the point, it had been staged by the students of the Inner Temple, who were the great rivals of Gray's Inn.

Gorboduc was an original play about a British king who divided his realm between his two sons. The younger brother killed the elder. Out of revenge, the Queen killed her surviving son. The common people rose up in rebellion and slew their King and Queen. The nobility annihilated the rebels but then fell out among themselves. Civil war raged and for many years the realm became a waste land. The story is found in Geoffrey of Monmouth's popular history of British kings, although the primary inspiration for *Gorboduc* appears to have been the plays of the Roman writer Seneca, whose drama stressed the malevolent force of fate and who had a fondness for unhappy endings, where injustice, cruelty and tyranny are triumphant. The drawback to Seneca's tragedies is that they were written not to be performed but to be recited – something Seneca's Elizabethan admirers were wholly unaware of. His drama was essentially static and self-contained, lacking any interaction with an audience.

Gorboduc was the first English play to be written in blank verse. In another innovation, its five acts were each prefaced by a simple "dumb show", symbolically representing without dialogue what the play was about. The first dumb show is described as follows:

> First, the music of violins began to play, during which came in upon the stage six wild men, clothed in leaves. Of whom the first bare on his neck a fagot of small sticks, which they all, both severally and together, assayed with all their strength to break; but it could not be broken by them. At the length, one of them pulled out one of the sticks, and brake it: and the rest plucking out all the other sticks, one after another, did easily break them, the same being severed; which being conjoined, they had before attempted in vain. After they had this done, they departed the stage, and the music ceased. Hereby was signified, that a state knit in unity doth continue strong against all force, but being divided, it is easily destroyed; as befell upon Duke Gorboduc dividing his land to his two sons, which he before held in monarchy; and upon the dissension of the brethren, to whom it was divided.

When the play was performed at the Inner Temple in 1562 Gascoigne may well have been present. He almost certainly saw the text of the play, which was published for the first time in 1565 – a year before the writing of *Jocasta*. Although it remains only as footnote in the history of early English drama, Norton and Sackville's play was a minor classic of sorts. "Of all the early plays following Senecan play structure," comments John Gassner, "*Gorboduc* was the most vigorous even if it too suffered from Senecan rhetoric and from the customary substitution of lengthy and turgid Messengers' reports for actual stage action."[27]

The *Phoenissae* was also a good choice for competing with *Gorboduc*, in so far as it was also a sententious play, full of wise sayings. Both dramas were played before an audience largely comprised of lawyers and legal trainees and enshrined in a ceremonial way the ideal majesty and spectacle of the law and the law courts. Solemn speeches are given by figures of authority. Arguments are made in a slow, stately manner. Human destinies and lives may be at stake but there is no hurry. The drama has a static quality; it is drama which is oddly undramatic. *Jocasta*, even more than *Gorboduc*, is a sententious play, with constant appeals to authority. A typical example is: "wise is he, that doth obey the Gods" (III.ii.74) Sententiousness carries an essentially conservative and unthreatening message. In the closing words of Oedipus: "every man must bear with quiet mind / The fate that heavens have earst to him assigned". Gabriel Harvey thought this kind of cracker barrel wisdom was wonderful and hailed

Jocasta as "An excellent Tragedie: full of manie discreet, wise, and deep considerations".[28]

Gascoigne's intention in *Jocasta* was clearly to surpass *Gorboduc* both in its language and its spectacle, and he succeeded on both counts. The language of *Jocasta* is both more dramatic and more ornate and consciously poetic than that in *Gorboduc*. A typical speech by the Chorus in Sackville and Norton's play runs as follows:

> Oft tender mind that leads the partial eye
>   Of erring parents in their children's love
> Destroys the wrongly loved child thereby.
>   This doth the proud son of Apollo prove,
> Who, rashly set in chariot of his sire,
> Inflam'd the parched earth with heaven's fire. (I.ii.452-7)

The moral that a parent's indulgence towards a child can lead to that child's destruction is illustrated by an example drawn from Book Two of Ovid's *Metamorphoses* – Phaethon was permitted to drive his father's chariot of fire but lost control of it, causing enormous destruction and losing his life. The language is stately and formal and the classical allusion tamely conventional. There's a flatness of tone here, reinforced by the rhyme scheme. The speech has a repetitive and faintly narcotic quality. Listening to it, a modern audience would quickly nod off.

Gascoigne's use of language for the Chorus in *Jocasta* is very much livelier:

> O fierce and furious God, whose harmful heart
> Rejoiceth most to shed the guiltless blood,
> Whose heady will doth all the world subvert
> And doth envy the pleasant merry mood
> Of our estate that erst in quiet stood,
> Why doest thou thus our harmless town annoy
> Which mighty Bacchus governed in joy?
>   Father of war and death, that doest remove
> With wrathful wreck from woeful mother's breast
> The trusty pledges of their tender love,
> So grant the Gods that for our final rest
> Dame Venus' pleasant looks may please thee best,
> Whereby when thou shalt all amazed stand
> The sword may fall out of thy trembling hand. (II.iii.1-14)

This is vigorous, rhythmic verse, energised and amplified by four voices speaking in unison. Alliteration and monosyllables thump home the thunderous address to Mars, the god of war. There is no danger of the audience's concentration slackening. This verse immediately engages the listener's ear.

At the level of spectacle *Jocasta* also superseded *Gorboduc*. Here Gascoigne's choice of Greek play was pertinent as the *Phoenissae* has the biggest cast of any Greek tragedy. Its structure offered the opportunity for a lavish blockbuster production. H. D. F. Kitto has described Euripides' play as a "pageant" and "very good cinema".[29] No information about the staging of *Jocasta* at Gray's Inn has survived but it is reasonable to assume it was in the largest appropriate building on the site, which would have been "the hall of Graies Inne" mentioned in a Close Roll entry.[30] The stage may have been a temporary construction or something more permanent. Over the years the regular staging of plays must have resulted in the opportunity for increasingly sophisticated productions. Forty years earlier the poet's distinguished grandfather, Sir William Gascoigne, may have been present when the students of Gray's Inn performed two moralities, *Lord Governaunce* and *Lady Publicke Wele*, for Cardinal Wolsey. Wolsey was angered by them, detecting satire. Over subsequent decades productions were known to be extravagantly ornate, attracting courtiers and other members of Tudor London's elite to their audience.

Jocasta provided an opportunity for lavishly painted scenery and impressively modelled scene-setting. The play is set against the backdrop of the royal palace of Thebes. Access to and from the stage was provided at three points. A gateway, probably located centre-stage, provided entry to the palace and two other gates – the Electra Gate and the Homoloydes Gate – represented the boundaries of the city. These stage features are not found in Dolce and were clearly tailored to the conditions of the production in the great hall at Gray's Inn.

Jocasta is a play in slow motion, which utilises these three gateways to the full. Aside from the dumb shows preceding them, the five acts basically consist of lots of solemn, stately entrances, long solemn speeches, and solemn, stately exits. After the first dumb show the play begins with twelve male attendants emerging from the palace, escorting Queen Jocasta. Trumpets blow as the Queen comes into view. Eight ladies in waiting follow. The procession of twenty-one actors does one tour of the stage, then Jocasta turns to Servus (Latin for "slave" and a character who appears in neither Dolce nor Euripides) and the play begins. When the Queen and her entourage return inside the palace at the end of the first scene, four of the ladies in waiting remain on stage as the Chorus, "where they continue to the end of the Tragedie".

Apart from the involvement of Francis Kinwelmershe and the perfunctory contribution of Christopher Yelverton, *Jocasta* involved collaboration on a grand scale with the community at Gray's Inn. There were speaking parts for seventeen actors, including the four Theban women who comprise the Chorus.[31] All the women's parts – Queen Jocasta, her daughter Antigone, the prophet Tiresias's daughter Manto, and the Chorus – were, of course, played by men.

The play's writers may have involved themselves in the performance, with Yelverton reading his epilogue and Kinwelmershe taking on the role of one of the characters whose lines he was exclusively responsible for (Servus, perhaps, or Bailo). As events at Kenilworth in 1575 were to show, Gascoigne was not bashful when it came to putting on a performance, and one suspects he would have picked at least one of the play's plum roles for himself (Jocasta herself, perhaps, or either Eteocles or Polynices doubled up with Oedipus). But this can only ever be a matter of speculation.

There were non-speaking roles for eighty identified figures as well as miscellanous "ladyes and dames". Even allowing for doubling-up, this was, by any theatrical standards and particularly those of 1566-7, a massive cast, unequalled by any other Tudor drama. At the level of sheer spectacle *Jocasta* was obviously intended to make *Gorboduc* seem thin by comparison.

Visually, the key area of competition was in the dumb shows. In *Gorboduc* the five dumb shows had in turn featured the same format of a short symbolic tableau related to the play's themes of bloody ambition and disunity. The shows were enacted to music which fell silent at the end, as follows:

> (i) Violin music. Six wild men clothed in leaves appear. They attempt to break a bunch of small sticks, fail, then succeed in breaking the individual sticks and depart.
> (ii) The music of cornets. A king with attendants appears and sits on a throne. He is then twice offered a cup of wine, the second one containing poison which kills him.
> (iii) Flute music. A company of mourners dressed in black pass around the stage three times and then depart.
> (iv) The music of hautboys. Three furies wrapped in snakes, with snake wigs and wearing lurid black costumes painted with blood and flames, emerge from beneath the stage. One carries a snake, one a whip, one a burning firebrand. Each drives before them a king and queen.
> (v) Drums and flutes sound. A company of harquebusiers and other armed men in battledress march on to the stage and discharge their weapons. They march around the stage three times, then depart.

The five symbolic dumb shows in *Jocasta* involve many more musical instruments, more actors, a spectacular wheeled stage prop and even special effects involving fire and moving scenery:

> (i) Music is heard: "a dolefull and straunge noyse of violles, Cythren, Bandurion, and suche like". Four kings wearing crowns pull on to the stage "a Chariote very richely furnished" in which sits a fifth king "with an Imperiall Crowne upon his head, very richely apparelled, a Scepter in his

right hande, a Mounde with a Crosse in his left hande". The chariot is pulled twice around the stage, then the kings depart.

(ii) Flute music, "very dolefull". Eight pallbearers carry two covered coffins on to the stage, followed by eight mourners. Next, "after they had carried the coffins about the stage, there opened and appeared a Grave, wherin they buried the coffins and put fire to them, but the flames did sever and parte in twaine, signifying discord... After the funerals were ended and the fire consumed, the grave was closed up again, the mourners withdrew them off the stage".

(iii) A "very dolefull noise of cornettes, during the which there opened and appeared in the stage a great Gulfe". Six gentlemen in doublets and hose walk onstage, carrying baskets filled with earth on their shoulders. They throw the earth into the abyss, attempting to fill it in, "but it would not so close up nor be filled". Miscellaneous "ladyes and dames" enter and attempt to close the chasm by tossing in their chains and jewels. When this also fails "came in a knighte with his sword drawen, armed at all poyntes". The knight walks by the abyss "twise or thrise", staring into it. Then, "after solempne reverence done to the gods, and curteous leave taken of the Ladyes and standers by, sodeinly lepte into the Gulfe the which did close up immediatly".

(iv) Trumpets sound, drums beat, fifes play, "and a greate peale of ordinaunce was shot of". Three armed knights enter from the Electra Gate, and three from the Homoloydes Gate, each group being accompanied by seven other armed men. They march about the stage, "the one partie menacing the other by their furious lookes and gestures". While their attendants stand by and watch the two groups of knights draw their swords and engage in combat. Two knights in one group are killed and the survivor runs off, pursued by the first, second and then third member of the other group, who he kills one by one in single combat. The solitary victor "triumphantly marched aboute the Stage with hys sword in his hand...After that the dead carcasses were carried from the Stage by the armed men of both parties, and...the victor was triumphantly accompanied out also".

(v) Stillpipes sound a mournful melody. Four noblemen pull a chariot on to the stage, in which sits a woman dressed in white, her lap full of jewels. She is wearing headgear which shows a fair, smiling face at the front and a black, malevolent one with blindfolded eyes at the back. Her legs are naked and her feet rest on a great round ball. In her right hand she holds a string attached to two crowned kings, in the other string attached to two poor slaves in rags. After a circuit of the stage she changes the strings over, takes the crowns and regal clothes from the kings and places them on the slaves and makes the kings wear their rags. The chariot is then pulled off the stage.

Dazzling as this all must have been, it did not in the end make *Jocasta* a successful play. Special effects in themselves are not enough. As a tragedy *Jocasta* is not rooted in individual psychology and the characters are too stereotypical; they lack individuality. Their world is one of curses, inescapable destiny and doom. There is no real room for human freedom or choice. Its popularity was restricted to its time and it probably had at most only one more performance. When the Earl of Leicester paid an official visit to the University of Oxford in 1569 the entertainments included "a playe or shew of the destruction of Thebes, and the contention between Eteocles and Polynices for the government thereof". E. K. Chambers has suggested that this might have been *Jocasta*.[32] If so, it provides a possible early connection between Gascoigne and one of the most distinguished and powerful literary patrons in England. It is equally possible that Robert Dudley was in the audience at Gray's Inn for the play's premiere. Coincidence or not, Gascoigne became one of Leicester's leading writers and performers for the entertainments put on for the Queen when she stayed at Kenilworth Castle the following decade.

Forty years later Shakespeare mocked the sententious tradition in the comic pomposity of *Hamlet*'s Polonius. He may however have glanced at *Jocasta* when writing *The Tempest*. Prospero's famous lines about "The cloud-capp'd towers, the gorgeous palaces" which "like this insubstantial pageant faded, / Leave not a rack behind" (IV.i.152, 155-6) seem to carry a distant echo of *Jocasta*'s palace with "The chambers huge, the goodly gorgeous beds, / The gilted roofs, embowde with curious work" (I.ii.9-10) and the Theban chorus's image of the ultimate collapse of palatial splendour and towers: "Thy gorgeous pomp, thy glorious high renown, / Thy stately towers, and all shall fall a down" (I. iv. 53-54).

Jocasta's own pageant faded into obscurity. The beginnings of popular commercial theatre in the late 1570s saw English drama take a different path. *Jocasta* fails because action and spectacle are divorced from the dialogue. The high drama of the individual dumb shows is followed by the anti-climax of each slow-moving act. The speeches, though highly wrought, are essentially static and sometimes far too long (in Act II, Jocasta takes eighty-three lines to tell Eteocles to cast aside ambition). The action – the fight between Eteocles and Polynices, the death of Jocasta – is never seen, merely reported at second hand. With these flaws, and with its ponderous and archaic speeches, it is impossible to imagine *Jocasta* being performed today, other than perhaps as a curiosity piece before an audience of renaissance scholars.

Supposes

The same cannot be said of Gascoigne's other entertainment presented to his Gray's Inn audience. Whereas *Jocasta* was a solemn and stately production which would have been watched with awe, *Supposes* is a boisterous, racy comedy in prose about disguised identities. Attending the performance of *Jocasta* would have been like being in church or at a coronation, requiring a respectful silence. But *Supposes* was fun. It positively encouraged a vocal reaction from its audience. The plot hinges on a young nobleman, Erostrato, swapping his name and social position with his man Dulippo, in order to find employment as a servant in the household of Damon and thereby woo his daughter, Polynesta.[33]

No one knows the dates on which Gascoigne's Gray's Inn plays were performed or which came first. *Supposes* was in the spirit of the election of lords of misrule and the traditional pranks of their followers on Candlemas Night, 2 February, which is a possible occasion for its performance. It is the best known of Gascoigne's plays, partly because it is the first English comedy in prose and partly because Shakespeare borrowed from its plot, characters and text in writing *The Taming of the Shrew*. As every modern edition acknowledges, Shakespeare's Lucentio and his servant Tranio are versions of Gascoigne's Erostrato and Dulippo, and Lucentio's wooing of Bianca replicates Erostrato's pursuit of Polynesta. Likewise Shakespeare's Baptista is based on Damon and old Gremio is a version of Gascoigne's Cleander.

Supposes was not on the massive scale of *Jocasta*, nor did it require special effects. It has a cast of twenty, though three are non-speaking parts and with actors doubling-up for the minor characters it would be possible to use fewer. The play was Gascoigne's unaided translation of Ludovico Ariosto's *I Suppositi*, which was first written in prose for the carnival season in Ferrara. *I Suppositi* is set in that city around the year 1500. Although Gascoigne retained the Ferrara setting he cut the play's references to specific locations in the city. Ariosto was an ex-law student and the play's provocatively barbed comments about lawyers and legal chicanery made it an attractive choice for Gascoigne to put before a Gray's Inn crowd. Lines like these were perfect for a hall packed with barristers and trainee law students:

> CLEANDER: The trade of Law doth fill the boisterous bags,
>   They swim in silk, when others roist in rags.
> PASIPHILO: O excellent verse! Who made it? Virgil?
> CLEANDER: Virgil? Tush, it is written in one of our glosses.
> PASIPHILO: Sure, whosoever wrote it, the moral is excellent and worthy to be written in letters of gold. (I.ii.54-9)

There are jokes about drinking, whoring, and preferring sex to studying books. There are lines of sexual innuendo ("he little remembreth that his daughter's purse shall be continually empty unless Master Doctor fill it with double duck eggs" – "purse" signifying the vagina and "double duck eggs" testicles pressed against it during penetration). Young Erostrato's scorn for the aged barrister

Cleander – "the silly doctor with the side bonnet, the doting fool" – may involve an in-joke about the formal garb of the Gray's Inn elders. The "Master Doctor" is portrayed as a bumbling old fool who, "old as he is, and as many subtleties as he hath learned in the law" (III. i. 43-4) is no match for his much younger rival in love. *Supposes* invited a response from its witty, cynical, sophisticated metropolitan audience and no doubt got one – laughter, catcalls, applause.

If the local colour is often Gascoigne's, the play's comic energies were Ariosto's. The Italian was an experienced man of the theatre, involved in play production at the Ducal court. He was familiar with plays by Plautus and Terence, which influenced his own approach to comedy. Ariosto acknowledged *I Suppositi*'s debt to Terence's *Eunuchus* ("The Eunuch") and Plautus's *Captivi* ("The Captives"). It was Ariosto's second comedy and was first performed on 6 February 1509, at the palace of Duke Alfonso I d'Este. Ariosto spoke the prologue himself and the play was apparently very successful. It was subsequently performed before Pope Leo X in Rome on 6 March 1519. For this performance the prologue was rewritten and the backdrop, showing a view of the city of Ferrara, was painted by Raphael. The Pope apparently hugely enjoyed the play's madcap and at times somewhat risqué humour. Ariosto later rewrote the play in verse and this version was published in Venice in 1551 and in a collection of Ariosto's plays from the same publisher in 1562. Ten editions of the prose version appeared between 1525 and 1542. It is clear that Gascoigne had copies of both the prose and verse editions in adapting the play. Some critics who have compared *Supposes* only with Ariosto's original prose version have attributed to Gascoigne changes which were in fact made by Ariosto himself in the later verse adaptation. Generally, Gascoigne's adaptation is closer to Ariosto's verse version than to the prose original.

Gascoigne made very minor adjustments to the cast list. Psiteria he defined as "an old hag" and Litio as an innkeeper. He slightly changed the names of most of the characters. Cleandro, for example, becomes Cleander. Caprino is changed to Crapino (unintentionally comic to modern ears; "crap" meaning "defecate" does not exist before the mid-eighteenth century). Gascoigne gave the name "Petrucio" to one of the un-named servants of the Sienese man. This was subsequently borrowed by Shakespeare, who used it for the hero of *The Taming of the Shrew*; he also borrowed "Litio" for Hortensio's bogus identity as a lute teacher.

*

The editors of the most recent modern edition of *Supposes* describe Gascoigne's translation as "accurate and reliable".[34] While acknowledging slight variations and the use of English idioms, they argue that these "make no changes to the substance or drift of the original". Gascoigne's adaptation was however a richly imaginative one which idiosyncratically recast the drama on his own terms.

G. W. Pigman notes that

> In fact, "translation", if encumbered with modern notions of verbal fidelity, gives a poor idea of what Gascoigne is doing. Gascoigne rarely translates Ariosto closely but rather paraphrases or adapts him, often expanding on his originals, less frequently condensing them, and occasionally changing the sense completely...Gascoigne's modifications...run from small details to substantial addition and revision. In fact Gascoigne changes so many details that sometimes it appears that he does so for the simple pleasure of being different... Gascoigne's characteristic way of changing Ariosto is to expand him. He adds something to every scene in the play.[35]

The titles themselves register the difference between the Italian original and the English adaptation. *I Suppositi* means "the pretenders" or "the impersonators" and Ariosto uses "supporre", "supponere" and "supposizione" in the sense of "substitution" (Dulippo the servant switching identities with his master Erostrato and the Sienese stranger acting the part of Erostrato's father). There is an additional erotic pun on "sub ponere" (meaning "placing under"). Although Gascoigne does briefly use "suppose" in the sense of "substitution" he usually prefers the common English meaning of "assume" or "accept as probable". Beecher and Butler see in this a key contrast between the two styles of theatre:

> That Gascoigne emphasized supposition or misleading assumptions on the part of the various characters as a thematic motif, as opposed to substitutions or exchanges of identities through disguising and pretending, represents a major shift in emphasis and may tell us something about the basic differences between Italian and English conceptions of comic theatre. The former stresses disguise, trickery and illusion, the latter comic irony, errors of judgement, and rectification of confusion through experience.[36]

Gascoigne's Prologue milks the word "suppose" for all it is worth and offers a parody of a lawyer's nitpicking, pedantic argumentation. Just as Ariosto himself performed the role for the first Italian performance, there can be little doubt that Gascoigne also appropriated this speech for himself. As if addressing a judge or jury, the speaker steps out on to the stage and introduces the play. "I *suppose*", the speaker remarks, "you are assembled here *supposing* to reap the fruit of my travails" [labours]. "To be plain," he continues – in a speech which quickly becomes far from plain, about a play where all is confusion – "I mean presently to present you with a comedy called *Supposes*". Gascoigne then lets rip:

> the very name whereof may peradventure drive into every one of your heads a sundry *Suppose*, to *suppose* the meaning of our *supposes*. Some percase

will *suppose* we mean to occupy your ears with sophistical handling of subtle *Suppositions*. Some other will *suppose* we go about to decipher unto you some quaint conceits, which hitherto have been only *supposed* as it were in shadows: and some I see smiling as though they *supposed* we would trouble you with the vain *suppose* of some wanton *Suppose*. (my italics)

This is comic overload – a device to elicit groans, hoots, catcalls and laughter from an audience of young men all too well acquainted with the sophistry of a barrister's special pleading. Anyone knowing the original Italian would have laughed that extra bit louder, detecting in Gascoigne's vague mention of "shadows" (meaning pictures) an echo of Ariosto's specific allusion to Giulio Romano's *I Modi* ("The Positions"). This was a notorious series of sixteen explicit drawings depicting couples having sex, which were subsequently scandalously reproduced in engravings by Marcantonio Raimondi. As for the "vain suppose of some wanton Suppose": that was a muted echo of Ariosto's reference to the Elephanti, a legendary collection of ancient pornography.

Having apparently exhausted the comic possibilities of repetition, Gascoigne adopts a plain speaking idiom and goes on to summarise the plot of the play in a single sentence:

But understand, this our Suppose is nothing else but a mistaking or imagination of one thing for an other: for you shall see the master supposed for the servant, the servant for the master: the freeman for a slave, and the bondslave for a freeman: the stranger for a well known friend, and the familiar for a stranger.

"Supposed" here lacks Ariosto's sense of "substituted for". As a summary of the play it omits any explanation *why* these false "suppositions" have occurred, although this does start to become clear in the opening scene that follows.

"But what?" adds the speaker, lapsing back into a pastiche of the clotted language of the law:

I *suppose* that even already you *suppose* me very fond, that have so simply disclosed unto you the subtleties of these our *Supposes*: where otherwise indeed I *suppose* you should have heard almost the last of our *Supposes*, before you could have *supposed* any of them aright. (my italics)

The speaker suggests that the audience must think him very foolish ("very fond") to give away the plot but asserts that without this information they would themselves have been fooled by the play's deceptions. "Let this then suffice" he concludes, with a clarity in sharp distinction to what has gone before. This wittily terminates the comic use of the word "suppose" and the play begins.

*

Supposes hinges on two crises, in which deception is threatened with exposure. Firstly, the play begins with Polynesta pregnant and her father's imminent discovery of her secret relationship with Erostrato. Secondly, Philogano's unexpected arrival in the city means that Dulippo will be unmasked in his pretence that he is his master Erostrato. From these two crises the comedy flows: the elderly lawyer Cleander's desire for the supposedly chaste Polynesta, Damon's horror at discovering his daughter's pregnancy, the imprisonment of Erostrato and Dulippo's desperate attempts to maintain his bogus identity as Philogano's son. The false "supposes" are exposed but all ends happily. Philogano discovers that Dulippo has not, after all, murdered his master and is reconciled with his son. Cleander is reconciled to the loss of Polynesta by the discovery that Dulippo is his long-lost son. Damon is reconciled to his daughter's pregnancy by the revelation that Erostrato is not, after all, a servant but a wealthy nobleman who will marry her.

The play is fast-moving, funny and effective. Two of its comic highlights involve additions by Gascoigne, not found in the original. With his Gray's Inn audience obviously in mind he significantly amplified dialogue about injustice and corruption in the law and the tricks of lawyers:

> LITIO: Sir, he that will go to the law must be sure of four things: first, a right and a just cause, then a righteous advocate to plead, next favour *Coram Judice* [before the judge] and above all a good purse to procure it.
> FERRARESE: I have not heard that the law hath any respect to favour. What you mean by it I cannot tell.
> PHILOGANO: Have you no regard to his words; he is but a fool.
> FERRARESE: I pray you, sir, let him tell me what is "favour".
> LITIO: Favour call I to have a friend near about the Judge, who may so solicit thy cause as if it be right, speedy sentence may ensue without any delays. If it be not good, then to prolong it, till at the last, thine adversary, being weary, shall be glad to compound [settle out of court] with thee.
> FERRARESE: Of thus much, although I never heard thus much in this country before, doubt you not, Philogano, I will bring you to an advocate that shall speed you accordingly.
> PHILOGANO: Then shall I give myself, as it were, a prey to the lawyers, whose insatiable jaws I am not able to feed, although I had here all the goods and lands which I possess in mine own country, much less being a stranger in this misery. I know their cautels [deceptions] of old; at the first time I come they will so extol my case as though it were already won, but within a sevennight or ten days, if I do not continually feed them as the crow doth her brats, twenty times in an hour, they will begin to wax cold and to find cavils in my cause, saying that at the first I did not well instruct them, till at the last

they will not only draw the stuffing out of my purse but the marrow out of my bones. (IV.viii.41-67)

This no doubt had everyone in the great hall in stitches. This cynicism about the legal process was for comic effect but it indicates an underlying disillusion with the profession. Gascoigne was not, of course, interested in legal reform. Rather, the law was something he began studying, gave up, went back to – probably in a perfunctory way – and then gave up again. Its only use to him was in enabling him to meet other young intellectuals and in supplying him with material for his writing. How far a legal training assisted him in the law suits in which he was himself involved is open to question. In the case of his disputed marriage it appears that what counted most of all was indeed "favour *coram judice*" – or at any rate, the friendly intervention of Sir Nicholas Bacon.

Supposes ends with a scatological joke not found in Ariosto's play. After the reconciliation between fathers, sons and daughter the main characters troop off the stage, leaving Nevola and Damon alone together. Nevola shows his master the fetters and bolts which had been used to restrain Erostrato and asks what he is to do with them:

DAMON: Marry, I will tell thee, Nevola. To make a right end of ours *supposes*, lay one of those bolts in the fire and make thee a *suppository* as long as mine arm, God save the sample. (V.x.44-6, my italics)

On this witty, earthy pun the play ends.

*

Great claims have been made for *Supposes*. Donald Beecher and John Butler have argued that "this work contributes perhaps more directly than any other to the founding of the European drama, and to the shaping of the English stage".[37] But others have been puzzled by its lack of influence. A. R. Humphreys commented that "During the next twenty years little of promise evolved from this lone example [of dramatic prose aspiring to art]".[38]

Gascoigne was perhaps too far ahead of his time. At the end of the century plays with an Italian setting became very popular – a trend embodied in plays by John Marston, Webster, Tourneur and Ford, not to mention *Romeo and Juliet*, *Othello* and *The Merchant of Venice*. But Gascoigne played down the Italian setting. The characters may have Italian names but the idiom and local colour are distinctly that of England in the 1560s.

Of Gascoigne's three plays, *Supposes* is the one which remains eminently stageable. The problem for any modern audience, however, is that its members would be likely to feel they had seen it all before. This is the consequence of the enormous impact *Supposes* had on Shakespeare. The modern cultural hegemony of Shakespeare means that his creative asset-stripping makes Gascoigne seem reminiscent of him rather than the other way round. The extensive indebtedness of *The Taming of the Shrew* to *Supposes* is acknowledged by every modern edition of the play. Shakespeare himself briefly signalled his debt to Gascoigne in Tranio's remark that "supposed Lucentio / Must get a father, called supposed Vincentio" (II.i.400-1) and Lucentio informing his new father-in-law that "counterfeit supposes bleared thine eye" (V.i.106).

But Shakespeare's *Taming of the Shrew* is different from *Supposes* in two ways. It is a play with a softer comic focus, which does not in itself make it a better play. Gary Taylor has acerbically remarked,

> What I personally admire about Plautus and other writers like him is what Shakespeareans so regularly deprecate: hardness, toughness, exuberant and fantastic amorality. And what I dislike about Shakespeare's comedies – and tragedies – is their softness, their central mushiness, their inevitable "love interest", their wholesomeness.[39]

Just such toughness is what we find in *Supposes* but not in *The Taming of the Shrew*. In Shakespeare there is no pre-marital sex, no unexpected pregnancy. In Shakespeare's play Katherina and Bianca are chaste; there is no sex until marriage. Nor are there any blistering attacks on corrupt judges, greedy and devious lawyers and the injustice of the legal system. There are no jokes about holes and arses in the *Shrew*. At the end Shakespeare supplies what he always supplies: reconciliation and closure. Gascoigne, by contrast, brusquely bids farewell to his audience with a joke about a huge suppository.

Irrespective of that difference we are still likely to feel that *The Taming of the Shrew* is a better play. Shakespeare's blank verse is a richer instrument than Gascoigne's racy vernacular prose. Secondly, Shakespeare's play is more complex. It gives us two plots, *Supposes* only one. Gascoigne's main plot becomes Shakespeare's back story. And Shakespeare cares more for the dramatic life of his female characters than Ariosto/Gascoigne. In *Supposes* Polynesta dominates the opening scene, then never says another word throughout the play. Familiarity with Shakespeare's plays is likely to lead a modern reader to expect speeches from Polynesta and Erostrato at the end. There are none. Having vanished from the play after Act 3, Scene 2, Erostrato re-appears in the penultimate scene and utters just two words: "O father".

The influence of *Supposes* upon Shakespeare seems to have been profound. The general assumption is that he first encountered it on the printed page in the 1587 edition of Gascoigne's *Whole woorkes*. Brian Morris believes *The Taming of the Shrew* was written "only a year or so" afterwards.[40] We do not know where Shakespeare was on 8 January 1582 but he would not have been in the audience for the performance of *Supposes* put on that day at Trinity College, Oxford. However he discovered it, and in whichever edition, it was a play which Shakespeare came across at the very beginning of his career as a dramatist, possibly before he had ever written a play. Damon's description of his daughter as "a collop of my own flesh" (III.iii.63) is echoed by Joan of Arc's father in *Henry VI, Part One*: "God knows thou art a collop of my flesh" (V.iv.8), just as Vincentio's abusive "crack-hemp" (glossed as "a rogue that deserves to be hanged": *The Taming of the Shrew*, V.i.40) seems to originate in a half-remembered conflation of Gascoigne's "crack-halter" (I.iv.4) and "hempstring" (IV.ii.19).

Supposes was also a play which Shakespeare either remembered very clearly in later years or went back to and re-read. He clearly appreciated the dramatic potential of the scene in which Philogano, Litio and the Ferrarese bang on the door of Erostrato's house and have difficulty in getting anyone to open the door:

FERRARESE: Lo you, sir, here is your son Erostrato's house. I will knock.
PHILOGANO: Yea, I pray you, knock.
FERRARESE: They hear not.
PHILOGANO: Knock again
FERRARESE: I think they be on sleep.
LITIO: If this gate were your grandfather's soul, you could not knock more softly. Let me come. Ho! Ho! Is there anybody within?
DALIO: What devil of hell is there? I think he will break the gates in pieces.
(III.iii. 52-71)

This scene is recycled in *The Taming of the Shrew* (I.ii.5-42 and V.i.7-14) but it surely also supplies the germ of the famous knocking-on-the-gate episode in Act 2, Scene 3 of *Macbeth*. Similarly, the badinage between the young woman Polynesta and her nurse Balia is oddly reminiscent of that between Juliet and her nurse.

One passage added by Gascoigne, involves a dialogue between the false Dulippo and another servant. Crapino's style of response and his wilful interpretation of "find" in its secondary sense of "support" or "maintain" much resembles the quibbling between the gravedigger and Hamlet:

DULIPPO: Ho, Jack pack, where is Erostrato?
CRAPINO: Erostrato? Marry, he is in his skin.
DULIPPO: Ah, whoreson boy, I say, how shall I find Erostrato?
CRAPINO: Find him? How mean you? By the week or by the year?
(I.iii.98-9-iv.1-3)

*

The link between Gascoigne's law training, Gray's Inn and the choice of *I Suppositi* is straightforward. But was there any other biographical significance in his choice of that play or method of adaptation? Ariosto's play was about two men in pursuit of the same woman and in that sense it replicated the rivalry between Boyes and Gascoigne, but the differences are far more striking than that loose parallel. Much more intriguing is Damon's long, mournful speech in Act 3, Scene 3, triggered by his discovery of Polynesta's pregnancy, apparently by a mere servant. It is the longest speech in the play and virtually none of it is found in Ariosto. C. T. Prouty concluded that it was a direct autobiographical reflection on Gascoigne's situation in 1566 and was addressed to Sir John Gascoigne:

> it seems that in this reflection on the duties of parents, the longest original addition to his translation, Gascoigne was indirectly reproaching his own father for neglecting to guide his life aright and for failing to provide a suitable marriage.[41]

This is not persuasive. Damon's speech is from the perspective of the parent, not the child, and its anxieties could just as easily be read as voicing Gascoigne's feelings about fatherhood and his recently born child. Damon expresses the misery of a betrayed parent, not the complaint of a badly treated child. His speech is about wanting revenge on a diabolical third party and bitterly regretting the restraints imposed on a man by the need to observe the laws of the land. It is fuelled by a dark, powerful sense that an event has occurred which can never be undone and which Damon has partly brought upon himself:

> the thing once done can not be undone. My daughter is deflowered and I utterly dishonested, how can I then wipe that blot off my brow? and on whom shall I seek revenge? Alas, alas, I myself have been the cause of all these cares and have deserved to bear the punishment of all these mishaps.
> (III.iii.30-35)

He blames himself for putting his daughter in the care of her old nurse, "for we see by common proof that these old women be either peevish or too pitiful: either easily inclined to evil or quickly corrupted with bribes and rewards". He remembers his dead wife who, had she lived, would surely have prevented the catastrophe. He reflects on the child's duty to be obedient to its parents and the binding ties of parents to their child:

> first to beget them, then to bring them forth, after to nourish them, to preserve them from bodily perils in the cradle, from danger of soul by godly education, to match them in consort inclined to virtue, to banish them all idle

and wanton company, to allow them sufficient for their sustentation, to cut of excess the open gate of sin, seldom or never to smile on them unless it be to their encouragement in virtue, and finally to provide them marriages in time convenient, lest neglected of us, they learn to set either too much or too little by themselves. Five years are past since I might have married her, when by continual excuses I have prolonged it to my own perdition. Alas, I should have considered, she is a collop of my own flesh, what should I think to make her a princess? Alas, alas, a poor kingdom have I now caught to endow her with. It is too true that of all sorrows this is the head source and chief fountain of all furies. The goods of the world are uncertain, the gains to be rejoiced at, and the loss not greatly to be lamented. Only the children cast away cutteth the parent's throat with the knife of inward care, which knife will kill me surely. I make none other account.

Pigman believes that Damon's speech may involve "another reminder to Elizabeth, in the midst of the succession controversy, of the importance of her marrying and producing an heir".[42] Perhaps, though Elizabeth surely never saw the play. Besides, Damon's problem is not that his daughter has failed to produce an heir but rather the reverse.

Damon's long speech resists the extrapolation of a single meaning; his mind constantly shifts its focus as he articulates his rage, misery and frustration. What is striking about it is its tone. In a play which is essentially fast-moving, light-hearted and brightly comic Damon abruptly slows down the pace. His dark, sombre speech seems jarringly out of key with the surrounding comedy as it plumbs the depths of his shock and despair. His words belong more to a tragedy than a sparky comedy where nothing is quite as it seems and everything works out happily in the end. Every commentator on *Supposes* senses that there is something going on here which is surplus to Damon's situation or to the play's dramatic requirements. That Gascoigne was, through Damon's voice, venting his own powerful emotions about something seems very probable. But that it was anything to do with his father or the Queen's single status is unlikely.

One possibility is that it concerns a shocking event in his life which had happened in the recent past and of which he never spoke directly. What it was became clearer when Gascoigne was accused of "greate crymes" in the year he fled abroad.[43] But that was several years away. For the present everything, on the face of it, was going spectacularly well in his life. His bigamous marriage had been sorted out in his favour, he had a wealthy wife and a handsome new house in Walthamstow, and he was the father of an infant boy. Back at Gray's Inn he was the man of the moment and the driving force behind two stunning plays, one a spectacular epic tragedy, the other a zippy comedy.

But something went wrong. After these two plays, nothing happened. Neither drama was put on at court. No one sought Gascoigne's services. No patrons appeared on the scene for him to dedicate his writings to. George Gascoigne remained where he had been a decade earlier: an outsider at court, a man on the margins of the cliques that controlled the state and the royal household.

It is an odd and unexplained fact that the fruits of comedy and acting – laughter and applause – are associated by Gascoigne with humiliation. At the end of the poem beginning "Despised things may live, although they pine in pain" the speaker emerges from misfortune and betrayal and vows "to clap my hands, / And laugh at them which laughed at me: lo thus my fancy stands".[44] Even more searing are the last two lines of "And if I did what then?" The poem ends with a vision of men who have deceived and betrayed the speaker tossed by time "on the shelf" (meaning a sandbank):

> And when they stick on sands,
> That every man may see:
> Then will I laugh and clap my hands,
> As they do now at me.

A sense of betrayal and humiliation and dreams of revenge are, of course, what fuel Damon's long speech. Something bitterly personal seems to be swirling around below the surface of these lines, linking Gascoigne's private life with his brief involvement with the world of theatre. After what would seem to have been two dazzling productions Gascoigne gave up theatrical production. Gray's Inn asked for no more revels penned by Gascoigne. Perhaps the actors let Gascoigne down; perhaps, as Richard Madox grumbled when *Supposes* was re-staged at Trinity College, Oxford, the play was "handeled...indifferently".[45] Maybe the playwright was invited on stage, only to be mocked and jeered at. We are unlikely ever to know what it was that upset Gascoigne so deeply. Whatever it was it did not discourage him entirely from playwriting. In the following decade he tried his hand at writing his own play but the result was, as the productions of *Jocasta* and *Supposes* just may have been, a dismal failure.

15: "My muse is tied in chains"

Back at the Gascoigne ancestral home at Cardington Manor, the fortunes of the poet's father seemed to be in spectacular decline. Events at Cardington eventually sucked in George Gascoigne, with devastating consequences.

In 1565 Sir John Gascoigne became involved in a bitter year-long legal dispute with his neighbour, Lord Latimer. According to Sir John, his Lordship's men went by night to Cardington Wood and cut down timber, which they then put on Latimer's side of the boundary. Sir John called the constable and peaceably took the timber back. The matter eventually reached the Star Chamber where, in Prouty's words, "a great array of witnesses was marshalled and everyone called everyone else a riotous and lying fellow".[1] Before the dispute was settled Sir John was involved in another boundary dispute, this time with Reginald Grey, later Earl of Kent.

In 1566 Sir John's fortunes hit rock bottom when he was imprisoned for debt. The episode is an obscure one. Whether or not George helped his father out in this crisis is not known but the debt seems to have been paid off. What wasn't paid was the cost of Sir John's board and lodging, and it wasn't for another three years that the sum of one pound, four shillings and eight pence was handed over "to the Jaylor of Bedford for the dett of Sir John Gascoigne when he was in the Jayle".

The following year father and son sold the manor of Eastcotts to Thomas Colby and his wife. However, it was not theirs to sell. Technically Sir John was only holding the property on behalf of his daughter-in-law, having already sold it to her uncle Francis as a jointure for Elizabeth. That same month – November, 1567 – Sir John was ill, so the sale might have been the act of a man putting his affairs in order and trying to build up his fortune. Colby paid £940 for the manor. Although Gascoigne co-operated in the sale it later became clear that he was unhappy with what his father had done.

Sir John's death, when it came, was not wholly unexpected, for he made his will on 2 April 1568 and died two days later. The poet seems not to have been present and was probably in London at this time. The funeral would have been a grand one and George Gascoigne was surely there as chief mourner, along with his mother. Dame Margaret presumably played the role of grief-struck widow, but may have been quietly pleased to be relieved of the burden of her unfaithful husband's presence. She chose not to be buried with him when she died, but as far away from Cardington as possible.

Sir John's two other children, relatives and friends, along with servants, neighbours and local dignitaries would also have been in attendance (but not, perhaps, Lord Latimer or Reginald Grey). With the Gascoigne coat of arms displayed in black banners, the slow, stately procession would have made its way slowly from the big manor house up the lane to St Mary's for the funeral service and the interment.

In his will, Sir John Gascoigne requested that he be buried in the north chapel of St Mary's, against his father's tomb. He left £6.13s.4d towards the cost of repairing the north chapel and the purchase of a "forebell". This instruction was presumably carried out and the burial was probably recorded on Sir William's tomb. Over time, however, Sir John received a graceless payback from the church authorities for his gift. The inscription for the brass and Sir William's children is missing. All trace of Sir John Gascoigne's grave has vanished.

Sir John's will came as a great shock to the poet. As the eldest son, George Gascoigne expected to inherit the bulk of his father's wealth. It was more than wishful thinking, for Gascoigne was specifically identified as Sir John's "son & heir apparent" on the indenture selling Eastcotts Manor to Colby. Only one day before the will was proved, confident of his inheritance, Gascoigne arranged to sell off a large slice of the family estate.

It was an unpleasant surprise, therefore, when it turned out that what he'd been left amounted to Cardington Manor and a quarter part of the barony of Bedford, which were collectively worth an annual £21.6s.11d. To a man like Gascoigne, this was an insultingly small sum. In fact the situation was not quite as bad as it seemed. C. T. Prouty calculated that altogether the poet inherited property from his father's estate with an annual value of £135, as well as lands of his mother's worth £60 a year.[2] But to Gascoigne this was still a lot less than he'd been expecting. He remained bitter about the settlement to the end of his life. In later years he even claimed he'd been disinherited. This was an exaggeration which contained a painful grain of truth. As Prouty noted, Sir John Gascoigne "although leaving him a considerable patrimony, did not bequeath as large an amount as his heir might have expected".[3]

The will also contained other unpalatable terms. Sir John died owing £62 to three creditors, an unspecified sum to a man named Wynche and seven quarters of barley to "Mr Gosticke of Bedford" (perhaps John Gostwick of Willington Manor). George Gascoigne was required to discharge all Sir John's debts and legacies and to make sure the funeral expenses were paid. An annuity of £20 granted to Anna Drewrie, Sir John's former mistress, was to be compounded and paid. The servants Richard Lambe and Lewis Mathew were to receive £10 each, and every other servant in the house a quarter's wages. Sir John's nephew William Curzon Esquire of Bylaugh, Norfolk, the will's sole executor, was to receive £40. Dame Margaret was to receive "300 marks' worth of household stuff". Second only to Sir John's widow was the bequest "To Robt. 'Carpendo' 100 marks", though the identity of this lavishly-rewarded individual is obscure. These obligations were to be met within one year. If George Gascoigne failed to do so then Sir John's executor was required to meet them by selling the "manor lands tenements and hereditaments" bequeathed to him.

On the face of it, Sir John made it obvious that he had little faith in his son executing the terms of his will without the threat of punitive sanctions. He was also apprehensive about his son's evident fury with Colby over the sale of Eastcotts Manor. Further sanctions were threatened if Colby "be any ways troubled or molested" by George Gascoigne over "any lands" which he'd bought jointly from George and Sir John.

The will has always been regarded as evidence of Gascoigne's volatile and bellicose character, but it is equally possible to interpret it another way. The will had only one executor, William Curzon, who benefited from it to the tune of £40. The executor was "to give Thos. Colby every assistance" and Colby was made "supervisor". The will was witnessed by the servants Lewis Mathew and Richard Lambe (who each got £10), by Robert Bray (another servant, whose wife Sir John allegedly owed the staggering sum of £50), John Wolriche and none other than Thomas Colby himself. Those involved in drawing up the will in the apparent absence of Sir John's chief heir were not without vested interests of their own and Colby's concern about being "troubled" by George Gascoigne may indicate that he knew very well that the poet would be enraged by the provisions of the will. Gascoigne certainly had reason to be angry. The lease of the parsonage of Fenlake Barns was bequeathed to his younger brother, John. Fenlake Barns was also known as Cardington Priors and, like Cardington Manor itself, originally belonged to Newnham Priory. This lease gave its owner control not simply of the parsonage building but also of valuable land and income, namely "all manner of glebe lands meadows and pastures...and almoner of Tithes as well of Corn hay and wood as of wool and Lamb within the whole parish of Cardington". But George Gascoigne believed that this lease was not his father's to bequeath. The poet asserted that it already belonged to him. He claimed that in return for meeting a debt of £200 of Sir John's, his father had given him the lease of the parsonage by an indenture dated 15 June 1562.

Sir John Gascoigne's will had spectacular consequences. It left his eldest son embittered for the rest of his life. But it also tore the Gascoigne family apart. The issue of who really owned Fenlake Barnes resulted in an angry and unforgiving dispute between the poet and his mother and brother John.[4]

*

It is quite likely that this family fissure had been present before Sir John's death, with Gascoigne and his father on one side and his mother and younger brother on the other. In a society in which the major part of any inheritance went to the eldest male child there was often little love lost between that fortunate individual and his siblings. While George Gascoigne was away in London, living it up at the Inns of Court and at court, his younger brother John remained behind in Bedfordshire, among what the poet once contemptuously called "country louts".[5] In this situation it was perhaps natural that the wife of an unfaithful husband should bond most closely with her second son, rather than with her spouse or her absent first child.

There is the possibility that John and Dame Margaret exerted pressure upon Sir John as he lay dying. If so, it would not have been the first or last time that an elderly and confused or frightened person was persuaded to make some last-minute adjustments to their will, benefiting those suggesting those changes. The poet, it seems, was not present for the final days of his father's life. This might not have been callousness but simply ignorance. If Dame Margaret and her second son were plotting against the heir, they would have been in no hurry to call him home to Cardington.

According to John Gascoigne his father declared "on his death bed that [his eldest son George] had nothing at all to do with the said lease or parsonage". Not only did he make it clear that he wanted John to have Fenlake Barnes but he also said that he "had some suspicion" of George's "evil doings". The only witness to this damning conversation was John himself. However, he also recalled that Sir John had warned both him and Dame Margaret "to take good heed and to beware of [George] saying if they did not so [he] would them beguile which thing by experience they have now found true".

In fact, George Gascoigne's claim to Fenlake Barnes seems to have been legitimate. Accordingly within days of his father's death George Gascoigne took control of "the said parsonage with the premises and was thereof lawfully possessed". Soon afterwards, on St Mark's Day (25 April) Gascoigne, acting within his rights as the new property owner, did "quietly and peaceably gather the tithe lambs of the inhabitants of Cardington aforesaid being then due…as in his right to the said parsonage". Altogether, there were about 64 tithe lambs. These Gascoigne branded with his mark, as he was entitled to do. But although the poet was taking a keen personal interest in his land and his property rights, he was probably an absentee landlord who delegated the day to day running of affairs to others. Documents for the period reveal that he was "of Grayes Inn" (1566-68) and "of Walthamstowe, Essex" (1569) and "of Walthamstow Tony, Essex" (1569).

Matters came to a head on 20 September 1568 when John Gascoigne retaliated by stealing his brother's sheep. John and seven other "lewd and evilly disposed persons" assembled at Cardington "in very Riotous and disordered manner" and then "did Riotously chase course and disturb the said flock of sheep". In fact the sheep were the tithe lambs which Gascoigne had taken possession of as owner of the lease of Fenlake Barnes. When Gascoigne's shepherd intervened he was attacked by John with a long staff, knocked down and badly beaten. The stolen sheep were driven away and sold at the market in Leighton, allegedly for only half their true worth. Gascoigne requested writs of subpoena against his brother and five of his men to account for their actions in the Court of Star Chamber.

John Gascoigne's defence was that the sheep belonged to Dame Margaret and he was merely acting on his mother's behalf to regain her property. He denied riotous behaviour and said they were unarmed – he and two of the men only having "a little walking stick" and the other two their shepherd's hooks. This provoked George into a furious reply. The frenzied and obsessive detail of his response makes it clear that he genuinely believed he was the injured party.

He recapitulated the history of the ownership of Fenlake Barnes – back to the time of the dissolution of the monasteries. He revealed that this was not the first time the accused had stolen his tithe lambs. A month or so after Gascoigne first took possession of the lambs they had been stolen by his brother and his associates and put in a pasture of Dame Margaret's "commonly called the park". Gascoigne "did at sundry times and by sundry means in most obedient humble and submissive manner beseech the said Dame Margaret being his mother to redeliver the said lambs". This she failed to do because of "some unnatural disposition…and of an unmeasurable love and affection that she hath conceived towards…her younger son". It so happened that the park was adjacent to a pasture of Gascoigne's known as Somerfeild and one day the sheep broke through the hedge into Gascoigne's land. Upon going to see whose sheep they were he discovered that some belonged to his mother but that others were the stolen tithe lambs, bearing his own brand. He therefore took back the lambs and returned the other sheep to the park. On 20 September, John and his men stole the lambs back yet again, this time selling them. Gascoigne begged the court to take possession of the parsonage and determine the rightful ownership "to avoid disorders and that a brotherly concord may ensue".

We can be confident that Gascoigne's pious wish for the breach to be healed remained unfulfilled. His account of the disputed lambs happening to wander through the hedge is clearly bogus but the central thrust of his complaint seems to have been accurate. Gascoigne attempted to deal with the problem by direct action, and when that failed he went to law. By the sound of it, his younger brother was a bellicose and aggressive man. Under further questioning John Gascoigne admitted that two of his men were armed with daggers and that the "walking sticks" were hawking staves. He was also evasive over the ownership of the lambs and claimed not to know how much they were sold for. In the end, all the evidence points to George Gascoigne having won his case in the Star Chamber.

Gascoigne was less fortunate in his dealings with the executor of his father's will, namely his cousin William Curzon of Norfolk. Curzon, aided by "the advice of Thos. Colby supervisor of Sir John's will", said that Gascoigne had failed to pay the legacies, debts and annuity under the terms of his father's will. He therefore moved swiftly to make a sale of corn, cattle, sheep, pigs and horses, which brought in £114.15s.10d. Out of this he paid the debts (perhaps no more than £65 in all). Whether or not Sir John's old mistress Anna Drewrie received her annuity is unclear. One suspects she did not. From the money received, William Curzon disbursed £102.11s.4d. That figure included legal charges and travelling expenses, which Thomas Colby was no doubt only too happy to approve.

Gascoigne was in no position to argue with what Curzon and Colby had done, since he had not met his obligations under the will. In law, he was unquestionably the guilty party. But over the circumstances and provisions of his father's will there hang some large question marks, and the motivation and roles played by Curzon, Colby, the witnesses to the will, and Gascoigne's mother and brother should surely be scrutinised with some scepticism.

*

The second half of the 1560s was a period in the poet's life overshadowed by a tangle of litigation and growing financial problems. To George Gascoigne it must have seemed as if he was under attack from all directions. Elizabeth's lawful re-marriage had not put an end to the couple's difficulties with Edward Boyes. When his relationship with Elizabeth had broken down he'd evidently made off with over £300 in cash as well as plate, jewels, clothes "and household stuff". Following their divorce he was no longer entitled to retain possession of any of this and should have returned it either to Elizabeth or to the safe custody of Thomas Seckford, one of the Masters of Requests. Boyes had not done so. Legally, he had no grounds for holding on to this property since by now there was "none appeal strife demand or other question hanging or depending" between his ex-wife and himself.

Boyes retorted that the action had no basis in law, since it had been brought by Richard, Nicholas and Thamar Breton, who were all minors. In any case the property consisted of legacies due to the children when they were older. What's more the case had been initiated by George Gascoigne for no other reason than to cause him "great vexation". No one has so far discovered any documentation showing what ultimately happened. The probability is that it was resolved in favour of the Breton children as a Chancery Bill of 1566 concerning the case is addressed "To the right honourable Sir Nicholas Bacon knight, Keeper of the great seal of England". Bacon is unlikely to have felt any sympathy for Boyes in prolonging Elizabeth's difficulties.

If the children's property was returned (as seems to be the case) it was now threatened by other predators, namely their mother and their stepfather. Following William Breton's death in January 1559, there should properly have been an *inquisition post mortem* to determine inheritance matters. But neither Elizabeth nor her second or third husbands seem to have been in any hurry to effect it. In March 1567, perhaps as a result of the wrangle with Boyes, an order was given for one to be held, which was duly done on 27 October 1567. The following year Gascoigne and Elizabeth were summoned to the Guildhall for a Lord Mayor's enquiry into the children's property. Subsequently, on 17 February 1569, Gascoigne was granted the wardship of Richard Breton and an annuity of £15 from the Breton estate, back-dated to the time of William Breton's death. Perhaps Sir Nicholas Bacon was exerting friendly pressure from behind the scenes on behalf of the poet, for as Jean Robertson observes, "It is difficult to see how he could be entitled to this, and even harder to understand how the manor of Burgh, which William Breton had left to Nicholas, has come to be included in the list of Richard's property entrusted to the custody of George Gascoigne."[6] In fact the tangled affair of the Breton estate continued in the courts until the end of Gascoigne's life, without apparently ever being decisively concluded.

Meanwhile the case brought by Sir Ambrose Jermyn on behalf of the Ashefeilde children dragged on through the courts. The matter was still unresolved in July 1565 when a provisional award of 100 marks to the Ashefeildes was being argued over. No further documentation in the case has surfaced but the probability is that Gascoigne lost.

In 1568, some two or three years after Gascoigne had quit Willington Manor, he found himself being sued by its owner. John Gostwick claimed that he had been tricked by Gascoigne into transferring all the contents of the manor house to the poet, who had eventually walked off with them. Gascoigne retorted that Gostwick had agreed to the transfer to avoid an action for damages and slander resulting from Elizabeth Gostwick's theft of goods and chattels which the poet was responsible for under the terms of the inventory of contents. He had also been paying "a great yearly rent" for the furnished property and had agreed to support the Gostwicks and permit them to stay in the house in return for taking control of the contents. The line "my swains eat up my gains" (i.e. my rustics devour my profits) could conceivably be a laconic reference to the expense of supporting the Gostwicks.

Ironically, Gascoigne now found himself accused of the very thing that the Breton children had sued Edward Boyes for – the appropriation of what didn't belong to him. Who won is not known. In an earlier dispute over the possession of Goldington Manor, Gostwick was described as "being a man of great simplicity and having little or no understanding". By the sound of it Gostwick was a man who had what we would now call learning difficulties and who had no one to look after his interests. Like many others involved in transactions with Gostwick, Gascoigne was probably guilty of sharp practice. However, as someone grounded in law, he did not necessarily lose this case.

A separate action against Gascoigne over the same agreement with Gostwick was brought by Sir Richard Verney. Upon the death of his stepmother Anne, who was also John Gostwick's mother, Verney discovered that property which was rightfully hers under the terms of the will of her first husband, Sir William Gostwick, had passed into Gascoigne's possession. Verney asserted it now belonged to him and he wanted it back. Quite probably it was Verney who encouraged Gostwick in his own action for the recovery of the contents of Willington Manor. To Verney's charge the poet replied that Anne Gostwick's inheritance had been settled long ago and there was no case to answer. The outcome of this case, like all the others, is not known. But property in Bedfordshire proved to be an increasing source of vexation for Gascoigne during the second half of this decade.

Complicated litigation involving George, his brother, his mother and others dragged on until the end of the decade. The Earl of Bedford brought an action against the poet, which the Earl won. It was probably a land dispute and may have been about the lease of Cardington Manor. Gascoigne retaliated with a writ of "audita querela", which sought to re-open the case on the basis of new evidence. Meanwhile the ubiquitous Thomas Colby brought an action against five people, including the poet, his servant John Rogers and Dame Margaret Gascoigne, to get hold of documents about Eastcotts Manor. Colby was evidently successful in gaining lawful control of the property.

Gascoigne seems to have been in growing financial difficulty over the period 1566-70. C. T. Prouty calculated that the poet gave bonds amounting to £2,600 and 1,500 marks during these years and that the likeliest explanation is that these were debts.[7] In June 1569 the poet was informed by Gray's Inn that he must pay his debts or "be put out of the fellowship of the house". Evidently he was unable to do so. Quite why Gascoigne was plunged into insolvency is far from clear, other than the obvious reason that his expenditure exceeded his income.

The expense of maintaining a substantial house in Walthamstow must have been considerable. At the same time he was an intermittent resident of Gray's Inn for many years. His expenses would have included fashionable clothes, entertainment, horses, servants' wages, lawyers' fees and a host of expenses associated with other activities such as travel, deer hunting, falconry, shooting, fencing and music. He also accumulated a library of books at a time when these were luxury items. Presumably litigation ate into his fortune and the old jokes about lawyers in *Supposes* now had a bitterly personal edge.

Bedford prison

The nadir of the poet's fiscal misfortunes seems to have been reached in the first year of the new decade. A Chancery decree dated 21 April 1570 revealed that Gascoigne "lieth in Bedford gaol upon an execution". In this context the term "execution" meant the seizure of a debtor in default of payment. The poet owed someone serious money and couldn't pay it back on time. From being a dashing young man of the metropolis he'd suddenly sunk to being shut up behind the walls of a prison in a provincial market town. George Gascoigne was perhaps 35 years old. It marked a new low in his life.

Gascoigne was probably writing very little during this period. But, as at the time of his bigamous marriage, a crisis in his life provoked some of his rare religious poetry. Gascoigne wrote only three religious poems, and two of them were probably produced around the time of his imprisonment at Bedford. The first, "Gascoigne's good morrow", even addresses itself at one point to "you whom care in prison keeps".[8]

The title refers to a cheery greeting – the Tudor version of "hi!" or "good day". The poem takes the form of a greeting to all those who have "spent the silent night / In sleep and quiet rest". These sleepers are invited to rise up with him and greet the dawn of a new day with a hymn of praise to the Lord. The poem's quiet simplicity of language is strikingly successful:

> The rainbow bending in the sky,
> Bedecked with sundry hues,
> Is like the seat of God on high…
>
> The little birds which sing so sweet
> Are like the angels' voice,
> Which render God his praises meet
> And teach us to rejoice:

It has all the appearance of a traditional hymn, but even though set to music it never became one. The poem's lyrical sweetness co-exists uneasily with a Christianity which is not so much muscular as explosively militant:

> The carrion crow, that loathsome beast,
> Which cries against the rain,
> Both for her hue and for the rest,
> The Devil resembleth plain:
> And as with goonnes we kill the crow   [guns]
> For spoiling our relief,
> The Devil so must we overthrow
> With goonshot of belief.

This is the battle against evil fought out from the perspective of a Bedfordshire landowner with a shotgun tucked under his arm – or at any rate a harquebus. The devil is a pest who must be shot. In *The Pilgrim's Progress* we encounter matters from the very different point of view of a landless Bedfordshire author. There, it is landowners who are in league with Satan. At one point Evangelist warns Christian that he is "not yet out of the gun-shot of the Devil".[9]

Curiously, the devil in Gascoigne's poem resembles a black female carrion crow. Possibly the poet was subconsciously thinking of Dame Margaret and the mourning clothes she would have worn at her husband's funeral. There is a visceral disgust in these lines and a real anger. The lines are out of keeping with the rest of the poem, which is a song of exuberant release. It may have been written soon after Gascoigne left prison. The poem joyously praises day after night, light after darkness, and sunshine after rain:

> ... joy to see the cheerful light
> That riseth in the East:
> Now clear your voice, now cheer your heart,
> Come help me now to sing:
> Each willing wight come bear a part,   [person]
> To praise the heavenly king.
>
> And you whom care in prison keeps
> Or sickness doth suppress,
> Or secret sorrow breaks your sleeps,
> Or dolors do distress:
> Yet bear a part in doleful wyse,   [manner]
> Yea think it good accord,
> And acceptable sacrifice,
> Each sprite to praise the Lord.   [spirit]
>
>   The dreadful night with darksomeness
> Had overspread the light,
> And sluggish sleep with drowsyness
> Had overpressed our might:
> A glass wherein we may behold
> Each storm that stops our breath,
> Our bed the grave, our clothes like mould,
> And sleep like dreadful death.
>
>   Yet as this deadly night did last
> But for a little space,
> And heavenly day now night is passed,
> Doth show his pleasant face:
> So must we hope to see God's face

Perhaps being incarcerated in Bedford prison was a painful and shocking experience for Gascoigne – truly a "dreadful night". A later Bedford prisoner, albeit someone of very different temperament and character, emerged from that experience to write *The Pilgrim's Progress*. Gascoigne's imprisonment was hardly comparable to Bunyan's either in terms of its length or its conditions but to a sensitive, cultured man it may still have come as an unpleasant surprise. How long he remained there is not known but it was probably not for long. Almost certainly his "deadly night did last / But for a little space". His wife Elizabeth or one of his associates would have rallied round and arranged for the debt to be paid – if necessary by taking out another loan.

There was no particular stigma about a gentleman being put in prison. Later in the century Gascoigne's imprisonment was even seen as something rather admirable. When Thomas Nashe was mocked for having been thrown into the London prison known as the Counter for debt, he wittily replied:

> I yield that I have dealt upon spare commodities of wine and capons in my daies, I have sung George Gascoignes Counter tenor; what then? Wilt thou peremptorily define that it is a place where no honest man, or Gentleman of credit, ever came?
> Heare what I say: a Gentleman is never thoroughly entred into credit till he hath been there; & that Poet, or novice, be hee what he will, ought to suspect his wit, and remaine halfe in doubt that it is not authenticall, till it hath beene seene and allowd in unthrifts consistory.[10]

Imprisonment was more a kind of house arrest than a punishment. Gentlemen were often allowed the company of their servants. Food could be sent out for. Nevertheless the experience seems to have provoked some soul-searching on the poet's part. Gascoigne wrote a gloomy sequel entitled "Gascoigne's good night", in which the emphasis is less on the Lord's joyous presence in the fields and skies of Bedfordshire than on death and last things.[11] Its central image is of a man lying in bed, half asleep. Perhaps the accommodation at Bedford prison was less than satisfactory:

> The hungry fleas which frisk so fresh, to worms I can compare,
> Which greedily shall gnaw my flesh, and leave the bones full bare.

The bed "which soft and smooth is made" sounds more like the kind of bed Gascoigne was used to, but now the poet imagines himself in a dark room where

> of my bed each sundry part in shadows doth resemble
> The sundry shapes of death, whose dart shall make my flesh to tremble,
> My bed itself is like the grave, my sheets the winding sheets,
> My clothes the mould which I must have to cover me most meet

This is a nightmare image and inside it may lurk the experience of lying on a dirty prison bed in rumpled, days-old clothes. The poem advises everyone to search inside themselves and call to God for mercy for their sins – though the barrister in Gascoigne cannot quite resist the possibility that his client (a much-victimized poet, shall we say?) is entirely free of guilt:

> though thy find nothing amiss, which thou can'st call to mind

But even the spotlessly innocent need to think about God, says Gascoigne. Any complacency about his agreeable life as a gentleman ("My daily sports, my paunch full fed") has gone. Now even a man's bed is a *memento mori*. But Gascoigne still manages to bounce back from these sombre thoughts with characteristic optimism. Earthly justice might not always have been on his side but he's confident of what a higher court will decide:

> So hope I to rise joyfully, to Judgement at the last.
> Thus will I wake, thus will I sleep, thus will I hope to rise,
> Thus will I neither wail nor weep, but sing in godly wyse.   [manner]
> My bones shall in this bed remain, my soul in God shall trust,
> By whom I hope to rise again from death and earthly dust.

Sir Walter Ralegh was so impressed by this poem that he adapted its last two lines for his poem "Even such is time", supposed to have been written the night before his execution:

> And from which earth and grave and dust
> The Lord shall raise me up I trust.

But then Ralegh was in a position to appreciate the poem from the perspective of a man in prison. And as someone who met Gascoigne he may even have known something of the poem's origins and remembered it many years later as he lay in his cell in the Tower of London.

*

Though Gascoigne was keen to give thanks to God and warmly anticipate a favourable verdict on the Day of Judgement, he did not neglect lesser judicial figures who might be able to assist him before that time arrived. One such person was Lewis Dive, who was a distant relative and close associate of Lord Grey of Wilton. When in 1564 the Privy Council ordered a check on the nation's Justices of the Peace to see whether or not they were loyal to the government in matters of religion, the Bishop of Lincoln reported that in Bedfordshire Sir John Gascoigne was among the "hinderers" but that Lewis Dive was "earnest in religion".[12]

Dive was an important figure on the Bedfordshire scene and was frequently employed as a person of good repute to take the depositions of witnesses. Gascoigne's imprisonment meant that the poet was temporarily unable to put in an appearance for one of the hearings into the long-running dispute between his brother and himself as it dragged on interminably through the courts. "Lewis Dives and Robert Newdigate esquires" were therefore instructed to visit Gascoigne in prison "to take the answer of the defendant". Gascoigne clearly found Dive someone worth cultivating. It is quite possible that he wrote his paired "good morrow" and "good night" poems with half an eye on Dive's approval and patronage. Dive's daughter-in-law Douglas certainly knew of Gascoigne's writing, for she requested that he write some verses for "*a booke wherein she had collected sundry good ditties of divers mens doings*".[13]

Gascoigne diplomatically described her personal anthology as being "fraughte with learned verse" and modestly explained that he lacked the skill to match it. He could have fobbed her off with something short and bland. Instead he gave her a substantial slab of "*councell*" (i.e. advice) 84 lines long, in rhyming couplets. The poem compares the falcon (Douglas herself) with the puttock or scavenging kite (the poet). With his mind still on the law, Gascoigne describes Douglas Dive as "without empeach or crime", but also notes that apart from chickens, which it devours,

> I cannot see who can accuse the kite for felony.

As is often the case, Gascoigne cannot resist a spot of self-promotion. Gascoigne the kite is almost as innocent as the falcon – or guilty only in the tiniest and most inconsequential way. This illicit aspect of a kite's diet is in sharp contrast to the pampered, dainty diet of the falcon, which feeds on partridges, quails, pigeons, plovers, ducks, drakes, heron, lapwings, teals and water rail. Moreover the kite is a useful scavenger, eating worms in corn and seeds, killing moles and devouring the filth in the streets. The kite advises the falcon

> Serve thou first God thy Lord, and praise him evermore,
> Obey thy Prince and love thy make, by him set greatest store. [maker]
> Thy Parents follow next, for honour and for awe,
> Thy friends use always faithfully, for so commands the law.

After these conventional pieties the poem changes gear and becomes increasingly and unexpectedly bizarre as Gascoigne considers Douglas Dive and her potential for sin. He warns her against self-love and in so doing penned what is surely the only poem in the whole of English literature that attempts to rhyme "etymology" with "surquedry" (a word derived from French, meaning pride or arrogance). Gascoigne the scavenging kite continues:

Thus can I weed the worm, which seeketh to devour
The seeds of virtue, which might grow within thee every hour.
Thus can I kill the mole, which else would overthrow
The good foundation of thy fame, with every little blow.
And thus I can convey, out of thy comely breast,
The sluttish heaps of peevish pride, which might defile the rest.

Quite what Douglas Dive made of this is difficult to imagine. The image of Gascoigne as a filth-devouring kite poking around inside her for worms or searching her "comely breast" for pride – he means her interior morality but it is difficult to resist the image of him exploring her cleavage – manages to combine gothic grotesquery with an unmistakeable sexual charge.

It gets worse.

Perhaps some falcons fly, which will not greatly grutch
To learn thee first to love thy self, and then to love too much.
But I am none of those, I list not so to range,
I have man's meat enough at home, what need I then seek change.

In other words: "perhaps there are some men around who wouldn't mind teaching you to appreciate yourself and who would then seduce you, but I'm not like that, I don't seduce women, anyway why would I need to have sex with you when I can get all the sex I want at home?" As G. W. Pigman comments, with some understatement, "Gascoigne is taking the stance of the plain-speaking, vice-reproving counsellor rather far...in language hardly respectful of his own wife".[14]

Evidently conscious that he might have overstepped the mark, Gascoigne goes on breezily to remind Douglas that she commissioned the poem in the first place, and should she "chance to fall on construing, whereby some doubts may grow" she should make the effort to read it two or three times before condemning it. In another idiosyncratic image he asks

Do not as barbers do, which wash beards curiously,
Then cut them off, then cast them out, in open streets to lie.

This supplies an unusual image of a rarely discussed Tudor litter problem – barbers thowing hair out into the street. But while the comparison between the sheet of parchment on which the poem was written and a beard is very original it is also preposterously inept. And it is unlikely that Douglas Dive, daughter of Sir Anthony Denny, felt flattered to be compared to a male barber.

Gascoigne then thinks of an even better excuse. It is quite a plausible one for it suggests that some of this poem (or perhaps all of it) may have been composed within the dark walls of Bedford prison itself:

> Remember therewithal, my muse is tied in chains,
> The goonshot of calamity hath battred all my brains.   [gunshot]
> And though this verse scape out, take thou therat no mark,
> It is but like a headless fly, that tumbleth in the dark.

Douglas Dive clearly knew of her father-in-law's visit to the poet in Bedford prison. Whether or not she felt Gascoigne's ordeal excused his faintly risqué poem is another matter. Gascoigne himself was obviously anxious on that score, for he adds "It was thine own request, remember so it was".

The poem ends by reworking an image of "a bush of thorns amongst sweet smelling flowers" with which it began. The bush represents the sharp advice of the poem; the sweet flowers are Douglas Dive. Gascoigne develops the image in a truly bizarre way for his final lines:

> Yet take this harmless thorn, to pick thy teeth withal,
> A tooth pick serves some use perdie, although it be but small.
> And when thy teeth therewith be piked fair and clean,
> Then bend thy tong no worse to me, than mine to thee hath been.

"Clean out your mouth before telling me what you think of this poem" is one way of reading this strange conclusion. The instruction to "bend thy tong" simply means "speak" – but the notion of them bending their tongues to each other carries a faint sexual charge and perhaps an implied image of French kissing. There are some odd themes sloshing around in the sub-text of this poem – hunger, picking clean, eating filth, worms, comely breasts, sexual meat, severed beards, teeth, tongues and a headless fly, frantically zig-zagging around in the dark. It's a psychoanalyst's treasure chest. It's also perhaps Gascoigne's final Bedfordshire poem. A phase in his life was over. After his release from prison he headed for the capital, where a new set of unexpected adventures and disasters was waiting to unfold.

PART FOUR: CONSPIRACY AND WAR

16: The Italian Connection

After his release from prison, the likelihood is that Gascoigne retired to his big house in Walthamstow to lick his wounds and take a long hard look at where his life was going. His links with Gray's Inn had been decisively severed. His family connections in Bedfordshire had broken down and would never be repaired. In future he avoided endless litigation and complicated property deals. It was time to try something new.

By now the idea of publishing a collection of his writings was probably beginning to take shape in Gascoigne's mind. Publication was partly an expression of Gascoigne's strong sense of self. But it also provided a source of ready cash. Although the poet later stoutly denied ever receiving any payment this denial should be taken with a large pinch of salt. Charles Nicholl is surely right to say that "Money problems probably prompted another decisive step, a most 'ungentlemanly' one: in 1573 he published his first collection of poetry."[1] For a collection of his writings, Gascoigne could hope for a sizable one-off payment from a publisher. His manuscripts so far amounted to two plays and perhaps around 65 of the poems which appeared in "The Devises of Sundrie Gentlemen", as well as the material which underpinned *The Adventures of Master F.J.*

Gascoigne's poem to Douglas Dive, which invites her to "licence it to pass / Into my breast again, from whence it flew in haste", shows he was simultaneously thinking of publication, state censorship and the potential offence his writing might cause.[2] Douglas Dive's "licence" was merely to express her own opinion. If she disliked his poem there would be no greater sanction than tearing his poem into shreds and throwing it out into the street as a barber might the hair from a trimmed beard. But the verb alludes to the Tudor system of licensed publication. Deep down, Gascoigne knew that some of his lines had a great capacity to offend anyone who didn't share his fondness for irreverent satire and sexual innuendo. His novel also contained erotically suggestive material and explicit sex scenes.

Between Gascoigne's poem to Douglas Dive – almost certainly written in 1570 – and its sequel – another poem of "councell" or advice, this time to the poet's good friend Bartholmew Withypoll – lies a two year gap. The second follows on from the first in the order in which the poems appear in *A Hundreth Sundrie Flowres*, underlining the probability that Gascoigne took a break from versifying when he left Bedfordshire. Because no manuscript survives, we don't know when Gascoigne wrote *The Adventures of Master F.J.* A reasonable scenario is that it began as one of his earliest pieces of writing, a cluster of lyrics, sonnets and love letters emanating from his affair with a married woman at Gawthorpe Hall. He then kept the material and only returned to rework it a decade or so later, after his career as a playwright had fizzled out.

The 1560s was the decade when there was an explosion of interest in Italian literature among the English intelligentsia. Baldesar Castiglione's *Il cortegiano* (*The Book of the Courtier*) appeared in an English translation, *The Courtyer*, by Sir Thomas Hoby in 1561. An even more popular Latin translation, by Bartholomew Clerke, was published in London in 1571. It was a book perfectly pitched for the new Elizabethan court. The fashionable icon of the age was no longer the knight in armour but the courtier. Castiglione's book is all talk. Set in a palace, it consists of courtiers exchanging ideas and observations. Basically it was a guide to style and good behaviour, though as the book's modern translator notes, "As a handbook for gentlemen, *The Courtier* conceals the most shameless opportunism under the cloak of a tiresome refinement".[3] *The Adventures of Master F.J.* is an obvious variation on Castiglione's work. Its leisured aristocratic characters while away the time in conversation, cards and dancing, and rarely move beyond the confines of a big country house. But unlike Castiglione, Gascoigne exposes the hypocrisy and sexual intrigue beneath the civilized veneer.

William Painter's translations of Italian fiction appeared in 1566 and the critic Leicester Bradner has suggested that Gascoigne found inspiration for *The Adventures of Master F.J.* in his reading of such novellas, while conceding that though he "had many models, his use of them shows great independence in combining materials". Bradner points to works by Boccaccio, Bandello, Cinthio and in particular the *Opusculum de duobus amantibus Eurialo et Lucresia*, written by Aeneas Sylvius Piccolomini, later Pope Pius II. It was translated into English in 1549, 1560 and 1567 under the title *The goodli History of the most noble and beautifull Lady Lucres of Scene in Tuskan and of her lover Eurialus, verye pleasaunt and delectable unto the reader*.

> This is a work of some fifty pages which relates the adulterous intrigue of Eurialus, a member of the Emperor's court, with Lucrece, the wife of a nobleman of Siena. The story has been obviously influenced by the Troilus and Cressida legend. In it the intrigue is opened by letters, as in Gascoigne, and in both cases the women first reject love but continue to receive letters. In both cases there are tricks to convey letters and in both cases a letter is torn up and then pieced together again. In both cases after the lovers accept each other the letters are dropped and the story is continued in direct narrative.[4]

Whether or not Gascoigne knew and was influenced by Piccolomini's fiction, it seems likely that his knowledge of Italian literature was heightened by a personal visit to Italy. The English interest in Italy was growing throughout the poet's adolescence and manhood. William Thomas's *Italian Dictionary* had appeared in 1549 and his *Italian Grammar* in 1550. Mary Augusta Scott, author of *Elizabethan Translations from the Italian*, was in no doubt that Gascoigne had been there, concluding that he was one of those "'Italianated' travellers, whose literary work reflects a personal knowledge of foreign lands".[5]

Tudor attitudes to Italy were ambiguous. Italy was the country of such admired figures as Ariosto, Petrarch, and Castiglione. But it was also stereotyped as a nation of poisoners and sexual deviants and the native country of the monstrous cynic and atheist, Machiavelli. Roger Ascham cautioned against the threat which Italian vice posed to young Englishmen, and these prejudices continued to the end of the century and beyond. Gascoigne's long poem of advice to Bartholmew Withypoll "*a little before his latter journey to Geane* [Genoa]. 1572" is in this vein of English xenophobia. He warns Withypoll against Italian thieves and a range of other tricks played on unwary travellers. The implication is that Gascoigne himself knows Italy all too well and is speaking from experience. There is also a strong suggestion that Gascoigne has been there in the past with his friend:

Remember *Batte* the foolish blinkeyed boy
Which was at *Rome*, thou knowest whom I mean[6]

This is a private reference between friends. Far from bothering to explain what he meant, when the poem was republished Gascoigne laconically appended the marginal comment "A Misterie". This is a writer who quite explicitly enjoys teasing the reader by withholding the information needed to make sense of something. Again, his influence on *Shakespeare's Sonnets* should not be underestimated.

That Gascoigne had visited Rome seems more than likely. In a later piece of writing he drew a comparison between the contorted shapes of corpses and the scenes shown on what he called Michelangelo's "tables of Doomsday".[7] This can only be a reference to the painter's fresco "The Last Judgement", on the altar wall of the Sistine Chapel in the Vatican Palace. In Gascoigne's day there were no reproductions of Michelangelo's masterpiece. The only way he could have known it was to have travelled to Rome and seen it with his own eyes.

It is easy enough to understand how the poet never forgot Michelangelo's massive painting, with its graphic images of the damned tumbling from Charon's barge into hell. But what Gascoigne saw was not the painting we see today. He saw it when it was a relatively new painting, long before it was transformed by time and restoration. Even Michelangelo's images changed with the passage of the years as aspects were deemed offensive by the church authorities. In 1565 loin cloths were painted over some of those muscular, nude male figures.

Adventures in paratext

At some point in the years leading up to the publication of *A Hundreth Sundrie Flowres* Gascoigne had the idea of prefacing a collection of his own poems with the novel *The Adventures of Master F.J.* and presenting both as having been organised by an editor, "G.T." That moment probably arrived around 1570-1571. A visit to Italy and a passion for the Italian novella may well have given Gascoigne the impetus to complete *The Adventures of Master F.J.* But even if he'd finished the novel earlier in his career, it was probably only now that he began to think of its role in the overall structure of a personal anthology.

G.T. is not simply involved in assembling the materials of the novel – F.J.'s poems and the letters which pass between Elinor and F.J. He also supplies a linking narrative which describes what happens and comments both on the protagonists and F.J.'s verse. From this fiction springs much of the imaginative energy of the book as the world-weary cynicism of G.T. is levelled against the ardent, courtly Petrarchan posturing of F.J.

The novel and the collection of poems are prefaced by an address to the reader by H.W. and a letter sent to H.W. by G.T. This is what we would now call paratext – text which exists outside a piece of writing but which frames it and shapes the way we read it. Paratext is often anonymous and is frequently the work of the author (for example, the author's description or the précis of a book's contents which appears on the jacket). But paratext is also all that other material on the jacket (recommendations by celebrity authors, quotes from rave reviews) as well as author interviews and letters which shed light on the writer's intentions and opinions.

What the material prefacing *A Hundreth Sundrie Flowres* shows is Gascoigne's shrewd awareness of an aspect of publishing then virtually unrecognised, namely marketing and promotion. The address to the reader describes how the material came to be in H.W.'s possession and why he decided to urge a publisher – A.B. – to print it. Its basic purpose is to obscure Gascoigne's sole authorship of the volume by defining what follows as a miscellaneous anthology by various gentlemen. It also attempts to hide his responsibility for the book's publication by pretending that two other men were the ones who determined that these "divers discourses and verses" should be printed. H.W. also claims to have thought up the title *A Hundreth Sundrie Flowres*.

This bogus scenario is then further attested to by G.T. in his letter to H.W. dated 10 August 1572, which, tongue in cheek, describes the effort involved in obtaining from "Master F.J. and sundry other toward young gentlemen, the sundry copies of these sundry matters". The more the diversity and variety of the "discourses", verses and authors is insisted upon the bigger grows the joke. This army of authors is a phantom army; their "sundry copies" are penned by a single hand. *A Hundreth Sundrie Flowres* is an anthology only in the sense of including different types of writing, not in the primary sense of a collection from various authors. It is as if Tottel's *Songes and Sonettes* was a clever hoax, with the writings of "Henry Howard, Earl of Surrey, Sir Thomas Wyatt, the Elder, Nicholas Grimald, and Uncertain Authors" all the work of a single author, who was also masquerading as "Tottel".

The bogus introductions also function as a form of paratext which even today remains an important part of book publishing – namely, the blurb. Instead of having a celebrity to eulogise his book, Gascoigne had to do it himself. Thus H.W. finds the contents "right commendable for their capacity" ("capacity" meaning "ability") and "thought it worthy to be published". G.T. concurs, modestly intimating that the collection is equal to any "notable volume…by poets of antiquity" or the works of Chaucer. G.T. also maintains the fiction of unwilling authorship by mentioning "two notable works" by F.J. which might never see the light of day if the publication of his *Adventures* goes ahead without first obtaining his permission. These works – *Sundry lots of love* and *The climbing of an eagle's nest* (this second title a metaphor for risky ambition) – probably did not exist anywhere except in Gascoigne's imagination. If they did, which is unlikely, they have not survived. But as titles they sound suspiciously similar to the actual contents of *A Hundreth Sundrie Flowres*, which contained a rich variety of love poems, was a big, ambitious volume containing a dangerously risqué novel, and which concluded with a lengthy but incomplete poem, "Dan Bartholmew of Bathe".

G.T. further explains that he has spoken to Master F.J. and the other "sundry…young gentlemen" who explained to him the circumstances and causes "that then moved them to write". From this he plunges straight into the action of the novel, prefacing the first of F.J.'s letters with a single sentence that sets the scene:

> The said F.J. chanced once in the north parts of this realm to fall in company of a very fair gentlewoman whose name was Mistress Elinor, unto whom bearing a hot affection, he first adventured to write this letter following.

In biographical terms, F.J. is the young Gascoigne and G.T. is the older and wiser Gascoigne (Gascoigne Talking; Gascoigne Teasing). F.J. is both Gascoigne the naïve and inexperienced youth who was ill-prepared for an entanglement with a cool, calculating, promiscuous married woman and Gascoigne the poet of Petrarchan cliché. G.T. represents the fictional voice of experience: Gascoigne the failed law student and disillusioned courtier. G.T. is also Gascoigne the more accomplished writer and the ironist, who has moved away from imitating Petrarch. The two personae are not entirely distinct in their chronology; rather they are modes of voice. F.J. is innocence; G.T. is experience, cynicism, irony. The experiences which F.J. has at the country house are a part of what will one day make him into G.T.

G.T. emphasizes the authority of his version of events. Of Elinor's letter to F.J. voluptuously offering "to do for you any pleasure" he comments "This letter I have seen, of her own handwriting". He acknowledges that his information depends entirely on letters, poems and what others have told him, and that he doesn't know everything ("how all parties took rest that night I know not" – meaning by that – with a sly wink – who slept with whom).

G.T. presents himself as a detached critic. He notes, accurately, that Elinor writes less well than her "secretary". But he is less reliable when it comes to judging F.J.'s verse. The feeble sonnet "Love, hope, and death, do stir in me such strife" was, we are informed, "highly commended, and in my judgement it deserveth no less...it is both pretty and pithy." He is more defensive when it comes to the song "In prime of lusty years, when Cupid caught me in", where he notes a technical objection (too many verses) and the poem "A cloud of care hath covered all my cost" ("but a rough meeter...written in rage...*F.J.* himself had so slender liking thereof, or at least of one word escaped therein, that he never presented it"). G.T. acknowledges that the reader "percase...will not like" the song "Dame Cynthia herself that shines so bright" and that "some will accompt it but a dyddledome" [trifle]. He defends it on the grounds that anyone "who had heard *F.J.* sing it to the lute, by a note of his own devise, I suppose he would esteem it to be a pleasant dyddledome". This is perhaps less G.T. in his role as fictional narrator and more Gascoigne wryly commenting on his own youthful effusions for a coterie audience of Gray's Inn young bloods. G.T.'s posture as a sexual innocent who cannot fully describe the pleasures of F.J. and Elinor on the gallery floor "for lack of like experience" was surely designed to provoke sniggers.

G.T. is more critical when it comes to the sonnet "The stately dames of Rome their pearls did wear", grumbling that it contains "a little too much praise" of the lady (as indeed it does, absurdly so: Elinor is described as being "formed of none other mould / But ruby, crystal, ivory, pearl and gold"). But G.T. is less objective than he might seem to be. His claim that F.J. "is no borrower of inventions" is flagrantly contradicted twenty pages earlier when he recalls how F.J. explained that "he borrowed th'invention of an Italian" for the sonnet "Love, hope and death do stir in me such strife". Likewise "The stately dames of Rome" is "but a translation". However, he is nearer the mark when he observes of the feeble sonnet "With her in arms that had my heart in hold" that "it is somewhat too general".

The equivocal objectivity of G.T. is also exposed by his treatment of the "secretary". He laconically conveys F.J.'s almost incoherent fury concerning his sexual rival, Elinor's existing lover. G.T. emphasizes that his description is "by report of my very good friend":

He was in height the proportion of two pigmies, in breadth the thickness of two bacon hogs, of presumption a giant, of power a gnat, apishly witted, knavishly mannered, and crabbedly favoured, what was there in him then to draw a fair lady's liking? Marry, sir, even in all, a well-lined purse, wherewith he could at every call provide such pretty conceits as pleased his peevish fantasy... This manling, this minion, this slave, this secretary...

G.T. can see that this is a caricature which stems from a jealous rage. But his narrative nevertheless colludes in F.J.'s version of the man by holding him at a distance. The man is never named; he remains a mere shadow.

The term "secretary" is one of calculated abuse. He is clearly not (as most commentators assume) a servant, any more than F.J. is when Elinor addresses him as "servant". The "secretary" is another wealthy member of the gentry. Unlike F.J. he is unable to write "pretty conceits" to impress his mistress – he has to pay someone else to supply them. But he is nevertheless a better writer than Elinor, and a willing participant in what at first is a game of deception played out against F.J. It is only later, when the man goes off to London, that Elinor becomes sexually available and F.J., having now understood the realities of the situation, thinks he is now in with a chance. But the whole tone of the narrative is coloured by what at this stage has not yet happened: Elinor's return to her old lover. The description of the man may be absurd and unconvincing but it is never subsequently amended in any way.

Sex and violence

F.J. is represented as shallow and insincere. His first letter shows him as the purveyor of the worst kind of hackneyed Petrarchan sentiment ("I have found fire in frost... I feel a continual frost in my most fervent fire... let this poor paper (besprent with salt tears, and blowen over with scalding sighs) be saved of you..."). Mistress Elinor feigns bafflement, "that (as at delivery thereof, she understood not for what cause he thrust the same into her bosom), so now she could not perceive thereby any part of his meaning..." F.J.'s sexually charged act of pushing his letter "into her bosom" is the first of many moments of sly innuendo, emphatic double entendre or explicit sex in the novel. It also supplies the first of a string of associations between "pen" and "penis" / writing and fucking. Not only does Elinor's "secretary's" pen write her early love letters for her, his penis also competes with that of F.J. It transpires that he was her bedmate before F.J. arrived on the scene, and becomes so again after Elinor has broken off the relationship with F.J. When the "secretary" goes to London, Elinor lacks his "eloquence" (meaning both his letter-writing skills and his skill as a lover) and F.J. determines "to lend his Mistress such a pen in her secretary's absence, as he should never be able at his return to amend the well writing thereof" (meaning he, F.J., will be so much more accomplished in bed that

Elinor won't want to go back to having sex with that other man). It's a piece of double entendre Shakespeare echoes in *The Merchant of Venice*. When Nerissa says she'll sleep with the doctor's clerk, Gratiano retorts,

> Well, do you so. Let me not take him then!
> For if I do, I'll mar the young clerk's pen. (V.i.236-7)

Later, when Master F.J. has cured Elinor's symbolic nosebleed with a quack remedy involving a phallic hazel stick and knife she thanks him for having "so clerkly steynched my bleeding" – "clerkly" meaning "learnedly" but with a play on the sixteenth-century sense of "with great penmanship".

The comedy in the novel springs from the naïvety of F.J., the insincerity of both protagonists, and the gap between pretty romantic sentiment and calculating sexual appetite. When Frances remarks to Elinor that "not only I but all the rest had occasion to judge that your curtesie was his chief comfort" her compliment is double-edged, with "curtesie" simultaneously meaning both "ladylike behaviour and love" and "vagina" (with a play on "cut" for "cunt"). When F.J. tells the Lord of the castle that "the great curtesie of the gentlewomen was such as might revive a man although he were half dead" he is not consciously indulging in double entendre but Gascoigne as author very definitely is. No doubt sentences like these provoked tremendous belly laughs when he read the manuscript aloud to friends at law school or at court.

F.J. might like to see himself as a combination of David, Solomon, Hercules and Sampson but he is really just a young man in search of sex. He also fails to note that those famous lovers were doomed men. His "Bathsheba" will turn out to have a heart of stone and to want only sex, not love or romance. But what destroys their relationship is not the gap between romantic posturing and physical appetite but F.J.'s unfounded jealousy. His immaturity makes him feverishly suspicious that Elinor has once again taken up with her "secretary" upon his return from London. This is not true but in his jealous rage F.J. rapes her, ensuring the end of their relationship and that what he has most feared does indeed come true. Not only that, she is unashamed of the fact. "If I did sleep with someone else, so what?" is her cool attitude – something which teaches F.J. that the high-minded gestures of the Petrarchan sonnet are no guide to life and that any possibility of renewing his relationship with Elinor is finally at an end.

The novel's comedy lies in the ironic distance between F.J.'s courtly postures and the earthy realities of what is going on. The two most basic contrasts with F.J.'s expressions of Petrarchan sentiment are the language of innuendo and the disturbing emphasis on physical force as underlying the passion. F.J. may feel that writing poetry leaves his heart "eased of swelling" but the reader is well aware that there is another swelling which is also eased by Elinor. The narrative is sexualized by repeated double entendre, ranging from such overt and notorious episodes as that of F.J.'s "naked sword" under his nightgown and the hunting scene with the cuckolded husband to suggestions of the beginnings of a fresh erection after ejaculation ("unspeakable comfort...to revive a man half dead").

The physical force used by the characters is strikingly at odds with the rarefied language of F.J.'s love verses. Frances mockingly "caught hold of his lap, and half by force led him by the gallery unto his Mistress chamber" – symbolically dragging F.J. along by his penis. Love is warfare in which prisoners are "enforced to yield" and "vanquished". When the lovers quarrel in bed G.T. suggests that all it would take to make them friends again would be "but only one push of the pike". (The word "pike" is used for "penis" in a speech by Falstaff in Shakespeare's "Gascoigne" play, *Henry IV, Part Two*, II.iv.49-53.) Elinor becomes in the end like the hunted deer, "stricken: and so in the end forced to yield". But at first she is even more assertive than Frances. When he is in bed she smacks F.J. with a willow branch and later climbs on top of him, "pressing his breast with the whole weight of her body, and biting his lips with her friendly teeth". C. T. Prouty felt that such moments established the autobiographical basis of the novel, on the grounds that "no one would relate to another the details of this passage". From a twenty-first-century perspective this argument appears naïve and prim but Prouty is almost certainly correct in perceiving such moments as rooted in Gascoigne's own sexual experience. How far this autobiographical aspect extends is more problematic and, to a contemporary sensibility, more troubling.

The undercurrents of violence terminate in what for modern readers is the most disturbing moment in the novel: F.J.'s rape of Elinor. Having been falsely accused of renewing her relationship with her previous lover, Elinor declines to have sex with the furiously jealous F.J.:

> the Dame denied flatly, alleging that she found no cause at all to use such courtesy unto such a recreant, adding further many words of great reproach: the which did so enrage *F.J.* as that having now forgotten all former courtesies, he drew upon his new professed enemy, and bare her up with such violence against the bolster, that before she could prepare the warde, he thrust her through both hands, and etc. whereby the Dame swooning for fear, was constrained (for a time) to abandon her body to the enemy's courtesy. At last when she came to herself, she rose suddenly and determined to save herself by flight, leaving *F.J.* with many despiteful words, and swearing that he should never (eftsoones) take her at the like advantage, the which oath she kept better than her former professed good will: and having now recovered her chamber (because she found her hurt to be nothing dangerous) I doubt not, but she slept quietly the rest of the night: As *F.J.* also persuading himself that he should with convenient leisure recover her from this hagger

conceit, took some better rest towards the morning, than he had done in many nights forepast.

G.T. is both evasive and nonchalant about this violent assault. He abbreviates its crude physical realities in two brisk, dismissive words (one of which is itself an abbreviation): "and etc." The reader's imagination is left to improvise.

G.T.'s breezy assertion that "she found her hurt to be nothing dangerous" invites the obvious question: *how does he know?* His assumption that Elinor "slept quietly the rest of the night" seems equally as offensive and complacent as F.J.'s definition of the rape as a "hagger conceit" (meaning wild behaviour, after an untamed or "haggard" hawk). But it was an attitude which would have been shared by the novel's male readers in the sixteenth century. The extent to which Gascoigne shared it is difficult to judge. The word "courtesy" is bitterly ironic in the context of rape ("constrained...to abandon her body to the enemy's courtesy"), and supplies a vicious, violent, physical conclusion to F.J.'s pseudo-Petrarchan courtship and all its "courtesy" or crypto-knightly and ostensibly chivalric behaviour.

There is more authorial distance here than in, say, the fourth of Philip Sidney's "Certaine Sonets" in which Sidney unequivocally trivialises rape and portrays it through a soft focus. In Sidney's poem extreme sexual violence is represented as simply the work of a "strong hand" and Philomena's complaint is not that her tongue had been cut out or that she has been the victim of multiple rapes by Tereus but merely that "her will" has been broken. Like Elinor, it's her pride that has been dented, nothing more. But Sidney goes much further than Gascoigne. His poem asserts that a man who can't obtain sex has a lot more to complain about than a woman grumbling she's been raped. There is no reason to doubt that this is what Philip Sidney himself believed.

What is striking about Gascoigne's account is its realism and psychological plausibility. It is a scene which is utterly convincing in its transition from female desire, male sulkiness, argument, quarrel and sudden violence. Afterwards Elinor flees but she keeps silent about her rape. She can do little else, in terms of her reputation, sixteenth-century law or hegemonic patriarchal assumptions about rape. Even today F.J. would stand a high probability of being acquitted of raping a woman who had come to his room at night to have sex with him, lain on top of him, engaged in foreplay, removed all her clothing – and then said she didn't want sex.

The rape scene is followed by a digression by G.T. on the subject of the cause of F.J.'s quarrel with Elinor, namely the return of her "secretary". The man returned from London expecting to resume his relationship with Elinor but was repeatedly fobbed off by her. G.T. tells us that "At the last these new accidents fell so favourably for the furtherance of his cause, that he came to his Mistress presence, and there pleaded for himself." This implies that Elinor's discarded lover has at the very least got wind of her falling out with his replacement, or even knows something about the rape. That G.T. should describe the quarrel and the rape as "accidents" underlines his breezy evasiveness about the reality of what happened.

The "secretary" challenges Elinor about the rumours; she, it seems, denies ever having taken F.J. as lover. G.T. comments: "Now, if I should at large write his allegations, together with her subtle answers, I should but comber your ears with unpleasant rehearsal of feminine frailty." By "frailty" G.T. means "moral weakness" or "deception" but his pious condemnation seems preposterously pompous. It is possible to read "frailty" as "physical weakness" and read the entire sentence as unintentionally ironic (from G.T.'s point of view) and intentionally ironic (arguably from Gascoigne's point of view and certainly from a modern feminist perspective). Underlying G.T.'s bluster is the fact that Elinor was faithful to F.J. and that his jealous rage was entirely without substance. This in fact is what F.J. finally acknowledges: "that if his mistress were not faulty [i.e. unfaithful], then had he committed a foul offence in needless jealousy". He nevertheless still believes that a renewal of the affair is possible and that he can recapture her affections much as a hawk set loose in falconry can be called back: "hoping that when his lure was new garnished, he should easily reclaim her".

In fact the rape simply propels Elinor speedily back into the arms of her previous lover. In spite of G.T.'s caricature of the man as this "minion" he is clearly more mature and altogether less violent than F.J. Their sexual relationship, it later becomes clear, is renewed the morning after the rape. Its renewal releases a flood of double entendre on G.T.'s part:

> It fell out that the Secretary having been of long time absent, and thereby his quills and pens not worn so near as they were wont to be, did now prick such fair large notes, that his Mistress liked better to sing farburden under him, than to descant any longer upon *F.J.* plain song: and thus they continued in good accord, until it fortuned that Dame Frances came into her chamber upon such sudden as she had like to have marred all the music.

The passage provides a good example of the way Gascoigne's imagination is triggered by a single word, from which flow a variety of associations. The phallic "quills and pens" make him think of "prick", "prick" makes him think simultaneously of tumescence, of a thrusting penis causing cries of orgasmic pleasure and of pricksong or contrapuntal music. Contrapuntal music makes him think again of the female orgasm and of Elinor lying beneath her lover while he fucks her and she pleasurably sings "farburden", which is literally an undersong or accompaniment which is deep, humming and continuous. This, Elinor finds, is preferable to her descant or counterpoint sung above the plain song of the tenor (i.e. F.J.). These images hint that the Secretary gives her greater sexual satisfaction than F.J. and that Elinor mounted F.J. during sex, symbolising her dominance of her inexperienced lover. We might wonder how G.T. can possibly know such intimate details about both of Elinor's lovers. Possibly F.J. told him, but equally possibly the information comes from Frances, who maintains an obsessive surveillance of Elinor's sex life.

Frances, though represented by G.T. as a chaste maid, seems in fact every bit as sexually voracious as Elinor. She tries to discourage F.J. from sleeping with Elinor by telling him about her previous lovers. When that fails she lets the affair take its course but watches keenly (even voyeuristically) every development. Once she perceives that the relationship is at an end she makes clear her own desire to have sex with F.J. She offers to "trim up" his bed "in the best manner that I may" but he declines. Next day when F.J. says, "I must crave the help of your assured friendship", she replies, "Thereof you may make accoumpt" (i.e. "account" punning on "a cunt").

When F.J. discovers for himself that Elinor really has renewed her sexual relationship with the "secretary" he challenges her over her "treachery". Her instinct is to deny it but in the end she acknowledges it. Her response is a curt, "And if I did so, what then?" F.J. writes one last poem, then departs. G.T. terminates the novel on an equally brusque note: "It is time now to make an end of this thriftless History".

This final poem, "And if I did what then?", is quite different to those that precede it. It is written in a plain, mostly monosyllabic style, with no literary allusions. There is a single controlling metaphor of a fisherman on the shore wanting the sea to be his alone to fish. It is by far the best of the poems in *The Adventures of Master F.J.* and is one of Gascoigne's most anthologised works. It reads like a later version of his poem "Despised things may live", which is about a lover dumped by his mistress in favour of a new man. That poem may have been inspired by the real-life affair which seems to have inspired the novel and uses the hackneyed Chaucerian analogy of Diomede, Criseyde and Troilus. "Despised things may live" uses similar marine imagery to express the turning wheel of fortune ("The roots of rotten reeds in swelling seas are seen, / And when each tide hath tossed his worst, they grow again full green").[9] It also ends, like the poem in the novel, with a jeer at those who laugh at the rejected lover:

> I now wish change that sought no change but constant did remain
> And if such change do chance, I vow to clap my hands,
> And laugh at them which laughed at me: lo thus my fancy stands.

This is less Christian resignation and forgiveness than the expression of a belligerent certainty that all women are faithless and that every lover will one day suffer rejection. The novel ends on the same sour note:

And with such luck and loss
I will content my self:
Till tides of turning time may toss
Such fishers on the shelf.

And when they stick on sands,
That every man may see:
Then will I laugh and clap my hands,
As they do now at me.

This is a bleak, desolate vision of every man's love as fated to end in failure. But it is one which affords F.J. enormous satisfaction, as it supplies a consolation for his rejection by Elinor. It is also framed by the prospect of ecstatic revenge. When other lovers are eventually rejected by their mistresses (and especially, implicitly, the "secretary") Master F.J. will squeal with delight and break out into laughter and applause.

This is *Schadenfreude* with a vengeance – but one from an imagined moment in the future. It indicates that when F.J. departs he is filled with bitterness and hatred. Nor is he prepared to console himself sexually with Mistress Frances. His rejection by Elinor requires in turn a grand, haughty gesture of rejection on F.J.'s part of the castle and everyone in it. There is literally nothing more to be said. He departs. The story is over. What happened to Elinor and the "secretary" or to Frances or even to F.J. is something we can never know. Gascoigne does not describe the scene as F.J. leaves the castle for the last time but to a twenty-first-century reader it is easy to imagine and implicitly cinematic: a lone horseman riding away into the distance across a deserted landscape.

The first English novel

Is *The Adventures of Master F.J.* a novel? Clearly it is. It has characters, a plot, a beginning, a middle and an end. It has a chronology and moves from spring to autumn. In sum, it is a psychologically plausible account of a young man's infatuation with an experienced, sexually predatory married woman. It even belongs to what is nowadays a recognisable genre – the country-house novel. But it is also a comic novel, playing off the conventions of chivalry and rarefied Petrarchan lyric against earthy physical appetite. Its language is double-edged, sharp with sexual innuendo and wit. It also has a technical feature associated with the novel form in a much later incarnation, namely an unreliable narrator.

To deny *The Adventures of Master F.J.* the status of a novel, as some have done, is to have a very narrow conception of the form. Judged by the standard of the nineteenth-century novel, of course, the narrative is a failure. As Milan Kundera has laconically noted, two centuries of psychological realism have created some nearly inviolable standards: (1) A writer must give the maximum amount of information about a character: about his physical appearance, his way of speaking and behaving; (2) he must let the reader know a character's past, because that is where all the motives for his present behaviour are located; and (3) the character must have complete independence; that is to say, the author with his own considerations must disappear so as not to disturb the reader, who wants to give himself over to illusion and take fiction for reality.[10]

Gascoigne does none of these things. We learn that Elinor and Frances are "fair" but we are told nothing more about their physical appearance, or that of F.J., or of anyone else. We know almost nothing of their pasts. But as Kundera points out, serious and important novelists do this, including Musil, Broch and Kafka – or for that matter, Cervantes:

A character is not a simulation of a living being. It is an imaginary being. An experimental self. In that way the novel reconnects with its beginnings. Don Quixote is practically unthinkable as a living being. And yet, in our memory, what character is more alive?

The same might be said of Gascoigne's characters: Elinor, cool, sensual, duplicitous but capable of a kind of fidelity; F.J., youthful, passionate, confused, jealous; Frances, feisty, observant, sexually hungry.

What is striking about *The Adventures of Master F.J.* is just how sophisticated it is as narrative. This is something which has only belatedly been recognised after some four centuries, encouraging much critical commentary in recent years. As Colin Burrow remarks, it "has rightly been regarded of late as Gascoigne's finest work".[11] It resembles nothing so much as those great works of modernism which are simultaneously "about" a recognisable social world while being highly self-conscious games-playing fictional artefacts. Its claims to being the first English novel are legitimate. It may even be the first modern novel.

The word "novel" bears the meaning "of a new kind; strange; previously unknown" as well as "fictitious prose narrative" and, though it drew on materials from different sources, *The Adventures of Master F.J.* was, in its totality, quite unique for its time. If we ask why that should have been the answer seems to lie in Gascoigne himself. He had a sense of his own importance and worth, and of the importance and worth of those experiences transmuted into art. There was a powerful egotism here, but one attractively tempered by a comic sensibility. In *The Adventures of Master F.J.* he sought out a different form to the prevailing cultural one – lyric verse – in which to express himself. If Gascoigne's narrative was novel in the sense of new, it also sensed the dangers that could bring. *The Adventures of Master F.J.* matches everything Frederick R. Karl has to say about the origins of the form:

> From its start, the English novel has represented an adversary culture. Although it seemed to bow to the tastes and needs of the new bourgeoisie, it also stood for new and often dangerous ideas, criticized the predominant culture, and displayed what were often subversive forms of behaviour. It upset familiar assumptions, questioned realistic suppositions, and tested out, however sparingly at times, new ideas, forbidden desires, secret wishes.[12]

But in English culture the impact made by *The Adventures of Master F.J.* was muted by ecclesiastical censorship and the bowdlerised edition which Gascoigne produced in response to that censorship. The first, radically original version dropped from sight. It was then further marginalised by Gascoigne's unexpected death, the growing centrality of theatre in late Tudor culture, and the rapid decline in its author's reputation during the seventeenth century. It marked, in Bradner's words, "the end of any realistic portrayal of English upper class life in the novel for years to come".[13] By the time what we think of as the first English novels began to appear in the eighteenth century – *Robinson Crusoe* (1719), *Pamela* (1740), *Joseph Andrews* (1742), *The Life and Opinions of Tristram Shandy* (1759-67) – George Gascoigne was a totally forgotten figure and his novel had been out of print for over a century.

17: "A Spie, an Atheist and godlesse personne"

"You may not care about foreign policy," Trotsky is supposed to have said, "but foreign policy cares about you". In 1572 international affairs impinged on Gascoigne's life in a way which he could not possibly have anticipated at the start of that year.

The remarkable events which later embroiled him began in an innocuous enough way. He was commissioned to write a masque for a double wedding between a son and daughter of "Lord Mountacute" – better known as Anthony Browne, Viscount Montague – and a daughter and son of Sir William Dormer. It was an arranged marriage between two prominent Catholic families, each marrying off their male heirs. Gascoigne explained the background to the commission:

> *There were eighte gentlemen (al of bloud or alliance to the saide Lord Mountacute) which had determined to present a mask at the day appointed for the sayd marriages, and so farre they had proceeded therein, that they had alredy bought furniture of silks. Etc and had caused their garments to be cut of the Venetian fashion. Nowe then they began to imagine that (without some speciall demonstracion) it would seeme somewhat obscure to have Venetians presented rather than other countrey men. Whereupon they entreated Master Gascoigne to devise some verses to be uttered by an Actor wherein mighte be some discourse convenient to render a good cause of the Venetians presence.*[1]

Gascoigne had himself been an invited guest at a wedding celebration at Montague House, probably in 1566. On that occasion he was most likely there as his father's heir and someone presumed to be a good Catholic. Six years later it may have been via Anthony Kinwelmershe, Gascoigne's old Gray's Inn associate and brother of his collaborator on *Jocasta*, that the poet renewed his association with the Montague family. Kinwelmershe was a very close friend of Robert Dormer, one of the quartet being married at this double family wedding. Dormer himself had been admitted to Gray's Inn in 1567 and was probably a member of that set among whom Gascoigne's manuscripts circulated.

In fact weddings seemed at first to be the keynote of that year. On 4 May Gascoigne's eldest stepchild, Richard, married Katharine Geste, spinster, of Walthamstow in Essex. The wedding presumably took place at the local church, St Mary's. The celebrations would not, however, have been on the spectacular scale of that planned by the Montague family.

In the preamble to his masque Gascoigne explained that remembering that there was "*a noble house of the Mountacutes in Italie*" and knowing that Viscount Montague quartered the coat of "*an ancient english gentlemen called*

Mountherner, and hath the inheritance of the sayde house", he therefore devised a plot about a boy of about 12-14 years. The boy was a Montague on his mother's side and a Monthermer on his father's. His father having been killed by the Turks at the siege of Famagusta,

> *He was recovered by the Venetians in their last victorie, and with them sayling towards Venice, they were driven by tempest uppon these coasts, and so came to the marriage...*

The boy then steps forward and tells his story to the assembled wedding guests. Since he is supposed to have arrived by boat, the implication is that the wedding celebrations were put on at Montague House in Southwark, rather than the Viscount's country seat at Cowdrey Park in Sussex. This is confirmed by the boy's remark that *"London* is not far".[2]

Gascoigne's masque was not one in what later became the commonly understood sense of the word. There was no dumb show, choreographed dancing, singing, stage machinery or any dramatic exchanges of dialogue. Instead, flanked by four torchbearers, the child orator simply narrated a 376-line narrative poem in rhyming couplets. It was essentially a recitation, not a visual feast of colour and movement. Its only dramatic moment came at the end when the child cries, "lo now I hear their drum", and the eight Montague men enter in their extravagant Venetian costumes. There may have been scenery but none is mentioned in the text's marginalia, which describes the role of the four torchbearers and the Montague token in the child actor's cap.

If the poem was learnt off by heart it was an impressive achievement for a child. There's a joke at the end about not having learned many words, which could be taken either way. It might be a self-deprecating comment by a precocious Montague child or a professional child actor who'd learnt the entire script. Or it might simply mean that the child held the manuscript in his hand and had only managed to learn parts of it.

The poem itself is a rattling good yarn about the boy's adventures among the heathen Turks. He describes how his father's ship was blown by a storm into the middle of the siege of Famagusta and how his father was killed in the fighting. The boy is taken prisoner but shortly afterwards rescued by Venetians at the battle of Lepanto. His rescuers turn out to be from the noble house of Montague. Blown off-course (rather remarkably, in terms of geography), they all end up off "the Chalkie Clyves [cliffs] upon the Kentishe coast". Sailing up the Thames, they land just in time for the wedding celebrations.

Tudor wedding celebrations were clearly full-blooded affairs, for the boy's tale is expressed in very broad brush strokes. Turkish atrocities are described with lip-smacking relish. The Turks "glut" the "greedy fish" with "gobs of Christian carcases, in cruel pieces cut", engage in buggery and mass rape – "the foul abuse of boys in tender years...maids ravished, wives, women forced by fear" – and slice off the ears of the town's governor. Thankfully there were brave and noble Christians on hand to redress these outrages:

> The good *Venetian* general did charge upon the same.
> At length they came aboard, and in his raging pride
> Stroke off this Turkish captain's head, which blasphemed as it died.
> ...His head from shoulders cut, upon a pike did stand,
> The which *Don John* of *Austria* held in his triumphant hand.

Gascoigne's narrative superimposed the fictitious adventures of a fictitious child Montague onto real, contemporary events. The siege of Famagusta and the battle of Lepanto had occurred less than a year earlier, in 1571. The first accounts and memoirs of these major historical engagements were just beginning to appear in print, and Gascoigne drew on them to give authenticity to his lurid re-telling of the facts.

But though the Montague masque is a tale of modern European history, it also had a personal dimension. The masque is unexpectedly protracted before it reaches its *raison d'être* – the moment when the eight costumed gentlemen make their appearance. Gascoigne's enthusiasm for the commission perhaps got the better of him, releasing some of his own obsessions into the text. The boy explains that in an earlier battle his father had been captured and forced to sell his lands to meet the ransom demand. The child says he bears his father no ill will for the loss of his inheritance:

> Believe me now my lords, although the loss be mine,
> Yet I confess them better sold, than like a slave to pine.
> For lands may come again, but liberty once lost
> Can never find such recompense as countervails the cost.
> Myself now know the case, who like my father's lot,
> Was like of late for to have lost my liberty god wot.
> My father (as I say) enforced to leave his land
> In mortgage to my mother's kin, for ready coin in hand...

In these lines is surely an echo of Gascoigne's own recent past and his scorchingly painful experience of being incarcerated in Bedford prison. There's perhaps a suggestion that whatever it cost him to be released was well worth it, even if it did involve the loss of his lands. It reads like a displaced form of apology to his son, William, who was perhaps by then about eight years old. The loss of a man's liberty can never be adequately compensated, Gascoigne says. There is nothing sweeter than freedom. A father's freedom is even worth the loss of one's inheritance. In the original published text lines 49 and 50 ("For lands may come again, but liberty once lost / Can never find such recompense as countervails the cost") were even highlighted typographically at the beginning of the lines to stress their importance.

With the money left over from his ransom, the boy's father "rigged up a proper *Barke*, was called *Leffort Brittayne*" and sails off "some great exployte to finde". His ship may just symbolize the sturdy Briton, bravely going off into the unknown, though the potential pun on "Brittayne" and "Breton" could conceivably involve a risqué allusion to Gascoigne's wife, Elizabeth ("he boarded *le fort* [the strong] Breton and hoisted his sails"). If there was a deliberate pun it was an oblique one – more a matter of winks and nudges among close friends than something to be flaunted.

Viscount Montague was evidently delighted with Gascoigne and his masque. Even before it was performed he had used his influence to ensure that the poet was elected Member of Parliament for Midhurst, a small Sussex town close to his vast estate at Cowdrey Park. Gascoigne may have even asked for the favour as payment for the masque. The poet undoubtedly would have had no interest whatever in the affairs of Midhurst, but as the town's MP he enjoyed one valuable perk. When Parliament was sitting an MP could not be pursued by his creditors. This immunity from prosecution was a jealously guarded privilege among members of the house – and a source of great vexation to anyone they owed money to.

Many years later there was one other person who was impressed by Gascoigne's masque. As a narrative poem about a lost child and human destiny shaped by storm-tossed vessels and shipwrecks it held an obvious interest to a playwright such as Shakespeare. But even the language of the poem haunted him. Gascoigne's description of a "glittering golden gite"[3] [gown] – a phrase recycled from his earlier "lovely nutbrown face" sonnet – reappears in *The Rape of Lucrece*, where Time smears with dust the "glitt'ring golden towers" (945). When Shakespeare came to write *Romeo and Juliet* he remembered the masque's use of Italian Montagues. Gascoigne's reference to the "*Capels*" (Capulets) and his line,

For ancient grutch which long ago tween those two houses was[4]

reappears in the third line of the Prologue to the play:

Two households, both alike in dignity
 In fair Verona, where we lay our scene,
 From ancient grudge break to new mutiny

Roger Prior has located over thirty borrowings from Gascoigne in both *Romeo and Juliet* and *A Midsummer Night's Dream*, concluding that "the Montague masque was an important source for both plays".[5] He believes these borrowings indicate that the plays were written as a pair and at much the same time, with *A Midsummer Night's Dream* probably written first.

*

While Gascoigne was writing about a siege in Cyprus and a naval battle in the Gulf of Patras, events nearer home were closing in. They centered on a Florentine banker named Roberto Ridolfi, who had for many years been resident in London.

Some Catholics dreamed of overthrowing Elizabeth, replacing her with Mary Queen of Scots and returning the realm to the old faith. The Roman Catholic mass had been made an illegal rite in 1559, and with every year that passed Protestantism strengthened its grip. Disappointingly, the Pope had said nothing about the church under Elizabeth. Mary had fled Scotland and was now living in England, and she had a strong case for being next in line to the throne. But some Protestants believed that the threat posed by Mary could be defused if she was married off to the country's leading Catholic peer, Thomas Howard, Duke of Norfolk.

Norfolk was the son of the poet Earl of Surrey, who had been executed for treason. Like his father, he had a haughty sense of his own importance and somehow believed that he could never be made accountable for his actions. Like his father, he was capable of acting rashly and impulsively, with a reckless disregard for the consequences. Norfolk, who by September 1567 had been widowed for the third time, described Mary as a "notorious adulteress and murderess" – but he was privately very keen on the marriage. The Earl of Leicester secretly offered Mary a deal. If she married Norfolk she would be put back on the Scottish throne but in return she had to accept a Protestant establishment in Scotland and an alliance with England. In June 1568 Mary agreed to these terms. Any power and any throne were better than none.

But no one told Elizabeth I, and in Scotland there was little enthusiasm for Mary's return to power. Worse, the plan now began to assume the shape of a political conspiracy, using Roberto Ridolfi as an intermediary in an attempt to get support from France, Spain and the Pope. The plotters dreamed of a bloodless coup d'état involving a Franco-Spanish trade embargo against England, the imprisonment of Cecil and a restoration of Catholicism under Mary. Instead Elizabeth got to hear of what was going on. Mary was placed in secure custody and Norfolk was imprisoned in the Tower. In the north of England there was an uprising involving the three great Catholic families – the Percys, the Nevilles and the Dacres. The Pope offered to send money via Ridolfi but his support arrived too late. The rebellion in the north began to fizzle out. It was now, in December 1569, that Viscount Montague and his son-in-law the young

Earl of Southampton had to take an agonizing decision. Should they head north and support the rebels or cross the Channel and seek sanctuary and support abroad? They decided to set sail for Flanders, but were turned back by strong winds. It was at this point that Montague's nerve broke. He went to straight to court, pledged his allegiance to Elizabeth and was reconciled with her. His decision not to support the northern earls in their rebellion was a wise one. The rising had little support and was easily crushed.

But the dream of a Catholic queen was far from over. In February 1570 Pope Pius V issued the bull *Regnans in Excelsis*, formally excommunicating Elizabeth and freeing English Catholics from their loyalty to her. By May it was known in England. Someone attached a copy to the door of the Bishop of London. Ridolfi arranged for copies to be printed for distribution in England. In August 1570 Norfolk was released from the Tower. Foolishly, he now became involved in another conspiracy. Ridolfi's new idea was for an invasion of England from the Low Countries, where growing Protestant dissent against Spanish rule had encountered ruthless repression from an army under the Duke of Alva. Philip II of Spain cannily said that an invasion could only come *after* a Catholic uprising in England. Alva himself was unenthusiastic about the banker's fantasy, contemptuously describing Ridolfi as a *gran parlaquina* or chatterbox.

Although Mary was still prepared to marry Norfolk, she grew tired of his ceaseless indecision and procrastination regarding an English Catholic uprising. Armed intervention by Spain to overthrow Elizabeth was now her preferred option. The plot thickened. A plan was hatched to free Mary from her confinement. Another scheme involved hurrying Mary away to the east coast. But by 1571 Burghley had got wind of this new conspiracy and in September it was all finally brought out into the open. It was revealed that Norfolk had continued to communicate with Mary. A letter in his name promised an army of "twenty thousand foot and three thousand horse", which forty leading English Catholic families would muster to put her on the throne.[6] On 7 September he was once again arrested and put in the Tower. Ridolfi had the good fortune to be in Spain when he learned that the game was up. Wisely, he did not return. Three other major conspirators were also imprisoned – the Earl of Arundel, the Earl of Southampton and Lord Lumley.

A fourth conspirator was Gascoigne's patron, Viscount Montague. But he was too powerful to touch when so many other leading Catholics had been seized. It had to look like a legitimate judicial exercise, not a witch hunt. Pragmatism dictated policy. Viscount Montague was left at liberty.

The trial of Thomas Howard, Duke of Norfolk, began in January 1572. A fortnight before it began two Catholics, Edmund Mather and Kenelm Berney, were caught plotting to assassinate either Burghley or Elizabeth herself. They hoped killing one of these figures would be enough to inspire an insurrection that would put Mary on the throne.

Norfolk faced three charges, of which the most serious was that he'd conspired to overthrow the Queen and change the constitution. He was found guilty but Elizabeth showed herself indecisive about authorizing his execution. Norfolk had still not been executed when Parliament opened on 8 May, and MPs were furious. In his opening speech to the new assembly Lord Keeper Bacon said that it was generally agreed that existing legislation was inadequate to deal with the great treasons and notable conspiracies recently revealed through the providence of God. The Speaker, alluding to Mary, said that anyone who committed a felony should die, irrespective of who they were. One speech put the detailed case against Mary. The Ridolfi plot was described and angrily denounced. MPs demanded Mary's exclusion from the succession. Many wanted her execution.

One isolated voice was raised in her defence. It belonged to Gascoigne's old associate Arthur Hall, who coolly informed the house that Mary might one day rule over them. "You will hasten the execution of such whose feet hereafter you would be glad to have again to kiss." There was outrage and pandemonium. Hall was subsequently arraigned before the house and forced to submit.

A Spy, an Atheist and a Killer

The events in Gascoigne's life which occurred at this time cannot be understood outside the context of the mood of anti-Catholic hysteria which swept the country in 1572. Firstly, he came from a Catholic family and his father was a stubborn adherent of the old faith, judged as a "hinderer" in matters of religion.[7] Secondly, the poet was an associate of the Montagues, who were deeply implicated in the Ridolfi conspiracy. Thirdly, he was a protégé of Viscount Montague himself, who had arranged for him to become the MP for Midhurst. Fourthly, he had written a masque celebrating the virtues of the Montagues, both at home and abroad. Worse still, his masque was a celebration of glorious victories by Catholic powers. The battle of Lepanto was a victory of the Venetian, Spanish and papal fleets under the command of Phillip II's half brother, Don John of Austria. Finally, Gascoigne was an old associate of Arthur Hall, who was an outspoken supporter of Mary Queen of Scots.

In the face of these facts, who could possibly doubt that if Gascoigne himself was not directly involved in the Ridolfi conspiracy, then it nevertheless had his full support? But who knows? Perhaps he was personally involved!

That was the extraordinary suggestion made in a letter sent to the Privy Council. It accused him of being "a spie". At this moment in English history such an accusation meant only one thing. Gascoigne was part of the great Catholic conspiracy which was working against the state. A spy was someone like Roberto Ridolfi, flitting here and there with messages and money. A spy was the kind of person who hung around with the Montague set and accepted their patronage. A spy travelled around a lot. A spy was someone who, perhaps as Gascoigne had done not all that long ago, made mysterious trips to Rome. Gascoigne the writer was a master of fake identities and shifting perspectives. In his own way he was perhaps not all that different to a man like Ridolfi, who remains an ambiguous figure of uncertain allegiance.

The "spie" letter – an anonymous denunciation – is unsigned and undated.[9] It was sent to the Privy Council. The main thrust of the letter was that Gascoigne was unfit to be an MP. It was written some time between Gascoigne's election and the start of Parliamentary proceedings on 8 May. If the letter was written in April its author – who shows some knowledge of Gascoigne's unpublished work – might in theory have known something of the poet's masque, which includes material from a publication which appeared after 23 March 1572. However, Gascoigne's other associations were quite enough to damn him in the eyes of his denouncer, irrespective of the wedding poem.

The anonymous letter reads as follows:

> *To the righte honnorable the Lordes of the Privie Cownsaile.*
>
> *Certaine objections why George Gascoigne oughte not to be admitted to be a Burgesse of the Parliament*
>
> *First he is indebted to a greate number of personnes for the wch cause he hath absented him selfe from the Citie and hath lurked at villages neere unto the same citie by a longe time, and nowe beinge returned for a Burgesse of Midehurste in the Countie of Sussex, doethe shewe his face openlie in the dispite of all his Creditors.*
> *Item he is a defamed person and noted as well for Manslaughter as for other greate crymes.*
> *Item he is a common Rymer and a deviser of slaunderous Pasquelles againste divers personnes of great callinge.*
> *Item he is a notorious Ruffianne and especiallie noted to be bothe a Spie, an Atheist and godlesse personne.*
> *For the wch causes he is not meete to be of the Cownsaile of High Courte of ye Parliament.*

This denunciation raises a number of questions. Who wrote it? Why? Were any of these accusations true? And what effect did this letter have?

Gascoigne's most obvious enemy was Edward Boyes, perhaps still nursing a grudge after his divorce. But the letter's author was clearly not Boyes. Gascoigne's accuser's main motive was to prevent him being an MP, thereby removing his immunity from action to recover a debt. In other words, this was someone Gascoigne owed money to. Not only was the poet evading repayment, he was now apparently displaying a swaggering you-can't-touch-me-I'm-an-MP posture.

The anonymity of the denunciation indicates some apprehension about what the consequences might be if the identity of the accuser was known. It shows that the accuser was not someone with powerful friends and that he was afraid of reprisals, either from Gascoigne himself or a powerful ally. Its anonymity perhaps indicates that the writer knew Gascoigne had at least one friend on the Privy Council (Viscount Montague – and perhaps Lord Keeper Bacon).

Gascoigne's other most obvious enemy was his own brother, John, who by 1569 was in London, ostensibly studying law at Staple's Inn. But John would surely have known about the poet's connections with Walthamstow. The anonymous accuser knows that Gascoigne has been spending a lot of time outside the city limits but seems unsure where. The claim that he "hath lurked at villages neere unto the same citie by a longe time" sounds like someone who is unaware of Gascoigne's precise whereabouts and knows nothing of Thorpe Hall.

All in all it sounds very much like a shopkeeper, trader or city merchant. The writer knows something of Gascoigne's life but not everything. He even knows something of the manuscripts which Gascoigne has circulated among his friends and acquaintances. But to this man Gascoigne is nothing more than "a common Rymer" – a phrase which expresses the sturdy disgust and contempt of a tradesman for such namby-pamby stuff as love sonnets. He also knows that Gascoigne is "a deviser of slaunderous Pasquelles". A pasquiler is one who pokes fun at authority; a pasquinade is a lampoon or a coarse satire. The description indicates that the complainant knew something of works like "Gascoigne's Recantation" or *The Adventures of Master F.J.*, even if only by hearsay. But whoever he was, he was not one of the easy-going Inns of Court crowd. He was someone with a streak of Puritanism in his make-up. He was someone easily shocked and appalled by what he had heard of Gascoigne's comic writing.

To call Gascoigne "a Spie, an Atheist and godlesse personne" was about the worst accusation that could be made in Tudor England (a bit like nowadays accusing someone of being a terrorist *and* a paedophile). The "spy" slur was clearly connected to Gascoigne's associations with the Montagues. So, too, was the accusation of atheism and godlessness. Papistry and atheism were often conflated by fundamentalist Protestants. What's more Gascoigne, who had perhaps recently visited Italy, was in the process of celebrating the connection between the Italian Montagues and their English relatives. But Italy was a land of depravity. It corrupted innocent young Englishmen. Even Italians were shocked by their sinful behaviour. According to Roger Ascham, the Italians had a phrase for it: *Inglese italianato è un diabolo incarnato* ("an Italianate Englishman is the devil incarnate").[10] "Atheist" was a useful insult because it was guaranteed to make those in authority sit up and take notice and at the very least investigate the charge. Its lethal properties were demonstrated later in the century when the identical charge was levelled against both Christopher Marlowe and Sir Walter Ralegh.

The accusation that Gascoigne was "a godless person" was clearly not true in its most literal sense. He obviously genuinely believed in God and an after-life. But it had a grain of truth in it in so far as the poet's religious affiliation appears to have been at times remarkably flexible. His religion was of the easy-going, comfortable, untroubled sort. He was born into a staunch Catholic family, perhaps fell under the influence of a radical Protestant reformer at university, became a moderate Protestant under the moderate regime of Elizabeth, but then pumped out an implicitly pro-Catholic masque for a Catholic patron. Nowadays we might call these kinds of changes opportunism, but the charge is largely meaningless in an era like the sixteenth century. Most people bent with the wind, and as Gascoigne well knew even such a committed reformer as Cranmer was prepared to adjust his religion according to circumstance. Those who stuck doggedly to religious principles which flouted the governing orthodoxy risked having their homes ransacked and their books burned, while they themselves might expect a range of sanctions and punishments which at their most extreme might include imprisonment, torture or execution.

It is difficult to imagine Gascoigne as a regular or enthusiastic worshipper, though on the face of it he put in his weekly appearance at his local church as required by law. He and Elizabeth were listed as not attending St Mary's, Walthamstow, on 19 June and 2 September 1572. On the second occasion he was abroad and in fact there were many Sundays not listed when he was away elsewhere. Temperamentally the poet was a sceptic, with a strong sense of irony and self-deprecating humour. Religious orthodoxy requires a one-dimensional mind – absolute, unswerving belief in a particular creed. But Gascoigne was a pluralist, alive to the shifting meanings of a letter, a word, a line of verse. His implicit mockery of Cranmer must have seemed shocking to anyone of a devout Protestant sensibility. And of course he had written some scandalously risqué poems about love as well as a tale about adultery in an aristocratic household. In the eyes of someone who took their religion seriously and who despised rich layabouts who wasted their time on something as worthless and ephemeral as literature, such a man was clearly not fit to represent decent people in Parliament.

The final allegation, that Gascoigne was "a defamed person and noted as well for Manslaughter as for other greate crymes" and "a notorious Ruffianne", is intriguing, as nowhere else is there any record of the poet having once killed someone. The word "defamed" could mean anything from "disreputable" to "infamous" – and clearly Gascoigne's accuser would have preferred the more extreme interpretation.

Had Gascoigne once killed a man? No documentary evidence has ever surfaced to confirm this, but the answer is probably yes. The claim was surely true. There would be little point in accusing him of such a very specific offence if it had never occurred. The anonymous denunciation exaggerates and distorts but its variegated fury has a foundation of fact. Gascoigne is "noted for Manslaughter and other greate crymes". Clearly, there were no other "great crimes" because if there were the denouncer would have enthusiastically and indignantly listed them. Instead, Gascoigne's accuser used what was known and accepted – that Gascoigne was guilty of killing a man – as a foundation stone for broader, vaguer and baseless accusations.

If Gascoigne was a killer, who and how did he kill and when and where did the killing take place? The commonest locations for Tudor manslaughters were ale-houses and taverns. Ownership of daggers and rapiers was widespread. Alcohol and gambling supplied a ready source of heat-of-the-moment quarrels, brawlings and stabbings. The age's most famous victim was Christopher Marlowe but there were many other examples. Tybalt's killing of Mercutio in *Romeo and Juliet* was behaviour well known to the citizens of Tudor London. Violent death was perhaps less shocking in a society where the plague killed thousands at a time and when all kinds of illness had deadly consequences in the absence of effective medicine or healthcare. Ben Jonson killed an actor who had himself murdered another man. Shakespeare's close friend and associate John Heminges married the sixteen-year-old widow of an actor killed by a fellow actor.

But a bar-room brawl does not fit with what we know of Gascoigne. He does not seem to have been a quarrelsome man and his friends were many and diverse. There is an occasion and a location which seems far more probable – namely the skirmish in Red Cross Street on 30 September 1562. That Gascoigne killed one of Edward Boyes's men seems entirely plausible. If Boyes led his men to his former home to reclaim it and his wife, then Gascoigne could reasonably have claimed to be acting in self-defence. If the man had died on the spot then Machyn would surely have heard about it and recorded the fact. If this *was* the occasion, then the probability is that Gascoigne wounded one of Boyes's men with his sword, and the man died some days later of his injuries. If, as seems likely, the author of the anonymous denunciation was a London merchant or tradesman, then he might well know about this killing in the capital. He would have been less likely to have known about Gascoigne's involvement in manslaughter had it occurred in Bedfordshire or somewhere else far from the city. It might also explain why Gascoigne and Elizabeth evidently gave up the big house on Red Cross Street and moved away, first to Willington and then to Walthamstow. After being pardoned for committing manslaughter in Walthamstow, Edmund Withypoll moved to Ipswich. Probably there was always a fear of reprisals in cases like these.

If a servant of Boyes died from wounds sustained on Red Cross Street there must have been an inquest, followed by the burial of the victim. In an episode such as manslaughter resulting from self-defence a formal pardon would have been issued in the Queen's name and the case would thereafter have been closed. It is quite possible that documentation from such a case still survives. Sixteenth-century archival material is patchy, widely dispersed and often incomplete but is nevertheless extensive. The case of Christopher Marlowe shows just how long it can take for primary evidence of this sort to be rediscovered. Marlowe was stabbed to death in 1593 but it was not until 1925 that the papers of the coroner's inquest were finally located and brought into the public domain.

There are two moments in his writing when Gascoigne may obliquely acknowledge killing a man. The third part of his final work *The Grief of Joy* takes "The faults of force and strength" as its theme. Stanzas 10-17 deal with ideas of strength, weakness, excess and the haphazard nature of death. There are images of sudden blows, fencing, fighting, blood-stained blades and "doompes of deepe repent" (stanza 10) (i.e. a deep, remorseful depression). The weakling who sits "buzzing at his book" is praised as superior to strong men who "roonethe after riot" (stanza 14). Gascoigne looks back at his younger days when he was lusty and strong and energetic:

But lo: beholde; my mery daies amydd,
One heady deede, my haughty harte did breake,
And since (full oft) I wisht I had bene weake. (Stanza 12)

What this "heady deede" or impulsive action was, the poet does not elaborate. It happened in his "mery daies" – his twenties? – and it was related to pride and superior strength. The deed broke his heart and he has always regretted it. What it was is impossible to decipher from *The Grief of Joy* alone, but if Gascoigne did kill a man, either in the brawl on Red Cross Street or in a duel on some other occasion, then these lines probably refer to it.

There is also that strange moment in *Supposes* which has always puzzled critics of the play. This is the passionate, remorseful speech by Damon, which Gascoigne greatly expanded from the original Italian (III.ii.22-71). Its dark and sombre tone is strikingly out of key with the light-hearted tone of the rest of the play. The speech expresses Damon's horror at the discovery that his daughter is pregnant by "Dulippo", apparently a mere servant. It follows his order that Dulippo be bound hand and foot and imprisoned in a dungeon in the cellar.

Damon's long speech conveys his swirling feelings about crime, punishment and duty. At its heart lies one terse, bitter, haunting sentence: "The thing once done can not be undone". Damon is referring both to the loss of his daughter's virginity and to her pregnancy. Could Gascoigne also have been referring to an irrevocable act of his own – namely the killing of a man in a street skirmish? The matter can only be speculative, but it is interesting that the speech contemplates the consequences of killing a man: "to such detestable offences no punishment can seem sufficient, but only death". Although Damon blames

Dulippo for the catastrophe which has ruined him he blames himself more: "Alas, alas, I myself have been the cause of all these cares, and have deserved to bear the punishment of all these mishaps."

It is, of course, impossible to prove that Damon's speech is a projection of Gascoigne's own sense of guilt and remorse for killing a man. All one can do is note that the emotions of the speech seem far in excess of what is dramatically required at this point and that the speech touches on matters of crime, punishment, revenge, killing, remorse and death. Damon is even haunted by a memory of a dead person – his wife, "that now liest cold in the grave". Everyone who has analysed this passage has felt that it is about more than its ostensible subject and that Gascoigne is alluding to something outside the play itself. *The thing once done cannot be undone*: that that touches on an act of manslaughter by Gascoigne himself is at the very least a possibility.

*

Technically the letter should have been sent to the Parliamentary authorities, not the Privy Council. But someone powerful took these anonymous complaints seriously. Although the letter described Gascoigne as "nowe beinge returned for a burgesse of Midehurst" he had only been elected. He had not yet taken his seat. Nor did he. As G. W. Pigman notes, "Gascoigne's name was crossed out on a list of MPs, probably drawn up before the opening of Parliament, 8 May 1572; on another list, tentatively dated to the week before Parliament opened, his name does not appear... On the first day of the session, Thomas Cromwell wrote in his journal, 'This oration [Lord Keeper Bacon's opening speech] ended the petitions for Gascoyne and Guyan *etc.* were red'. Was this a petition for Gascoigne to take his seat?"[11] If so, it failed. Parliament was now a body in which radical Protestants had a stronger voice than ever before. The previous year's Parliament (2 April-29 May) was the first to sit under the act requiring subscription to the oath of supremacy. The Catholic influence was waning.

Gascoigne did in fact appear at Westminster a month after the Parliamentary session started, but not as an MP. On 9 June he was present to give evidence on behalf of his father's old enemy Reginald Grey, 5th Earl of Kent, in a land dispute with Lord Henry Compton. Compton might have expected to find Sir John's son on his side and was enraged to find that this was not so. Having been cheated of his seat in Parliament, Gascoigne was evidently in an uncompromising mood.[12]

In short, the anonymous denunciation worked. Many of its accusations were wild and exaggerated but in the hysterical atmosphere surrounding the Ridolfi conspiracy, Gascoigne's patronage by Viscount Montague was probably enough to damn him. It was guilt by association. The angry creditor's timing was perfect. The mood of Parliament was indicated by its petition requesting Mary's execution and its demand that Norfolk be brought to the block before the end of the session. Elizabeth temporized on the first but not even she could resist the overwhelming desire for vengeance against that other prominent and treacherous Catholic. On Monday 2 June 1572 Norfolk was executed on Tower Hill, just as his poet father had been a quarter of a century earlier.

18: Minding your P's and W's

Bartholomew Withypoll is a shadowy figure in Gascoigne's life, who inspired one of his liveliest poems. If Withypoll hadn't known one of the finest writers of his age he would be utterly forgotten. He was just another young man from an affluent Tudor family. He had a good education; he travelled; he had ample money to fund his life of leisure. It is far from clear what Bartholomew *did*, if anything. But then the same objection could have been levelled against George Gascoigne. He was born into wealth and privilege; he owned land and a fine country house. But apart from a brief stint as an MP and some tenant farming, he'd so far done nothing which would have satisfied a Puritan sense of a hard-working life. All he'd really done was write, and in that sense he was merely a kind of amateur entertainer. He'd produced two plays to amuse the Gray's Inn crowd and he'd circulated poetry and prose among courtiers and law students. As Shakespeare later understood, to be an entertainer was of no lasting significance. It might make a playwright and a theatre-owner money but it was a transient activity, of no lasting cultural value.

Gascoigne was different. He had a very modern concept of himself as *a writer*. He also had a very modern sense of the book as simultaneously a cultural and commercial product. In that respect he was way ahead of Shakespeare. Gascoigne had half an eye on immortality and half an eye on turning himself into a best-selling author and celebrity. Even more, over two centuries before the great Romantic poets, he had a towering sense of self. His life and personality was something to be written about and marketed as a thing interesting and important in its own right. This was much more than being simply proud of his ancestry. To be a Gascoigne gave him pride and confidence. But Gascoigne was not interested in promoting himself as the latest bearer of the family coat of arms. He was not *a* Gascoigne but *the* Gascoigne: a Gascoigne for all time.

In the absence of all those things which we now take for granted – promotion, publicity, celebrity and marketing – he had to do it all himself. He became his own commentator, nudging the story along with the remarks of a variety of invented critics. When "G.T." discusses one of the poems by "F.J." he comments that "it was in the first beginning of *his writings*, as he was no *writer* of any long continuaunce"[1] (my italics). "G.T." not only offers a critical commentary on the merit of "F.J."'s work, he also links it to his private life ("it cannot be written lesse than six or seven yeres before he knew *Hellene*").[2] Later, when Gascoigne's best-seller status had been achieved, he even arranged for his portrait to be engraved for his next book.[3]

Gascoigne's poem to Bartholomew Withypoll[4] takes us way beyond Petrarch and his imitators. It gives us a wholly new tone of voice in English literature, far removed from Surrey and Wyatt. The voice speaking in "*Gascoignes councell given to master* Bartholmew Withipoll *a little before his latter journey to Geane.*

1572" is relaxed, self-confident and conversational. Although the title suggests that it is a sequel to the poem of advice or "councell" to Douglas Dive, the poem's timbre is entirely different. Gascoigne's tone of voice addressing Douglas Dive is a cacophonous mix of respectful deference, bizarre imagery, innuendo and a nervous awareness that he might have overstepped the mark (but with a "and if I did, what the hell" swagger attached). Douglas Dive was a gentlewoman; the daughter of a knight. Gascoigne wasn't entirely sure where he stood with her. Perhaps she wanted an affair with him? Perhaps he wanted an affair with *her*? They meet in Gascoigne's poem like people blundering around in the dark, uncertain of everything. But then again perhaps it's all just the feverish fantasy of a man in prison, driven half mad by the shock of his imprisonment.

With the "councell" to Bartholomew Withypoll (the poet evidently pronounced his friend's first name in three syllables, dropping the second "o"), Gascoigne has recovered his poise. The Withypoll poem is addressed to someone who was his equal; someone who was a very good friend. Someone, in short, much like himself. Gascoigne knows exactly where he stands with Bart Withypoll. The tone is jaunty, comic, mocking and utterly relaxed. It's a style we hardly come across again in English literature until Byron published *Don Juan*.

The poem's title refers to Withypoll's second trip to "Geane" or Genoa. His father had made a financial provision which entitled him, as the second surviving son, to claim money invested in the Bank of St George, Genoa, once he reached the age of 25. Quite possibly Gascoigne accompanied him on his previous Italian visit. The poem speaks knowingly of shared experiences there:

> Remember *Batte* the foolish blinkeyed boy
> Which was at *Rome*, thou knowest whom I mean,
> Remember eke the pretty beardless toy,
> Whereby thou foundst a safe return to *Geane*,
> Do so again: (God shield thou shouldst have need)[5]

This is coterie literature with a vengeance, utterly obscure to anyone who isn't in on the story. What foolish boy with the twitching eyes? Exactly what crisis propelled Withypoll from Rome back to Genoa on his last visit? And what does a "pretty beardless toy" mean? A girl? A boy? A male whore? These are lines pronounced with a wink and a nudge. To ram the point home Gascoigne appended the marginal note "A Misterie" to line 50 in the second publication of the poem. Marginalia traditionally explains or summarises the writer's argument. But Gascoigne turns even that tradition on its head.

Later in the poem he wonders,

>   if it fall out so,
> That *James a Parrye* do but make good that,
> Which he hath said: and if he be (no, no)
> The best companion that long *George* can find,
> Then at the *Spawe* I promise for to be
> In August next, if God turn not my mind

More in-jokes. It is impossible to know what James a Parrye promised to do or whether "(no, no)" is an affectionate jest or sneering sarcasm. And no one has ever plausibly tracked down who James a Parrye was. This is a poem which talks about *knowing* and *saying* while denying the reader that knowledge or what was said. The *Spawe* was the town of Spa, now in Belgium. It was the first town to become popular as a resort for people in search of the health-giving qualities of water from mineral springs. Gascoigne almost certainly didn't meet up there with Withypoll in August 1572.

It is easy enough to understand how excited Shakespeare might have been when *The Whole woorkes of George Gascoigne Esquyre* was published in 1587 at the very start of his career as a playwright. In Gascoigne he would have found someone who pioneered dramatic monologues in verse. In "*councell given to master* Bartholmew Withipoll", Withypoll is almost tangibly present as Gascoigne addresses him. When Gascoigne makes a blunt remark, he hears his friend's amused response: "What? laughest thou *Batte*, because I write so plain?"

The poem may have been written in April or May 1572, soon after the anonymous denunciation of Gascoigne to the privy council. Gascoigne speaks of praying "for *Batte*, / And for *Pencoyde*", and appears to imply that Sir William Morgan of Pencoyde was going with Withypoll on the Genoa trip. Morgan may not have gone at all or he may have only gone a little of the way, for by the last week of May he was fighting in the Low Countries. The poem was written around the same time as the Montague masque and the first two lines of the poem to Withypoll:

>   Mine own good *Bat*, before thy hoise up sail,   [hoist]
>   To make a furrow in the foaming seas

is a variation on the masque's

>   How so it were, the winds now hoisted up our sails,
>   We furrowing in the foaming floods[6]

Apart from the in-jokes between friends, the poem has two dimensions of meaning hidden below its zestful surface. Firstly, it refers to an aspect of the Withypoll family history that connects to that of the Gascoignes, namely a common link with Cardinal Wolsey. The poet's grandfather was Wolsey's treasurer, and the Cardinal's chaplain, Thomas Lupset, was tutor to Bartholomew's father, Edmund. Lupset was a scholar, letter writer and theologian, and among his works was a treatise of godly advice dedicated to young men in general and Edmund Withypoll in particular. This work, *An Exhortacion to yonge Men, perswadinge them to walke in the Pathe way that leadeth to Honeste and Goodnes* (1530) proved very popular (more, one suspects, as gifts from parents to children than among the recipients). It was republished in 1534, 1535, 1538, 1540 and 1544.

The Lupset treatise was full of ponderous advice from the earnest young theologian. Withypoll was advised to read the New Testament in a reverential spirit: "Presume not in no case to thynke, that there you understonde ought: leve devisinge thereupon: submit your selfe to the expositions of holy doctores: and ever conforme your consent to agre with Christes church". The child was also advised to read Chrysostom and Jerome, Aristotle's *Ethics* and Book VII and VIII of his *Politics*, as well as Plato, Cicero and the works of Seneca, Xenophon's *Oeconomicus* and Epictetus's *Enchiridion*. But a healthy and wholesome body was every bit as important as a mind crammed with wisdom. "Be temperate in your lustes…For this part I wolde you reade, as your leiser shalbe, a little worke of Galen *De bona valetudine tuenda*."

Gascoigne's "councell" to Bartholomew Withypoll is obviously intended as parody of the famous advice to his father Edmund. Lupset warned Edmund Withypoll to take heed of three things in due order: the soul, the body, and the substance of this world. For his part, Gascoigne cautions against three things beginning with "P" – poison, pride and papistry – and three things beginning with "W": wine, women and wilfulness. But Gascoigne's advice is jocular and easy-going:

> First in thy journey, gape not over much,
> What? laughest thou *Batte*, because I write so plain?

Here "gape" doesn't mean "stare" but is Tudor slang for "fuck" (punning on "gape" meaning "open wide" or "open-mouthed" and "gap" meaning "fissure" or "passage"). This is frank advice indeed, but presumably Bartholomew was sometimes fond of "Women, such as haunt the stews" [brothels] (139) and wine "which may enflame thy blood" – hence his "staggering steps" are perhaps comically literal as well as emblematic of his faltering moral progress.

Gascoigne doesn't in fact forbid his friend to sample Italian whores and wine; he merely warns him to "exceed not" in his enjoyment of them. It might be best to avoid them, but if not then "temper them always". This is scarcely advice on a par with Lupset's. Even the first two lines contain suggestive innuendo: "before thy hoise up sail / To make a furrow in the foaming seas" could mean lifting up a woman's skirt in order to have sex with her. Tudor women of all classes did not wear knickers. To make a furrow is to plough, and Shakespeare used this as a metaphor for fucking ("He ploughed her, and she cropped" – *Antony and Cleopatra*, II.ii.234).

Gascoigne's poem is in the sixteenth-century tradition of English xenophobia about Italy. He portrays Italy as a land of rogues and poisoners, up to all kinds of tricks which the poem inventories with lip-smacking relish. But Gascoigne's attitude is different to Roger Ascham's. Ascham was genuinely horrified by Italian vice and sophistication and the threat it posed to innocent young Englishmen. Gascoigne's satire is fuelled not by anger or disgust but affectionate amusement. He refers to Ascham's notorious description of corrupted English youth, but in a breezy manner:

Believe me *Batte*, our countrymen of late
Have caught such knacks abroad in foreign land,
That most men call them *Devils incarnate*,
So singular in their conceits they stand:

The phrase remained popular. The dying Falstaff is reported to have denounced women as "devils incarnate" (*Henry V*, II.iii.29).

Gascoigne knows that Englishmen are far from innocent. His "countrymen" are also "cunt-ry-men" and what stands "singular" (like the digit one) in "conceits" (or cunts) is an erect penis. It wasn't only Gascoigne's idea of a pun. As Stephen Booth notes, "Like any word beginning with *con*, *conceit* is always open to sexual joking in Shakespeare".[7] A "knack" can mean a "toy" – presumably one of "the pretty beardless" sort. The erotic meaning is confirmed by Gascoigne's vision of his friend returning from Italy "in queynt araye" – i.e. "in cunt clothing" (meaning fashionable clothes intended to make him irresistible to women).

Beneath its chatty surface, "*councell to master* Bartholomew Withypoll" is actually a very tightly structured poem with a regular rhyme scheme and a multiplicity of puns and hidden meanings. But more than being just a technical achievement, it's also very funny. This is Gascoigne's vision of the Tudor equivalent of what a Kinks' song once called a dedicated follower of fashion:

Your brave *Mustachyos* turned the *Turky* way,
A Coptanckt hat made on a Flemish block,
A nightgown cloak down trailing to your toes,
A slender sloppe close couched to your docke,
A curtold slipper, and a short silk hose:
Bearing your rapier point above the hilt,
And looking big like *Marquis of all Beef*

A moustache shaped the Turkish way was presumably curled up at the ends in an exaggerated manner. A "Coptanckt" hat was high-crowned and shaped like a sugar loaf. A "slender sloppe" is a contradiction in terms, meaning slender baggy trousers, and "close couched to your docke" means "clinging tightly to your buttocks". This is the Englishman as a buffoon, a pompous ass in thrall to foreign fashion who swaggers around like a minor aristocrat with an inflated sense of his own importance.

Apart from expressing a satirical response to Lupset's solemn tome, Gascoigne's poem has a second concealed dimension. It expresses his response to the letter of denunciation sent to the Privy Council. His anonymous accuser had called him "a common Rymer". Gascoigne picks up the accusation and throws it back. In a long, clever, complex rhyming poem he casually apologises for his "dogrell rime". As for the allegation that he is "a spie; an Atheist and godlesse personne", Gascoigne makes his allegiance clear:

> next to GOD, thy Prince have still in mind,
> Thy country's honour, and the common wealth:
> And flee from them, which fled with every wind
> From native soil, to foreign coasts by stealth:
> Their trains are trustless, tending still to treason,
> Their smoothed tongues are lined all with guile,
> Their power slender, scarcely worth two peason,
> Their malice much, their wits are full of wile:
> Eschew them then, and when thou seest them say,
> *Da, da,* sir *K*, I may not come at you,
> You cast a snare your country to betray,
> And would you have me trust you now for true?

This is a description of Catholics involved in the Ridolfi plot. Among those who "fled with every wind" were, of course, Viscount Montague and his son-in-law the young Earl of Southampton – until the wind blew them back to England. Gascoigne is making it crystal clear he is a loyal servant of his "Prince" (i.e. Elizabeth – the term was used to mean queens as well as kings). He rejects the very thought of even talking to such Catholics, were Bartholomew to bump into any of them on his European travels.

To reinforce the point, Gascoigne makes a blistering attack on papists and papistry, which defile both body and soul and are "foul". Some Englishmen return home from Italy as papists,

> Or else much worse (which is a heavy loss)
> Drowned in errors like an *Atheist*

An atheist and a godless person? Gascoigne emphatically denies the charge.

Consistency was never Gascoigne's strongest point. In his "*councell to Douglasse Dive*" he praises toothpicks as useful instruments; in "*councell to master* Bartholmew Withypoll" he mocks them as foolish foreign imports. In his masque he salutes the Montague clan and the victories of European Catholic powers, while almost simultaneously denouncing papists and the Ridolfi plotters in his Withypoll poem. The most telling objection to the anonymous letter of denunciation against Gascoigne is that it accuses him of treasonable and heretical beliefs, whereas in fact, far from being a man driven by ideology, he believed in almost nothing. Or to put it another way, he could see the funny side of almost anything, which sapped his willingness to believe in anything very strongly. Gabriel Harvey grumbled that "vanity" and "levity" were "his special faultes, & the continual causes of his misfortunes"; "nothing fadgeth [succeeds] with him, for want of Resolution, & Constancy in any one kind".[8]

*

Gascoigne never mentioned Gabriel Harvey in his writing. But the two men seem to have known each other through their mutual friendship with Daniel and Bartholmew Withypoll. Harvey is a minor figure on the Elizabethan literary scene, nowadays best known for his association with Edmund Spenser and his acrimonious exchanges with Thomas Nashe.

When Gascoigne knew him Harvey, born c. 1550, was a young Cambridge scholar from an affluent family in Walden, Essex (now better known as Saffron Walden). In 1572-3 Harvey's father was Treasurer of Walden, roughly the same as being mayor. Harvey entered Christ's College, Cambridge, in June 1566. When he graduated he expected to be made a Fellow, but was not elected. Through patronage he managed to get a fellowship at Pembroke Hall. However, there was an attempt to block the award of his M.A. degree and Harvey fell out with a number of the Fellows. He emerged victorious and the 1570s were a good decade for him. In 1573 he was appointed both Lecturer in Greek and Bursar, in 1574 he became University Praelector in Rhetoric and, in 1575, Senior Treasurer. His lectures drew large audiences of up to 400.

Harvey was a considerable scholar, a great reader and an enthusiastic and prolific annotator of the books in his library. *Gabriel Harvey's Marginalia* (1913) provides a selection from twenty-three volumes. He owned copies of Gascoigne's *Posies* and *The Steel Glass*. Gascoigne shocked him and he didn't really approve of him, but even Harvey couldn't help liking and admiring him. It is just possible that he introduced Edmund Spenser to Gascoigne, and it is very probable that he made Spenser aware of Gascoigne's writings. Spenser was certainly aware of Gascoigne's work by the time his first book was published in 1579, since it acknowledged him as "the very chefe of our late rymers".

Harvey's copy of the *Posies* was peppered with criticisms of the poet's inconsistencies and irreverent humour. Whereas Gascoigne was easy-going and full of cheerful contradictions, Harvey seems to have been more intense, introverted and academic. A biographer remarks that "he seems to have lacked the art of being convivial in a relaxed way among groups of his contemporaries",[9] an accusation no one could level against Gascoigne. Harvey's career as an academic and a writer was marred by his involvement in petty squabbles and bickering. They may not have been all his fault but they left an impression of a difficult and argumentative man. That Gascoigne got on well with two of the most quarrelsome men of his age – Arthur Hall and Gabriel Harvey – is a considerable tribute to his genial temperament.

19: Flushing Frays

During the early summer of 1572 George Gascoigne's life took a dramatic new direction. He went off to the Low Countries to join the English soldiers fighting alongside the native forces against the Spanish colonial army.

Two years earlier Ridolfi had promoted the idea of a Spanish invasion of England after the decisive defeat of the Dutch Protestant insurgency. But the Duke of Alva's savage repression had failed to subjugate the rebellious population and the conflict dragged on. Elizabeth I was under pressure at home to back the Dutch Protestants but declined to do so formally. However, she was prepared to lend her tacit support to the cause, as had been demonstrated when Spanish treasure ships sought refuge from pirates in English ports. They were carrying a large consignment of new-minted money borrowed in Genoa. The money was seized on the spurious grounds that it did not lawfully belong to Spain but to Genoese financiers. Alva responded by seizing English property in the Low Countries. England retaliated by confiscating Spanish ships and Spanish and Flemish property. There was a major diplomatic crisis but neither Philip II and Alva nor Elizabeth wanted a war. For England, France was just as much of an anxiety as Spain.

In April 1572 the struggle for Dutch independence flared up again when the Sea Beggars – Dutch privateers under the command of La Marke – captured the city of Brielle. They were so called because the Spanish scornfully referred to the Dutch as beggars; the insult was proudly absorbed and thrown back into the teeth of the occupying forces. Other towns, including Flushing (now known as Vlissingen), overcame their Spanish garrisons and came out in support of the Dutch rebel leader, William of Orange. Flushing, on the island of Walcheren, was a port of major strategic importance. It lay at the mouth of the estuary leading to Antwerp; one contemporary called it the "gate which opens and shuts up the entrance into Zealand".[1] William appointed Jerome Tzeraerts (or Saras) as governor of Flushing and Lieutenant Governor of Walcheren.

At the end of May 1572, a company of 300 volunteers under Captain Thomas Morgan was mustered at Greenwich before the Queen. They reached Flushing at the end of the first week in June. Gascoigne was clearly not with Morgan's force because he was present in the House of Commons on 9 June. He most likely went with a second group, which left in July under the command of Sir Humphrey Gilbert. This consisted of ten bands, numbering some 1,500 men. Gilbert (born c. 1538) was the half-brother of Walter Ralegh. He was known to his contemporaries as "a man of higher stature than the common sort and of complexion cholericke".[2] In the previous decade he'd served as a Colonel in Ireland, under Sir Henry Sidney. As a commander there he was impulsive, brave, foolish, and brutal. Thomas Churchyard approvingly described an atrocity committed by Gilbert in Munster:

His maner was that the heddes of all those (of what sort soever thei were) which were killed in the daie should be cutte of from their bodies, and brought to the place where he encamped at night, and should there be layd on the grounde by each side of the waie leading into his owne Tente, so that none could come into his Tente for any cuase, but commonly he must passé through a line of heddes, which he used *ad terrorem*...and yet did it bring greater terror to the people, when they sawe the heddes of their dedde fathers, brothers, children, kinsfolk and friends.³

When Spain protested about the arrival of English volunteers in the Low Countries, Elizabeth I blandly explained that they had no official backing and were present in purely a personal capacity.

Why did the George Gascoigne go to the Low Countries? Men like Gilbert went to fight because they enjoyed soldiering and enthusiastically believed in the Protestant cause. Not Gascoigne. In a poem written after his return he breezily explained he'd hoped warfare would make him rich:

He shoots to be a soldier,
Mistrusting all the virtues of the mind,
He trusts the power of his personage.
As though long limbs led by a lusty heart
Might yet suffice to make him rich again⁴

But in what sense would soldiering make the poet rich? Gascoigne doesn't explain. Gascoigne went as a gentleman volunteer, which makes it unlikely that anyone on the English side was offering him any financial inducements. By going he established himself as a loyal English Protestant (and not a spy or an atheist). It created the foundation of possible future patronage by prominent English Protestants who favoured such intervention and also, perhaps, that of a grateful Dutch Protestant establishment. Less high-mindedly, he may have contemplated the attractive prospect of spoils of war from looting. Another traditional way of making money out of sixteenth-century warfare was to capture a high-ranking enemy officer and obtain a handsome ransom.

Money may have been present as a motive in an altogether different sense. The letter of denunciation makes it clear that Gascoigne had at least one angry creditor on his tail. Having had his hopes of becoming an MP dashed, Gascoigne may conceivably have been even more determined not to pay up. Disappearing abroad was an excellent way of evading any debts he was either unable or unwilling to meet. If the experience of imprisonment in Bedford for debt had been an acutely painful one then he had a powerful motive to avoid repeating the experience.

In following the poet's adventures there it needs to be remembered that the

Netherlands in 1572 was not geographically the same as it is today, in name or form. In the sixteenth century the Low Countries were a sprawling Spanish colony made up of what we now know as the Netherlands, Belgium, Luxembourg and a part of north-east France that included Dunkirk, Arras and Cambrai. Physically, as well as politically, much has changed over the centuries. Land reclamation has altered the configurations of this ragged, low-lying coastline of estuaries, islands, ditches and dikes.

The men under Sir Humphrey Gilbert, arrived at Flushing on 10 July. At first Tzeraerts was reluctant to admit the English troops. They spent the first night waiting outside the walls dressed in their armour. Pressure from the town's civilian population soon forced Tzeraerts to give way, but it was an inauspicious beginning.

George Gascoigne was in the Low Countries for approximately four months, and almost certainly returned with Gilbert in November. Gascoigne described his adventures there in four stanzas (95-98) of his poem entitled (in part) *The fruites of Warre, written upon this Theame, Dulce Bellum inexpertis*. It was his longest poem: 1,479 lines plus a preamble, letter of dedication, posy and postscript. In these stanzas he briefly mentions the actions in which he was involved, including skirmishes in the vicinity of Flushing, a night's march from Aardenburg to Bruges and back, a seven days retirement at Aardenburg and trench warfare outside Tergoes (Goes). These were all quite close to each other and Gascoigne's entire experience of the Low Countries in 1572 was restricted to an area which roughly makes up a square some 25 miles long each side, around the modern border between north Belgium and the far south of the Netherlands in the region now known as Zeeland.

Gascoigne's surprisingly perfunctory account of his martial exploits is easily explained. They were inconclusive and ultimately rather pointless, with no spectacular victories. The war in the Low Countries at this time and at this location boiled down to brief, half-hearted sieges of fortified towns and cities and skirmishing between elements of the two rival armies. It was a haphazard affair with no decisive engagements on either side. Gascoigne was a member of a rag-tag army made up of volunteers recruited at home and by the deputies of Flushing, together with experienced soldiers who had fought in France, Ireland and Scotland. They were up against the most powerful and experienced military force in Europe. Their leadership was often poor and there was little to celebrate. In *Anna Karenina*, Tolstoy, who knew a lot about professional soldiering, portrayed Russian volunteers going off to fight for their Serbian comrades as largely made up of drunkards, loudmouths and boasters. And in that novel even Vronsky only goes off to fight as a form of escape from the haunting memory of Anna's terrible end. The English volunteer army was likewise clearly not without problems relating to professionalism and motivation. Gascoigne said he was not one of those who "pinch the painful soldier's pay, / And sheer him out his share in ragged sheets"[5] – meaning "steal the wounded soldier's pay and fleece him out of his share of the spoils by giving him rags".

There was a recurring problem with the men plundering villages they passed through. On 19 July a proclamation was read out to the troops instructing them to leave the local population alone. It seems to have had little effect, for in August the Privy Council wrote to Sir Humphrey Gilbert severely condemning the looting carried out by some English troops. According to Gascoigne there were officers who confiscated plundered property, expressed great anger at the perpetrators then kept these spoils for themselves.[6] In fact looting seems to have been both widespread and regarded as quite acceptable. Gascoigne himself cheerfully owned up to having "fleest in *Flaunders* eke among the rest"[7] – meaning "pillaged in Flanders just like everybody else".

The army's military exploits were equally inglorious. On 16 July Sir Humphrey Gilbert and Tzeraerts launched an attack on Flanders. A force of 1400 Englishmen, 400 Walloons and Flemings and 600 French, crossed the water to Flanders. Some 800 troops – almost certainly including Gascoigne – arrived at the town of Sluis, half way to Bruges. Sluis was of interest as a town of strategic value if the Spanish ever decided to launch an invasion of England. The town was well defended by a citadel, a wall and a wide moat but it was caught unawares by the English, with its gates open. The town's governor intimated that he would deliver the town and its castle to the besiegers but in reality he was only playing for time. He successfully fooled them into waiting there for four days until Spanish troops arrived. Expecting to enter the town in triumph, the English troops instead found themselves under an artillery bombardment. They beat a hasty retreat to Aardenburg.

On the night of 20 July they marched on to Bruges. Gascoigne laconically wrote of what happened next:

The bragge of *Bruges*, where was I that day?
Before the walls, good sir, as brave as best,
And though I marched all armed withouten rest,
From *Aerdenburgh* and back again that night,
Yet mad were he that would have made me knight.[8]

In this context the word "bragge" is double-edged, and Gascoigne used it with his tongue firmly in his cheek. It can mean either "brave challenge" or "boastful folly". The second meaning was the most appropriate. The professional soldier Roger Williams was present and described what happened:

At the breake of day, Sir *Humfrey* sent his trumpet to summon the towne. The trumpeters horse was kild with a shot from the Rampier: and they made answere vnto diuers gentlemen, who were approached neare the walls, that the Count *de Reux* desired all our troupes to stay where wee were; assuring vs, either within foure and twenty hourses the Count would deliuer vs the towne, or finde meanes to hang vs all, at the least our confederates in the towne. *Sir Humfrey* was in great choler; swearing diuers oaths, that hee would put all to the sword, vnlesse they would yield. After staying some sixe or eight houres, *Saras* vnderstanding the warrs better then Sir *Humfrey*, perswaded him to retire: withal assuring him, vnlesse hee would doe it quickly and in good order, hee and his troupes would repent it.[9]

Sir Humphrey Gilbert's bluster and empty threats got him nowhere and his army trudged straight back to Aardenburg. As Gascoigne sardonically noted, in such a futile endeavour the person who knighted the poet for it would truly have been mad. The comment had a barbed edge, though. As the son of Sir John Gascoigne, the writer might well have expected to have been knighted in his turn, according to tradition. But Elizabeth I, unlike her predecessors, was notoriously stingy about handing out honours. Gascoigne may have dreamed of finally being awarded a knighthood as a reward for heroic soldiering in the Low Countries, but none of the actions in which he was involved brought credit to the English army. After a few days at Aardenburg they ambushed a convoy on the way to Bruges, killing many of the troops and seizing artillery and supplies. Then news arrived that a large body of Spanish troops under the command of Juliano Romero was marching into Flanders. The English hurriedly retreated. It was all very different to Agincourt, the heroic myths of knighthood and chivalry, or for that matter the fabulous adventures of *Orlando Furioso*.

Gascoigne said he had seen "full many a *Flushyng* fraye",[10] probably referring to what happened next. From Aardenburg they travelled back to the coast, where ships took them up the Honte of Westerschelde, disembarking them at Baarland on the southern tip of Zuid-Beyeland. The plan was to take the town of Goes (which Gascoigne called "Tergoes" and Williams "Tergoose"). Gilbert and Tzeraerts believed its garrison only amounted to 100 troops and were soon to receive an unexpected surprise. The Spanish force was much greater, saw the enemy ships long before the troops disembarked, and lay in ambush nearby. As the English drew close "they deliuered a hotte volley of shot…and withal charged with some 100 pikes".[11] Panic broke out and men turned and ran, only to be cut down in the confusion by other English troops. Others jumped into ditches and tried to swim to safety. Having inflicted a stunning blow on the attackers, the Spanish force retreated to Goes. The next morning the English advanced to within half a mile of Goes but successful initial skirmishes were not followed up. Williams fumed at Gilbert's incompetence, commenting that "a Commander that enters the enemies countries, ought to know the places that he doth attempt: If not, he ought to be furnished with guides; especially in coming to besiege a towne. But we were so ignorant, that we knew not our owne estate;

much lesse the enemies."[12]

The siege of Goes was abandoned and the English force retired to Zoutelande, a coastal village some five miles north of Flushing. Now it was the Spaniards' turn to underestimate the strength of the enemy. Believing that the English had suffered heavy losses the Spanish launched an attack, only to be routed: "our men gaue the enemie a full oeurthrow, driuing them cleane out of the Campe, and following them in defeate halfe way to *Middleburgh*. After, our men hung a number of them with their owne haulters. This piece of seruice was one of the best and worthiest encounters that our men had from that time to this hower, in all their warres of the *Lowe Countries*."[13] However, the defenders "scaped not scot-free for wee had slaine and hurt about two hundred and fifty; many of them Officers; and amongst others the Captaines *Bouser*, *Bedes*, and *Bostocke* English".[14] The first of these captains is almost certainly the same man who inspired the only epitaph Gascoigne ever wrote, "*Gascoignes Epitaph upon capitaine* Bourcher *late slayne in the warres in* Zeland, *the whiche hath bene termed the tale of a stone as followeth*".[15]

The epitaph purports to be told by Bourcher's gravestone, which is personified as "Marmaduke Marblestone". It describes the soldier's many qualities and tells how he fell in the thick of battle "with bloudy sword in hande". Lying wounded in bed after the battle Bourcher heard new fighting break out and cried for a weapon:

I will to field (quoth he) and God before.
Which said, he sailed into more quiet coast,
Still praising God, and so gave up the ghost.

Bourcher died a hero and a good Christian. An epitaph could say no less.

The rout of the Spanish encouraged Gilbert and Tzeraerts to make another attempt on Goes. This time a combined force of 3,000 English, French and Walloons disembarked and set up a base at Biezelinge, south-east of the town. A night-time march took them to within a mile of Goes, and an attack began at dawn. The Spanish troops surrendered the fort beyond the walls and hurriedly retreated into the town. A siege now began in earnest, lasting from 29 August until 1 October. Gascoigne wrote:

I was again in trench before *Tergoes*,
(I dare not say in siege for both mine ears)

The allied forces excavated trenches close to the city walls and shelled the bulwarks. Gascoigne's denial that it was a siege was a canny acknowledgement that this military action had only the tacit, not the official, support of Elizabeth I. His metaphor alludes to the penalty for sedition and slander: the slicing-off of both ears. Its comic tone expresses the confidence of a privileged member of Tudor English society. Punishment by amputation or branding of body parts was a common sight in the streets of London but not something George Gascoigne was ever in serious danger of undergoing. But it also hints at the fatally flawed nature of the enterprise. It was not a siege because it was botched. Sir Humphrey and the Dutch commander quarrelled bitterly about tactics. Worse still, a nighttime attempt to scale the town walls was beaten off with massive loss of life. Williams described the disaster:

> After midnight, we dislodged from our quarter some two thousand of our best men, all in Camisadoes with scaling ladders, God knows like ignorant souldiers: else we would neuer haue attempted a scalado on such a troupe. For lightly a scalado neuer takes place, vnlesse it bee on a simple troupe, or a negligent guarde, hauing a rampier or fort to defend. Notwithstanding ambition and courage so pushed vs on, that Sir *Humfrey* and *Saras* being approached, aduanced vp their ladders: so did a great number of Gentlemen and souldiers on sundry ladders. The enemy politickely kept close vntill many were ready to enter. Then they discharged a voley of shot full in our faces, killing many. And withal, their armed men aduanced to the push of the Pike; In such sort, that they dismounted the most without ladders. At which terror we retyred without commandement, vntill wee came vnder the dike where the enemies shot could not hurt vs.[16]

The end came when the attackers were outflanked by unexpected Spanish reinforcements. On the night of 20 October, in a brilliant thrust, the elderly veteran Cristóbal de Mondragon, assisted by a local guide, led a double column of 3,000 troops on a night-time march at low tide across the shallow waters of the "Verdronken Lands". Breast-high in water, they had just six hours to wade some eleven miles to the island of Zierikzee before the tide came in – a mission which was accomplished with the loss of just 9 men. Williams blamed what he bitterly described as *"the negligence and ignorance of our Gouernour"*[17] (i.e. Sir Humphrey Gilbert) for the debacle because, if a proper watch had been kept, Mondragon's force could have been annihilated. As it was, the besiegers fled in disarray, pursued by the Spanish:

> Wherefore our disorder was great, in seeking meanes to escape into our nauy; which anchored within a harquebush shot of the fort. A great number were drowned, besides those that were slain; and some yielded vnto the enemy... Thus ended our ignorant poor siege. And but for the skuts and small boats which came hard by the shore to recieue vs in, all had been lost. Our blowe was so great, that Sir *Humfrey* and the most of our men not being acquainted with such disasters, sought all meanes to returne into *England*.[18]

Sir Humphrey Gilbert sailed home on 5 November 1572, with around 800 men. His biographer concluded that "As a leader of men, Gilbert was not a success. Failure and disappointment met him on every hand."[19] Gascoigne did his best to put a brave face on the defeat, concluding:

> Yet surely this withouten bragge or boast,
> Our English bloudes did there full many a deed,
> Which may be Chronicled in every coast,
> For bold attempts, and well it was agreed,
> That had their heads been ruled by wary heed,
> Some other feat had been attempted then,
> To show their force like worthy English men.[20]

This was whistling in the wind. The expedition had largely been a shambles, which had achieved very little. Moreover, Gascoigne's criticisms of the military strategy and Sir Humphrey Gilbert are so muted as to be barely noticeable. But his long poem on the theme "Dulce bellum inexpertis" ("war is attractive to those who have no experience of it") makes it clear that he viewed war as largely an absurd and futile business. Gascoigne was one of the first English war poets and also one of the first anti-war poets. It is an historic irony that those English troops who found themselves floundering in muddy trenches in the same region some 345 years later had probably never heard of Gascoigne or his Flanders verses.

Old Babe

After describing the end of the prolonged and fruitless assault on Goes, Gascoigne wrote:

> Since that siege raised I roamed have about,
> In Zeeland, Holland, Waterland, and all,
> By sea, by land, by air, and all throughout,
> As leaping lots, and chance did seem to call,
> Now here, now there, as fortune trilde the ball[21]   [rolled]

Gascoigne's image of himself as a kind of winged entity flitting here and there across the watery Low Countries omits the mundane fact of his presence in England on at least one occasion before his return to the wars. But the image – penned some two or three years later – embodies the sheer excitement of this phase of his career. The next twelve months were to be the most important in his writing life. The imagery and erratic word order aptly express the mobility and elusiveness of his movements at this time.

It is possible but unlikely that Gascoigne slipped away from the siege of

Goes back to London to take charge of his masque at the Montague double wedding. The wedding evidently took place some time between 15 September and 6 October. We know this because of a complaint by Thomas Giles of London who was appalled at possible damage to royal property resulting from the Yeoman of the Revels renting out royal costumes. That was what he said, anyway. In fact what really enraged Giles, who was a haberdasher, was that his own trade was being damaged by the Yeoman's sideline in cheap rentals. He grumbled that between those dates was rented out "to the maryage of the dawter of my lorde Montague…the coper clothe of golde gownes".[22]

It is a massive irony that Gascoigne's masque in praise of Catholic military victories in foreign lands should have been performed at the very moment he was in a Flanders trench fighting the papists. It is just possible, of course, that part of his motive for volunteering for military service was precisely to put some distance between himself and the Montagues. Foreign service provided him with the perfect excuse for not attending the wedding. What the Montagues thought of this is another matter entirely – always assuming that they knew what he was up to on the other side of the North Sea.

*

That summer an event occurred which horrified Protestant Europe. In Paris, on St Bartholomew's Day, 24 August 1572, some 4,000 Protestants were butchered by Catholic mobs. It supplied another strong motive for the poet to seek support in other quarters than those of Catholic lords. It may not be entirely a coincidence that once back home in England Gascoigne next sought the patronage of one of England's most ardent Protestant aristocrats.

This man was Arthur Grey, fourteenth Baron Grey de Wilton (otherwise known as Lord Grey of Wilton). He is mainly remembered now for his two years as Lord Deputy of Ireland and for his association with Edmund Spenser. Spenser cast him as the figure of Artegall in *The Faerie Queene* and wrote a dedicatory sonnet to him, calling him "the pillar of my life". But those connections developed after Gascoigne's death. When Gascoigne knew him Lord Grey was simply an aristocrat whose star was rising at court. He was under consideration as a suitable future governor of Ireland, and in June 1572 was installed as a Knight of the Garter. Grey came from a distinguished family and was a particularly zealous Protestant. A letter dated 19 September 1572 has survived in which Grey alludes to the recent Paris massacre and invites Lord Burghley to "gess of th'encrease of my grief by the late horrible and tirannicall dealings in Fraunce" (adding ominously that he hopes "hyr Majestie may have the wysedoome too follow and magnitude to execute the thynges that maye divert the same from hence"). But, unlike Grey, Elizabeth I was a cautious pragmatist, not a fundamentalist hardliner.

Gascoigne spent part of the winter of 1572-3 with Lord Grey – an experience which inspired him to write one of his finest poems. The invitation probably came about as a result of the mutual friendship of both men with the Dives of Bedfordshire. Grey was presumably aware of Gascoigne's abilities as a writer, though he may only have seen the poet's more respectable output. Grey's estate at Whaddon in Buckinghamshire was just twenty miles west of Cardington Manor. Gascoigne must have stayed with Grey at his large country mansion, then named Whaddon Hall. The Hall (which still exists, though the current building is a nineteenth-century one, built on the site of the older hall) occupied an imposing site on a hilltop above the village, with spectacular views of the surrounding countryside. Elizabeth I twice stayed at Whaddon Hall during royal progresses. A few minutes' walk away were the village and, on another hilltop, the twelfth-century church of St Mary's. Beyond that, to the south, was the large expanse of forest and parkland known as Whaddon Chase. It was this landscape which had brought Gascoigne to Whaddon Hall, for he was here to hunt. Whaddon Chase was a deer park and Lord Grey, who was Keeper of the Chase, was an enthusiastic huntsman. Hunting, in the form of falconry, was embodied in his coat of arms, which showed a falcon on a glove.

Lord Grey seems to have enjoyed Gascoigne's company and to have taken a liking to him. On the face of it the friendship was an unlikely one, yet he was to become Gascoigne's most important literary patron. Gascoigne was the poet of love and erotic innuendo and a mocker of the concept of heresy; Grey was a sober, zealous Protestant who loathed the old religion. For Gascoigne to shift from the patronage of the ardent Catholic Anthony Browne, Viscount Montague, to that of Arthur, Lord Grey of Wilton, was truly to jump from one end of the sixteenth-century theological spectrum to the other. But Grey had probably not seen Gascoigne's more risqué productions. He may even only have seen the religious verse. What endeared Gascoigne to Grey, apart from the fact that they were both of the same generation, was perhaps less literature, hunting or religion than military matters.

Grey was born at Hammes, in the English Pale in France, in 1536. He was the eldest son of William, Lord Grey de Wilton. As a child he was trained to take an interest in soldiering and warfare, and he first saw active service at the battle of St Quentin in 1557. He was also present with his father at Guisnes (or Guînes) when it was besieged and captured by the French. Grey was released from a short captivity and returned to England to raise the massive ransom demanded for his father's release. This accomplished, he joined his father on a military intervention in Scotland in 1560. In a skirmish at Leith he was wounded. On the death of his father in 1562 he succeeded to the title and retired to Whaddon, where he concentrated on his duties as chief magistrate for Buckinghamshire. Grey wrote an account of his father's military career and the siege of Guisnes for the Tudor historian Holinshed, parts of which were incorporated more or less verbatim in the *Chronicles* (1571). The manuscript was rediscovered in 1844 and subsequently published as *A Commentary of the Services and Charges of William Lord Grey of Wilton, K.G.*

Gascoigne's own exploits as a soldier fighting for the Protestant cause in the Low Countries would have been of keen interest to Grey. As military men they doubtless exchanged war stories in the timeless manner of old soldiers. When Gascoigne returned from the Low Countries a few months after his first visit to Grey he wrote a second poem to him, which concludes with the promise of an exciting update of the military situation there:

> And I shall well my seelly self content   [poor]
> To come alone unto my lovely Lord,
> And unto him (when rhyming sport is spent)
> To tell some sad and reasonable word,
> Of *Holland's* state, the which I will present,
> In charts, in maps, and eke in models made[23]   [also]

The warmth of that word "lovely" (meaning "charming" or "attractive") is striking. Gascoigne is starting to purr with pleasure at Lord Grey's patronage. He wants to see him again, and soon. More, he wants to see him "alone". He has charts, a map, he's even made models (presumably of forts). No trouble is too much where Lord Grey is concerned.

The poem which Gascoigne wrote about his first visit to Grey's estate is one of his most popular and has often been anthologised, usually under the title "Gascoigne's Woodmanship" (which abbreviates the wordy introduction to the poem).[24] Some critics have even hailed it as his masterpiece. Addressed directly to a named person and consisting of 150 lines, it bears some resemblances to his poem to Bartholomew Withypoll, which is just four lines longer and has an identical rhyme scheme. But whereas his "councell" to Withypoll takes the form of a jaunty speech to someone who is his equal, Gascoigne's address to Lord Grey is altogether more deferential and, though at times comic, it entirely lacks the suggestive innuendo and risqué allusions to boozing, whoring and syphilis found in the first poem. To Withypoll, Gascoigne offers witty advice; to Lord Grey, merely a rueful summary of his own life.

"Gascoigne's Woodmanship" whimsically describes the poet's incompetence as a huntsman. The title involves a little grovelling on Gascoigne's part. As the poem's prose preface explains, it refers to Lord Grey humorously calling him "one of his wodmen" (i.e. one of the forest workers who assisted in a deer hunt). The poet, who normally had a haughty insistence on his status as an *Esquire* or knight's son, deferentially identifies himself as "master Gascoigne". It is most unlikely that Gascoigne was an incompetent hunter, although he may well have missed when firing an unfamiliar crossbow. Equally likely he may tactfully have let his host make all the hits. The poet uses Lord Grey's skill as a foil for his own comic incompetence.

Although there are no topographical details to indicate the setting, the background to the poem is undoubtedly Whaddon Chase. The poem describes how Gascoigne fires his crossbow at passing deer and repeatedly misses. He then commits a *faux pas* by hitting a deer which is "but carren" (i.e. a doe with young, unfit for eating). Gascoigne then uses the conceit of himself as a hopeless shot to explain that his whole life has been one of missed targets. His "wanton wits went all awry" and he "shot sometimes to hit Philosophy" – presumably at Trinity College, Cambridge. At Gray's Inn "he shot to be a man of law". When that failed he tried the life of a courtier, but there too "he shot awry". Only recently he has tried the life of a soldier,

But flussing frays have taught him such a part, [Flushing]
That now he thinks the wars yield no such gain.

Gascoigne requests the help of his noble friend "To train him yet into some better trade". The poet then describes his own lack of ruthless ambition, his unwillingness to beg in the street or to steal from simple soldiers and the way others who lack his education or experience seem to succeed where he always fails. Returning to the image of the shot doe, Gascoigne suggests it may be a symbol from Jehova (or God):

And when I see the milk hang in her teat,
Me thinks it sayeth, old babe now learn to suck,
Who in thy youth could never learn the feat
To hit the whites which live with all good luck.

This faintly grotesque metaphor of Gascoigne as an "old babe" sucking on a teat and drinking milk merges with the image of hitting the white circle at the centre of an archer's target. It brings the poem back to its beginning with a daringly bizarre conceit more akin to that of the metaphysical poetry of the early seventeenth century than that of the Tudor age. What Gascoigne is hinting here is that God has brought him to Lord Grey's estate to demonstrate how much this good-hearted bungler needs a change in his fortunes. That change, implicitly, will only occur with the help of the noble Lord himself. It is an appeal for patronage, or to put it another way, perhaps the finest begging letter in the history of English verse.

By now the "old babe" was some 38 or 39 years old. By the standards of the age he was well into middle age. Behind "Gascoigne's Woodmanship" lies the shadow of another poem written at about the same time, namely the epitaph to Captain Bourcher. Gascoigne quite probably didn't know the Captain particularly well. Bourcher was simply an admired professional soldier, cut down in his prime. It's more than likely that he didn't get the marble gravestone imagined by Gascoigne but was simply tossed into a mass grave along with the other corpses. "*Bourcher* is dead, whom each of you did know," the poet wrote, addressing his fellow soldiers, "Yet no man writes one word to paint his praise." The thought must surely have occurred to Gascoigne that had he died in Flanders, who would have written his epitaph? And how would anyone have summed up his life and death, "the valiant acts, the fame"?

In writing "Gascoigne's Woodmanship", the poet was weighing up his life so far, and what he saw was a farce of comic misadventures. As an account of his life it was highly partial, of course. There was nothing about his childhood or his distinguished ancestry or his amours. His marriage is not mentioned, unless obliquely in the passage which compresses the years between 1561 and 1572 into just four lines[25] and states: "the taste of misery, / Hath been always full bitter in his bit". If this is an allusion to his years as a married man (and it is hard to see how else to interpret these lines) the images of a horse being restrained and of a sour taste in the mouth are hardly flattering to Elizabeth Breton.

Gascoigne was spending less and less time at Walthamstow during this period of his life. Four months away in the Low Countries, a winter interlude with Lord Grey, and then in March 1573 he was off again across the North Sea. Evidently his appeal to Grey for patronage had worked, for his next poem[26] described the "*voyage into* Hollande" and was "*written to the ryghte honourable the Lorde Grey of* Wilton". Quite what patronage meant in these circumstances is elusive, as this was a delicate matter among gentlemen. It could involve some form of employment, or hospitality, or a recommendation to some other influential figure. Ideally, it meant a gift of money.

Whatever it was, Gascoigne was pleased. At 360 lines the new poem for Grey was more than twice the length of the previous one appealing for patronage. As a narrative poem "*Gascoignes voyage into* Hollande, An. 1572" (old style dating) tells a dramatic, true-life tale of a journey to Breyll (nowadays known as Brielle, in the Netherlands). Gascoigne describes leaving Gravesend on 19 March 1573 for a ship moored off Queenborough (a port on the Isle of Sheppey, at the mouth of the Thames estuary). The ship set sail the next day but ran into difficulties on 21 March. It found itself in dangerously shallow water off the treacherous Dutch coast and hit the bottom. The helm was damaged, the vessel became impossible to steer and then the keel split, causing water to pour in. While some manned the pumps, others desperately tossed freight overboard. The ship began to tip over and in a panic some of the passengers jumped into the sea, only to be crushed and drowned as it righted itself. The ship's lifeboat was launched but was overloaded. Gascoigne opted to remain on board, which turned out to be a wise decision. The lifeboat was swamped by waves and sank, drowning its twenty or so occupants. At that point the wind changed, the foresail filled and the ship began to lurch out to sea. The anchor was thrown overboard but then the anchor rope was quickly severed as the ship threatened to split in two. Someone had the bright idea of firing off the vessel's big guns as a distress call. A small sailing ship steered a path to them, saw the trouble they were in – and sailed away. On the pier at Brielle the Dutch watched the scene with indifference until some Englishmen forced them at swordpoint to effect a rescue. Recovering on land, the visitors later discovered that the ship's Dutch pilot had made off with its cargo of "powder, shotte, and all our best araye".

It's a racy, vibrant work which captures the excitement and drama of this near-disaster. Charles Nicholl has called it "a superb action-poem, a crackling story…that races over its rhyme-scheme like something by Browning".[27] But Gascoigne cannot resist turning it into a moral fable designed to appeal to Lord Grey's sombre Protestant sensibility. At first he penitently presents it as a kind of fable of his younger days:

> Vouchsafe my Lord (*en bon gré*) for to take   [in good worth]
> This trusty tale the story of my youth,
> This Chronicle which of my self I make,
> To show my Lord what healplesse happe ensewth,
> When heady youth will gad without a guide,
> And raunge untied in leas of liberty

But this is just window-dressing. The analogy is implausible as Gascoigne is simply a passenger on a boat which strays into shallow waters as a result of the pilot's incompetence. Free will doesn't come into it. More pointedly, it is seen as an example of what happens

> when bare need a starting hole hath spied
> To peep abroad from mother Misery,
> And buildeth castles in the welkin wide,
> In hope thereby to dwell with wealth and ease.

This reprises the message of "Gascoigne's Woodmanship". The poet delineates himself as a poor, impoverished wretch reduced to "bare need" (but too proud to beg in the streets). He is like a hunted animal, who spots a hiding place ("a starting hole") and uses it to survey the surroundings, from a perspective of all-embracing misery. The image combines that of a wounded animal with, perhaps, an unhappily married man. This figure lurking in the undergrowth then turns into a dreamer, building castles in the air. Gascoigne dreams of attaining "wealth and ease" – but then look what happens. His ship founders! But fortunately God was on hand to hear his prayers and save him. Thanks to the Lord he has been spared and he can't wait to see Lord Grey again to tell him all about the state of things in Holland, "If God of heaven my purpose not prevent".

We can be quite confident the God of heaven did not prevent it. In fact in Gascoigne's poem the Lord of creation and the Lord Grey of Wilton are almost equals, easily confused. Gascoigne clearly had the measure of his aristocrat Protestant patron and adjusted his self-image accordingly. When things go wrong for the ship there are solemn prayers, followed by a second set when the ship goes aground. Gascoigne is anxious for his patron to know how he personally rose to the occasion:

> As for my self: I here protest my Lord,
> My words were these: O God in heaven on height,
> Behold me not as now a wicked wyght,   [person]
> A sack of sin, a wretch ywrapt in wrath,
> Let no fault past (O Lord) offend thy sight,
> But weigh my will which now those faults doth loath,
> And of this mercy pity this our plight.

And much more, in this wearisomely pious vein. Gascoigne narrates in a tone of complete incredulity that there were those on board who instead of praying for divine assistance put their faith instead in the hand pumps:

> Alas (quod I) our pump good God must be
> Our sail, our stern, our tackling, and our trust.

It is hard to forgive Gascoigne for such shamelessly opportunistic – and highly implausible – lines as these. But then it is equally painful to see the poet failing to resist a terrible pun on "pilot" and "(Pontius) Pilate". Arthur, Lord Grey of Wilton may have proved a valuable patron to Gascoigne but it cannot be said that he always brought out the best in the poet. "*Gascoignes voyage into Hollande*" is a broken-backed poem in which a searingly vivid and compelling tale of a near-shipwreck is padded out with slabs of piety and anti-papist rhetoric designed to appeal to Grey's narrow religious sensibility. His patron's name in fact seems all too unintentionally symbolic. Xenophobia bubbles up again in this poem, and Gascoigne supplies the noble Lord with plenty of material to flatter his prejudices – cowardly Dutchmen of every variety, an incompetent, thieving pilot who may have been bribed by the Duke of Alva, the Governor of Brielle in a drunken stupor amid his sleeping sluttish mistresses, old nuns who are pimps and young nuns who are whores.

Grey was evidently delighted by the poem. Years later he seems to have drawn it to the attention of his young protégé Edmund Spenser. Spenser's gushing dedicatory sonnet to Grey, which prefaces *The Faerie Queene*, apologises for its "Rude rymes", much as Gascoigne deferentially shrugged off his own "worthless verse" and "ranging rhyme". Spenser's invitation to Grey to "Vouchsafe, in worth, this small guift to receave" is clearly an allusion to Gascoigne's "Vouchsafe my Lord (*en bon gré*) [in good worth] for to take / This trusty tale". Edmund Spenser was diplomatically keen to signal his knowledge of, and admiration for, his predecessor in his patron's favour.

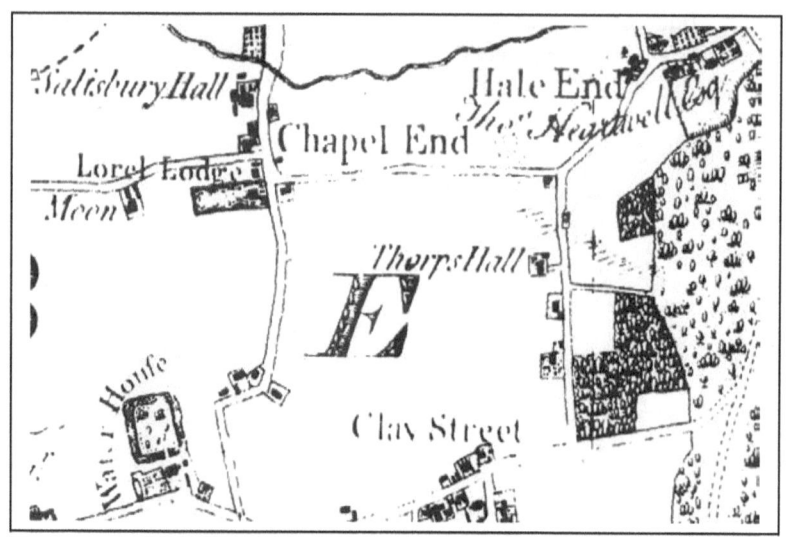

Plate 23. "Thorps Hall" (Thorpe Hall) in the eighteenth century, with Salisbury Hall in the top left corner, just south of the River Ching.

Plate 24. The site of Gascoigne's Thorpe Hall garden, looking east towards Epping Forest.

Plate 25. The Gascoigne memorial (with inaccurate year of birth) on Forest Road, Walthamstow, close to the site of Thorpe Hall, where his major writing was produced.

Plate 26. The coat of arms of William Lord Grey of Wilton, K.G., father of Arthur Lord Grey of Wilton.

20: Waterland

Gascoigne, perhaps unsurprisingly, did not stay long in the Low Countries. The following month he seems to have been back in London, at that place of mixed memories, Red Cross Street. On 17 April 1573 at St Giles, Cripplegate, was held the funeral of Reginald Grey, 5th Earl of Kent. It was recorded that among those present was the Earl of Bedford's servant, Gascoigne. This might just conceivably have been the poet's brother, John. But the strong likelihood is that it was George Gascoigne. Grey (who was unrelated to Arthur, Lord Grey of Wilton) had been one of the poet's contemporaries at Gray's Inn and the year before Gascoigne had given verbal testimony in the House of Commons in support of Grey in his land dispute with Lord Henry Compton.

The description of Gascoigne as a servant of the Earl of Bedford is revealing. The legal dispute between them three years earlier had evidently been resolved and forgotten. The poet would later dedicate a weighty theological treatise to the Earl, as well as a moral tract to Lewis Dive. With lip-smacking anti-papist verse such as the "*voyage into* Hollande" and as someone in the process of reinventing himself as, literally, a soldier for Christ, it seems that George Gascoigne was now becoming a favoured son of the Bedfordshire establishment and some of the country's leading Protestants. But though pandering to those of a pious disposition, Gascoigne was about to blot his copy book in a spectacular fashion. 1573 was the year that saw the publication of *A Hundreth Sundrie Flowres*. It would create a scandal and, to those able to identify its true author, would shatter any image of him as a humble, devout, God-fearing man.

*

The preface "to the reader" by "H.W." at the beginning of *A Discourse of the Adventures Passed by Master F.J.* explains that he first encountered the book's contents when he was loaned the manuscript by his "familiar friend Master G.T." the previous August. "H.W." explains that he entreated his friend "A.B." to print it "as one that thought better to please a number by common commoditie then to feede the humor of any private parson by needlesse singularitie". Seeking pardon for his "rashnes", "H.W." signs off, "From my lodging nere the Strande the .xx. of January. 1572."

The dating is almost certainly old style. The story put forward in this bogus preface with its invented characters suggests that Gascoigne finally contemplated publishing the writings of a lifetime during his first experience of warfare in the Low Countries. Significantly, August 1572 was the month Captain Bourcher died. If Gascoigne identified in any way with this professional soldier, he might well have wondered about the fate of his own manuscripts after his death. (His anxieties were probably justified. When he died he apparently left unpublished work, which subsequently vanished.) Publication also offered the prospect of an agreeable lump sum payment from a publisher.

In 1573 – quite possibly in January, the same date as "H.W."'s preface – a publisher struck a deal with Gascoigne and printing of the book began. It was almost certainly published before the end of the year, although we cannot be absolutely certain of this since the official Stationers' Register containing book entries from July 1571 to July 1576 has disappeared. The business of publication was on the face of it fairly straightforward. A writer sold a publisher a manuscript in return for a single sum of money. There were no royalties payable. The publisher, who was often also the printer, profited from sales of the book. Copyright did not exist in the form we know it today but the fact that all titles were supposed to be registered gave the publisher certain proprietorial rights.

Gascoigne's publisher was Richard Smith and the printer was Henry Bynneman. They were both major figures in contemporary Tudor publishing. By the standards of the time, *A Hundreth Sundrie Flowres* was a big book, a quarto printed from 52 sheets, producing a maximum of 416 pages. Bynneman's total work output for 1573 has been calculated at 466 sheets or 1.55 sheets per working day – a fairly standard production rate for a shop with three presses. All the signs are that, very unusually, *A Hundreth Sundrie Flowres* was printed over a period of many months, with production halted once or possibly even twice. One of the reasons for this is probably that the contents of the book had not been fully settled when printing began. A second complicating factor in understanding the form the volume took is that the author was not around for its completion. At least one glaring error in the book went unnoticed.

The bibliographer Adrian Weiss made a special study of the problems posed by the first edition of *A Hundreth Sundrie Flowres*.[1] After examining the fonts used for emphasis, headings and quotations, Weiss concluded that Bynneman farmed out some of the printing to Henry Middleton and his partner Thomas East, who were responsible for 18 sheets (or around one third of the book). Weiss reconstructed a printing schedule lasting at least eight months, with long delays in production. His argument that "A delay in printing…may indicate belated delivery of copy in segments" seems plausible if printing began some time in January or February, before Gascoigne's March voyage to Brielle.

It is conceivable that Gascoigne frantically wrote – or rewrote – *The Adventures of Master F.J.* during the spring of 1573, though it probably belongs to an earlier phase of his career. Most of the poetry in the volume had clearly been written long before. The only verses definitely composed in 1573 are the two poems dedicated to Lord Grey. The long, unfinished narrative poem "Dan Bartholmew of Bathe" may also have been written at this time, though it is equally possible that it consists of early material hastily revised and tossed into the volume at the very last moment.[2] It is also possible that the garden poems were written at this time. "The Printer to the Reader", though obviously composed by Gascoigne, must have been a late addition to the collection. The two letters by "G.T." and the address to the reader by "H.W." may also have been written around this time. Delays in receiving author's copy could then have been compounded by other factors. Weiss suggests that completion was a low priority for Bynneman and that *A Hundreth Sundrie Flowres* may well have been set aside to allow him to print topical theological or political texts which couldn't wait.

Weiss believes that the bibliographical evidence shows that copy was delivered at intervals to Bynneman in some six to eight separate manuscript segments between late January and mid-May 1573. He speculates that the novel was written at this time. He also asserts that "Gascoigne neither was involved in the printing of the book nor saw any printed sheets." However, this last point has been convincingly challenged by Pigman,[2] who notes a proof correction in *Supposes* which is most unlikely to have been anything other than authorial. But that Gascoigne did not see the proofs in the later stages of production is not in serious doubt.

With the whole (or almost the whole) of *A Hundreth Sundrie Flowres* with his publisher, Gascoigne once more returned on military service to fight the Spaniards. He probably went in the second half of May, with the ten companies under the command of Colonel Thomas Morgan. He'd been promoted and now enjoyed the rank of captain.

After his unimpressive experiences the previous year and his near-shipwreck in March, why did Gascoigne return to the Low Countries? He may have still been on the run from his creditors and determined to avoid another spell of imprisonment. More credibly, he was now evidently enjoying the favour of two prominent Protestants, and there could hardly be a better way of pleasing the Earl of Bedford and Lord Grey of Wilton than by heading off again to support the brave Protestants of the Netherlands in their righteous struggle against papist oppression. Quite possibly he missed the excitement of warfare. Winter turned to spring, and though strolling up and down his "close walk" in Walthamstow was an agreeable leisure activity, perhaps he longed once more for the thrill of action. Gabriel Harvey thought that restlessness was a central feature of the poet's temperament. At the end of the "Weedes" section of his copy of the *Posies* he wrote that "in his studies, & Looves, [Gascoigne] thowght upon ye Warres; in the warres, mused upon his studies, & Looves".[3]

Gascoigne may well have been musing about love during his early weeks back in the Low Countries. We first hear of him at The Hague in July 1573, when an anonymous letter described the presence of Captain Gascoigne and his men. According to the letter, Gascoigne did not fight at Haarlem, which capitulated on 12 July 1573 after heroically holding out for seven months against a massive Spanish force of 30,000 troops. It was at The Hague that Gascoigne became involved in some way with a local woman. Like the lover in the poet's enigmatic sonnet "When steadfast friendship (bound by holy oath)",[4] he gave her a miniature of himself. He may have had "meat enough" at Thorpe Hall, but clearly once he was far from home his eye began to wander. Gascoigne's marginal note to "the *Haghe*" in *The fruites of Warre* (stanza 126) gushes that it is "The pleasauntest village (as I thinke) that is in Europe" – indicating that he had very happy memories of his time there.

"Looves" was also the theme of one last contribution to *A Hundreth Sundrie Flowres*, which Gascoigne may have been working on at this time and sent back across the North Sea to his publisher. It could broadly be said that the poetry in *A Hundreth Sundrie Flowres* gets more impressive and versatile as the collection progresses. But that all comes to a messy end with "Dan Bartholmew of Bathe". This long, ramshackle poem in twelve sections reads like discarded early verse which has been hastily patched together and updated.[5] Quite why Gascoigne wanted to include it is far from clear. Possibly it had occurred to him that the poems in *A Hundreth Sundrie Flowres* did not actually add up to one hundred in number. But even with "Dan Bartholmew of Bathe" it is impossible to get the contents to add up to one hundred in a straightforward way. Should one count the poems in *The Adventures of Master F.J.*? If not, should the single-line Latin motto on the stone in Gascoigne's garden be counted? Is "Dan Bartholmew of Bathe" one poem or twelve poems? It is possible to arrive at a total of one hundred poems but only by selectively fiddling the figures.

"Dan Bartholmew of Bathe" tells the story of a young man's searing first love for a woman who is disguised under the name Ferenda Natura ("nature must be endured"). It purports to have an objective narrator named "The reporter", who in parts one, three and twelve sets the scene and comments on the love affair, putting a frame around Bartholmew's outpourings. But the objectivity of "The reporter" is wafer thin. There is little difference between his tone and that of Bartholmew. At the end, Bartholmew dies of a broken heart and "The reporter" muses on woman's faithlessness.

The situation which the poem develops very loosely resembles the one in *The Adventures of Master F.J.* but it lacks the concrete social setting of the novel. The town of Bath gets a perfunctory mention as the scene of Bartholmew's passionate suffering, but it could be anywhere. The title "Dan Bartholmew of Bathe" may be an attempt to suggest that the poem is a kind of male version of Chaucer's *The Wife of Bath's Tale* (or at least *The Prologe of the Wyves Tale of Bathe*). But equally Gascoigne may have had in mind the contemporary expression, "Go to Bath!" meaning "You're crazy!" There's certainly no shortage of derangement in the poem once Bartholmew has broken up with Ferenda and bemoans his fate with "rolling eyes" and "raving rhyme".[6] The poem received the enthusiastic endorsement of one nineteenth-century critic, William Minto, who praised its "abundance of comic vigor and mad rollicking humor" but it has since fallen into obscurity.[7]

"Dan" is not an abbreviation of "Daniel" but is an archaic form of "sir" or "master", and a rough English translation of the Spanish "Don", as in *Don Quixote*. But the hero's full name sounds suspiciously like a collage involving some kind of private joke between Gascoigne and his two friends Daniel and Bartholomew Withypoll (and "Bath" might itself pun on "Batt" or some other abbreviation of Bartholomew). The type of erotic reference found in the poem of advice to Bartholomew Withypoll recurs here. We learn of Bartholmew's eventual sexual success with Ferenda:

> The prick of kind can never be unplaced,
> And so it seemed by this dainty dame,
> Whom he at last with labour did reclaim.[8]

Bartholmew's "labour" is, of course, sexual intercourse. Here "kind" is used in the old sense of "nature". But Gascoigne is also punning on a now obsolete meaning of the French word "la nature" as the vagina. "Kind" also plays on "cunt", with the echo more pronounced in Tudor pronunciation than in modern usage. Gascoigne was not alone in using the word "kind" for sexual innuendo. Stephen Booth suggests that when Shakespeare wrote "thy deep kindness" in Sonnet 152 he intended "some genital reference...suggested by the consonants of *kind*-, and/or by the surface relationship between *kindness* and 'deed of kind' (*Merchant of Venice*, I.iii.80)".[9]

In short, Ferenda Natura could mean "Ferenda Cunt" – or "Cunt must be endured". There is a great deal more in this vein, which was presumably intended to have the Withypoll brothers in stitches. The old "queynt array" or "cunt clothes" joke is wheeled out again. Sir Bartholmew duly spends lingering days in trifling toys, he whets his tools to carve his content, he wearies his web, his pleasures are pent in a pinfold, he lodges in pleasure's princely port.

But Gascoigne's heart perhaps wasn't entirely in it. There is a sense of him going through the motions. The tone is sometimes horribly wrong, as in Bartholmew's melancholy memory of the time he triumphed in love's war, "When first I got the Bulwarks of thy breast".[10] This is supposed to be heroic and stately but it's hard not to laugh. Elsewhere the erotic innuendo co-exists uneasily with the high-minded Petrarchan passion which dominates the poem. When Ferenda dumps him for someone else Bartholmew moans with dismay, freezes in hope, swelters in chilling heat, melts in tears and suffers the pain of a swelling heart. These stale Petrarchan clichés are taken to their logical conclusion as Bartholmew wastes away, grows prematurely old and dies. But somehow it is difficult to feel touched by his demise.

Even Shakespeare, who normally found Gascoigne inspirational and well worth pilfering from, was unmoved. If the mocking lines in Sonnet 130 –

> My mistress' eyes are nothing like the sun (1)
>
> If hairs be wires, black wires grow on her head (4)
>
> I have seen roses damasked, red and white,
> But no such roses see I in her cheeks (5-6)

– parody a specific source, it is surely these excruciating lines in praise of Ferenda's beauty:

> First, for her head, the hairs were not of gold,
> But of some metal far more fine,
> Whereof each crinet seemed to behold,   [hair]
> Like glistring wires against the sun that shine,
> And therewithal the blazing of her eyne,
> Was like the beams of *Titan*, truth to tell,   [Titan = the sun]
> Which glads us all that in this world do dwell.
>
> Upon her cheeks the lily and the rose
> Did entremeete, with equal change of hue[11]

The removal of Feranda's Petrarchan charms from Bartholmew's bed releases floods of Petrarchan suffering. But perhaps there is an erotic joke here too:

> These thoughts (dear sweet) within my breast I bear,
> And to my long home, thus my life it hasteth.
> Herewith I feel the drops of sweltering sweat,
> Which trickle down my face, enforced so,
> And in my body feel I likewise beat
> A burning heart, which tosseth to and fro.
> Thus all in flames I cinderlike consume,
> And were it not that wanhope lends me wind,
> Soon might I fey my fancies all in fume,
> And like a ghost my ghost his grave might find,
> But freezing hope doth blow full in my face,
> And cold of cares becomes my cordial,
> So that I still endure that irksome place,
> Where sorrow seethes to scald my skin withal.[12]

This is not just Petrarchan cliché. It is also a thinly disguised account of the symptoms and conventional sixteenth-century treatment for the pox (a term which encompassed any kind of venereal disease, including gonorrhoea and syphilis). This primarily involved inducing sweating by immersing the patient in very hot water, though some medical practitioners used mercury ointment and an oral comforter which mixed milk and syrup. In short, Bartholmew's sufferings and treatment are "enforced" by having contracted the pox from Ferenda. Hence, perhaps, the bitter reflection that "The prick of kind can never be unplaced" (or "what's fucked can't be unfucked").

If Bartholomew Withypoll ever read these lines – and he may well not have done – he presumably smiled ruefully. Gascoigne's poem of *"councell given to master* Bartholmew Withipoll" implies that his friend is someone who frequents brothels and cautions him against whores. The name Bath in the poem's title puns both on the standard cure for the pox and the associations between the town and such matters, explaining why Dan Bartholmew "thether had recourse".[13] A contemporary document mentions that the approval of two J.P.s was required to "License diseased persons (living of almes) to travel to *Bathe* or *Buckstone*, for remedy of their griefe".[14]

Though Shakespeare appears to poke fun at the rhetorical excesses of Gascoigne's initial description of Ferenda, his own sequence of love poems ends up in the same place as Dan Bartholmew. Notoriously, sonnets 153 and 154 play with equations of fiery passion and hot water in sweating tubs used to cure venereal disease. Whether or not the bard's mention of "a seething bath", "the bath for my help" and "a bath and healthful remedy" triggered thoughts of Bath in the minds of contemporary readers remains something that is, so to speak, hotly debated.

*

Another possibility is that the poem is not rooted in the life and sufferings of Bartholomew Withypoll but is rather about Gascoigne himself. But if "Ferenda Natura" is supposed to be Gascoigne's wife Elizabeth, then the portrait is hardly a flattering one. There are lines in part 4, "*Dan Bartholmews Dolorous discourses*", which could conceivably be about the poet's bigamous marriage:

Did not I hazard love yea life and all,
To ward thy will, from that unworthy man?[15]

So laboured I to save thy wandring ship,
Which reckless then, was running on the rocks[16]

Yet hauled I in, the mainsheet of thy mind,
And stayed thy course by anchors of advice,
I won thy will into a better wind,
To save thy ware, which was of precious price.
And when I had so harboured thy bark,

> In happy haven, which safer was than Dover,
> The *Admiral*, which knew it by the mark,
> Straight challenged all, and said thou wert a rover:
> Then was I forced in thy behalf to plead,
> Yea so I did, the judge can say no less,
> And whiles in toil, this loathsome life I lead,
> Camest thou thy self the fault for to confess,
> And down on knee before thy cruel foe,
> Didst pardon crave, accusing me for all,
> And saydst I was the cause, that thou didst so,
> And that I spoon the thread of all thy thrall.[17]   [spun]

The "unworthy man" could be Edward Boyes, and it is a striking coincidence that Ferenda has to be rescued from Dover, which is in Boyes's Kent and not all that far from his home town of Nonnington. The nautical imagery also calls to mind the possible pun on *Leffort Brittayne* in the Montague masque. The *Admiral* accuses Ferenda of piracy (i.e. Boyes names her as a bigamist). If it *is* about that moment of crisis in the couple's life then it reveals that Elizabeth Breton's first instinct was to go down on her knees before Edward Boyes and blame Gascoigne for pressuring her into an unlawful marriage. The scenario is a perfectly possible one, reinforcing the impression that Gascoigne himself was at first unaware that his marriage was bigamous. Perhaps, as the years went by, old and smouldering resentments resurfaced in his verse.

But in the context of the poem as a whole it is impossible to develop any kind of sustained parallel between Ferenda Natura and Elizabeth Breton or between Don Bartholmew and George Gascoigne. The poem is a compendium of fragments, riddled with narrative inconsistencies. In any case, the radiant young woman of the early part of the poem is hard to square with the older woman with five children whom Gascoigne married. The probability is that "Dan Bartholmew" is a composite figure constructed out of events in the lives both of the author and of his two friends, Dan and Batt, with the occasional dash of invention. As a joke between friends it may have evoked laughter but to anyone else it looks like a slapdash, self-indulgent production.

The only moment when Gascoigne's imagination truly catches fire is in part nine, which presents a disillusioned lover's bitter parody of a conventional last will and testament ("Then let the youngest sort be set to ring Love's bells, / And pay repentance for their pains, but give them nothing else").[18] Gascoigne's creative fatigue is evident in the lacklustre final three sections. In the end he didn't even finish the poem. It ends abruptly in mid-stanza and in mid-line, followed by a short note breezily explaining that the author hasn't handed over the rest of it. But not to worry, as what the reader holds in his or her hand "*amounteth to a good rounde vollume*".[19] From the laconic tone, it was obviously written by Gascoigne, though implicitly it's a final address from "H.W." to the reader. With this, *A Hundreth Sundrie Flowres* was complete. All that remained now was for the book to be published.

*

If Gascoigne did complete his book in the Low Countries, that might go some way to explaining the unsatisfactory materials and structure of "Dan Bartholmew of Bathe". The conditions of warfare may have made it impossible for him to get the peace and quiet he needed in order to write. Alternatively, with this final narrative poem, possibly boredom and creative exhaustion set in. The vast project of putting together a lifetime's writing in publishable form was just about over and maybe he just wanted it finished with. Or perhaps he was simply overtaken by events. In The Hague he was involved in some kind of relationship with a local woman. And before long, he was called away to fight.

He was sent south, back to his old stamping ground on the island of Walcheren. The Dutch had lost a big naval battle in May and Haarlem had fallen, but all was far from lost. Gascoigne and his men were sent to assist in the capture of Ramykins (Rammekens, sometimes also known as Zeeburg). This was a citadel built on the dike between Flushing and Spanish-held Middelburg and usually had a large garrison because of its commanding position. Here, as Gascoigne put it, "I was in rolling trench".[20] This remarkable machine was perhaps the world's first rudimentary tank – or at any rate, armoured vehicle. It consisted of a line of large carts covered in musket-proof boards, with fixed positions for "sundry field pieces". Its purpose was to allow troops to get close to defensive walls, without injury.

> Being all joined together, I mean in one, it might cover at the least three hundred men. This sconce [miniature fort] was to be drawn with horses on both sides, and in the middest, until we were engaged with the enemy's small shot; then to be pushed with poles by the force of men.[21]

Using the rolling trench the troops succeeded in putting a mine under the wall of the fort, which quickly surrendered. Gascoigne said that "little shot was spent" and that "gold and groats" won an easy victory. Others attributed it to the cowardice of the fort's commander and the poor morale of the troops inside, who had inadequate supplies of gunpowder, were out-manned by the enemy and had discovered that there would be no help coming their way from Middelburg.

Gascoigne explained what happened next:

> Next that, I served by night and eke by day,
> By sea, by land, at every time and tide,

Against *Mountdragon* whiles he did assay
To land his men among the salt sea side,
For well he wist that *Ramykins* went wide, [knew]
And therefore sought with victual to supply
Poor *Myddleburgh* which then in suddes did lie. [sands]

   And there I saw full many a bold attempt
By seelie souls best executed aye, [poor]
And bravest bragges (the foemen's force to tempt) [advances]
Accomplished but coldly many a day,
The soldier charge, the leader lope away,
The willing drum a lusty march to sound,
Whiles rank retirers gave their enemies ground.

   Again at sea the soldier forward still,
When mariners had little lust to fight,
And whiles we stay twixt faint and forward will,
Our enemies prepare themselves to flight,
They hoist up sail (o weary word to write),
They hoist up sail that lack both stream and winds,
And we stand still so forced by frowarde minds.[22] [perverse]

These three stanzas about events in August 1573 sum up the essence of the Dutch war of independence, which was destined to drag on for generations and is now known as the 80 Years War (it ended in 1648 with the Peace of Münster). Each side skirmished and manoeuvred for local victories. But the motivation of many of those fighting was mixed, with varying degrees of commitment, and morale was often poor. Gascoigne's complaint is the perennial one of the infantryman. He and his comrades fought bravely but were let down by poor leadership, cowardice and the inadequacies of other services.

   His description conflates skirmishes outside Middelburg (where Mondragon had once again arrived to save the day for the Spanish on Walcheren) with a naval battle which occurred off the island later that month. Gascoigne describes ships sailing off "with riches full yfraughte" and grumbles that he and his men were left to "Take up the worst when all the best are fled".[23] He seems to mean that thanks to lazy and incompetent sailors they were cheated of valuable plunder – though in the previous stanza, with characteristic inconsistency, he offers a high-minded denunciation of "greedy minds" which desire "spoil and prey" and "golden heaps". Claiming that he could no longer serve in a regiment "where no good rules remain…Where discipline shall be but deemed vain", Gascoigne fell out with Colonel Morgan and resigned his commission.[24] It seems likely that his genuine disgust at the sloppiness of the military organisation was magnified by a sense of fury at having missed out on valuable booty.

Gascoigne wanted to get back to England, "With full intent to taste our English ale" – oh, and for sound patriotic reasons: "I longed much to see our Queen". That high-minded motive is tacked on five lines later, as if Gascoigne realised that going home to drown his sorrows wasn't quite reason enough. A different kind of writer would have deleted the line about the ale, but it is part of Gascoigne's charm that he cheerfully leaves his contradictions intact. *The fruites of Warre* was quite probably written at high speed, and at times it resembles a garrulous monologue by someone who has indeed tasted a little too much English ale.

But although he was now effectively a civilian, the poet felt obliged to explain to the man in charge why he was quitting:

Then went I straight to *Delfe*, a pleasant town,
Unto that Prince, whose passing virtues shine,
And unto him I came on knees adown,
Beseeching that his excellence in fine
Would grant me leave to see this country mine:

I craved leave no longer but till *Yule*,
And promised then to come again *Sans fail* [25]

The Prince was William of Orange, otherwise known as William the Silent (after the Dutch word "schluwe" which actually meant "cunning" or "careful"). Born in 1533, he was about Gascoigne's own age. He was the first great national leader to be thrown up by the rebellion against Spanish rule and he was successful in sustaining this opposition and holding Philip II's army at bay. He is now regarded as the founding father of Dutch independence and is widely honoured in the Netherlands. With engaging crassness, Gascoigne makes a point of stoutly denying what contemporary rumour said about William: "The slandrous tongues do say thou drinkst too much". Happily, Gascoigne was able to call God as a character witness to refute this scandalous slur.

The poet had another reason for wanting to return to England, apart from his own taste in ale or his supposed yearning for a glimpse of Elizabeth I. *A Hundreth Sundrie Flowres* was entering the last stages of production and Gascoigne probably wanted to be there, partly to check the proofs and partly for the excitement any writer feels when a work finally appears in bound and published form.

William agreed to the poet's request and gave him a passport signed with his seal. Gascoigne was all ready to go and had his bags packed when at the last moment he was asked to stay. Colonel Morgan had arrived at the court and the Prince seems to have wanted to hear his side of the story and to effect a reconciliation between the two quarrelsome soldiers. Regrettably, "wicked wrath had some so far enraged, / As by no means their malice could be swaged [assuaged]" (or: *it was all Captain Morgan's fault, he was the one who wouldn't be reasonable, blame him*).[26] There is some evidence that Morgan was indeed a haughty, stubborn man, quick to take offence and reluctant to make up. On the first expedition to the Low Countries in 1572, Morgan had fallen out with Gilbert: "Morgan considered himself insulted, and wanted to withdraw from Sir Humphrey Gilbert's command; but…the matter was too trivial to be called an insult…"[27] Another time even William fell out with Morgan, although the two men made it up. But on this occasion the Prince of Orange was unable to calm Morgan down.

At this point "the Spaniards came so near / That *Delfe* was girt with siege on every side".[28] The poet explains that he could have escaped by ship but decided it simply wouldn't be right to leave William "in such distress".[29] Gascoigne may genuinely have liked William and felt this way. Equally, he may well have cannily thought it politic to make a stand alongside the outstanding Protestant military leader of the age. Such a posture would do him no harm at all in the eyes of Lord Grey or the Earl of Bedford and would further discredit the accusations contained in the anonymous letter to the Privy Council.

It was now that a shadow fell over Gascoigne. The Burghers of Delft suspected him of treachery. It was a reasonable suspicion, in so far as many of the foreign troops fighting on the Protestant side were mercenaries. These men were motivated by their pay and by what they could get from looting. No one who knew Gascoigne at all well could have seriously believed that he was motivated by a passionate commitment to either the Protestant cause or Dutch independence. The Dutch war did not yet have the official sanction of Elizabeth I, therefore an Englishman who worked for the Spaniards could not properly be called a traitor. Changing sides was not unknown among the English soldiers. Sir Roger Williams happily went over to the Spanish and served under Mondragon between 1575 and 1577. Gascoigne's associate Rowland Yorke, mentioned in "*Gascoignes voyage into* Hollande", also served on the Spanish side, returned to the Protestant cause, and then betrayed Zutphen to his old masters.

As Gascoigne explained it, the suspicion stemmed from his affair with the "virtuous Lady" at The Hague. Gascoigne was apparently keen to retrieve his portrait and the woman sent him a love letter saying he'd have to come and get it himself. But the arrival of the woman's maid with a packet for an Englishman made the Burghers wonder if Gascoigne was involved with the Spaniards, as The Hague was now in the enemy's hands. They watched to see what Gascoigne would do with the letter.

In fact the packet included something far more explosive than just a love letter. It contained a passport signed by Francisco de Valdes, giving Gascoigne safe passage through the Spanish lines. As the Spaniard commanded the forces then besieging Delft, the Burghers' suspicions of Gascoigne were not unjustified. (It seems clear that the Burghers had opened the packet, then re-sealed it.) Who knows, perhaps Gascoigne's urgent desire to depart from Delft had something to do with his treachery? William gave the poet permission to write back to the lady but not, pointedly, to visit her. Meanwhile, the Burghers kept Gascoigne under permanent surveillance and gave instructions that he was banned from every port and not permitted to board a vessel to any destination.

Gascoigne was left angrily trapped at Delft, raging against "the Bowgers" (i.e. "the buggers", punning on "Burghers"):[30]

> Well thus I dwelt in *Delfe* a winters tyde,
> In *Delfe* (I say) without one penny pay[31]

He had good reason to be furious. His hopes of a romantic assignation at The Hague and of getting back his "counterfayte" had been dashed. There was now no chance of returning to England. He had missed his last opportunity to correct the proofs of *A Hundreth Sundrie Flowres* and the book had been published (possibly in November) in his absence. Possibly he hadn't even seen a copy yet. But if letters from England were reaching him, he was about to get some very bad news. The burial register for the year 1573 for St Margaret's Church, Ipswich, gives the blunt, melancholy facts:

> Bartholmewe Wythypoll, the sonne of mayster Edmunde Wythipoll esquyer, and of maystres Elsabeth hys wyf was buryed yn thys churche the xxvi daye of the moneth of November beiynge thursdaye

If Gascoigne learned this news at Delft it must have come as a stunning blow and helped to make it perhaps the worst Christmas of his life. His friend almost certainly never saw a copy of *A Hundreth Sundrie Flowres* with the poem about him in or learned that his old travelling companion was about to become the leading writer of the day.

Bartholomew's death at the age of about 34 puts a new perspective on "Dan Bartholmew of Bathe". There is a possibility that his brother Daniel, some two years younger, was already dead at this time. Perhaps Bartholomew was already ill and dying the last time George Gascoigne saw him, shortly before the poet headed off to the Low Countries. This can only be speculative, but if it was so it would make "Dan Bartholmew of Bathe" a kind of jaunty composite elegy to both brothers and Bartholomew in particular:

> Amongst the rest I most remember one
> Which was to me a dear familiar friend,

> Whose doting days since they be past and gone
> ...I will be bold (by his leave) for to tell,
> The restless state wherein he long did dwell.³²

Syphilis may well have been the cause of his friend's death, if Gascoigne's writing about him can be regarded as being grounded in fact. The "*councell*" poem punningly offers Bartholomew "grave advice" which will help him "prolong his youthful years" – advice which perhaps came too late and which in any case Bartholomew would seemingly have ignored.

On the face of it, it seems odd that Gascoigne should have written an elegy to Captain Bourcher, who was probably no more than a passing aquaintance, but not one about his old friend Bartholomew Withypoll. But the Bourcher poem was perhaps as much about Gascoigne's own state of mind as about the fallen captain, and with "Dan Bartholmew of Bathe" and his "*councell*" poem the poet may have felt he'd paid adequate tribute to his dead friend. In the revised version of the advice poem, written after Withypoll's death, Gascoigne changed the third deadly "P" from "papist" to "pox" and introduced new references to sexual infection, including "Spanish buttons", those who "by sweat" have to "learn to live and last", and "*Guydoes* pype" (possibly referring to a doctor who treated V.D.).³³ These alterations are clumsy and strained. Why Gascoigne made these revisions is an open question. The Ridolfi affair was ancient history by 1575, so he may have felt it was no longer necessary for him to trumpet his anti-papist credentials. But he may also have been sending a melancholy signal about the manner of his friend's death.

*

With time on his hands in Delft, Gascoigne began writing the long poem *The fruites of Warre*, which was then "*written by pecemeale at sundrye tymes, as the Aucthour had vacaunt leysures from service*". With characteristic ingenuity Gascoigne managed to make it both an anti-war poem and an appeal for future military service. It was not finished until he was back in England, by which time the poet's motivation was not simply to describe his adventures as a soldier.

At the end of December 1573 William travelled to Flushing and the focus of the war once again became the island of Walcheren and the sea around it. Gascoigne claimed that in recent months he had fought bravely for the ungrateful Dutch, and that

> It did one day the Prince (my chieftain) please
> To ask me thus: *Gascoigne* (quoth he), you dwell
> Amongst us still: and thereby seemeth well,
> That to our side you bear a faithful heart,

For else long since we should have seen you start.

But are (said he) your soldiers by your side?[34]

Gascoigne explained to William that his men had long since gone off with Colonel Morgan. He offered no comment on the notion that he'd remained in the Low Countries because of his faithful adherence to the cause, which was in glaring contradiction to the previous description of how he was confined to Delft by order of the Burghers of the town. Instead he asserted his firm intention to fight for William's cause to the end, to which end he requested "some fisher boat, / To show my force among this furious float".[35] The Prince liked Gascoigne's fighting spirit and supplied him with a hoy, which the poet captained during three days of battle with Spanish ships. This was a small, very manoeuvrable craft capable of carrying small cannon and ideal for fighting in the shallow, treacherous waters off Walcheren. According to the poet, William watched these nautical skirmishes from the pier at Flushing. The aim was to prevent the Spanish from re-supplying Middelburg.

Now, after the defeats for the Dutch side at Haarlem and The Hague, the tide seemed to be turning. Alva had been dismissed and replaced as governor-general by Don Luis de Requesens but the change in command brought no improvement to the Spanish position. Mondragon negotiated a civilised surrender of Middelburg on 19 February 1574 and departed from the town on 22 February. Gascoigne claimed that he dined out in the town a day before the Spanish departure, trusting entirely to Mondragon's good faith. William was so pleased by his victory that he rewarded Gascoigne with his pay and a generous bonus of 300 guilders (worth somewhere between £20-£30 in sixteenth-century currency).[36]

William's generosity was motivated by Gascoigne's desperate straits (though in the same breath he claims they were "uncraved" and not the result of special pleading). The poet hadn't been paid during the time he was at Delft and now he was "so prest, / At such a pinch" – and even the weather was against him on that "dismal day". The Prince felt sorry for him. The cash gift came in the nick of time. Just as his "fortune fell" his "credit still was saved" and his "scores were paid".[37]

Gascoigne's gloom at this moment of victory may have owed something to the news from England. *A Hundreth Sundrie Flowres* had by now been published and had had a mixed reception. It had created a sensation (good) but also a scandal (bad). Sophisticated Londoners loved the book; those of a more sober and devout disposition were appalled by it. Of all the contents of the volume the one which seems to have caused the most interest was *The Adventures of Master F.J.* It was read as an account of a true scandal involving persons of high social standing. Tongues wagged, winks were exchanged – and persons of godly character were scandalised by its raunchy language and shockingly explicit scenes. There seems little doubt that the book was called in by the state's major censorship body and that those copies which had not already been eagerly snapped up were destroyed. How much of all this Gascoigne knew at the time is far from clear.

He may not even have seen a copy of the book until his return to England later in the year. If he had been sent a copy he is unlikely to have been entirely pleased. Not all of the book's oddities can be attributed to cultural change and the passage of time. The first anomaly is the very odd placing of the two plays in the ordering of the book's contents. It is perplexing to begin with a preface entitled "The Printer to the Reader" which refers to H.W.'s letter "in the beginning of this worke", which is then followed by *Supposes* and *Jocasta*, and only then by "H.W. to the Reader". Any reader is likely to deduce that something has gone horribly wrong with the sequencing of the volume's contents.

C. T. Prouty concluded that Gascoigne never meant the two plays to be included at all and that the printer Henry Bynneman put them in to make the volume more saleable.[38] Prouty therefore left them out of his 1942 edition. That was a very large and very questionable assumption which resulted in the most influential twentieth-century text of *A Hundreth Sundrie Flowres* being substantially incomplete. In fact it is much more likely that Gascoigne intended *Supposes* and *Jocasta* to come at or near the end of the volume, not at the beginning. What *was* unequivocally left out were the 88 lines of "Gascoigne's *De profundis*".[39] Instead the printers mistakenly assumed that the prefatory sonnet[40] was the complete poem. But some errors were noted: between "The printer to the reader" and *Supposes* is a full, crammed page of "Faultes efcaped" and their "correction". On page 441 there was an acknowledgement that the correct order of the poems in "Dan Bartholmew of Bathe" had been muddled. "This should have bin placed in the dolorous difcourfe, before the Supplication to Care in Folio. 430" the reader is informed, by way of a preface to sections 3 and 12. This muddle may indicate that the poem sequence was a last-minute, rushed appendix to the volume. In addition the book's pagination goes haywire. Page 36 jumps to page 45 and page 164 jumps to page 201. In one copy (held in the British Library) page 293 jumps to page 297. Blank pages occur without warning or explanation. Finally, at the end of *A Hundreth Sundrie Flowres*, any reader is likely to be surprised by the way it concludes with an unfinished poem and to wonder whatever happened to the translation from Ovid promised on the book's title page.

As Pigman notes, Gascoigne's ideas about the contents of the book probably changed during the long production schedule.[41] Quite possibly the pages used for "Dan Bartholmew of Bathe" were originally allocated to an earlier draft of *The Complaynte of Phylomene*. Whatever the truth of these matters, it is a fair bet that Gascoigne's initial excitement at handling his book turned to rage when he saw how its layout had been horribly botched.

*

In March more English volunteers arrived and Gascoigne reverted to his rank as a captain. He and other officers with a total of 500 men under them were given the task of defending the new fort of Valkenburgh, some three miles north-west of Leiden in South Holland. But the fort was unfinished and had inadequate supplies of ammunition and victuals. At this point a force of at least 3,000 Spanish troops turned up. First, the Spaniards attacked nearby Fort Alphen, some ten miles away. A conference was held among the men and officers whether or not to stay and defend the half-built fort. While they were discussing the situation a messenger from Alphen arrived and advised them to leave or be massacred. (This was good advice; some 300-400 troops died at Alphen, which was better defended.) As the retreat began, the enemy arrived on the scene, and soon there was total confusion and panic.

> In this retire three English miles we trod,
> With face to foes and shot as thick as hail,
> Of whose choice men full fifty souls and odd
> We laid on ground, this is withouten fail,
> Yet of our own we lost three by tale:
> Our foes themselves confessed they bought full dear
> The hot pursuit which they attempted there.[42]

Finally the English soldiers reached Leiden, which hurriedly shut its gates against them. They were left stranded out in the open and spent the night there. At dawn on 27 May they were woken by the sound of approaching Spanish drums. Gascoigne and his associate Captain Sheffield went forward to negotiate with two Spanish officers. The two Englishmen requested that their force be allowed to surrender and return to England. This was agreed, and after twelve days in captivity the English volunteers were sent home. But Gascoigne and the other officers were imprisoned at Haarlem for four months. They were well treated and eventually released.

That was Gascoigne's version of what happened. In the Netherlands, however, it was widely believed that he and the other officers had been bribed by the Spanish to surrender. The English volunteers also suspected treachery and returned to England claiming that the reason Gascoigne and the others stayed behind was to claim their reward. It is perfectly possible that that is what happened. Gascoigne's motives for his involvement in Holland and Zeeland in 1573-4 were personal and mercenary, not patriotic or religious. If Gascoigne did take a bribe then it means his account of being "In pryson pent"[43] was a lie. However, none of the contemporary documentation from Dutch or Spanish sources contradicts Gascoigne's account. In the absence of any tangible evidence, Gascoigne must be acquitted of the charge of treachery.

A year or so later, the poet later opened up his heart to a young admirer and would-be writer named George Whetstone. Gascoigne revealed that he had an explosive manuscript about his experiences in the Netherlands, which was only to be published after his death. When that happened, "men will say, that *Gaskoign* wrote of *Zeale*".[44] If there was such a manuscript, it was lost or destroyed. No such posthumous publication ever appeared.

Whetstone wrote an elegy for Gascoigne in which the dying poet addresses his friend and recounts his bitter experiences in Zeeland:

What hart can bide, in bloody warres to toile:
when carpet swads devour ye Soldiers spoile?

I am the wretch, whom Fortune flirted soe,
These men, were brib'd, ere I had breth to speak:
Muse then no whit, with this huge overthrowe,
though crusshing care my giltless hart doth break.[45]

The first two lines reiterate Gascoigne's sense of resentment about being cheated out of his due share of plunder ("carpet swads" are men not directly involved in the fighting – perhaps commanders who hang back and let the ordinary soldier do the dangerous work). The next lines appear obliquely to touch on events at Valkenburgh and Leiden. It is not clear whether or not "These men" refers to the "carpet swads" or "ye Soldiers" but either way Gascoigne appears to admit that there *was* bribery but that it took place before he had a chance to express an opinion. If that is what happened, then perhaps Gascoigne felt obliged to stay silent out of loyalty to his fellow officers. But it was not his decision and he felt outraged to be blamed.

The "huge overthrowe" could be read as the destruction of Gascoigne's reputation and honour. This episode, in which he was guiltless, broke his heart. It's a plausible scenario, though it cannot be proved. This is Gascoigne's voice but mimicked by a ventriloquist. Whetstone wrote these lines after the poet's death. However, there is no reason to believe that he wasn't passing on information confided in him by Gascoigne. In that ever-changing war of shifting allegiances, religious hatred, high principle, low greed, treachery and paranoia, truth was often elusive. The Low Countries were geographically, militarily and often morally, a quagmire.

*

It may well have been during his four months at Haarlem that Gascoigne wrote a group of five linked poems on the theme of war and imprisonment – literally *The fruite of Fetters*.[46] It's a patchy and uneven sequence in which Gascoigne once again reviews his life. The first poem is full of sighs, grief, torment and windy generalisations about misfortune, though it does provide a brief glimpse of his confinement:

> My quiet bed, which I for solace sought,
> Doth irk mine ears, when still the warlike crew
> With sound of drums, and trumpets braying shrill
> Relieve their watch, yet I in thraldom still.

This does not prove that Gascoigne was in prison; merely that he was disturbed by the noise of the Spanish army. If there were "fetters" they were probably metaphorical rather than literal. His imprisonment, if it occurred, would have been of the agreeable, comfortable sort. Those who suspected him of treachery no doubt believed he was simply remaining with the Spaniards until the heat had died down.

In *The fruites of Warre* Gascoigne explained that at Delft the Dutch dubbed him "die groene Hopman" ("the green captain") – apparently meaning "naïve" or "inexperienced". The poet cheerfully accepted the moniker, but converted it to the slightly grander, mock-chivalric "the green knight". Now he took up the nickname again in "The complaint of the greene Knight".[47] As Charles Nicholl notes, "This Green Knight is not the implacable axe-man of medieval romance, but the disappointed face of George in the mirror."[48] The poem is another "dreary doleful tale" of bad luck and growing old. Green no longer stands for innocence but for misery: "green, because my greeves [griefs] are always fresh and green".

The green knight tells of his first love, Cosmana, who died, and of her replacement, Ferenda. But now what he misses more than anything is "a peerless firelock piece". It is not hard to see in all this a kind of allegory of Gascoigne's life. Cosmana is his first love, the woman who inspired *The Adventures of Master F.J.*, Ferenda is Elizabeth Breton and the beautiful gun – "A piece so cleanly framed, so straight, so light, so fine.../ And though I bent it night and day the quickness never failed" – is the woman at The Hague. But as in "Dan Bartholmew of Bathe" the tone is jarring. The sniggering sexual innuendo and the jokes about meat and cuts make the knight's sighing, grieving and floods of brinish tears seem unintentionally preposterous. Delicate, sensitive melancholy can't convincingly exist alongside lads' cunt jokes.

The fruite of Fetters is another rambling poem which begins with several stanzas of double entendre about big balls, guns which are stiff, straight and stout, spitting pellets, and pieces which which provoke moans of sorrow. It moves on to some moralizing reflections about the value of imprisonment, and ends with a denunciation of "Fansie", meaning dreams or ambition. It serves as a bizarre preface to one of Gascoigne's finest poems, ""The Green Knight's Farewell to Fancy"". Mercifully free of sexual innuendo, this poem is a melancholy overview of Gascoigne's life, every bit as good as "Gascoigne's Woodmanship". It is as partial in its account as that other, longer poem, but in some ways fuller. Gascoigne looks back and reflects upon himself as fancy's fool ("in my hat full harebrayndly, thy flowers did I wear"), as a deluded lover (stanza two), as a vain courtier (stanza three), as a failed farmer (stanza four), as a foolish huntsman (stanza five), as a popular poet (stanza six), as a singer and musician (stanza seven), as a gardener in thrall to fashion (stanza eight) and as a soldier (stanza nine). In the last stanza Gascoigne bids a final farewell to fancy and appeals to reason, God and "comfort of Philosophy" to improve his lot. A short *"Epilogismus"* of 14 lines wraps the sequence up with the astonishing and unexpected suggestion that, after all, "Fancie hath not yet his last farewell" and the laconic observation

When foxes preach, good folk beware your geese

After the poem is the posy *Tam Marti, quàm Mercurio*, meaning "As much for Mars as for Mercury". From now on, this was to become Gascoigne's motto. He was as much for the god of war as for the god of eloquence, or to put it another way, as much a soldier as a poet. It became his slogan and his brand identity in the great market-place of Tudor opportunity. He reinvented himself as both a skilled writer and a brave warrior, associate and servant of Prince William of Orange and militant upholder of the Protestant cause. He was someone who could do service to the state. He wanted patronage. He was happy to do any job at all – soldier, writer, messenger. You only had to ask. George Gascoigne was your man. As a brand logo *Tam Marti, quàm Mercurio* seems to have been a success, judging by the way it was later adopted by Walter Ralegh, echoed by George Whetstone, Robert Naunton and Barnabe Rich, and used ironically by Ben Jonson in *The Poetaster* (1601).[49]

Gascoigne said he did not know why he and the other officers were kept in confinement for almost four months and then released, evidently in late September or early October 1574. An accepted convention was a prisoner exchange, but if Gascoigne was swapped for some Spanish officer prisoners he evidently knew nothing about it. He speculates that they were kept that long because their captors were trying to find out if they were worth ransoming. However, no money seems to have changed hands. Whether or not he was permitted to visit The Hague, see the virtuous lady there and get back his portrait, is unclear. Gascoigne is silent on the subject, so perhaps he was simply escorted to the nearest port and put on a ship back to England.

> And home we came as children come from school,
> As glad as fish which were but lately catched,
> And straight again were cast into the pool.⁵⁰

The tone is light-hearted and relaxed, with perhaps an echo of an idyllic childhood in the garden of Cardington Manor. Gascoigne explains that the prisoners were "right gently used". It was evidently a very different experience from Bedford prison.

PART FIVE: THE RUNNING MAN

21: "offensive... and... scandalous"

Upon his return to England in the autumn of 1574, Gascoigne presumably went home to Walthamstow to see his long-suffering wife Elizabeth and their child William (now aged around ten or eleven). He may conceivably have made a melancholy journey into East Anglia to visit poor Bart Withypoll's grave and commiserate with his family. His friend was probably the first Withypoll to be buried in the family's massive high table tomb which was erected in the centre of the chancel of the Church of St Margaret, Ipswich, in 1574. It was really intended for Edmund Withypoll, who wanted to be sure that when he died he was buried in a tomb of appropriate dimensions for someone as locally important as himself. The church authorities however later came to regard it as a nuisance, as it prevented some sections of the congregation from seeing the minister at the communion table. It was removed in the eighteenth century. Today its site is marked by a stone in the floor and a marble slab from the tomb stands against the west wall of the north transept.

Back home in England Gascoigne was faced by two problems. The first was the rumour spread by the volunteers who served under him about his treachery at Valkenburgh (not to mention his quarrel with Colonel Morgan and the difficulties at Delft). The second was the controversy surrounding the publication of *A Hundreth Sundrie Flowres*.

The first scandal Gascoigne dealt with in *The fruites of Warre*, indignantly refuting the allegation in some detail in stanzas 143-188. Self-justification, in fact, is a major aspect of the poem which, significantly, was begun at the moment Gascoigne was suspected of treachery at Delft. The poem has passages of narrative brilliance but also many longueurs. As Gascoigne put it in the prose preface addressed to Lord Grey of Wilton, "*The verse is roughe. And good reason, sithence it treateth of roughe matters, but if the sence be good then have I hyt the marke which I shote at.*" It breaks down into a number of sections. Stanzas 1-93 reflect upon the theme "Dulce bellum inexpertis" (or "war is attractive to those who have no experience of it"). Here Gascoigne solemnly calls upon all sections of society to avoid greed, rancour and strife and cites a wide range of examples from history and the classics to prove his thesis that war is "the scourge of God". Stanzas 94-98 describe his experiences in Zeeland in 1572 and stanzas 99-192 his return to fight in the Low Countries in 1573 and the events which climaxed with the evacuation of Valkenburgh and surrender outside Leiden.

The poem moves to a conclusion with a peroration to a variety of influential figures from Elizabeth I downwards (stanzas 193-207). This exercise in feverish name-dropping shows Gascoigne at his most shamelessly deferential and opportunistic as he attempts to ingratiate himself with just about everyone who matters in the English ruling class. The tone is reminiscent of a worried Soviet artist desperately pleading, flattering and abasing himself before Stalin. As the lines about Gray's Inn reveal, Gascoigne was anxious to claim a connection not to those closest to him there but to those who were the most respectable and influential: William Lovelace (a serjeant-at-law), William Rugge (Dean of the Chapel at Gray's Inn in 1570) and Christopher Yelverton (Lent reader in 1574).

Finally, an envoi of 30 lines rounds off this vast, ramshackle poem. Astonishingly for what purports to be an anti-war poem, the last two lines put in a bid for future military service:

If drums once sound a lusty march in deed,
Then farewell books, for he will trudge with speed.

The fruites of Warre is Gascoigne's longest poem and his third to be dedicated to Lord Grey of Wilton. This time the noble lord was given the benefit of an expansive "Epistle Dedicatory". In it Gascoigne nervously notes that by now Grey will have

> *thoroughly perused the booke* [i.e. *A Hundreth Sundrie Flowres*], *which I prepared to bee sent unto you somewhat before my coming hither* [i.e. return to England from the Low Countries], *and therewithal I doe likewise conjectour that you have founde therein just cause to laugh at my follies forepassed. So that I am partly in doubte whether I were more overseene in my first devising, or in my last directing of the same? But as fantasticall humours are common imperfections in greene unmellowed braines: So hope I yet that your good Lordshippe wyll rather winke at my weakenesse in generallitie, then reprove my rashnesse in perticularitie. And because I would be glad, to drawe your Lordshippe into forgetfulnesse thereof, by fresh recorde of some more martiall matter, as also for that I would have your Honour perceive that in these lingering broyles, I doe not altogether passe over my time in ydlenesse: I have therefore thought meete nowe to present you with this Pamphlete written by stelth at such times as we Loytered from service. And the subject thereof being warre, I could not more convenientlye addresse the same unto any Marshiall man, then unto your good Lordshippe: Whome I have heard to be an universall patrone of all Souldiours, and have found to bee an exceeding favourour of mee your unworthy follower.*

Lord Grey certainly had plenty of time to peruse Gascoigne's volume as in 1574 he was incarcerated in the Fleet prison. His disgrace arose out of a long-running dispute with his neighbour, Sir John Fortescue (b. 1533), owner of Salden Manor. Although Fortescue was lower in rank, the two men were social equals. In 1559, soon after becoming Queen, Elizabeth put Fortescue in charge of her ceremonial outfits, appointing him Keeper of the Great Wardrobe. In 1572 Fortescue was elected MP for Wallingford in Oxfordshire, where he also owned land.

Sir John accused Grey's servants of "hunting my warren [i.e. land for breeding rabbits], breaking my hedges, and disturbance of mine inheritance at Salden".[1] When he put his complaints to Lord Grey in the Presence Chamber at court, he claimed that Grey used "uncivil language", snapping, "Tush, a Lord in your teeth, I will hunt it." Two days later the antagonists met again in the gallery at the rear of the Queen's lodging at Westminster. This time Grey was more conciliatory and the two men made up. But the problem continued. Grey's servants continued to hunt in Fortescue's warren grounds. The keeper's boy was a persistent offender. Fortescue accused him of having "broken divers gaps, and plodding at my conies". In response the boy gave him "lewde words". Another regular trespasser was John Savage, Lord Grey's ranger. Lord Grey's position was simple: where Fortescue's land was concerned, "He had, would, and must hunt." Matters climaxed with Savage and fifteen others invading Fortescue's land, armed with bows, forest bills and long staffs. In a pitched battle four of Grey's men "were very evil hurt" and one died from his injuries.[2] Now it was Grey's turn to be indignant. The matter came before two local Justices of the Peace and then the Privy Council. Grey explained that deer frequently crossed from the Chase on to Fortescue's estate and that it was "a continual custom, time out of mind (as hath been and is well to be proved), the keepers, with hound and horn, to hunt and to make in the same, without any resistance". He accused his adversary of having said that "he also knew what the Lord Grey was". Indeed, "Mr Fortescue himself is a rioter".

The judges in the case were evidently unsympathetic to Grey. He therefore took matters into his own hands. A deposition by Fortescue vividly depicts what happened next. On 30 November 1573, in London, Lord Grey

> came by at ix of the clock, accompanied with xii serving men of purpose, and tarried in the shop of one Lewes, a cross-bow maker, above one hour, sending out diverse times a lackey to bring word of my coming; his men were laid divided on every side of the street a little beneath Temple Bar, towards the Court, and at x of the clock, or rather after, I came out of Chancery Lane on horseback, with v men…whereupon they, all ready, my L. suffering me to pass, strake me on the head so sore, that I was astouned [stunned], and fell from my horse, saying, as the standers do repeat, "You have spoiled me:" Whereupon he answered, "Nay, villain, I will have my pennyworth of thee; thou shalt not scape so:" with many other like speeches; striking, when I was down, divers blows, which partly were by me with mine arm and cloak borne, and diverse broken by a serving man called Harry Clerke, who took the crab-tree truncheon out of the Lord Grey's hand, and brake a thrust that one of the L. Grey's servants, called Tymothie, cast to

have slain me withal: Some of the servants of one Hearne plucked me up, and pulled me into an entry, where Zowche thrusting at me, I had been slain, had not the said Hearne's man broken the bow with a yard, where I staggered, and, not able to come to myself, was pulled into the house, nor could see, or discern any man, a pretty space: His men, all provided [armed], set upon my servants, and ii of them are very dangerously hurt, and had been presently slain, if the rescue of the street had not been: All this, with many other circumstances of the matter may be perfectly known to your Honors by the testimony of diverse gentlemen and inhabitants of the said street.[3]

Temple Bar was a wooden gateway marking the western limit of the City, at the end of Fleet Street. Beyond it lay the Strand, Charing Cross and the "Holbein" Gate to Whitehall Palace. The attack on Fortescue evidently occurred at the east end of the Strand, just beyond the gateway.

Fortescue's account has the ring of truth to it and provides an insight into the character of Gascoigne's patron. Like most religious fundamentalists, Lord Grey had a dogmatic, unyielding personality, underpinned, no doubt, by his aristocratic background. The courts might say he was in the wrong and Fortescue's complaints were legitimate; if so, Grey didn't care. If the courts wouldn't punish Sir John, then he would.

The scene is an ugly one. Grey made sure his own retinue outnumbered Fortescue's. He loitered for over an hour, with malice aforethought, armed with a cosh. It is interesting that Grey waited in the shop of a cross-bow maker. This was evidently a weapon in which he had a keen interest. It was the very same weapon which Gascoigne portrayed himself as being ham-fisted with in "Gascoigne's Woodmanship". Gascoigne shrewdly understood that in botching his own hunting abilities, he flattered Grey's. Although he was far away in the Netherlands when this episode occurred, Gascoigne probably knew all the participants in Grey's ambush. "Zowche" is Sir John Zouche. He was a relative of Grey's first wife, Dorothy. He may well have been present when Gascoigne stayed at Whaddon Hall the previous winter. Gascoigne certainly knew him, describing him as "good *John Zuche*" in "*Gascoignes voyage into* Hollande".[4]

As far as the Privy Council was concerned an assault on a person of Sir John Fortescue's standing was unacceptable. Worse, it had taken place in broad daylight in one of London's busiest streets. Worse still, Grey had planned what was effectively a very cowardly ambush. Even worse, it concerned a matter in which the judgement had previously gone against Grey. Fortescue begged the Privy Council's assistance, "for that I am farther informed, that the said L. Grey hath appointed another compact for the murdering of me and my servants".[5]

Grey's punishment was to be clapped in the Fleet prison. He was probably put there in December 1573 and remained several months. He was there in March 1574, when he wrote to Lord Burghley. By 1575 he had been released.

His confinement there would have been quite comfortable, with rented chambers, fine food and the opportunity to entertain family and friends. The Warden of the Fleet permitted some prisoners their freedom for anything between a half-day and a week, though the privilege was paid for and required the company of a keeper. It was during his imprisonment that Grey probably devoted himself to writing his memoir of his father.

Lord Grey's imprisonment must have unexpectedly benefited Gascoigne. Since Lord Grey was out of favour with the court and the Privy Council he is unlikely to have been disturbed by the furore surrounding *A Hundreth Sundrie Flowres*. If readers were decoding *The Adventures of Master F.J.* as a *roman à clef* then one might have expected Grey to perceive the book as possibly being set at Whaddon Hall, but clearly the thought never crossed his mind. Nor does he seem to have been troubled by Gascoigne's associations with the Catholic Montagues. His tolerance was probably encouraged by Gascoigne's representation of himself as the Tudor analogue of a born-again Christian. The poet's writings testified to his sinful past but now all that was behind him and he was truly penitent. In Grey's eyes, Gascoigne was perhaps also, like himself, being victimized by a harsh, unfair establishment. Gascoigne's plea that Grey forgive him his "*rashnesse in perticularitie*" and his mention of "*lingering broyles*", "*stelth*" and having "*Loytered*"[6] seems imbued with a canny knowledge of Grey's own weaknesses on this point. There was also the remarkable coincidence that while Grey was in prison in London, Gascoigne was pent up in Delft and later incarcerated by the Spanish. Fate seemed to turn Gascoigne into Grey's shadow.

By now Gascoigne was all too well aware that his book had caused offence. He was now beginning to search for excuses to explain away what he had done (convincingly so, as even in the second half of the twentieth century some scholars convinced themselves that the book had been published without the poet's permission). Hazlitt was in no doubt that Gascoigne's writings in *A Hundreth Sundrie Flowres* "found their way to the press in an imperfect shape without his authority or knowledge".[7]

One of Gascoigne's major lines of defence was that he had only published his licentious writings as an awful warning to the younger generation not to go astray in the same way. This argument was clearly pitched as much at his patron as at the state censors. Tied in with that was his reinvention of himself in the image of a penitent sinner, who deeply regretted the excesses of his past and was now humbled, God-fearing and liberated from frivolity and lust. Thirdly, he was a man of the only true religion, a loyal soldier in the Protestant cause, who had fought bravely across the seas against the papist army. Evidently Lord Grey himself was happy to accept Gascoigne's deferential explanations and excuses. The poet presumably hoped for another substantial pay-off and he cannot have been disappointed, for yet more dedications followed.

*

That the contents of *A Hundreth Sundrie Flowres* possessed the power to offend and shock was evident both from contemporary responses to it, the confiscation of the second edition and censorship which continued to occur even as late as the twentieth century. As previously noted, the *Oxford Book of English Verse 1250-1900* (1900) silently censored the only contribution by Gascoigne. According to C. T. Prouty, writing in 1942, Gascoigne's "Phillip sparrow" poem was "omitted from the anthologies" (American as well as British, perhaps) because of its sexual content.[8] Prouty himself, writing in a more puritanical and censorious age, could only bring himself to speak of the poem in a discreetly muted fashion, remarking with cloudy vagueness that "One thinks of Catullus and Skelton...It is such a poem as would have delighted the members of the Scriblerus Club".[9] The kind of outrage expressed by Frederick Gard Fleay M.A., when he railed against Gascoigne's poems, which were "far more filthy in expression"[10] than anything produced by his contemporaries, was perhaps never stronger than in the sixteenth century itself. To Gabriel Harvey, the poet could be summed up in two words: "Lewd Gascoigne".[11]

The desire to annihilate writing which upset powerful churchmen or the sovereign stretched back decades. The censorship of books in Tudor England was at first focused on religious texts which the state regarded as subversive. The continental reformation threatened the English church with dangerous new ideas, and many of the radicals were printers, able to circulate these ideas to a mass audience. Reformers pointed out that nowhere in the Bible is there mention of a Pope, or bishops, or a hierarchical church. They wanted the Bible translated into English, so that ordinary people could read it and form their own judgement about religious truth. But the idea of the common people reading the Bible for themselves, rather than having it explained to them by priests, horrified the church establishment. Wolsey issued a commission in 1521 to the bishops to search for heretical books. William Tyndale provides the outstanding example of a Tudor writer who was killed for no other reason than that his work was unacceptable to the church and religious fundamentalists like Thomas More. In September 1546 Bishop Bonner oversaw the burning of heretical books, including the biblical translations of Tyndale and Coverdale.

As a young man Roger Ascham produced a beautifully handwritten manuscript of an elegantly composed Latin translation of a tenth-century commentary on the Epistle to Titus. He dedicated it to the conservative Archbishop Edward Lee and took it to London to present it in hope of some tangible reward. Lee read it and returned it with an objection to the commentary's mention of married clergy. Ascham felt obliged to write two grovelling letters of apology expressing abject remorse for his blunder.

The publication of any book was affected by the power wielded by prickly and difficult men like Lee, who were always sharply on the lookout for deviations from conservative orthodoxy. In September 1554 the printer John Day made literary history when he published blank verse for the very first time, namely the Earl of Surrey's fourth book from Virgil's *Aeneid*, "translated into English, and drawn unto a straunge metre". But the following month he was imprisoned in the Tower of London "for pryntyng of noythy bokes" ["naughty books", i.e. heretical texts].[12] Day did not return to printing until 1557. The chronicler John Stow, famous for his *Survey of London*, was regarded in some quarters as a dangerous subversive because of the troubling printed matter he'd accumulated. His house was searched by order of the Bishop of London, who sent William Cecil an inventory of "his unlawfull bookes". Among the Bishop's shocking discoveries was Thomas Stapleton's translation of Bede's *Ecclesiastical History*. Cecil pragmatically let the matter drop.

What is striking about George Gascoigne's career is that he appears to be the first important imaginative writer of the Tudor era to fall foul of the censors. He was a poet, a novelist and a playwright, not a political or a religious thinker. But he was subversive because he lacked deference or reverence for the prevailing ideology. He wrote about sex, he poked fun at martyrdom and recantation, he exposed life inside the ruling class as one of duplicity and lust. But he had no desire to overthrow the state or reform or change its official religion. Gascoigne accepted the status quo; his heresy lay in his humour. He was not like John Stubbs, who in 1579 wrote a blistering attack on the Queen for considering a marriage to Francis, Duke of Alençon and Anjou. Stubbs was found guilty of "seditious libel" and he and the book's distributor had their right hands amputated.

What George Gascoigne transgressed was the church's monopoly on morality and decency. Worse, he was the first important writer to circulate his scandalous verse and fiction to a mass audience in book form. Lynda E. Boose has suggested that in the sixteenth-century state

> censorship orders are provoked not by the writing of a book nor even by the reading of a work in circulated manuscript, in which case the text in question reaches only an elite audience. What the state proscribes is the circulation of certain works among the proverbial masses. It is at this juncture that such works are imagined – and the metaphor here changes little from the sixteenth to the twentieth century – as acquiring a pervasive contagion that threatens the entire social body.[13]

Boose is surely right and her argument fits neatly with what happened to Gascoigne. Most of his verse and possibly his novel had almost certainly circulated in manuscript for some considerable time before they were eventually published. But writings that were tolerated when they circulated in private among courtiers and the young men of the Inns of Court became suddenly intolerable when they reached a wider audience. Partly this was because they now became accessible to those of a religious disposition, who may have previously been unaware of their existence. To the narrow, humourless sensibility of an ecclesiastic Gascoigne's work was deeply offensive, irrespective of its readership. But the offensiveness of his writing was magnified when it reached a broader readership through the medium of print. It was still an elite audience (the high cost of a large book like Gascoigne's ensured that commoners would never buy a copy) but a more diverse one – students at Oxford and Cambridge, perhaps; city merchants and gentlemen.

To a later generation, and perhaps to Shakespeare in particular, Gascoigne became the archetype of the silenced writer. He was the forerunner of all those later cases involving the suppression of imaginative writing or the punishment of authors, ranging from the imprisonment of Ben Jonson for co-writing a "seditious" comedy to the public burning of Marlowe's translation of Ovid's *Amores*. Gascoigne was thinking of the system of Tudor state censorship at the time he wrote his poem to Douglas Dive, and he did so in relation to the theme of literature's power to offend. If she doesn't like his poem, says Gascoigne,

> then licence it to pass
> Into my breast again, from whence it flew in haste[14]

By "licence" Gascoigne meant "approve". The metaphor refers to the licensing system set up to control book publishing. Under Henry VIII a text had to receive some form of official authorisation and approval before it was allowed to be published. But the explosion in printing and book publication eventually made pre-print censorship impractical. In 1557 Queen Mary granted a royal charter to the London Company of Stationers. This body represented London printers and henceforth every book title had to be registered with it. In return the Company issued a licence which gave exclusive publishing rights. As Boose notes, "the apparatus of regulating censorship...was explicitly designed to control printers, not authors".[15] This had the effect of liberalising the publication of imaginative writing, which could now be published without state or church approval. The only books which still required the sanction of a greater authority before publication were translations, foreign language titles, or those explicitly to do with political or religious matters. But this system was far from foolproof. Some books were simply brought in from abroad and avoided the censorship process altogether. Others were privately printed, with the author paying the printer and then distributing the books himself. Some books attempted to evade the registration process by being published anonymously, with no identification of the printer.

But within the licensing system was a contradiction, and it was one which

Gascoigne's work came up against. A book could be officially licensed, published and still fall foul of censorship. The same year that Mary granted a charter to the Stationers' Company she also set up Her Majesty's Commissioners in Causes Ecclesiastical. This was a body with wide-ranging powers to suppress books and it was this body which evidently disliked Gascoigne's masterpiece.

A Hundreth Sundrie Flowres appears to have been a licensed publication. It was produced by a leading printer, Henry Bynneman, and sold by a reputable publisher, Richard Smith. Gascoigne later denied accepting money for the publication of his manuscript but this denial lacks credibility. His finances were only intermittently in a sound state and it is hard to imagine him spurning an agreeable lump sum for publication of what was, in effect, his life's work. The registration of the harmless-sounding *A Hundreth Sundrie Flowres* seems unlikely to have attracted any attention, and it presumably at first evaded censorship by virtue of its ostensible innocence as an anthology of writings by various gentlemen, including two distinguished plays which had been staged at Gray's Inn.

But 1573 was not a good year to put out an offensive book. The previous summer the anonymously published *An Admonition to Parliament* had upset Elizabeth I and caused outrage. The situation had worsened when the secret Puritan press put out *A Second Admonition* in November 1572. The Bishop of London was put in charge of suppressing these books. The authors were caught and imprisoned but copies still circulated. As late as 1578 a bookseller, Thomas Woodcock, was imprisoned for selling a copy of the *Admonition*. A proclamation of 11 June 1573 bitterly criticised the book and required "al and euery Printer, Stationer, Booke bynder, Marchaunt" and anyone else who might hold copies to surrender them. 1573 was also the year that the *Treatise of Treasons* was republished in an abridged form. It vexed Lord Burghley because of its personal abuse against himself and his brother-in-law, Nicholas Bacon. The pamphlet, first published in Louvain the previous year, was the work of an anonymous Catholic. It has been summarised as a "mixture of moral indignation and xenophobia, of religious condemnation, social prejudice and personal abuse".[16]

The suppression of *A Hundreth Sundrie Flowres* and its second edition also took place against a background of theatrical censorship. The traditional Mystery plays had lingered on under Elizabeth, even though many Protestants regarded any visual representation of God as blasphemy. In 1572 there was one final performance of the processional Pater Noster play in York, albeit in a heavily amended form. Archbishop Grindal asked to see a copy of the play and did not return it. There were no more performances, even though the town council maintained the pageant wagons and went on fruitlessly requesting permission until 1580. In Chester, in 1574, "the whitsun playes" were staged, in defiance of an ecclesiastical ban. The town's mayor was hauled before the Privy Council and there were no more performances. In Wakefield in 1576 the approval of the secular authorities for the performance of a cycle of traditional religious plays was countermanded by the Diocesan Court of High Commission, which prohibited them on the grounds that they "tende to the Derogation of the Majestie and glorie of god the prophanation of the Sacramentes and the maunteynaunce of superstition and idolatrie".[17]

The publication of *A Hundreth Sundrie Flowres* evidently also caused a scandal, but it was one which in terms of surviving documentation is registered nowhere but in Gascoigne's own writing. Tudor England was a culture without newspapers or magazines, where diary-keeping was almost non-existent and where those letters which survive tend to be formal and unrevealing of the minutiae of everyday life. Our knowledge of this scandal depends entirely on three prefatory letters which Gascoigne wrote in defence of the second, revised edition of *A Hundreth Sundrie Flowres*, which appeared two or three years later under the title *The Posies of George Gascoigne Esquire*.

The first of the "Prefatory Letters" is addressed "*To the reverende Divines, unto whom these Posies shall happen to be presented, George Gascoigne Esquire (professing armes in the defence of Gods truth) wisheth quiet in conscience, and all consolation in Christ Jesus.*" Gascoigne deferred to the "grave judgementes"[18] of these unidentified religious figures and wrote that it was his intention to explain his motive in publishing *The Posies of George Gascoigne Esquire* and "the depth and secrets of some conceytes, which (being passed in clowdes and figurative speeches) might percase both be offensive to your gravitie, and perillous to my credite".[19]

The reason why Gascoigne felt it necessary to engage with churchmen and to defend his writings becomes clearer later in the letter. These men "hathe thought requisite that all ydle Bookes or wanton Pamphlettes should bee forbidden".[20] Although there is no concrete evidence that *A Hundreth Sundrie Flowres* became a banned book, the clear implication is that it did indeed attract the attention of ecclesiastical censors and that copies were seized. Although not in itself proof of seizure it is suggestive that very few copies of *A Hundreth Sundrie Flowres* seem to have survived. A print run for a book of this sort is likely to have been around 1,000 copies. Today, fewer than twenty copies are known to exist.

These powerful but unidentified "grave and graye headed Judges" were almost certainly Her Majesty's Commissioners in Causes Ecclesiastical, who by 1570 were more commonly known as "the High Commission" or "the High Commissioners". Any documentation that may have existed concerning the suppression of *A Hundreth Sundrie Flowres* has not survived. The Commission was abolished in 1641 and most of its records appear to have been deliberately destroyed during the English revolution – "registry books, act books, immense files of pleadings and lawyers' briefs, and bales and sacks of papers...in short, of every scrap of evidence great and small connected with the Court".[21] Ironically, it was the Commission's powers of censorship which eventually led to its termination during the English revolution. Its efforts to censor militant Puritan literature and burn books by John Bastwick and William Prynne inflamed popular opinion and resulted in the Commission's abolition on the grounds of its illegality and "great and insufferable wrongs and oppression of the King's subjects".[22]

The Commission had its origins in the break with Rome and in the time of Henry VIII was concerned with heretics who denied the royal supremacy. Edward VI had used commissions to uphold the Book of Common Prayer and the Forty-Two Articles; under Mary they were employed to remove the Edwardian bishops, reinstate the priests and banish the Book of Common Prayer in favour of the mass and images. Elizabeth then used them to reinstate the Book of Common Prayer.

The earliest commissions were small, temporary investigations and the first general commission was probably not formed until 1549. In the decades that followed the scope of the commissioners widened to deal with a broad range of matters which threatened the established order. These included those who refused to attend any part or all of a church service, the threat to peace posed by vagabonds and masterless men, immorality at the Inns of Court, and offensive publications.

In 1557 Queen Mary issued a commission to twenty-two commissioners "for a severer way of proceeding against heretics". The Patent declared that many false rumours and seditious books had been set forth and that misdemeanours and enormities had been committed to the disturbance of the peace and disquieting of the people. To prevent this the Crown authorized

> full power and authority unto you and three of you, to enquire, as well by the oaths of twelve good and lawful men, as by witnesses, and all other means and politic ways you can devise, of all and sundry heresies, heretical opinions, Lollardies, heretical and seditious books, concealments, contempts, conspiracies, and of all false rumours, tales, seditious and clamorous words or sayings, raised, published, bruited, invented, or set forth against us, or either of us; or against the quiet governance and rule of our people and subjects, by books, letters, tales, or otherwise, in any country, city, borough, or other place or places within this our realm of England and elsewhere.[23]

Powers included the searching of premises, "to give and award such punishment to the offenders by fine, imprisonment or otherwise". Though ecclesiastical in name the commission was, in Gascoigne's lifetime, controlled and directed by the State. The jurisdiction of the commission was determined by the Privy

Council, although sometimes its remit was so vague as to allow for great flexibility. An examination of "all abuses and enormities of religion" could easily, for example, take in such offensive material as "Gascoigne's Recantation". That *The Adventures of Master F.J.* might attract the commission's attention is no real surprise, bearing in mind that in 1581 Her Majesty's Commissioners for Causes Ecclesiastical were sternly ordered by the Privy Council to bring about "a reform of the morals of the Inns of Court".

The strong probability is that *A Hundreth Sundrie Flowres* fell foul of the Commissioners for Causes Ecclesiastical in the Province of Canterbury and was condemned by some of those who served on its 1572 commission (which was almost certainly still operating in 1573). These commissioners were usually men who were resident in London and the scope of their business was very broad; "the Province of Canterbury" covered half the country. The 1572 commission was the first big commission in the body's history. Membership had previously been limited to twenty-seven at most but now its numbers were substantially increased, greatly enlarging its scope and power.

The names of the sixty-eight individuals entitled to sit on this commission have survived[24] and they break down into four groups: bishops and other senior ecclesiastics (16), judges and lawyers (10), senior state figures (13) and a miscellaneous group of gentlemen including knights, Bachelors and Doctors of Divinity, and Aldermen of the City of London. (29). It was, in other words, a broadly representative slice of the Elizabethan ruling class. However, the real power undoubtedly lay with the most senior members of the Commission, and twenty-eight members of the Commission of 1572 were only permitted to exercise their authority in the dioceses. In order to transact its business the 1572 Commission required a quorum of twenty-five. The composition of this quorum was weighted in favour of the bishops and lawyers. It is therefore most unlikely that all or even a majority of the Commission's members were involved in the suppression of *A Hundreth Sundrie Flowres*. The investigation of an allegedly scandalous book may well have involved only two or three commissioners. Quite possibly a single person was delegated to read it and report back.

The question arises of how *A Hundreth Sundrie Flowres* came to be investigated by the Commissioners for Causes Ecclesiastical in the first place. The history of the commission suggests either that the Commissioners were specifically instructed by the Privy Council or that the book was drawn to the Commissioners' attention during some kind of wider investigation of immorality or "clamorous words or sayings". Gascoigne's reference to the forbidding of "all ydle Bookes or wanton Pamphlettes" suggests a general clampdown on immoral literature. In his Second Prefatory Letter to *The Posies of George Gascoigne Esquire* Gascoigne referred to "grave Philosophers" who "have thought meete to forbid the publishing of any ryming trifles which may serve as whetstones to sharpen youth unto vanities".[25] Again, it is unclear whether *A Hundreth Sundrie*

Flowres was singled out for special attention or simply fell foul of a general suppression of immoral literature.

Censorship was always a part of the Commission's work and its power was extensive. As Usher notes, the Letters Patent "invested the commissioners with an almost unlimited jurisdiction". The Letters Patent of 1559 reinforced earlier powers of censorship in a slightly re-worded form, giving the Commission broad powers to crack down on any printed material which took the form of "heretical opinions", "seditious books" or "slanderous words".[26]

The timing of the assault on *A Hundreth Sundrie Flowres* is suggestive. Since Gascoigne was denounced to the Privy Council in 1572 it seems highly likely that whoever had seen his work in manuscript and complained that the poet was "a common Rymer and a deviser of slaunderous Pasquelles againste divers personnes of great callinge" would have been enraged to find the poems and *The Adventures of Master F.J.* actually appearing in print. *A Hundreth Sundrie Flowres* purported to be an anonymous anthology of writings by various gentlemen and therefore on the face of it there would be no immediate reason for the Privy Council to connect it with the earlier complaint against Gascoigne. But someone clearly had it in for the writer. Was it simply a creditor, a jealous, double-dealing acquaintance of Gascoigne's, or was it someone on the Commission itself?

Of the 68 names on the 1572 Commission one is quite remarkable. Could the Commission's "Edward Boys, B.D." be the same Edward Boyes (also spelt Boys) who married Elizabeth Bacon Breton in the spring of 1559, who fought with Gascoigne on Red Cross Street in September 1562 and who then became enmeshed in a long-running legal action with the poet? In a Chancery Bill of 1566 Boyes is described as "gent" and at the time of his death in 1599 he was identified as "Edward Boyes Esq." Edward Boyes had every reason to hate George Gascoigne, who was the man who had not only bigamously married his wife but who had also emerged triumphantly in possession both of Elizabeth and her fortune. But did he also graduate with the degree of Bachelor of Divinity and if so was he the man of that name who sat as a member of the Commissioners for Causes Ecclesiastical in the Province of Canterbury in 1572? If Boyes and Boys are the same man then we need look no further for the individual who had a violent animus against Gascoigne and who was active in suppressing *A Hundreth Sundrie Flowres*. Edward Boys, B.D. also sat on the 1576 Commission, which is likely to have been the one which spurned Gascoigne's apologies and which ordered the seizure of the revised edition in its new guise as *The Posies of George Gascoigne Esquire*.

That "Edward Boys, B.D." is the same man as the Edward Boyes who fell out with Gascoigne is possible. Boyes was typical of the kind of man chosen to sit on a commission and he was also a leading member of the Kent gentry, which would strengthen the likelihood of him serving on the Canterbury commission. In 1577 he was appointed Sheriff of Kent. When *The Whole woorkes of George Gascoigne Esquyre* was published in 1587 it seems to have attracted no attention from the commission, despite having the same contents as the two earlier volumes which had caused offence. But by this time "Edward Boys" was no longer a member. Besides, any personal animosity on Boyes's part must by then have faded, in the knowledge that Gascoigne was ten years dead.

Gascoigne may have had some inkling of a personal vendetta against his book. In his second Prefatory Letter he suggests that even the most wholesome and delightful matter can be picked on and wrongfully accused: "so the malicious Spider may also gather poison out of the fairest floure that growes".[27] The metaphor was a commonplace one but the notion of *malice* is reiterated in the third Prefatory Letter ("the good writer shall be sure of some to bee maliced").[28] The reverend Divines had a humourless and moralistic agenda but there was nothing personal about their suppression of Gascoigne's book. Others may have been working from quite different motives.

If "Edward Boys" and "Edward Boyes" are the same man, then a great deal is explained about how Gascoigne's book came to be banned. However, that identification, though possible, is not proven. A B.D. was a standard undergraduate degree in theology, though it was commonly done after an Arts degree, and seven years of dedicated study is perhaps hard to square with the Edward Boyes who brawled in the street and appears to have been keenly interested in the acquisition of material riches. "Boyes" was a common surname in Kent and the similarity of names may just be a coincidence. Either way, "Edward Boys, B.D." did not by himself have the power to ban books. That formidable right lay with the senior members of the Commission. In considering who was responsible for banning *A Hundreth Sundrie Flowres* we need look no further than the important churchmen. Edward Boys, B.D. may have brought the book to the Commission's attention, and may even have produced a report on its contents, but it was the senior ecclesiastics who would have supplied the moral outrage at Gascoigne's sometimes facetious attitude to matters of religion and his scandalously explicit treatment of sex and adultery. That *The Adventures of Master F.J.* consisted of "slanderous words" was surely self-evident.

No personal animus was needed to motivate a strong distaste for the contents of *A Hundreth Sundrie Flowres* among men like John Aylmer, Archdeacon of Lincoln, Nicholas Bullingham, Bishop of Worcester, Richard Cox, Bishop of Ely, Richard Curteys, Bishop of Chichester, William Day, Dean of the Chapel Royal, Richard Dayves, Bishop of St David's, Edmund Freak, Bishop of Rochester, Thomas Godwin, Dean of Canterbury, Gabriel Goodman, Dean of Westminster, Robert Horne, Bishop of Winchester, Alexander Nowell, Dean of St Paul's, William Overton, Bishop of Coventry and Lichfield, Matthew Parker, Archbishop of Canterbury and Robert Weston, Dean of Wells. These fourteen men are "the reverende Divines" whom Gascoigne pleaded with in his first Prefatory Letter (not knowing that the composition of the 1576 Commission would slightly change).

It is surely significant that included in the peroration of *The fruites of Warre* is a stanza of sycophantic salute to the elders of the English church:

> Right reverend, of *Canterbury* chief,
> *London*, and *Lincoln*, Bishops by your name,
> Good Dean of Paul's (which lend a great relief
> To naked need) and all the rest of fame,
> In pastors' place: with whom I were too blame,
> If *Nevynson* my master were not placed,
> Since by his help I learning first embraced.[29]

Matthew Parker, Archbishop of Canterbury, and Alexander Nowell, the Dean of St Paul's Cathedral, both served on the Commission, and Gascoigne was anxious to stress his religious orthodoxy. Mentioning Stephen Nevynson was a shrewd way of underlining his Protestant credentials, as Nevynson was an honoured and loyal servant of the reformed church.

From what little is known of the workings of the Commission it is likely that only a handful of commissioners would have been involved with the banning and seizure of *A Hundreth Sundrie Flowres*, if that is indeed what occurred. A gathering of just three commissioners possessed full legal authority and it was not uncommon for such small groups to investigate particular cases. Indeed, "examinations of witnesses and minor inquiries were conducted by two or even by one commissioner".[30] Commissioners were entitled to hold their sittings wherever they wished, and duly did so – in churches, palaces, dining-rooms and even gardens. The standard procedure simply seems to have involved commissioners questioning a suspect or witness. In Gascoigne's case, interrogation of the offender was not possible as he had left the country to fight in the Low Countries. Presumably what happened is that the book was banned and copies seized in his absence. By the time he returned to England there was no need to question the author, for the matter was over and dealt with. But it is just possible that Gascoigne was himself seized in connection with the offence his book has caused. The dedication to the next work that Gascoigne published contains an oblique hint that he may have been briefly imprisoned in the Tower of London.[31]

Although "the reverend Divines" were technically in a minority on the Commissioners for Causes Ecclesiastical in the Province of Canterbury it is most unlikely that there would have been any opposition to their wish to ban and seize copies of an apparently scurrilous book like *A Hundreth Sundrie Flowres*. The assumption that *The Adventures of Master F.J.* was about real members of an aristocratic family would have been quite enough to damn the book in the eyes of secular members of the Commission, even assuming that they were involved in discussing it. The seizure of Gascoigne's book was essentially a very minor matter in relation to the broader work of the Commission. Heresy and attempts to subvert the Protestant state were matters of far greater consequence than a book which, by the narrow standards of the time, was guilty only of immorality.

There is no other motive for Gascoigne subsequently bothering to address the censors than that he wished to see his writings back in the public domain again. Nor is there any conceivable reason why Gascoigne would bother revising and re-arranging the contents of *A Hundreth Sundrie Flowres* if it *hadn't* been banned. What would be the point? His intention, clearly, was to defuse the accusations which had evidently been levelled against the book.

Gascoigne claimed to have been out of the country when *A Hundreth Sundrie Flowres* was published and to have returned after "verie neare two yeares past", only to discover that

> at my returne, I find that some of them have not onely bene offensive for sundrie wanton speeches and lascivious phrases, but further I heare that the same have beene doubtfully construed, and (therefore) scandalous.[32]

Gascoigne expresses his shock at the misreading and misunderstanding of his book which has occurred during his absence from England while "in service with the virtuous Prince of Orenge [*sic*]". Having established his credentials as a Protestant patriot fighting the papists in the Low Countries, Gascoigne goes on to insist that he is both a gentleman and a man of middle age, remote from the follies of "greene youth". He indignantly denies that there was a financial motive in seeking publication or that he did anything as vulgar as accept "great summes of money for the first printing of these Posies...it is moste true (and I call Heaven and Earth too witnesse) that I never receyved of the Printer, or of anye other, one grote or pennie".[33]

Gascoigne gives five reasons why he chose to publish *A Hundreth Sundrie Flowres*. Firstly, poetry has never been banned in any society and is something of intrinsic merit ("in all ages Poetrie hath beene not onely permitted, but also it hath beene thought a right good and excellent quality"). Secondly, Gascoigne's own writings are patriotically English and avoid "borrowing of other languages, such as Epithetes and Adjectives as smell of the Inkhorne". Thirdly, possessing "those giftes wherwith it hath pleased the Almighty to endue [endow] me", Gascoigne was anxious to put them in the "publike recorde...To the ende that thereby the virtuous might bee incouraged to employ my penne in some exercise which might tende both to my preferment, and to the profite of my Countrey". Fourthly, although one or two items in the book might be objectionable he had "written sundry things which coulde not chuse but content the learned and Godlye Reader", proving even to "the light minded" that he "coulde aswell sowe good graine, as graynes or draffe". Finally, while "the better sort" of the book's contents might "purchase good lyking with the honourable aged" so "in the worst sorte" the writing "might yet serve as a myrrour for unbridled youth, to avoyde those perilles which I had passed".[34]

Pursuing the theme of the possible moral value of writing which may describe unsavoury matters, Gascoigne modestly aligned himself with Theodore Beza (1519-1605). Beza was a scholar appointed to head a college of higher education for Protestants set up in Geneva by Calvin in 1559. He later became Calvin's successor and to English Protestants Beza was a distinguished and greatly admired figure. In 1548, before his conversion, Beza published a collection of neo-Latin poems. His enemies later used these to make exaggerated accusations of personal immorality. Gascoigne wrote:

> I delight to thinke that the reverend father Theodore Beza, whose life is worthily become a lanterne to the whole worlde, did not yet disdaine too suffer the continued publication of such Poemes as he wrote in his youth. And as he termed them at last *Poëmata castrata*, So shal your reverend judgements beholde in this seconde edition, my Poemes gelded from all filthie phrases, corrected in all erroneous places, and beautified with addition of many moral examples.[35]

Gascoigne also noted that offence had been taken at "certaine wanton wordes and sentences" in *The Adventures of Master F.J.* and that the narrative had commonly been read as a true and scandalous account of "some worthie personages". He acknowledged the justice of the first complaint but firmly rejected the second. *The fable of Ferdinando Jeronimi and the Lady Elinora de Valasco*, like its original version, featured "no living creature":

> And for the rest you shall find it now in this second imprinting so turquened and turned, so clensed from all unclenly wordes, and so purged from the humor of inhumanitie, as percase you woulde not judge that it was the same tale.[36]

Modern critics agree that the second version of *The Adventures of Master F.J.* is indeed not "the same tale" but they also consider it vastly inferior to the original. The wider credibility of Gascoigne's claims to have purged his writings of unsavoury matter, and the High Commission's response, is something to be considered later. In 1573 *A Hundreth Sundrie Flowres* may have caused uproar, but Gascoigne was safely overseas, away from the fuss. It would be another two years, perhaps three, before a new edition appeared.

*

Although members of the High Commission regarded *A Hundreth Sundrie Flowres* as scandalous and disgraceful, other readers clearly enjoyed the book enormously. These divisions went right to the heart of the Tudor ruling class. On the face of it there is a puzzling contradiction between *A Hundreth Sundrie Flowres* being apparently banned in 1573 or 1574, Gascoigne's employment by the Earl of Leicester to entertain the Queen in 1575, and the confiscation of the book's second edition at almost exactly the same moment that he received state employment from Lord Burghley and Francis Walsingham. What these contradictions show is that the Tudor ruling class was far from homogenous. England at that time resembled certain modern states today, where power is in conflict between repressive religious fundamentalists and more liberal, pragmatic, secular forces. Put simply, *A Hundreth Sundrie Flowres* offended the forces of religious conservativism. It probably did not shock the court or men like the Earl of Leicester; on the contrary, they probably loved the book. Leicester supported his own company of players and was constantly protecting the profession from busybodies who thought acting and theatre were immoral and subversive. Eleanor Rosenberg points to the Earl's defence of the recusant Sebastian Westcote as a sign "that Leicester was actually more concerned about drama than about religious convictions".[37] But though a powerful statesman could protect acting companies he was associated with, it was the fundamentalists who had the power to suppress books. They avidly used that power, in the name of all that was decent and godly.

Not surprisingly, what shocked elderly churchmen seems to have thrilled young male readers (and quite possibly female ones as well). Gascoigne's manuscripts probably circulated among groups of readers and involved an element of performance. But a book could be consumed in private, alone in a room. And what could be more fascinating than writing that was funny, clever, and irreverent, with lots of sex? By the standards of the time *A Hundreth Sundrie Flowres* seems to have been what we would now call a bestseller, and its impact on other writers was extensive. Gascoigne couldn't quite resist supplying his own blurb for the second edition, boasting in the second Prefatory Letter that "the first Copie of these my Posies hath beene verie much inquired for by the yonger sort".[38] When Gascoigne later wrote of a time when he enjoyed his fame, "To hear it said, there goeth *the Man that writes so well*",[39] he is unlikely to have been exaggerating. But even among those who enjoyed the book there were those who didn't understand it in the way Gascoigne wanted them to. In the revised edition Gascoigne followed up his address to the High Commission with two more prefatory letters, one "To al yong Gentlemen, and generally to the youth of England" and "To the Readers generally a generall advertisement of the Authour".

The second Prefatory Letter clarifies the objections of the High Commission to *A Hundreth Sundrie Flowres*. If the most overtly offensive work in the book was *The Adventures of Master F.J.* the Commission's greatest anxiety was the bad influence that it and the other writings might have on impressionable young men. The "greatest offence that hath beene taken thereat, is least your mindes might hereby become envenomed with vanities," Gascoigne informed "the youth of England".[40]

Displaying a cool indifference to the finer feelings of High Commission members, Gascoigne rounds on

> three sortes of men which (beeing wonderfully offended at this booke) have founde therein three maner of matters (they say) verie reprehensible. The men are these: curious Carpers, ignorant Readers, and grave Philosophers. The faultes they find are, *Iudicare* in the Creede: Chalke for Cheese: and the common infection of Love. Of these three sortes of men and matters, I do but very little esteeme the two first. But I deeply regarde the thirde.[41]

Gascoigne's regard for the "grave Philosophers" on the Commission seems a little perfunctory as he rages against the blockheads who have criticised *A Hundreth Sundrie Flowres*. He compares his critics to "the spawne of a Crab or Crevish" – crabs and crayfish being regarded in Tudor times as unnatural and ridiculous creatures with a foolish method of locomotion. He also lashes theological pedants and obsessives of the type who, "when they can indeede finde none other fault, will yet think *Iudicare* verie untowardlye placed in the Creede". To hammer home the point he also mentions the famous Renaissance story about the nit-picking cobbler who complained about inaccuracies in a painting by the legendary master, Apelles.

Gascoigne supplies specific examples of textual misreadings. He complains that "Gascoigne's Arraignment" and "Gascoigne's Libel of Divorce" have been "mistaken in sad earnest" by readers who failed to grasp that they were comic poems, "written in jeast". He refers to an abusive exchange of poems between Thomas Churchyard and Thomas Camel and claims that one "blockheaded reader" thought the dispute involved two neighbours, one of whom had a camel which strayed into a churchyard. He alleges that the Earl of Surrey's poem "In winters just returne", in which a "poore" and "simple" shepherd tells how he came upon a suicidal, broken-hearted lover, was assumed by some naïve readers to have actually been written by a shepherd. Likewise, others believed that Lord Vaux had penned his poem beginning "I loathe that I did love" (anthologised under Tottel's title "The Aged Lover Renounceth Love") when he was actually dying, not understanding the artifice involved in the creation of this poem, with its mention of "A pickaxe and a spade, / And eke a winding sheet". Lastly,

Gascoigne mentions the naïvety of those readers who believed that "the Soulknill of M. Edwards was also written in extremitie of sicknesse", although which poem he has in mind is obscure.[42]

The odd one out in this inventory of misreadings is the Churchyard/Camel example, which appears merely to involve the misunderstanding of a book's contents on the basis of its title – the book in question being *The Contention between Churchyard and Camell upon David Dycers Dreame* (1560). It is not a very persuasive line of argument for Gascoigne to take, bearing in mind that *A Hundreth Sundrie Flowres* had a very misleading title – not to mention its bogus editorial apparatus deliberately designed to fool the reader.

But apart from that anomaly the thrust of his argument is clear. Many readers are incapable of distinguishing between a writer's persona and the writer himself. The complaint both is and is not justified. In one sense Gascoigne was right to insist on the comedy in his writing and the naïvety of those who failed to detect his use of irony and comic hyperbole (and presumably such dull-witted readers also missed out on the extensive double entendres). But to some extent Gascoigne only had himself to blame for the misreadings of his text. The linking prose passages of "The Devises of Sundrie Gentlemen" suggested that the poems were indeed about real people in real situations.

The titles also indicated that the verses were inspired by actual people and that an entity named "Gascoigne" was the star of the show. The point was hammered home time and time again: "Gascoigne's Anatomy", "Gascoigne's Arraignment", "Gascoigne's Passion", "Gascoigne's Libel of Divorce", "Gascoigne's Praise of his Mistress", "Gascoigne's Lullaby", "Gascoigne's Recantation".

It is strangely contradictory, then, that in his third Prefatory Letter addressed "To the Readers generally" Gascoigne denied that most of his poems were autobiographical, insisting "that the most part of them were written for other men".[43] This is wildly implausible and underlines Gascoigne's scattergun response to criticism. Throughout the three letters Gascoigne constantly shifts his ground. He squirms, blusters, pleads and adopts a variety of voices: quietly pious and Bible-quoting, jeering and angry, mocking and sarcastic, solemn and moralistic.

He had little choice. He was a Tudor writer and his life's work had been banned. If he wanted to see his writing in print again he had to put on a good show. He needed to persuade the censors that he was a reformed character and that his book was cleansed of offence. Only time would tell if he'd pulled it off.

22: The Fox and the Geese

Gascoigne's solution to censorship and scandal was to pick up his pen and try to write his way back into favour. He was clearly determined to see his life's work back in print. To that end he retreated to Walthamstow, revised *The Adventures of Master F.J.* and re-arranged the order of the contents of his book. He was also at work on new material to be included in a second edition. He penned his three prefaces apologising for any offence caused and insisted that his book had been misunderstood. Better still, he was a truly reformed character – penitent, devout, anxious only that his more offensive writing serve the worthy purpose of deterring modern youth from making the same mistakes that he'd made. These arguments were contradictory, but self-contradiction never bothered George Gascoigne. He thought fast and wrote fast. He danced playfully between different points of view. He was determined to batter his critics into submission. Any argument, any writing, would do.

To demonstrate his newfound piety he composed what was probably his first publication after *A Hundreth Sundrie Flowres*, a play entitled *The Glass of Government*. The play was never performed in Gascoigne's lifetime, nor has it been since. Nor is it ever likely to be. It is a seriously flawed work, which is more mental theatre than something viable for the stage. No doubt it was written in the poet's study at Thorpe Hall, most likely in the spring of 1575. The play is set in the Low Countries and probably owes something to an early sixteenth-century Dutch humanist tradition of Latin drama about the education of young men and prodigal sons. Gascoigne may well have bought copies of such plays while at The Hague or in Delft. But his conception of *The Glass of Government* was also heavily coloured by his practical experience of *Jocasta* and *Supposes*. The play attempts to blend the sententious stateliness of the former with the knockabout comedy of the latter.

Gascoigne found a different publisher for this work. It was printed "by H M for Christopher Barker at the signe of the Grassehopper in Paules Churchyarde". The play is prefaced by a woodcut about the size of a matchbox, showing a figure raising an axe above a tree stump, apparently chopping pages. Above it is the couplet

> A Barker if ye will,
> In name but not in skill.

The publisher was evidently enjoying a private joke about his name, tree bark, paper and publishing. But despite the self-deprecating comment, the play was competently produced, with only seven "Faultes escaped in the printe", all trivial (such as the inadvertent omission of the definite article).

Barker explained that "This worke is compiled upon these sentences following, set downe by mee C.B."

Feare, God, for he is just.
Love God, for hee is mercifull.
Trust in God, for he is faythfull.

This was followed by another eight numbered sections, with invocations to obey royal authority, "Adventure thy life in defence and honor of thy cuntrie, for the quarrel is good", honour priests, respect magistrates, honour your parents, respect the old and "Be holie, for thou art the Temple of God".

By the sound of it, Barker was a publisher with strong religious tendencies. What he meant by "compiled" and "set downe by me" is ambiguous. It could mean he commissioned Gascoigne to write the play, or that he was simply providing a handy summary of its profound moral worth. The "quarrel" might be the Dutch war and a sign that Gascoigne had impressed upon him his personal involvement in that noble cause. In short, Barker may have been a completely gullible man, easily outfoxed by someone as slippery as George Gascoigne, Esquire. He may not even have realised that Gascoigne was the presiding genius behind the scandalous *Hundreth Sundrie Flowres*. Barker thought he was getting a solemn religious play from a respectable soldier in the war against papistry; Gascoigne was happy to use Barker to further his reinvention as a man of quiet religious respectability. That scenario is entirely speculative but is at least a possibility in helping to explain an oddity like *The Glass of Government*.

Gascoigne no doubt kept an entirely straight face at Barker's emphasis on the importance of honouring "thy cuntrie". The title "the glass of government" means "the mirror (or shining example) of wise authority/self-restraint and good behaviour" and the play contrasts the educational fortunes of the youngest and oldest sons from two close and wealthy families. The two younger sons Phylotimus and Phylomusus, both aged nineteen, are diligent, virtuous and hardworking. Their older brothers, Phylosarchus and Phylautus, are twenty, and far more interested in pleasure and entertainment than hard work and education. A schoolmaster named Gnomaticus attempts to inculcate all four brothers with the finest teachings and moral examples. But the two older brothers become involved with a whore named Lamia and her associates Dick Drum, Pandarina and Eccho (*sic*). At the end of the play Phylosarchus and Dick Drum are executed for carrying out a robbery and Phylautus is banished for fornication and given a severe whipping.

Gascoigne described the play as "A tragicall Comedie" but that uneasy definition points to one of the play's many problems. *Jocasta* and *Supposes* were quite different types of theatre and mixing slow-moving Greek tragedy with racy Italian comedy was a challenge too great for him. The commercial theatre of Marlowe and Shakespeare did not yet exist and Gascoigne's only practical experience of audiences and how they responded was at Gray's Inn.

But what entertained law students, well used to lengthy disquisitions, nit-picking arguments and solemn citations of legal authority, was not what necessarily pleased the majority who lived their lives outside this narrow world.

Gascoigne also wrote best when he wrote about himself and his own preoccupations. He lacked the true dramatist's gift of empathy. In *The Glass of Government* the brothers are not rounded, individual characters and the reader's sympathies are not engaged. It is hard to care about any of them. The two younger brothers are nauseatingly virtuous prigs and the fate of the older brothers is likely to leave the reader unmoved. The play, which is firmly on the side of good behaviour, is more likely to evoke yawns than laughter or tears.

The faults of *Jocasta* are duplicated in *The Glass of Government*, which has far too many lengthy speeches and far too little action.[1] The chorus of "four grave Burghers" is also likely to induce drowsiness as it troops in to offer sententious reflections at the end of each act. Perhaps surprisingly for someone involved in producing a comedy by Ariosto, Gascoigne had a poor sense of dramatic potential. A key moment near the end of the play, when Lamia, Pandarina and Eccho are seized by an officer, is described, not staged. When one of the characters complains that "there are too many strange names for me to remember" it is not an opinion the reader is likely to dissent from, faced with a play whose leading characters include Phylopaes, Phylocalus, Phylotimus, Phylomusus, Phylosarchus and Phylautus.

The language of the play really only comes alive when it captures the reality of everyday Tudor life – as in Dick Drum's grumble that his coat is so old and "hath cleft so long to my shoulders that a louse can not well climb the cliffs thereof without a pitchfork in her hand". But moments like that are few. Much commoner are Gnomaticus's ponderous recommendations of the importance of being acceptable to God, pleasing to the world, profitable to oneself and respectful to one's parents.

Ronald C. Johnson has suggested that in its treatment of the prodigal son theme, *The Glass of Government* had an indirect influence on *All's Well That Ends Well*.[2] The comic character Parolles (who in some ways is the ancestor of Falstaff) is at one point called "Good Tom Drum" (V.iii.315), and elsewhere there is a reference to "John Drum's entertainment" (III.vi.36), which may echo Gascoigne's Dick Drum. True or not, Shakespeare certainly read Gascoigne's play. Phylosarchus' naïve description of the whore Lamia (whom he believes to be respectably virtuous) – "and the sweetness of her heavenly breath, surpasseth the spiceries of *Arabia*" (III.iv) – surely lingered in Shakespeare's memory and imagination, to be recycled as "all the perfumes of Arabia will not sweeten this little hand" (*Macbeth*, V.i.48; First Folio text).

C. T. Prouty believed that the play was a sign of Gascoigne's "moral reformation".[3] It was certainly an attempt to impress upon those who had the power to censor books that its author was a devout Protestant who was firmly opposed to vice and believed in the importance of wise authority. "Blessed are they that fear the Lord, their children shall be as the branches of olive trees round about their table" is the pious message of the book's title page. The play was duly passed by the ecclesiastical censors and Gascoigne was keen to stress this fact. *Seen and allowed, according to the order appointed in the Queenes majesties Injunctions* boasts the title page. That the play shows Gascoigne to be a man transformed is very questionable, however. "The fox can preach sometimes, but then beware the geese," intones the chorus at the end of Act Four, reworking the cynical line from the epilogue to *The fruite of Fetters*. *The Glass of Government* makes more sense as a botched attempt to write another play for the Gray's Inn crowd, while simultaneously and clumsily trying to ingratiate itself with *"the reverende Divines"*. The play's imagery shows that it was composed at the same time that Gascoigne was re-structuring the contents of *A Hundreth Sundrie Flowres* as flowers, herbs and weeds:

For even as weeds, which fast by flowers do grow,
(Although they be with comely colours clad:)
Yet they are found, but seldom sweet of smell,
So vices brag, but virtue bears the bell. (Chorus, Act 3)

But in fact Gascoigne's horticultural strategy was a fraud and his pious distinction was essentially meaningless. To him, weeds *were* flowers. It is hard to believe that he really shared the play's condemnation of the "strange and unaccustomed slackness" evinced by Phylosarchus and Phylautus, who turn out to have "spent the time in writing of loving sonnets and...verses in praise of martial feats and policies" (IV.i).

There is one other oddity about this publication. It was dedicated to "the right worshipfull Sir Owen Hopton, knight, hir Majesties Lieutenant in hir tower of London", of whom Gascoigne claimed to be "by alliance your poore Kinsman". By "alliance" Gascoigne perhaps meant that he was related to Hopton in some way through his wife Elizabeth. However, a very distant ancestor of Hopton's had married a Mary Scargill, so just possibly the name-dropping poet was trumpeting that probably tenuous and inconsequential connection with Gascoigne's mother. A greater and more interesting enigma is what Gascoigne meant by the statement that he was Hopton's "debter" and that the Lieutenant had taken "exceeding travayles" on his behalf:

I am become yours bounden and assured. So that it shall bee my part with full indevour so to employ my time, as I may either coũtervaile or deserve some part of your bountifull dealings. And because I find mine estate (presently) not able any other way to present you, I am bold to dedicate this my travaile unto your name.

Although exaggerated flattery was a standard convention of any Tudor dedication to a social superior, Gascoigne was clearly deeply grateful for *something* that Hopton had done on his behalf. But what? He is not someone who had appeared in Gascoigne's life before this date, or did so again. It seems unlikely that he patronised Gascoigne as a writer, and if the poet thought that *The Glass of Government* made an appropriate work to dedicate, it suggests that Hopton was of a dour, respectable, religious temperament. Could it, one wonders, have been something to do with Hopton's role as Lieutenant of the Tower? Upon his return to England, was Gascoigne seized at the behest of a vengeful ecclesiastic on the Queen's Majesty's Commission and briefly clapped in the Tower? One commentator regarded the poet's defensive letter to the Commission as displaying an "almost abject fear".[4] Did Hopton treat him well and help to get him released? If something like this occurred it explains a good deal about why Gascoigne was motivated to write a dull, one-dimensional play about good behaviour after publishing such a complex, ironic masterpiece as *A Hundreth Sundrie Flowres*. However, there is not a scrap of evidence that any such thing happened, so the matter must remain a mystery. Whatever Gascoigne was so grateful for, the moment evidently quickly passed. Though he promised Hopton that he would not make the play the "last harvest wherof you shall reap the fruites" he didn't dedicate anything else to the Lieutenant. Instead he turned his attention once again to his most reliable and generous benefactor, Lord Grey of Wilton.

The Complaynte of Phylomene

Gascoigne's dedication of *The Glass of Government* was dated 26 April 1575. Presumably the play was published soon afterwards. That same month he began writing a verse satire with a similar title: *The Steel Glass*. However (as he later explained to Lord Grey), as soon as he had written the "*Exordium*" or first part, in which he compared his "case to that of fair Philomene, abused by the bloudy king her brother by law", he remembered his abandoned long poem entitled *The Complaynte of Phylomene*.[5] What seems to have happened then is that he stopped work on *The Steel Glass*, which has a dedication dated 15 April 1576, and set about completing his old poem, which he implies was finished by 16 April 1575.

The story of Philomena, raped by her brother-in-law, who then violently mutilated her to prevent her speaking or writing of what had happened, seems to have held a special appeal to Gascoigne. He evidently enjoyed identifying himself with this legendary victim, both as someone cruelly betrayed and abused by another, be it a lover or a bigamous woman, and as someone transformed by suffering into a melodious, lamenting nightingale. This identification took on a new force after the Queen's Majesty's Commission banned *A Hundreth Sundrie Flowres*. Now his voice had been, in its printed form, quite literally silenced.

Presumably by "*Exordium*" Gascoigne was referring to the first 160 lines of

The Steel Glass. Here the poet reprises the Philomena story by casting himself in that role as *Satyra* (or satire) and her sister as *Poesys* (or poetry). The figure of *vayne Delight* marries *Poesys* but later ravishes *Satyra* and

> Cut out my tong, with *Raysor* of *Restraynte*[6]

Gascoigne's motives in this cloudy allegory are mixed. Partly he is apologising for the licentious aspects of *A Hundreth Sundrie Flowres*, which Lord Grey had graciously deigned to overlook in the face of the poet's repentance. But partly the poem is also a howl of rage against the ecclesiastical censors:

> And yet, even as the mighty gods did deign
> For *Philomele*, that though her tong were cutte
> Yet should she sing a pleasant note sometimes:
> So have they deigned, by their divine decrees,
> That with the stumps of my reproved tong,
> I may sometimes, *Reprovers* deeds reprove,
> And sing a verse, to make them see themselves.[7]

What follows is a blistering satire on the state of Tudor England. But Gascoigne says he is licensed to make this attack, by which he perhaps means that his criticism is made from an honest Christian perspective. Nevertheless his tongue has been cut; all he has to sing with are stumps. In one sense this bitter complaint is justified. Nothing he wrote after *A Hundreth Sundrie Flowres* matches the vigour, versatility and daring of that volume. *The Steel Glass* is often credited as being the first non-dramatic poetry of any length in blank verse before *Paradise Lost*, but that in itself is simply a formal achievement. Much of Gascoigne's writing in the years 1575-6 was hack work, written to please powerful individuals or groups. Only rarely does it burst into life. The old creative freedom was gone.

Gascoigne seems to have stopped work on *The Steel Glass* before launching his satire on the state of the nation and concentrated instead on completing *The Complaynte of Phylomene*. The word "complaynte" in the title carried greater force in the sixteenth century than it does today. It signified both a wail of protest and a melancholy lament. This long poem provides a more literal rendition of the legend than the allegorically inclined version in the introduction to *The Steel Glass*. But as a symbol of the censors' assault on his creative freedom, Gascoigne was keen to milk the legend for all it was worth. Tereus takes a knife and cuts out Philomene's "guiltless tong":

> The tong that rubbed his gall,
> The tong that told but truth,
> The tong that moved him to be mad[8]

This "tong" (or tongue) is in a symbolic sense the language of *A Hundreth Sundrie Flowres* – the brash, bawdy, satirical true-to-life voice of a cynical, experienced lover and a disrespectful satirist. Tereus is the maddened, narrow, vicious power of hypersensitive ecclesiastical censorship. Like an outcast, dissident writer of the Stalinist era Gascoigne was reduced to an oblique revenge. Clever, embittered, brilliant, he was getting his own back.

*

At some point in 1575, Gascoigne was probably involved in helping to produce and publish *A Smale handful of fragrant Flowers*. This was a first volume of fragile lyric poetry "By N.B." – almost certainly his stepson, Nicholas Breton. It was published by Richard Jones and "Dedicated for a Newe-yeeres gyft, to the honourable and virtuous Lady, the Lady Sheffeeld". Nicholas was by then probably aged about nineteen or twenty. The book is in every way saturated in Gascoigne's influence, including the use of a bogus commendation by "John Parcel" and the use of the cryptic pseudonym "G.T." There were no later dedications to Lady Sheffield, so presumably she declined to become Breton's patron.

By the following year Nicholas had probably moved out of Thorpe Hall and gone to live in the city, eventually settling in the parish of St Giles without Cripplegate, where he'd earlier lived as a child. He appears to have spent most of the rest of his life there. His first book was quickly followed by two more – *A Floorish vpon Fancie* and *The workes of a young wyt, trust vp with a Fardell of pretie fancies*, both published in the spring of 1577 and similarly crammed with echoes of Gascoigne's verse.

Gascoigne's *oeuvre* casts a long shadow over Breton's own. Nicholas was clearly intoxicated by his stepfather's fame and success and, like most young writers, he set out to imitate what he most admired. Gascoigne presumably used his own influence to help Nicholas get his first three books published. What is hard to establish is the nature of their relationship, and what makes it hard is Nicholas's silence. He wrote an epitaph for Spenser and elegies for Philip Sidney but had nothing at all to say about the death of his stepfather. There are moments when his writing *might* be about Gascoigne but only obliquely, never overtly. His "Letter of a Batchelor to a rich Widow"[9] could be about his stepfather, and the description of the faithless, man-hungry widow in "The Uncasing of Machivil's Instructions"[10] reads very much like a blistering satire on his mother, Elizabeth. If so, Breton had a lingering sense of loyalty to the memory of his dead father and a resentment that was directed much more against his mother than her third husband.

*

Gascoigne completed *The Complaynte of Phylomene* but does not seem to have gone back to *The Steel Glass* until many months later. What happened next is that he received another commission. This was from a patron even more powerful and important than Lord Grey of Wilton. More to the point, it was from someone who was not shocked by erotic innuendo or a risqué tale of adultery. This man was someone whose own life was mired in innuendo and scandalous rumour. He had clearly read *A Hundreth Sundrie Flowres* and enjoyed every word of it. What's more he not only wanted to hire Gascoigne as a scriptwriter for one of the most spectacular entertainments of the age, he also wanted him as a performer. Years earlier, he may have been in the audience at the great hall of Gray's Inn and seen *Jocasta* and *Supposes*. He offered George Gascoigne, Esquire, the opportunity of displaying his talents at the very heart of Tudor power and influence.

This man was Robert Dudley, Earl of Leicester, and the audience he was offering Gascoigne was none other than that of Elizabeth I, Queen of England and her court. The highlight of Elizabeth's royal progress that summer was to be a stay at Kenilworth Castle. Leicester intended to provide her with the most spectacular entertainment she had ever seen, all set against the stunning background of the castle and its great lake. Money was no object, and some of it seemed to be coming Gascoigne's way. In June 1575 he signed a recognisance to pay £500 arrears on lands of William Breton.[11]

It is easy to understand Gascoigne's excitement at the Earl of Leicester's commission.[12] He abandoned *The Complaynte of Phylomene* yet again, left *The Steel Glass* unfinished, and turned his mind to the forthcoming entertainments before the Queen. But at the same time he was working on another book, the history of which became entangled both with the poet's difficulties with the censors and with his forthcoming trip to Kenilworth.

The Deer Hunter

The story of George Gascoigne involves a remarkable bibliographical oddity. This is the fact that one of his books has for centuries been attributed to another writer. Even today this book has never been published under the name of its true author, George Gascoigne.

The book is *The Noble Arte of Venerie and Hunting*. The title was influential in so far as it inspired the once popular phrase used to describe hunting, although "the noble art of venery" has now largely fallen into disuse, along with the sport itself. The book, 250 pages long (with an appendix of four unnumbered pages which describe 17 varieties of hunting calls, with musical notation) is a practical hunting manual.[13] It is mostly in prose but includes eleven poems and 53 illustrations (the first one, on the title page, in colour). Much of it is translated from a French hunting manual. First published anonymously in 1575, *The Noble Arte of Venerie and Hunting* has been misattributed to George

Turberville for more than three and a half centuries. Neither of Gascoigne's two American biographers realised that the book was his work. John W. Cunliffe, editor of *The Complete Works of George Gascoigne* (1907-10), included one poem from the book but nothing else.

The error stemmed from the fact that Gascoigne's book was commonly bound up with George Turberville's *The Book of Faulconrie, or Hawking*, which was first published by Christopher Barker in the same year, 1575. This was the same publisher who produced *The Noble Arte of Venerie and Hunting*. The books were obviously commissioned at the same time. But because Gascoigne's book was published anonymously (and secondly in the single volume) it was naturally assumed that this companion piece to Turberville's book about falconry was the work of the same author. Once paired in this way, the error became institutionalised. The second edition of Turberville's book, published by Thomas Purfoot in 1611, was also bound up with the second edition of *The Noble Arte of Venerie and Hunting*. In fact a careful reading of Gascoigne's book indicates that its author cannot be Turberville. *The Noble Arte of Venerie* puts forward the view that as a sport hunting is superior to hawking. Beside it is the laconic marginal note, "*The Falconer sayth no.*"

Hazlitt seems to have understood who was responsible for the book, describing it as "a compilation by Gascoigne".[14] However, it was not until 1942 that Jean Robertson pointed out that the authorship of *The Noble Arte of Venerie* was indicated by George Whetstone's 1577 elegy for Gascoigne.[15] In it the poet is made to say

> My Doomes day Drum, from sin dooth you awake.
> For honest sport, which dooth refresh the wit:
> I have for you, a book of hunting writ.[16]

The first line refers to Gascoigne's theological translations, collectively published in 1576 under the title *The Droomme of Doomes day*. Underlining the fact that these lines refer to two separate published books are Whetstone's printed marginal annotations. The first reads "Drum of doomsday" and the second "Hunting". Robertson concluded: "There is little doubt that Gascoigne was responsible for both the poetical interludes and the prose translations of *The Noble Arte of Venerie and Hunting*; and an edition of his works that omits this book cannot be called complete."[17]

Her attribution of this title to Gascoigne is now widely accepted as accurate in academic circles. However, the book has not been republished for almost a century and has yet to appear in print with his name on the title page. At the present time *The Noble Arte of Venerie and Hunting* is Gascoigne's most obscure and least accessible work and it remains popularly associated with George Turberville, who is often still stated to be its author.

*

In "Gascoigne's Woodmanship" the poet represented himself as a comically incompetent hunter. His lack of skill with an unfamiliar crossbow may have been true enough but it is most unlikely that he was quite such a bad huntsman as he pretends. On the contrary, he was almost certainly a very good one. As the son of Sir John Gascoigne, the poet was brought up to hunt on the large family estate south of Bedford. Gascoigne's expertise with a crossbow cannot be known but there is no reason to think that he wasn't a highly experienced and accomplished equestrian, huntsman, archer and user of firearms. In "The Green Knight's Farewell to Fancy" Gascoigne treats his days as a hunter as being of equal significance to his experiences at court, or as a writer and soldier:

> In hunting of the deer, my fancy took delight,
> All forests knew my folly still, the moonshine was my light:
> In frosts I felt no cold, a sunburnt hue was best,
> I sweat and was in temper still, my watching seemed rest:
> What dangers deep I passed, it folly were to tell,
> And since I sigh to think thereon, *Fancy* (quoth he) *farewell*.[18]

Someone who hunts by moonlight is clearly not a bumbling amateur. In the section on coursing with greyhounds in the *Noble Arte* Gascoigne added a passage which is not in the original French text about this thrilling variation:

> There is another kinde of coursing which I have more used than any of these: and that is at a Deare in the night: wherein there is more arte to be used than in any course els. But because I have promised my betters to be a friend to al Parkes, Forests, and Chaces, therefore I will not here express the experience which hath bene dearer unto me, particularly, than it is meete to be published generally.[19]

Gascoigne cannot quite resist boasting about how *his* method of deer hunting is more exotic, unusual and (surely) dangerous than the ordinary sort. In short, sexier. But, characteristically, he adds a dash of mystery. Some things are not "meete" (i.e. "proper") to be discussed generally. This is coterie literature for aristocratic hunters. His book is not entitled "The *Noble* Arte of Venerie" for nothing.

In the sixteenth century, hawking and hunting were enjoyed by all levels of society, although as with most things these were largely masculine pursuits. But deer hunting was the preserve of the ruling class – almost literally a sport for the nobility. So, in many ways, was writing (or at any rate the enduring variety we call English literature). Like his contemporaries, Gascoigne in his writing frequently draws on hunting and hunting terminology, sometimes for literal but mostly for figurative purposes. The problem for modern readers is that a whole dimension of experience has been lost to us, just as contemporary literary references to familiar objects like cars and computers and the internet, with their own specialised vocabulary, would seem baffling to anyone in a society which made no use of them. When Gascoigne describes in *The Adventures of Master F.J.* how Elinor's husband "gan assaye to rechate"[20] no modern reader is likely to know that this refers to a huntsman blowing a series of notes on a horn to call the hounds. Analogies between erotic pursuit and hunting are a little more obvious:

> as the perfect hound, when he hath chased the hurt deer, amid the whole herd, will never give over till he have singled it again

> ...ceased not by all possible means, to bring this Deer yet once again to the Bows, whereby she might be the more surely stricken: and so in the end enforced to yield.[21]

The hunting references in Gascoigne's writing indicate great familiarity with the sport, so it is logical that he should have produced a book entitled *The Noble Arte of Venerie or Hunting. Wherein is handled and set out the Vertues, Nature, and Properties of fiveteen sundrie Chaces togither, with the order and maner how to Hunte and kill every one of them. Translated and collected for the pleasure of all Noblemen and Gentlemen, out of the best approved Authors, which have written any thing concerning the same: And reduced into such order and proper termes as are used here, in this noble Realme of England.* It was intended to be a comprehensive guide to all types of hunting in Tudor England – everything from the royal sport of deer hunting to "conies" (rabbits), hares, foxes, otters, badgers, wild goats, wild boar, and coursing with greyhounds.

The reason Gascoigne chose anonymity is easy enough to understand. Firstly, producing a manual of this sort didn't fit the pious image which the poet had recently put forward in his apologetic letters prefacing *The Posies of George Gascoigne Esquire*. God's work was not furthered by helping others improve their hunting skills. Secondly, Gascoigne surely only produced the book for money. It was commissioned by a publisher with his eye on the growing market for Tudor self-improvement manuals. Essentially, for Gascoigne, it was hack work. But in his letter to the Reverend Divines he had indignantly refuted the scandalous suggestion that he had ever accepted money for *A Hundreth Sundrie Flowres*. Anonymity ensured that his cover story would not be blown. Gascoigne cheerfully owned up to his authorship to his young fan and confrère George Whetstone but the fact seems not to have been generally known. The book was omitted from Gascoigne's *Whole Woorkes* published after his death.

Christopher Barker was also, of course, the publisher of Gascoigne's *Glass of Government*. That Gascoigne was anxious to humour Barker's solemn religious sensibility is indicated by two aspects of *The Noble Arte of Venerie and Hunting*. Firstly, he omitted de Fouillox's poem about a love affair – or as Gascoigne put it, "certayne unseemely verses, which bycause they are more apt for lascivious mindes, than to be enterlaced amongst the noble termes of Venerie, I thought meete to leave them at large, for such as will reade them in French". Secondly, explicit descriptions of the mating habits of some animals were silently left out. That Gascoigne was commissioned by Barker and translated the book purely for financial reasons is further indicated by the fact that the book was dedicated by the publisher, not Gascoigne. The dedicatee, Lord Clinton, was someone with whom Gascoigne had no connection.[22] On the face of it, the ideal person to dedicate the book to would have been Arthur, Lord Grey of Wilton. But having portrayed himself to Lord Grey as a bungling amateur huntsman, Gascoigne perhaps reflected that it would be glaringly inconsistent to reveal his expertise. One suspects he never told Grey about the book.

Though adopting a cautionary anonymity as the work's translator, Gascoigne breezily supplied a poem in his own name commending the noble sport of hunting. Obviously with the busybodies on the High Commission in mind, Gascoigne emphasized the virtuous and Godly qualities of hunting:

> It occupies the mind, which else might chance to muse
> On mischief, malice, filth and frauds, that mortal men do use.

Even better, it helped to maintain health, stimulate wit, reduce pride and combat sloth. The huntsman rises early – unlike those who sleep sluggishly on at the mercy of lechery and lust. In short, hunting was the perfect vocation "for Men of Noble kind". Who on the High Commission could possibly object to that?

The poem "George Gascoigne, in the commendation of the noble Arte of Venerie", does not recommend the book but the sport. It is followed by a poem "T.M.Q. in praise of this book". This showers praise on the volume and concludes,

> A book well bought, God grant it so be sold
> For sure such books are better worth than gold.

And who was T.M.Q. who had such high regard for Gascoigne's book? All too clearly the poet himself, playing more games with capital letters (this time toying with his motto "Tam Marti quàm Mercurio"). To hammer the point home Gascoigne concluded with the Latin motto *Latet, quod non patet* – "What is not obvious is concealed".

Those twentieth-century's leading Gascoigne scholars Charles and Ruth

Prouty were shocked by the poet's cynicism. "What a deal of levity and vanity are here!" they commented.²³ Charles Prouty, in his other incarnation as Gascoigne's biographer, believed that Gascoigne underwent a profound moral conversion after *A Hundreth Sundrie Flowres* fell foul of the censors. But it is just as plausible to see Gascoigne's games as a tart response to the humourless blockheads of the High Commission. Like a principled Soviet artist under Stalin, his response to the tyranny of the state over creative expression was mockingly oblique, not full-frontal.

*

The Noble Arte of Venerie and Hunting is derived from *La Vénerie de Jacques du Fouilloux*, published in Paris in 1573. That publication combined two hunting books, du Fouilloux's *La Vénerie* and extracts from a classic medieval work on hunting, *Le Livre de Chasse* by Count Gaston de Foix. Gascoigne's version was a reasonably faithful translation, which included du Fouilloux's 63 chapters on hunting, the de Foix material and "Receptes pour guarir les Chiens de Plusieurs Maladies" ["Recipes for curing dogs of various maladies"]. However, Gascoigne periodically re-arranged the order of the original, occasionally added material and rewrote two short sections (one dealing with hunting terms). He also added six original poems (the two commendatory poems, a long poem about a royal picnic, and poems expressing the point of view of a hare, an otter and a fox). The three animal poems contradict the glowing praise for hunters in the first commendatory poem. The hare asks why he is hunted when he is of no value. The fox complains that men are more destructive than foxes and that he is only hunted because hunters need variety. The otter denounces mankind for gluttony. "The Hare, to the Hunter" carries a message which any animal rights protester would agree with:

> Are minds of men become so void of sense
> That they can joy to hurt a harmless thing?
> A silly beast, which cannot make defence?
> A wretch? A worm that cannot bite, nor sting?
> If that be so, I thank my Maker then
> For making me a beast and not a man.

Compared to men, even the lion shows compassion and discrimination. Hunters just want to kill anything that moves. They are not content with hunting harts, hinds, bucks, roe deer, goats, boars and bears but

> Must yet seek out me, silly harmless hare,
> To hunt with hounds, and course sometimes with care. [keen attention]

Gascoigne acknowledges that some animals damage a farmer's crops. The hart and buck break down hedges and spoil corn. The roe deer "doth he harm in many a field and town". Goats pull up plants and vines. Pigs ruin grassland.

> But I poor beast, whose feeding is not seen,
> Who break no hedge, who pill no pleasant plant:
> Who stroy no fruit, who can turn up no green,
> Who spoil no corn to make the ploughman want:
> Am yet pursued with hound, horse, might and main
> By murdering men, until they leave me slain.
>
> *Sa how* sayeth one, as soon as he me spies,
> Another cries *Now, now*, that sees me start,
> The hounds call on, with hideous noise and cries,
> The spur-galled jade must gallop out his part:
> The horn is blown, and many a voice full shrill
> Do whoop and cry, me wretched beast to kill.
>
> But what meanest thou man, me so for to pursue?
> For first my sin is scarcely worth a plack, [a Dutch coin]
> My flesh is dry, and hard for to endue, [use]
> My grease (God knoweth) not great upon my back,
> My self, and all, that is within me found
> Is neither good, great, rich, fat, sweet, nor sound.
>
> So that thou showest thy vaunts to be but vain,
> That bragg'st of wit, above all other beasts,
> And yet by me, thou neither gettest gain
> Nor findest food, to serve thy glutton's feasts:
> Some sport perhaps: *yet grievous is the glee*
> *Which ends in blood*, that lesson learn of me.

*

The Noble Arte of Venerie and Hunting contained fifty-three illustrations, made up of thirty-two different woodcuts (some used up to five times). Of these, twenty-seven were copies of the ones used in the French edition and five were original. Of these five, four appear to be the work of the same artist. Three of these portray Elizabeth I hunting, the fourth (on the title page) shows huntsmen with their dogs. It is possible that these four woodcuts are the work of George Gascoigne (the fifth woodcut, showing an otter eating a fish, is quite different to all the others and was probably a last-minute filler derived from some other source).

Hazlitt believed that three of these original woodcuts showed Gascoigne, and Charles and Ruth Prouty likewise noted "a certain resemblance between the huntsman and the portrait of Gascoigne on the reverse of the title-page of *The Steele Glas*".[24] That Gascoigne produced them is certainly possible. In one the huntsman presents the Queen with a knife, to make the first cut of the flesh of the dead deer. In the second a huntsman kneels before the Queen as she enjoys a picnic in the woods. In the third a huntsman displays fewmishings – a selection of deer droppings – for Her Majesty's attention. (She was supposed to scrutinise the relative merits of the excrement and use her expertise to decide which deer best merited pursuit.)

The unidentified figure presenting the Queen with a knife bears some resemblance to the portrait used in Gascoigne's book published the following year. The hair, beard and moustache are the same style. Perhaps the most striking similarity is that of the long slender nose. It may be significant that three of these woodcuts show a bearded figure kneeling before the Queen, the centre of her attention. That is precisely the arrangement used for the pen and ink drawing which Gascoigne did of himself and Elizabeth for the manuscript which he gave her on New Year's Day 1576.[25]

*

The Noble Arte of Venerie not only lacks a named author, it also lacks a year of publication. However, the letter of "The Translator to the Reader" is dated "From my chamber this xvi of Iune 1575". That may indicate that Gascoigne had the book wrapped up and finished before he ever set foot in the grounds of Kenilworth Castle. If so, that would mean the woodcuts showing hunting scenes with Elizabeth, if indeed his own work, were either entirely imaginary or derived from Gascoigne's presence at some earlier royal deer hunt.

But Kenilworth was clearly on Gascoigne's mind as he worked on his translation. In the text of Du Fouilloux instructions are solemnly given as to how a hunters' picnic should be arranged. Gascoigne converted the French prose into a long, original poem in poulter's measure. This developed into what Charles and Ruth Prouty call "a masque,"[25] involving a dramatic confrontation between a butler, a cook and their supporters. It ends with a huntsman kneeling before the Queen and reciting a poem (aptly, in rhyme royal) in which he invites her to hunt "As great a Hart as ever yet bare breath":

This may be seen (a Prince's sport indeed)
And this your grace shall see when pleaseth you:
So that vouchsafe (O noble Queen) with speed,
To mount on horse, that other may ensure,
Until this hart be roused and brought to view.

> Then if you find that I have spoke amiss,
> Correct me Queen: (till then) forgive me this.

The great hart – or heart – was Robert Dudley. There was more to this invitation than the pleasure of hunting a deer. And by becoming involved in the Earl of Leicester's private schemes, Gascoigne was entering dangerous territory and risking the wrath of no lesser person than the Queen herself.

Plate 27. The site of the Great Mere, beyond the perimeter wall of Kenilworth Castle.

Plate 28. The ruins of Kenilworth Castle today, with Leicester's Building on the right.

Plate 29. The remains of the Great Hall at Kenilworth Castle.

Plate 30. The coat of arms of William Patten, on The Old Church of St Mary's, Stoke Newington.

23: Kenilworth

In July 1575 something happened which would be remembered hundreds of years afterwards. Every biography of Queen Elizabeth I mentions it. So, too, do many biographies of William Shakespeare. And George Gascoigne is to be found at the very centre of this event.

On Saturday 9 July 1575 Elizabeth arrived at Kenilworth Castle in Warwickshire. The Queen stayed at the castle for 19 days, witnessing the costliest and most dazzling entertainment of her long reign. Among the crowds of local people who gathered to watch the fabulous variety of spectacle, music and song put on to entertain the Queen may have been an eleven-year-old from Stratford-on-Avon, just fourteen miles away. William Shakespeare unambiguously included a memory of the Kenilworth festivities in *A Midsummer Night's Dream* and this may well have derived from his life rather than his reading. If, as almost all his biographers believe, Shakespeare *was* present he would have witnessed the most extravagant theatrical show of Elizabeth's entire reign. It is easy to understand the enormous impression which it must have made upon him. It may even have been the transforming experience of his childhood, giving him the drive and motivation to become an entertainer himself.

John Brandard, a Victorian lithographer, created a rich, dense, much-reproduced picture which portrays the moment that the Queen reached the castle. Beneath a pale blue sky, Elizabeth rides through a vast crowd of onlookers. A firework explodes like a gigantic white fern above the ancient castle's battlements. The Queen sits side-saddle on her magnificent stallion, banners fluttering behind her, a white, virginal goddess dominating a colourful sea of admirers. Royal authority and dignity are aligned to the tradition and history represented by the castle in the background. Power is framed by the adulation of the common people and the impressive spectacle of state power. The colourful costumes and the glorious weather signify the impending, joyous carnival.

The lithograph perfectly expresses a popular image of the long, golden summer of Elizabeth's early reign – a carefree, merry England of gorgeous spectacle, affluence, tranquillity and good cheer. But the image is bogus. It wasn't like that at all. As she approached the castle the Queen was not greeted by fireworks. She did not ride a magnificent stallion but a palfrey – a dull, safe, plodding horse for ladies. Elizabeth was late getting to the castle and there was no blue sky or sunshine. It was so dark that the welcoming plaque above one of the gateways was illegible. The Queen's mood seems to have been prickly. When someone dressed up as a figure from Arthurian legend welcomed her and granted her dominion over the castle and its grounds, Elizabeth snapped back that it was hers already and she'd have a word with the actor later.

The scene was set for a replay of the incident at Grafton, not long before. Arriving hot and thirsty after her journey, Elizabeth was enraged to discover there was "not one drop of good drink for her" but only ale so strong it was about as thirst-quenching as sweet wine. It "did put her very far out of temper".[1] Now things were set to get much, much worse than that. In the days that followed there would be impertinent challenges to the Queen's authority, bad weather, and a calculated attempt to lecture her on her failings as a monarch, climaxing in a sudden, furious halting of the festivities. The Spanish ambassador would even report a failed assassination attempt. And George Gascoigne was at the heart of that strange matter, too.

*

Kenilworth is situated on the road between Warwick and Coventry and even today, with much of the castle in ruins and the great lake gone, it remains an impressive and imposing site. The Domesday Book of 1086 records Kenilworth as a small settlement inside the Forest of Arden. Though there was a castle at Kenilworth in Saxon times the massive expansion of the site did not occur until the twelfth century, under Geoffrey de Clinton, when the deep outer moat and the large keep known as Caesar's Tower were constructed. In later years the outer curtain wall and towers were added, enclosing a seven acre site. Outside this perimeter small streams to the south and west were dammed to create a massive artificial lake (sometimes known as the Great Mere). This was over a mile long, to the south and west of the castle, with a broad moat on the other two sides. It was the largest artificial lake in the kingdom and covered over one-hundred acres.

In the late fourteenth century, under John of Gaunt, the fortress was converted into a palace and enlarged. The Great Hall was built, with the largest span of any timber hammer-beamed roof in England. The last person significantly to develop the site was Robert Dudley. In 1563 the castle was returned to him by Elizabeth, after its ten-year confiscation following his father's involvement in the plot to put Lady Jane Grey on the throne. A year later the Queen made him Baron of Denbigh and Earl of Leicester.

Over a decade Dudley transformed it from a medieval fortress into a Tudor palace, using material from the demolished Kenilworth Abbey. Large rectangular windows were installed in the Norman keep and a columned gallery was built to link it to a rectilinear ornamental garden containing walks, plants, flowers, an aviary, an obelisk and a fountain with statuary of antique marine gods. The great Gatehouse on the northern side, which had originally formed the rear of the castle, was enlarged, modernized and turned it into the entrance. In the south-east, at the head of the lake, two new towers were constructed – Mortimer's Tower and the Flood Gate or Gallery Tower, which stood at one end of the tilt yard and included a large observation room for watching displays of Tilting and Barriers. Dudley also had a large, luxury apartment block with tall mullioned windows built overlooking the lake.

A timbered bridge fourteen feet wide and six-hundred feet long, led from the castle to The Chase on the north and west side of the castle. This was an extensive area of parkland and forest, stocked with red deer and other game, as well as containing many walks, arbours and bowers.

Leicester had two motives in staging the Kenilworth entertainments. One was to impress Elizabeth with a sixteenth-century attempt at the greatest show on earth. He wanted to dazzle her with day after day of spectacle and entertainment the like of which she had never seen before (and would, in fact, never see again). The other was more personal. He wanted to send her a message. Two messages, really. They would be above the heads of the common people, but Elizabeth and her courtiers would understand. One would be to do with politics and military matters; the second and most important one would be strictly personal.

These mixed motives required various kinds of hospitality. The first was feasting. Here, Leicester could hardly hope to surpass the food put before her by any other grand lord in the land. Elizabeth was well used to lavish banquets. But for the others he had one great advantage: Kenilworth and its grounds. One of the Queen's favourite pursuits was stag-hunting on horseback, and the Chase supplied an extensive stretch of woodland, kept well stocked with game. The castle itself was more a palace than a fortress, and more a fantasy playground and holiday hotel than a home. The Great Mere provided a huge watery stage for floating pageants, as well as a vast mirror to intensify the impact of sophisticated fireworks displays. An Italian specialist was hired to orchestrate this crackling celestial extravaganza. The fireworks could be enjoyed by the local population, who'd flock to the shores of the lake to watch in wonder. Underlining his role as benevolent and generous ruler of the locality, Leicester arranged that the common people could be admitted to the castle grounds to enjoy bear-baiting, celebrate a rustic wedding and watch a performance of the annual Hock-Tuesday Play from nearby Coventry.

But the most important component of the entertainments was to be the speeches, masques and pageants, which utilised to the full the dramatic real-life theatrical props supplied by the castle and its grounds. These would be learned and serious entertainments, using the talents of many actors. They would include elements of folklore, Arthurian legend and myths and tales from the Greek and Latin classics familiar to every educated person. To produce the scripts for these dramas the Earl assembled a team of writers which included William Hunnis, Master of the Children of the Queen's Chapel, John Badger, "Superior Beadle of Divinity" at Oxford University, George Ferrers, co-author of *A Mirrour for Magistrates*, Richard Mulcaster, high-master of St Paul's School, William Patten, and Harry (or Henry) Goldingham.[2]

These figures, apart from Goldingham, had substantial past connections with the Court. Some were writers and some were experienced in the field of pageantry and royal entertainment. But arguably the leading member of the team was George Gascoigne – the year's most sensational, controversial and fashionable writer. That, at least, was the image the poet chose to project when he later assembled his anthology of Kenilworth material: Gascoigne was the man at the creative centre, whose writing dominated the Queen's attention.

Gascoigne's position was akin to that of a serious novelist who is invited to do a Hollywood screenplay. The consequence for the writer's *oeuvre* and for literature may be small but the material rewards can be substantial. Gascoigne's writing for the Kenilworth entertainments was hack work but it gave him a powerful new patron, an entrée into the very heart of the court and state, and, best of all, the opportunity to promote not only Leicester's interests but his own. And as far as the Queen's entertainment at Kenilworth was concerned, he not only wrote key parts of the script but he made sure he had a prime part in the movie, as actor and performer. In 1575 he must have felt he was on a roll. The work poured from his pen.

*

After it was all over and Elizabeth had departed from the castle, Gascoigne put together a collection of the Kenilworth scripts and had them printed as *The princelye pleasures at the Courte at Kenelwoorth. That is to say; the Copies of all such Verses, Proses or Poeticall inuentions, and other deuices of pleasure as were there deuised by sundry Gentlemen, before the Qvene's Maiestie: in the year 1575*. It was published anonymously in March 1576, and the only copy that survived into the nineteenth century perished in a fire at the Birmingham Free Library in January 1879. Fortunately the text was reprinted in the 1587 edition of *The Whole Woorkes of George Gascoigne Esquire*, which unambiguously asserted what internal evidence otherwise suggested, that it was indeed Gascoigne's work. Gascoigne's pamphlet puts his own work centre-stage. It excludes texts by other members of the team, omits the popular entertainment put before the Queen and in its totality provides only a very sketchy and incomplete narrative of her nineteen-day visit.

A far racier and more substantial account of events at Kenilworth is contained in *A Letter: whearin part of the Entertainement untoo the Queenz Maiesty, at Killingwoorth Castl in Warwik Sheer, in this Soomerz Progress, 1575, iz signified: from a freend officer attendant in the Coourt, unto his freend a Citizen and Merchaunt of London*. This was an anonymously published 18,000-word prose description of the Queen's visit, and supplies the human interest behind the monologues, song and drama. As its title indicates, it takes the form of a chatty letter, apparently from a minor court official named Robert Langham to a friend in London.

George Gascoigne mentioned another account entitled *The Pastime of the Progress*. This has traditionally been regarded as a third record of the festivities, but it is possible that the reference is to *A Letter*,[4] which appears to have been suppressed shortly after publication and which Gascoigne may have heard of but never seen. If it did exist it might well have clarified some of the contradictions and ambiguities of the other two accounts, but no copy is known to exist. From *The princely pleasures* and *A Letter*, together with one or two incidental manuscripts, it is possible to reconstruct much, but not all, of what happened at Kenilworth and George Gascoigne's central role in both the planned and wholly unexpected dramas which occurred.

*

On Saturday 9 July 1575 the Royal Progress north halted at Long Itchington, on the main highway from Banbury to Coventry. Here, some ten miles south-east of Kenilworth, a vast, palatial marquee had been erected, subdivided into rooms. A solitary statistic has survived to indicate its size: putting it up required seven cartloads of tent pegs.

Here the Earl of Leicester welcomed Elizabeth to his domain and gave her a suitably lavish dinner. By way of entertainment the parents of a local prodigy proudly displayed their "great Chyld" – apparently a young man of restricted growth with learning difficulties and a "simpl and childish" disposition. It's more than likely that Gascoigne, too, was present. Also there in the assembly of guests and onlookers would likely have been Leicester's nephew Philip Sidney and his close friend Edward Dyer, who would both become literary stars of Elizabeth's court in the 1580s. Sidney's mother was there, and so too was his 15-year-old sister, Mary, who would many years later achieve her own literary fame as the editor of her brother's *Arcadia* and who, as Countess of Pembroke, was a patron of several writers, including Gascoigne's stepson, Nicholas Breton.

A Royal Progress was a leisurely affair. There was no hurry. After dinner the royal party went off hunting and did not reach the grounds of Kenilworth until mid-evening. As Elizabeth moved through the park on the approach to the castle she was diverted by the sudden spectacle of ten sibyls or pagan prophetesses. The sibyls appeared out of an arbour in the park, in suitably classical costumes. According to the strict conventions of the age, the actors playing the part of these women, and all the others in the masques and pageants that followed, would have been males. By now it was around 8 p.m. and the daylight was slowly starting to fade.

"All hayle, all hayle, thrice happy Prince!" Clad in a robe of white silk the chief sibyl stepped forward to address the Queen. It's a line that resonates. Coincidence, or was the eleven-year-old Shakespeare present, drinking it all in? The "All hail, Macbeth!" cries of the three witches in *Macbeth* certainly sound like a black echo of that moment in the park at Kenilworth. But though the Kenilworth sibyl claimed to have stared into what Banquo calls "the seeds of time" the visionary insights were not cataclysmic but turgidly conventional. The prophetess mouthed some conventional platitudes about the "tenne thousand" rejoycings at Elizabeth's visit. Reassuringly, "vertue", peace and happy days were what the future had in store.

Elizabeth benignly accepted this flattering doggerel, which had been penned (and the tableau choreographed) by William Hunnis. Then she passed on from the Brays and through the first gate of the castle towards the Gallery Tower. There she encountered a remarkable sight. Silhouetted against the battlements were six gigantic figures holding, in Gascoigne's words, "huge and monstrous Trumpettes".

As Elizabeth approached, these silk-swathed giant trumpeters seemed to blow a fanfare of welcome from their silver instruments. It was a trick, of course. The giants were dummies and so were their trumpets. The real trumpeters were hidden behind them, out of sight. Gascoigne, remembering *Jocasta*, called it a "dum shew",[5] and like the dumb shows of early Tudor theatre it conveyed a symbolic meaning. Everyone knew that Kenilworth Castle had historical associations with King Arthur, and everyone also knew that in Arthur's day men were much, much bigger in size than they were in the sixteenth century. The message trumpeted from above was therefore simple: the castle was still safely in the hands of King Arthur's heirs and their servants. In case the Queen hadn't understood, the meaning was explained to her in a masque two days later:

> And what meant those great men
> which on the walles were seene?
>   ...they served
> King Arthur, man of might,
> And ever since this castle kept
> for Arthur's heirs by right.[6]

As Elizabeth entered the gateway of the Gallery Tower she was confronted by a lesser giant. It was Hercules, the mythic figure embodying strength and courage. He was present as guardian and warden of the castle. This time the giant was no dummy but someone "tall of parson, big of lim and stearn of coountinauns, wrapt also all in sylk, with club and keyz".[7]

In a speech purporting to be spontaneous but actually written beforehand by John Badger, Hercules pretended to be amazed and disturbed by all the fuss. "What stirre... is here?" he cried, attempting to hold back the royal party. But then he spotted "faire Dames" and "daintie darlings". These were the Ladies in Waiting. But there was ("oh God") one face more beautiful and astonishing than all the others – "a peereles Pearle". Hercules was literally disarmed by the presence of this beautiful, gracious, heavenly, majestic figure. The lengthening inventory of banal adjectives climaxed with Hercules falling to his knees, laying down his weapon and handing over the castle keys. Free passage was granted to the royal party. The Queen, graciously accepting Hercules' apologies for his ignorance and impatience, passed under the arch. Another fanfare blew from the battlements.

The trumpet blasts continued to sound as Elizabeth, still on horseback, entered the Tiltyard and rode slowly across it. The Tiltyard ran along the top of the Mere dam, to Mortimer's Tower, which formed the real entrance to the castle. She passed through the next archway and entered the base court of the castle. Here an even more dazzling spectacle awaited the Queen. Some distance away, on the darkening waters, was a floating island, lit by blazing torches. The flickering torchlight illuminated three magical figures in silken garments. As the Queen watched, the island began to move towards her. As it drew close to the castle the figures resolved themselves into "a Ladie" and her two attendant nymphs.

As the island reached the shore, the Lady called out, begging Elizabeth to wait and hear her story:

> I am the Lady of this pleasant lake
>   who since the time of great King Arthur's reign
> That here with royal court abode did make
>   have led a louring life in restless pain
> Till now that your third arrival here
>   doth cause me come abroad, and boldly thus appear.[8]

In a rhyming verse of forty-two lines, the Lady of the Lake told her sad tale. For centuries she had hidden herself away, avoiding the changing and turbulent fortunes of the castle and timidly keeping away from its fearful owners. But now the spell was broken. Elizabeth's third visit "doth bode thrice happy hope and voids the place from fear".

> Wherefore I will attend while you lodge here
>   (most peerless Queen) to court to make resort,
> And as my love to Arthur did appear
>   so shalt to you in earnest and in sport.
> Pass on, Madame, you need no longer stand:
>   The lake, the lodge, the Lord, are yours for to command.

It was at this point that something occurred to indicate that the Queen's mood that night was not entirely genial. She thanked the Lady of the Lake, but tartly added "we had thought the lake had been ours, and do you call it yours now?"[9] As sovereign, Elizabeth theoretically owned the entire land. She did not like someone presuming to challenge her authority in matters of land ownership, even if that person was just a fantasy figure in a masque. "We will herein commune more with you hereafter," she added, ominously. It may, at best, only have been badinage, but it was not the sort to make whoever was playing the role of the Lady feel very comfortable.

After this prickly exchange, the mood was lightened by "a delectable harmony" of "loud music". Hautboys, shalms (a kind of oboe, with a double reed enclosed in a globular mouthpiece) and cornets played as Elizabeth moved on across the great drawbridge. This was a permanent fixture some 20 feet wide and 70 feet long. It had wooden railings and the planks were covered in gravel. Along the sides of the bridge had been arranged gifts from the gods: a pair of wire cages containing bitterns, godwits, ducks and other "dainty birds", a pair of silver bowls containing apples, pears, cherries, pomegranates and sundry other fruits and nuts; a pair of silver bowls containing wheat, barley, oats, beans and peas; a bowl of grapes; pots of white wine and claret; trays of seafood including oysters, salmon, eel and herrings.

Beyond these lay gifts from Mars, the god of war. A pair of silver staves had been fashioned in imitation of the ragged staff shown on the Earl of Leicester's coat of arms. These were displayed to support a collection of armour, including shield, head piece, gorget, corselet, spears, swords, bows and arrows. Finally, two branches of bay were adorned with offerings from Phoebus, the god of music: lutes, viols, shalms, cornets, flutes, recorders and harps.

As the Queen rode between the offerings an actor dressed as a poet recited a Latin verse, telling how this homage had been commanded by Jupiter and explaining what each gift signified. What was not spelt out but which was implicit in the display of armour was Dudley's desire for a military command. As a Protestant, he not only wanted to see Elizabeth commit herself to the war in the Netherlands, but he also wanted to command troops there himself. That was his first message to her. The second and most important one would come later.

Having passed the last of these symbolic gifts, Elizabeth rode on into the inner court of the castle. Here she was greeted by the sound of "sweet music" from drums, fifes and trumpets. At last she was able to dismount from her palfrey and was led away upstairs to her lodgings.

The night climaxed with "a great peal of gunz" and a grand fireworks display. It was said that the "noyz and flame" were seen and heard twenty miles away.[10]

*

The next day, Sunday, began quietly. In the morning there was a service at the parish church, and in the afternoon music and dancing for the ladies of the court and their partners. Back at Walthamstow, the shocking absence of George Gascoigne and his wife from St Mary's church was solemnly noted, so it's just possible he took Elizabeth with him to Kenilworth.[11]

At night there were fireworks even more elaborate and spectacular than the ones the night before. This display utilised the Great Mere as a backdrop and even an old theatrical impresario like Gascoigne was impressed. The fireworks were, he wrote, "both strange and well executed: as sometimes passing under the water a long space, when all men had thought they had bene quenched, they would rise and mount out of the water againe, and burne very furiously untill they were utterlie consumed".[12]

The blueprint for the Kenilworth displays has survived, describing spectacles such as "serpents of fire", "lifelike birds flying about in the air scattering fire everywhere", "wondrous scented wheels of fire of various colours" and "A dragon as large as an ox... which will fly two or three times as high as the towers of San Paulo [St Paul's], and at that height will be completely consumed by fire, while suddenly from its whole body will issue dogs, cats and birds which will fly and scatter fire everywhere".[13] The thunderous explosions went on until well after midnight – extravagantly late by the standards of Tudor society.

The third day was hot and Elizabeth stayed indoors until 5 p.m. She then rode out with the hounds on a royal deer hunt in the Chase. Courtiers galloped after her, while the "varlets" in charge of the hounds ran alongside, trying to keep up. The hunt seems to have lasted for at least three hours. A deer was eventually found by the hounds and broke cover. Horns blew to signal the start of the pursuit. But to the frustration of the royal hunting party the deer "took soil"[14] – the hunting jargon for escaping into water. The terrified deer ran into the Great Mere and swam desperately away. It glided through the water, its antlers reminding one watcher of a stately sailing ship. The hounds swam after it. What happened next isn't clear, but "the hart waz kyld".[15] The accepted convention in such a situation was that someone rowed out in a boat and cut the creature's throat.

The Queen and her party returned on horseback through the Chase. But before they reached the castle Robert Dudley had arranged another tableau for her. Elizabeth came to a part of the woods lit by torchlight. Here she was greeted by England's most prominent and controversial poet and novelist, George Gascoigne, dressed as a wild man of the woods. This mini-masque drew on native English folklore rather than classical mythology. The wild (or green) man signified uncorrupted pastoral innocence – the spirit of elemental nature as opposed to the fallen, artificial world of human society.

This "Savage Man" was wearing an outer garment of moss and ivy and carrying an oak sapling "pluct up by the roots in hiz hande".[16] (Presumably Gascoigne's face was suitably daubed for the part, too.) Gascoigne later wrote that he'd been commanded to produce this mini-drama "upon a very great sudden".[17] It was clearly something the Earl of Leicester had dreamed up on a whim and at its heart was a simple message to Elizabeth: *marry me.*

This message in fact was everywhere at Kenilworth that July. The clock on Caesar's Tower had been deliberately stopped at two o'clock to underline Leicester's unsubtle message that he and Elizabeth ought to be paired. The courtship had been going on now for some seventeen years and Dudley had had enough of it. He was growing old. He wanted a decision, one way or the other. He was pulling out all the stops and giving her the greatest show on earth. If that didn't do it, nothing would. And the Earl was determined to press his suit in the most explicit ways possible.

As the Queen approached, Gascoigne began a loud half-rhyming forty-line monologue.[18] Addressing "Thundring Jupiter" he demanded to know why "all these worthy Lords and Peeres" were assembled in the Chase. And not just noblemen, either, but also

> glorious Dames
> As kindle might in frozen breasts
> a furnace full of flames.

But Jupiter was silent in the face of Gascoigne's questions, so instead he called on "Echo" to help. "Echo" – an actor concealed in the undergrowth – duly answered his plea. What followed was an ingenious dialogue in which Gascoigne spoke twenty-five stanzas of verse, with Echo repeating the last word of each stanza.[19] The poem – hardly Gascoigne's most distinguished literary production – offered a racy reprise of the entertainments previously presented to the Queen. But its purpose was more than descriptive. Having reminded Elizabeth of what she'd already seen – the sibyls, the giant trumpeters, Hercules the porter and the Lady of the Lake – the Savage Man interrogated Echo about the objects displayed on the drawbridge. Were they

> sent from the Gods
> As presents from above?
> Or pleasures of provision
> as tokens of true love?

Echo answered: *true love*. Robert Dudley, Earl of Leicester, was making his pitch. But the Savage Man hadn't finished yet. "And who gave all those gifts?" he innocently asked – although, remarkably, he seemed to know the answer:

> Was it not he? Who (but of late)
> this building here did lay?

Echo duly echoed the desperately creaky pun in those last two words: *Dudley*.

The Savage Man then thundered the message which was at the heart of the Kenilworth entertainments and which would be repeated until Elizabeth grew sick of it:

> O Dudley, so me thought:
>   he gave himself and all,
> A worthy gift to be received,
>   and so I trust it shall.

It shall, affirmed Echo, confidently. But in fact it never was. The moment when Elizabeth might have wed Robert Dudley had long since passed. The "gift" of his hand in marriage would be spurned, yet again. But that defining moment had not yet been reached. For the present Elizabeth was merely being courted. Combining a memory of Sunday's stupendous fireworks display with the hot/cold antithesis which had become the standard template of the Petrarchan love lyric, the wild man went on to ask:

> What meant the fiery flames
>   which through the waves so flew?
> Can no cold answers quench desire?
>   Is that experience true?

True, agreed Echo. But in spite of Gascoigne's sponsored optimism the "cold answers" would continue and Leicester's "desire" would collapse almost overnight. Besides, the Earl was driven not by desire but by ambition. It was all more to do with power and status than sexual attraction. And the final collapse of Leicester's hopes was just nine days away.

At this point the wild man pretended to discover the proximity of the Queen and fell to his knees. It seems to have been at this moment that Gascoigne did something which caused the Queen's horse to rear up, nearly unseating her. George Gascoigne came very close to going down in history as the man who broke her neck. This mishap is mentioned in most popular biographies of Elizabeth. The only source that we have for it is in *A Letter*:

> Az this Savage for the more submission brake his tree asunder, kest the top from him, it had almost light upon her highness hors hed: whereat he startld and the gentlman mooch dismayd See the benignitee of the Prins, as the footmen lookt well too the hors, and he of generositee soon callmd of him self, no hurt no hurt quoth her highness.[20]

In other words, Gascoigne made the theatrical gesture of snapping his oak branch in two and hurling one half away. Unfortunately it flew past the head of

353

the Queen's horse, startling it. The assembled courtiers gasped in horror and footmen rushed forward to seize the horse. But the upset was only momentary; the animal quickly settled down. Elizabeth, an expert horsewoman, was unruffled by the incident. "No hurt, no hurt,"[21] she called out, probably seeking to calm the fussy, exaggerated displays of concern from the assembled sycophants. The incident was quickly over. The show went on.

The self-styled "wild and savage man" – the description now coloured with unintended comic irony after Gascoigne's clumsiness – continued with a monologue. After more platitudes about the Queen's intelligence, beauty and glory, Gascoigne informed her of a forthcoming attraction later in the week – "sundry gladsome games". Bidding the now silent Echo farewell, the wild man departed.

In *The princelye pleasures at the Courte at Kenelwoorth* Gascoigne made no mention of the incident with the branch, which is hardly surprising since the publication consisted largely of scripts. The only noteworthy feature of the savage man masque which he thought worth mentioning, apart from his writing and acting role, was that he produced it all "upon a very great sudden". But news of the incident quickly filtered out to those who weren't present. Don Antonio de Guaras, the Spanish Ambassador, wrote a week later that "it is said that whilst she was going hunting on one of the days, a traitor shot a cross-bow at her... The bolt passed near the Queen but did her no harm, thank God!"[22] This seems to have been nothing more than a garbled, exaggerated account of Gascoigne's over-exuberant breaking of the oak branch.

*

"The next thing that was presented before her Majesty was the deliverie of the Lady of the Lake," says Gascoigne, after his account of the wild man's speeches.[23] What this remark reveals is the poet's indifference to the popular entertainment that was staged and his willingness to marginalise material not produced by himself or the other leading members of Leicester's writing team. Gascoigne sought to ingratiate himself with those who enjoyed high status and influence and to cast himself as a figure of central importance in entertaining Her Majesty. Although in some ways a rebel and an innovator, Gascoigne remained at heart bound by the interests and prejudices of his class, for whom self-advancement was a fundamental impulse.

Gascoigne's account of proceedings at Kenilworth is unreliable but this is simply another aspect of his relentless self-promotion. In fact the Lady of the Lake did not re-appear for another week, during which time a variety of amusements were set out for Elizabeth. There was dancing, a stroll in the castle grounds and across the bridge into the Chase, and music played from a barge on the lake. There was another deer hunt, when once again the deer fled into the water. It was captured and "the watermen held him up hard by the hed, while at her highness commaundement he lost his earz for a raundsum, and so had pardon of lyfe".²⁴ Even bloodier entertainment was on offer the next day, when thirteen bears were assembled in the inner court and a pack of mastiffs in the outer. The dogs were then set on the bears, going for their throats while the bears slashed the dogs' scalps – "a sport very pleazaunt".²⁵ To round off the day's fun there was a display by an Italian acrobat and more fireworks, interspersed with cannon fire.

At the weekend there was " a solem brydeale of a proper coopl"²⁶ – a so-called "country wedding" of two commoners which was permitted to take place in the great court. This involved a procession and celebrations that included morris dancing and tilting at a wooden quintain, after which the couple and their guests marched out of the Northgate and into the town. It was followed by what is usually called "the Coventry play" – a festive history play dating from 1416, which celebrated the overthrow of the Danes. It was a "Hock Tuesday" play, referring to a local custom whereby on Hock Monday men were entitled to "hock" or capture women and demand money from them. On Hock Tuesday the roles were reversed and women were allowed to seize men. It licensed much horseplay and embracing, with the ostensibly socially respectable goal of collecting money for community projects such as church repairs. The play involved mock battles between Danes and English horsemen until at last, defeated, the captive Danes were led off in triumph by the women of Coventry. More than that we do not know, as no text has survived.

In the evening, after supper, another play was put on. It lasted over two hours. Who wrote it and what it was about remain, like the subsequent show put on that evening, an enigma. Gascoigne doesn't mention it and *A Letter* merely says it was "of a very good theam" and was entertaining and well performed. It was followed by a spectacularly lavish banquet with three-hundred different dishes. While they ate, those at the feast were entertained by a masque, "for riches of array, of an incredibl cost". It went on late into the night.

*

What happened the next day at Kenilworth supplied the second of two moments from the July festivities which are remembered above all others. The first – Gascoigne's mishap with the oak branch – involved the Queen. The second is famous for its intriguing suggestion that William Shakespeare was present. In *A Midsummer Night's Dream*, Oberon, King of the Fairies, remarks:

My gentle Puck, come hither. Thou rememberest
Since once I sat upon a promontory
And heard a mermaid on a dolphin's back

Uttering such dulcet and harmonious breath
That the rude sea grew civil at her song,
And certain stars shot madly from their spheres
To hear the sea-maid's music?

And Puck replies:

I remember. (I.i.148-156)

Was Shakespeare expressing his own memories of the evening of Monday 18 July 1575? It was a sweltering hot day. Around 5 p.m. the Queen went hunting in the Chase. Once again the deer fled into the water. Returning from the hunt, Elizabeth was crossing the bridge back into the castle when a trumpet blast blew, attracting her attention with a "sound very shrill and sonorous".[27] It was Triton, servant of the sea god Neptune, riding a boat shaped like a gigantic mermaid, eighteen feet long.

Triton put down his trumpet, which had been made to look like a giant whelk shell, and navigated the mermaid-boat closer to the bridge where the Queen watched from her horse. The actor then narrated the sad tale of the Lady of the Lake. Merlin had been incarcerated in a rock by the Lady "for his inordinate lust" and his cousin, Sir Bruce, had come seeking revenge upon the virtuous virgin. Neptune had intervened to save her by surrounding her with water. Merlin had prophesied that the Lady of the Lake would never be set free until a maid even finer and more virtuous showed herself at the lakeside. That moment had now arrived. The wicked knight Sir Bruce and his bands of men could be defeated and the spell broken if Elizabeth would but take in hand the Lady's cause.

Triton then sounded his trumpet again and commanded the winds to fall silent and the "waters wilde" to turn calm. The Lady of the Lake, liberated by Elizabeth's presence, now appeared with her two attendant nymphs. The three figures floated across the water (supported "upon heapes of Bulrushes")[28] and the Lady made a short speech of thanks to Elizabeth. As a token of her thanks she presented the Queen with the gift of Arion, sat on a dolphin's back. The dolphin – which presumably now sailed into view – was another disguised boat or barge, some 24 feet in length. It contained rowers, whose oars were made up to look like fins, as well as six musicians concealed out of sight in the beast's belly. When Arion began his song the mask seems to have got in the way: "finding his voice to be very hoarse and unpleasant when he came to performe it, he teares of his Disguise, and swears he was none of Arion not he, but eene honest Harry Goldingham; which blunt discoverie pleasd the Queene better, then if it had gone thorough in the right way".[29]

Was Shakespeare really present when all this took place? He describes a *mermaid* on a dolphin's back. A childhood memory may have become blurred, or perhaps he thought a mermaid seemed dramatically more effective. Even those who were present were sometimes confused. Gascoigne wrongly identified the figure on the dolphin's back as Proteus. The show presumably took place as night was falling or had fallen. Shakespeare wrote *A Midsummer Night's Dream* some twenty years after Kenilworth. The line about the stars which "shot madly from their spheres" was obviously inspired by the fireworks, but no fireworks seem to have accompanied the Lady of the Lake masque. However, "The rude sea grew civil at her song" unambiguously echoes Triton's speech.

Oberon's words to Puck provide a poetic and imaginative précis of that spectacle on the Great Mere and other Kenilworth festivities. This does not, of course, prove that Shakespeare was present, but on balance it is highly likely that he was. And if he was, its impact on him was surely enormous. Kenilworth was not just an entertainment but the most stunning theatrical display of Elizabeth's reign, in a fabulous setting. If anything fired Shakespeare's imagination and made him want to become involved in theatre and entertainment, it was surely this experience. To a child it must indeed have seemed like "a midsummer night's dream".

A Midsummer Night's Dream rewrites some of the central features of the Kenilworth entertainments. The solemn theme of love and marriage is burlesqued by the "lamentable comedy" of Peter Quince and his associates, just as the coarse, brash country wedding seemed to at least one person present an unintended parody of Leicester's courtship of Elizabeth.

The opening lines of *A Midsummer Night's Dream* focus on desire which is frustrated and put off to another day. Theseus presents Hermia with the stark choice of marriage

> Or on Diana's altar to protest
> For aye austerity and single life. (I.i 89-90)

Even the mighty Theseus is made to wait and grumbles about "how slow / This old moon wanes! She lingers my desires" (I.i.3-4). Demetrius pursues Hermia but is rejected by her. Helena pursues Demetrius and is equally rejected. And the workings-out of the human drama in the foreground are mirrored by the "moonlight revels" (II.i.141) of the fairies. In fact Puck is almost like a version of Gascoigne's wild man of the woods – an elemental force of nature, emerging from the trees to do his master's bidding.

A Midsummer Night's Dream is one of the few plays which Shakespeare wrote which did not overtly draw on another, already existing narrative. This reinforces the probability that he drew on his own experience and memories for a play which often seems to echo what occurred at Kenilworth. The entertainment planned by Theseus matches the ambition of Leicester:

> A fortnight hold we this solemnity
> In nightly revels and new jollity. (V.i.359-60)

The solemn theme of marriage is counterpointed by the comic sub-plot involving Hermia, Helena, Lysander and Demetrius and the shambolic play put on by Peter Quince and his associates seems to echo the country wedding.

Hippolyta recalls a hunt in a Cretan wood

> With hounds of Sparta. Never did I hear
> Such gallant chiding, for besides the groves,
> The skies, the fountains, every region near
> Seemed all one mutual cry. I never heard
> So musical a discord, such sweet thunder. (IV.i.113-17)

Did the boy Shakespeare witness the Queen hunting with dogs in the Chase? These lines are not based on anything Shakespeare found in classical mythology but were added by him. These intriguing parallels are suggestive. What is striking about the play is how it seems suffused with a memory of the Kenilworth fireworks. There is "hail" and "heat" and "showers of oaths" (I.i.244-5), and Cupid's "best arrow with the golden head" (I.i.170). And there is Lysander's sense of the powerful forces which perpetually threaten love,

> Making it momentany as a sound,
> Swift as a shadow, short as any dream,
> Brief as the lightning in the collied night (I.i.143-5)

Even more impressively there is fate, which annihilates human achievement:

> The jaws of darkness do devour it up.
> So quick bright things come to confusion. (I.i.148-9)

At least some of these similes and metaphors seem to be rooted in the experience of seeing fireworks. It is highly improbable that Shakespeare ever read *A Letter*. Gascoigne's perfunctory description is unlikely to have made quite the same impact that actually seeing them as a child would have done. And here I can only judge the matter by my own experience of life. When I was the same age that Shakespeare would have been at Kenilworth my parents took me on a trip to Paris. I remember little of that holiday. But what I do remember is the visit to Versailles. We stood beside the ornamental lake at night and watched a stupendous and spectacular fireworks display. After the passage of many years the experience is still vivid.

*

The next day, Tuesday 19 July, the Coventry play was put on again. Elizabeth apparently had only seen part of the earlier performance. Evidently she enjoyed this straightforward rough-and-tumble entertainment involving real horses and the expulsion of a foreign enemy. *A Letter* describes "her highness myrth and good acceptauns, and reward unto them, and…their rejoysing thereat".[30]

On Wednesday morning another feast in a marquee or "fayr pavilion" had been arranged at "Wedgenall" or Wedgenock Park, three miles west of the castle. The major feature of the day was to be "a devise of Goddessez and Nymphes" presented to the Queen "in the Forest".[31] It included special effects, such as Mercury descending in a cloud and Iris coming "downe from the Rainebowe sent by *Juno*".[32] Written by Gascoigne, the "devise" was a short, untitled play of two acts and seven scenes. The *dramatis personae* consisted of Diana, goddess of chastity, and three attendant nymphs, Mercury the messenger of Jove, and Iris the messenger of Juno. The plot concerned what had happened to one of Diana's nymphs, lost to her many years before. Between the acts "a man cladde all in Mosse" was to appear, explaining that he was the savage man's son, Audax.[33] This may have been Gascoigne himself, once again losing no opportunity to put himself centre-stage.

The play had been rehearsed and was ready to be performed. But suddenly that morning there was turmoil. The feast at Wedgenock Park was abruptly cancelled. The play was called off despite (as Gascoigne plaintively put it) "being prepared and redy".[34] The Queen was evidently furious about something. The author of *A Letter* hints at Elizabeth's rage, coolly remarking "this day also waz thear such earnest tallk and appointment of remooving that I gave over my noting, and harkened after my horse".[35]

Gascoigne explained that the reason his play wasn't performed was "lack of opportunitie and seasonable weather".[36] But this reasoning was threadbare and implausible. The play was the problem, not the weather. Evidently that Wednesday morning the Queen discovered in advance the content of Gascoigne's play. Presumably someone who appreciated exactly what it signified had discovered the inflammatory theme of the production and reported to Elizabeth just what was to be set before her later that day. Whoever that person was it had to be someone powerful, discreet and with access to the Queen. The likeliest candidate in such a scenario is Lord Burghley. But however Elizabeth came to find out about the play there was no ambiguity about the consequences. The result was an explosion of royal displeasure.

Her wrath was directed not at the play's author, George Gascoigne, but at the person who had clearly solicited this insulting piece of theatre. The Earl of Leicester's hand in the affair was unmistakeable. It was an almost identical repeat of what he'd done to her at court a decade earlier. On that occasion he'd staged a play involving an argument between Juno, goddess of marriage, and Diana, goddess of chastity. Diana lost. The Queen is reported to have turned to the Spanish ambassador next to her and said, "This is all against me."[37] But in 1565 Elizabeth's mood was more playful and light-hearted. Flirtation was acceptable. Oblique, symbolic games with figures from Greek mythology were relatively harmless fun. Marriage was a much stronger possibility in those days.

Now the atmosphere had changed. Elizabeth required deference, not symbolic instruction about her supposed inadequacy. Besides, the relationship between the two principals was much cooler now. Ten long years had passed. The sexual electricity was gone. What was left was a tense, edgy relationship which mingled friendship with antipathy. The Earl of Leicester was insufficiently deferential. He undiplomatically and egotistically regarded himself as her equal and still the only obvious candidate for her husband. But by sponsoring Gascoigne's drama he had over-played his hand. The name of the lost nymph, "Zabeta", was all too obviously, all too publicly, a version of "Elizabeth". That Zabeta was lost "neere seventeene yeares past"[38] clinched the identification. It was 17 years since Elizabeth had become Queen and in so doing become "lost" to her passionate friend and admirer, Robert Dudley. Just in case anyone had missed the analogy, Mercury steps forward to explain what Zabeta has been up to since the time of Elizabeth's coronation:

> For first these sixteen years
> She hath been daily seen
> In richest realm that Europe hath,
> A comely crowned Queen.[39]

The most offensive part of Gascoigne's play was its final scene. Iris, messenger of the goddess of marriage, arrives with a lecture about "How necessary [it] were / for worthy Queens to wed". In an ingenious argument worthy of the trainee lawyer in Gascoigne, Iris asks what the goddess of chastity ever did for Elizabeth in the period before she became Queen:

> Were you not captive caught?
>   were you not kept in walls?
> Were you not forced to lead a life
>   like other wretched thralles?
> Where was Diana then,
>   why did she you not aid?[40]

The closing lines of the play are addressed directly to Elizabeth. Iris passes on a blunt message from the goddess of marriage. Juno's advice isn't simply *get married* but *get married now to the Earl of Leicester*.

>   she bade me say
> That where you now in Princely port
>   have passed one pleasant day
> A world of wealth at will
>   you henceforth shall enjoy
> In wedded state, and therewithal
>   hold up from great annoy
> The staff of your estate:
>   O Queen, O worthy Queen,
> Yet never wight felt perfect bliss
>   but such as wedded been.[41]

But joining the royal sceptre or staff to the staff on the Dudley coat of arms was the last thing on Elizabeth's mind. This time the Earl had pressed his suit too hard and too often. She exploded in rage.

Precisely what happened next is unclear. *A Letter* refers to "earnest tallk & appointment of remooving"[42] and its account of the festivities comes to an abrupt halt. Gascoigne says that his play "never came to execution" and goes on to describe "The Queenes Majestie hasting her departure from thence…"[43] The Queen left Kenilworth on a Wednesday, but not, apparently, for another week. Did she gallop away in a rage on 20 July before being persuaded back by Burghley and the others who had influence over her? If, as seems to be the case, Elizabeth stayed on for another week, then it looks very much as if she stayed in her chambers, sulking. After twelve days of spectacle and amusement, the festivities ground to a sudden halt.

The author of *A Letter* clearly understood the role of Gascoigne's play in this sudden upset. He blandly referred to its "ingenious argument" but evasively declined to discuss the particulars, ostensibly for fear of misrepresenting the play's "beauty". Gascoigne himself appreciated the potential for offence in his play's final speech. In passing on the marital advice from Juno the actor playing the part of Iris makes a point of saying

> Forgive me, Queen, the words are hers,
>   I come not to discuss.
> I am but messenger[44]

Gascoigne could have said the same thing. It was Leicester who'd put him up to it; Leicester who'd surely sketched the plot for Gascoigne to put into verse. He was no more at fault than the player at Elsinore, mouthing Prince Hamlet's explosively provocative "speech of some dozen or sixteen lines".

Did Gascoigne fully appreciate the offence which his play had caused? At first, perhaps not. He was present at Kenilworth as an entertainer, not a courtier.

He was not a member of that exclusive inner circle which comprised the Queen and her attendants, Leicester and his associates, and Lord Burghley and other members of the Privy Council. Gascoigne and his actors seem to have hoped that the suddenly cancelled play might yet be performed. He describes the show as "redy (every Actor in his garment) two or three dayes together",[5] which suggests that the troupe waited in vain for the Queen to show herself.

Gascoigne was happy to see the unperformed play published and equally happy to take total credit for it ("This shewe was devised and penned by M. Gascoigne").[46] But he took the precaution of ensuring that the collection of Kenilworth scripts was published anonymously, making it appear as if it had been edited by an unidentified third party. He was even prepared to drop that all important *Esquire* after his name to distance himself from the work.

In fact by the time *The princelye pleasures* appeared in print the storm had long since blown itself out. On the surface the book was nothing more than a harmless collection of masques and verses. Since they had been sponsored by one of the most powerful men in the land, who could possibly take offence? The only person likely to have been offended by its contents was the Queen, but she is unlikely ever to have seen a copy.

There was one final entertainment put before Elizabeth prior to her departure. It was written by Gascoigne, who once again gave himself a leading role. After apparently sulking in her room, Elizabeth eventually emerged to go on one last deer hunt. Gascoigne was waiting for her. He was once again dressed up in a folklore costume, clad like "Sylvanus, God of the Woods". Presumably the garb, though green and leafy, was a little less primitive and a little more regal than that of the Savage Man.

The Queen had obviously taken some time to extricate herself from her black mood, judging by Gascoigne's heartfelt and slightly barbed comment that he had "continually awaited these 3. dayes to espie when your Majestie would (in accustomed manner) come on hunting this way".[46]

This time the script was less inflammatory. "Right excellent, puissant and most happy Princesse!" cried Gascoigne, offering to guide her safely through the woods and recount "certaine adventures" while she rode on. The Queen gave her consent, and set off, with Gascoigne jogging alongside. After lots more wooden flattery, Gascoigne explained that he was sent as a messenger from the gods, "to beseech your Majestie that you would here remaine".[47]

Evidently by this time Gascoigne was beginning to sweat and pant. He was, after all, in his early forties, and by Tudor standards was a man well into middle age. "Here her majestie stayed her horse to favour *Sylvanus*, fearing least he should be driven out of breath by following her horse so fast."[48] But Gascoigne was tall and probably fit. Evidently he was proud of his stamina – or was yielding to the *gascon* in the family name: "*Sylvanus* humbly besought her Highnesse to goe on, declaring that if hys rude speech did not offend her, he coulde continue this tale to be twenty miles long."

So the Queen rode on, and Gascoigne ran on with her. It was like a symbolic expression of Gascoigne's lifelong quest for patronage, as he panted after wealth and power, pouring out words. But Gascoigne could be cheerfully brash, as well as sycophantic (and it is part of his charm that deep down he really didn't care what people thought, no matter who they were). Provocatively, he returned to the story of Zabeta. In this account, Diana's nymph was someone who had turned "sundry famous and worthy persons...into most monstrous shapes and proportions".

Gascoigne pointed to a massive oak. That, he explained, was Constance – a faithful follower and trusted servant of hers, turned into a tree by "a strange and cruel metamorphosis". It sounded dangerously close to being some sort of parable about Elizabeth's treatment of Leicester. But Gascoigne moved on – literally – and defused the tale, making it blandly unspecific. Near the mighty oak was Inconstancy, turned into a poplar tree, "whose leaves move and shake with the least breath or blast". A nearby ash tree represented Vainglory – the first plant to bud "and the first likewise that casteth leafe". As for "that busie elfe *Contention*" – Zabeta had turned him into a bramble bush. And so it went on, with Gascoigne pointing to trees and explaining what each one meant. Ambition was a branch of ivy; "Due Desert" a laurel.

But there was a twist in the tale. This botanical disquisition was a prelude to the Earl of Leicester's final and rather more muted attempt to entice Elizabeth to stay on at Kenilworth. Gascoigne led the Queen to "a close Arbor, made all of Hollie, and whiles Sylvanus pointed to the same, the principall bush shaked". This trembling bush represented Zabeta's transformation of Deep Desire – a "wretch of worthies and yet the worthiest that ever was condemned to wretched estate". Deep Desire was obviously supposed to be Robert Dudley, who was making his last pitch as a devoted lover after the style of Petrarch. He was such a man, explained Gascoigne, "as neither any delay could daunt him: no disgrace could abate his passions, no tyme could tyre him, no water quench his flames". The bush shook in furious agreement.[49]

Gascoigne claimed that his speech to the Queen was extempore and there is no reason to disbelieve him. The published text, then, is a reconstruction after the event, and not an exact account. Gascoigne presumably polished and revised his prose before seeing it into print. It seems unlikely that he really told the Queen that there were male and female varieties of holly and that "the she *Holly* hath no prickes".[50] Bawdy innuendo like that would surely not have amused the Virgin Queen.

Sylvanus suddenly realised that the holly's animation indicated "that Deepe desire hath gotten leave of the Gods to speake unto your excellent Majestie...me thinks I hear his voice". Gascoigne then stood aside and let Deep Desire do the talking. Although the voice booming out of the holly represented Leicester, it clearly wasn't the Earl crouching in an undignified posture behind the prickly bush. Desire spoke of Leicester in the third person as "the Knight". There was a cryptic reference to grieving and tears "these five dayes past and gone" – ostensibly at the news of the Queen's impending departure but perhaps a tacit acknowledgement of her recent sulks and fury. Though the message hadn't really changed, the invitation to marry Dudley was implicit rather than explicit ("Live here good Queene, live here, / you are amongst your friends"). There was no attempt to lecture her; no mention of Juno. On the contrary, "Diana would be glad / to meet you in the Chase".

Musicians hidden behind the bush began to play and Deep Desire sang a melancholy song of farewell:

> Come, Muses, come, and help me to lament,
>   come woods, come waves, come hills, come doleful dales...

The song ended; the music ceased. Gascoigne stepped forward to wrap the proceedings up. The metamorphosis of Deep Desire into a holly bush was, he emphasized, "very lamentable". He humbly craved that the Queen intervene on his behalf with the gods or at the very least consent to transform him back into human form,

> Whereat your highnesse may be assured that heaven will smile, the earth will shake, men will clap their hands, and I will always continue an humble beseecher for the flourishing estate of your royall person.[51]

The Queen presumably nodded and perhaps gave a glacial smile at this last, muted attempt to promote Leicester's cause. Then she rode on her way. The great Kenilworth extravaganza was finally over.

24: Authorship and a Hermit

Shakespeare seems to have understood clearly that Kenilworth signalled the annihilation of Leicester's fantasy of marrying Elizabeth. In *A Midsummer Night's Dream*, Oberon recalls the time he saw

> Flying between the cold moon and the earth
> Cupid all armed. A certain aim he took
> At a fair vestal thronèd by the west,
> And loosed his loveshaft smartly from his bow
> As it should pierce a hundred thousand hearts;
> But I might see young Cupid's fiery shaft
> Quenched in the chaste beams of the watery moon,
> And the imperial votaress passed on
> In maiden meditation, fancy-free. (II.i.156-164)

In other words, Cupid (alias Robert Dudley) shot his arrow at Elizabeth and missed. The passage also seems suffused with memories of the fireworks – an arrow/rocket soaring across the sky, "a hundred thousand hearts", a "fiery shaft / Quenched". The metaphors express an historical truth: the brilliant display was in vain. Elizabeth was untouched by it. She moved on, shunning his advances. It marked the end of Leicester's royal marriage fantasy. Three years later he secretly married Lettice Knollys.

Shakespeare was perhaps not the only one to perceive Kenilworth as a failure. One problem in understanding the reality of events at Kenilworth Castle that summer involves the authorship and interpretation of that anonymous publication, *A Letter*, which appeared in the aftermath of the Queen's departure. Its text takes the form of a chatty communication about events at the castle during the Queen's visit. But the authorship of *A Letter* is disputed, as is its purpose. The traditional reading is that *A Letter* is exactly what it purports to be – a straightforward account of the Queen's visit. However, a dissident reading proposes that the ostensible authorship is spurious and that the work is a veiled satire on the Kenilworth revels. This obscure scholarly debate is of some relevance to Gascoigne biography in so far as the alternative reading brings him into focus as the object of envy and mockery.

A seam of sarcasm and comic irony certainly appears to percolate the narrative. The author seems to take delight in describing everything that went wrong, including Elizabeth's ill-tempered rejoinder to the Lady of the Lake and Gascoigne's bungled throwing of the oak branch. The cupbearer at the country wedding is "unhappily infested" with flies and the "ill smelling" bride, "not very beautifull indeed but ugly fooul ill favord".[1] What's more, the wedding "had not the full muster waz hoped for".

The "princely pleasures" seem far from princely. The bridegroom blows his nose and wipes his face with his father's borrowed jacket. When a lavish banquet of 300 dishes is set before the Queen *A Letter* makes a point of telling us that "Her majesty eat smally or nothing" and that the meal became a shambles with the food "disorderly wasted and coorsly consumed".[2]

A Letter was written to Humphrey Martin, a friend of the writer's. Although there is no name on the title page at various points in the text the author of *A Letter* identifies himself as Robert Langham. He is readily identifiable as the Robert Langham (c.1535-1580) who was admitted to the Mercers' Company in 1557. However by 1572 Langham was no longer a mercer but "Keeper of the Council Chamber" – a minor position at court which involved him in furbishing rooms where the Privy Council met with cushions, flowers and materials for maintaining a fire in the fireplace. Humphrey Martin, recipient of the letter, was himself a mercer (i.e. a dealer in cloth or textile fabrics). He was the son of a former Master of the Mercers' Company and by 1575 was an affluent London merchant, probably in his mid-twenties.

A Letter was long viewed as being exactly what it purports to be: a private communication between friends. However in 1977 two scholars, Brian O'Kill and David Scott, independently arrived at the conclusion that the work was a hoax – specifically, a satire intended to mock its putative author.[3] O'Kill and Scott each identified the real author as William Patten, who was a member of Leicester's entertainments team present at Kenilworth that summer. They argued that Patten had impersonated Robert Langham for reasons unknown, but which might be reasonably conjectured.

One of the foundations of this radical reinterpretation of the authorship of *A Letter* was a long-overlooked letter written by Patten to Lord Burghley, dated 10 September 1575. It concerned "hoow the book waz too be suppresst for that Langham had complaynd upon it, and ootherwize for that the honorabl entertainment be not turned into a jest".[4] The conclusion reached by O'Kill and Scott was that "the book" was *A Letter*, that "the honorabl entertainment" referred to the festivities at Kenilworth and that turning them into "a jest" indicated that the book was intended to mock the entertainments, as well as poke fun at Robert Langham.

The question of the text's authorship remains contested. The most recent edition of the *Oxford Dictionary of National Biography* supports both interpretations, with the entry for Langham regarding him as the probable author, engaging in "self-mockery", while the entry for William Patten asserts that he was "almost certainly" its true writer. The book's modern editor, Elizabeth Goldring, is emphatic that only Robert Langham could have been its author, insisting that key information conveyed in *A Letter* was rooted in private, personal knowledge.[5] Arguments of this kind have a long pedigree. George Orwell's classic reports "A Hanging" and "Shooting an Elephant" are ostensibly autobiographical but continue to divide biographers. They may be genuine accounts of personal experience. They may equally be brilliant fictions which ventriloquise incidents in the lives of others. To this day the truth remains elusive, hidden among the many mysteries of Orwell's five years in Burma.

Irrespective of such conjecture, the "Langham" whose voice is heard in *A Letter* is garrulous and boastful. If that persona bears any relationship to the man himself then there is no logical reason to believe that the letter's contents could not have been known to someone who knew Langham and who was present at Kenilworth that July.

Much hinges on the significance of that word "jest" in Patten's September 1575 letter to Burghley. As a noun it signifies something ludicrous and amusing, the object of laughter. Interestingly, Shakespeare used it repeatedly in the subsidiary sense of "the contrary to earnest; what is not meant as it was pretended".[6] The word "jest" in the letter of 10 September 1575 appears to indicate that the thrust of *A Letter* was not self-advertisement or an attempt to profit financially from a behind-the-scenes account of a royal visit but rather mockery.

In short, a "straight" reading of the text, in which Langham represents himself as smug, boastful, opinionated and crassly lacking in self-awareness seems less plausible than that the text is a brilliant tongue-in-cheek effort by a malicious master-ironist. A reading of the text as satire seems to make far more sense of its many oddities than one which treats it as honest reportage by a man happy to represent himself as "self-satisfied"[7] and displaying "conceit and self-importance".[8]

Read as a satire, *A Letter* targets three people in particular. The book is prefaced by three not very good lines of Latin, no doubt coined by its author.[9] They present conventional pieties contrasting Elizabeth's happy days among her people with the chaos of neighbouring kingdoms. But even this ostensibly harmless salutation is razor-edged: "genialibus" can simply mean "genial days" or, more explosively "days pertaining to marriage". *That*, of course, was what all the trouble was about: Kenilworth represented a last-ditch effort by Leicester to entangle Elizabeth in matrimony.

Arbitrarily tacked on at the end of these lines to her illustrious majesty is a sudden spurt of venom: *Rumpantur et ilia Codro* – "May Codrus's innards burst!" (slightly modified from "invidia rumpantur et ilia Codro" in Virgil's *Eclogues*, vii, 26). In Latin literature Codrus was the archetype of a talentless poet. Who did the author have in mind in those final, not quite grammatical, and slightly hysterical Latin words? The answer is surely George Gascoigne. Gascoigne had authored the most offensive of the masques intended to be put before the Queen – the one that lectured her on her inadequacy as a single woman. Not that the author of *A Letter* really cared about whether Elizabeth married or stayed single. The animus towards Gascoigne was personal, not political.

Some of the details of the description of the grotesque bridegroom at the country wedding sound very much like a dig at Gascoigne. The man is clumsy and ridiculous and "brake hiz spear" at quintain, though he "had no hurt as it hapt, but only that hiz gyrt burst, and lost his pen and inkhorn that he waz redy to weep for".[10] The scene reads like a calculated mockery of Gascoigne's mishap with the oak branch, complete with the exact phrase used by the Queen, *no hurt*. The jeering description of how the bridegroom had "a pen and inkhorn at his bak, for he woold be knowne to be bookish"[11] makes one wonder if Gascoigne was already proudly showing people the engraved portrait used to preface *The Steel Glass*, published the following year. It shows the poet with a pen and a pot of ink dangling from a bookshelf behind him.

The digression about the "aunciient minstrel"[12] whose "ridiculoous devise" was never performed also sounds suspiciously like a skit at Gascoigne's expense, particularly as it immediately follows the account of how his play about Zabeta was aborted. The preposterous minstrel has a "smugly shaven" beard every bit as trim as Gascoigne's, and his "side gooun of kendall green"[13] may mockingly allude to Gascoigne's self-representation as "the green knight". The minstrel also sports "a green lace" and wears "a Schoochion, with metall and cooler resplendaunt upon his breast of the aunciient armez of Islington".[14] This, too, was perhaps intended to mock the intolerable pretensions of George Gascoigne Esquire, pictured in his armour.

But Gascoigne gets off lightly compared with the book's two other targets. The biggest was the Earl of Leicester himself, and here the author had to be very careful in conveying his disdain for Dudley and all his works. Pretending to be deliberately obtuse, the *Letter*'s author describes the clock with its hands stopped at two and pretends to wonder what this freezing of time can mean. He concludes that it's Leicester's way of signifying that visitors are welcome at any time, early or late, "whither cum they to stay and take cheer, or straight to returne: too see or too be seen: cum they for duty to her Majesty or love too hiz Lordship, or for both".[15] This description is far from innocent. It hints at the Earl's delusions of grandeur in regarding himself as the Queen's equal. The fact that some visitors may be there simply "to be seen" points to their shallow vanity. And why would anyone arriving at this magnificent castle wish "straight to returne"? Underneath this magnificent entertainment something is horribly wrong.

A Letter puts forward a discreet, comically alternative meaning to everything on display. What else but a lampoon of the Earl of Leicester is the "great Chyld of Leyceter shyre...of a foour foot and four inches hy...simpl and childish"?[16] The extensive description of the grotesque country wedding ridicules the solemn marriage theme which the Earl was keen to promote, and the remark that "it woold have moved sum man too a right meery mood, though had it be toold him hiz wife lay a dying"[17] is clearly a barbed allusion to the scandal surrounding the mysterious death of the Earl's wife Amy Robsart. To Leicester's enemies "the "thing that coold not be hidden from ony" was not, as *A Letter* mock-naïvely goes on to explain "hoow careful and studious hiz honor waz" in amusing Elizabeth, but the cold fact of his ruthless murder of Robsart in order to make himself available as the Queen's prospective husband. Passages like these are the verbal equivalent of giving someone a friendly handshake – and squeezing until it hurts. Some nine years later another "letter" was published anonymously. The *Copy of a Letter Written by a Master of Arts of Cambridge to his friend in London* was a ferocious assault on Leicester's reputation, accusing him of serial adultery and the murder of his wife. Anonymous tracts of this sort appeared with such regularity that they amount to a genre.

Twentieth-century scholarship tended to downplay the possibility that Amy Robsart was killed, subscribing to the theory that she suffered from terminal cancer and that a fall might easily have resulted in her death. However, the most recent scholarly analysis of her mysterious end, based on newly discovered contemporary documents, including the coroner's report, concludes that murder remains a distinct possibility.[17] While it is highly unlikely that Robert Dudley commissioned the killing of his wife it is entirely possible that she was killed by one or more members of his retinue, who perceived her, correctly, as an impediment to his marrying Elizabeth. The coroner's jury was far from impartial and it came under pressure to arrive at a verdict which would satisfy both the Earl and the Queen. Dudley was informed of the verdict in advance, privately. But though he was exonerated publicly the rumours of his involvement in his wife's death pursued him to the end of his life. *A Letter*, read as satire, is further evidence of widespread scepticism about his innocence, which lingered for many years afterwards.

A Letter notes the "immens and profuse a charg of expens" involved in the festivities and with wide-eyed mock innocence asks "what may this express, what may this set oout untoo us?"[18] The obvious answer would be that it expressed the Earl's extravagance, vanity and overweening ambition and the exact opposite of "a magnifyk minde, a singular wizdoom, a prinsly purs, and an heroicall hart". The author tacitly concedes as much, adding (with a verbal wink) after the conventional, safe response, "yet coold I say a great deel more".

A Letter competes with Gascoigne by punning on the Earl of Leicester's name. But whereas the Savage Man's *did lay/Dudley* dialogue with Echo was flattering, *A Letter* is sarcastic, describing the Fates accompanying the Queen on her grand entry to Kenilworth being "duddld with such varietee of delights".[19] "Duddld" – an obvious play on "Dudley-ed" – was, even in the sixteenth century, an extraordinarily obscure word, meaning "confused" or "muddled". What they see at the castle leaves the Fates "gigling" – hardly a very deferential response to the Earl's munificence and effort.

If *A Letter* is indeed a satire then its third target is its implicit author, Robert

Langham, described at the end of the book as "Clark of the Councell chamber doore". There was a minor court official of that name but his title was "Keeper of the Council Chamber" and his role was not to control access but merely to furnish the Privy Council's committee room with flowers, fire-tongs and other minor comforts. Since the supposed recipient of *A Letter* was a friend of the putative author there would be no point in fabricating a false job title to impress him, which raises the question of why, if Robert Langham was really the author, he chose to misrepresent that title. Sir Walter Scott used *A Letter* as source material and wrote that "There has seldom been a better portrait of the pragmatic conceit and self-importance of a small man in office".[20] He portrayed Langham in his historical novel *Kenilworth* as a buffoon whose appearance "seemed to body forth a vain, harebrained coxcomb, and small wit".[21] That is certainly how Langham comes across – vain, pompous and self-regarding.

That the real author of *A Letter* was William Patten, a member of the Earl's own team of Kenilworth writers, accords with the author having knowledge of the content of Gascoigne's unperformed play. It would also explain his knowledge of details such as the trumpets having a diameter of over 16 inches, indicating someone involved with the organisation of the entertainments rather than a court official.

Other features of the book strengthen the case for Patten's authorship. The extraordinarily idiosyncratic, phonetically based orthography (or spelling) of *A Letter*, with its proliferation of "z"s and disinclination to use one "o" when two could be slotted in, is paralleled by the identically bizarre style of Patten's *A Calendar of Scripture* and his 1580 elegy for the twelfth Earl of Arundel. This strange-looking language has sometimes mistakenly been assumed to have been a local Warwickshire or Nottinghamshire dialect. In fact *A Letter*'s distinctive style is totally synthetic. It is also revealing that the word "duddld" is found nowhere else in writing of this period except in another of Patten's works. But if William Patten did write *A Letter*, what were his motives in attacking a minor court official, his writing associate George Gascoigne, and his patron, Robert Dudley?

Patten, who was born around 1510, seems to have had some legal training. In the 1540s he was secretary to the Earl of Arundel and through the patronage of the Earl of Warwick was appointed to be one of the two "Judges of the Marshalsey"; the other judge was William Cecil, later Lord Burghley. Patten clearly kept up his connection with this increasingly powerful and influential figure, and it may well have been Burghley who persuaded Leicester to let him assist at the Kenilworth entertainments. Patten's interests included antiquarianism and authorship. His *Expedition into Scotland* (1548) was an account of Protector Somerset's raid on Scotland in August-September 1547. The diary format and rambling digressions much resemble the style of *A Letter*. Later works included *The Calendar of Scripture* (1575), a biblical glossary enlivened by Patten's numerological obsessions (which re-appear in *A Letter*). Over the years Patten moved up the social ladder, receiving a number of lucrative state and church appointments, becoming Lord of the Manor at Stoke Newington and sending his eldest son to Trinity College, Cambridge. But in the period 1568-1570 he fell into debt and in 1573 all his remaining estates and offices were sold or forfeited. Brian O'Kill has conjectured what may have happened next:

> A possible situation takes shape: Patten, still brooding over his disgrace and the apparent injustice of the world, returns to Court and finds an idiotic upstart mercer flaunting his little brief authority as Keeper of the Council Chamber. Robert Langham now takes precedence over William Patten, grand-nephew of a Lord Chancellor and Archbishop, true gentleman and devoted friend of great men! So the faithful servant of the old order rails against the newcomer who denies him his place, as Kent against Oswald in *King Lear*.[22]

This is plausible, if unprovable. But why was Patten so angry with Leicester and his protégé Gascoigne? After all, Leicester had hired him to help write the entertainments for Her Majesty. Why the sour grapes?

Pride and hurt feelings, one suspects. Of the seven members of the writing team, Patten, though at sixty-five the oldest, was probably also its most junior. Compared to the others, he was a bankrupt nobody. In a society as hierarchical and status-driven as Tudor England the others may not have bothered to conceal their disdain for Patten's lowly status. Whatever the truth of the situation, Gascoigne made sure that in recording what happened at Kenilworth the lion's share of the writing was all his own work. He also represented himself as having had a starring role in the proceedings. By contrast, Patten was marginalized. His only contribution to the entertainments that we know of is the Latin verse on the board above the gate, which the Queen was unable to read because it was too dark.

In *The princelye pleasures* Gascoigne gives writing credits to Hunnis, Ferrers and Harry Goldingham, but is strikingly offhand and casual about Patten's contributions to the entertainments. Describing the moment that the Queen passed along the drawbridge he quotes a Latin verse by Mulcaster, adding: "other verses to the very selfe same effect were devised by M. *Paten*, and fixed over the gate in a frame. I am not verye sure whether these or master *Patens* were pronounced by the Actor, but they were all to one effect."[23] In his anthology of the entertainment's scripts, Gascoigne didn't even bother including Patten's contribution. If Patten himself hadn't reproduced it in *A Letter* – which is another incidental reason for assuming his authorship – it would have been lost to posterity. He not only quoted it in full but clearly instructed the printer to give it typographical prominence. Patten's verse is italicised and eye-catchingly set with narrow margins at the top of page 14. In his own way he was as proud of his work as Gascoigne, and just as keen to promote its importance.

Wiliam Patten was surely the classic outsider, silently consumed by private discontents. Worse, Patten had to tolerate the presence of the most successful writer of the day, and there is nothing quite like someone else's success to bring home to a failed writer the acuteness of his disappointed hopes. Patten's literary career had, in truth, been undistinguished. His antipathy to Gascoigne probably wasn't personal so much as professional – sheer jealousy and envy. And in a sense Patten's equation of Gascoigne and Codrus was not unjustified. There was nothing particularly memorable about the lines which Gascoigne penned at Leicester's command. It was hack work. Patten would probably been able to produce speeches that were just as good – but he wasn't asked.

Nor was Patten the only person present at Kenilworth that July who may have felt a pang of jealousy regarding Gascoigne's success and reputation as a writer. Philip Sidney was present at the entertainments and can hardly have been unaware of Gascoigne's dominant presence. But Sidney himself never said a word about Gascoigne. Sidney was probably in the audience for *Jocasta* and *Supposes*, yet from the writings of Philip Sidney you would never know that George Gascoigne had ever existed. After Sidney's exposure to Gascoigne in the summer of 1575 his subsequent absolute silence about his literary achievements seems curiously eloquent.

That Sidney and Gascoigne did not enjoy each other's company is hardly surprising. Gascoigne was handsome, easy-going, extrovert, fond of a bawdy quip, whereas Sidney, by all accounts, was priggish, uptight and solemnly "serious". Ben Jonson disliked Sidney intensely and described him as "no pleasant man in countenance, his face being spoiled with pimples and of high blood and long".[24] Sidney's biographer calls him "a hot-tempered, arrogant, and in many ways 'difficult' young man, who was not liked by all his contemporaries".[25] Sidney was a haughty aristocrat who disdained the vulgarity of publication. When he died in 1586 none of his poetry, fiction or critical prose had appeared in print. But if, as seems very likely, Sidney and Gascoigne fell out with each other at Kenilworth, they each may have taken an oblique revenge on the other. Sidney revenged himself on Gascoigne by expunging him from the record of English literary achievement in *The Defence of Poesie*. But Gascoigne, too, seems to have retaliated. One of the illustrations to *The Noble Arte of Venerie* shows the Queen picnicking during a hunt, surrounded by courtiers. Katherine Duncan-Jones has suggested that the two bearded courtiers with garters on their left legs may be Sidney's father and Leicester. She adds,

> A group of courtiers sitting and picnicking to the right ought, if precise identifications are intended, to include Sidney. The most noticeable of the

group, and the youngest-looking, bears some slight resemblance to the 1577 portraits of Sidney. He is shown, unglamorously, about to stuff a large piece of meat into his mouth.[26]

Duncan-Jones's hunch is certainly a possibility. In fact the Sidney figure is duplicated by that of a boy in the foreground, who is also pushing a large chunk of food towards his open mouth. If the identification is correct, Gascoigne was satirising the haughty aristocrat as coarse and infantile. It may not be entirely a coincidence that a bearded male figure leans towards the gluttonous child and is shown pouring wine from a flagon. The thin, stylized jet of liquid makes it look very much as if the man is symbolically pissing in the boy's direction. This may be reading too much into the scene, but sly humour like this would be perfectly in keeping with Gascoigne's temperament. If the resemblance was intentional (and in the original the illustration is far too small for certainty) it was a private joke on the poet's part, but no more than that.

As for William Patten. The abrupt way in which *A Letter's* description of proceedings at Kenilworth terminates on Wednesday 20 July 1575, a week before the Queen departed, strongly suggests that his services were dispensed with. All the more reason, then, for Patten to return to London, smouldering with sundry discontents, bent on his revenge.

Woodstock

From Kenilworth the royal progress crawled north to Lichfield. After Lichfield it headed to Chartley Park in the valley of the Trent, then on to Stafford Castle. From there it went south to Chillington Hall and Dudley Castle. On 29 August it arrived for a month-long stay at the Queen's estate at Woodstock in Oxfordshire. Here the entertainments were managed by Sir Henry Lee, who was both the royal champion and Lieutenant of the Royal Manor of Woodstock.

Whether or not Gascoigne tagged along too is not known. That he accompanied the court on its travels as a hanger-on is perfectly plausible. Or, like Philip Sidney, family matters may have taken him away, to return later. Whether or not he returned to Walthamstow after Kenilworth, by the time the progress had reached Woodstock George Gascoigne, like Philip Sidney, was certainly present. But this time it was Gascoigne who was reduced to the role of spectator and others who put on the entertainments. From Sir Henry Lee's perspective, Gascoigne was heavily implicated in the debacle at Kenilworth. Sir Henry's agenda was simple, which was to flatter, not lecture, the Queen. But even in this unfavourable situation Gascoigne managed to press matters to his own advantage.

On her very first day at Woodstock the Queen was presented with an entertainment which was seen visibly to excite and move her. Indeed, although the festivities put on by Sir Henry Lee could hardly hope to compete with the grandeur and extravagance of Leicester's, it's clear that Elizabeth was altogether happier at Woodstock than at Kenilworth. Pointedly, she stayed there an extraordinarily long time, arriving in late August and not departing until 3 October.

The show that thrilled her was a romantic tale of thwarted love and self-denial told by an actor dressed up as a hermit. (It is just possible that George Gascoigne was allotted this role, but if he was he never mentioned or alluded to it.) The Queen was led into woodland on the estate, as usual still on her horse. There she was confronted by the spectacle of two knights in armour having a sword fight. As she approached, a hermit stepped forward and called out, "No more, most valiant knights!" The fight was halted.[27]

By 1575 hermits had virtually ceased to be a part of contemporary life. They belonged to the middle ages and existed in late Tudor times largely as folklore. The hermit announced that his name was Hemetes – itself a play on the word "heremyte" and tantamount to calling himself "Hermit the hermit". The actor playing Hemetes was dressed in a lavish costume which was felt to be right for the part, loaded down "with beads and other such ornaments of his profession".

"Violence must give way to virtue, and the doubtful hazard you be in, by a most noble help, must be ended," cried the hermit. The knights dutifully lowered their swords and kneeled. Hemetes turned to Elizabeth, hailing her as "bound to the immortal gods" and announcing that he would tell her an instructive tale. It went like this:

> *Not long ago, in the country of Cambaya, situated near the mouth of the River Indus, lived Duke Occanon, who was its ruler. His only heir was his fair daughter, Gandina. She fell in love with a poor but noble and honourable knight named Contarenus, and he with her. When the Duke discovered his daughter's secret love he said nothing but was nevertheless determined to separate the lovers. At his bidding, and for a fabulous sum of money, an enchantress caused Contarenus to be swept into the air and carried to the furthest boundaries of the ocean. Depositing the knight on the ground again the enchantress advised patience, promising him that before seven years had passed his dearest wish would come true. But before that happened he would first see "the worthiest lady in the whole world" and have to do combat with its "hardiest knight". At the same time Contarenus would also have to help a blind hermit who would recover his sight at the very same moment as his wish came true.*
>
> *Gandina, meanwhile, grew restless. Eventually she discovered what the Duke had done. "Farewell, unhappy country and most cruel father!" she cried, and set off to find her lover, accompanied only by a single maid. Dressed in simple clothes they fled over the border and eventually arrived at Sibyl's grotto, where they encountered the noble knight Loricus. Loricus*

explained that the lady he loved regarded him as unworthy of her and that he was travelling the world to win a great reputation and impress her.

The Sybil told Gandina and Loricus that their destinies were linked and that they would not be parted until they came to a place where the men were strong, the women very fair, the land fertile, the people wealthy, the government just and the sovereign most worthy. There Gandina would find that which would content her and Loricus that which would comfort him.

The hermit then interrupted his tale to explain his own role in the story. Though old and wrinkled in appearance and "cast into a corner" Hemetes revealed he was himelf once a knight. Not only a knight but one known and accepted with the best in the world, who resided at a famous court among many knights and ladies of great worth and virtue. There Hemetes had fallen in love with a lady who, alas, kept changing shape when touched. When Hemetes embraced her she finally metamorphosed into a terrible tigress and he had to let go.

In the face of such a doomed love Hemetes went on a pilgrimage to the temple of Venus on Cyprus. Entering the temple, Hemetes was suddenly struck blind. He was ejected from the temple for his folly and presumption, and told that Venus was not honoured by "parted affection". Weeping and sighing, Hemetes begged Apollo for help. Apollo's priest took Hemetes by the hand and told him that the god was sympathetic to his plight and had granted him the gift of foreseeing the destiny of every lover. What's more Hemetes would recover his sight but only when, in a wonderfully tranquil land, two very valiant knights would fight, two of the most constant lovers would meet, and the most virtuous lady in the world would appear. Until that happy moment Hemetes must live as a solitary hermit in the wilds. As the priest's words ended, Hemetes found himself suddenly transported to a nearby hill, where he'd subsequently spent many winters in seclusion from the world.

While the hermit was talking, Gandina presumably silently entered and joined the other three actors in the masque. Hemetes now dramatically announced that the prophecies of the Sibyl and Apollo's priest had both come true. The two knights had fought. The most constant lovers in the world had met. And he, Hemetes, had recovered his sight. And all thanks to the presence of her gracious and most virtuous majesty!

More flattery – but there are no signs that the ageing Elizabeth (just days away from her forty-second birthday) ever grew tired of being praised for her great beauty, virtue, wisdom, learning or benignly transformative presence.

The hermit's tale may have owed something to Greek romance. Six years earlier Thomas Underdowne's English translation of Heliodorus's *Aethiopian Historie* had introduced the tradition to Tudor London. But the tale was also a bit like one of those sub-plots in *Orlando Furioso* about true love thwarted by magical forces. The main characters in the tale had been brought face to face, and their destinies transformed. But the climax was oddly inconclusive. Just as at the end of Ariosto's cantos you were left wondering *what happened next*. Elizabeth was not to be disappointed by the twist in the tale – but she'd have to wait. Her enthusiasm and impatience were evident. The impact of her first day at Woodstock was so great that the Queen let it be known "that the whole in order as it fell, should be brought to her in writing".

Apologising for tiring the Queen's "noble ears" with the length of his tale, the hermit beseeched her to honour his home with her presence. He then offered to lead the way and began to stagger off, evidently weighed down by his beads "and other such ornaments". Perhaps the actor playing the part of this old and wrinkled hermit was himself elderly. Whatever the reason, Elizabeth then did something extraordinary. *She got off her horse and walked*. She was evidently in a bubbly, animated mood. As the hermit escorted her through the trees to his home she "fell into some discourse and praise of his good tale". The romantic tale of Gandina and Contarenus had evidently struck a chord. Elizabeth was keen to know more. The story was thrilling but, frustratingly, "was not ended, or rather scarce fully begun". As the Queen chatted to the actor, the crowd of privileged onlookers, including the French ambassador and George Gascoigne, trooped after them.

But the conversation between her majesty and the actor was brief. Almost at once they reached the poor hermit's home amid the trees. Here the hermit explained that the hour approached when he had to say his prayers, according to a vow he had sworn never to break. He bade her farewell, and left her to enjoy the comforts of his "simple hermitage". The actor slipped away, and presumably Sir Henry took over as Elizabeth's guide.

The hermitage was hardly in keeping with the bleak, ascetic tradition of the hermit in his stony, inhospitable cave. A 200-yard perimeter of ornamental latticework surrounded a spectacular ivy-draped entrance. The entranceway was decorated with loose gold plate on strings, creating a fabulous shimmering effect. Once through the entrance, the Queen walked along a pathway made from fresh turf. Railings draped with flowers and ivy offered protection as the grassy path ascended some forty feet off the ground. At the top Elizabeth came to the hermit's home: a cavern of greenery fashioned from an oak tree. The tree's topmost branches had been bent over and tied down with ropes, forming a curving roof of natural foliage.

At one end of this fantastic green room was a table in the shape of a half moon. The tablecloth was made of freshly cut turf and on it was enough food for a royal banquet – scores of fish and meat dishes, pastries and delicacies. At the other end was a round table with a chair covered in crimson velvet and embroidered with a leaf design enclosing scenes of wild beasts and trees. On the "walls" hung allegorical paintings of noblemen and other worthies.

The Queen then sat down to eat – presumably in the velvet chair, at her own table. Sir Henry and the other chief guests sat down at the other. Numbers were probably limited and George Gascoigne Esquire is unlikely to have been high enough in the pecking (or gobbling) order to rate inclusion. But presumably food was laid on outside the hermit's "house" for the hosts of hangers-on.

During or after the feasting another entertainment was put on – described, vaguely, as a "pageant". More costumed actors and speeches of banal flattery, one suspects. There was one other diversion. Philip Sidney's new friend Edward Dyer hid in the oak tree and elegantly wailed his "Despair" at his sad neglect. The Queen was evidently in an ebullient mood. Dyer's request for preferment was granted. A little over three months later he was granted a "licence to pardon and dispense with tanning of leather" – a lucrative monopoly. Sidney, too, got something out of his attendance at the progress. He was made a royal cupbearer – a worthwhile post but disappointingly badly paid by the standards of a member of the ruling class.

George Gascoigne received nothing so tangible but he'd made his mark. His social rehabilitation was almost complete. The following year was to show that he was regarded as someone whose talents were worth deploying on behalf of the Tudor state. Like the characters in the masques which were always set before Elizabeth, his proximity to the Queen really had transformed him. He was no longer the scandalous author of a lewd and offensive volume of verse and prose. He'd become *respectable*.

*

Meanwhile, back in London, the publication of *A Letter* had had predictable repercussions. If Patten had used a fictitious pseudonym he would probably have got away with his satire but in adopting the persona of a real person he'd caused a minor scandal. The real Robert Langham had evidently not been amused to discover he was the supposed author of a book which portrayed him as a hard-drinking, philandering, self-satisfied fool and poked fun at the Kenilworth festivities.

Patten was quickly unmasked as the culprit. Although *A Letter* had appeared anonymously the book's use of a particular design of decorated initial "A" enabled the printer to be identified. On 10 September William Patten wrote a letter to his old associate and patron Lord Burghley (who was still with the court at Woodstock) saying he had just received an answer from Thomas Wilson, one of the four Masters of the Court of Requests, "hoow the book waz too be supprest for that Langham had complaynd vpon it, and ootherwize for that the honorabl entertainment be not turned into a iest". This single tantalising letter is all that is left of a chain of correspondence about *A Letter* involving Lord Burghley and other court officials. It suggests that Langham, having become aware of the book, not only complained about it to senior figures on the Privy Council, but tried to lay his hands on every copy he could get hold of in order to prevent others reading it. It was, essentially, a storm in a teacup. If Leicester had become involved then Patten might have been in much more serious trouble, but Leicester, away from London, is unlikely to have known about *A Letter*. Likewise Gascoigne probably never saw a copy of the book. If he did, he was probably unaware that he was one of its satirical targets. The book's clotted surface texture must surely have deterred casual readers from venturing very far into the text or its oblique ironies. On the face of it the joke was strictly at the expense of Robert Langham and it requires a much sharper eye to see the broader satire at work or the sustained, double-edged quality of the narrator's posture of garrulous, wide-eyed innocence. Burghley intervened to have the book suppressed. Though Patten might be said to belong to the Burghley faction at court there is no reason to suppose that anyone but William Patten was responsible for the hoax. Burghley, though he might well have privately smiled at a satire on Leicester's overweening egocentricity and pretensions, would hardly have involved himself in such surreptitious manoeuvring. His role in the affair was to soothe Langham's ruffled feelings, suppress the book and protect his own slightly eccentric protégé.

That *A Letter* was successfully suppressed in 1575 is clear. Only three copies of the probable first edition survive, and they were most likely ones left in Patten's own possession. Fourteen copies of the second edition survive. This seems to have been a pirated edition, though given the murky circumstances surrounding the publication of *A Letter* Patten may well have been perfectly happy to see his book re-appear through a third party at a later date when the fuss had died down. Robert Langham died around 1579-80, by which time republication would have been a much safer bet.

Back at Woodstock, Elizabeth had to wait just over three weeks for the climax to the thrilling story of Gandina and Contarenus. This was set before her on 20 September in the form of a play. The long wait indicates that the play may have been hurriedly written to order to answer those questions left unresolved at the end of the tale. Gascoigne seems not to have been involved in the composition of this play. Its style is wooden and banal, and had he been in any way involved as a co-author he would surely have trumpeted the fact and arranged for the work's publication.

There are various possibilities why he might have been excluded – professional jealousy at an outsider who wasn't part of Sir Henry Lee's set or simply caution on Lee's part because the poet's Kenilworth play had upset the Queen. Gascoigne may of course have remained aloof for reasons of tact and self-interest. He was a protégé of the Earl of Leicester and owed him everything for being able to put himself centre-stage at Kenilworth. Although Sir Henry Lee was ostensibly a member of the Earl's faction at court, ruthless self-interest clearly figured when the chance came to ingratiate oneself with Elizabeth. The striking thing about the Woodstock play is that it is very obviously a retort to

Gascoigne's aborted masque about Zabeta. It climaxes with Gandina suppressing her passion for Contarenus and giving him up out of duty to the state. Sir Henry substituted a tale of romantic self-denial for Leicester's waspish critique of Elizabeth's status as a spinster, and the Queen was delighted. Lee's flattery was spot on. There was a reflection of her contorted, difficult relationship with Dudley in the drama, but it was a safe, soothing one. It told her she was right to remain single. Not just right but thrillingly and nobly self-sacrificing. It reinforced her deepest beliefs and imbued them with poetry. It was an entertainment which surely meant much more to her than Kenilworth's elaborate contrivances involving fireworks and floating dolphins.

*

On Tuesday 17 October 1575, Lady Margaret Gascoigne died at Cardington Manor. The breach between Gascoigne and his mother had not been healed by the time of her death. The only aspect of her decease which seems to have interested him was the provisions of her will, which he unsuccessfully contested. It made no mention of George Gascoigne or his wife Elizabeth. The disaffection between mother and son evidently continued to the bitter end. Lady Margaret's property went to her youngest son, John, and relatives in the north from the Scargill and Conyers families. The will's executor was John Conyers of London, Gentleman, who received a very generous legacy.[28]

The will made provision for the transportation of Lady Margaret's body to the parish church of Whitkirk, and directed her executors to pay the expenses of those who accompanied the cortège from Bedford to Yorkshire. Lady Margaret's body was conveyed north to Thorpe Hall, prior to being interred in the parish church of Whitkirk on Tuesday 6 December 1575. Neither of her sons attended her funeral. The chief mourner was her daughter-in-law, Jane Gascoigne, wife of John. The funeral was evidently a lavish affair and was directed by the York Herald of Arms, William Dethick.

Gascoigne returned to Walthamstow that autumn aware of a new opportunity to promote himself at court. The Queen had publicly requested a written account of the first day's entertainment at Woodstock. He would do better than that. He would supply her with a beautifully produced manuscript presentation copy of the hermit's tale. This was a conventional way of ingratiating oneself with the monarch; decades earlier Thomas More presented Henry VIII with a lavishly decorated copy of a Latin poem he'd written celebrating his coronation.

"The Tale of Hemetes the Heremyte" was not, as is sometimes assumed, an original piece of writing by Gascoigne. He nevertheless decided to stamp it as a distinctively Gascoignean production in other ways. Since the Queen admired and respected learning, he produced a multi-lingual manuscript in 38 folios. It is quarto size, 8¾ inches x 6½ inches – about the size of a modern notebook. It even resembles a notebook, in so far as Gascoigne only filled half of it. The remaining 38 folios are blank. It has commonly been assumed to have been produced by a scribe on the poet's behalf but there seems no real authority behind this belief. It is just as likely to be entirely Gascoigne's own painstaking work.

The narrative is accompanied by his own translations of the tale into Latin, Italian and French. In addition, the versions of the tale are divided by three emblematic pen-and-ink drawings accompanied by verses in Latin, Italian and French. Gascoigne claimed that his Latin was "rustye" and "over long yeared", his French "forgrowne" and "owt of fashion" and his Italian "mustye" and "to lately lerned" but his modesty was merely conventional. The Italian was "Gascoigne's best, both in its use of idiom and in fluency. However, the Latin and the French reveal a certain degree of skill, indicating that Gascoigne had a good knowledge of both."[29]

On the first page another quasi-emblematic drawing portrays the poet presenting "The Tale" to the Queen. It is followed by a sonnet and a prose address "To the Queen's Most Excellent Majesty", ending with an 18-line rhyming epilogue. The prose preface amounts to a request for employment. Gascoigne concedes his "youth myspent", his "follys laughed att" and other errors, but the key item in his list of personal failings isn't really a failing at all: "my trewth unemployed". What he wants is patronage and sponsorship, and he isn't too choosy whether it's for his writing or his soldiering:

> Behold here (learned pryncesse) nott *Gascoigne* the ydle poet, writing trifles of the green knighte, but *Gascoigne* the *Satyricall* wryter, meditating eche *Muse* that may expresse his reformation/ fforgett (most excellent lady) the poesies which I have scattered in the world, and I vowe to wryte volumes of profitable poems, wherewith your majesty may be pleased/ Only employ me (good Quene) and I trust to be proved as dillygent as *Clearchus*, as resolute as *Mutius*, and as faythfull as *Curtius*/ Your majesty shall ever fynde me with a penne in my righte hand, and a sharpe sword girt to my lefte side, *in utramaque paratus*/ as glad to goe forwards when any occasion of your service may dryve me, as willing to attend your person in any calling that you shall pleas to appoint me/ my vaunting vayne being nowe pretyly well breathed, and myne arrogant speeches almost spent, lett me most humbly beseche your highness, that you may vouchsafe to pardon my boldness, and deigne to accepte this my simple new yeres gifte/

The Queen did design to accept it and today this unique and priceless manuscript is held at the British Library.[30] The preface is dated "this first of January 1576" and it is commonly assumed that the manuscript was presented to Elizabeth I on this date, although there is no concrete evidence of this.

It turned out that Patten's *Letter* was not the only questionable text to emerge from the royal progress of 1575. Someone managed to get hold of either the original or a copy of Gascoigne's gift to the Queen, and transcribed the English and Latin versions of the hermit's tale. Falsely attributed to "Abraham Fleming" they appeared, with surrealistic incongruity, bound up with a tract by Synesius of Cyrene entitled *A Paradox, Proving by reason and example that Baldnesse is much better than bushie haire*. Gascoigne would no doubt have protested bitterly about this pirated edition but it did not appear until 1579, by which time he was dead.

The handsome manuscript was also signed by Gascoigne. A graphologist could no doubt read much into Gascoigne's autograph. Each time he signed himself "G Gascoigne" he wrote the first "G" backwards and looped it through the second "G", like a pair of linked keyrings. It was an idiosyncracy he shared with Thomas Churchyard, whose signature also used a double initial letter. Gascoigne's signature is big and bold, as if indicating his confidence that the Queen knew exactly who he was. He wasn't, like Robert Dudley, addressing her as an equal, but neither was he beseeching her favours as an unknown outsider. Indeed, in the prefatory sonnet he even seems to have been reminding her of the mishap in the Chase at Kenilworth:

Behold (good Queen) a poet…

In doubtful doompes, which way were best to take
with humble heart, and knees that kiss the ground
presents himself to you for duty's sake.
And thus he saith, no danger (I protest)
shall ever let this loyal heart I bear
    to serve you as may become me best
in field, in town, in court, or anywhere.

Gascoigne is referring to the pen and ink drawing of him kneeling and presenting the manuscript. But indirectly he seems to be echoing that moment when, as the savage man, he startled Elizabeth's horse. He is, as he says, down in the dumps or depressed and uncertain about "which way were best to take". The Queen's cry "no hurt" seems to reverberate in the poet's insistence that "no danger" will attend his future service on her. As an actor he rather botched the job. What, then, of the future? Gascoigne puts forward the "strange sight" of "a poet with a spear" who is simultaneously

A soldier armed, with pencil in his ear,
with pen to fight, and sword to write a letter,
his gown half off, his blade not fully bound

The Gascoigne portrayed in the drawing is an armed warrior. But he is also a poet and he presents, as Hamlet was to do, an artfully dishevelled appearance. This is a man of possibilities, multi-talented, equally at home on the battlefield or in the study. By "pencil" Gascoigne means an artist's brush – something used in drawing (the modern meaning doesn't begin until the eighteenth century). He is, and is not, a soldier, a writer, an artist.

This drawing is much reproduced in books about the Tudor age, as if it was the sixteenth-century analogue of a photograph. Ironically, modern monochrome reproduction has the effect of making the picture seem sharper and fresher than the original, which has a faded brown-grey appearance.[31] The caption usually reads something along the lines of "George Gascoigne presenting Elizabeth I with the gift of a book." But this is not really true. What the drawing expresses is George Gascoigne's *fantasy* of himself presenting the Queen with the manuscript of "The Tale of Hemetes the Heremyte". The scene shown is an extremely stylized one. Prouty rightly comments that "the drawing is practically an emblem".[32] The Queen, wearing her crown, sits on her throne beneath a fringed canopy. A winged griffin with naked female breasts squats beside her like a guard dog. Elizabeth ceremonially clutches her orb and sceptre, almost as if she was undergoing her coronation all over again. Gascoigne kneels before her. In his left hand he holds what he called "a spear" (but is really a small lance) and his right hand his manuscript. The line of the drawing brush tucked behind his left ear parallels that of his sword. In the margin at the right-hand base of the page – and sometimes either missed out or indecipherable in reproductions – are the words "Biholde good".

Although obviously intended to feature the interior of one of the royal palaces, the whole scene is intensely theatrical. It's almost like a two-person dumb show from a static, gloomy play like *Jocasta*. Elizabeth and Gascoigne are pictured entirely alone (a wildly improbable scenario), as if on a small stage. They appear to be facing each other but on closer examination the perspective is wrong. The enthroned Queen is tilted to her right and Gascoigne, his right shoe resting (oddly) on the right corner of her outermost robe on the floor, is actually positioned looking to the left of the griffin.

Two steps lead up to this stage-like room, which is viewed from about the height of Gascoigne's head. Flagstones or tiles stretch to the rear of the room, where an open doorway set in a curtained partition reveals a cloister-like scene of pillars receding into the distance along a walkway or corridor. To the right another open doorway shows a tiny part of an apparently deserted antechamber. The ceiling of the room consists of exposed crossbeams. From a large black hole cut in the beams an outsize hand dangles the snake-like arm of an ornamental hook. From it dangles an elaborate frame bearing the words of Gascoigne's motto *Tam Marti quam Mercurio*, with a tassel drooping beneath it. Above Gascoigne's head, like a saint's halo, floats a crown of laurel leaves.

The artificiality of this frozen, strangely exaggerated, theatrical scene is accentuated by an outer frame of elaborate scrolled patterning. It looks like a three-dimensional scene on a page from a book – which is, of course, exactly what it is. The circumstances were probably quite different to those portrayed in Gascoigne's fantasy drawing. The room – whether at Whitehall or Greenwich or one of the other royal palaces – was probably bigger, less intimate, crowded with ladies in waiting and courtiers and other servants of the royal household. Gascoigne is hardly likely to have been admitted to Elizabeth's presence armed to the teeth, gripping a lance. It must nevertheless have been an odd moment when the Queen took delivery – almost like one of those strange tales of receding realities by Jorge Luis Borges. She accepted a manuscript showing her accepting the manuscript in a drawing which even portrayed the brush used to draw the drawing of her accepting the book which she held in her hand.

From a biographical point of view the most interesting feature of the scene is Gascoigne's representation of himself. We only have two conclusive images of the poet – this one and the portrait printed in *The Steel Glass*. The second image shows a lean, trim man in armour. Age is creeping up on him. The eyelids droop down over the eyes. There are lines under the eyes. He looks wary. This is a man who has experienced much and who wears it in his face. There are curving vertical white lines along the right cheek and temple which may simply indicate bone structure and frame the shadowed part of the face. But the line across the right cheek might almost be a scar – the mark of a slashing sword, perhaps.

It is a portrait which lives up to the book's title: the steel mirror – the mirror that reflects the hard, realistic, unembellished truth. The image, "a fine woodcut",[33] is not attributed but Gillian Austen plausibly suggests that "With its simple lines and the intense stare, the slight misalignment of the eyes, it is almost certain that this is actually a self-portrait, done in front of a mirror."[34]

Since *The Steel Glass* portrait was apparently done at around the same time as the drawing in "The Tale of Hemetes the Heremyte" – possibly within weeks of each other, and almost certainly in the same twelve-month period – it is instructive to compare them. The image of Gascoigne in his self-penned drawing is similar but with revealing differences. In both he has a full head of hair, a moustache and beard. There is the same fine, sharp nose. But the Gascoigne who kneels before the Queen looks healthier and more robust. His hair is fuller, even curly. It comes down in an exaggerated fashion to just above his eyebrows, whereas in the portrait the forehead is much more expansive and the hairline higher, almost on the brink of receding around the crown of the head. The kneeling poet looks strong and vigorous, apt for a man seeking military service. The calf of his exposed right leg and the thigh of his left leg look muscular and strong – the legs of a regular horse rider.

The image is likely to have been a flattering, slightly exaggerated one. This is Gascoigne as he liked to imagine himself. Compared with the man in the portrait he looks unwrinkled and younger – a fine strapping man in his prime and surely no older than his thirties. But of the two images, the portrait is likely to have been by far the closer to the reality. Looking at the portrait it is not hard to believe that it shows a man in his early forties. It is a face which seems to combine a range of emotions: melancholy, suspicion, disapproval, perhaps. It is not a relaxed, happy face. The lines under the right eye indicate fatigue. The face is thin and taut. It is the image of a man who, whether or not he knew it, was moving towards his end. Barely two years after the wonders of Kenilworth, Gascoigne would be dead.

Plate 31. A dramatic, stylized representation of Gascoigne presenting Elizabeth I with the manuscript copy of "The Tale of Hemetes the Heremyte".

Plate 32. A woodcut of George Gascoigne reflected in a "steel glass" or mirror. The Latin motto translates "As much for Mars as for Mercury".

25: *The Posies of George Gascoigne Esquire*

When Gascoigne republished A *Hundreth Sundrie Flowres* in its revised form he was keen to claim credit for what was evidently a spectacularly popular and controversial book. The new edition was unequivocally entitled *The Posies of George Gascoigne Esquire* and abolished at a stroke the fiction that the previous edition was an anthology which incorporated the work of various writers.

There are two unsolved mysteries about the publication of *The Posies of George Gascoigne Esquire*. The first is when the book was published. The initial Prefatory Letter (to "the reverend Divines") is dated "this last day of Januarie. 1574", the second ("To al yong Gentlemen") is dated "the second of Januarie. 1575". If Gascoigne was conforming to the conventions of his age then the letters were, by modern dating, written in 1575 and 1576. It is very unlikely that the first letter was written in January 1574, at a time when Gascoigne was in the thick of fighting in the Dutch war. Logically, then, *The Posies* must have been published no earlier than 1576.[1]

However, Gascoigne's dating was not always consistent and he may have been ignoring accepted practice. There is also the puzzle as to why the second letter is dated one year after the first. Was this a fiction, a slip of the pen, a printer's error, or did a year really elapse between the writing of the two letters? The situation is further complicated by the fact that some copies of the book display an ornament bearing the date "jan.1574".

To add to these difficulties the dedication to *The Complaynte of Phylomene* is dated 16 April 1575 and refers to his "*Poesies*", as if they had already been published. But *The Complaynte* was not published until 1576, along with *The Steel Glass*. This last work is prefaced by a dedication dated 15 April 1576, indicating that Gascoigne was fond of spacing his introductions by a period of twelve months. This may have been because he liked the pattern or shape that suggested, not because the dates were necessarily true. No documentary material providing unequivocal evidence of the publication date has yet surfaced. On balance, the probability is that *The Posies of George Gascoigne Esquire* was published some time during 1575, but the first half of 1576 cannot entirely be ruled out.

The second puzzle is why the book is prefaced by a letter which appeals to the censors not to ban it, since by the fact of its publication the book had ostensibly been approved. Probably it was licensed by the Stationers' Company but not approved by the church censors. The strong implication is that the book was published without the busybodies on the High Commission knowing or ever having seen a copy. That would certainly explain why the suppression of the book seems to have occurred quite late in the day, when almost all copies had been sold. It seems more than likely that the dating of the prefatory letters was bogus and Gascoigne was up to his old tricks again. Cyndia Susan Clegg has suggested that Gascoigne wanted to give the misleading impression that the Commissioners had approved the text, and that the dating "represents an attempt to separate the two letters, suggesting that the first letter accompanied the manuscript to the official reviewers and some time passed between its submission, their approval, and the book's printing".[2]

Whether or not Gascoigne deliberately misled his publisher and the printers into thinking that his book had been passed by the Commissioners is unclear. The control and censorship of Tudor publications could be punitive and vicious but in some respects it was a ramshackle, inefficient, amateurish business.

A Continuation

A second edition offered Gascoigne the chance to complete "Dan Bartholmew of Bathe", which was now republished with two new sections and an envoi, totalling 448 lines. In the envoi Gascoigne comically dedicated the poem to "Sir Salamanke", ostensibly a jokey nickname for a crony from the Dutch wars (his fellow prisoner, Captain Sheffield?):

> Sir *Salamanke* to thee this tale is told,
> Peruse it well and call unto thy mind
> The pleasant place where thou didst first behold
> The rueful rhymes: remember how the *Wind*
> *Did calmly blow*: and made me leave behind
> Some leaves thereof: whiles I sat reading still
> And thou then seemst to hearken with good will.
>
>   Believe me now, hadst thou not seemed to like
> The woeful words of Bartholmew's discourse,
> They should have lyen still drowned in the dyke[3]

But "Sir Salamanke" may never have existed. Gascoigne's explanation that the poem was published incomplete because the final section of the manuscript blew away in the wind and fell into water could well be a comic fabrication. He claims to have reconstituted the lost ending from memory. True or not, the new ending adds little to the second-rate quality of the poem. In the version published in *A Hundreth Sundrie Flowres* Dan Bartholmew appears to be either dead or very close to death at the end. In the extended version a perfunctory opening section discovers him still alive and denouncing sensuality. Now, however, all references to Bath and the pox are gone, along with most of the sexual innuendo.

The third-person narrator then relates how, as Dan Bartholmew lies dying, a messenger arrives. He is bearing a letter from Ferenda written in blood, expressing her woe. Bartholmew immediately rallies and returns to London, where he is reunited with his lover. But soon Ferenda is up to her old, promiscuous tricks again. This time instead of sinking into despair Bartholmew decides to ride off in search of adventures. The narrator then reveals that Bartholmew is in fact the green knight, whose "heavy plaint" has been published. In other words, Bartholmew is George Gascoigne.

But the same objection to any neat biographical equation exists as before. Ferenda cannot straightforwardly be identified as Elizabeth Breton. There is no reason to believe that Gascoigne ever languished at a lodging house until revived by a letter written in blood from his wife, an old girlfriend or anyone else. Rather "Dan Bartholmew" is an all-purpose character, sometimes Bartholmew Withypoll (and perhaps his brother Daniel), sometimes Gascoigne, and sometimes a figure of pure imagination. This is coterie literature in its least attractive form, with passages obscure to any but those with personal involvement in it.

If there is an autobiographical message in the poem, it is an ugly one. "I do believe," the narrator concludes, "That once again he will be amorous", or to put it another way:

I coumpt him lost because I see him bent
To yield again where first his grief began.[4]

Here "grief" is slang for "ejaculation" (and "coumpt" plays on "cunt"). This could mean "he is going to have sex once again with Ferenda". But in the overall context of the complete poem it could signify "he is going to a brothel to have sex with a whore, which is where he had his first sexual experience". Put in its crudest form, the autobiographical sub-text of the poem might read something like this: *Bartholmew Withypoll screwed around a lot in brothels and caught the pox. He died. I, George Gascoigne, am my friend reborn. I, too, don't believe in love. I am going to yield to my sexual impulses and take the same risk.*

What Gascoigne's wife Elizabeth made of all this, or his involvement with a woman in The Hague, is anyone's guess. Perhaps Gascoigne laughed it off as comic fantasy. Or perhaps he simply didn't care.

Certayne notes of Instruction

The Posies of George Gascoigne Esquire included a striking new ingredient to that volume's rich mix of contents: a non-fiction essay about how poetry should be written. *Certayne notes of Instruction concerning the making of verse or ryme in English* has gone down in literary history as the first ever essay on English prosody.

Its sixteen numbered sections comprise a practical discussion of the mechanics of writing a poem. A good poem, Gascoigne argues, should begin with "some fine invention" – meaning some clever and original idea, not a cliché. The poet should avoid obscurity, keep to the same metre, understand the importance of ordering words according to stress, avoid words of many syllables and favour monosyllables and beware rhyme for the sake of it. The poet should also avoid too much repetition, eschew strange words, keep to ordinary English and not set the adjective after the noun, and take care with the placing of caesuras (or pauses). He should also grasp accurately the structure of metrical forms. These include native English forms such as Poulter's measure, found in the commonest sort of contemporary verse. "Riding rhyme", used by Chaucer in *The Canterbury Tales* is "best for a merry tale" and rhythm royal is "fittest for a grave discourse". Gascoigne also discusses foreign metrical forms, mostly French:

> Ballades are best of matters of love, and rondlets most apt for the beating or handling of an adage or common proverb; sonnets serve as well in matters of love as of discourse: Dyzaynes and Syxaines for short fantasies: Virelays for an effectual proposition, although by the name you might otherwise judge of Virelays, and the long verse of twelve and fourteen syllables, although it be nowadays used in all themes, yet in my judgement it would serve best for psalms and hymns.[5]

Gascoigne's essay has been variously hailed for its acute understanding of metre and language, accused of being superficial and confused, and praised for raising the central issues which subsequently dominated four centuries of English prosody.[6] Such contradictory responses underline how much prosody is itself a contentious subject. Understanding Gascoigne's ideas is complicated by changes in the pronunciation of words and the question of what he meant by such terms as "measure", "number" and "emphasis". But in general terms, *Certayne notes* forms part of that wider movement, exemplified by William Tyndale's translation of the New Testament, Thomas Wilson's *The Arte of Rhetorique* (1553) and Roger Ascham's *The Scholemaster* (1570), which resisted foreign words ("inkhorn terms") and syntax and promoted the value of ordinary, everyday English.

Gabriel Harvey admired Gascoigne's division of the subject into precepts of "Invention" and "Elocution", commenting "He doth prettily well: but might easely have dun much better, both in the one, & in the other: especially by the direction of Horaces, & Aristotles Ars Poetica."[7] But that comment says as much about Harvey's prickly pedantry as it does about Gascoigne's understanding of prosody.

All writers who set out literary manifestoes invariably put forward a notion of best practice which just happens to fit their own kind of writing and interests and "Certayne notes of Instruction" is no exception. It began a tradition which later included such notable examples as Wordworth's Prefaces to *Lyrical Ballads* (1800 and 1802) and Mayakovsky's *Kak delat' stikhi? [How are Verses*

Made?] (1926). But manifesto writers are usually driven by a burning passion to explain, persuade and convert the reader to their great literary cause. Gascoigne's essay has an altogether more relaxed tone. "Certayne" simply means "some", modestly indicating that it does not pretend to be a comprehensive guide. It is written in a casual, genial, chatty style: "I write moved by good will, and not to show my skill". In fact it very probably was written casually, in a single draft. Section 16 breezily begins, "I had forgotten a notable kind of rhyme, called riding rhyme..." Gascoigne is not bothered by formal elegance but just pops his digression in as it stands. He does not bother to go back, rewrite the essay, and locate it where it more properly belongs, in section 14.

Certayne notes purports to be written "at the request of Master Edouardo Donati", who made Gascoigne promise to write down for him some "instructions" (or advice) about how to write English verse or rhyme. Donati sounds Italian but no one has ever managed to track down such a person and it seems more than likely that he never existed. If he was Italian, then why should Donati wish to seem "the truer Englishman"? And why would he need to be told in section 14 that the Italian word "Ballare" means "to dance"? It sounds like another one of Gascoigne's games.

What motivated the essay is debatable. When a previously unknown writer is acclaimed as a dazzlingly original talent or becomes a bestseller there is usually a rash of imitators. Why did *that* book succeed where scores of others sank without trace? What's the writer's secret? Perhaps *Certayne notes of Instruction* was Gascoigne's affable response to all those young bloods of the Inns of Court who longed for his success and acclaim and who begged for tips from the *maestro*. Perhaps "Edouardo Donati" was invented to give a faintly exotic tinge to the production, or simply to avoid the charge of being patronising.

It is possible to find examples of Gascoigne contradicting his own advice but broadly speaking in *Certayne notes* he is describing his own practice in *A Hundreth Sundrie Flowres*. It is only in his later work that he shows signs of forgetting his own injunctions against repetition and cliché, and above all that timeless pearl of wisdom for any writer to

> avoid prolixity and tediousness...and knit up your sentences as compendiously as you may, since brevity (so that it be not drowned in obscurity) is most commendable.[8]

Gascoigne's essay excited Gabriel Harvey more than anything else the poet wrote, if we measure that emotion by quantities of marginal jottings. In that he was four centuries ahead of his time. Only in recent years has "Certayne notes" attracted a substantial amount of academic commentary. For centuries it lay in the shadows of a much better known work. Philip Sidney's *Defence of Poesie* (also known by the title *An Apology for Poetry*) is the best known work of literary criticism of the Elizabethan age. This is partly due to the massive public relations campaign orchestrated by the Earl of Leicester after his nephew's early death in the Low Countries, and partly due to a later cultural ignorance of the Latin writings of the age. For example, Henry Dethick's *Oratio in laudem Poëseos* [*Speech in Praise of Poetry*] is probably a work of the 1570s but in common with most Elizabethan criticism has lacked recognition by virtue of having been written in Latin.

What has never been acknowledged is that *The Defence of Poesie* is almost certainly an attempt to denigrate and marginalize Gascoigne, without ever actually mentioning him by name. *Certayne notes* is dedicated to an Edouardo Donati, who is almost certainly bogus. Sidney's essay begins with a mention of a different Edward, "the right vertuous *Edward Wotton*" – who very definitely *did* exist – and *John Pietro Pugliano* – a famous Italian, an equestrian master, whose student Sidney was. An Edward and a prestigious Italian. Coincidence? Possibly. But possibly also an aristocratic squashing of the upstart Gascoigne.

The Defence of Poesie was probably written some five years after Gascoigne died. It makes the exaggerated and silly claim that poetry "from almost the highest estimation of learning is fallen to be the laughing-stocke of children".[9] This is the sixteenth-century version of an editorial in a tabloid newspaper, whipping itself into a froth of outrage. Sidney demands to know "why *England* (the Mother of excellent mindes) should bee growne so hard a step-mother to Poets". The very earth itself laments the fact "That Poesie...embraced in all other places, should onely finde in our time a hard welcome in England".[10]

Sidney then constructs a highly contentious English poetic tradition to prove his point. He makes the patronising observation that "*Chaucer*, undoubtedly, did excellently in hys *Troylus and Cresseid*...Yet had he great wants, fitte to be forgiven in so reverent antiquity".[11] He admires the anthology *The Mirrour for Magistrates* (1559). He gushes over the Earl of Surrey's lyrics, finding in them "many things tasting of a noble birth, and worthy of a noble minde". He approves of *The Shepherd's Calendar* (1579), which Spenser had dedicated to Sidney, but ticks the poet off for the "framing of his stile to an old rustick language". Apart from these writers, says Sidney, there is no modern English poet of worth.

The claim is ludicrous. Sidney excludes Wyatt. He disdains to mention Tottel's hugely popular and influential *Songes and Sonettes*. And most of all, of course, he excludes the most popular and outstanding poet of the 1570s, George Gascoigne. When Sidney says of poetry, "base men with servile wits undertake it: who think it enough if they can be rewarded of the Printer" this could conceivably be a dig at Gascoigne.[12]

Gascoigne himself modestly disavowed "the name of an English Poet" in his grovelling letter to the Reverend Divines.[13] A poet was implicitly superior to a mere versifier or rhymer (terms which in themselves drew an ancient technical distinction between *versus* or quantitative verse and *rithmus* or stressed verse), but in Gascoigne's eyes there was no real difference. Modesty, not any sense of technical inferiority, encouraged him to avoid claiming the status of poet. In "The Green Knight's Farewell to Fancy" he describes how he was driven "to wryte in verse and rime", but gave up, "since I see, what Poetes bee".[14] Gascoigne is not making a serious technical distinction between poets, versifiers and rhymers. He simply avoids the word "poet" to bypass the charge of vanity or pretension. But to Sidney, Gascoigne was surely one of those "Poet-apes, not Poets" who gave the profession a bad name. Sidney was keen to distinguish between poets and mere "versifiers".

As a prig, Sidney, who abhorred "scurrility, unworthy of any chast eares",[15] was no doubt appalled by Gascoigne's erotic innuendo. Sidney's air-brushing of Gascoigne from literary history conceivably extended to the writer's drama. Sidney sweepingly condemns all English tragedy and comedy for "observing rules neyther of honest civilitie nor skilfull Poetrie" except *Gorboduc* (adding "of those that I have seene").[16] He makes no mention of *Jocasta* or *Supposes*. But while finding himself unable to mention George Gascoigne's diverse achievements even once, Sidney twice mentions the utterly forgotten Scottish writer George Buchanan (1506-82), heaping glowing praises on his "piercing" wit and expressing "divine admiration" for his tragedies.[17] Buchanan wrote in Latin and was certainly highly regarded in the sixteenth century but posterity's verdict has been brutal: "an intellectual mediocrity".[18]

Sidney's poetic practice also seems like a deliberate attempt to spurn Gascoigne and all he stands for. His "Certaine sonnets" have a variety of line-lengths, rhyme schemes and stanza forms and ostentatiously shun Gascoigne's strict definition of the form. The basic foundation of *Certayne notes* is the recommendation that the "making of a delectable poem" requires that it be grounded "upon some fine invention". But as Pigman notes, "The first sonnet of Sidney's *Astrophil and Stella* reads like a refutation of Gascoigne's advice in [his opening] paragraph".[19] A consciously deliberate and calculated refutation, one might add. Sidney complains that he studied "inventions fine" and they were no help at all. He takes Gascoigne's advice and it gets him nowhere. His muse tells him he is a "Foole".

Sidney's sister Mary collaborated in the project. Her version of Psalm 130 has been seen as stemming from "a determination to respond to Gascoigne's stanzaic virtuosity".[20] She borrowed a pair of his rhymes and much else, in order to re-write Gascoigne and produce a new and competitively superior version of his poem. In Eriksen's words, "The influence of Gascoigne's earlier attempt is felt almost throughout [her] psalm, in her choice of stanza, metaphors, and of rhymes, but not so much in terms of plagiarism as in terms of a pervasive desire to outwit her precursor at his own game."[21]

*

When he wrote his first Prefatory Letter addressing "the reverende Divines" who had banned *A Hundreth Sundrie Flowres* Gascoigne could not have known that the Commission's membership would change. The Letter is dated the "last day of Januarie. 1574" but if this meant 1575 then by that date the work of the Commission which banned *A Hundreth Sundrie Flowres* was presumably over, or coming to an end. The new body of Commissioners for Causes Ecclesiastical in the Province of Canterbury was not set up until 1576.

The later Commission had a number of new members including Edmund Grindal, the new Archbishop of Canterbury, John Mullins, Archdeacon of London, John Pierse, Bishop of Rochester, John Whitgift, Dean of Lincoln, and John Watson, Bishop of Winchester. It no longer included "the reverend Divines" William Overton, Matthew Parker or Robert Weston. However, these and other changes can have made little difference. None of these sober ecclesiastics is likely to have been enthused by *The Posies of George Gascoigne Esquire*. And if commission member Edward Boys was indeed Elizabeth's former husband and Gascoigne's old rival then he would have made sure that these senior ecclesiastics were informed that the new edition retained highly offensive material.

Gascoigne ended his first Prefatory Letter with the pious hope that with the publication of *The Posies of George Gascoigne Esquire* "all men might see the reformation of my minde".[22] He concluded with an appeal for employment from these "reverende Divines":

And for full proofe of mine earnest zeale in Gods service, I require of you (reverende) most instantly, that if hereby my skill seeme sufficient to wade in matters of greater importance, you will then vouchsafe to employ mee accordingly…The God of peace vouchsafe to governe and product [sic] you, and me, and all his, in quiet conscience, and strength of spirit. Amen. From my poore house at Waltamstow in the Forest, this last day of Januarie. 1574.[23]

Among those bowled over by the poet's eloquence was the twentieth century's greatest Gascoigne scholar, C. T. Prouty. Professor Prouty was in no doubt that the year 1575 saw a shattering moral transformation in the writer: "That Gascoigne was sincere I do not doubt." He believed that the objections levelled against *A Hundreth Sundrie Flowres* and his various failures as a writer, farmer and soldier

> impressed on his mind the inexorable truth that his way of life had been wrong. He had followed the way of the world, only to find it a snare and delusion; therefore, he sought out the way of the spirit, which might justify

life and bring the rewards hitherto denied. That Gascoigne was sincere I do not doubt; that his reformation was in tune with his times seems clear, and his writings after his final return from the Dutch wars seem to me to testify to the sincerity of his transformation, as well as to the fruits of the new spirit.[24]

It is difficult to share this simplistic vision of a miraculous transformation wrought in Gascoigne in the year 1575, after which all his work was imbued with a "new spirit".

Examined critically, Gascoigne's letter "To the reverende Divines" is a mixture of bluster, special pleading and superficial piety designed to appeal to narrow-minded, humourless religious fundamentalists and to convince them that the new edition of his writings had duly taken note of their objections. These grey, sombre heresy-hunters had the power to seize and ban books, and it was therefore necessary for Gascoigne to accommodate their prejudices if he wished to see his life's work remain in print. Grovelling dedications and sycophantic effusions of admiration and the desire to serve powerful and influential patrons were basic requirements of Tudor writers seeking advancement in this period. In Gascoigne the tradition received a new twist by his direct engagement with the forces of ecclesiastical censorship. It is characteristic of him that he should even cheekily offer his services to the Commission while pulling its members' legs about the moral transformation of his writing.

It is hard to take Gascoigne's claims of reformation and revision very seriously. In the first place *A Hundreth Sundrie Flowres* contained virtually no explicitly "filthie phrases" – though Gascoigne did decide to change "arse" to "etc" in the republished *Supposes* (III.i.11). The only major revision was the deletion of certain passages in *The Adventures of Master F.J.* and its recasting as a mock-Italian novel. But even here the rewriting was often perfunctory and a good deal of sexual innuendo remained. Gascoigne jumbled up the previous order of his poems for their reappearance in *The Posies* but he retained those most likely to cause offence, including "Gascoigne's Recantation", "A Riddle" and "The Praise of Philip Sparrow". To say that the *The Posies* differed from *A Hundreth Sundrie Flowres* by being "beautified with addition of many moral examples" was just not true. None of the new material – the final stanzas of "Dan Bartholmew of Bathe", *The fruites of Warre, The fruite of Fetters: with the complaint of the greene Knight, and his Farewell to Fansie* or *Certayne notes of Instruction concerning the making of verse or ryme in English* – was remotely religious or piously moral in content.

In writing his three prefatory letters Gascoigne clearly had in mind Theodore Beza's prefatory letter to his 1569 edition of *Theodori Bezae Vezelii Poematum Editio secunda, ab eo recognita*. But Gascoigne's attempt to draw parallels between himself and Beza was grossly misleading. It was true that the poems

Beza wrote as a young man were regarded in some quarters as licentious. For example, Beza wrote passionate lines in praise of his mistress's feet and his verse can reasonably be compared with those of other neo-Latin poets of the renaissance such as Bonefonius (who wrote of the sensual charms of his mistress's breasts), Ioannes Secundus (who wrote of rape and seduction) and Gilles Ménage (whose Latin poems to Domina Laverna embody an almost masochistic sensuality which is lacking in his French and Italian poems to her).[25] But it is not true, as Gascoigne claimed, that Beza "did not yet disdaine too suffer the continued publication of such Poemes as he wrote in his youth",[26] for in his second edition he omitted all his love poetry. Nor did Beza ever use the phrase "Poëmata castrata", as Gascoigne asserts.

Gascoigne's strategy was clearly to muddy the waters by bringing in a figure whom the "reverende Divines" would be bound to admire, just as he muddied the waters by pretending that *The pleasant Fable of Ferdinando Jeronomi and Leonora de Valasco* was translated out of the Italian riding tales of Bartello, which combined a non-existent Italian author with the double entendre implicit in "riding tales". The superficial nature of many of these changes expresses an inherent contempt for the censors. Gascoigne assumes that the reading of his book will be half-hearted and lazy. His contradictory presentation of the new version of his novel as both a revision of an immoral tale *and* a translation from an Italian original assumes a certain stupidity and ignorance on the part of the censors.

In his second Prefatory Letter addressed "generally to the youth of England" Gascoigne defends himself against the "grave Philosophers" on the High Commission who have objected to his "doings at the common infection of love".[27] Gascoigne offers a moral excuse for his writing in the face of their objections:

> I must needes alledge suche juste excuse as may countervayle their juste complaints. For else I shoulde remayne woorthie of a severe punishment. They wisely considering that wee are all in youth more apt to delight in harmefull pleasures, than to disgest wholesome and sounde advice, have thought meete to forbid the publishing of any ryming trifles which may serve as whetstones to sharpen youth unto vanities.[28]

He then goes on tacitly to acknowledge that his book may contain "the most stinking weede"[29] but argues that, properly handled, "weedes are right medicinable".[30] He is, in short, a mirror to youth, a warning against shipwreck, a gardener with a rich variety of plants, some good, some bad.

Gascoigne rounded off his defence of *A Hundreth Sundrie Flowres* with a third Prefatory Letter, "To the Readers generally a generall advertisement of the Authour". It begins with pious Biblical references from Paul's Epistle to the

Romans (15, 4) and Paul's first Epistle to the Corinthians (9, 20-23), designed to justify the presence in the *Posies* of "some verses more sauced with wantonnesse than with wisedome".[31] It goes on to drag in Terence, Paracelsus and the proverbial "one which dwelt at Billingsgate, that coulde help all men"[32] in order to offer more rambling justifications for retaining some of the material which offended the censors in the first place.

Gascoigne distanced himself from his love poetry, claiming that hardly any of it was autobiographical. On the contrary, most of the poems were commissioned: "the most part of them were written for other men. And out of all doubt, if ever I wrote lyne for my selfe in causes of love, I have written tenne for other men in layes of lust."[33] But this was surely just more bluster. Gascoigne had a great sense of self. Writing about other people and their emotions wasn't his style at all. The love poems are about George Gascoigne and the women in his past. He only denies it in order to make himself seem the more respectable.

What the "lustie Gallants" and "yong blouds" or that elusive entity the general reader made of this special pleading is anyone's guess. Probably no one took the extravagant declarations of dedications and prefaces very seriously. At this juncture Gascoigne's most important readers were the commissioners themselves. They read what he had to say and were not persuaded. This is not really surprising.

The new title was as inaccurate as the first one. "Posies" implied that the volume was a collection of poems. In fact, just like the earlier edition, it contained two plays, a short novel and a miscellaneous collection of poems. However, it also included additional material and involved various revisions of the earlier work. Apart from the revisions what was new were three prose "Prefatory Letters", twenty-two "Commendatory Poems", the rest of the previously unfinished poem "Dan Bartholmew of Bathe", the long poem *The fruites of Warre* on the theme "Dulce bellum inexpertis", five poems about a "green Knight" and an essay on prosody, *Certayne notes of Instruction*. In this respect *The Posies of George Gascoigne Esquire* is less like a second edition than a different work altogether.

Much of the content of *A Hundreth Sundrie Flowres* was barely altered at all, so far as text is concerned. In the case of *Supposes* Gascoigne added two words, altered seven others and – evidently correcting typesetters' errors – made nine alterations to the spellings of words. He also added new stage directions and was presumably responsible for twenty-six marginal annotations which emphasized each "suppose" that the play contained (a new twenty-seventh one consisted of the bitter, heartfelt comment, "Lawyers are never weary to get money"). Beecher and Butler plausibly suggest that the "suppose" marginalia was added because he felt "a need to underline the significance of the title with its many shades of meaning and to mark the principal deceptions upon which his plot was based".[34] With the single exception of the substitution of "etc" for "arse", the motivation for all these changes was clearly to improve the text rather than to respond to the disapproval of the Commission. Even that alteration was perfunctory since the joke confusion of "Erostrato" with "Roscus or arsekiss" was not changed (II.iv.79), and "cackabed" ["bed-shitter"] also remained (IV.vii.45).

Of the previously published material, three poems were omitted.[35] These were "A translation of Ariosto allegorized", the poem which had opened the collection of "Devises of Sundrie Gentlemen", the sonnet beginning "When steadfast friendship (bound by holy oath)", and "Either a needless or a bootless comparison between two letters". Gascoigne probably dropped the Ariosto translation out of deference to the High Commission and to the moral panic about licentious Italian literature and *Orlando Furioso* in particular. If Gascoigne had learned that Edward Boyes was on the 1572 Commission that would explain the dropping of the "two letters" poem. But irrespective of that it is probable that Gascoigne's wife objected to his courtship poem, with its erotic innuendo about him having played "a little with [her] *B*." She may also have objected to the sonnet, or Gascoigne himself may have decided to drop verse which seems to have touched on something very personal.

Gascoigne jumbled up the sequence in which his poems had formerly appeared in "The Devises of Sundrie Gentlemen", re-assembling them in a different order under three new categories: 28 in "Flowers", 18 in "Hearbes" and 12 in "Weeds".[36] This horticultural distinction was intended to signal aesthetic and moral value. Herbs were wholesome, flowers attractive to the eye and weeds unwholesome but of cautionary value. Though a little precious to modern eyes, such floral categories made a kind of sense. In practice, however, these distinctions were fuzzy and incoherent. In what sense is "The praise of brown beauty" a herb and not a flower? Likewise, why is a powerful religious poem such as "Gascoigne's *De profundis*" categorised as a flower and not a herb? What is *Certayne notes of Instruction* doing among the weeds? And what on earth is a piece of obscene innuendo like "A Riddle" doing among the herbs?

Though Gascoigne's categorisation was largely meaningless it was not entirely so. The location of "The praise of Phillip Sparrow" among the weeds confirms a reading of the poem as an exercise in sustained sexual innuendo. Likewise, placing the bowdlerised version of *The Adventures of Master F.J.* among the weeds, under its new title *The fable of Ferdinando Jeronimi and Leonora de Valasco*, acknowledged the offence it had caused. It also cannily removed the text from its earlier placing before the poems and relocated it nearer the end of the book, where, hopefully, a sour-eyed humourless ecclesiastical censor with a short attention span would be less likely to spot its potential to offend.

Gascoigne also took the opportunity to make textual changes to the poems as well as to the novella.[37] These were on a much smaller scale and involved occasional stylistic changes, the correction of minor typographical errors, the addition of intermittent marginal notes and a re-titling of some poems.

By far the most striking change was to the novella. The changes show that Gascoigne chiefly responded to the two main charges against it: that it was obscene and that it was about a contemporary English aristocratic household. The narrative was substantially bowdlerised. Gascoigne's intention was similar to that of Henrietta Bowdler herself, whose *Family Shakespeare* "endeavoured to remove every thing that could give just offence to the religious and virtuous mind" (literally so, since in the sixteenth century "thing" could mean either a penis or a vagina).[38]

The biggest cut Gascoigne made to the text was the section involving the return of Elinor's husband, the hunting episode with its double entendre about horns and bugles, and the suggestive sonnet beginning "As some men say there is a kind of seed / Will grow to horns if it be sowed thick".[39] Also deleted was the sex scene on the gallery floor between Elinor and F.J. The rape of Elinor was rewritten and rendered obscure, its previously unambiguous detail replaced by a vague description of how F.J. "having now forgotten all former curtesies, he assayleth his enemies by force".[40] The character Pergo was eliminated. There were many other minor changes designed to rid the novel of both its overtly sexual scenes and its recurrent erotic innuendo.

By re-titling the novel *The pleasant Fable of Ferdinando Jeronimi and Leonora de Valasco* and by claiming that it was a translation from the work of "Bartello", Gascoigne blocked off the possibility that the narrative might be interpreted as being about English men and women. "Bartello" was an invented name obviously intended to echo that of the most famous author of the Italian novella, Matteo Bandello, whose work was popular in England. The prefatory material by G.T. and H.W. was removed, as was G.T. as narrator. In its place was a much more relaxed, expansive, omniscient introduction:

> In the pleasant country of Lombardy (and not far from the city of Florence) there was dwelling sometimes a Lord of many rich seignories and dominions, who nevertheless bare his name of the Castle of Valasco: this Lord had only one son and two daughters: his son was called (during the life of his father) the heir of Valasco, who married a fair gentlewoman of the house of Bellavista named Leonora: the elder daughter of the Lord of Valasco was called Francischina, a young woman very toward, both in capacity and other active qualities.

What vanish are all the teasing mysteries of *The Adventures of Master F.J.* Elinor's mysterious lovers H.D. and H.K. are identified as the faintly preposterous-sounding Hercule Donaty and Haniball de Cosmis.

In *The pleasant Fable of Ferdinando Jeronimi and Leonora de Valasco* everything is explained. Ferdinando Jeronimi is a young gentleman from Venice "of a very good parentage...not only rich but adorned with sundry good qualities". The Lord of Valasco has invited him to the castle with the specific intention of getting him to marry his daughter Francischina. The narrative which follows is the same as in the earlier version but less sexually explicit. At the end Gascoigne tacks on a moralizing ending in which Ferdinando Jeronimi spends the rest of his days "in a dissolute kind of life", Leonora continues her life of "wicked lust" and the virtuous Francischina sinks into misery and dies of consumption. The story concludes with the pious hope that it "may serve as example to warn the youthful reader from attempting the like worthless enterprise".

Compared with its earlier incarnation *The pleasant Fable of Ferdinando Jeronimi and Leonora de Valasco* is strangely flat and inert. Gascoigne's own heart wasn't really in this inferior expurgated edition. At the end of the story "Leonora" carelessly metamorphoses back into "Elinor". The invented Italian author "Bartello" sounds very much like a pun on Gascoigne's alter egos "Bartholmew" and "Bart". At a number of points the tale signals that it is not authentically Italian. Florence is not in Lombardy but in Tuscany. Frances translates into Italian as Francesca, not Francischina. The narrator's absurd insistence that Florence in the south is colder than Venice in the north signals that this Italian fiction is a spoof. Nor is the text quite as innocent as Gascoigne pretended. The suggestive passage about Elinor singing in counterpoint to her lovers was not excised. The claim that the work is a translation from "riding tales" introduces new innuendo ("riding" in the sense of "sexually mounting" and "tales" punning on the sixteenth-century sense of "tail" as penis or vagina). The setting of the story "In the pleasant Countrie of Lombardie" sounds suspiciously like a pun on "cunt".

Commendatory Poems

As if to bolster his three apologetic prefatory letters, Gascoigne included nineteen commendatory poems – Shakespeare's First Folio made do with four – and a short piece of commendatory prose in Italian. The contributors were identified only by their initials.

None of these verses were particularly distinguished. "E.C." congratulated Gascoigne on not taking any money for his "great treasures". "M.C." applauded the fact that "the bad" in *A Hundreth Sundrie Flowres* had now been "culled and cast away". "A.W." confessed that when he heard "what slander says" about Gascoigne, "my heavy heart it bleeds". "I.B." remarked that "they did him double wrong, / Which F. and J. misconstrued have so long" (*sic*). These moving testimonials[41] might be more touching if it wasn't for the very strong suspicion that Gascoigne wrote them himself. G. W. Pigman suggests that Gascoigne was also "M.A." of Perugia, who effusively saluted the poet in Italian as a worthy rival of Boccacio, Aretino and every other excellent and famous poet of the age.[42]

Seven of the poems were in Latin and one in French. Some of the commendatory poems were undoubtedly written by real people – "T.Ch." is almost certainly Thomas Churchyard, "R.S." is possibly the bookseller Richard Smith, and "T.B." may be Thomas Bedingfield, translator of *Cardanus Comforte*, which contained a commendatory poem by Gascoigne. "G.W." is almost certainly a young fan of Gascoigne's named George Whetstone, whose poem obligingly praises Gascoigne for the effort he put in "to glean the bad from best" and defends him from the charge of treachery in the Low Countries. "G.H." could well be Gabriel Harvey. The identities of the other contributors – "P.B.", "I.D.", "I. de B.", "H.M.", "B.C.", "K.D.", "P.W." and "E.H." – are uncertain and a matter of continuing conjecture.[43]

*

In the end, Gascoigne's revisions satisfied no one. Modern critics rightly regard *The Posies* as decidedly inferior to *A Hundreth Sundrie Flowres*, and clearly the High Commissioners were as displeased by the second edition as by the first. All Gascoigne's revisions and re-arrangings, and all his Prefatory Letters with their displays of piety, argument and laboured horticultural imagery had been in vain. The second edition, like the first, was banned. On 13 August 1576 his publisher Richard Smith was obliged to return "half a hundred of Gascoignes poesies" to the Stationers' Hall "by appointment of the Q.M. Commissioners".[44] That late date arguably strengthens the possibility that the book was not published until the spring of 1576.

The demand for the return of books did not in itself signify a permanent ban. Two other titles were returned at the same time as *The Posies* but later given back to the booksellers. These were 225 copies of *A Handful of Delights* and 200 copies of *Restorities to love*. The three titles were each on sale at three bookshops next to each other in Paul's Cross Churchyard, indicating that the censors were on the lookout for offensive amatory literature. But *The Posies* was probably not redelivered. As Pigman notes, no books by Gascoigne were recorded in the inventory of Henry Bynneman's stock made after his death.[45]

The small numbers of copies seized strongly suggests a case of a stable door being slammed shut long after the horse had bolted. The workings of Tudor censorship could sometimes be cumbersome and slow. Gascoigne may have temporarily skipped past the censors with his combination of charm, bluster and laconic insolence but others were not so fortunate. Much later in the century Thomas Nashe and Gabriel Harvey also fell foul of the ecclesiastical censors. The notorious order issued by Archbishop John Whitgift and Bishop Richard Bancroft on 1 June 1599 included the command that "all Nasshes and Doctor

Harvyes bookes be taken wheresoever they maybe found and that none of theire bookes bee ever printed hereafter". Nashe and Harvey were silenced as effectively as any writer sent to the Gulag by Stalin.

Gascoigne was luckier. He probably had more confidence in his ability to ride out the storm. He was, after all, *George Gascoigne, Esquire*. He had connections. He was not a man easily crushed by adversity. If the print run for the *Posies* had been around one thousand copies, or even several hundred, then clearly almost all had been quickly snapped up by the young men of the Inns of Court and anyone else who enjoyed reading a controversial and risqué book. Fifty copies sounds very much like a small unsold stock of leftovers.

But there would be no third edition of Gascoigne's book in his lifetime. Gascoigne may have temporarily outwitted the censors but he did not defeat them. With the seizure of both the first and now the second edition of what was effectively his life's work, the game was up. Having produced the most extraordinary work of fiction written by any sixteenth-century English writer, Gascoigne now abandoned the genre. There were to be no more novellas. Nor did he ever again write witty, double-edged erotic love lyrics. A range of artistic impulses inside him had been smothered. Censorship did not stop Gascoigne from continuing to write but it diverted his energies into less dangerous and less original material. It forced him out of the market-place by preventing his wares from being sold there. He was obliged to seek patronage in whatever quarter he could seek it, and patronage brought its own constraints. What happened between 1573 and 1576 unquestionably restricted his creative freedoms, blighting the rest of his writing career.

PART SIX:
THE SUNDRY SHAPES OF DEATH

26: A Man with a Gun

In the winter of 1575 George Gascoigne went to call on Sir Humphrey Gilbert at his home at Limehouse. Gilbert had moved there in 1573, not long after his marriage to the heiress Anne Ager, daughter of Sir Anthony Ager, Marshal of Calais. Ager had died fighting the French, when they recaptured the city in 1558.

According to Gascoigne, he asked his old commander "howe he spente his time in this loitering vacation from martiall stratagemes".[1] By way of reply Gilbert took him upstairs to his study and showed the poet "sundrie profitable and verie comendable exercises, which he had perfected painefully with his owne penne: And amongs the rest this present *Discoverie*". This was a reference to the manuscript dated 30 June 1566. Gilbert explained that he had written it to persuade his sceptical older brother John of the merits of an expedition to find a quick route from England to Cataia (China).

Knowing that his kinsman "M. Fourboiser" (i.e. Martin Frobisher) was also interested in finding a new route, Gascoigne asked if he could take the manuscript away with him for a few days. Humphrey granted the request but made it clear that he did not regard the manuscript as publishable. Gascoigne "at good leasure perused it" (presumably at Thorpe Hall). He was deeply impressed. He checked Sir Humphrey's theory against the facts set out in "the Tables of *Ortelius*, and by sundrie other *Cosmographicall Mappes* and *Charts*". Gascoigne was convinced that Sir Humphrey's manuscript should be published:

> I seemed in my simple judgement not onely to like it singularly, but also thought it very meete (as the present occasion serveth) to give it out in publike. Whereupon I have (as you see) caused my friends great travaile, and mine owne greater presumption to be registred in print.

Sir Humphrey's letter "sent to his brother, Sir John Gilbert, of Compton, in the Countie of Devon Knight, concerning the discourse of this Discoverie" duly appeared, with Gascoigne's preface, as *A Discourse of a Difcouerie for a new Paffage to Catai*. The title page of the booklet, which was printed by Henry Middleton for Richard Jones, is precisely dated 12 April 1576.

The "new passage to Cataia" was the dream of a northern passage across America linking the Pacific and Atlantic oceans. We now know that it was an empty fantasy but at the time it was a hugely enticing one because it offered a convenient route from Europe to Cataia or Cathay (as China was then known), avoiding areas under the domination of Spain and Portugal.

Many believed the waterway existed, including geographers and mapmakers like Mercator and Ortelius, John Dee, and sailors like Cabot and Gilbert. There were disagreements about its precise location and form but generally it was believed that it ran from north-east to south-west, with the Atlantic entrance situated in a higher latitude than its exit into the Pacific.

What the dream of a new passage to China illustrated was the existing ignorance of world geography. Twenty years earlier sailors had dreamed of a route around northern Europe and Asia to China. When that dream died a new one took its place. But men like Frobisher and Gilbert were whistling in the dark. What motivated them was the dream of acquiring great wealth, not any kind of interest in impartial scientific discovery. But sixteenth-century navigators had no means of assessing longitude and English long-distance navigational skills lagged well behind those of the Spanish. The first English manual of navigation, William Bourne's *Regiment for the Sea*, had only recently been published, in 1574. It was largely plagiarised from a Spanish publication.

Gilbert's booklet, which is unpaginated, consists of 66 pages in which the author proves with the aid of Plato and Aristotle and "al the best moderne Geographers" that America is an island, and that "there lyeth a great Sea betweene it, Cataia, and Grondland, by which any man of our countrey, that will give the attempt, may with final danger passe to Cataia, the Moluccae, India, & al other places...in much shorter time, then either the Spaniard, or Portingale". To reinforce his wealth of documentation and learned authorities, Humphrey included "a universall Map" proving his theory. It portrays a roughly accurate outline of the U.S.A. Unfortunately north of it, in place of Canada, is an ocean, narrowing to a strait which emerges into the Pacific. Canada is shown but consists of a tiny island east of the north-east tip of America. To modern eyes it is clear that Gilbert's vision of a short-cut to China was based on a patchy and inadequate knowledge of Canada's eastern seaboard. Its eventual impact on Gilbert's contemporaries, however, was prodigious. As one of his biographers remarked,

> This treatise, with its false arguments and false deductions, was yet a remarkable compilation for that time, and had far-reaching effects upon the course of English adventure.... Having once set themselves the task of finding of North-West-Passage, the English never gave up the search. One expedition after another was prepared, thousands upon thousands of pounds spent, and hundreds of valuable lives lost in this vain pursuit.[2]

Gascoigne claimed that he would have liked to write more about Sir Humphrey Gilbert, but he was afraid of being accused by him of flattery. He therefore kept his praise muted, simply remarking that he was a gentleman with a noble mind, courageous and valiant in martial affairs, "endowed with sundry great gifts of the mind, and generally well given to the advancement of knowledge and virtue". Small praise indeed.

The "Prefatory Epistle" has frequently attracted the attention of biographers of Walter Ralegh who, knowing nothing of Gascoigne's fondness for promotional games-playing, have taken its claims at face value. But the idea that

Gascoigne published Gilbert's pamphlet without his permission can safely be discounted. One biographer of Ralegh has even painted a picture of four jolly adventurers – Ralegh, Frobisher, Gascoigne and Gilbert – hanging out at Limehouse watching the ships go by while Ralegh, "so much the youngest of the four friends, planned with them the discoveries and conquests they themselves would make, and not only at sea".[3] This scene is one that belongs to historical fiction, not biography.

The poet's insinuation that Sir Humphrey's theory was so compelling that it simply had to be shared with everyone was just spin. The pamphlet was propaganda designed to assist Gilbert and Frobisher in getting support for an expedition. Long-distance voyaging required both the permission of the Queen and the Privy Council and financial support from investors. Gilbert had been promoting his cause for many years, putting it in person to the Privy Council and offering the manuscript of his *Discourse* to anyone who might be prepared to finance it.[4] Gascoigne may of course have personally believed in the northern passage. But it is just as likely that he was humouring Gilbert. Gascoigne was a man who kept his options open.

The claim that "George Gascoigne had put every penny he could raise into the expedition, and intended to embark on it himself"[5] seems completely without foundation. It is possible that he invested in it, though there is no evidence that he did. That he ever intended to sail on it personally is highly improbable. When Frobisher did eventually set sail later that year, Gascoigne was not among the crew. The poet knew from bitter experience that Sir Humphrey Gilbert was an impulsive and mediocre military commander. There is no hard evidence that Gascoigne's support ever went further than his Epistle and the attached feeble "Prophetical Sonnet" upon Gilbert's "commendable travaile" set out in his pamphlet. Judged on purely literary grounds, his heart wasn't in it. One suspects his money wasn't either.

But the publication of the pamphlet almost certainly helped the project. Permission and financial support was duly obtained and on 7 June 1576 Frobisher set sail in search of his passage to Cataia. Not surprisingly, he got no further than Canada. Ironically, his ship's library contained a copy of Sir John Mandeville's *The Travels*. This book would soon lose all credibility when the great age of exploration got under way but in 1576 it was still taken very seriously as an accurate account of long-distance travel. Mandeville claimed to have visited both China and India and to have met the fabled emperor Prester John. In fact it was a book based on what was probably an authentic visit to the Middle East which was then padded out with legends borrowed from a variety of previously published sources.[6]

Though Gilbert's treatise was based on a delusion, in the course of embellishing it he put forward the first proposal for setting up an English colony in the New World. It was Gilbert who "first crystallized the indefinite, and made of it a concrete proposition" and in so doing he created "the germ from which sprang...the United States".[7] Since Gascoigne was instrumental in promoting Gilbert's treatise, his role in the eventual founding of the U.S.A. ought not to be overlooked.

Gilbert's pamphlet was not the only publication which Gascoigne publicly praised that year. As the leading writer of the day his assistance was solicited in helping sell other people's books. He duly contributed a wooden commendatory sonnet to Claudius Holyband's self-help manual *The French Littleton. A Most easie, perfect and absolute way to learne the frenche tongue*.[8] He contributed an equally dull one to Thomas Bedingfield's *Cardanus Comforte*, which was the translation of an Italian book which supplied "examples from classical authors of reactions to distressing events, offering comfort for mental or emotional distress".[9]

The Steel Glass

After the excitements of Kenilworth and Woodstock, Gascoigne devoted much of the following year to writing. He remained, as he told Lord Grey on 15 April 1576, "amongst my bookes here at my poore house in Waltamstowe, where I praye daylie for speedy advauncement".[10] It is surprising Gascoigne did not seek further patronage from the Earl of Leicester. The fact that he did not perhaps indicates that the Earl associated Gascoigne with the debacle of the Queen's departure. It was the message of Gascoigne's play that had tipped her over the edge and perhaps Leicester haughtily chose to blame the messenger rather than himself.

In April 1576 Gascoigne completed *The Steel Glass*, which he dedicated to Grey. This lengthy, meandering, moralizing poem purported to be a satire on the state of the nation. The title alludes to the changing fashion in mirrors. Mass produced glass mirrors from Venice were gradually displacing the older, traditional form of mirror made from a plate of polished silver, gold or steel. In place of "the crystal glass" – the ordinary glass mirror, which Gascoigne represents as an instrument of vanity and self-deception – he held up "the steel glass". Informed by Christian example, this offered a tough, uncompromising reflection of the true state of things. Such a message was well calculated to appeal to a man like Grey. But perhaps the satire also partly expressed Gascoigne's sense of growing old. The sturdy, solid mirrors of his youth were being displaced by fashionable fragile glass imports. Herbert Grabes notes that "In Gascoigne, mirrors of steel and glass are qualitatively juxtaposed in terms of the golden past and the corrupt present."[11] The poem has been seen as one of the most complex contemporary explorations of what was becoming an increasingly popular metaphor.

But as a satire, the poem is far too keen to ingratiate itself with power to be successful. It lacks a compelling narrative structure and is crammed with repetitive generalisations. *The Steel Glass* is pitched at Lord Grey, who is intermittently invoked as the auditor of Gascoigne's moralising narrative. It is all too clearly designed to flatter Grey's theologically hardline prejudices. *The Steel Glass* denounces the wicked world which wallows in sin. It mocks Catholics. It criticises corrupt rulers – but hastens to assure the reader that no reference at all is intended to Queen Elizabeth. It attacks courtiers who swagger around in expensive wool – but quickly exempts English courtiers from this attack, noting that English wool is the finest in the world. It humbles itself before bishops, archdeacons, deans and other ecclesiastics. It bravely lashes the many-faceted failings of foreigners, including the Spanish, the French, the Portuguese and Italians.

All told, it's a sprawling, rambling work, full of pious generalisations about greed, lust, ambition and every other human failing. But its lack of focus and failure of nerve makes it essentially a toothless satire. *The Steel Glass* was highly regarded in the nineteenth century, although that may be because its wealth of classical allusions made it an agreeable read for those who'd had a public-school education and who liked their satire religious but woolly. In 1893 Schelling said that of all Gascoigne's writings, it was the one "on which his claims to remembrance have hitherto chiefly depended",[12] but it has attracted relatively little attention among modern scholars. Its claustrophobic and monotonous moralising makes it an apt sequel to *The Glass of Government*. But, like the play, it only comes alive when it leaves banal generalities behind and pays attention to ordinary, everyday life.

Perhaps the finest section of the poem, which is fragmented into around 100 stanzas of wildly uneven length, comes at the end, where Gascoigne works himself into a fury at the frauds and incompetence of Tudor tradesmen. In four blistering, repetitious stanzas the poet rages against thieving tailors and tanners, fraudulent cutlers who pass off old, rusty, cracked blades as new, tinkers, thatchers, colliers, brewers, lazy labourers, bungling blacksmiths, bakers, dirty butchers, horse dealers, weavers, mercers, vintners, hatters, goldsmiths, upholsterers, drapers, surgeons – and many others.[13] This is the Tudor gentleman at bay, raging against a thieving underclass. But perhaps the most eloquent of all the listed vices of the age, far worse than sinks of filthy sin, belongs to printers, whose proof-reading is dismal and who allow errors in their books. This was Gascoigne truly speaking from the heart.

Lord Grey had Puritan tendencies and disapproved of style and fashion, judging by Gascoigne's attack in the Epilogue on "monsters" with angels' faces:

Behold, behold, they never stand content,
With God, with kind, with any help of art,
But curl their locks, with bodkins and with braids,
But dye their hair, with sundry subtle sleights,

> But paint and flick, till fairest face be foul,
> But bumbast, bolster, frizzle and perfume: [pad out]
> They mar with musk the balm which nature made[14]

What are they? Gascoigne asks, appalled. Are they men? Boys? Women dressed up as men? He invites his Lord to share in his horror at these threatening, hellish creatures of uncertain gender.

These are lines which tap a deep vein of anxiety about cross-dressing, effeminate men and homosexuality. It's all a bit rich coming from the author of "Phillip Sparrow" but presumably Gascoigne had a shrewd sense of what he had to do to stoke the fires of Lord Grey's enthusiasm and to loosen his purse strings.

The Steel Glass was prefaced by three commendations. "N.R." commended the poet for the diversity of his talent. Seneca wrote "rousing verses" in his tragedies; Catullus wrote epigrams; Archilocus was an innovator famous for his iambic poetry; Plautus wrote peerless comic verse; Naso (i.e. Ovid) and Tibullus wrote elegies and wanton love verse without parallel; Lucilius and Horace wrote sharp satire:

> Thus diverse men, with diverse veins did write,
> But Gascoigne doth in every vein indite.[15]

The poet could hardly have put it better himself. But then perhaps he did. "N.R." may conceivably have existed, or he may just be Gascoigne wearing another of his masks. A nineteenth-century critic who had a rare grasp of Gascoigne's essential slipperiness was Alexander Chalmers, who detected "a vein of sly sarcasm" in the satire of *The Steel Glass*.[16] That slyness may well have extended to this dedication.

A young fan supplied the second commendation. This was "Walter Rawely of the middle Temple". Ralegh was then in his early to mid-twenties and only just beginning to write the poetry which would turn out to be one of his many claims to fame. The two men probably became acquainted through Ralegh's half-brother, Sir Humphrey Gilbert. Following the same cultural trajectory as Gascoigne and thousands of other young gentlemen, Ralegh had attended university (Oriel College, Oxford) and then moved on to the Inns of Court. He was listed in the registers of the Middle Temple on 27 February 1575: "Walter Rawley, late of Lyons Inn, Gent. Son of Walter R. of Budleigh, Co. Devon, Esq."

Ralegh had obviously listened sympathetically to Gascoigne's complaints about his enemies. His poem attacks "spyteful tongs" – possibly those soldiers who regarded Gascoigne as a traitor and Humphrey Gilbert as incompetent – and defends the versatility of his writing and the lapses in his private life:

> Sweet were the sauce would please each kind of taste,
> The life likewise were pure that never swerved[17]

He also defended Gascoigne against the envy of lesser talents, in lines which have often been seen as hauntingly appropriate to Ralegh's own eventual tragic destiny:

> For who so reaps renown above the rest
> With heaps of hate shall surely be oppressed.[18]

The commendation had a literary significance of its own, as Ralegh's first published verse. Charles Nicholl notes that Ralegh's "own later *contemptus mundi* poems owe much to Gascoigne's vision"[19] and Michael Schmidt calls Gascoigne "his first poetic mentor. His [commendation of *The Steel Glass*] reveals Ralegh's preference for plain style and brusque, masculine utterance".[20]

The third commendation consisted of a sonnet by Nicholas Bowyer, Bowyer's praise is laced with presumably unintended irony as he noted that the poet "seeks the gravest to delight":

> Lo this we see is Gascoigne's good pretence,
> To please all sorts with his praiseworthy skill.[21]

That is the crux of the matter. Did Gascoigne's writing after *A Hundreth Sundrie Flowres* express the penitence of the genuinely remorseful sinner or was he just putting on mask after mask, attempting to please anyone who might further his career? The second seems more likely. The anonymity of *The Noble Arte of Venerie* indicates a wish not to be associated with a book which might be regarded in some quarters as frivolous in its concentration on a leisure activity. And the risqué message of the extended "Dan Bartholmew of Bathe" is very hard to square with the pious moralizing of *The Steel Glass*.

Gascoigne supplies an explanation of sorts in his poem "The Author to the Reader", which follows the three commendations:

> To vaunt were vain, and flattery were a fault,
> But truth to tell, there is a sort of fame
> The which I seek, by science to assault,
> And so to leave remembrance of my name.
> The walls thereof are wondrous hard to climb
> And much too high for ladders made of rhyme.
> Then since I see that rhymes can seldom reach
> Into the top of such a stately tower,
> By reason's force I mean to make some breach,

> Which yet may help my feeble fainting power
> That so at last my muse might enter in
> And reason rule, that rhyme could never win.
>
> Such battring tyre this pamphlet here bewrays   [discovers]
> In rhymeless verse, which thundreth mighty threat,
> And where it finds that vice the wall decays,
> Even there (amaine) with sharp rebuke it beats.   [with full force]
> The work (think I) deserves an honest name,
> If not? I fail to win this sort of fame.[22]

Gascoigne never so nakedly expressed his own literary ambition as here. He wants fame but he wants more than fame. He wants immortality. And he remembers his participation in the siege of Goes in autumn 1573. The night assault on the walls with men swarming up ladders had been a complete shambles. To Gascoigne, that military disaster was paralleled by the response to *A Hundreth Sundrie Flowres* and *The Posies of George Gascoign Esquire*. Both books were suppressed. The enemy, in the shape of the humourless Commissioners in Causes Ecclesiastical, had won. He had been silenced as effectively as poor Captain Bourcher. But Gascoigne also knew that victories on both sides could be temporary affairs. He would therefore use "science" or something akin to military strategy to make another attempt. If his bid for fame using "ladders made of rhyme" had ended in disaster, he would try something else. He therefore offered up a satire "in rhymeless verse". He wanted "this sort of fame" – the sort that leaves "remembrance" of a name. To a sixteenth-century reader the military dimension would have seemed more obvious because of the printer's use of a long "s" (with its similarity to the letter "f"); in the original text Gascoigne seeks "a fort of fame".

In retrospect we know that Gascoigne got it wrong. He is mainly remembered for the contents of his first book, not for *The Steel Glass* or his other late work. But in one way he got it brilliantly right. He made a point of using an engraving of himself, which was printed at the back of the title page. It ensured that with Gascoigne we have something that is lacking for many of his contemporaries, including Shakespeare: an image made from life, not something copied or made from memory. It gives us for all time a face to go with the voice; a unique individuality and an artefact of immeasurable value in a later culture which prizes images every bit as much as language.

Was this Gascoigne engraving a self-portrait? Gillian Austen believes that its simple lines, Gascoigne's "intense stare" and the slight misalignment of the eyes indicate that "it is almost certain that this is actually a self-portrait, done in front of a mirror... Gascoigne's self-portrait was calculated to demonstrate to Lord Grey his commitment to self-scrutiny and, by inference, to self-improvement or reformation".[23] She sees it as deliberately designed to invoke an older, wiser Gascoigne, whose suffering is written on his face.[24]

In the poem Gascoigne piously expressed a wish

to see my self in deed,
Not what I would, but what I am[25]

He claimed to "like this trusty glass of steel". It matched the sombre contents of his satire and his reinvention as a reformed prodigal:

Wherein I see a frolike favour frounst	[merry appearance frowns]
With foul abuse of lawless lust in youth:	
Wherein I see a Sampson's grim regard	
Disgraced yet with Alexander's beard:	
Wherein I see a corps of comely shape	[body]
(And such as might beseeme the court full well)	[become]
Is cast at heel by courting all too soon:	
Wherein I see a quick capacity,	
Berayde with blots of light inconstancy:	[disfigured]
An age suspect, because of youth's misdeeds.	
A poet's brain, possessed with lays of love:	
A Caesar's mind, and yet a Codrus might,	
A soldier's heart, suppressed with fearful dooms:	
A philosopher, foolishly fordone.	[undone]
And to be plain, I see myself too plain,	
And yet so much unlike that most I seemed,	
As were it not that reason ruleth me,	
I should in rage this face of mine deface,	
And cast this corpse down headlong in despair,	
Because it is so far unlike itself.[26]	

If the image is not a self-portrait but a commissioned drawing then, despite his claims of wanting a warts-and-all portrait, it sounds very much as if it was a shock for Gascoigne to see himself through someone else's eyes. He thought he had a cheerful countenance but the portrait shows a rather serious, frowning face. Two deep scowl lines descend from his brow to the beginning of his nose. It's the look of a man on his guard: world-weary, experienced, faintly suspicious. He looks, as Gascoigne glumly acknowledges, "grim".

If it is a commissioned portrait then the pose is conventional for its time. The sitter is positioned at a slight angle from the artist. Gascoigne turns his head a little to the right to face the person who is drawing him. The nose seems disproportionately long. A deep line runs down his right cheek, but this is presumably the artist's attempt at shading rather than a massive scar from a sword slash. The poet's ruff is small and practical – nothing like the preposterously large one in the famous Droeshout engraving of Shakespeare, which was probably a copy of a painting done years earlier. Gascoigne is dressed in the field armour he presumably wore in the Low Countries – gorget, shoulder guards and breast plate. The gorget, which protected the throat and neck, consists of three lames, or strips of steel. The sections were united by a loose-working rivet on one side and joined by a turning pin on the other. The picture also shows the leather harness which held the other armour in place as well as etched and probably gilt decoration. Dressed like this, it would have been clear on the battlefield that he was a gentleman.

Gascoigne seems to have been oddly embarrassed about his beard. "Disgraced" might mean "shamed" or "humiliated". Scrutinised closely, it looks much bushier at the tip of his chin than beneath his lower lip. It's a close-cropped beard and there seems to be bare skin between the near side and the moustache above it. Gascoigne's self-consciousness is underscored by a marginal annotation: "Alexander magnus [i.e. the Great] had but a smal beard." The moustache itself is, despite the poet's earlier mockery of "brave *Mustachyos* turned the *Turky* waye", fashionably long and curled.

"I regarded not my comeliness in the May-moon of my youth," he confessed to Lord Grey in his "Epistle Dedicatory", "and yet now I stand prinking me in the glass, when the crow's foot is grown under mine eye". Gascoigne was perhaps forty-one years old when this portrait was made. The flesh above his left eye has begun to sag in one corner; under the other eye there are two thick lines, suggesting exhaustion and lack of sleep. This is a fatigued and ageing but lean, watchful face – not quite haggard or wasted, but not plump or comfortable with the world either. Looking at himself, Gascoigne sees his life written in it. His "quick capacity" or natural ability has been ruined by "light inconstancy" – which might mean anything from sexual infidelity to fickle opinions.

In the background Gascoigne's new motto *Tam Marti Quàm Mercurio* is given visual expression. To the right are a wooden bookshelf and a row of books, with a pen and a container of ink dangling down beneath. On the other side is Gascoigne's handgun. It hangs downwards, with two dangling flasks. Both the shelf of books and the gun are fixed to a wall but they seem to hang in space, parallel objects of affection. The curving lines of the bookshelf support mirror the sinuous lines of the gun and reciprocate the contours of Gascoigne's head and face. This is the man of action and the man of contemplation given literal expression and brought together in a single figure. This is a man who is equally at home with a gun as a book. Indeed, two of his poems – "The complaint of the greene Knight" and *The fruite of Fetters* – celebrate firearms in some technical detail.

The gun is a matchlock harquebus or petronel, of a type which is now extremely rare.²⁷ Gascoigne described petronels as "perfectest and better than the rest".²⁸ The deeply curved stock is characteristic of a group of guns of this period and allowed the user to shoot with the stock resting on the chest rather than the shoulder. It has its serpentine on its left side, indicating that Gascoigne was left-handed. Used in the heat of battle it would have been for firing off a single musket ball. Presumably its virtues were akin to those of the gun which Gascoigne described as

> A piece so cleanly framed, so straight, so light, so fine,
> So tempered and so polished, as seemeth work divine...
> A peece which shot so well, so gently and so straight,
> It neither bruzed with recoil, nor wroong with overweight.²⁹

Sometimes such weapons were used in conjunction with pistols, also used for single shots. The large powder flask would have contained the rough, crude powder used for packing the musket ball in the barrel. The smaller flask was for finer powder, used for igniting the touch hole. Probably, like the protective armour, it was a relic of Gascoigne's time in the Low Country. If it was used in battle it was a weapon usually quickly discarded in favour of a sword. In a close-quarters engagement there was simply no time to re-load. But sometimes these guns were more for personal protection than use in battle. And armour was sometimes discarded in favour of a leather coat, which offered almost as much protection against these crude, low velocity primitive firearms. Gascoigne was proud of his weapon. He is the first English writer to pose with a gun – a Hemingway of the sixteenth-century lyric tradition.

The picture shows a man who is the leading writer of his age. But Gascoigne is not happy with what he sees. When he looks at his portrait all he can remember is what's gone wrong with his life. He was "cast at heel by courting all too soon". Is that an oblique and bitter reference to his marriage to Elizabeth Breton? Perhaps – but not necessarily. Gascoigne may have simply been using the verb "to court" in the sense of "to try to please" or "to seek favour by blandishments".

Others may have seen the portrait differently. Nicholas Breton wrote

> Say coyne can make a painter draw a face,
> He cannot give it life, do what he can:
> And though that coyne can give an outward grace,
> It cannot make a knave an honest man

Breton may have been borrowing his stepfather's pun on "coyne" and "Gascoigne" and turning it back against him. These lines come from his last publication, *Pasquils Mad-cappe, Throwne at the Corruptions of these Times*

(1626). The work has an energy and an anger that is rare in Breton, whose writings tend to be soft-centred and sentimental. But as always it is difficult to tell what Breton's attitude to his stepfather really was. These lines are preceded by a stanza about a man of "valiant heart" who leaves his house, children and wife to go abroad and fight. That, too, could be Gascoigne. Quite possibly both descriptions are specific and express Breton's contradictory feelings towards the man who inspired his own career as a writer, but who also grabbed some of his stepchildren's inheritance.

Gascoigne's own dissatisfaction with his lot is given vivid expression in the letter of dedication to Lord Grey:

> I am derided, suspected, accused and condemned: yea more than that, I am rigorously rejected when I proffer amendes for my harme. Should I therefore dispayre? Shall I yeelde unto jellosie? Or drown my days in idleness, because their beginning was bathed in wantonnesse.
>
> ...(alas my lorde) I am not onely enforced stil to carie on my shoulders the crosse of my carelesslnesse, but thereewithall I am also put to the plonge too provide newe weapons, wherewith I maye defende all heavy frownes, deepe suspects, and dangerous detractions.
>
> ...our saviour himselfe hath encoraged me, saying that I shal lacke neither workes nor service, although it were noone dayes before I came into the Market place.[30]

Who exactly were Gascoigne's accusers? The poet is unlikely to have had in mind the letter denouncing him to the Privy Council. That was now four years in the past. Probably he was thinking both of the rumours of his treachery in the Low Countries and the banning of *A Hundreth Sundrie Flowres*. Perhaps, too, the process of seizing copies of *The Posies of George Gascoigne Esquire* had already started. The rigorous rejection of his proffered "amendes" sounds very much like a reference to the Commissioners spurning his wheedling letter of apology and his bowdlerisation of *The Adventures of Master F.J.*

But though Gascoigne was down he was very far from out. He may have luridly seen his sufferings as on a par with Jesus bearing his cross to the place of crucifixion, and his reputation as no more than that of "a Codrus" or worthless scribbler, but he also, in his own eyes, combined some of the virtues of Julius Caesar, Sampson and Alexander the Great. Silence for such a man was not an option. He would go on writing, putting out whatever books or pamphlets he could sell in the market-place, to whomever might buy them. In that sense nothing had changed.

Gascoigne's ghost

Sonnet 66 of Shakespeare's sonnets reads as follows:

> Tyr'd with all these for restfull death I cry,
> As to behold desert a begger borne,
> And needie Nothing trimd in jollitie,
> And purest faith unhappily forsworne,
> And gilded honour shamefully misplast,
> And maiden virtue rudely strumpeted,
> And right perfection wrongfully disgrac'd,
> And strength by limping sway disabled,
> And arte made tung-tide by authoritie,
> And Folly (Doctor-like) controuling skill,
> And simple-Truth miscaled Simplicitie,
> And captive-good attending Captaine ill.
> Tyr'd with all these, from these would I be gone,
> Save that to dye, I leave my love alone.

This sonnet seems to draw on *The Steel Glass* and on one stanza in particular:

> But now (aye me) the glasing crystal glass   [glazing]
> Doth make us think that realms and town are rich
> Where favour sways the sentence of the law,
> Where all is fish that cometh to the net,
> Where mighty power doth over rule the right,
> Where injuries do foster secret grudge,
> Where bloody sword makes every booty prize,
> Where banqueting is compted comely cost,   [counted]
> Where officers grow rich by princes pens,
> Where purchase comes by couyn and deceit,   [coin / fabrication]
> And no man dreads but he that cannot shift,
> Nor none serve God, but only tongtide men.

The technique of repeated words or phrases at the beginning of a sequence of lines is one for which the technical term is anaphora. It produces an insistent, thumping, assertive effect, reminiscent of a preacher hammering home a point to his congregation. The analogy is apt in so far as both *The Steel Glass* and Shakespeare's sonnet involve a moral denunciation of their age.

Helen Vendler notes this sonnet's "generalizing lack of specificity", something which owes everything to the template which shapes it, which is guilty of the same vice.[31] Or as Colin Burrow puts it, sonnet 66 reads "like a survey of abstract ills"[32] – which is largely what *The Steel Glass* amounts to.

Shakespeare's inventory of abuses is different to Gascoigne's but there is some overlap. Gascoigne attacks extravagant banquets; Shakespeare attacks worthless people in ostentatious clothes. Gascoigne attacks mighty power over-ruling right; Shakespeare supplies four variations on this theme as he attacks folly controlling skill, art censored by authority, strength disabled by weak authority and the enslavement of good by what is bad. Gascoigne attacks secret grudges, Shakespeare attacks the slander of perfection. Gascoigne gives us men punished for unbending principle; Shakespeare denounces undeserving honour, truth described as stupidity and vows broken or betrayed.

There are differences. Shakespeare mentions women and the poor; Gascoigne mentions neither (though Shakespeare's "needie Nothing" is probably an echo of Gascoigne's "needy lacke" which is found in the second stanza after the one quoted above). Gascoigne draws on his own experiences to attack judicial corruption, corrupt officers of the state and false "purchase" (perhaps a dodgy land deal). Shakespeare's description of "captive-good attending Captaine ill" may be a distant echo of Gascoigne's experiences in the Low Countries, which the poet himself alludes to in his reference to a bloody sword and booty. Captain Gascoigne had both been taken prisoner and accused of treachery. John Kerrigan glosses "captive" as in one sense a noun signifying "prisoner-of-war".[33] By the time *Shakespeare's Sonnets* were published the rank of captain had long since become associated with beggars and confidence tricksters making bogus claims of military service. Finally, "arte made tung-tide by authoritie" is not some vague, general reference to censorship. It picks up Gascoigne's own use of the word "tongtide" and re-applies it to the fate of the poet. The ninth line of sonnet 66 transmits Shakespeare's understanding of what happened to the career of George Gascoigne.

27: Doomsday and Drunkards

Towards the end of his life, George Gascoigne was a changed person. He had failed both as a soldier and a writer. After 1575 he was transformed into a repentant sinner – a transformation underlined by his later, graver writings.

This, at any rate, was the conclusion of the twentieth century's leading Gascoigne scholar and biographer, C. T. Prouty: "He had followed the way of the world, only to find it a snare and delusion; therefore he sought out the way of the spirit, which might justify life and bring the rewards hitherto denied. That Gascoigne was sincere I do not doubt..."[1] The final section of Prouty's biography is titled "The Moralist" and is dedicated to delineating the poet's new identity as "a bitter and disillusioned Puritan".[2]

In the late spring of 1576 Gascoigne published his longest single work, *The Droomme of Doomes day* (i.e. "The drumbeat of doomsday"). As an intense work of theology warning sinners that the Day of Judgment awaits them it is, for secular readers, probably his least interesting book. In the Cambridge University Press edition of Gascoigne's collected works it amounts to 232 pages. Most of it is not original and consists of a translation from the Latin writings of Pope Innocent III and others. This book and a much shorter theological tract which also appeared this year in Gascoigne's name, Prouty saw as emerging from a time of sober and intensive work and "sincere moral purpose".[3]

The book is prefaced by a gushing letter of dedication addressed to Francis Russell, 2nd Earl of Bedford (but also saluting the Earl's "good Ladie"). In it Gascoigne describes himself as Russell's "faithful servaunt and follower". He apologises for the time he has wasted in the past "in penning and endightyng sundrie toyes and trifles". Whether by accident or design the title page design of *The Droomme of Doomes day* bears a striking resemblance to that of *A Hundreth Sundrie Flowres*, with a frame of repeating swirling patterns in three layers. It is as if the poet was wiping the slate clean, supplying a sober religious sequel to a scandalous original.

Gascoigne solemnly explains that almost a year ago he was

> Pricked and much moved, by the grave and discreete wordes of one right worshipfull and mine approved friend, who (in my presence) hearing my thryftlesse booke of *Poesyes* undeservedly commended, dyd say: That he liked the smell of those *Pœsies* pretely well, but he would lyke the Gardyner much better if he would employ his spade in no worse ground, then eyther Devinitie or morall Philosophie.

This friend could conceivably have been someone of the same dour disposition as Arthur, Lord Grey of Wilton or may have been invented to suit Gascoigne's purpose or, as Gillian Austen suggests, could well have been his new patron,

Francis Russell, 2nd Earl of Bedford.[4]

Many other friends, Gascoigne claimed, had praised his book and said he deserved a laurel garland (of the same sort, no doubt, as that which Gascoigne had brazenly placed above his own head in his self-portrait with Elizabeth I). But on due reflection he realised that the first friend was right. Someone with a gift for writing "ought also to bestowe and employe the same in some worthie and profitable subjecte or travayle". It so happened that "not manye monethes" ago, Gascoigne

> tossyng and retossyng in my small Lybrarie, amongest some bookes which had not often felte my fyngers ende in xv. yeares before, I chaunced to light upon a small volumne skarce comely covered, and wel worse handled.

Gascoigne claimed not to know who the author was.[5] His description of how he came to put *The Droomme of Doomes day* together is given more precisely in a much shorter moral work written soon afterwards. In *A delicate Diet, for daintiemouthde Droonkardes* he explains that the earlier work was constructed out of "sundry Pamphlets". The word "pamphlet" signified something more substantial than it does today.

Gascoigne's theology book is comprised of four parts. The first, "Of The View of Worldly Vanities" is a translation of a corrupt edition of *De miseria humane conditionis* ("On the Misery of the Human Condition") by Lothario dei Segni, otherwise known as Pope Innocent III (c.1160-1216). This was a late twelfth-century text which remained popular in Europe for four centuries. It is quoted in *Piers Plowman*, mentioned by Chaucer (who did a lost translation of at least part of it), and it was almost certainly known to Montaigne, Dante, Erasmus and Rabelais. The text's modern editor describes it as "a work of...unmitigated gloom" which emphasizes "only the pessimistic side of Christian dualism".[6]

The original authors of the second and third tracts – "Of The Huge Greatness and Enormity of Sins" and "The Needle's Eye" – are not known. A final section "which doth teach remedies against the bitternesse of Death" purports to be written "by I.B. unto his familiar friend G.P." Although by implication also translated out of Latin it is most likely an original work in English by Gascoigne himself. The twelfth commendatory poem in *The Posies* is also by "I.B.", who probably existed nowhere outside the poet's imagination.

Gascoigne explained to the Earl that he had assembled these tracts together under the title *The Droomme of Doomes day* with the Christian soldier in mind. The military analogy was not meant literally but metaphorically: "Thinking my self assured that any Soldier which meaneth to march under the flagge of gods favour, may by sounde of this droomme be awaked, and called to his watch and warde with right sufficient summons."

This is muscular Christianity for the Puritan end of the Protestant spectrum. That there was a market for material like this was underlined by a second translation of Pope Innocent's text, which appeared the same year, translated by Henry Kerton under the title *The Mirror of Mans lyfe*. Kerton and Gascoigne worked independently; neither seems to have read or been influenced by the other's translation.[7] Gascoigne emphasized that he had had his translation checked and corrected by certain "learned Devines", to make sure he had committed no theological faux pas. He did not say which ecclesiastics he meant. In theory Stephen Nevynson would be one obvious possibility, though one would have expected Gascoigne to trumpet the co-operation of such a prestigious collaborator, had he ever obtained it. If the claim was true it was a wise decision in such a zealous, theologically disputatious, nitpicking age.

Gascoigne's new patron was perhaps a surprising one since he and the Earl had been involved in a legal dispute over land in Bedfordshire in 1570.[8] Evidently six years later this was no longer a cause for any ill-feeling between them. Francis Russell, 2nd Earl of Bedford, was a leading nobleman, a soldier, an ardent Protestant, a Knight of the Garter, a member of the Privy Council, and a literary patron: "Of the thirty volumes dedicated to him in his lifetime, almost exactly one-third were works of overtly religious propaganda, and if to these are added the collections of sermons and biblical works, the proportion reaches a half."[9] By dedicating *The Droomme of Doomes day* to the Earl, Gascoigne moved further to the radical Protestant centre of power and influence in Elizabethan England.

From the biographical point of view this publication is also revealing for the insight it supplies into Gascoigne's keen interest in proofreading. At a time when Latin remained the chosen language of the intelligentsia and when many poets scorned the vulgar act of publication, Gascoigne took a direct, personal interest in the appearance of his books. Against the grain of the age, he wrote in English and produced virtually nothing in Latin. Against the indifference of a poet like Dyer or, later, Shakespeare, to publication, Gascoigne was acutely interested in the appearance of his words as printed text. A note at the start of *The Droomme of Doomes day* explains that Gascoigne would normally have visited the printers regularly "to attend the dayly proofes". Owing to illness, he was obliged to send a servant instead. Unfortunately the man was "not so well acquainted with the matter as his maister was" with the result that "there have passed some faultes much contrary unto both our meanings and desires". There follows a long column of 49 typographical errors accompanied by the correct text.

This inventory of corrections supplies a fascinating insight into the nature of a Tudor typesetter's misreadings of an author's manuscript. These include the complete reversal of meaning ("revolveth" for "revolveth not" and "ever faile" for "never fayle"), basic misreadings ("many" for "might"), the omission of complete lines, the misreading of individual letters ("degrees" instead of "decrees"), the omission of individual words ("that despiseth" for "that he despiseth"), the deliberate and unauthorised revision of the author's text, the inadvertent insertion of new words ("it is not" for "is not"), a baffled attempt to cope with a rare word ("in an hillate" for "adnychilate", which was an archaic spelling of "annihilate") and a wide range of minor mistranscriptions stemming from Freudian slips or the misreading of one word for one only marginally different in appearance (of which the most ironic example is "carefulnesse" for "carelessenesse"). Reading this list of errors and corrections makes it all the easier to understand how plausible it is that the First Folio's notorious "for his Nose was as sharpe as a Pen, and a Table of greene fields" (*Henry V*, II.iii.16) should really be "for his Nose was as sharpe as a Pen, and a babeld [a'babbled] of greene fields" (the capital letters being the work of the compositor, not Shakespeare).

The Droomme of Doomes day is also of biographical significance for supplying evidence that Gascoigne was suffering from an illness during April 1576, and possibly earlier. He explains that he was prevented from visiting the printers by "sickness", and his effusive letter of dedication to the Earl of Bedford ends, "From my lodging where I finished this travayle in weake plight for health as your good L[ord]: well knoweth this second daye of *Maye*. 1576." Gascoigne's prefaces and dedications are, of course, often exercises in mystification, obfuscation or exaggeration, as well as outright fabrication, but there is no real reason to suppose that he was inventing this tale of having suffered from sickness. The fact that he would be dead of an unspecified illness before the end of the following year underlines the likelihood that he had genuinely been unwell. What this illness was, and if it was connected to his death, is impossible to deduce from Gascoigne's own sketchy references. However, Gillian Austen cautions against the assumption that intimations of mortality motivated the book, since the chronological record indicates it was largely completed before Gascoigne fell sick.[10] She sees canny opportunism rather than devotional piety as the poet's probable motivation. The book was essentially hackwork: "As a translation it is not innovative or experimental, and its subject matter is entirely conventional."[11] Gascoigne's shrewdness as a writer anxious to satisfy any market open to him is not in doubt and G. T. Prouty's image of the poet broken by circumstance and reborn as a devout and remorseful man now seems naïve. Nevertheless it is perhaps reasonable to conclude that illness may well have given a certain edge to Gascoigne's account of the vanity of worldly things.

Which edition of *De miseria humane conditionis* Gascoigne used is not known but it was evidently the same corrupt text as that used by Kerton. It was substantially the same as the original text but not quite complete. Gascoigne's version tactfully omits, for example, section XXIV of Book Two, "On Unnatural

Intercourse". Gascoigne's translation is a single, intimidating slab of prose, lacking the reader-friendly arrangement of the original text into three short books organised into brief sections.

The Droomme of Doomes day has a strong emphasis on man's vulnerable, human, earthly nature as a creature which "bringeth forth nitts, lyse & worms...maketh excrements of spettle, pisse, and ordure" and "belcheth, breaketh wynde and stincketh". The first part, which recycles numerous Biblical texts, lashes the frailty of man in full-blooded, vigorous prose. Its thumping, repetitive nature (the book's title is apt) is likely to quickly make it a wearisome read for anyone uninterested in biblically based preaching, but as a rhetorical exercise Gascoigne probably enjoyed writing it. The section which humours the puritan taste for plain, simple clothing is typical:

> Marke what our Lorde god doth threaten against the superfluitie of apparel by the Prophet Esay saying: For asmuch as the daughters of Syon are puffed up with pryde, & alke with bare neckes layd out, and bridling in their gate, therfore the Lord will make bauld their bushy locks, & will take of the hayre from the daughters of Sion. In those daies the Lord will take away the ornaments of their shoes, and their hoope ringes, chaynes, carkenets, bracelets, & Jewels. Their calles, & their frisled & curled perwyckes, their small chaynes, theyr pomanders, their eare ringes, & the precious stones, hanging upon their forheads, their short clokes & shifts of garments, their fine linen & their needleworks, their glasses, their lawne partlets, their fillets, and their fine skarfes & vayles. And in steed of sweet smels, they shall have stynch, in steed of their fayre purses and girdles, they shall have a small corde to bynde theyr coffyne, and in steade of frysled hayre, they shall have a bare and balld skull.

This is theological *Schadenfreude*: a lipsmacking relish at the thought of inevitable death. But it is the sombre moralising of an Old Testament prophet adapted to the women's fashions of Tudor London of the mid-1570s. Translated, it expresses the Puritan loathing of extravagant fashion combined with a fear of women's tempting sensuality. It is a vein Bunyan later mined more effectively in the form of prose narrative. And it is a message which can still be heard more than four centuries later not all that far from where Gascoigne worked at his translation, as preachers in Walthamstow's town square wave their Bibles and harangue the Saturday crowds passing by on their way to such centres of sinful vanity as the local hair salons and clothes shops.

Theological anxiety about sin and punishment achieves its most vivid expression in *The Droomme of Doomes day* in the form of a single, extraordinary woodcut. It appears in the first part as an illustration "Of the unspeakable perplexitie of the damned". It may well be a woodcut that the printer had already used elsewhere, though it is just possibly an original work by Gascoigne himself. The scene it portrays is quite literally hellish. A naked, long-haired woman raises her arms in terror and supplication as a squat, bending, hairy, bearded devil with horns, a hooked nose, claw feet and a spiky back drags her towards the mouth of hell using a chain looped around her waist. She is escorted on one side by a devil with a large phallus, whose right arm raises a stick with two large hooks attached (evidently to slash her with). On the other side of her is another monstrous figure, a major devil whose hideous face is barely distinguishable from its wings, which form a vast webbed membrane enclosing it like a nightmarish ruff. In the far distance stands a building. It looks like the front of a large, twin-spired cathedral or minster and signifies the Heavenly Jerusalem.

To the right are, quite literally, the jaws of hell. A stretched wide-open mouth in a gigantic, porcine Bosch-like face waits to swallow the woman. Between its teeth lie flames and a confused crowd of devils and the damned. To anyone believing in hell and damnation this woodcut supplies a terrifying image of the horrors awaiting a sinner. The design is not original, however, but based on standard late-medieval representations of Hell-mouth. English art typically represented this as a gaping mouth, usually on the right as it is viewed. Varieties of devils, hooks and the chain are equally conventional. Sometimes particular vices are distinguished within Hell, but apparently not here.

After Freud, iconography like this can plausibly be interpreted as a cluster of symbols representing sexual anxiety. The woman is bound and in a passive sexual position, with her legs apart. The devil with the thick phallus wants to sink his hooks into her. The smaller demon has his fingers around a chain which he is pulling and which much resembles the tip of an erect penis rising from a scrotum. The open mouth is the classic *vagina dentata*. In Tudor terms, entering a vagina of fire meant contracting a sexual disease. The very act of sex threatened a man.

However one chooses to decipher this image (and with its nudity, gaping orifice, fire, hooks, spikes and phallus, a psychological explanation is compelling), it vividly expresses anxiety about human frailty, flesh and divine punishment. But how far does *The Droomme of Doomes day* express Gascoigne's own beliefs? The second and third parts, though by different authors, belong to the same genre as Innocent's text. What the second part calls "base earthly and carnal things" are repeatedly condemned with the aid of a vast repertoire of quotations and allusions from the Bible and other authorities such as St Augustine. The third part piously asks

> such as doe dayly follow vanities, laughyung, bablyng, sportyng, dallying, wandring here and there, and accustoming them selves to all lightnesse, and in the meane whyle doe very seldome or never repent or amend, how can

they choose but become culpable also of great enormities?

It is hard to believe that Gascoigne himself, who not long before had produced a guide to hunting, really believed in a life of devout simplicity. Or perhaps he believed in it while translating these lines, on the basis that it could be discarded when it suited him. He was a man who after all was cheerfully capable of embracing large contradictions, as shown by his anti-war poem in which he put himself forward for future military service.

Gascoigne himself is likely to have been on automatic pilot when he produced the translation. At the level of language it is colourful and richly resonant, and one does not have to share its harsh, extreme theology to enjoy what Roland Barthes once famously called "the pleasure of the text". But it is doubtful if Gascoigne himself was seriously vexed by women's fashion or any of the other aspects of modern life which made Puritans froth with indignation. *The Droomme of Doomes day* was essentially a hack job, a theological sequel to the secular *Noble Art of Venerie*. It was done for material advantage, not from passionate conviction. Lynda E. Boose has suggested that after the confiscation of the *Posies* Gascoigne "seems to have become a grovelling court toady".[12] But that is to take his effusions of moral repentance and deference at their face value. Grovelling to those who had power, wealth and influence was a game that had to be played by anyone of ambition. It would be truer to say that in the face of a humourless and repressive system of state censorship Gascoigne was a slippery survivor who wore many masks – he was a driven man but with a sly, irreverent attitude to authority.

The one section of *The Droomme of Doomes day* where Gascoigne steps out from behind his masks to reveal something of himself is in the final part, "A letter written by I.B. unto his familiar frende G.P. teaching remedies against the bytternesse of Death". It is a kind of sequel to *Certayne notes of Instruction concerning the making of verse or ryme in English*. Like the essay on prosody, this short prose essay purports to have been written at the request of a friend, "G.P." This could, just possibly, have been George Puttenham or someone else but may have been as fictitious as Master Edouardo Donati seems to have been.

"I.B." – who is almost certainly Gascoigne – explains that his friend asked him to write "a meditacion of contented death, or at the least to diminish the desire of long lyfe". It was a request that with a suspicious neatness coincided with Gascoigne's translation work for *The Droomme of Doomes day* and the poet's own sickness. Just as *Certayne notes* offered a practical guide to the writing of poetry, Gascoigne's short religious essay concerns itself with "the science of dying wel, to be learned with tyme, meditacion, and exercise" (meaning spiritual exercise or task). About the same length as the essay on prosody, "remedies against the bytternesse of Death" argues that death is "no plague, but benefyt".

There are three reasons, Gascoigne argues, why men are loath to die. One is because nature itself resists death and "abhorreth dissolucion". The second is because few people really believe in "the mervailous promises of incomparable blysse" which God and the Christian religion hold out. The third and greatest reason is that life itself is sweet and no one wants to be parted from "the goods and commodyties of the same". Only one force is able to make a man "content to forsake his goods, his living, him selfe and his life" and that force "is love & nothing else". Gascoigne proves his point by drawing on his memories of the Low Countries. It was no other thing:

> So many captains & souldiers willingly & wittingly to goe to their death, but love: They lovid something better then lyfe, the wisest their coũtry and frendes whome they would preserve, thither fame, and as they called it immortalitie the lightesy vayne estimacion & glory, but every one somewhat wherewith they were ledde.

These memories reinforce the argument that a man needs to make Christ his captain, put on the strong buckler of faith and be prepared to receive the assault of death with a good heart and conscience. A man must live in continual meditation of death, "neither troubled with inordinate desire of high estate...neither affrayde to be in meaner [position] than he is".

The essay is written in a plain prose style which is in stark contrast to the dense, encyclopaedic style of the preceding three parts of *The Droomme of Doomes day*. It offers simple and quiet reflection in place of the full-blooded, hectoring Old Testament-based preaching which precedes it. There are a handful of references to ancient history and Aristotle, Cicero and Marcus Aurelius but otherwise "remedies against the bytternesse of Death" is free of the dense networks of allusion which characterise the prose texture of the other tracts. From it one can deduce that Gascoigne was not naturally drawn to the Bible as a source of inspiration or authority. His sole religious essay indicates that his sickness in the late spring of 1576 may have been serious enough to make him think that he faced the very real possibility of death. It opened up a gloomy image of what that might mean:

> I leave here unsaid, that health and strength of bodie may impayre by sickenesse, wife be lost by death, & friends turne to enimyes, goods and revenewes casuall, suche as may decay, or without desert be taken away to ye occasion of great heaviness & sorrow, of al which so maketh otherwise his accompte is farre deceived...

But, characteristically, Gascoigne's response to sickness and possible death was to pick up his pen and attempt to deal with his latest misfortune in words. Death might be "not loss, but gaine" but while he remained in the material world George Gascoigne did not really want to be in a meaner position than he was. He would continue to seek patronage in whatever quarter he could find it.

A delicate Diet, for daintiemouthde Droonkardes

On 10 August 1576 George Gascoigne was once again absent from Walthamstow and lodging in London. We know this because this was the date and location appended to his letter of dedication to a pamphlet published later that month, piously entitled *A delicate Diet, for daintiemouthde Droonkardes. Wherein the fowle abuse of common Carowsing, and Quaffing with hartie draughtes, is honestlie admonished*. It was published by Richard Jones on 22 August 1576, and was frankly acknowledged as the work of "George Gascoyne Esquier".

The pamphlet was dedicated to Sir Lewis Dive of Bromham in Bedfordshire, who Gascoigne hailed as a "synguler good friend". This was the same man who had visited and advised Gascoigne in Bedford prison and who was the father-in-law of Douglas Dive, to whom Gascoigne had addressed his idiosyncratic poem of advice. Dive seems to have been a dour Protestant and Gascoigne was keen to emphasize his moral reformation after his "wanton (and worse smelling) Poesies". He indicated, quite untruthfully, that they had been published without his permission ("they came forth sooner then I wyshed"). But now after "the lost time" frittered away on sinful work Gascoigne was a reformed man: "I have of latter dayes used al my travaile in matters both serious and Morall."

Gascoigne explained that he had recently devoted himself to works "both Morall and Godly", including *The Glass of Government*, *The Droomme of Doomes day*, *The Steel Glass* and *The Complaynte of Phylomene*. (He made no mention, however, of his two anonymous productions – the Kenilworth entertainments and his hunting manual, which were focused on pleasure and earthly things.) The writer ruefully acknowledged that he hadn't sent a copy of any of those pious publications to his dear friend. This was partly because he'd had very few copies himself and partly because even when he had set one aside to send with his "brother" John Dive (Lewis's son and husband to Douglas) "at the very instant of his departure it was not redie". This sounds like a reversion to the dissembling Gascoigne of old.

To make up for it, the poet explained he was offering up his pamphlet to Dive's "name and patronage", adding that he was presenting it along with copies of all those other titles:

I knowe you, and the world hath always esteemed you, for a paterne of Sobryetie, and one that doth zealously detest the beastlie vyce of droonken-nesse: This small worke is therefore so much the meeter to bee dedicated unto you.

A delicate Diet, for daintiemouthde Droonkardes is a title with a faintly sarcastic edge. "Diet" means both "food" and "course of treatment", "delicate" could signify "fine", "tender" or "delicious" and "dainty" carries the sense of "pleasing to the palate", "enticing" or "fastidious". The pamphlet's message is to avoid intoxication. In other words, the most delicious food for drunkards is the spiritual sustenance offered by the Bible – or not to drink at all. It is not a message any alcoholic is likely to have wanted to hear but it may well have made Lewis Dive chuckle at Gascoigne's wit.

It was a fact that in the rest of Europe, from early in the sixteenth century, the English had a reputation for being drunkards. In *Othello* Shakespeare played to the groundlings by exploiting the stereotype with a joke about the Englishman's fondness for alcohol. Drunkenness seems to have been very common in Elizabethan England. It was particularly associated with the soldiers and captains returning from the Low Countries; one popular explanation blamed it on their contact with Germans. But in more refined circles public displays of drunkenness were frowned on.

Gascoigne's short pamphlet falls into three parts. A short introduction explains how, while working on the "sundry Pamphlets" which formed the basis of his translation of *The Droomme of Doomes day*, the poet came across a letter of St Augustine's written against drunkenness. Recognising that drunkenness was spreading through the realm, not least through the popularity of the "continuall custome of cheering, and banqueting", Gascoigne thought it timely to translate Augustine's epistle. He decided "to adde some Aucthoryties and examples for the more speedy extirpation of this monstrous plant, lately crepte into the pleasaunt Orchyardes of Englande".

Gascoigne explains that his general proposition is that all drunkards are beasts. Some are merely turned "into a certaine jocunde myrth, and dallyaunce", making them "delighted with everie fonde toye, and trifle". Others are turned by drink into brawlers and quarrellers. The lecherous drunkard "wyll spare neyther Sex, Age, Kyndred, nor companion, in the filthy hate of his lewde concupiscence". The proud, vain drunkard parades in the street in his fine clothes, "never abashed, tyll hee fall downe in the channel". The consequence for all these drunkards is always the same: they

> lye vomiting and belching with great griefe, and greater offence, or else they become Asses, and sluggishly consume in sleepe, that Golden tyme which is lent us to use and bestowe to the honour of God, and for our own avayle.

No doubt Lewis Dive's head nodded in vigorous approval of such a colourful, stern and pious admonition.

Augustine's epistle against drunkenness, which follows, is in fact not a teetotal tract, merely a recommendation of moderate drinking. It is drunkenness which is "a great evyll, and an odious sin unto God", not drinking *per se*. What vexed Augustine was social drinking which involved encouraging others to consume alcohol who might not really want to. Every man should be left alone "to drinke as much and as lytle as hee lysteth: that if he wyll needes make him selfe droonken, he maye perishe alone and not both of you bee cast away".

Gascoigne then added his own short treatise, citing examples of drunkenness and degradation drawn from the Old Testament and the Greek and Roman classics. This inventory gives way to a lively account of the contemporary alcohol problem. The previous examples might seem bad, says Gascoigne, but modern drunkenness is far worse:

> We doo so much exceede al those that have gone before us, that if they might seeme as men transfourmed into Beasts, we shal rather appeare as Beasts misshapen & changed into Devyls.

The Germans have always been notorious drunkards, says Gascoigne, but now "our newfangled Englyshe men" are just as bad. Every dinner invitation is accompanied by a toast, resulting in excessive "Quaffing, Carowsing, and tossing of Pots". And when preachers condemn the practice it is replaced by "a harty draught" which is "five tymes worse". But the problem is not restricted to well-born dedicated followers of fashion. The lower classes are just as bad:

> Let us but consider this one thing: in what civyll Realme or dominion, where the people are taught and exercised in the commandementes and counsels of God (England onely excepted) shall we see the unthriftye Artificer, or the labourer, permitted to syt bybbing and drinking of Wine in every Taverne? Or what woman (even amongst the droonken *Almaines*) is suffred to followe her Husbande unto the Alehouse or Beerehouse? But it were folly to stand so much upon these meane personages, who for lacke of wytte or good education, maye easily be enclyned to thinges undecent.

But if the common people are bad, the gentry are little better, being addicted to hearty draughts and endless pledges and toasts. Worse still is the sheer variety of alcohol available to the English. The drunken Germans are satisfied with small Rhenish wine or a cup of beer. The English have March beer, "dooble dooble Beere", dagger ale, "bragget" (ale and honey fermented together), Rhenish wine, white wine, French wine, "Gascoyne wine", sack, Canary wine, Greek wine "& al the wines that may be gotten". Gascoigne was not exaggerating. Some 56 different varieties of French wine were available as well as 30 brands of Italian, Greek, Spanish and Canary wine. But worse still, wine was commonly flavoured with sugar, lemon "& sundry sorts of Spices", further encouraging drunkenness.

The sheer variety of alcohol on offer, combined with the fashion for toasts, had lamentable consequences:

> And well wrote hee which sayd, that the first Cuppe quenched thirst, the second enduced myrth, and rejoysing in hart, the third voluptuousnesse, the fowrth droonkennesse, the fifth wrathfulnesse, the syxt contenciousnesse, the seventh furiousnesse, the eyght sluggishnesse, and the ninth, extremetie of sycknesse.
> But with us, nyne draughts: yea, nineteen draughts: nay, sometime nine & twenty doo not suffice.

The pamphlet ended with Gascoigne in effect on his knees, praying for the reformation of a self-indulgent nation. He concluded with some Biblical quotations and the pious wish that the authoritative examples he'd cited would deter anyone from "falling into this swinish and filthye abhomination". If not, all he could do was "praye unto God, that some better learned, and more eloquent then I, maye (by assistance of his holy spyrite) be made able to set downe such wholesome lessons for the avoiding thereof..."

It is reasonable to assume that Lewis Dive enjoyed Gascoigne's tract. It was obviously pitched at his Puritan sensibility and designed to assure him of the poet's own personal reformation. The magic word "patronage" in the dedicatory letter to Dive hints at Gascoigne's hope of some tangible reward. In that sense *A delicate Diet, for daintiemouthde Droonkardes* was a calculated work, not an outpouring of Gascoigne's own indignation about drunkenness. He may well, as a gentleman, have found the sight of public drunkenness and women in alehouses offensive. But it is debatable whether or not the subject vexed him as much as it evidently vexed Lewis Dive. The descriptions of drinking and drunkenness find a parallel in the fourth part of "Dan Bartholmew of Bathe", where the heartbroken hero finds solace in spiced wine. He goes on a bender, collapses, falls into a trance and succumbs to "dayly drinke" and "bottells that were fylled to the brinke".[13] It may or may not be autobiographical but it indicates that Gascoigne was used to the spectacle of a man drowning his sorrows in drink. On that occasion it aroused melancholy sympathy rather than the hot-blooded religious outrage of *A delicate Diet*. Drunks puking in the street or brawling probably offended Gascoigne but it is doubtful if he really cared as much about the topic as he pretended to Lewis Dive. In writing the pamphlet he surely had other motives than a devout wish to reform the morals of the nation.

28: The Spanish Fury

On 22 August 1576, Gascoigne promised Sir Lewis Dive that "soone after Mighelmas (by Gods leave) I wyll see you".[1] But that meeting cannot have taken place. Michaelmas, or the Feast of Michael and All Angels, is what used to be known as a quarter day, signalling the start of a new season. It falls on 29 September and on 15 September of that year the poet was in Paris. He remained abroad until mid-November.

The reason for his broken promise is plain. In the autumn of 1576 Gascoigne finally received the state employment he craved. He was sent by Sir Francis Walsingham to France and the Low Countries to report on the political situation there. Walsingham was a former English ambassador in Paris, who in 1573 had been made Secretary of State. He is famous as the man who established England's first intelligence service – the Tudor equivalent of MI5 *and* MI6. But this service really only developed in the 1580s, in response to plots by Catholic conspirators to overthrow Elizabeth. In the 1570s Walsingham's network of informers was in its infancy and he was largely involved in acquiring information that might be useful in determining the Privy Council's foreign policy.

Who recommended Gascoigne to Walsingham is not known. Walsingham was close to the Earl of Leicester, so there may be a link with Gascoigne's presence at Kenilworth. Gascoigne's military service in the Low Countries, his patronage by Lord Grey of Wilton, and his pose as a reformed prodigal and author of pious Protestant literature, might have made him an attractive or at any rate ideologically sound figure. Or perhaps Sir Nicholas Bacon put in a good word. The fact of his employment indicated that Gascoigne was regarded as loyal, trustworthy and reliable.

By September 1576 George Gascoigne was in France, at the royal court. He was there to report on the latest situation and thinking there. He was an official government spy in the secondary sense of that term. He was there to report on the activities of a foreign power. But he was not a secret agent. He was there under his own name, an English gentleman among French gentleman. He reported back to Lord Burghley, sending ostensibly straightforward letters of reportage, in that ragged, spidery, now barely legible style known as secretary hand. It is possible that some of the contents were coded but if so their meaning is now lost to us.[2]

Two of these letters survive in the Public Record Office.[3] On 15 September Gascoigne wrote to Burghley from the French court at Paris. His flair for the dramatic extended even to this bureaucratic item: he asked Burleigh to pardon his hasty script, "for I wryte att mydnyght beying returned butt this afternoone". The letter is a mixture of military information and gossip. He reported that the latest news from Flanders had been celebrated with excitement by the French military. Twenty-five cornets reiters (i.e. cavalry officers) were stationed at Châlons, in Champagne, brought there by the Duke Casimir. The Duke of Montmorency, Monsieur de Sories (the King's favourite) and 500 gentlemen remained in the lower parts of Germany and their return was long overdue. The King's brother was at Tours and many captains, gentlemen and soldiers passed between them. The King and his brother were friends and had sent a commissary to Germany for levies. Danville's wife had spoken with the King and Queen Mother, not without great suspicion. The King had still in readiness about him 7,000 infantry. Gascoigne said he intended shortly to travel on to Flanders and see for himself what was happening there. He added a postscript: frost and hail had wreaked havoc on French vineyards; wine would surely become very expensive this year.

The letter supplied a mix of raw information; it was up to someone like Walsingham to process its significance. And Gascoigne was just one of many informants who sent information to London. Sir Amias Paulet reported back to Burghley the following month. He wrote that outwardly the French King and Queen, and the Queen Mother, appeared friendly to England but that the treasons and dissimulations of the Court were as deep and dangerous as they'd ever been.

On 7 October 1576 Gascoigne wrote again to Burghley. The signatures on both these letters hint at Gascoigne's high spirits. A flourish beneath the first "G" plunges down the page, loops back up, loops down again, then jerks away, forming a long straight line that frames and underlines a second, more complexly patterned flourish. This second flourish is formed by an outsize "c" which curls downwards beneath the "o" and "i" in "Gascoigne", then forms three or four lengthy loops which extend beyond the end of the signature. The dot above the "i" is never a dot, always a swirl, resembling a backward "s". The individual letters are not so much joined as brushing up against each other. Gascoigne clearly wrote his signature in four separate stages: the first, reverted "G", the second "G" together with the "a" and "s", then the outsize "c" with its attendant flourishes, and finally the "o", "I", "g", "n" and "e". Sometimes he included a second horizontal underlining. These flourishes, known as ascenders and descenders, were common enough in handwriting of the period. But though conventional the autographs suggest boldness, self-confidence, a strong ego.

Gascoigne informed Burghley that he was anxious that he keep Walsingham informed of what he was up to: "maye I beseche yor L[ordship]: to make mr Secretarye acqueynted with this my good wyll to discharge my dewtye". The letter crackles with excitement and urgency. Paris was evidently abuzz with rumours of military action. French intervention in the affairs of the Low Countries was more and more being talked about. The King and the Queen Mother had left Paris, the King ostensibly for pleasure and the latter to see "Monsieur" (i.e. his brother). The King's reiters (cavalry equipped with swords and firearms) were on the march. They were already beyond Verdun, which was the most direct route towards the Netherlands. The money to pay their wages was borrowed upon credit and the Duke of Arschot's agent was involved. This man left the house which he'd been living in for over a year at short notice, in a great hurry. His secretary stayed behind but seemed very worried. Two companies of footmen had been levied, to go towards the Low Countries. The Duke of Guise was expected to lead the reiters and had gone to join them.

Gascoigne announced that he intended to depart for the Low Countries the next day, to see what was going on for himself. He was clearly anxious not to be left behind in Paris if the action was moving elsewhere. He intimated that Walsingham knew of the possibility of him going there: "I meane to spend this winter (or as long as shalbe thought meete) yn service of my coũtrye. I beseche your honour to confer with Mr Secretarye who can more att large make you pryvye to myne entent." But there was also a personal matter which he drew to Burghley's attention. Since he was obliged to be away from England on the Queen's business, he requested a stay of process in a suit "in the Cowrte of warde before yor honor concernying an accoũpt for Brettones lande". This indicates that Gascoigne was still apparently involved in some kind of legal dispute with one or more of his stepchildren, but the details are obscure. Jean Robertson believed that "This suggests that the Breton children did sue Gascoigne to recover their property, but there is no trace of any bill; possibly they never got any satisfaction owing to the death of Gascoigne."[4]

Atrocity in Antwerp

On 8 October 1576, Gascoigne left Paris for Antwerp, arriving there some twelve days later. He was back in the Low Countries for the first time since his ignominious return to England as a liberated prisoner of war two years earlier. But now he was there as a civilian, not a soldier.

He reached Flanders just as the war of independence was entering a new and ugly phase. On 20 October Maastricht fell to a besieging Spanish army. This was followed by bloody reprisals against those inside the town. At the same time the situation in Antwerp was reaching boiling point. Events there were to result in Gascoigne writing *The Spoyle of Antwerpe*, one of the great works of Tudor journalism in a genre which then barely existed.[5] It supplies a classic, dramatic eye-witness account from a reporter on the spot, who not only unfolds a tale of horror but also attempts to provide an objective framework of explanation.

Paris and Antwerp were the only two European cities with populations greater than 100,000. Antwerp was the chief city of Vlaanderen (Flanders) and Europe's second biggest port. It owed its ascendancy to patronage from the Emperor Maximilian and his successor Charles V and was an important centre for diamond cutting, printing and European trade in general. Thomas Cromwell had been a merchant in Antwerp before he entered the service of Henry VIII.

The city was cosmopolitan, largely Protestant and a centre of the new humanism. Sir Thomas More's *Utopia* begins there, with a scene set in the Onze Lieve Vrouwekathedraal (Cathedral of Our Lady). This was the biggest church in the Netherlands, established in 1352 but not completed until the sixteenth century. Its massive spire dominated the city skyline.

Gascoigne went to stay at the English House at the Hof van Liere on the Prinsstraat. The English House was first granted by the city to the Merchant Adventurers in 1474. It was something like a consulate, and a lodging house for Englishmen. Antwerp's English House is famous for its associations with the Biblical translator and Protestant martyr, William Tyndale.[6] In Tyndale's day the English House was situated near the "Old Bourse" (or "English Bourse"). In 1553 the Merchant Adventurers relocated to a new address, which is the one where Gascoigne lodged. This was a relatively palatial complex which still exists and today forms part of the University of Antwerp.

In the pamphlet which he later wrote about the events he witnessed, Gascoigne claimed that he was there "upon certain private affairs of mine own". He also refers cryptically to "weighty business" which he had to transact there. But this appears to have been Gascoigne's first and only visit to Antwerp. It is doubtful if he was there for any reason other than to report on the situation and as someone who could be trusted to deliver messages back to Burghley and Walsingham. The pamphlet was published anonymously, so probably the private business was simply a front to disguise his true purpose and to make him sound like any other travelling merchant.

Gascoigne's Antwerp was a city of brooks, moats and canals. Narrow cobbled lanes led to open squares, and around the Grote Markt was a labyrinth of alleyways. A handsome Stadhuis (Town Hall) was completed in 1566, a symbol of the city's commercial supremacy. But that was also the year that sectarian tensions between the Catholic priesthood and the local population exploded, with Protestant guildsmen smashing up the interior of the cathedral. As the Dutch war of independence gathered pace Antwerp was in a position of uneasy neutrality – an open city with a large, free-thinking Protestant population under the watchful eye of a Spanish garrison in a citadel overlooking the quays and the town centre. Designed by two fashionable Italian architects, the citadel (usually referred to as the castle) was built at a cost of 1,400,000 florins between October 1567 and early 1568. It had five bulwarks and was protected by ditches 100 feet across and 12 feet deep, and an external wall.

Gascoigne arrived on or around 22 October, just as matters started to come to a head. The Spanish garrison in the citadel had not been paid and was surviving on sparse rations. The soldiers had to endure the daily sight of a thriving, prosperous city of well-fed heretics. Friction between the resentful occupiers and their religious adversaries was growing. After the sacking of Maastricht some residents of Antwerp began to leave the city. To protect it, the estates sent from Brussels a protective force of 3,000 infantry and 1,000 cavalry. They arrived on Friday 2 November at a port on the west side of the city. The city authorities permitted them to enter the city the following day. Masked by mist, the Dutch forces hastily erected barricades and trenches at the end of five streets which led from the castle yard, fortifying the city from any sudden attack by troops in the castle. By midnight the trenches were, in Gascoigne's admiring words, "as high as the length of a pike". Work also started on a counterscarp linking these defences, but it was unfinished by the next fateful day.

The Dutch expedition was known to the Spanish authorities, who hastily sent their own force to Antwerp. The town gates were closed, so Gascoigne was unable to get out of the city to see the Spaniards approach. But he talked to them afterwards and they told him what had happened. Early the next day, Sunday 4 November, they approached Antwerp from the east, then went to the southwest side of the town ditch. There the horsemen and footmen entered at a gate called the Windmill. Meanwhile the Spaniards' German mercenaries marched round and found a way in through a small side entrance by the river, on the east side of the castle. The two groups rendezvoused at the castle at 10 a.m., where they were joined by the soldiers inside. The combined force of 5,000 troops then stormed the defences set up by the Dutch forces.

At dinnertime (i.e. midday) some English merchants came out of the town and dined in Gascoigne's chamber, telling him that "a hot scarmouch was begun in the castle yard" and that the fighting was getting more intense. In the middle of dinner someone brought news that the amount of cannon fire and gunfire was now so thick that smoke blotted out the houses, the streets and the people. The Spanish, it seemed, were on the brink of taking the trenches. Gascoigne sprang from the table and ran upstairs to the top of a high tower which rose above the English house.

From here the poet stared across at the smoke rising from the area around the Grote Markt. The trenches were defended by German mercenaries and Walloons, without any relief from reinforcements or re-supply. The reports reaching the English House were accurate. The Spanish broke into the trenches by midday. At every crossroads the Spanish sent a barrage of musket fire down the street ahead until resistance died out, then they pursued the fleeing defenders, executing anyone they caught up with. The troops were followed by lackeys and pages who set fire to the houses.

Gascoigne took his cloak and sword and headed for "the Bource". By this he may have meant the "Old Bourse" (otherwise known as "the English Bourse"). This was a market for international trading supervised by the city and established in the fifteenth century. The Oude Beurs was close to the Grote Markt and the castle and still exists today at #15 Hofstraat. On the face of it, this is where Gascoigne went, to the heart of the action. However, it is unlikely that he would have referred to the "English Bourse" simply as "the Bourse". It is just as likely that he was referring to the New Bourse which was built in 1532 outside the old city walls, between the Meir and the Lange Nieuwstraat (two of the most desirable addresses in the expanding city). The English merchants continued to trade their cloth at the Old Bourse first thing in the morning, and then go over to the New Bouse for other trading, particularly financial deals.

Beyond the English House the streets were full of fleeing soldiers and citizens standing by their doors with what weapons they had. He went on to the far side of "the Bource", where he encountered

> a great troupe coming in greater haste, with their heads as close together as a school of young fry or a flock of sheep, who met me on the far side of the Bourse, toward the market place. And having their leaders foremost (for I knew them by their javelins, borespeares and staves) bare me over backwards, and ran over my belly and my face, long time before I could recover on foot. At last when I was up, I looked on every side, and seeing them run so fast, began thus to bethink me, *What in God's name do I here which have no interest in this action? Since they who came to defend this town are content to leave it at large and shift for themselves*. And whiles I stood thus musing, another flock of flyers came so fast that they bare me on my nose and ran as many over my back as erst had marched over my guts. In fine, I got up like a tall fellow and went with them for company, but their haste was such as I could never overtake them, until I came at a broad cross street which lyeth between the English house & the said Bourse.

The identity and location of this "broad cross street" is ambiguous. To get to either the English Bourse or the New Bourse from the English House, Gascoigne would have had to cross three streets. If he was returning from the New Bourse then he may have been referring to the Keizerstraat, the Kipdorp or the Lange Nieuwstraat. If he was coming back to the English House from the English Bourse then he may have meant the Minderbroedersui, a particularly broad avenue where a stretch of medieval wall had formerly stood.

Wherever exactly he was, Gascoigne surely exaggerated the situation for dramatic effect. That he might have been barged aside and fell is quite likely. That he was knocked down by a crowd which ran over his stomach and face, got up, and was then knocked down by another crowd which ran over his back, seems unlikely. It seems redolent of a scene from a slapstick silent movie.

That he was touching up an already colourful reality is confirmed by his claim that he "passed through five hundred shot, before I could recover the English house". That musket balls were whizzing through the air is not to be doubted. But *five hundred*? It hardly seems possible. No one could pass through a hail of five hundred bullets and not be hit. In any case, in 1576 there were no automatic weapons. All guns of whatever type were single shooters. Once fired, they needed re-loading. Five hundred musket shots required five hundred armed soldiers.

Gascoigne regained the safety of the English House. Some of the merchants were standing outside. Gascoigne went straight to Thomas Heton, the governor, and urged him to get everyone inside and shut the gates. But before Gascoigne could shut and bar the gates the Spanish were outside and opening fire.

In fact musket shot was a lot less dangerous than modern bullets. The velocity was relatively slow and the range limited. This was underlined by the way in which, once back inside the English house, Gascoigne witnessed the Spanish troops "bestowing five or six musket shots at the grate where I answered them, whereof one came very near my nose, and piercing through the gate, struck one of the merchants on the head, without any great or dangerous hurt". A dangerous situation quickly resolved itself as the troops ran on in pursuit of the fleeing Dutch soldiers.

By 3 p.m. it was all over and the Spanish wandered back into town, the victors. What happened next was to shock Protestant Europe and motivate Gascoigne to publish his account of it in *The Spoyle of Antwerpe* (i.e. the plunder of Antwerp).

The Spanish troops annihilated the city's defences and sent the Dutch troops packing through a combination of professionalism and courage. Gascoigne later estimated that 600 on the Spanish side had died in taking Antwerp. But in victory they were not magnanimous. Instead, the soldiers turned into an undisciplined rabble who stormed through the city, killing, seizing plunder and trashing buildings. Gascoigne estimated that 17,000 men, women and children died. This was undoubtedly an exaggeration but it expressed his sense of being overwhelmed by the sight of dead bodies everywhere. The troops ran riot for three long days, plundering Antwerp's public buildings and private mansions. It was the greatest atrocity in the history of sixteenth-century Europe.[7] The civilian death toll was massive and even after the passage of more than four hundred years "the Spanish fury" is still remembered in Antwerp. Modern historians put the number of dead at around 8,000 – lower than Gascoigne's total but still shockingly high. The major part of the city was also burned to the ground.

The atrocity was remembered for long afterwards. Some time between 1594 and 1600, the Lord Chamberlain's Men performed *A Larum for London, or The Siedge of Antwerpe*, an anonymous play believed by some scholars to have drawn on Gascoigne's account. This drama, first published in 1602, presents a lurid account of Spanish brutality, including the callous stabbing to death of a blind man's two small children. Its hero is a one-legged lieutenant, who bravely protects the innocent from the cowardly and fiendish Spaniards. This melodrama is thin in plot, language and characterisation, and is clearly not Gascoigne's work. It has at various times been superficially ascribed to Thomas Lodge and, with wild improbability, as the collaboration of Marlowe and Shakespeare or

John Marston and Shakespeare, but its real author remains unknown. Scholars are divided as to whether it owes anything to Gascoigne's pamphlet.[8]

*

The Spoyle of Antwerpe offers a vivid, lively account of events as witnessed by an intellectual with first-hand knowledge of combat. In that respect it is a kind of Tudor *Homage to Catalonia*. Killing in the heat of battle was one thing. What angered Gascoigne was that an indiscriminate massacre took place long after the city had fallen to the Spaniards:

> For age and sex, young and old, they slew great numbers of young children, but many more women more than four score years of age. For time and place, their fury was as great ten days after the victory, as at the time of their entry. And as great respect they had to the church and churchyard (for all their hypocritical boasting of the catholic religion) as the butcher hath to his shambles or slaughter house. For person and country they spared neither friend nor foe – Portuguese nor Turk. For profession and religion the Jesuits must give their ready coin, and all other religious houses both coin and plate with all short ends that were good and portable. The rich was spoiled [plundered] because he had & the poor were hanged because they had nothing. Neither strength could prevail to make resistance nor weakness move pity to refrain their horrible cruelty.

Gascoigne went out into the streets and saw the carnage for himself. He talked to "sundry" Spanish soldiers, getting details of how they'd attacked Antwerp and asking them to justify their burning of the Town Hall and the city's records. They told him it was the place where "evil policies" were agreed.

By the castle the defensive trenches of William's forces were piled high with corpses. In the new town to the east were "huge numbers" of dead:

> a man might behold as many sundry shapes and forms of man's motion at time of death as ever *Mighel Angelo* did portray in his tables of Doomsday. I list not to reckon the infinite numbers of poor Almains [German mercenaries fighting for the Dutch], who lay burned in their armour, some the entrails scorched out & all the rest of the body free, some their head and shoulders burnt off, so that you might look down into the bulk & breast and there taken an anatomy of the secrets of nature. Some standing upon their waist, being burnt off by the thighs & some no more but the very top of the brain taken off with fire, whiles the rest of the body did abide unspeakable torments. I set not down the ugly & filthy polluting of every street with the gore and carcases of men and horses, neither do I complain that the one lacked burial

and the other flaying, until the air (corrupted with their carrion) infected all that yet remained alive in the town.

The Spanish demanded 500 crowns from an English merchant who was the employee of a rich businessman. He managed to sell his master's goods for 300 crowns, so the Spaniards hanged him until he was half-dead, then cut him down. The weeping merchant promised on bended knees to get the other 200 crowns. When he was unable to do so he was executed. A total of four English merchants who were lodging elsewhere in the city were killed and many others "they most cruelly & dangerously hurt". Some paid a ransom as many as three times to have their goods spared – only to have them then plundered.

Even though the English House had diplomatic immunity "under safe conduct, protection and Placard of their King" (i.e. Philip II of Spain), it was not spared. Spanish troops threatened to burn it down if the gates and doors were not unbolted and their entry permitted. Having been admitted, the troops then demanded a ransom of 12,000 crowns from the governor, Thomas Heton. When he replied that the House held less than 4,000 crowns they menaced him with their swords and daggers, threatening death. At this point Gascoigne intervened and saved the day:

> I will not boast of any help afforded by me in that distress, but I thank the Lord God, who made me an instrument to appease their devilish furies. And I think that the governor and all the company will confess that I used mine uttermost skill and aid for the safeguard of their lives, as well as mine own.

But although Gascoigne's fluency in languages and experience of Spanish soldiery evidently calmed an explosive situation, he was not able to prevent the demand for a ransom:

> But in the end, all eloquence notwithstanding, the governor being a comely aged man and a person whose hoary hairs might move pity and procure reverence in any good mind (especially the uprightness of his dealing considered), they enforced him with great danger to bring forth all the money, plate and jewels which was in the house & to prepare the remnant of twelve thousand crowns at such days and times as they pleased to appoint.

Others fared much worse than this. For days afterwards, anyone identified as a Walloon (i.e. a Dutch soldier from the French-speaking south) was killed on the spot. On Sunday 11 November, Gascoigne himself witnessed three people killed in the street "because they were pointed to be Walloons". In fact one was quickly identified as a local civilian, "a poor artificer" who had never handled weapons. Gascoigne wrote that he himself "did often escape very narrowly because I was taken for a Walloon".

There were also sexual assaults on the women of Antwerp:

> Neither can I refrain to tell their shameful rapes & outrageous forces presented unto sundry honest dames & virgins. It is a thing too horrible to rehearse that the father and mother were forced to fetch their young daughter out of a cloister (who had thither fled as unto sanctuary, to keep her body undefiled) & to bestow her in bed between two Spaniards, to work their wicked and detestable will with her.

Gascoigne estimated that 5,000 of the dead were massacred because they were unable to pay the ransom required by their captors.

He was able to get out of Antwerp on Monday 12 November, carrying with him letters, including one from Thomas Heton. He left behind him a city in ruins. The destruction included "the wilful burning and destroying of the stately townhouse & all the monuments and records of the city".

> Within three days, Antwerp, which was one of the richest towns in Europe, had now no money nor treasure to be found therein, but only in the hands of murderers and strumpets. For every *Dom Diego* must walk jetting up & down the streets with his harlot by him in her chain and bracelets of gold. And the notable Bourse, which was wont to be a safe assembly for merchants and men of all honest trades, had now none other merchandise therein but as many dicing tables as might be placed round about it all the day long.

On 12 November Gascoigne left Antwerp and returned to London "to solicit their rueful causes" and "to deliver the same unto her Majesty and council in such sort as I beheld it there".

On Wednesday 21 November 1576, Francis Walsingham noted in his journal: "Mr Gascoigne came out of the Low Countries with letters."[9] Gascoigne was duly rewarded for his work as a messenger:

> Paid upon a warrant signed by Mr Secretaire Walsingham dated at Hampton Court xxi November 1576 to George Gascoigne gent for bringing of L[etter]'es in post for her Ma[jes]ties affaires frome Andwarpe to Hampton Courte. XX[10]

His reward – £20 – was evidently the going rate for intelligence/courier work in the Netherlands. It was sufficient to sustain a gentleman for about four months.[11]

One of the letters he brought with him, from Thomas Heton, referred Walsingham to the poet's account of what had happened at Antwerp:

The discourse of these tragedies we omit, and refer the same to be reported to your lordships by this bearer, Master George Gaston [*sic*], whose humanity in this time of trouble we, for our parts, have experimented.[12] [experienced]

Gascoigne's anonymous description of events in Antwerp is identified as having been "Written the 25 day of November 1576 by a true English man, who was present at this piteous massacre." *The Spoyle of Antwerpe* was presumably an expanded version of his report to Walsingham, with the added drama of his personal experiences in the city. It was published by Richard Jones, who'd done Nicholas Breton's first book, the *Discourse of a Difcouerie for a new Paffage to Catai* and *A delicate Diet, for daintiemouthde Droonkardes*. Gascoigne, perhaps still smarting from the seizure of the *Posies*, was keen to emphasize that the publication was, as it says on the title page, *seene and allowed*. Its topicality was stressed by the publication date on the title page: "Nouem. 1576."

Today it is the rarest of any of Gascoigne's published works, with only two copies known to exist, one held in the strong room in the vaults of the British Library, the other at the Bodleian. Both are incomplete, since they lack the plan of Antwerp which Gascoigne included.[13] Its rarity probably testifies both to its popularity – read and re-read until it fell apart – and to the low regard given to pamphlets. It is the tiniest of all Gascoigne first editions, about the size of a modern reporter's notebook. *The Spoyle of Antwerpe* was the Tudor equivalent of a cheap paperback, rushed out to cash in on a burning topical issue.

Gascoigne was careful to adopt the pose of impartial reporter. Politics was religion and there was nothing more potentially explosive than to stray into that dangerous area where the old and new faiths clashed. He nervously acknowledged that some people (i.e. Catholics) might think that Antwerp got what it deserved and that "the wickedness used in the said town, do seem unto the well disposed reader, a sufficient cause of God's so just a scourge and plague". But all the same "the fury of the vanquishers do also seem more barbarous and cruel then may become a good Christian conqueror". Gascoigne was anxious to stress that he was simply an impartial observer, attempting to draw a worthy conclusion from the dreadful spectacle he'd witnessed:

> let these my few words become a forewarning on both hands: and let them stand as a lantern of light between two perilous rocks: that both amending the one and detesting the other, we may gather fire out of the flint and honey out of the thistle. To that end, all stories and chronicles are written: and to that end I presume to publish this pamphlet: protesting that neither malice to the one side, nor partial affection to the other, shall make my pen to swerve any jot from truth of that which I will set down & saw executed... mine only intent is to set down a plain truth...

Gascoigne's posture as a sturdy man of the middle ground was undoubtedly influenced by the confiscation of his *Posies* just three months earlier. He was anxious not to upset anyone, whether Catholic or Protestant. His anonymity raised another shield against attack. Besides, a racy eye-witness account of an atrocity did not quite fit in with his new image as a devout, sombre, penitent writer. That supplied another reason to conceal his authorship.

That *The Spoyle of Antwerpe* gives a reasonably objective account of what Gascoigne himself witnessed is entirely plausible. But the framework of explanation and analysis which he fitted around it is much more open to question. Gascoigne plucked at his readers' heartstrings with a sorrowful account of the poor, suffering Dutch: "their accusations without cause, and condemnations without proof, might enable a dumb stone to talk of their troubles, and fetch brinish tears out of the most craggy rock". Here he was surely thinking not just of the Dutch but also of himself.

Gascoigne the soldier marvelled that a mere 5,000 Spanish troops and mercenaries had managed to take a city with trenches and barricades "of such height as seemed invincible", defended by some 15-16,000 well armed fighting men. Not only that, but the speed of the victory over Antwerp and its consequences were breathtaking: "it was charged, entered and won in three hours. And before six hours passed over, every house therein sacked or ransomed at the uttermost value."

Gascoigne was torn between thinking that the collapse of Antwerp was a punishment from God and his admiration for the professionalism of the Spanish soldiery in overwhelming the city and its defences: "it was the very ordinance of God for a just plague and a scourge unto the town, for otherwise it passeth all men's capacity to conceive how it should be possible. And yet the disorder and lack of foresight in the Walloons did great help to augment the Spanish glory and boast."

In fact the basic problem was that the defenders lacked an effective and co-ordinated command. The citizens of Antwerp stood by their doors and many died there fighting bravely while the Walloons and high Dutchmen fled. The defenders were brave but lacked direction. "For those which came to supply & relieve the trenches came straggling and loose". Some staggered out "from drinking and carousing, who would scarcely believe that any conflict was begun". Essentially, the city's defences were complacent and disorganised. Gascoigne included a plan to illustrate the military situation but this has since vanished from the two surviving copies of the pamphlet.

In the aftermath of the massacre, Elizabeth held an emergency meeting of the Privy Council. English subjects were advised to remove their goods from the city. The Spanish agent in London, Antonio de Guaras, was later arrested, and wrote "She and her Council desire to expel the Spaniards from Flanders, more than the Flemings themselves." Gascoigne's prose, which Charles Nicholl has described as "a crackling piece of front-line journalism",[14] may well have had a powerful impact on the thinking of the Privy Council.

The "Spanish fury" was a catastrophe which ended Antwerp's commercial supremacy. The city's shattered economy was further weakened by mass emigration. Skilled workers went north. The following year Philip's soldiers were ejected from the city but it was too late to reverse the city's slow, steady decline.

The Grief of Joy

Gascoigne's last known work is a collection of four elegies (or "songs") collectively entitled *The Grief of Joy*. It was dedicated to Elizabeth I and given to her in manuscript as a New Year's Day present on 1 January 1577. The manuscript (38 folios followed by 38 blank folios) is a presentation copy.[15] The word "Queene" is written throughout in gilt, as is "Elizabeth", "peereles Queene" and "sweete Queene". It is conventionally assumed to have been in Gascoigne's hand but if he was the transcriber he was unusually careless, making around a dozen errors, mostly small but some glaring. In the second line of stanza seven of the First Song the word "little" has been clumsily inserted as a late correction. The sixth and seventh lines of the first stanza of the Third Song, in Latin, garble a comment about Hercules made in Plato's *Phaedo* (although Gascoigne's source was probably Erasmus's *Adagia*).

This long poem remained unpublished for almost three-hundred years, finally appearing in William Hazlitt's *Complete Poems of George Gascoigne* (1869-70). Sadly, it is no late masterpiece. Its motive was to seek Elizabeth's patronage. Gascoigne took his inspiration from Petrarch (not least in the title's oxymoron). He said that just as Petrarch had recounted "the uncerteine Joyes of men in severall dialogues" in *De remediis utriusque fortunae* [Remedies against both types of fortune] so he had "distributed the same into sundrie songes" in these elegies. But Gascoigne did not use the technique of a dialogue. In fact he took little from that work of Petrarch's, apart from some ideas for themes.[16]

Gascoigne explained to Elizabeth that he wanted her to witness how he passed "the *Interims* and vacant hours of those days which I spent this summer in your service". That description is slightly puzzling, as the only firm evidence we have of the poet's official status as an English intelligence agent and messenger locates him abroad in the period September-November 1576. On 10 August Gascoigne was in London, but perhaps he went off to Paris shortly afterwards. The poem ends abruptly, hinting that it was interrupted by the arrival of Spanish troops. This implies that it was finished at Antwerp in November. Elizabeth was plainly being reminded of his recent service abroad.

Although its form is superficially different, *The Grief of Joy* in many ways resembles *The Steel Glass*. It is prefaced by a sycophantic dedication, pitched at his hoped-for patron's sensibilities. Aware of the Queen's love of blood sports, Gascoigne uses hunting metaphors to make the point that this is a moral work:

> Yea as hunters do soonest kill their chase which (standing on a clear wind) can find the same at feed, even so those dangers do soonest entrap us, which lurk in the fair pretence of our fading pleasure, and lie closely wrapped up in the mantle of our posting felicities [rapidly passing joys]

Gascoigne skittishly postures as Petrarch to Elizabeth's Laura. (At this date they were both in their forties.) She is "the comeliest Queen that ever was", she is "peerless," she has "heavenly eyes" – and so on, *ad nauseam*. From time to time he addresses her as the auditor of his monologue. And just as the pen and ink drawing accompanying "The Tale of Hemetes the Heremyte" fantasized about the pair of them alone together, so, too, does *The Grief of Joy*. Gascoigne envisaged a scene in which

> she hath laid her mighty mace aside
> And strokes my head and biddeth God me guide.[17]

In fact, though Gascoigne hoped that "My gracious Queen (I trust) will not refuse, / To weigh my words", we do not know if she ever read this gift. Quite probably she did but if so what she felt about it is unknown. Likewise, how far Gascoigne's intimations of a flirtatious friendship between them are accurate or are merely fantasy and projection is also a mystery. The extent to which Elizabeth registered Gascoigne's presence among the crowd of sycophants at court and how much of his work she knew is equally an enigma. But whatever element of truth there may have been in Gascoigne's poem some of it was plainly imaginary. We can be confident Elizabeth never ran her hands through the poet's hair or whispered uplifting advice in his ear.

Like *The Steel Glass*, Gascoigne's last poem is full of generalisations and abstractions. The first section, 43 stanzas on "The griefs or discommodities of lusty youth" is about passing time and the transience of youth and contains such banal nuggets of wisdom as:

> All is not gold, which glistereth fair and bright,
> Nor all things good, which fairest seem in sight.

The 68 stanzas of "The vanities of Beauty" are packed with flattery of the ladies of the court, including Elizabeth's personal attendants. It amounts to a tired inventory of names and stale compliments ("Russell and Audley, Sheffield, Shandose, Sands, / All Barons' wives, of beauty rare and bright"). It also includes some excruciating wordplay: Mary Hopton, "poor wench, Hopt on:

though not in haste".[18]

In the middle of this list appears a crowd of angry women. These are Gascoigne's lovers, come to rail at his faithlessness. At their head is Ferenda Natura, who addresses him as Bartholmew and weeps at his faithlessness. Perplexingly, Ferenda is an "oft Reviving Death" (playfully insinuating an erection), a "right and last Relief" (which sounds like an orgasm), a "Hollow tree" (a vagina), a "banishment to Bath" (which might be the pox) but also "My Livia, my love, and my delight". Her polymorphous perversity – or at any rate diversity – is followed by a Dutch woman, Petronella de Alquemade (a joke pseudonym, perhaps, for the woman at The Hague). Seven other foreign "Dames of price" are named, though that description is highly ambiguous and could be interpreted as meaning prostitutes. The statement that "coũtrie comes / nay Coũtries mo then one" is dangerously close to blatant punning on "cunt".[19] The poem then moves on to safer territory, reflecting on time's inevitable annihilation of beauty. But Gascoigne hastily makes it clear that he is not condemning beauty. On the contrary,

> Dame Beauty dressed with garments made of grace
> Deserves such fame as Time cannot deface.[20]

The third section, "The faults of force and strength", consists of 38 stanzas. Having dealt with womankind in the previous section, Gascoigne now turns his attention to men, the dangers of physical strength and time's weakening effect, "To prove how frail the fruits of forces be".[21] This is the section which contains the poet's enigmatic reference to having committed a single "heady deed" in his younger days, associated with physical strength, which he now bitterly regrets and wishes he "had been weak".[22]

In a final section of 46 stanzas Gascoigne turns his attention to "The vanities of activities", meaning leisure activities. In many ways this is the finest part of *The Grief of Joy*, as the poet looks nostalgically back over his heady, younger days and his love of song, music and dancing. But as in *The Steel Glass*, ponderous moralizing spoils the poem as Gascoigne solemnly wags his finger at the naughtiness of such indulgence. Dancing, he says, is just a cover

> for Sin,
> To tempt the best, that ever yet hath been
> A cleanly cloak to cover (often times)
> The sly pretence of many subtle crimes.[23]

He moves on to show the vanity of gambling, wrestling and riding. But Gascoigne's wooden moralizing is in stark contrast to the liveliness of the scenes of everyday Tudor life:

> To see someone sit scratching at his head
> (Yea tear his beard sometimes) when he hath lost,
> Another chafing till his cheeks be red,
> And both wax warm to countervail their cost,
> To see the cards and dice about house tossed
> Till anger vex both father, kin, and brother:
> Is it not madness? Sure it is none other.[24]

The vanity of horse-riding perhaps brought Gascoigne up against the recognition that this was one of Elizabeth's favourite occupations. As he brashly remarks, "riding is of nobles much desired, / And what can be brought in against the same?"[25]

The poet starts to contemplate the danger (rather than the vanity) of riding a horse, before breaking off in mid-line:

> For sett asyde, the danger of a fall,
> (Which so maye chance, that (woulde wee ride or no,)
> Agaynst owre wylles, at last wee must or shall,
> When with a broken legg wee cannot goe)
> I can rehearce yet many myschieves mo,
> And sundry greeves, that &c. &c.
>
> *Left unperfect for feare of Horfmen/*

These are Gascoigne's final lines. The implication is that they were written in Antwerp at the very moment that Spanish horsemen came clattering down the street outside the English House. This is unlikely to have been true. It is just a little too neat that lines about horse-riding and danger should have been dramatically interrupted in such a thematically apt manner. In any case, Gascoigne had plenty of time to finish the poem before he delivered it over one month later. The urgency of the ending might be more convincing if it was an original manuscript, not an elegant transcription in italic hand.

It is far more likely that Gascoigne just grew bored with the poem. Creative fatigue set in and he had no real drive to go on listing the vices of the age, describing the inevitability of passing time and continuing with the kind of hackneyed material found in *The Grief of Joy*.[26] Much better to pack the whole thing in on a dramatic note that reminded the Queen of his service to the state. The poem ends with another pitch for patronage and employment. Its very last words are Gascoigne's motto "Tam Marti quàm Mercurio". George Gascoigne remained eager to benefit his Queen and country – and not least himself.

29: A Burial at Stamford

Gascoigne once imagined his own death. It was a romantic, significant event.

> My latest leave of thee I taken have:
> And unknown coasts which I must seek with care
> Do well divine that there shall be my grave:
> There shall my death make many for to moan,
> Scarce known to them, well known to thee alone.
>
> This boon of thee (as last request) I crave,
> When true report shall sound my death with fame:
> Vouchsafe yet then to go unto my grave,
> And there first write my birth and then my name:
> And how my life was shortened many years,
> By women's wiles as to the world appears.[1]

But this was a fantasy. When death at last came, it was nothing like that. Those lines are the extravagant poses of a young man. George Gascoigne's grave was to be located in an English churchyard in the provinces, not abroad. But there was no gravestone and no inscription. And though troubles piled up for Gascoigne in his later years, "women's wiles" were the least of his worries.

The year 1577 began well for Gascoigne. His high spirits are captured in an ebullient letter which he sent to Sir Nicholas Bacon, dated 1 January 1577.[2] It is the only personal letter of Gascoigne's known to exist, and one of only three letters in his hand to have survived. Its content coincided with the climax to *The Grief of Joy* in so far as it indicates horses and riding were on Gascoigne's mind. He represents himself as a frisky colt which has at last accepted "the bridle of discretion" and hopes "to be well placed in a prince's stable". The letter, in short, is another attempt to ingratiate himself with an influential figure and to stress his moral reformation.

What Gascoigne wanted, as he bluntly put it, was sustenance from "Her Majesty's storehouse". Yet again he sought patronage and money, and he hints that his situation is getting desperate: "without some speedy provision of good provender I shall never be able to endure a long journey". The metaphors of the wild and the tamed horse are used to put a witty gloss on what is really a begging letter. Gascoigne evidently used New Year's Day as an excuse to shower similar letters on others at court. Quite possibly they were more or less identical.

> My verie favourable good Lorde, beinge latelye received into Her Majesties service (wherein I hope to recover my decayede estate) I devisede

to presente all my lordes and good frendes in Cowrte with certayne *Emblems* for their Newyeres gyftes, an exercyes (as I judge) neyther unplsante nor unprofitable. Att leaste my meaninge is therby to showe prooffe that my penn cann aswell be paynfull in morall *poetrie* as itt hathe bene hitherto over curious in expressinge of lighte affections.

And my resolutione beinge suche, I coulde not chuse but proffer your Lordship the lyke presennte. An objecte not altogether corespondente to the gravite of your judgmente, and yet voyde of any vanitie which may justlie offende your honourable disposicion, and in full hope thereof, I have put in hazarde to sende you the same, beseachinge your Lordship thus to understande. I kept my koltish trickes muche longer then was eyther for my credytte, or for my proffytte. I friskede, I flange, I refused the brydell of discretione, and ran still at lardge in the fenns of sondrye follyes. At laste it hath pleasede God to make reasone my ryder, and he havinge firste corectede me, I begynne to beare the bridle pretelye well, and hope so to goe forwardes as I may deserve inthende to be well placed in a princes stable.

But (my good Lorde) my colltyshe and jadishe trickes have longe sythens broughte me so owte of fleashe, as withowte some spedye provysione of good provender I shall never be able to endure a longe jorneye, and therefore am enforcede to neye and braye unto your good Lordship and all other which have the keye of Her Majesties storehowse, beseachinge righte humblie that you will voutchsaffe to reamember me with some extreaordynarye allowaunce when it fallethe. God preserve your Lordship to the comoon proffytte & my perticuler comforte this firste of January 1577 and ever.

Your Lordships redye at commaunde G. le Gascoigne.[3]

The letter and the accompanying "emblem" (something like a home-made New Year's Day greetings card) were kept among the family papers of the Bacon family. Of the others sent to Gascoigne's "Lords and good friends" at Court, none is known to have survived. It has been suggested that likely recipients could have been Walsingham, Burghley, the Earl of Leicester, the Earl of Bedford, Lord Grey of Wilton, the Earl of Warwick and probably several others.[4]

Sir Nicholas's emblem is headed by an original Latin tag – *Aliquando tamen proficit qui sero sapit* ("A man who becomes wise, even though he is late in doing so, sometimes gains thereby"). The drawing shows on the left a groom with a raised stick holding what is presumably intended to be an unbroken colt which wears a simple bridle. On the right the colt is saddled and ready for service and is being ridden by a gentleman with a flat-topped riding cap. The picture repeats the message of Gascoigne's accompanying letter, and is itself reiterated by a six line poem beneath it:

Before the sturdye colte will byde the bytt,
he beares oftymes the broont of many blowes
But when at laste he letts his ryder sytt
he learnes to rayne and forwarde then he goes.
Some men be coltes: they friske & flynge at firste
yet onse well broke suche men prove not the worste.

The image in fact is a little at variance with Gascoigne's interpretation; the unbroken colt looks rather docile. Whether the poet's appeal to Bacon and other powerful figures at Court for "speedy provision of good provender" was successful or not is unknown.

*

Gascoigne published nothing during 1577, which is strange for a writer who had become quite prolific, who was well connected, and who had evidently no difficulty in composing at speed when required. It is possible that he had irritated the Queen, who then declined to grant her consent to publication of a new work. In *The Grief of Joy*, Gascoigne had promised Elizabeth that "withowt confirmation of your favourable acceptauns" he would "never presume to publishe any thing here after" – an astonishing and highly risky pledge. Worse, he coolly informed his prickly and hypersensitive sovereign that "Princes mindes (somtymes) mistake ye right". The idea that even a Queen can sometimes be wrong about what is right is unlikely to brought anything other than a scowl of displeasure to her face.[5]

When the winter was over, Gascoigne once again set out on his travels but if it was on state service is an open question. Without royal patronage Gascoigne gloomily forecast that he would "never be able to endure a longe jorneye". That long journey was about to come to a sudden end much sooner than he could possibly have anticipated when he sent his greetings to the Lord Keeper of the Great Seal.

Stamford

One day in 1577, perhaps on a summer's day in late June or early July, George Gascoigne rode into Stamford, in the county of Lincolnshire. The route he followed hasn't changed in centuries. Now known as the Old Great North Road, it still follows a long, straight line, gently descending towards the valley of the Welland. On the right hand side, as it approaches the town from the south, the road is bordered by a long wall. This marks the edge of a large country estate. Today, as in the sixteenth century, this is the western perimeter of Burghley Park. Beyond the wall and trees, a mile to the east, lies Burghley House, the vast mansion built to demonstrate the wealth and importance of the town's most famous resident, Lord Burghley. In 1577 they were finishing the west wing.

Entering Stamford, the road suddenly becomes much steeper, dropping down to a stone bridge over the River Welland. This part of the town, lying to the south of the river, is known as Stamford Baron. In 1577 both sides of this steep hill were heavily built. This was a sign of Stamford's importance on the country's most important north-south route, which later became known as the Great North Road. It is now more mundanely identified as the A1 and Stamford has long since been by-passed.

Its key location on England's main route between London and the north would have made Stamford in the sixteenth century seem a busy, prosperous, bustling place. In fact it was a market town in decline. In the past it had been important for pottery, wool, cloth, and as a centre of quarried stone. Stamford (from "Stane-ford" or "the stone-paved ford") owed its supremacy in the middle ages to its location between two important regions of wool production and its river. The River Welland was navigable to the sea and wool merchants took their produce to the great market at Calais. Economic affluence gave Stamford numerous churches, religious communities and schools. But by 1577 the wool trade was long in decline. It was still a town of medieval walls and gateways. But the river was silted up, the population remained static and the number of parishes was reduced to six.

Today Stamford is an unspoiled, undeveloped town of handsome Georgian buildings, used as a backdrop for an acclaimed BBC TV adaptation of *Middlemarch*. Its oldest buildings, including five medieval churches, were built from limestone quarried at nearby Barnack. One of these, St Martin's, is the parish church of Stamford Baron. As Gascoigne rode past in 1577 work was continuing on Lord Burghley's effigy in what is now the Burghley Chapel on the north of the chancel. Death was something affluent Christian gentlemen gave considerable attention to. Convinced of immortality in the next world, they were also keen to ensure it in the one they left behind. Burghley's ornately carved and painted effigy shows him in armour, his head resting on a pillow of gold brocade. He lies on his marble and alabaster tomb, wearing the scarlet mantle of the Garter. His right hand grasps his wand of office and a lion is curled at his feet. This magnificent effigy is believed to be the work of the sculptor Cornelius Cure and has strong stylistic resemblances to his monument to Mary Queen of Scots in Westminster Abbey.

Burghley's material interest in his last resting place was not a concern shared by George Gascoigne. As he ambled past the Church of St Martin, George Gascoigne was probably unaware that he was entering the town where he would shortly die. In fact as he descended the hill towards the river he was now in sight of the place where he would be buried.

The big puzzle is: why was Gascoigne in Stamford? What was he doing in a town with which he apparently had no connection whatsoever?

There are at least four reasons why Gascoigne might have travelled to Stamford. The first is to do with property. His stepson Nicholas had been left property by his father at Burgh le Marsh. This is located some 55 miles northeast of Stamford. In theory, Gascoigne might have been on his way there. But this seems the least likely of the various possibilities.

Another possibility is that Gascoigne was there to see Lord Burghley. Although Burghley's business was largely transacted at court and at meetings of the Privy Council, he did sometimes conduct business at Burghley House. In the summer of the following year Richard Topclyffe, the Queen's torturer (and a figure who rarely appears in popular accounts of her reign), accompanied the royal progress through Suffolk and Norfolk, then went on to Burghley House. Since Gascoigne had worked directly for Burghley the previous year it is plausible that he went to Stamford in connection with another mission of state. But there is no documentary evidence of this. In any case in early June Burghley was with the court at Greenwich, a much closer place for Gascoigne to go to from Walthamstow.

The third reason is connected with the fact that Gascoigne was not alone at Stamford. He was with a much younger man, George Whetstone. Today, Whetstone is most often remembered in connection with *Measure for Measure*. In the year following Gascoigne's death, Whetstone published *The Right Excellent and famous Historye of Promos and Cassandra: Devided into two Comicall Discourses*, a play which was never performed but which Shakespeare borrowed extensively from for his own play. Many editions of *Measure for Measure* reprint substantial extracts from Whetstone's play to show the striking similarities of character and situation.

Young would-be writers sometimes try to connect with celebrity authors they admire. Charlotte Brontë wrote to the poet laureate Robert Southey, sending him a sample of her work. She received a notoriously cold, patronising and sexist response. More successful was the young Samuel Beckett, who in his early twenties became part of the James Joyce set and was soon helping with research for *Finnegans Wake*. George Whetstone chose to attach himself to a man whose name bore a faint resemblance to his own and who was then the most prominent and notorious writer in Tudor England. Whetstone was with Gascoigne at Stamford that year and we must be grateful that he was, for he left the only account of the poet's death there. It is always possible that Gascoigne had arranged to meet him there but it seems more likely that the two travelled up from London together. As George Gascoigne descended the hill into Stamford, we can be fairly sure that at his side rode his young admirer, Whetstone.

In the summer of 1577 George Whetstone was 27 years old. If George Gascoigne was the man who nearly went down in history as the man who caused Elizabeth I to break her neck, George Whetstone was the son of the man who some historians believe saved her life. Robert Whetstone was the foreman of the jury which in April 1554 found Sir Nicholas Throckmorton not guilty of treason. It was the reaction of the London crowd, shouting for joy and throwing their caps in the air, that persuaded the Privy Council it would be most unwise to behead the Princess Elizabeth, who was then imprisoned in the Tower of London. Queen Mary was reported to be so upset at the jury's verdict and the crowd's reaction that she was ill for three days afterwards.

Twenty-three years later, what was one of Robert Whetstone's sons doing in Stamford with the poet George Gascoigne? George Whetstone was christened on 27 July 1550 at St Lawrence in the Old Jewry, not far from the Guildhall. His father, Robert Whetstone, was a rich haberdasher. Robert Whetstone died at Wells in Somerset when his son George was just seven years old. His widow subsequently married Robert Browne.

In Whetstone's elegy for Gascoigne, the dying poet addresses his friend and says that he "long my life did know... Yea *Whetston* thou hast knowen my hidden hart".[6] But how long was that? Whetstone's biographer is sceptical that the friendship was either deep or of long duration. He notes that the documentary evidence indicates "an acquaintance extending only over some two years".[7]

It may have been much longer. As a child, George Whetstone lived close to Gascoigne in the parish of St Giles without Cripplegate. The subsidy roll of 1562-3 lists both George Gascoigne and "Mr Browne which maryed Whetstons wife". George Whetstone had four brothers, four sisters and one step-brother (five of whom had died by 1572). The brother closest to George was Barnard, born in 1547. But although in theory George Whetstone might have known Gascoigne as a child, or later through his brother Robert, who was admitted to Gray's Inn in 1552, by far the likeliest possibility is that he met the poet through Barnard.

At his father's death, Barnard inherited the manor of Woodford in Essex. This was just a short distance from Thorpe Hall, Gascoigne's Walthamstow residence. Today, just as "Walthamstow" merges the five separate hamlets of Gascoigne's time, "Woodford" is the collective name for Woodford Wells, Woodford Green and South Woodford. In 1572 there were riots when Barnard Whetstone attempted to fence in part of the forest. It is more than probable that Barnard Whetstone and George Gascoigne knew each other as neighbours, and that George Whetstone became acquainted with the writer when he was visiting Woodford. When Whetstone wrote of "*Gascoignes* Garden plot, a passing pleasant soil",[8] he was alluding to the flowers, herbs and weeds of the *Posies*, but he may also have been signalling his personal acquaintanceship with the agreeable and stylishly laid out grounds of Thorpe Hall.

George Whetstone's relationship with Gascoigne is easy enough to identify. He was an adoring young fan. Whetstone was evidently a law student at

Furnivall's Inn, one of the Inns of Chancery in Holborn. But he seems to have abandoned his studies and did not go on to any of the Inns of Court. As a naïve young student who had inherited land and property in London worth one hundred marks a year, Whetstone had fallen into the hands of a dishonest scrivener. This man, George Craycoll, together with Lawrence Barton, persuaded Whetstone to lease his property to Richard Harker. The men then tricked Whetstone into signing a bogus indenture and leased the property to a fourth conspirator, George Butler, who assigned it to Roger Wetherell of Lincoln's Inn.

In return for being cheated out of a valuable inheritance Whetstone found himself in possession of just £30 in cash. Worse, if he died, the conspirators stood to inherit the property. They therefore paid people to pick fights with Whetstone, so that "for A certeyne space [he] Coulde not gooe nor Rest in quiet, but contynually was Assaulted, and often tymes by mere straungers, In which Assaultys he was verie sore wounded and hurte". His right hand was maimed in one of these attacks. Whetstone went to Star Chamber in an attempt to get his property back.[9] Whether or not he succeeded is unclear. The matter seems to have dragged on, and in *A Touchstone for the Time* (1584) he complained of "three yeares & more of costly sute" and sought release from "the toile of Law".

In his first book, *The Rocke of Regard* (1576), Whetstone wrote a fictionalised account of the affair, which probably occurred in 1574. It tells the story of "Paulus Plasmos" (Whetstone), who falls into debt after squandering his money on a faithless woman, Laymos. Plasmos is then tricked out of his inheritance by Liros (Barton), Frenos (Craycoll), Caphos (Harker) and Pimos (Wetherell). When Plasmos sues them, their defence is that he is "an unthrift, a quarreler, a proude and prodigall person". But God's justice "worthily cut off" Plasmos's enemies. Some became "sterke beggers", others did "dye soudenly, and miserably". (Richard Harker died in 1575 and Roger Wetherell was buried on 26 June 1576.) Plasmos repented that "the instruments of his mishap" had been "Wanton Comedies, Tragedies, and discourses".

It was probably around this time that Whetstone encountered George Gascoigne, controversial writer and supposed penitent. It was the perfect psychological moment for Whetstone, who evidently wanted to be a writer, to attach himself to an admired older man who also felt he'd been cheated out of his inheritance and regarded himself as being victimized by rumour-mongers and slanderers. In fact George Whetstone was just the kind of wannabe that *Certayne notes of Instruction concerning the making of verse or ryme in English* had been written for. And fans have their uses. The ninth commendatory poem to *The Posies of George Gascoigne Esquire* is entitled "G.W. In prayse of Gascoigne, and his Posies".[10] There can be little question that its author was George Whetstone and, as with Ralegh's commendatory poem for *The Steel Glass*, it is generally accepted as his first publication.

It is clear that Gascoigne himself shaped the contents of Whetstone's poem. It had an important propaganda function. Firstly, it echoes Gascoigne's bogus claim that he had purged the volume of offensive material ("Now weeds of little worth are culled from out the rest, / Which he with double pain did work to glean the bad from best"). Secondly, it insists on the moral worth and instructive value of poems about bad behaviour ("In every gallant flower, he setteth forth to show, / Of *Venus* thralls, the hap, the harm, the want, the weal, the woe.") Thirdly, it praises "his stately style in prose" (i.e. the bowdlerized *Adventures of Master F.J.*). Finally, Whetstone salutes his achievements as a soldier in the Low Countries and dismisses the rumours about the poet's treachery:

Wherewith to *Mars* his might, his lusty limbs are knit,
(A sight most rare) that *Hector*'s mind should match with *Pallas* wit.
By proof of late appeared (how so reports here ran)
That he in field was foremost still, in spoil the hindmost man.
No backward blasts could bruise the valour of his thought,
Although sly hap forestood his hope in that he credit sought.

George Whetstone was twenty-four or twenty-five when he penned these rather wooden lines. His career as a writer was to prove an undistinguished one, prematurely terminated by his violent death. Ironically, in later centuries his most reprinted work turned out to be his poem about Gascoigne's death at Stamford.

Friendship with Gascoigne bought an entrée into his world and connections. Nicholas Bowyer, who wrote one of the commendatory poems for *The Steel Glass*, obligingly repeated the favour for Whetstone and praised *The Rocke of Regard* (1576). The "T. Ch." who wrote the eighth commendatory poem "*In prayse of Gascoignes Poesies*" is generally agreed to be the minor writer Thomas Churchyard, and it seems highly likely he is also the "T.C." who supplied an introduction to Whetstone's *Censure of a Loyall Subject*. Thomas C. Izard conjectured that the "I.B." who wrote "In commendation of Gascoigne's *Posies*" might be the "Ioannes Botrevicus" who supplied Latin verse in praise of both Whetstone's *Heptameron of Civill Discourses* and *Mirour for Magestrates of Cyties*.[11] Whetstone may have enjoyed an introduction to Francis, Earl of Bedford. At any rate, he put in a bid for patronage from the family with a solemn elegy on the Earl's death. Whetstone also dedicated a poem in *The Rocke of Regarde* "To "Maistresse M[ary] H[opton] now Brydges", whom Gascoigne had praised in *The Grief of Joy* and to whose father he had dedicated *The Glass of Government*. Izard suggested that the "R.B." who contributed a prefatory verse for Whetstone's *English Myrror* might have been Gascoigne's stepson, Richard Breton, brother of Nicholas.[12]

Whetstone's second publication, *The Rocke of Regard*, appeared in 1576. It was evidently published when Gascoigne was abroad, for all the dedications are dated 15 October 1576, "from my lodging in Holborne". *The Rocke of Regard* is a miscellany of verse and prose, and in both form and content the influence of Gascoigne and his *Posies* is everywhere. Whetstone divided the book into four parts: "The Castle of Delight", "The Garden of Unthriftiness", "The Arbour of Virtue", and "The Orchard of Repentance". These classifications, however, are almost as meaningless as the distinction between flowers, herbs and weeds in Gascoigne's book. The book is prefaced, as was Gascoigne's *Posies*, by an address "To all the young Gentleman of England". In a second preface Whetstone solemnly suggests that his book should be a warning to the youth of the day:

> and thinke that my beginning with delight, running on in unthriftines, resting in vertue, and ending with repentaunce, is no other than a figure of the lustie yonkers adventures; who beginneth to seeke preferment with delightful braverie, and being entred into the hie way of unthriftiness, findeth his journey so pleasaunt that, ere he is a ware, he posteth his poore purse out of hart with prodigality: so that (unlesse he meane to tyre him to death) he must rest both his purse and raunging fancies, with some virtuous and stayed determination of life; and yet, when all is done, late repenatunce must recover his, and his purses surfet.[13]

This posture of world-weary wisdom might have been more convincing had its author not been in his mid-twenties. In fact Whetstone is not really talking about himself but about George Gascoigne. The influence of the older author permeated every aspect of his book, even down to the repeated use of a Latin posy (*Formae nulla fides* – "There is no confidence in beauty").

Essentially *The Rocke of Regard* is a miscellaneous bundle of bits and pieces, dense with Gascoigne's presence. The verse titles are reminiscent of the *Posies* and so too are lines like "And so escape the trains of trustless men". The "dolerous discourse" of Dom Diego and "Dom Diego His Triumphe" were an attempt to imitate "Don Bartholmew of Bathe". *The Discourse of Rinaldo and Giletta* ("first written in Italian by an unknowne authour") is an obvious pastiche of *The Pleasant Fable of Ferdinando Jeronimi and Leonora de Valasco* but reinstating the chivalry that Gascoigne originally satirised, and supplying a happy ending. A section of part four, entitled "The Honest Minded Mans Adventures, His Largesse, and His Farewell to the World", is a version of Gascoigne's life (the speaker fails to find advancement at court, tries his hand unsuccessfully at soldiery and farming, and in the end is saved by religion). A "Caveat to G.W. at His Going into Fraunce" by "R.C." blatantly imitates *"Gascoignes councell given to master* Bartholmew Withipoll". But the Gascoigne who influenced George Whetstone was the man keen to promote himself as a reformed sinner, not the witty, bawdy poet of *A Hundreth Sundrie*

Flowres.

Gascoigne must have generously suggested that his young admirer seek patronage in the same quarters as himself. The third part of *The Rocke of Regard* is dedicated to "Lady Jane Sibilla Greye, now of Wilton" and is about honourable ladies, their beauty and piety, and the value of fidelity. Lady Jane Sibylla Grey was the wife of Arthur, Lord Grey of Wilton. Whetstone also praised her in a poem addressed to "the right H. the Ladie I.S.G. of Wilton". A second poem is addressed to "My L.E.R." – probably Lady Elizabeth Russell, wife of John, Lord Russell, the second son of the Earl of Bedford. A third describes the virtues of "My L. Cecil of Burleigh" – Mildred, the wife of William Cecil, Lord Burghley. She and Lady Elizabeth Russell were sisters.

Walcott Hall

George Whetstone did not require Gascoigne's assistance to make a bid for patronage from the Burghleys. He had a connection of his own which might explain his presence in Stamford, and which certainly explains why the final and longest part of *The Rocke of Regard* was dedicated to Thomas Cecil, Burghley's eldest son by his first wife, Mary Cheke. By 1577 Thomas Cecil had been MP for Stamford during three Parliamentary sessions. In his dedication to Cecil, Whetstone gushed that knowing "how deeply bothe my good mother, and all her children are bounde unto you for received friendships, among the rest (acknowledging your desire of my well doing) I have sought howe (for such benefites) to avoyde the vile vice of ingratitude".[14]

Whetstone's mother, Margaret, had known the Cecils for many years. They were her neighbours. Her second husband, Robert Browne, owned Walcott Hall in the parish of Barnack, then in Northamptonshire. After Browne's death in 1572, she married a third time, and continued living at Walcott Hall with her new husband, Francis Ashby. Barnack lies four miles south-east of Stamford and in the Middle Ages its stonepits supplied limestone to the great buildings of England. Its most famous export was a hard, durable limestone known as "Barnack Rag", which was used for many abbeys, including the great Benedictine Abbey of Peterborough, as well as in the building of Windsor Castle and locally in the construction of Burghley House, Stamford's churches and Barnack church. Barnack Rag Bed was exhausted before the end of the fifteenth century and much of the village is built on old quarry land, including the estate where Whetstone's mother lived.

Whetstone's mother lived in what was probably the largest local property after Burghley House. At one point the two estates almost touch, though some three miles separate the houses. Walcot Hall (as it is spelt today) still exists, hidden away in a substantial wooded estate just to the south of the famous "Hills and Holes" of Barnack. This topographical feature – a lunar landscape of grassy craters – forms a striking remnant of the abandoned medieval stone quarries.

The modern Walcot Hall, however, is not the one which George Whetstone knew. The house was demolished and rebuilt in the 1670s.

It is reasonable to assume that Gascoigne and his young friend rode out to Walcott Hall to pay a courtesy call on Whetstone's mother and his stepfather. But they were evidently not invited to stay (or at least Gascoigne wasn't). Whetstone's poem about the sickness and death of George Gascoigne is quite unambiguous on that point. George Gascoigne "deceased at Stalmford in Lincolne Shire",[15] not Barnack in Northamptonshire.

What Gascoigne and Whetstone were doing in Stamford in the summer of 1577 will probably always remain a mystery. In 1810 Alexander Chalmers suggested that "He had perhaps taken a journey to this place for change of air, accompanied by his friend Whetstone".[16] In a pre-industrial age the air quality of Stamford is unlikely to have been superior to that of Walthamstow but it is true that in the sixteenth century, just as today, mobility was one of the privileges of affluence. The poor stay put; the rich restlessly travel. Gascoigne is not someone who seems to have found life in Walthamstow irresistibly magnetic and he spent much of his later life on the move, and much of it away from home. His presence in Stamford could therefore have conceivably involved nothing more than a casual excursion to meet Whetstone's family.

If it was something to do with state business, requiring Gascoigne's presence at Burghley House, then it is remotely possible that a document may one day turn up giving proof of this. Since Gascoigne had the previous year found employment as a trusted messenger of state he may have gone to Stamford to collect a letter or to receive instructions. Whetstone's elegy is tantalisingly ambiguous on this point. In the poem's deathbed scene Gascoigne addresses his son William (then aged somewhere between twelve and fifteen years old), remarking:

First serve thou God, then use bothe wit and arte
thy Fathers det of service to discharge,
which (forste by death) her Majestie he owes[17]

The "debt of service" owed to Elizabeth might be a reference to some sort of official state business, interrupted by his sickness and death. But it might equally be an invitation to William to follow in his father's footsteps and seek out royal patronage. Realistically, William could not "discharge" any unaccomplished employment of his father's, since no one in their early teens would be used on state business. These lines may therefore simply be of a vague, general application.

Ultimately, the highly suggestive Burghley and Walcott Hall associations could just be a red herring and wholly irrelevant. Stamford lay on the main route between London and the north. Gascoigne may simply have been travelling to the north, or travelling back from the north, when he fell ill at Stamford. What he was doing in that town is one of the many things which George Whetstone's long elegy for his friend fails to enlighten us about.

Whetstone's Elegy

"A REMEMBRAVNCE of the wel imployed life, and godly end, of *George Gafkoigne Efquire, who* deceased at Stalmford in Lincoln Shire the 7. of October. 1577. *The reporte of Geor. Wheftons* Gent. An eye witness of his Godly and charitable end in this world" was entered in the Stationers' Register on 15 November 1577 and published by Edward Aggas. It was, in short, written at white heat. Whetstone had attached himself to the most controversial writer in Tudor England, only to find himself bearing unexpected witness to his death. Whetstone's elegy provided what was both a dramatic account of the poet's death and what is in effect his first biography. It was written fast, while everything was still fresh in his mind. Whetstone assumed he had been present at an important event. In that he was correct. His poem registers its impact and supplies invaluable information. But, frustratingly for a biographer, it also leaves many questions unanswered.

Whetstone's elegy consists of fifty six-line rhyming stanzas about Gascoigne's life and death, followed by an "Exhortatio" (or exhortation) in 8 six-line rhyming stanzas, concluded by an epitaph in the form of a sonnet. Unfortunately Whetstone cast the long first section in the idiosyncratic form of an address from Gascoigne to his young friend, only switching from the first to third person for the fiftieth and final stanza. This subsequently caused enormous confusion as early readers assumed that the poem was substantially by Gascoigne and not by Whetstone. Stanzas 35-40 appeared in the second and subsequent editions of the anthology *The Paradyse of Daynty Devises* (1580), attributed to Gascoigne, and were duly reproduced as Gascoigne's work in eighteenth- and nineteenth-century anthologies. The Victorian scholar William Carew Hazlitt also attributed them to the poet in his edition of Gascoigne's *Complete Poems* (1869-70). Only a single copy of the original "A REMEMBRAVNCE of the wel imployed life, and godly end, of *George Gafkoigne Efquire*" has survived, which is today in the Bodleian Library. It remains an obscure and little-read text. The last time the complete elegy was published was 1901,[18] which may explain modern misunderstandings. Even modern editors of Gascoigne have sometimes erroneously attributed Whetstone's elegy to the poet and described it as "a deathbed poem".[19]

The first part of the elegy can be divided into a number of sections. In the initial three stanzas, the dying Gascoigne begs Whetstone to tell his story and identifies him as a man who knows his "hidden hart". In stanzas 4-10, Gascoigne gives a potted history of his life, describing his disinheritance by his father, his days as a courtier and his service in the Low Countries. Stanzas 12-15 describe some of his books, including *The Posies*, *The Glass of Government*, *The Steel Glass*, *A delicate Diet, for daintiemouthde Droonkardes*, *The Droome of Doomes day* and *The Noble Arte of Venerie*. Stanza 16 refers to as yet unpublished writings, including a book about "Zeale" (i.e. Zeeland or the Netherlands). Whetstone hints that Gascoigne has chosen to hold this writing back. Stanzas 17-24 rail against envy, suspicion and care, and the "fooles" who misconstrued his "plain words". Stanzas 25-27 refer to the poet's "inward greef" and "wretched plaint". That "greef" means physical sickness is underlined by a marginal note to stanza 28: "No Phisicion could find out his greef." Stanzas 28-33 describe the physical symptoms of Gascoigne's illness. Stanzas 34-40 warn of the transience of all earthly things. In stanzas 41-49 the dying Gascoigne makes his will and commends himself to his Queen, his wife and his son. On his deathbed he bids farewell to his wife, son and friends. In stanza 50 he dies.

The second and third sections of the elegy lack the detail and interest of the first part. The "Exhortatio" is a banal, cautionary address to the elite of Tudor society and to the reader to "Prepare thy self eche houre for the grave". The equally undistinguished "Epitaph" pictures Gascoigne's soul in heaven, living in endless joy. It finishes with a celebration of his writings, describing how Gascoigne's appreciative readers (the wordplay is excrutiatingly crass) "devoured the sweet of all his sweat".

As a biography in verse, Whetstone's elegy reveals little about the poet that could not already have been gleaned from *The Posies of George Gascoigne Esquire*. Its mention of Gascoigne's days as a courtier is perfunctory, it passes over his years as a law student and his marriage and its account of his experiences in the Low Countries summarises the much more detailed rendition given in *The fruites of Warre*. But Gascoigne obviously enjoyed exaggerating his woes to a sympathetic listener. The claim that he was "Disinherited" was untrue but testified to his enduring bitterness about Sir John Gascoigne's will. Since Whetstone regarded himself as also having been cheated out of his inheritance the two men clearly had a strong mutual bond of indignation. The claim that in the Netherlands the poet "in prison vile was popt" was another exaggeration, easily contradicted by a reading of stanza 169 of "*The fruites of Warre*". But it is interesting that Gascoigne was still apparently vexed in 1577 by the rumours of his treachery in Holland three years earlier.

Whetstone's account of Gascoigne's writing is heavily skewed towards his late moral tracts. The *Posies* is justified by its author's claim that it was a wholesome volume intended to demonstrate "The woes of loove, and not the wayes to love". *A Hundreth Sundrie Flowres* is not mentioned. But Gascoigne did own up to authorship of the anonymous *Noble Arte of Venerie*, though he clearly put a favourable spin on it, justifying the subject as "honest sport, which dooth refresh the wit". What is most intriguing about this section is Whetstone's revelation of Gascoigne's unpublished work:

> Yet other woorks (I think) of more emprise,
> Coucht close as yet, within my cofers sleep.
> yea til I dy, none shall the same revele:
> So men wil say, that *Gaskoign* wrote of *Zeale*.[20]

One obvious unpublished work in the summer of 1577 was *The Grief of Joy*. But "emprise" is a word that can mean either "enterprise" or "an undertaking of danger". In the chests containing his manuscripts was, if Whetstone is to be believed, an explosive account of Gascoigne's experiences in Zeeland. Whether it was an erotic memoir or a blistering critique of the conduct of the war, and whether it was in verse or prose, is impossible to say.

Most probably it was a prose account of his experiences as a soldier and captain. Gascoigne seems to have understood it would be a controversial book, which is why he forbade publication until after his death. But no such book ever appeared. Every one of Gascoigne's working manuscripts has disappeared. The surviving manuscripts of *Jocasta*, "Hemetes the Heremyte" and *The Grief of Joy* are presentation copies. Gascoigne's final publication was his anonymous pamphlet *The Spoyle of Antwerpe*, which appeared some eleven months before his death. The next book bearing his name would not appear until 1587, after his widow's death. That was a reprint of previously published material. Whoever took charge of Gascoigne's chests after his death – and it was presumably his wife, Elizabeth – took no interest in getting his unpublished manuscripts into print. Whether this was from apathy or anger, and whether or not Gascoigne's account of his adventures in Zeeland was actively suppressed, can only be a matter of speculation, unless these enigmatic lost manuscripts turn out to have survived and are found and identified.

Gascoigne's Final Sickness

The main interest of Whetstone's elegy lies in what it reveals about Gascoigne's final sickness and death. The previous May, in his preface to *The Droomme of Doomes day*, Gascoigne had described himself as being "in weake plight for health". On that occasion he had evidently rallied and managed to journey to the continent and take an active role as a witness to the sack of Antwerp.

Whetstone supplies a psychosomatic explanation for the poet's fatal sickness. Gascoigne's heart has been "killed" by "privy foes" who sought "to tread [him] under foot". His true intentions were thwarted by "forged faults". Spiders turned his flowers into poison. His "plain words" were misconstrued by "fooles". A proper reward for his industry was held back by "fond tales". Within his breast he lacked "a cause to settle care" [i.e. "a matter to settle grief/anxiety"] (evidently a reference to the failure of *A Hundreth Sundrie Flowres* to win him patronage or due reward). Gascoigne was forced "to starve among his books" while dolts fed "uppon a booty". He toiled in bloody wars while "carpet swads" [rogues who took no part in the fighting] devoured "ye Soldiers spoile". "These men" – presumably the "carpet swads" – "were brib'd, ere I had breth to speak" (probably an allusion to the events surrounding the rumours of Gascoigne's treachery):

> Muse then no whit, with this huge overthrowe,
> though crusshing care, my giltless hart doth break
> But you wil say, that in delight doo dwell:
> My outward showe, no inward greef did tel.
>
> I graunt it true; but hark unto the rest,
> The Swan in songs, dooth knolle her passing bel:
> The Nightingale, with thornes against her brest
> when she might mourn, her sweetest layes doth yel
> The valiant man so playes a pleasant parte:
> When mothes of mone, doo gnaw upon his hart.[21]

Gascoigne remained strong in the face of adversity. Though battered by misfortune and wounded by malice he stayed silent about his suffering. But even a suit of armour can eventually be pierced by small, repeated attacks:

> But as oft use dooth weare an iron cote,
> as misling drops, hard flints in time doth pearse
> By peece meales, care so wrought me under foot
>   but more then straunge is that I now rehearse,
> Three months I lived, and did digest no food:
> When none by arte my sicknes understood.[22]

Perhaps Gascoigne himself believed in a psychosomatic explanation for his illness. That was what the dying Keats came to believe, blaming his sickness on his thwarted passion for Fanny Brawne. Whetstone's elegy ventriloquizes Gascoigne's voice and there is no reason to doubt its veracity as an expression of the poet's feelings about his life and fate. Gascoigne felt he had been trodden underfoot, thwarted, crushed, made poisonous, his heart broken, his heart killed, his breast made anxious, starved, and overthrown. Mental anxiety had provoked physical sickness. This supplied a framework of explanation for the physicians' bafflement about his illness. His inability to hold down food was a bodily expression of the way he'd been starved by misfortune. Gascoigne blamed a host of enemies for reducing him to a physical wreck.

That some illnesses can be psychosomatic in origin is not in doubt, but it seems highly unlikely that George Gascoigne was laid low by malicious tongues. He had a very strong sense of self and a natural resilience that seemed to let him bounce back from any misfortune. His illness seems far more likely to have had other origins, although it may well be the case that a dying man found psychological satisfaction in blaming his mystery illness on his enemies.

Whetstone reveals that in the final three months of the poet's life "none by arte [his] sicknes understood". The fact that no doctor was able to diagnose or effectively treat Gascoigne's mysterious sickness is not in itself significant. Medicine at this time was very primitive, with often damaging ignorance and superstition among those who called themselves doctors. Nicholas Breton wrote a vivid description of the type of predatory, bungling physician who was "a kinde of horse-leech, whose cure is most in drawing of bloud and a desperate purge, either to cure or kill, as it hits... Hee is never without old merry tales and stale jests to make olde folks laugh and comfits or plummes in his pocket to please little children... His discourse is most of the cures that hee hath done and them afarre off; and not a receipt under a hundredth pounds, though it be not worth three halfe-pence."[23]

A person's affluence and social importance was no guarantee of adequate medical attention, even in relation to the rudimentary competencies of the day. When someone as powerful and well connected as Thomas More fell ill from "fittes" in 1521 and experienced simultaneous sensations of being "hott & cold" the doctors were baffled and couldn't think of any appropriate treatment. More was saved by his well read, well educated adopted daughter, who recalled reading about such symptoms in Galen's *De differentiis febrium* and came up with a remedy. Fifty years later Tudor medicine had advanced no further. Nothing could be less surprising than that no one understood what was slowly killing George Gascoigne in the summer of 1577.

Whetstone describes an illness lasting three months, during which Gascoigne wasted away. Presumably he was in Stamford when he became too ill to return home to Walthamstow, and remained there throughout July, August and September 1577. Since he was buried in St Mary's parish, Gascoigne is likely to have been staying at one of the lodging houses in that small parish in the heart of Stamford – probably either on St Mary's Hill or St Mary's Street. It was a busy, noisy location, close to a market and with the regular passage of horsemen, carts and wagons and animals moving to and fro on the London road. August was when the last of the three great livestock fairs held in the town each year took place.

Whetstone seems to have stayed with the dying man, playing Joseph Severn to Gascoigne's Keats. At first Gascoigne was able to walk, though he looked like a dying man. But soon he took to his bed. In "Gascoigne's Anatomy" he had mocked the feverish lover of Petrarchan cliché and pictured himself physically worn away by love. Those lines now took on a bitter resonance as he began to lose weight.

It was a terrible end. What struck Whetstone most was the awful wasting away of Gascoigne's body. In three stark stanzas he supplies the symptoms of Gascoigne's terminal illness:

> You see the plight I wretched now am in,
> I look much like a threshed ear of corn:
> I hold a forme, within a wrimpled skin,
> but from my bones the fat and flesh is worne
> See, see the man, late pleasures Minion:
> pinde to the bones, with care and wretched mone
>
> See gallants see, a picture worth the sight,
> (as you are now, my self was heretofore)
> My body late stuft ful of manly might,
> As bare as *Job*, is brought to Death his doore.
> My hand of late, which sought to win me fame:
> Stif clung with colde, wants forse to write my name.
>
> My legs which bare, my body ful of flesh,
> Unable are to stay my bones upright:
> My tung (God wot) which talkt as one would wish,
> In broken words can scarce my minde recite.
> My head late stuft with wit and learned skil:
> May now conceive but not convay my wil.[24]

Any attempt at a retrospective diagnosis cannot possibly be conclusive, because it is forced to rely on George Whetstone's subjective descriptions of non-specific symptoms. A brain tumour could account for the loss of motor ability and mental confusion. Metastatic tumours in distant organs, which are derived from the primary tumour, could cause wasting and vomiting. Cancer seems unlikely, however, if Whetstone's description of "wrimpled skin" (i.e. wrinkled or puckered skin) is accurate. But almost anything debilitating could lead to the symptoms Whetstone describes, including weight loss and a swollen abdomen, exacerbated by poor hygiene and a lack of antibiotics.

Given the time in which Gascoigne lived the likeliest probability is that he had an infectious disease. One of the commonest was pulmonary tuberculosis (TB). It was a lethal disease which killed off millions until the mid-twentieth century and the advent of antibiotics. It has been described as the oldest disease on earth. Characteristically, the invading organism destroys lung tissue and symptoms include coughing up blood and a high temperature with prolonged sweating. Its most visible aspect is rapid wasting of the body, hence the Tudor name for the disease: consumption. Falstaff wittily uses it as a metaphor for his shortage of money: "I can get no remedy against this consumption of the purse;

borrowing only lingers and lingers it out, but the disease is incurable." (*Henry IV, Part 2*, I.ii.237-9) The long list of writers who died of TB includes Laurence Sterne, Tobias Smollett, John Keats, Ernest Dowson, D. H. Lawrence, Franz Kafka and George Orwell.

Gascoigne's symptoms match those of other writers who went to a lingering death from the disease. Keats first showed the symptoms in January 1820 and died, emaciated, thirteen months later. His death mask shows his sunken eyes and protruding cheekbones. In April 1924 Franz Kafka was taken to a sanatorium; tuberculosis had affected his epiglottis and prevented him from swallowing food or talking. He died two months later. George Orwell found the physical act of writing almost unbearable and complained of the extraordinary difficulty of composing consecutive sentences. In May 1948 his symptoms included exhaustion in his legs, aching knees, back pain, watery eyes and discomfort in his gums. By July he was able to leave hospital but suffered later relapses. Back in hospital, his diseased lung haemorrhaged on the night of 21 January 1950. He died at once, aged forty-six.

It has recently been suggested that Orwell may have contracted TB after he was injured fighting in the Spanish civil war, either from poor hospital hygiene or contaminated food. Gascoigne's adventures as a soldier in the Netherlands likewise made him open to illness. Adam N. McKeown paints a vivid picture of the atrocious conditions experienced by those who went on such expeditions; "Soldiers lived in crowded, wet, and often cold environments, where they were vulnerable to disease."[25]

Travel increased the possibility of infection. It may have been what brought the life of the infamous witchfinder Matthew Hopkins to a premature close,

> ashen and emaciated, his fatigue and dry cough having developed into a relentless fever punctuated by violent fits of expectoration. The familiar smell of pleural tuberculosis – the tang of onions – permeated the room. With each contraction of his lungs his stertorous breaths grew fainter, as the essence of his life was sucked away.[26]

Perhaps Nicholas Breton was present to see his stepfather in his final illness. In a poem published in the anthology *The Phoenix Nest* (1593) he, like Whetstone, ventriloquizes the voice of a man dying from a protracted illness. Death does him "double wrong, / To let me lie so long in such a fit... / Long was I dead, ere death would let me die". In *The Countess of Pembroke's Love* (1592) there are lines very reminiscent of Whetstone's elegy:

> Mine eyes are dim, my flesh, bare skin and bone,
> My sinews shrunk, and all my limbs are numb,
> Mine ears are deaf, but to the sound of moan,

My speech, is but to sorrow stricken dumb:
My blood dried up, my heart with sorrow soken,
Oh help the soul, before the heart be broken.

If Breton was present – and this will always be uncertain – then these two lines may be relevant:

Proverb: No extreme will hold long.
Cross Answer: Yes, weaknesse in a Consumption.[27]

Death

Gascoigne apparently insisted that he be buried in a common, unmarked grave:

I wish no pomp, the fame for to ingrave,
once buried corn dooth rot before it live.
And flesh and blood in this self sorte is tried:
Thus burial cost is (with out proffit) pride.[28]

This too is reminiscent of the desires of other dying writers, cheated of life in their prime. Keats requested that his gravestone simply portray a broken lyre and the inscription *Here lies One Whose Name was writ in Water*. A name written in water, of course, vanishes without trace and the gravestone attributes Keats's request to "the Bitterness of his Heart at the Malicious Power of his Enemies". George Orwell, too, resisted pomp and ceremony. He asked to be buried in the nearest convenient graveyard with a plain brown stone giving only his real name and the dates of his birth and death. He requested no memorial service and no biography.

In wanting a cheap, ordinary burial Gascoigne may well have been thinking of Burghley's ornate tomb then under construction inside nearby St Martin's. There is a bitterness in that request; a sense, perhaps, that his life has been "without profit" in more than merely a financial sense. Having finally worked his way into royal favour and found state employment it must indeed have been a bleak irony to be faced with imminent death. Exactly two years earlier he had been at the very centre of Tudor society and power, performing at Kenilworth Castle. Now he lay dying obscurely at Stamford.

The fact that Gascoigne lasted three months might indicate a fierce desire to live, an unwillingness to let go and slip away into oblivion. If so, he was no different to other writers in that melancholy situation. George Orwell acted as if his death was not really imminent, thinking of his next novel and planning to go to a sanatorium in Switzerland. One of Gascoigne's colleagues in the entertainments at Kenilworth may have been dying that summer, too. John Badger of Oxford, who'd written the Hercules speech to welcome the Queen, made his will on 15

July 1577. Since he'd graduated from Christ Church in 1553 he was probably, like Gascoigne, in his forties. Making your will was what you did as death approached. Gascoigne's was "quickly made", presumably because he was in no physical state to dictate or write a long one. Besides, his wealth was "small":

This short accompt (which makes me ill apaid)
My loving wife and sonne will hardly please.[29]

The word "accompt" means "reckoning" and these two lines seem to be a reference to the will rather than to Whetstone's account of his "wel imployed life". In other words, Gascoigne died poor and knew that his wife and son would be angry at how little had been left to them. No copy of the will has ever been located to clarify these matters.

Gascoigne's supposed words about "My loving wife whose face I fain would see" suggests that Elizabeth was not in Stamford to witness her husband's death. His teenage son William, however, perhaps was, if we are to take the line "Come, come deer Sonne, my blessing take in parte"[30] as a true account of the poet's final days or hours.

Summer was over. September, too – that month when "the Sunne begins to fall much from his height, the meadows are left bare...the windes begin to knocke the Apples heads together on the trees, and the fallings are gathered to fill the Pyes for the Houshold". It was now October and Gascoigne had just a few days to live. Outside his room was a world in which "the lofty windes make bare the trees of their leaves, while the hogs in the Woods grow fat with the falne Acorns...and kind hearts and true Lovers lye close, to keepe off cold: the Titmouse now keepes in the hollow tree, and the black bird sits close in the bottome of a hedge".[31] Gascoigne made his last farewells.

Overall, the deathbed scene that Whetstone evokes at the close of his "Remembraunce" is implausibly rhetorical. It seems highly unlikely that a man who was mentally confused and barely able to string a sentence together was able to make a solemn speech bequeathing his soul to Almighty God and praising his gracious sovereign Queen. The purpose of the address to Elizabeth quickly becomes clear, however. Whetstone is obligingly making a pitch for her sympathy on behalf of his dead friend with the message that his wealth was "but slender", so perhaps she could "aid" Gascoigne's widow and son. It seems very unlikely the Queen ever read this appeal, but even had she done so it is improbable that she responded to this request.

To the Tudor imagination, death struck you down with a dart or arrow. In "Gascoigne's Good Night" the poet envisioned

The stretching arms, the yawning breath, which I to bedward use,
Are patterns of the pangs of death, when life will me refuse:

And of my bed each sundry part in shadows doth resemble
The sundry shapes of death, whose dart shall make my flesh to tremble.[32]

As a law student in London Gascoigne would from time to time have seen Death literally walking the streets. Henry Machyn reported one such occasion, on the last day of January 1557. The Lord Treasurer's Lord of Misrule made his way through the city to the Lord Mayor, followed by a great carnival procession, including musicians and drummers. The figures included a devil shooting fire "and won was lyke Deth with a dart in hand".[33]

If Whetstone is to be believed, Gascoigne was in "good mood" as death approached. He managed to bid goodbye to those dearest to him: "Now farwell Wife, my Sonne, and Freends farewell." The list excluded his stepchildren, though it seems possible that Nicholas was present. Whether or not Gascoigne's wife, son and friends were gathered around his bedside as he died or whether he bid farewell to them in their absence is ambiguous. Next, the dying poet shook his fist at death: "Farewell O world, the baight of all abuse: / Death where is thy sting? O Devil where is thy hel?"[34]

There was surely a substantial amount of exaggeration in all this. Whetstone wanted to present his friend's end in the best possible light. In Tudor England it was commonly believed that a person who died in physical distress was exposing their sinful, perturbed, guilty character. Only someone who passed away peacefully was going to meet their maker with an untroubled and innocent soul. It was important to emphasize that a person had a tranquil end, and Whetstone did not disappoint his friend. The theatrical death bed scene leads up to, as the final stanza puts it, "an end worthy the showe":

Bereft of speech, his hands to God he heav'd:
And sweetly thus, good *Gaskoigne* went *a Dio*,   [to God]
Yea with such ease as no man there perciev'd
By struggling signe or striving for his breth
That he abode the paines and pangs of Death.   [foreshowed]

The dying poet seems to have undergone a final convulsion. Though weak, emaciated and unable to speak, Gascoigne managed to raise both hands. To Whetstone it was as if he was reaching out to God. "Heaved" could simply mean "lifted" but may carry a sense of forceful power or urgency. But Whetstone is anxious to deny the possibility of any uncontrollable physical disturbance or spasm. There was no struggle, no gasping for breath. Gascoigne reached out for his God and slipped quietly and sweetly away.

It was 7 October 1577. England's leading poet and most notorious writer was dead. He was probably forty-three years old.

Plate 33. The old Great North road running through the heart of Stamford, with The Church of St Mary the Virgin in the background.

Plate 34. The small, crowded graveyard of The Church of St Mary the Virgin, where George Gascoigne lies in an unmarked grave.

Plate 35. The decaying tomb of Gascoigne's patron, Arthur Lord Grey of Wilton, with now indecipherable lettering.

30: "When the Dirge is done"

Six days later, on Sunday 13 October 1577, Gascoigne was buried in the churchyard of St Mary's on the Bridge. The precise site of his grave is not known and the modern graveyard is smaller than it was in Tudor times (in 1804 a section was taken in order to widen the Wansford to Stamford turnpike).

The six days leading up to his interment would have allowed his wife Elizabeth enough time for her to be told the news and to travel up from Walthamstow. The month of October, her son once wrote, was "a Messenger of ill newes".[1] He meant that winter was on its way but it is possible that he may have also been thinking of his dead stepfather.

From its island site near the town centre, the medieval church of St Mary's with its 163-foot broach spire still dominates the southern approach to Stamford. During Gascoigne's funeral a "passing bell" would have sombrely tolled in his memory, but apart from that it was probably a low-key affair. The procession to the graveside likely consisted of the church choir, the priest, the corpse covered by a pall and borne on a timber frame with black coverings and then the mourners. The poet Richard Barnfield, who regarded Gascoigne as a major writer to be set alongside Chaucer, Gower, the Earl of Surrey and Sir Philip Sidney, described him as "tomb'd in stone". But that was just an imaginative assumption by someone writing more than two decades later. As a stranger to the town and someone of little social standing, Gascoigne was probably buried closer to the graveyard wall than to the church. The grave may have been marked by a simple wooden cross. Not that it mattered in the long run, as no Tudor graves survive in the tiny churchyard. The plots here have been used and re-used for centuries.

Even on 13 October 1577 the poet's wasn't the only burial that took place here. The old register of St Mary's records that on "1577, Octo. 13, Mr. Garskinge and Dennys Ashleye was buried".[2] Dennis Ashley was presumably a local man. The clerk may not have known or remembered "Garskinge"'s first name. He was an outsider in Stamford; his proud status as George Gascoigne *Esquire* went unrecorded.

In Tudor times death was a very much more visible and everyday matter than nowadays. The churchyard was right beside a market, and Gascoigne's funeral is unlikely to have been a tranquil occasion. In post-reformation England, Sunday markets thrived. Besides, St Mary's is right next to the London road. Gascoigne is likely to have gone to his grave accompanied by the cries of market vendors and the bustle and clatter of traffic and animals passing by just yards away.

The mourners would have included Elizabeth, the poet's teenage son William and George Whetstone. His stepchildren, locked in a law suit to get their inheritance back, are unlikely to have greatly mourned his passing or to have been present. Perhaps some of Gascoigne's London associates made the journey to Stamford. If so, only Whetstone was moved to write an elegy. Others who might have been expected to mourn the dead poet in print – Thomas Churchyard, Walter Ralegh – stayed silent. But one of Gascoigne's associates was touched by his unexpected demise, even if, characteristically, it only made him think about himself. On 6 November 1577 Sir Humphrey Gilbert completed *A Discourse How Hir Majestie May Annoy the King of Spayne*, in which he urged her to license an expedition "to discover and inhabyte some straunge place". That was Gilbert's particular obsession but not Queen Elizabeth's, and in order to make the proposal more attractive he offered her the prospect of the unofficial destruction of any Spanish shipping met with on such a voyage. He concluded with an urgent request that she not procrastinate: "But if yor Majestie like to do it at all, then would I wish yor highness to consider that delay doth often tymes prevent the perfourmance of good thinges: for the winges of mans life are plumed with the feathers of death".[3] *For the wings of man's life are plumed with the feathers of death*: Gascoigne's shocking death in his prime just the previous month surely reminded Gilbert of the need to achieve his own burning ambition before mortality put an end to it.

The shrewdest and most touching tribute to Gascoigne's personality, character and literary talents came from the pen of the Cambridge scholar, Gabriel Harvey. Harvey had only recently suffered the death of his good friend and patron Sir Thomas Smyth on 12 August 1577. He set about composing in Latin a sequence of elegies in Smyth's memory but his efforts were interrupted by a more urgent commission,

> a fewe delicate Poeticall Devises...extemporally written...in Essex, at the ernest request of a certain gentleman a worshipfull frende of his, and made as it were under the gentlemans owne person, immediatly upon the reporte of the deathe of M. Georg Gascoigne Esquier[4]

Who this gentleman was is unclear. He may simply have been a young man who admired Gascoigne's writing and who was deeply impressed that Harvey had known the great man. Harvey said that his elegy for Gascoigne was

> Published by a familiar frende of his, that copyed them owte praesently after they were first compiled with the same frends praeface of dutifull commendation and certayne other gallante appuretenances worth the readinge.[5]

By "published" he probably only meant "circulated in manuscript". No Tudor printed edition has ever surfaced and the text is known only in the manuscript that was eventually published in the nineteenth century under the title *The Letter-book of Gabriel Harvey A.D. 1573-80* (1884).

Harvey may have heard that Gascoigne was terminally ill at Stamford. His copy of *The Posies* is inscribed "Gabriel Harvey. Londini, Cal. Sept. 1577" (i.e. 1st September 1577), which is an enigmatic piece of dating, since the book had by then apparently long since been removed from sale. Perhaps news of Gascoigne's long illness and probable death prompted a fresh interest in his writing.

Harvey saluted Gascoigne's literary importance. He pictured him in the afterlife meeting Homer, chatting to Chaucer and – Harvey's imagination goes haywire at this point – being warmly entertained by Sir Thomas More.[6] Remembering Gascoigne made Harvey think of his two other dead friends, Daniel and Bartholomew Withypoll. They too are there among the more illustrious dead, waiting to greet "their odd copesmate" [companion]. But even in heaven Gascoigne is up to his old tricks and "gleekiste [mocks] many a lorde / And spees out maddames for the nonce / And sporte thyselffe with this and that / And specially with ther deinty bones". Gascoigne was, in short, "a merry mate" – which is perhaps the best tribute anyone can hope for.[7]

"Thus when the Dirge is done, let every man depart," Gascoigne once wrote.[8] But after the funeral, tradition required a dinner. Then, presumably, the mourners spent a night at their lodgings in Stamford before heading back to Essex and London in the morning. Alone of them, George Whetstone had an urgent mission: to complete his elegy and get it published. As a true admirer of Gascoigne's work he may have noticed that the poet unwittingly identified the day of his death in the line "As in *October* last upon the seventh day" in the Montague masque.[9] But there is nothing really to say about that other than to file it away as one of those curious and macabre coincidences of which life is sometimes capable.

Afterwards

After George Gascoigne's death, letters of administration were granted to John Campion, yeoman, of Woodford, Essex, on 2 December 1578. Who Campion was and why he effectively took control of the poet's estate remains obscure but it suggests that, contrary to the insinuation of Whetstone's "Remembraunce", Gascoigne died intestate. The arrangement seems to have been only a temporary one.[10]

In the month following Gascoigne's death his widow Elizabeth was listed as an outright recusant (meaning an unrepentant Catholic). Her disinclination to attend St Mary's church, Walthamstow, perhaps shows she was always inclined towards the old faith and no longer felt she had to conform to her late husband's more orthodox views. Perhaps, as for many people, religious belief took on a new force in the face of the death of close ones and of her own ageing. Elizabeth did not marry again. She survived Gascoigne by only a few years and was dead by 6 May 1585. After having spent twenty years in Walthamstow, the probability is that she is buried there, somewhere in the graveyard of St Mary's. No burial registers survive at the church and no Tudor graves are to be found in the graveyard.

Gascoigne and Elizabeth's son William became involved in the maritime adventures of Martin Frobisher and Francis Drake. He was one of 2,300 men who set sail on a 30-ship expedition under Drake's command on 14 September 1585. It is conceivable that William Gascoigne's departure stemmed from a desire for action after his mother's death earlier in the year. The expedition raided the Spanish coast, then headed for the Canaries and Cape Verde Islands. William Gascoigne died in his early to mid-twenties at Santo Domingo in 1586.

After Gascoigne's death his literary-minded stepson Nicholas published little or nothing for many years, suggesting to one commentator that "he felt his encouragement and support in authorship to have been removed".[11] Nicholas Breton described himself as a gentleman and seems to have studied at Oriel College, Oxford, and to have spent some time on the continent. He may have been instrumental in orchestrating the publication of *The Whole woorkes of George Gascoigne Esquyre: Newlye compiled into one Volume* on the tenth anniversary of the year of the poet's death. This edition consisted of the *Posies* (fragmented into three sections), *The Steel Glass* (in a new 1587 edition), *The Complaynte of Phylomene, The Pleasant Fable of Ferdinando Jeronomi*, the *princelye pleasures* retitled as *A briefe rehearsal, or rather a true Copie of as much as was presented before her majestie at Kenelworth*, and *Certayne notes of Instruction*. This "whole works" did not include *The Glass of Government, The Noble Arte of Venerie, The Spoyle of Antwerpe* or the two theological works. The publisher, Abel Jeffes, was located in Fore Street, which was literally round the corner from Red Cross Street, in Breton's home parish of St Giles without Cripplegate. Some copies appeared under the alternative title *The pleasauntest workes of George Gascoigne Esquyre*. The 1587 edition was considerably more slipshod than either *A Hundreth Sundrie Flowres* or the *Posies*, with erratic pagination and variable contents.[12] The letter of dedication to Grey is missing from *The fruites of Warre*. One edition of the *Whole woorkes* held by the British Library consists of the *Posies* (split into two parts), *A brief rehearsal, Certayne notes of Instruction, The Steel Glass, The Complaynte of Phylomene, The Glass of Government* and a new 1586 edition of *The Droome of Doomes day* (which was printed by John Windet for Gabriel Cawood).

Breton married Ann Sutton on 14 January 1593 and seems to have fathered at least five children, three of whom died young. Towards the end of the century Breton became a prolific minor writer, producing over fifty titles of verse and prose, including pastoral lyrics, satires, pamphlets, dialogues, letters and essays. Ben Jonson wrote a sonnet in praise of his *Melancholic Humours* (1600) and for a time he enjoyed the patronage of Philip Sidney's sister, the Countess of Pembroke. Breton's publications were exquisitely printed small editions with woodcut borders, which later enjoyed a great vogue among nineteenth-century book collectors. But according to his most recent editor "It looks as though Breton outlived his reputation as a writer, and was forced to do hackwork for booksellers in his latter years."[13] Thomas Nashe sarcastically apologised for being unable to match Breton's talent, remarking "my stile is some what heavie gated, and cannot daunce trip and goe so lively, with oh my love, ah my love, all my loves gone".[14] Nashe had a point. Breton's writing tends to be lightweight and saccharine, with rather too many passionate shepherds piping on dainty reeds. His description of women's breasts as "Balles of blisse" is memorable, but not for literary reasons. Nicholas Breton probably died in 1626, never having explicitly written anything at all about his illustrious stepfather.

Gascoigne's younger brother John lacked a male heir and by the early seventeenth century the Bedfordshire Gascoignes had become extinct in the male line and the family vanishes from local records. Cardington Manor remained in the Blundell family for more than 100 years, until it was purchased by Samuel Whitbread in 1779. Whitbread built up a famous brewing business and the Manor remained in the hands of the Whitbread family for almost two centuries. Then, on 24 January 1957 a brief note appeared in the magazine *Country Life*. Cardington Manor, "a moated house dating from the sixteenth century but with late Georgian Gothic embellishments" was to be demolished unless a purchaser was found. No buyer was found and the house where George Gascoigne was born and where he spent his childhood and adolescence was duly bulldozed.

Dame Margaret Gascoigne's family home, Thorpe Hall in Yorkshire, which inspired the name of Gascoigne's residence in Walthamstow, met a similar but ultimately more absurd fate which would surely have delighted the poet. Today its site is a strip of grass between the private road leading to Skelton Grange Power Station and the sludge beds of Knowstrop Sewage Works.

*

Seven months after Gascoigne's death, Elizabeth I set out on a long, slow, meandering Progress to Norwich. She was once again entertained by the Earl of Leicester, but it was an unremarkable affair, compared to Kenilworth. At the Earl's Wanstead residence she watched a masque written by Leicester's nephew, Philip Sidney. There is no reason to believe that the Queen herself treasured any fond memories of her last visit to Kenilworth, and any recollection of the savage man clad in ivy must surely have slipped further and further from her mind with each new entertainment. Of the same generation as Gascoigne, she outlived him by almost four decades, but ended her reign, as Germaine Greer has eloquently put it, "cruel, bald and rotten-toothed".[15] When Elizabeth died in 1603 after 44 years on the throne the national mood seems to have been one of relief rather than sorrow. The marble head on her tomb in Westminster Abbey, probably carved from a death mask, shows a face far removed from the flattering images of official portraits – plump-lipped, pudgy, "a rather coarse-featured woman with a large nose and a set mouth".[16]

None of the other great figures of the Court that Gascoigne knew lived as long as the Queen. The first to go was Sir Nicholas Bacon, who died unexpectedly on 20 February 1579. There was a sumptuous state funeral. Bacon left debts far greater than anyone had expected and his will resulted in an acrimonious squabble between the sons of his first and second wives.

The Earl of Leicester finally got his commission in the Netherlands but his military campaign there was a failure. There was also a personal bereavement. On 22 September 1586 his nephew Philip Sidney, who foolishly chose not to wear any thigh armour, was shot above the left knee during a skirmish at Zutphen. Sidney died at Arnhem on 17 October, probably from a combination of gangrene and septicaemia.

Leicester continued to reside at Kenilworth on and off until his death. He died in 1588, a puffy, bloated old man. Much of his castle home at Kenilworth was demolished in the English civil war, leaving the ruins which remain today. The great Mere which had acted as a striking backdrop to the glittering entertainments of 1575 was drained and turned into pasture.

Sir Francis Walsingham died two years after Leicester, having spent much of his private fortune on developing his extensive and very effective intelligence service.

Lord Burghley died in 1598 and went to his grand tomb in St Martin's church, Stamford, just half a mile from Gascoigne's unmarked grave.

*

Gascoigne's Cambridge "Master" Stephen Nevynson, like his pupil, might have expected to live longer than he did. He died in the summer of 1580. That same year the poet's greatest patron, Arthur, Lord Grey of Wilton, became notorious for his commanding role in the massacre of some 600 civilians and surrendered soldiers at Smerwick in Ireland. That act made him what we would nowadays call a war criminal. Ralegh and Edmund Spenser were also present at the atrocity. Grey's position as Lord Deputy of Ireland was terminated in 1582, and he returned to England. Lord Grey died in 1593, aged 57. He was buried in a large, plain tomb at the west end of the north side of the Lady Chapel in St Mary's Church, Whaddon. An inscription on the side once supplied a short biography of his life and glorious exploits but the words are now badly eroded and only fragments survive.

In June 1583 Sir Humphrey Gilbert set out once more to explore the New World. In a characteristically stupid gesture of bravado he made his flagship the tiny 10 ton pinnace the *Squirrel*. In September, north of the Azores, the fleet encountered stormy conditions and massive waves. One night about midnight the *Squirrel*'s lights were seen vanishing into a trough, from which they never emerged.

The following year, shortly before 2 p.m. on 10 July, William of Orange emerged from dining with his family in his Delft residence, the Prinsenhof. Crossing the hallway he paused to chat with three of his military bodyguards. One was Captain Roger Williams, who had fought alongside Gascoigne in the Low Countries in 1572. Another was Gascoigne's old adversary, the quarrelsome Thomas Morgan. As the Prince turned away to climb the stairs to his private chambers an assassin stepped forwards with a pistol and shot him three times. William collapsed and within minutes was pronounced dead. Roger Williams pursued the killer and was among those who caught him before he could escape. William was 52. He was buried in the New Church at Delft, where a baroque marble tomb was later erected, with a bronze image of him in his armour. He failed in his ambition of uniting the Netherlands but was instrumental in founding the province of Holland on the west coast. In Britain and elsewhere the name later came to be popularly used to refer to the Netherlands in its entirety.

*

Alexander Neville, one of that "fellowship" of six young men at Gray's Inn in the 1560s, was not inspired by Gascoigne's death to write an epitaph on his old associate, though a decade later he edited and contributed to the collection of elegies produced by the University of Cambridge on the occasion of Sidney's death. After a long life as occasional author, MP and secretary to three Archbishops, he died in 1614, aged seventy.

Of the others in that fellowship, John Vaughan and Richard Courtop vanished into obscurity. Francis Kinwelmershe, who collaborated with Gascoigne on *Jocasta*, was probably the "F. Ke" who translated Adrien Le Roy's *A briefe and plaine instruction to set all musicke of eight divers tunes in tablature for the lute* (1574). He was at most 41 years old when he died some time between 1575 and 1580. His brother Anthony Kinwelmershe lived on to see the new century in. In his will, dated 12 March 1600, he asked to be buried in Wing church, Buckinghamshire, near the family pew of his "singular good frende Sir Roberte Dormer", at whose wedding in 1572 Gascoigne's Masque had been performed. Arthur Hall finally published his translation of Homer's *Iliad* in 1581. It was not a success and was superseded by Chapman's far superior one in 1598. Hall spent much of his adult life quarrelling with others, self-publishing two slanderous pamphlets which he was forced to withdraw. He achieved the dubious distinction of being the first MP ever to be expelled from Parliament and replaced by a new member. Elizabeth I testily remarked that the Fleet Prison was a good place for Arthur Hall "and Bedlem a fytter".[17] He was imprisoned for debt between 1601 and 1604 and may have been back in the

Fleet Prison when he died on 29 December 1605, aged sixty-six. His final piece of writing was an unpublished treatise on transportable commodities.

Edward Boyes, who married Elizabeth Breton and fought with Gascoigne in Red Cross Street, seems to have returned to the county of his birth. The year Gascoigne died he was appointed Sheriff of Kent. He lived for another two decades and died in February 1599, aged seventy-one.

Two years after Gascoigne's death, Gabriel Harvey achieved literary immortality of his own as the wise rustic and poet "Hobbinoll" in Edmund Spenser's *Shepheardes Calender*. He gained an altogether different and deadlier kind of fame in his vitriolic exchanges with Thomas Nashe. Harvey also fell out with Robert Greene, a playwright and pamphleteer now best remembered for his blistering attack on the "upstart Crow" Shakespeare. When Greene died a sick man in September 1592, Harvey oozed with self-satisfied sympathy, remarking

> God helpe good fellows when they cannot help themselves. Slender reliefe in the predicamente of privations, and fained habits. Miserable man, that must pearish: or be succoured by counterfeite, or importente supplies. I once bemoaned the decayed and blasted estate of M. Gascoigne: who wanted not some commendable parts of conceit, and endeavour: but unhappy M. Gascoigne, how Lordly happy, in comparison of most-unhappy M. Greene.[18]

To have a worse end than George Gascoigne! Harvey can hardly contain his delight. Harvey gave up the life of a Cambridge scholar in order to practise as a lawyer in London but his career did not prosper. Harvey retired to Saffron Walden and spent the last thirty years of his life in relative obscurity. He died on 7 February 1631, aged about eighty.

In the short term, Sir Walter Ralegh fared best of all Gascoigne's admirers. The 1580s have been called Ralegh's decade. He was the kind of courtier Gascoigne had himself dreamed of becoming and Elizabeth showered him with money, jewels and land. His story has been told many times. Sometimes called "the last Elizabethan", he was executed on 29 October 1618.

Gascoigne's last friend and first biographer, George Whetstone, died in bizarre circumstances in mid-September 1587, close to the tenth anniversary of the poet's death. In those ten years Whetstone became a prolific minor author of fiction, non-fiction, drama and poetry. His writings were saturated in Gascoigne's influence, without ever enjoying his mentor's success. Probably through his friendship with the poet he got to know Sir Humphrey Gilbert and sailed with him on his poorly organised and fruitless 1578 expedition. After his Stamford "Remembraunce", Whetstone wrote other elegies, including two for influential figures with Gascoigne associations, Sir Nicholas Bacon and the Earl of Bedford. He followed in Gascoigne's footsteps by serving in the Low Countries, and was there in 1587 when Sidney received his fatal wound.

Whetstone's elegy for Sidney praised Captain Edmund Udall, who offered to lead Sidney's horse after his injury. In a strange quirk of fate Whetstone and Udall subsequently quarrelled and fought a duel outside the walls of Bergen op Zoom. Udall, a professional soldier, had little difficulty in despatching Whetstone, who was a mere commissary of musters. Thus the elegy for Sidney, published posthumously, praised the man who had killed its author.

Influence and reputation

As the most popular and fashionable writer of his day, Gascoigne's work made an enormous impression upon his contemporaries. His influence can be detected in the writings of Nicholas Breton, George Whetstone, Thomas Watson, Edward Dyer and Walter Ralegh, and perhaps also in some of the work of Philip Sidney, Edmund Spenser and William Webbe. His writing lived on in the Elizabethan age. *Supposes* was performed in the hall at Trinity College, Oxford, though the only spectator who left a record felt that the performance was mediocre. In a diary entry of 8 January 1582 the academic Richard Madox, a Fellow of All Souls, recorded how "We supt at the presidents lodging and after had the Supposes handeled in the haul [hall] indifferently."[19] Five years later Gascoigne's *Whole woorkes* was published, the title intimating that, like Chaucer, he was a classic English author.

Not everyone agreed. The year Gascoigne died, Thomas Blenerhasset complained that there was "a great inequalitie...betwixt Turberville and Tibullus, betwixt Golding and Ovid: betwixt George Gascoigne and Seneca". But this belonged to the scattergun school of criticism, as no one seriously regarded these last two writers as either equals or in any way alike. What happened in the years after Gascoigne's death has best been summarised by Charles Nicholl: "As a stylist Gascoigne was partially eclipsed by the successes of Euphuism and neo-Platonic sonneteering, but his virtues undoubtedly surface again, in the verse satires of Donne and Hall, in the pamphlets of Greene, Nashe and Dekker."[20] One beneficiary of Gascoigne's death was Philip Sidney. As Katherine Duncan-Jones has observed, "it is unlikely that he felt much regret at his passing...The cultural vacuum created by Gascoigne's death came at just the right time. Someone else was now needed to write and devise court entertainments for Leicester and the Queen..."[21] The romantic mythology which wildly distorted the actual circumstances of Sidney's wounding and death gave a huge boost to his public image and to the status of his posthumously published writings. It is hard not to see this deferential response as connected to the subsequent marginalising and undervaluing of Gascoigne's varied literary achievements.

In 1579, in the annotations to the "November" section of Edmund Spenser's *The Shepheardes Calender*, "E.K." (who may well have been Spenser himself), wrote of the mythic nightingale Philomela:

Whome the Poetes faine once to haue bene a Ladye of great beauty, till being rauished by hir sisters husbande, she desired to be turned into a byrd of her name. Whose complaints be very well set forth of Ma. George Gaskin a wittie gentleman, and the very chefe of our late rymers, who and if some partes of learning wanted not (albee it is well knowen he altogyther wanted not learning) no doubt would haue attained to the excellencye of those famous Poets. For gifts of wit and naturall promptnesse appeare in hym aboundantly.

William Webbe agreed that Gascoigne was "a wytty Poet"[22] and George Puttenham saluted Gascoigne "for a good meeter and for a plentifull vayne". Puttenham's *The Arte of English Poesie* (1589) identified ten poets "who have written excellently well", including Sidney, Ralegh, Dyer, Gascoigne and Nicholas Breton.[23] That same year Thomas Nashe wrote that "Master Gascoigne is not to bee abridged of his deserved esteeme, who first beat the path to that perfection which our best poets have aspired to since his departure."[24] Nine years later, in *Palladis Tamia*, Francis Meres drew up a list of 14 poets "the most passionate among us to bewaile and bemoane the perplexities of Love". It included Sidney, Ralegh, Dyer, Spenser, Shakespeare, Whetstone and Gascoigne.[25] Gascoigne remained popular until the end of the century, judging by Sir John Davies' satire of 1597, which poked fun at a flashy young man:

He weares a hat of the flat-crowne block,
The treble ruffes, long cloake, and doublet French;
He takes tobacco, and doth weare a lock,
And wastes more time in dressing than a wench:
Yet this new-fangled youth made for these times,
Doth above all prayse old *Gascoins* rimes.[26]

In 1615 there appeared *The Blazon of Jealousy*, a translation of an oration by Benedetto Varchi written for the funeral of Michelangelo in 1564. The translator's Epistle "To the Courteous Reader" praises Gascoigne and Turberville, "since they first brake the Ice for our quainter Poets, that now write, that they might the more safer swimme in the maine Ocean of sweet Poesie".[27] This view solidified in the twentieth century into the orthodoxy that Gascoigne was an influential literary pioneer and the most important writer between Surrey and Spenser but that this was a lacklustre period in English verse.

In the seventeenth and eighteenth centuries there was relatively little interest in Gascoigne, though Thomas Percy was impressed by "Gascoigne's beautiful Poem on Lady Bridges" and included it in his classic anthology *Reliques of Ancient English Poetry* (1765). At the start of the nineteenth century Alexander Chalmers remarked that "The life of this ingenious poet has long been involved in obscurity" and he complained that "the extreme rarity of Gascoigne's works has been the chief cause of his being so much neglected by modern readers". Chalmers had a high regard for Gascoigne, arguing that "In smoothness and harmony of versification he yields to no poet of his own time...As a satirist...he may be reckoned one of the first."[28] Interest revived with the publication of Hazlitt's *Complete Poems of George Gascoigne* (1869-70) and F. E. Schelling's pioneering biography. Hazlitt invited his readers to compare Gascoigne to his contemporaries "and observe his unmistakeable superiority", and he praised the works for "their personal and autobiographical allusions, their picturesque, vivid and delicate delineations of incidents and feelings" and their "unusual freedom from pedantry and affectation of style".[29]

Yvor Winters' high praise of Gascoigne as "a great master obscured by history", voiced in his book *In Defense of Reason* (1937), was a solitary modern reappraisal which anticipated the surge in interest in the poet in the last quarter of the twentieth century.[30] The changing temper of the times was best caught by Michael Schmidt, who wrote in *Lives of the Poets* (1998) that "Gascoigne's best poems are extraordinarily good" and argued, "His neglect is one of the not uncommon outrages in English poetry... Gascoigne for centuries has been more a footnote than part of the living text. He deserves as much celebrity at least as Surrey, as Ralegh – maybe even as Sidney."[31]

But perhaps the greatest tribute of them all came from the literary superstar of the Tudor age, who paid Gascoigne the compliment of reading and absorbing his work to an extent that even now has not been fully charted. William Shakespeare quite possibly saw Gascoigne perform in person at Kenilworth in 1575. That spectacular extravaganza may even have been the transforming experience of his childhood, giving him the desire and drive to become an entertainer himself. At the start of his own career as a playwright he encountered *The Whole woorkes of George Gascoigne Esquyre*, the lyrical, witty, bawdy contents of which were perfectly attuned to his own temperament. And if he knew anything of Gascoigne's life he may have felt a private bond with a man who'd married a woman several years older than himself.

It is quite possibly not a coincidence that Shakespeare refers to Stamford in a discussion about passing time and death in *Henry IV, Part Two*. The play was almost certainly composed in 1597, exactly two decades after Gascoigne's death. That was the year the theatres were closed by the Privy Council from July to October, in retaliation for the staging of Ben Jonson and Thomas Nashe's "very seditious and sclanderous" *Isle of Dogs*. Shakespeare's own career was now being affected by the kind of state censorship which had impinged upon Gascoigne's. The twentieth anniversary of the poet's death and the reality of censorship silencing artistic endeavour (whether by the confiscation of books or the forcible closure of theatre) could conceivably have put Gascoigne into

Shakespeare's mind at this time. In one respect the Lord Chief Justice in *Henry IV, Part Two* is a surrogate of the poet himself: a Gascoigne not afraid to offend authority. What is new about Sir William Gascoigne in Shakespeare's play is the importance given to him. He becomes a pivotal figure in the drama. That prominence is lacking in Shakespeare's sources or in other dramas about the reign.

Henry IV, Part Two is a death-haunted play. One critic has described it as "a prolonged meditation on time, death, age and the mutability of human affairs".[32] In the first scene of Act 3 the old king broods about passing time and change ("'Tis not ten years gone, / Since Richard and Northumberland, great friends, / Did feast together, and in two years after / Were they at wars. It is but eight years since, / This Percy was the man nearest my soul", III.i.57-60). This leads on to the scene in which Justice Shallow and Justice Silence reminisce about the good old days when they were young. Shallow remembers a fight behind Gascoigne's old Alma Mater, Gray's Inn. He thinks about how many of his old acquaintances are dead. The scene continues:

Silence. We shall all follow, cousin.
Shallow. Certain, 'tis certain, very sure, very sure. Death, as the Psalmist saith, is certain to all, all shall die. How a good yoke of bullocks at Stamford fair?
Silence. By my troth, I was not there.
Shallow. Death is certain. Is old Double of your town living yet?
Silence. Dead, sir.

Their conversation is rambling, inconsequential and comic. The sudden reference to Stamford fair seems quite arbitrary and pointless. *What's the price of two bullocks at Stamford fair?* Shallow asks. *Don't know. Wasn't there.* Silence replies. It's like a dialogue between a pair of drunks, the continuity slurred, going off at tangents. Dramatically, Shakespeare might have chosen any fair. But Stamford was where George Gascoigne died. Stamford saw the end of a censored, silenced poet and of the man who had helped orchestrate the brilliant entertainments at Kenilworth which may have so entranced an eleven year old boy from Stratford some twenty-two years earlier. In that sense, perhaps, he was nothing less than Shakespeare's "old Double" himself.

But all that lay in the future. On the Monday that Gascoigne died in Stamford, Shakespeare was just a schoolboy, trudging to school with all the enthusiasm that thirteen-year-olds usually greet the start of another school week. And he, too, in time, would die sooner and younger than he might have anticipated, in bed and ill.

For death is he which rides and breaks us all.[33]

Notes

In general I have modernised Gascoigne's poetry and occasionally silently changed the punctuation, while leaving the prose unmodernised. I have also abbreviated some of the lengthy and cumbersome original titles, modernising some but not all. My editorial practice is intended to make Gascoigne's writing readable for the non-specialist, while retaining some sense of the oddness and unfamiliarity of Early Modern English. For a discussion of Gascoigne's language, see Chapter 4.

Abbreviations

DNB *Oxford Dictionary of National Biography* (Oxford: Oxford University Press, 2004).

EA George Gascoigne, Esquire (ed. Edward Arber), *Certayne Notes of Instruction in English Verse, The Steele Glas, The Complaynt of Philomene* preceded by George Whetstone's *A Remembrance of the well imployed Life, and godly end of George Gascoigne Esquire, etc.* (London: A. Constable & Co, 1901).

GA Gillian Austen, *George Gascoigne* (Cambridge: D. S. Brewer, 2008).

GG C. T. Prouty, *George Gascoigne: Elizabethan Courtier, Soldier, and Poet* (New York: Columbia University Press, 1942).

HSF George Gascoigne (ed. with an Introduction and Commentary by G. W. Pigman), *A Hundreth Sundrie Flowres* (Oxford: Clarendon Press, 2000).

JWC John W. Cunliffe (ed.), *George Gascoigne: The Glasse of Government, The Princely Pleasures at Kenelworth Castle, The Steele Glas and other poems and prose works* (Cambridge: Cambridge University Press, 1910).

PHSF George Gascoigne (ed. with an Introduction and Notes by C. T. Prouty), *A Hundreth Sundrie Flowres* (Columbia: University of Missouri Press, 1942).

SCH F. E. Schelling, *The Life and Writings of George Gascoigne* (Philadelphia: Publications of the University of Pennsylvania, 1893).

In the notes that follow, numbers in bold (e.g. **4**) refer to the numbering of the contents of HSF (with line numbers as appropriate in normal type). The letter "P" followed by a number, both in bold (e.g. **P24**), signifies additional material from *The Posies of George Gascoigne Esquire* as it is reproduced in HSF. Other sources are abbreviated by author surname (or surname with a brief title if the author has more than one relevant publication, or there is more than one author with that surname) keyed to the author entries in the Bibliography.

Introduction

1   **4** For a discussion of this poem, see Chapter 29.
2   Beecher and Butler, p. 49.
3   Pooley, p. 7.

1: "Gascoigne"

1   **8**, 12, 14.
2   **70**, 15.
3   GA, p. 213.
4   SCH, p. 97.
5   GG, p. 9.
6   Cavendish, p. 100.
7   Ferguson, pp. 452-3.
8   Matusiak, p. 291.
9   Cavendish, p. 100.
10 Loughlin, p. 106.
11 The marriage had occurred by the time of the inquisition *post mortem* on her father, 10 October 1531. An inquisition *post mortem* was a local enquiry into the lands held by someone of status after their death, in order to discover what income and rights might be due to the crown. See Ward, p. 165.
12 **72**, 95-6.
13 See Eccles, "Brief Lives: Tudor and Stuart Authors", p. 55. Eccles confused his archives, however. The deposition – Letter Book V, f.225, duplicated in Journal 19, f.152 – has never been held at the Guildhall, as Eccles states, but is kept at the nearby Corporation of London Library.
14 Schelling concluded that the poet was most probably born between 1530 and 1535 (SCH, p. 5) on the (mistaken) basis of Gascoigne having been tutored by Stephen Nevynson at Trinity College, Cambridge, and his later admission to Gray's Inn in 1555. He did not know about the inquisition *post mortem* on Sir John Gascoigne, who died on 4 April 1568. This document states that at the time of his father's death Gascoigne was "vigenti sex annorum et amplius" – "twenty-six years and more" (GG, p. 287). If this is interpreted to mean "twenty-six years and some months" it would indicate 1542 as the year of birth. But that is impossible because Gascoigne was not a minor when he married in 1561, and he must therefore have been born before 1541. Prouty decided it signified that Gascoigne was aged about 26-28 and was therefore probably born in 1539. If Gascoigne was 34 in 1568 it is on the face of it puzzling that he was described as being "twenty-six and more". It becomes less puzzling in the context of what actually happened at an inquisition *post mortem*. These were held by an official known as an escheator, before a jury. The inquisition gave the name of the deceased and the date of death and was recorded in Latin, in a standard form. At the end, the next heir was identified, and an age given. If the heir was of age (over 21), the actual age given was often only an estimate. The likeliest explanation is that whoever gave Gascoigne's age on that occasion simply wasn't sure how old he was, and in terms of the document it was not important. All that mattered legally was to

establish that he was older than twenty-one. The deposition discovered by Eccles, "Brief Lives: Tudor and Stuart Authors", remains the most compelling piece of evidence, because it came from the poet himself.

2: Cardington Manor
1. Bunyan, pp. 176-7.
2. Moynahan, pp. 350-4.
3 **56**, 1-8.
4 A deed of 23 June 1563 lists "the manor house and moat with the fish in the moat": Whitbread Collection, Deeds, no. 52. For a valuable history of Cardington and its adjoining parish, see Wood.
5 JWC, p. 477.
6 GG, pp. 15-16.
7 EA, p. 107.
8 EA, p. 110.
9 Godber, p. 174.
10 *Ibid.*
11 DNB.
12 **39**.
13 HSF, p. 369.
14 Whitbread Collection, Deeds, no. 52.
15 GG, p. 225.
16 **62**.
17 **P**, 36.
18 In the Epistle Dedicatory to *The Steele Glas*, EA, p. 43.
19 **3**, 23-4.

3: Cambridge
1 Cited in Childs, *Henry VIII's Last Victim*, p. 318.
2 *Ibid.*, p. 317.
3 GG, p. 13.
4 EA, p. 77.
5 Stanza 199. HSF, p. 436.
6 Ryan, p. 88.
7 **72**, 18 .
8 EA, p. 77.
9 **72**, 114.
10 Ryan, p. 64.
11 *Ibid.*, p. 65.
12 **67**, 81-88.
13 Chadwick, p. 96.
14 **69**, 121, 123-4.

4: "A lady once did ask…"

1 HSF, p. 454.
2 Cooper, "Welcome to the House of Fame", p. 3.
3 Schmidt, *Lives of the Poets*, p. 152.
4 Benson, p. 376.
5 **9** See note, HSF, p. 603.
6 Honan, p. 45.
7 See Paulin.
8 **39**, 16.
9 Nielson and Skousen, cited in Moynahan, pp. 402-3.
10 Bolton, p. 301.
11 **43**.
12 HSF, p. 215.

5: "Cyphered words" and Master F. J.

1 Bradner, pp. 546-7.
2 GG, p. 191.
3 *Ibid.*, p. 201.
4 *Ibid.*, p. 198.
5 Hazlitt, vol. I, p. xxi.
6 Ward, *A Hundreth Sundrie Flowres From the Original Edition*. A second edition, with new material by Ruth Lloyd Miller, appeared in 1975. Captain Ward's theories have been widely discredited; see PHSF, pp. 19-28. Another conspiracy theorist is Kittle, whose account "Maintaining that the works of George Gascoigne were written by the Earl of Oxford" was published in 1930 by a vanity press. For a useful corrective to literary conspiracy theories involving the Earl, see Nelson.
7 Honan, p. 183.
8 HSF, p. 148.
9 HSF, pp. 362-3.
10 Fleay, p. 239.
11 Cited in Clegg, p. 118.
12 GG, pp. 193, 200.
13 PHSF, p. 247.
14 HSF, p. 364.
15 Shore, pp. 176, 168.
16 For example, George Orwell's animus against greengrocer Jack Bumstead of Southwold surfaced in *Nineteen Eighty-Four* in the scene, described with sadistic glee, in which a prisoner named "Bumstead, J" is viciously beaten up. See Binns, *Orwell in Southwold*, pp. 132-33.
17 **27**.
18 **45**, 14.
19 HSF, p. 363.

6: At Gray's Inn
1 GA, pp. 37-39.
2 Benjamin, p. 258.
3 Nichols, *The Diary of Henry Machyn*.
4 **21**.
5 **1, 21** and **39**.
6 See Chapter 11.

7: The Lawless Law
1 **72**.
2 Bowen, pp. 48-50.
3 **54**, 39-40.
4 HSF, p. 627
5 Nelson, p. 40.
6 **50**.
7 Emmison, Appendix E.

8: Five Thousand Days
1 HSF, p. 368.
2 HSF, p. 177.
3 Hazlitt, vol. I., p. xix.
4 **26**
5 **10, 11**
6 Arber, *Tottel's Miscellany*, p. 2.
7 HSF, p. lv.
8 HSF, p. 371.
9 The title page is reproduced as the frontispiece to GG.
10 HSF, p. 465.
11 Paterson, p. xii.
12 **42** and **61**.
13 **30** and **53**.
14 **49**, 10, 28.
15 **6 and 7**.
16 Ariosto, p. xiv.
17 Bayley, p. 104.
18 **1**, 33-8.
19 HSF, pp. 597-8.
20 HSF, pp. 187, 189, and 583, n. 184.23-4.
21 **57**, 29, 31-2.
22 Ariosto, p. 344.
23 **P24,** 11.

9: Under Mary
1 GA, p. 33.

2 **57**, 1.
3 **49**, **50** and **30**.
4 Strype, p. 391.
5 GG, p. 11.
6 *Ibid.*, p. 8.

10: At the Court of the Virgin Queen
1 **33**, **51** and **52**.
2 **61**, 1-14.
3 **61**, 32.
4 **14**.
5 **32**, 13.
6 Skidmore, p. 371.
7 MacCaffrey, pp. 71-85.
8 **14**.
9 **13**, 1.
10 **10**.
11 **12**.
12 **13**.
13 However, the overall sequencing of the collection, with the two plays being squeezed between the Contents page and *The Adventures of Master F. J.*, seems to have been arranged by the printer, mangling Gascoigne's own planned structure. See HSF, pp.liv, lvii and GA, p. 71.
14 **53**.
15 Duncan-Jones, *Shakespeare's Sonnets*, p. 50.
16 **61**, 1, 34. Gascoigne also uses "haste post haste" in **40**, **48**, **77**, *The Princely Pleasures at the Court at Kenilworth* and *The Drum of Doomsday*.
17 **13**.
18 **15**.
19 **43**.
20 **19** and **20**.
21 **56**.
22 Burrow, "Waves of Wo", p. 17.
23 Quoted in Stern, p. 189.
24 **22**.
25 GG, p. 283.
26 HSF, p. 364.
27 Wells, p. 157.
28 "Phyllyp Sparowe", 138-40.

11: "Elizabeth Brytane"
1 GG, p. 294.
2. *Ibid.*, p. 297.
3 Grosart, vol. I, p. xii. Apart from the introduction, Grosart's collection lacks

continuous pagination; my quotations of Breton from this work cite titles only.
4   GG, p. 297.
5   *Ibid.*, pp. 27-8.
6: **74,** 5-6.
7   GG, p. 297.
8   **39**.
9   GG, pp. 16-17.
10 **8,** 10.
11 PHSF, p. 262.
12 HSF, p. 601.
13 *Ibid.*, p. 620.
14 Flournoy, p. 266, believed that this was the house in the parish of St Giles that William Breton acquired on 4 December 1551.
15 Ward, "The Death of George Gascoigne", p. 36.
16 GG, p. 29.
17 EA, p. 99.
18 EA, p. 86.
19 HSF, p. 290.
20 GG, pp. 31-2.
21 See Eriksen.

12: A Great Fray in Red Cross Street
1   GG, pp. 29-30.
2   *Ibid.*, p. 30.
3   Public Record Office, E179/145/220
4   Nichols, *The Diary of Henry Machyn*, p. 293.
5   Flournoy, pp. 262-73.
6   GG, pp. 301-2.
7   **39**.
8   HSF, p. 226.
9   **13**.
10 HSF, p. 423, stanza 128.
11 Public Record Office, Chanc. Proc., Series II., 78/55. See GG, p. 302, n. 31.
12 The dates are 7 November, 9 December (twice), 12 December and 18 December. See GG, Appendix IV.
13 See GG, p. 307.
14 *Ibid.*
15 Close Roll Entries, 7 Nov 1562, 28 January 1563, 29 January 1563.
16 Material about Hall is drawn from Wright.
17 *Ibid.*, p. 170.
18 Prouty states that "in 1562 [Hall] was known as a tavern brawler, skilled in the use of the dagger" (GG, p. 26). Neither statement is true. Hall had no reputation as a brawler until his dispute with Melchisedech Mallory, which began on 16 December 1573. Subsequently Hall was accused of cowardice and of letting his servants do his

fighting for him.
19 GG, p. 308.
20 **P32**, 19.
21 **P32**, 20-24.
22 GG, p. 42.

13: "My poore house at Waltamstow in the Forest"
1 GG, p. 309.
2 *Ibid.*
3 Apart from works cited, material in this chapter is drawn from [Anonymous], *The Historical Monuments of Waltham Forest*; Reaney, *A History of Walthamstow and The Church of St. Mary, Walthamstow*; and Mander.
4 SCH, p. 50.
5 GG, p. 28.
6 Breton's will is reproduced and discussed in Grosart, vol. 1, p. xiiff.
7 Robertson, *Poems by Nicholas Breton*, p. xviii.
8 Evans, *Bygone Walthamstow*, "Introduction".
9 **P28**, 206. The poem is also known by its secondary title, "Dulce bellum inexpertis" ("war is liked by those who have no experience of it").
10 Reaney, *The place names of Walthamstow*, p. 39.
11 Cited in GG, p. 314.
12 HSF, p. 363.
13 GG, p. 28.
14 HSF, p. 363.
15 Quoted in Gwyn, p. 208.
16 See Gascoigne's preamble to **6**.
17 **P26**, 8-9.
18 **P26**, 321-6.
19 HSF, pp. 364-5.
20 Stewart, "Gelding Gascoigne", p. 148.
21 See Romig and Lawrence (1996).
22 Hill, p. 6.
23 **P32**, 43-48.
24 **73-6**.
25 HSF, p. 367.
26 **76**.
27 **75**.
28 Hill, p. 47.
29 **73**, 22-28.
30 **74**, 1-4.

14: Christmas Revels
1 GG, pp. 309-313.
2 HSF, p. 274.

3 **59**, 36-40.
4 **54**, 35-6.
5 **68**, 58.
6 It is just possible that Gascoigne's association with these five men began earlier, in the winter of 1562-3, when he was commuting from Willington. But the theatrical metaphors of his poem for Richard Courtop suggest that Gascoigne had *Jocasta* and the *Supposes* on his mind and that the friendship belongs to the summer and autumn of 1566. Austen (GA, p. 36) suggests a date of 1565 and believes that the sequence "almost certainly had a previous life in manuscript".
7 HSF, p. 274.
8 **58**.
9 Austen, p. 40, admires this poem's technical accomplishment, finding in it "a superbly confident display of literary skill" and remarking that "The extraordinary variety of registers Gascoigne incorporates into just seven stanzas is a virtuoso display". She suggests that four of the chosen themes were "provocative, as each comments to some extent on Gascoigne's own recent history and especially his mistakes" (GA, p. 37).
10 **60**, 1-3.
11 Marx, p. 896.
12 **62**, 15-16.
13 **63**, 19.
14 **62**.
15 Austen, p. 47, accepts Gascoigne's boast at face value and hails it as "a truly remarkable feat even for someone with an Inns of Court training and it would have attracted attention within Gray's Inn at least".
16 HSF, p. 657.
17 John Buxton, *Sir Philip Sidney and the English Renaissance* (1954) and Edmund Spenser, quoted by J. B. Steane in Nashe, pp. 28, 27.
18 Stern, p. 216.
19 **69**, 1.
20 **62**.
21 Nichols, *The Diary of Henry Machyn*, p. 221.
22 HSF, p. 59.
23 For an authoritative account of these variations, see HSF, 509ff.
24 Walton, p. xxv.
25 Stanza 202.
26 Beecher and Butler, *Supposes*, V.x.46-7.
27 Gassner, p. xx.
28 HSF, p. 519.
29 Walton., p. xxviii.
30 9 December 1562; GG, p. 306.
31 The list of *Dramatis Personae* includes "*Nuntii*, three messangers from the campe" but Nuncius appears to be the same character in the three scenes in which he appears, and speaks not as "we" but as "I".

32 W. W. Greg (ed.), *Collections II* (Oxford: The Malone Society, 1931), p. 146, cited in HSF, p. 513.
33 Confusingly, all published editions of the play list the *dramatis personae* and their speaking parts according to the fake identities; it is important to remember that on the printed page "Erostrato" is actually Dulippo and vice-versa.
34 Beecher and Butler, pp. 47, 66.
35 HSF, pp. 472-3.
36 Beecher and Butler, pp. 47, 66.
37 *Ibid.*, p. 22.
38 Humphreys, *Much Ado About Nothing*, p. 25.
39 Taylor, *Reinventing Shakespeare*, p. 400.
40 Morris, *The Taming of the Shrew*, p. 84.
41 GG, p. 171.
42 HSF, p. 495.
43 See Chapter 17.
44 **29**, 29-30.
45 Cited in HSF, p. 476.

15: "My muse is tied in chains"
1 GG, p. 36.
2 See GG, pp. 315-24.
3 *Ibid.*, p. 324.
4 *Ibid.*, 37ff.
5 **3**, 23.
6 Robertson, *Poems by Nicholas Breton*, p. xvi.
7 GG, p. 44.
8 **64**.
9 Bunyan, *The Pilgrim's Progress*, p. 123.
10 *Foure Letters Confuted* (1593), cited in SCH, p. 9.
11 **65**.
12 GG, p. 12.
13 **68**.
14 HSF, p. 651.

16: The Italian Connection
1 See Nicholl, "Rough but true", p. 884.
2 **68**, 75-77.
3 Castiglione, p. 17.
4 Bradner, pp. 547-8.
5 Scott, *Elizabethan Translations from the Italian*, p. xlvii.
6 **69**, 49-50.
7 Gascoigne, *The Spoyle of Antwerp* (discussed in Chapter 28).
8 GG, p. 198.
9 **29**, 7-8.

10 Kundera,, p. 33.
11 Burrow, "Waves of Wo", p. 18.
12 Karl, p. 5.
13 Bradner, p. 551.

17: "A Spie, an Atheist and godlesse personne"
1 HSF, 201.
2 **71**, 301.
3 **71**, 11.
4 **71**, 264.
5 Prior shows that Shakespeare's eye wandered across to the poem which followed the Montague masque, "The refusal of a lover", and used material from that, too. This indicates that Shakespeare's edition of Gascoigne was almost certainly the *Whole woorkes* of 1587 and not *A Hundreth Sundry Flowers*, where the poem is located (under a different title) much earlier in the volume than the masque. Shakespeare is unlikely to have been able to obtain a copy of the *Posies* more than a decade after it was suppressed.
6 Childs, *God's Traitors*, pp. 36-7.
7 GG, p. 12.
8 Childs, *God's Traitors*, p. 34.
9 Public Record Office, SP 12/86.
10 Quoted in Ryan, p. 259.
11 HSF, p. xxviii.
12 DNB.

18: Minding your P's and W's
1 HSF, p. 177.
2 *Ibid.*
3 See Chapter 26.
4 **61**.
5 **69**, 49-53.
6 **71**, 63-4.
7 Booth, p. 177.
8 Cited in Stern, p. 216.
9 *Ibid.*, p. 17.

19: Flushing Frays
1 Cited in Evans, *The Works of Sir Roger Williams*, p. 219.
2 Gosling, p. 74.
3 *General Rehersall of Warres* (1579), cited in *ibid.*, p. 49.
4 **72**, 62-6.
5 **72**, 76-7.
6 **72**, 81-4.
7 **P28**, stanza 95.

8 *Ibid.*
9 Evans, *The Works of Sir Roger Williams*, p. 100.
10 *Ibid.*
11 Evans, *The Works of Sir Roger Williams*, p. 113.
12 *Ibid.*, p. 114.
13 *Ibid.*, p. 116.
14 *Ibid.*
15 **70**.
16 Evans, *The Works of Sir Roger Williams*, p. 118.
17 *Ibid.*, p. 115.
18 *Ibid.*, p. 120.
19 Gosling, p. 278.
20 **P28**, 98.
21 **P28**, 99.
22 **77**, 351-56.
23 Quoted in GG, p. 173.
24 **72**.
25 **72**, 57-60.
26 **77**.
27 Nicholl, "Rough but true", p. 884.

20: Waterland
1 See Weiss.
2 HSF, p. lviii.
3 Moore Smith, p. 166.
4 **21**.
5 Eriksen, p. 4, puts forward the plausible suggestion that "In depth of hell I drowned was in deed" ("Dan Bartholmew of Bathe", part 7, l. 26) recycles an unused line from an earlier draft of "Gascoigne's *De profundis*.
6 HSF, p. 343, 219-20.
7 Cited in SCH, p. 80.
8 HSF, ll. 124-6.
9 Booth, p. 532.
10 HSF, p. 339, l. 78.
11 *Ibid.*, p. 330, ll. 57-65.
12 *Ibid.*, p. 344, ll. 247-60.
13 *Ibid.*, p. 330, l. 38.
14 Cited in Booth, pp. 535-6.
15 HSF, pp. 340-1, ll. 115-6.
16 *Ibid.*, ll. 141-2.
17 *Ibid.*, ll. 145-60.
18 *Ibid.*, p. 354, ll. 47-8.
19 *Ibid.*, p. 358.
20 **P28**, 102.

21 Williams, quoted in Evans, *The Works of Sir Roger Williams*, p. 128.
22 **P28**, stanzas 103-5.
23 **P28**, stanza 107.
24 **P28**, stanza 110.
25 **P28**, stanzas 114-5.
26 **P28**, stanza 120.
27 Gosling, pp. 95-6.
28 **P28**, stanza 121, ll. 1-2.
29 *Ibid.*, l. 6.
30 **P28**, stanzas 128, 131.
31 *Ibid.*, stanza 131, ll. 1-2.
32 HSF, p. 329, ll. 22-28.
33 HSF, p. 652.
34 **P28**, stanza 134, ll. 3-7, stanza 135, l. 1.
35 *Ibid.*, stanza 135, ll. 6-7.
36 *Ibid.*, stanza 141.
37 *Ibid.*, stanza 142.
38 PHSF, p. 18.
39 **67**.
40 **66**.
41 HSF, p. lvii.
42 **P28**, stanza 161.
43 **P28**, stanza 169
44 George Whetstone, "A REMEMBRAVNCE of the wel imployed life, and godly end, of *George Gafkoigne Efquire*" (1577), stanza 16, in EA, p. 20.
45 *Ibid.*, stanza 24, ll. 5-6, stanza 25, ll. 1-4.
46 **P29-33**.
47 **P28**, stanza 129 and **P30**.
48 Nicholl, "Rough but true", p. 884.
49 McKeown, p. 32.
50 **P28**, stanzas 171 and 169.

21: "offensive...and scandalous"
1 Clermont, pp. 314-16.
2 *Ibid.*, pp. 321-3.
3 *Ibid.*, p. 324.
4 HSF, p. 328, l. 344.
5 Clermont, p. 324.
6 **P28**, ll. 018, 021, 024.
7 Hazlitt, vol. I., p. xxii.
8 GG, p. 123.
9 *Ibid.*
10 Fleay, pp. 241-2.
11 Moore Smith, p. 189. In the sixteenth century "lewd" could mean "dissolute" and

"bad" as well as "indecent" or "lecherous".
12 Sessions, p. 268.
13 See Boose. For a different perspective, see Clegg's revisionist history. Clegg believes Elizabethan imaginative writers enjoyed considerably more freedom than has conventionally been supposed and that Gascoigne's book primarily upset members of the court but was not actually banned.
14 **68**, 75-77.
15 See Boose.
16 Beckingsale, p. 137.
17 Cited in Clare, p. 6.
18 **P1**, p. 359, ll. 6-7.
19 *Ibid.*, ll. 8-10.
20 *Ibid.*, p. 360, ll. 6-7.
21 Usher, p. 38.
22 *Ibid.*
23 *Ibid.*, p. 24.
24 Usher, p. 90, states that the 1572 Commission had a total membership of 71 but Appendix II of his book lists only 68. Commissions were set up in 1572 and 1576 but not for the years 1573-5. Most of those who sat on the 1572 Commission (which probably dealt with *A Hundreth Sundrie Flowers*) also sat on the 1576 Commission (which probably dealt with *The Posies of George Gascoigne Esquire*). Membership of the Commissioners for Causes Ecclesiastical in the Province of Canterbury in the period 1572-1576 was as follows (a single star indicates a member who sat only on the 1572 Commission and a double star one who sat only on the 1576 Commission): Robert Alcocke, B.D.; John Aylmer, Archdeacon of Lincoln; Nicholas Barham, Sarjeant-at-Law; William Bowyer, B.D.**; Edward Boys, B.D.; George Bromley, Attorney of the Duchy of Lancaster; Thomas Brumley, Solicitor-General; John Bullingham, D.D.*; Nicholas Bullingham, Bishop of Worcester; Sir Anthony Cooke; Richard Cox, Bishop of Ely (– also Almoner 1549 and 1551); William Crowmer, B.D.**; Richard Curteys, Bishop of Chichester; William Day, Bishop of Winchester; Richard Dayves, Bishop of St David's; John Dilmer, Archdeacon of Lincoln**; Christofer Ditton*; Christofer Draper, Alderman of London*; John Elder, D.D.; Thomas Fanshawe, Remembrancer of the Exchequer**; William Fletewood, Recorder of London; Edmund Freak, Bishop of Rochester (1572), Bishop of Norwich (1576); William Gerarde, Esq.*; Gilbert Gerrarde, Attorney-General; Thomas Godwin, Dean of Canterbury; Gabriell Goodman, Dean of Westminster; Edmund Grindal, Archbishop of Canterbury**; Lewys Gwyn, Chancellor to the Bishop of St Davids*; John Hamond, D.C.L., Master of Chancery; Rowland Heywarde, Alderman of London; Sir Owen Hopton; Robert Horne, Bishop of Winchester; Thomas Huett, D.C.L.*; Thomas Huick*; Edwarde Isaac, Esquire*; Thomas Ithell, D.C.L.**; Philip Johnson, B.D.**; Philip Jones, LL.B.*; John Kingsmill, D.C.L.; Sir Francis Knowles (Knolles), Treasurer of the Household; Henry Knowles, B.D.; Sir William Kyngesmill; John Langforde, D.C.L.*; Thomas Lawes, Commissary to the Archbishop of Canterbury; William Lewen, D.C.L**; David Lewis, Judge of the

Admiralty; Roger Manwood, Justice; John Marshe, Governor of the Company of Merchant Adventurers*; Henry Marvyn*; Sir Walter Mildmay, Chancellor of the Exchequer; William Moore, B.D.; Robert Mounson, Justice; John Mullins, Archdeacon of London**; Sir Henry Nevill; Sir Richard Norton; Alexander Nowell, Dean of St Paul's; Peter Osborne, Remembrancer of the Exchequer; William Overton, Bishop of Coventry and Lichfield*; Matthew Parker, Archbishop of Canterbury*; John Pierse, Bishop of Rochester**; Thomas Randolphe, D.C.L.**; Sir Henry Ratcliffe**; William Redman, B.D.**; John Rivers, Alderman of London**; Thomas Russell*; Thomas Sackford, Master of Requests; Sir Ralph Sadler, Chancellor of the Duchy of Lancaster; Nicholas Saint Leger, B.D.**; Miles Sandes; John Scott**; Sir Thomas Scott**; Sir Thomas Smith; John Southcott, Justice; John Still, D.D.**; Lyonell Suckett, Alderman of London**; Clemente Throckmorton*; John Walker, D.D.**; Henry Wallopp, Alderman of London; Francis Walsingham**; John Watson, Bishop of Winchester**; Thomas Watts, D.D.; Richard Wenslowe, Esquire*; Richard Weston, Justice*; Robert Weston, Dean of Wells*; Herbert Westphaling, D.D.**; John Whitgift, Dean of Lincoln**; Thomas Wilbraham, Attorney of the Court of Wards*; Lewis Williams, B.D.*; Thomas Wilson, Master of Requests; Henry Worley, D.C.L.**; Thomas Wotton, B.D.; Thomas Wrothe, Alderman of London*; Thomas Yale, D.C.L.

25 **P2**, p. 366, ll. 20, 26-28.
26 Usher, p. 93.
27 **P2**, p.366, ll. 37-38.
28 **P3**, p. 370, ll. 10-11.
29 **P28**, stanza 199.
30 Usher, p. 55.
31 *The Glass of Government*. See Chapter 22.
32 **P1**, p. 359, ll. 11, 13-16.
33 **P1**, p. 359, ll. 12, 2; p. 360, ll. 11, 15-17.
34 See **P1**, pp. 360-61.
35 **P1**, p. 361, ll. 31-38.
36 **P1**, p. 363, ll. 12-15.
37 Rosenberg, p. 301.
38 **P2**, p. 366, ll. 29-31.
39 **P 32**, 35.
40 **P2**, p. 365, ll. 6-8.
41 **P2**, p. 365, ll. 13-20.
42 **P2**, pp. 365-6.
43 **P3**, p. 370, ll. 32-33.

22: The Fox and the Geese

1 Intriguingly, the two plays are bound together in a copy held by the British Library. The pagination shows that the text of *Jocasta* was taken from *A Hundreth Sundry Flowers*, which might indicate that some copies of the book were cannibalised and recycled after it was banned.

2   Johnson, p. 157.
3   GG, p. 180.
4   Bowers, p. 23.
5   EA, p. 86.
6   EA, p. 52, l. 127.
7   EA, p. 53.
9   Letter 15 in Breton, *A Post with a Packet of Mad Letters* (1603).
10 Robertson, *Poems by Nicholas Breton*, p. 168, ll. 549-70.
11 Court of Wards, 9/266, f. 76. Cited in Robertson, *Poems by Nicholas Breton*, p. xvi.
12 Austen has suggested that *The Noble Art of Venerie* was what first drew Leicester's attention to Gascoigne: see GA, p. 107.
13 The last page is numbered 248 but the book's pagination briefly goes haywire, running after p. 202: 359, 358, 363, 362, before returning to an ordered sequence at p. 205.
14 Hazlitt, vol. I, p. xxv.
15 See Robertson, "George Gascoigne and *The Noble Arte of Venerie*", pp. 484-5.
16 Stanza 15, ll. 4-6: EA, p. 20.
17 Robertson, "George Gascoigne and *The Noble Arte of Venerie*", p. 485.
18 **P32**, 25-30.
19 Gascoigne, *The Noble Arte of Venerie* (1575), p. 248.
20 *The Adventures of Master F.J.*: HSF, p. 180.
21 *Ibid.*, p. 147.
22 GA, p. 107.
23 Prouty and Prouty, p. 654.
24 *Ibid.*
25 For further analysis of the woodcuts see GA, pp. 108-111.
26 Prouty and Prouty, p. 657.

23: Kenilworth

1   See Stewart, *Philip Sidney*, p. 145.
2   See Binns, *Elizabeth, Shakespeare and the Castle*, pp. 23-26.
3   GA, pp. 118-119.
4   See Binns, *Elizabeth, Shakespeare and the Castle*, pp. 128-132.
5   JWC, p. 92.
6   *Ibid.*, p. 98.
7   Kuin, *Robert Langham:A Letter*, p. 39.
8   JWC, p. 93.
9   Kuin, *Robert Langham:A Letter*, p. 41.
10 *Ibid.*, p. 43.
11 Binns, *Elizabeth, Shakespeare and the Castle*, p. 44.
12 JWC, p. 102.
13 Kuin, *Robert Langham:A Letter*, pp. 92-3.
14 *Ibid.*, p. 17.
15 *Ibid.*, p. 18.

16 *Ibid.*
17 JWC, p. 102.
18 *Ibid.*, p. 96.
19 *Ibid.*, pp. 97-100.
20 Kuin, *Robert Langham:A Letter*, p. 46.
21 *Ibid.*, pp. 20-21.
22 *Ibid.*, p. 91.
23 See JWC, p. 102.
24 Kuin, *Robert Langham:A Letter*, p. 21.
25 *Ibid.*, p. 23.
26 *Ibid.*, p. 26.
27 *Ibid.*, p. 41.
28 JWC, p. 104.
29 Kuin, *Robert Langham:A Letter*, p. 100.
30 *Ibid.*, p. 58.
31 *Ibid.*, p. 45.
32 JWC, p. 106.
33 *Ibid.*, p. 107.
34 *Ibid.*, p. 120.
35 Kuin, *Robert Langham:A Letter*, p. 59.
36 *Ibid.*
37 Binns, *Elizabeth, Shakespeare and the Castle*, p. 85.
38 JWC, p.106.
39 *Ibid.*, p. 114.
40 *Ibid.*, p. 119.
41 *Ibid.*, p. 120.
42 Kuin, *Robert Langham:A Letter*, p. 46.
43 JWC, p. 120.
44 *Ibid.*
45 *Ibid.*
46 *Ibid.*, p. 124.
47 *Ibid.*, p. 123.
48 *Ibid.*
49 *Ibid.*, p. 126.
50 *Ibid.*, p. 127.
51 *Ibid.*, p. 131.

24: Authorship and a Hermit
1 Kuin, *Robert Langham:A Letter*, pp. 50, 55.
2 *Ibid.*, p. 39.
3 See O'Kill, and Scott, "William Patten and the Authorship of 'Robert Laneham's *Letter*'". For a critique of O'Kill and Scott, see Kuin, "The Purloined *Letter*".
4 Binns, *Elizabeth, Shakespeare and the Castle,* p. 121.
5 See Goldring, 'The Authorship of the Kenilworth *Letter* Reconsidered". She argues

that the text "is infused with a first-hand knowledge of the mercers and their milieu". Thus "the lengthy and meticulous descriptions of clothing—with particular emphasis on the fabrics from which they are made—are exactly what one might expect to find in a missive written from one mercer to another". Moreover, *A Letter* uses a specialized technical vocabulary which only a mercer would have known: "flapet" ("a small flap"), "setting stik" (used to straighten the plaits of a ruff), "strouot" (used to shape the folds of a ruff). In short, "the vast majority of the statements made in the *Letter* correspond to objectively verifiable facts, many of which would have been known only to Langham". Towards the document's close Langham asks to be remembered to four mutual acquaintances: Thomas Pullison, Thomas Smith and two individuals who are almost certainly William Thorowgood and Thomas Denman. Golding believes this reinforces the case for Langham's authorship.

But this argument faces both the problem of Patten's letter of 10 September 1575 and the fact that Patten's fingerprints are all over *A Letter*. Goldring speculates that the reference to "the book" refers to "perhaps a now-lost first edition" which was a "version of the work we know as the *Letter*". She suggests that Patten was responsible for publishing this early version, without Langham's knowledge. She speculates that Langham had handwritten copies made of his *Letter* for private circulation among a select group of friends, which included William Patten. By implication Patten then abused the trust placed in him and arranged for an edited version to be published anonymously. Patten's hypothetical "editorial role" would explain "the similarities between the *Letter*'s orthography and that employed in some of Patten's writings". Moreover "a scenario in which Patten edited portions of the *Letter* would also help to make sense of the abrupt shifts in tone that have troubled some readers of the work". Goldring suggests two possible motivations behind Patten's involvement. One was self-advertisement. *A Letter* records the full nine lines of William Patten's Latin verse welcoming Elizabeth to Kenilworth, "fixed over the gate". Patten perhaps used Langham's letter to advertise his literary services. Secondly, publishing Langham's detailed behind-the-scenes scrutiny of a royal progress may have seemed to Patten a highly profitable endeavour for a man in financial difficulties. However, "That said, the Letter must surely be regarded as, fundamentally, the work of Robert Langham".

Both the arguments for and against the competing claims of Robert Langham and William Patten as author of *A Letter* rest on conjecture. That Patten was somehow involved in the production of *A Letter* is acknowledged by both camps; the disagreement rests on the nature, motive and extent of that involvement. Goldring accepts the possibility that Patten played an editorial role but evidently regards it as limited. She declines to speculate on the nature and extent of that involvement, although the text's unusual semi-phonetic orthography seems to indicate that it was substantial.

That Patten could not have known the personal information about Langham and mercery which is revealed in *A Letter* is debatable. As Goldring acknowledges, "Patten had longstanding ties to the Mercers' Company" and was "almost certainly" the "Mr patente" recorded as one of the important guests of honour at the mercers' banquet of 1564: "Patten, Langham, and [Humphrey] Martin…inhabited overlapping worlds". Patten was a man fascinated by language and there seems nothing especially outlandish about the idea that he would have had knowledge of the vocabulary of mercery. How well he knew Robert Langham is unknown. If he was, as Goldring suggests, a privileged recipient of a copy of a lost early version of *A Letter*, then either he was a close associate of Langham's or (far less likely, given his collapsed fortunes) someone who Langham felt it was worth cultivating.

Its author twice describes himself as the Black Prince. Goldring points out that the emblem of the Black Prince was associated with mercery and Langham may have traded under just such a sign. But at Kenilworth the association had a sour aspect. Leicester was heir to John of Gaunt, who was the last person before him to renovate the castle. But John of Gaunt's bitter enemy was the Black Prince. Introducing this historical figure into the text may furtively signal an antipathy to Gaunt's successor.

A Letter seems to drop a number of hints to the reader that all is not quite what it seems. A description of the Italian acrobat's agility – "such wyndings gyrings and circumflexions" – leads on to a reference to "men that can reason and tallk with too tongs". This is essentially what happens in *A Letter*, which can be read as a double-edged, many-tongued, slippery verbal performance. Twice the narrator casually asks, "perceyve ye me?" When "Langham" boasts "I have traded the feat of merchaundize in sundry Cuntreyz" the play on "cunt" is probably not innocent and there is clearly an obscene suggestion that he is a user of whores. Likewise his boast to his fellow "cuntreman" that he is a great success with the ladies, who adore "my running, my tyming, my tuning" and, suggestively, "my doobl release", seems to indicate that the writer had more than music in mind.

6 Schmidt, *Shakespeare Lexicon*, vol. I, p. 603.
7 Furnivall, p. x.
8 Walter Scott, cited in Binns, *Elizabeth, Shakespeare and the Castle*, p. 105.
9 See Binns, *Elizabeth, Shakespeare and the Castle*, p. 99.
10 Kuin, *Robert Langham: A Letter*, p. 30.
11 *Ibid.*, p. 27.
12 *Ibid.*, p. 46.
13 *Ibid.*, p. 47.
14 *Ibid.*, p. 48.
15 *Ibid.*, pp. 76-77.
16 *Ibid*, pp. 75-6.
17 Skidmore, pp. 357-372.
18 *Ibid*, p. 75.
19 *Ibid*, p. 68.
20 Binns, Binns, *Elizabeth, Shakespeare and the Castle*, p. 105.
21 *Ibid.*
22 O'Kill, p. 40.
23 JWC, p. 95.
24 Stewart, *Philip Sidney*, p. 127.
25 Duncan-Jones, p. xii.

26 *Ibid.*, p. 94.
27 My account of proceedings at Woodstock is drawn from Gascoigne, *The Queen's Majesty's Entertainment at Woodstock 1575*, and JWC, pp. 473-510.
28 GG, p. 15.
29 *Ibid.*, p. 225.
30 Royal Manuscripts, 18 A. XLVIII.
31 A blueish green ink has been used to colour in the laurel wreath above the poet's head and other features of the drawing, including the pen behind his ear. The most visible sign of this interference is around the Queen's lips, which have disappeared behind a clumsy smear of ink. Whether Gascoigne was responsible for this colouration is an open question; if he was, it may have been touched up by another hand at a later date.
32 GG, p. 223.
33 GA, p. 157.
34 *Ibid.*

25: The Posies of George Gascoigne, Esquire
1 See HSF, pp. xlv-lxv.
2 Clegg,, p. 108.
3 **P27**, ll. 421-430.
4 *Ibid.*, 388-9, 416-7.
5 **P34**, p. 462, ll. 2-9.
6 See Thompson, Hardison, Weismiller, and Berry.
7 Quoted in Stern, p. 173.
8 **P34**, p. 461, ll. 22, 29-31.
9 Sidney, p. 84.
10 *Ibid.*, p. 118.
11 *Ibid.*, p. 120.
12 *Ibid.*, p. 119.
13 **P1**, p. 360, l. 38.
14 **P32**, ll. 31, 36.
15 Sidney, p. 123.
16 *Ibid.*, p. 121.
17 *Ibid.*, pp. 118, 124.
18 See Smout, p. 172.
19 HSF, p. 733.
20 See Eriksen, p. 5.
21 *Ibid.*, p. 3.
22 **P1**, p. 363, l. 19.
23 *Ibid.*, ll. 24-28, 36-39.
24 GG, p. 239.
25 I owe this point to J. W. Binns (personal communication).
26 **P1**, p. 361.
27 **P2**, p. 366, ll. 20-21.
28 *Ibid.*, ll. 21-28.

29 *Ibid.*, l. 37.
30 **P2**, p. 367, l. 36.
31 **P3**, p. 369, ll. 30-31.
32 *Ibid.*, p. 371, l. 5.
33 *Ibid.*, p. 370, ll. 32-35.
34 **1, 21** and **39**.
35 Beecher and Butler, *Supposes*, p. 161.
36 Pigman provides a useful list of the contents of *Posies* keyed to thei original appearance.: ee HSF, pp. 741-2.
37 See PHSF, pp. 228-239.
38 See Taylor, *Reinventing Shakespeare*, 206ff.
39 HSF, p. 180.
40 See Pigman's discussion, *ibid.*, p. 553.
41 **P5**, 24; **P6**, 11; **P11**, 32; **P12**, 17-18.
42 HSF, p. 700.
43 *Ibid.*, pp. 697-698.
44 *Ibid.*, p. liii.
45 *Ibid.*

26: A Man with a Gun
1 Gilbert, Prefatory epistle.
2 Gosling, p. 64.
3 Irwin, p. 17.
4 McDermott, p. 95.
5 Irwin, p. 20.
6 See Milton.
7 Gosling, p. 64.
8 Austen suggests Gacsoigne may have learned Italian from Holyband: see GA, p. 153.
9 *Ibid.*, p. *152*.
10 EA, p. 45.
11 Grabes, p. 72.
12 SCH, p. 72.
13 EA, pp. 79-80.
14 EA, p. 82.
15 EA, p. 46.
16 Chalmers, p. 455.
17 EA, p. 47.
18 *Ibid.*
19 Nicholl, "Rough but true", p. 884.
20 Schmidt, *Lives of the Poets*, pp. 166-7.
21 EA, p. 48.
22 *Ibid.*
23 GA, p. 157.
24 GA, p. 158.

25 EA, p. 56.
26 *Ibid.*
27 Thom Richardson, Keeper of Armour at the Royal Armouries, Leeds, informs me that "We have only two matchlocks with deeply curved stocks, no. XII.1548, a little French harquebus or petronel of about 1590, which is of very much the same form as the gun in the portrait, but is lavishly decorated and XII.12, a larger French musket of the same date. These objects are very rare, and no collection has a great number of them." Both pieces are illustrated in Monaghan and Bound; the Alderney wreck they describe also included numerous examples of the powder flask and priming flask which are shown in the portrait hanging from the harquebus.
28 **P31**, 34.
29 **P30**, 159-60, 167-8.
30 EA, pp. 43-44.
31 Vendler, p. 310
32 Burrow, *The Complete Sonnets and Poems*, p. 512.
33 Kerrigan, p. 257.

27: Doomsday and Drunkards
1 GG, p. 238.
2 GG, p. 277.
3 GG, p. 270.
4 GA, p. 171.
5 Austen plausibly suggests that Gascoigne was deliberately avoiding acknowledging the Catholic source of this material: see GA, p. 175.
6 dei Segni, pp. xv, xx.
7 See GG, pp. 270-271.
8 GG, pp. 45-46.
9 GA, p. 172.
10 GA, p. 170.
11 *Ibid.*
12 Boose, p. 190.
13 HSF, p. 345, ll. 298-300.

28: The Spanish Fury
1 Dedicatory epistle to *A Delicate Diet for Dainty Drunkards* (1576).
2 Austen suggests that Gascoigne's sentence about vineyards and the cost of wine "is probably a coded message": GA, p. 185.
3 Public Record Office, SP For., Eliz, 70/139, fol. 169 and PRO SP For., Eliz., 70/140, fol. 23.
4 Robertson, *Poems by Nicholas Breton*, p. xvi.
5 Only two copies survive, in an incomplete form. See below.
6 This association is erroneous, however. When John Foxe wrote that Tyndale's host, Thomas Pointz, "kept a house of English merchants", he meant the private lodgings of a "freeward" of the Merchant Adventurers, not the English House itself. I am

indebted to Dr Paul Arblaster for this point.
7. The death toll at Antwerp exceeded those when Rome was sacked by the forces of the Holy Roman Emperor Charles V (4,000 civilians killed) and at the St Bartholomew's Day massacre in Paris (4,000 Protestants butchered). For the death toll and damage to the city see Van Gelderen, p. 47.
8. See Greg, and Taylor, "George Gascoigne: Some Problems". Austen notes that "None of the episodes of the play bear any resemblance to the events of Gascoigne's narrative" and points to key differences in their treatment of the humiliation of the English Governor and the role of Alba (GA, p. 179). McKeown, however, asserts that "clearly" the play borrows from Gascoigne and finds its chief character, Stump, "oddly reminiscent of Gascoigne himself" (pp. 94, 95). He devotes a chapter to the connection, arguing that the play amounts to more than simplistic propaganda (*ibid.*, pp. 83-101).
9. Martin, p. 29.
10. Cunningham, p. xxxi.
11. Gillian Austen notes that Robert Poley made twelve trips to the Netherlands, receiving payments which ranged from six to thirty pounds: see GA, pp. 183,. 215.
12. Gascoigne, *The Spoyle of Antwerp*, p. vi.
13. I have read only the copy in the British Library. For the Bodleian copy, see GA, p. 180.
14. Nicholl, *The Reckoning*, p. 172.
15. British Library, Royal Manuscripts, 18 A. LXI.
16. Austen describes the relationship between *The Grief of Joy* and Petrarch's *De remediis utriusque fortunae* as "tenuous at best" and sums up Gascoigne's text as "an extremely loose adaptation of Petrarch's main theme with scattered interpolations from his source": GA, p. 197.
17. The Second Song, stanza 63: JWC, p. 538.
18. The Second Song, stanzas 17 and 11: JWC, pp. 529, 528.
19. The Second Song, stanza 30: JWC, p. 532.
20. The Second Song, stanza 59: JWC, p. 537.
21. The Third Song, stanza 32: JWC, p. 546.
22. The Third Song, stanza 12. JWC, p. 542.
23. The Fourth Song, stanza 34: JWC, p. 554.
24. The Fourth Song, stanza 42: JWC, p. 556.
25. The Fourth Song, stanza 45: JWC, p. 557.
26. Austen sees the work in a more positive light, praising *The Grief of Joy* as "a closely planned and highly polished performance": GA, 200.

29: A Death at Stamford

1. 4, 26-36.
2. Hassell Smith and Baker, pp. 3-4. Gascoigne's letter to Sir Nicholas Bacon is wrongly dated 1 January 1578.
3. The manuscript is held at the Norfolk Record Office: Ray.25.
4. GA, p. 213.

5   See GA, pp. 201, 210.
6   George Whetstone, *A Remembraunce of the wel imployed life, and godly end, of George Gaskoigne Esquire, who deceased at Stalmford in Lincolne Shire the 7. of October. 1577.* (1577), stanzas 2 and 3: EA, p. 17.
7   See Izard, p. 228.
8   **P9**, 4.
9   See Eccles, "George Whetstone in Star Chamber".
10 **P9**.
11 Izard, p. 28.
12 *Ibid.*, p. 178. Izard suggests that "Whetstone's relations with the Bretons may conceivably have been quite intimate" and notes joint associations with both Lincolnshire and Holborn.
13 Quoted in *ibid*, p. 36.
14 *Ibid.*, p. 44.
15 EA, p. 15.
16 Quoted in Izard, p. 231.
17 EA, p. 26.
18 In Arber, *George Gascoigne, Esquire*.
19 Beecher and Butler, *Supposes*, p. 53.
20 EA, p. 20.
21 EA, p. 22.
22 Stanza 28, l. 6: EA, p. 22.
23 Breton, *The Good and the Badde* (1616).
24 Stanzas 31-33: EA, p. 23.
25 See https://www.theguardian.com/books/2018/jul/31/traces-on-george-orwell-letter-suggest-he-caught-tb-from-spanish-hospital and McKeown, p. 55
26 Gaskill, p.263.
27 Breton, *Crossing of Proverbs: Cross-Answeres And Crosse Humours* (1616).
28 Stanza 44, ll. 3-6.
29 Stanza 42, ll. 3-4.
30 Stanza 47, l. 1.
31 Breton, *Fantasticks* (1626).
32 **65**, 23-6.
33 Nichols, *The Diary of Henry Machyn*, p. 125.
34 Stanza 49, ll. 2-3.

30: 'When the Dirge is done"
1   "October" in Breton, *Fantasticks*.
2   Quoted in Brooks.
3   Quoted in Izard, pp. 19-20.
4   Stern, *Gabriel Harvey*, p. 33.
5   *Ibid*.
6   GG, p. 281.
7   *Ibid*.

8 "Dan Bartholmew of Bathe", Part 9, 'His last will and Testament': HSF, p. 354, l. 49.
9 **71**, 177.
10 HSF, p. xli.
11 Tappan, p. 225.
12 See SCH, p. 118.
13 Robertson, *Poems by Nicholas Breton*, p. xxxi.
14 *Ibid.*, p. xxiv.
15 Greer, p. 13.
16 Bassnett, p. 126.
17 Wright, p. 86.
18 Quoted in SCH, pp. 8-9.
19 Donno, p. 74.
20 Nicholl, "Rough but true", p. 884.
21 Duncan-Jones, *Sir Philip Sidney*, p. 138.
22 SCH, p. 103.
23 *Ibid.*
24 *Ibid.*
25 *Ibid.*, p. 105.
26 *Ibid.*
27 GG, p. 5.
28 Chalmers, pp. 447, 455.
29 Hazlitt, vol. I., p. xxviii.
30 Winters, p. 139.
31 Schmidt, *Lives of the Poets*, p. 146.
32 Billington, p. 23.
33 "The Grief of Joy", The First Song, stanza 22: JWC, p. 521.

Bibliography

PRIMARY SOURCES

Manuscripts

British Library:
Royal MS 18 A.xlviii, *The Tale of Hemetes the Heremyte*.
Royal MS 18A.lxi. *The Grief of Joye*.

Public Record Office:
SP Dom. 12/86, 59. "Agaynst George Gascoigne".
SP For. 70/139, fol. 169. Letter from George Gascoigne to Lord Burghley from Paris, 15 September 1576.
SP For. 70/140, fol. 23. Letter from George Gascoigne to Lord Burghley from Paris, 7 October 1576.
E179/145/220

The Record Office, Bedford:
Whitbread Collection, vol. 9, Estate Papers.

Norfolk Record Office:
Ray.25

Gascoigne Editions

Arber, Edward (ed.) *George Gascoigne, Esquire 1. Certain Notes of Instruction in English Verse 2. The Steele Glas 3. The Complaynt of Philomene, preceded by George Whetstone's A Remembrance of the well imployed Life, and godly end of George Gascoigne Esquire, etc.* (London: Constable, 1901).
Beecher, Donald and Butler, John. *Lodovico Ariosto, Supposes. Translated by George Gascoigne* (Ottawa: Dovehouse Editions, 1999).
Binns, Ronald (ed.) *George Gascoigne: Selected Poems, with "Certayne notes of Instruction concerning the making of verse or ryme in English"* (London: Zoilus Press, 2000).
Cunliffe, J. W. "The Queenes Majesties Entertainment at Woodstocke", *PMLA* 26, 1 (1911), pp. 92-141.
Cunliffe, J. W. *The Complete Works of George Gascoigne*, 2 vols. (New York: Greenwood Press, 1969).
Fleming, Abraham. *A Paradoxe, Proving by reason and example, that Baldnesse is much better than bushie hair, &c ... Hereunto is annexed the pleasant*

tale of Hemetes the Heremite, pronounced before the Queenes Majestie (London: H. Denham, 1579).

[Gascoigne, George]. *A hundredth sundrie Flowres bounde up in one small Poesie* (Anonymous, n. d.) [London: Richard Smith, 1573].

Gascoigne, George. *The Glasse of Government* (London: C. Barker, 1575).

[Gascoigne, George]. *The Noble Arte of Venerie or Hunting* [Anonymous] (London: C. Barker, 1575).

Gascoigne, George. *The Posies of George Gascoigne* (London: Richard Smith, 1575).

Gascoigne, George. *The Droomme of Doomesday* (London: G. Cawood, 1576).

[Gascoigne, George]. *The Spoyle of Antwerp* (London: Richard Jones, 1576).

Gascoigne, George. *The Steele Glas ... Together with The Complainte of Phylomene* (London: Richard Smith, 1576).

Gascoigne, George. *The Whole woorkes of George Gascoigne* (London: Abell Jeffes, 1587).

Gascoigne, George. *Gascoigne's Princelye Pleasures with the Masque intended to have been presented before Queen Elizabeth at Kenilworth Castle in 1575* (London: J. H. Burn et al., 1821).

Gascoigne, George. *The Princelye Pleasures at the Courte at Kenelwoorth* (London: F. Marshall, 1821).

[Gascoigne, George]. *The Queen's Majesty's Entertainment at Woodstock 1575* (Oxford: Clarendon Press, 1910).

Hazlitt, William Carew (ed.) *The Complete Poems of George Gascoigne*. 2 vols. (London: Roxburghe Library, 1869-70).

Pigman, G. W. *George Gascoigne: A Hundreth Sundrie Flowres* (Oxford: Clarendon Press, 2000).

Pooley, Roger (ed.) *George Gascoigne, The Green Knight: Selected Poetry and Prose* (Manchester: Carcanet New Press, 1982).

Prouty, C. T. (ed.) *George Gascoigne's A Hundreth Sundrie Flowres* (Columbia: University of Missouri Press, 1942).

Ward, B. M. (ed.) *A Hundreth Sundrie Flowres, From the Original Edition* (London: Etchells and Macdonald, 1926).

Other Editions

[Anonymous]. *A Guide to Kenilworth, containing a brief historical account of the Castle, Priory and Church* (Coventry: Merridew and Son, 1825).

[Anonymous]. *A guide to Kenilworth Castle, containing a brief account of its ancient history, with a particular description of the present state of its ruins. To which are added, historical and descriptive notices of the priory and the church, and lines on visiting the Castle* (Coventry: H. Merridew, 1834).

[Anonymous]. *The Historical Monuments of Waltham Forest* (Walthamstow, n.d., n.p.)

[Anonymous]. *Robert Laneham. A Letter*. Facsimile edition of *A Letter* [c. 1575] (Menston: Scolar Press, 1968).

Arber, Edward (ed.) *Tottel's Miscellany: Songes and Sonettes* (London: privately printed, 1870).

Ariosto, Ludovico. *Orlando Furioso*, trans. Guido Waldman (Oxford: Oxford University Press, 1998).

Benson, Larry D. (ed.) *The Riverside Chaucer* (Oxford: Oxford University Press, 1988).

Binns, J. W. *Latin Treatises on Poetry from Renaissance England* (Signal Mountain: Summertown, 1999).

Booth, Stephen (ed.) *Shakespeare's Sonnets* (New Haven: Yale University Press, 2000).

Braunmuller, A. R. (ed.) *Macbeth* (Cambridge: Cambridge University Press, 1997).

Breton, Nicholas. *A Post with a Packet of Mad Letters* (London: John Smethicke, 1602).

Breton, Nicholas. *The Good and the Badde, or Descriptions of the worthies and unworthies of this age* (London: John Budge, 1616).

Breton, Nicholas. *Crossing of Proverbs: Cross-Answeres and Crosse-Humours* (London: John Wright, 1616).

Breton, Nicholas. *Fantasticks* (London: Francis Williams, 1626).

Bunyan, John. *Grace Abounding to the Chief of Sinners* (London: The Religious Tract Society, 1912).

Bunyan, John. *The Pilgrim's Progress*, ed. Roger Sharrock (Harmondsworth: Penguin, 1965).

Burrow, Colin (ed.) *William Shakespeare: The Complete Sonnets and Poems* (Oxford: Oxford University Press, 2002).

Castiglione, Baldesar. *The Book of the Courtier*, trans. George Bull (Harmondsworth: Penguin, 1967).

Chalmers, Alexander (ed.) *The Works of the English Poets from Chaucer to Cowper*, vol. II (London: Johnson, 1810).

Chaucer, Geoffrey. *Troylus and Criseyde*, ed. Maldwyn Mills (London: Everyman, 2000).

Cunningham, Peter (ed.) *Extracts from the Accounts of the Revels at Court, in the Reigns of Queen Elizabeth and King James I* (London: Shakspeare (*sic*) Society, 1842).

Dasent, J. R. (ed.) *Acts of the Privy Council of England* (new series), vol. VIII (1571-1575) (Nendeln: Kraus, 1974).

Dasent, J. R. (ed.) *Acts of the Privy Council of England* (new series), vol. IX (1575-1577) (London: Eyre and Spottiswoode, 1894).

dei Segni, Lothario. *On the Misery of the Human Condition*, ed., Donald R Howard, trans. Margaret Mary Dietz (New York: Bobbs-Merril, 1969).

Donno, Elizabeth Story (ed.) *An Elizabethan in 1582: The Diary of Richard Madox, Fellow of All Souls* (London: The Hakluyt Society, 1976).

Duncan-Jones, Catherine (ed.) *Shakespeare's Sonnets* (London: Arden Shakespeare, 2010).

Evans, John X. (ed.) *The Works of Sir Roger Williams* (Oxford: Clarendon Press 1972).

Furnivall, F. J. *Robert Laneham's Letter* (London: Chatto and Windus,1907).

Gassner, John (ed.) *Elizabethan Drama* (New York: Bantam, 1967).

Gilbert, Sir Humfrey. *A Discourse of a Discovery for a new Passage to Cataia* (London: Richard Jhones, 1576).

Goldring, Elizabeth (ed.) *John Nichols's* The Progresses and Public Processions of Queen Elizabeth I*: A New Edition of the Early Modern Sources*, vol. 2 (Oxford: Oxford University Press, 2014).

Grosart, The Rev. Alexander B. (ed.) *The Works in Verse and Prose of Nicholas Breton* (Edinburgh: privately printed, 1875-79).

Greg, W. W. (ed.) *A Larum for London* (London: The Malone Society, 1913).

Hassell Smith, A. and Gillian M. Baker (eds.) *The Papers of Nathaniel Bacon of Stiffkey*, vol. 2 (Norwich: Norfolk Record Society, 1983).

Haydn, Hiram. *The Portable Elizabethan Reader* (New York: Viking, 1980).

Hill, Thomas. *The Gardener's Labyrinth*, ed. Richard Mabey (Oxford: Oxford University Press, 1988).

Holland, Peter (ed.) *A Midsummer Night's Dream* (Oxford: Oxford University Press, 1998).

Howard, Henry, Earl of Surrey. *Poems*, ed. Emrys Jones (Oxford: Clarendon Press, 1973).

Humphreys, A. R. (ed.) *King Henry IV, Part Two* (London: Methuen, 1966).

Humphreys, A. R. (ed.) *Much Ado About Nothing* (London: Arden Shakespeare, 1984).

Jonson, Ben. *The Sad Shepherd, The Fall of Mortimer, Masques and Entertainments*, ed. C. H. Herford, Percy Simpson and Evelyn Simpson (Oxford: Clarendon Press, 1952).

Kerrigan, John (ed.) *William Shakespeare:* The Sonnets *and* A Lover's Complaint (London: Penguin, 1999).

Kuin, R. J. P. (ed.) *Robert Langham: A Letter* (Leiden: E. J. Brill, 1983).

Lucie-Smith, Edward (ed.) *The Penguin Book of Elizabethan Verse* (Harmondsworth: Penguin, 1978).

Martin, C. T. (ed.) *The Journal of Sir Francis Walsingham* (London: The Camden Society, 1870).

More, Thomas. *Utopia*, trans. Paul Turner (Harmondsworth: Penguin, 1977).

Morris, Brian (ed.) *The Taming of the Shrew* (London: Arden Shakespeare,

1997).

Moseley, C. W. R. D. (ed. and trans.) *The Travels of Sir John Mandeville* (Harmondsworth: Penguin, 1983).

Nashe, Thomas. *The Unfortunate Traveller and Other Works*, ed. J. B. Steane (Harmondsworth: Penguin, 1984).

Nichols, John. *The Progresses and Public Processions of Queen Elizabeth I*, 3 vols. (London: John Nichols and Son, 1823).

Nichols, John (ed.) *The Diary of Henry Machyn, Citizen and Merchant-Taylor of London, from A.D. 1550 to A.D. 1563* (London: The Camden Society, 1848).

Paterson, Don (ed.) *101 sonnets by 101 poets: from Shakespeare to Heaney* (London: Penguin, 1999).

Patten, William. *The Calender of Scripture* (London: Richard Jugge, 1575).

Petrarca, Francesco [Petrarch]. *Canzoniere: Selected Poems*, trans. and ed. Anthony Mortimer (London: Penguin, 2002).

Pollard, Alfred W. *English miracle plays: Moralities and interludes. Specimens of the pre-Elizabethan drama.* (Oxford: Clarendon Press, 1965).

Puttenham, George. *The Arte of English Poesie*, ed. Gladys Doidge Willcock and Alice Walker (Cambridge: Cambridge University Press, 1970).

Ralegh, Sir Walter. *The Poems of Sir Walter Ralegh*, ed. Agnes M. C. Latham (London: Routledge and Kegan Paul, 1962).

Robertson, Jean (ed.) *Poems by Nicholas Breton* (Liverpool: Liverpool University Press, 1952).

Salzman, Paul (ed.) *An Anthology of Elizabethan Prose Fiction* (Oxford: Oxford University Press, 1998)

Sidney, Philip. *Defence of Poesie, Astrophil and Stella and Other Writings*, ed. Elizabeth Porges Watson (London: Everyman, 1999).

Skelton, John. *Selected Poems*, ed. Greg Walker (London: Everyman, 1997).

Spenser, Edmund. *Selected Poetry*, ed. A. C. Hamilton (New York: New American Library, 1966).

Spenser, Edmund. *The Faerie Queene*, ed. Thomas P. Roche and C. Patrick O'Donnell (Harmondsworth: Penguin, 1984).

Walton, Michael (ed.) *Euripides, Plays: One* (London: Methuen, 2000).

Webster, John. *The Duchess of Malfi*, ed. John Russell Brown (Manchester: Manchester University Press, 1997).

Williams, John (ed.) *English Renaissance Poetry: A Collection of Shorter Poems from Skelton to Jonson* (New York: Anchor Books,1963).

Wyatt, Sir Thomas. *The Complete Poems*, ed. R. A. Rebholz (Harmondsworth: Penguin, 1978).

SECONDARY SOURCES

Adams, Robert P. "Gascoigne's Master F.J. as Original Fiction", *PMLA* 73, 4 (September 1958), 315-326.
[Anonymous]. *Walthamstow Village Conservation Area* (London: London Borough of Waltham Forest, n.d.).
[Anonymous]. *Notes on the history of St. Giles' Church without Cripplegate, Barbican E.C.2.* (London: St Giles' Church, 1969).
[Anonymous]. *The Parish Church of St Mary the Virgin, Whitkirk, Leeds* (1992).
[Anonymous]. *The Church of St. Mary, Walthamstow* (London: Walthamstow Historical Society, 1997).
[Anonymous]. *St Giles' Church, Cripplegate* (2000).
[Anonymous]. *St Mary's Church, Whaddon* (2002).
Bassnett, Susan. *Elizabeth I: A Feminist Perspective* (Oxford: Berg, 1988).
Bayley, Peter. *Edmund Spenser: Prince of Poets* (London: Hutchinson, 1971).
Bayne, C. G. "The Coronation of Queen Elizabeth", *English Historical Review* 22, 88 (October 1907), pp. 650-73.
Beauregard, David N. "Isabella as Novice: Shakespeare's Use of Whetstone's *Heptameron*", *English Language Notes* 25, 4 (1988), pp. 20-23.
Beckingsale, B. W. *Burghley: Tudor Statesman 1520-1598* (London: Macmillan, 1967).
Benjamin, Walter. *Illuminations* ed. Hannah Arendt (Glasgow: Fontana, 1977).
Berry, Eleanor. "The Reading and Uses of Elizabethan Prosodies", *Language and Style* 14, 2 (Spring 1981), pp. 116-152.
Billington, Michael. "The old men's turn", *The Guardian* (1 July 2000), p. 23.
Binns, J. W. *Intellectual Culture in Elizabethan and Jacobean England: The Latin Writings of the Age* (Leeds: Francis Cairns, 1990).
Binns, Ronald. *Elizabeth, Shakespeare and the Castle: The story of the Kenilworth revels* (York: Zoilus Press, 2008).
Binns, Ronald. *Orwell in Southwold* (York: Zoilus Press, 2018).
Bolton, W. F. (ed.) *The English Language* (London: Barrie and Jenkins, 1975).
Boose, Lynda E. "The 1599 Bishops' Ban, Elizabethan Pornography, and the Sexualization of the Jacobean Stage" in Richard Burt and John Michael Archer (eds.), *Enclosure Acts: Sexuality, Property, and Culture in Early Modern England* (Ithaca, NY: Cornell University Press, 1994), pp. 185-200.
Bowen, Catherine Drinker. *Francis Bacon: The Temper of a Man* (Boston: Little, Brown, 1963).
Bowers, Fredson Thayer. "Notes on Gascoigne's *A Hundreth Sundrie Flowres* and *The Posies*", *Harvard Studies and Notes in Philology and Literature* 16 (1934), pp. 13-35.
Bradner, Leicester. "The First English Novel: A Study of George Gascoigne's *Adventures of Master F.J.*", *PMLA* 45, 2 (1930), pp. 543-52.

Brooks, E. L. "The Burial Place of George Gascoigne", *The Review of English Studies* 5, 17 (January 1954), p. 59.

Brownlow, F. W. *"The Boke of Phyllyp Sparowe* and the Liturgy", *English Literary Renaissance* 9, 1 (Winter 1979), pp. 5-20.

Burrow, Colin. "Waves of wo", *London Review of Books* 23, 13 (5 July 2001), pp. 17-19.

Buxton, John. *Sir Philip Sidney and the English Renaissance* (London: Macmillan, 1965).

Cavendish, George. *The Life and Death of Cardinal Wolsey*, ed. Richard S. Sylvester (Oxford: Oxford University Press, 1959).

Cawley, Robert Ralston. "George Gascoigne and the Siege of Famagusta", *Modern Language Notes* 43, 5 (May 1928), pp. 296-300.

Chadwick, Owen. *The Reformation*. (Harmondsworth: Penguin 1964).

Chambers, E. K. *Sir Henry Lee. An Elizabethan Portrait.* (Oxford: Clarendon Press, 1936).

Chandler, David (ed.) *The Oxford Illustrated History of the British Army* (Oxford: Oxford University Press, 1994).

Childs, Jessie. *Henry VIII's Last Victim. The Life and Times of Henry Howard, Earl of Surrey* (London: Vintage, 2008).

Childs, Jessie. *God's Traitors. Terror and Faith in Elizabethan England* (London: Vintage, 2015).

Clare, Janet. *"Art made tongue-tied by authority": Elizabethan and Jacobean Dramatic Censorship* (Manchester: Manchester University Press, 1990).

[Clarke, Ebenezer]. *The History of Walthamstow; Its Past, Present and Future* (Walthamstow: Joseph Shillinglaw, 1861).

Clegg, Cyndia Susan. *Press Censorship in Elizabethan England* (Cambridge: Cambridge University Press, 1997).

Clermont, Thomas Lord. *A History of the Family of Fortescue in all its Branches*, vol. II (London: Ellis and White, 1880).

Colman, E. A. M. *The Dramatic Use of Bawdy in Shakespeare* (London: Longman, 1976).

Cooper, Charles Henry and Thompson Cooper. *Athenae Cantabrigienses*, vol. 1 *1500-1585* (Cambridge: Deighton Bell, 1858).

Cooper, Helen. "Welcome to the House of Fame", *Times Literary Supplement* (27 October 2000), pp. 3-4.

Coote, Stephen. *A Play of Passion: The Life of Sir Walter Ralegh* (London: Macmillan, 1993).

Crawford, Charles. "Puttenham's 'Arte of English Poesie' and George Gascoigne", *Notes and Queries* 11 (November 1910), pp. 363-4.

Crosby, Allan James (ed.) *Calendar of State Papers, Foreign Series, of the Reign of Elizabeth, 1575-77* (London: Longman, 1880).

Daniell, David. *William Tyndale: A Biography* (New Haven: Yale University

Press, 1994).

Davies, Christopher. *A Guide to St Martin's Church, Stamford Baron* (n.p., n.d.)

Davis, Walter R. *Idea and Act in Elizabethan Fiction* (Princeton, N.J.: Princeton University Press, 1969).

Dovey, Zillah. *An Elizabethan Progress. The Queen's Journey into East Anglia, 1578* (Stroud: Sutton, 1996).

Duncan-Jones, Katherine. *Sir Philip Sidney: Courtier Poet* (London: Hamilton, 1991).

Eccles, Christine. *The Rose Theatre* (London: Nick Hern, 1990).

Eccles, Mark. "Brief Lives: Tudor and Stuart Authors", *Studies in Philology* 79 4 (Fall 1982), pp. 1-135.

Eccles, Mark. "George Whetstone in Star Chamber", *The Review of English Studies* 33, 132 (November 1982), pp. 385-95.

Edwards, Anthony S. G. (ed.) *Skelton: The Critical Heritage* (London: Routledge and Kegan Paul, 1981).

Emmison, F. G. *Elizabethan Life: Disorder* (Chelmsford: Essex County Council, 1970), Appendix E.

Eriksen, Roy T. "George Gascoigne's and Mary Sidney's Versions of Psalm 130", *Cahiers Élisabéthains: A Journal of English Renaissance Studies* 36, 1 (October 1989), pp. 1-9.

Evans, Brian. *Bygone Walthamstow* (Chichester: Phillimore, 1995).

Feldman, Abraham B. "Playwrights and Pike-trailers in the Low Countries", *Notes and Queries* 198 (May 1953), pp. 184-7.

Ferber, Stanley. "Peter Bruegel and the Duke of Alba", *Renaissance News* 19, 3 (Autumn 1966), pp. 205-219.

Ferguson, Charles. *Naked to Mine Enemies: The Life of Cardinal Wolsey* (London: Longmans, Green and Co., 1958).

Fieler, Frank B. "Gascoigne's Use of Courtly Love Conventions in *The Adventures Passed by Master F.J.*", *Studies in Short Fiction* 1 (1963-64), pp. 26-32.

Fleay, Frederick Gard. *A Biographical Chronicle of the English Drama, 1559-1642* (London: Reeves and Turner, 1891).

Flournoy, Fitzgerald. "William Breton, Nicholas Breton, and George Gascoigne", *The Review of English Studies* 16, 63 (1940), pp. 262-273.

Ford, Boris (ed.) *The Age of Shakespeare* (Harmondsworth: Penguin 1966).

Forster, Albert J. *Bunyan's Country. Studies in the Bedfordshire Topography of The Pilgrim's Progress* (London: H. Virtue and Co., 1901).

Gardner, John. *The Life and Times of Chaucer* (London: Granada, 1979).

Gaskill, Malcolm. *Witchfinders: A Seventeenth Century English Tragedy* (Cambridge, MA: Harvard University Press, 2006).

Geyl, Pieter. *The Revolt of the Netherlands, 1555-1609* (London: Benn, 1962).

Godber, Joyce. *History of Bedfordshire, 1066-1888* (Bedford: Bedfordshire

County Council, 1969).

Goldring, Elizabeth. "Portraiture, Patronage, and the Progresses: Robert Dudley, Earl of Leicester, and the Kenilworth Festivities of 1575", in Jayne Elisabeth Archer, Elizabeth Goldring and Sarah Knight, *The Progresses, Pageants, and Entertainments of Queen Elizabeth I* (Oxford: Oxford University Press, 2007), pp. 163-88.

Goldring, Elizabeth. "The Earl of Leicester's Inventory of Kenilworth Castle, c.1578", *English Heritage Historical Review* 2, 1 (2007), pp. 36-59.

Goldring, Elizabeth. "'A mercer ye wot az we be': The authorship of the Kenilworth Letter reconsidered", *English Literary Renaissance* 38, 2 (April 2008), pp. 245-269.

Goldring, Elizabeth. "Gascoigne and Kenilworth: The Production, Reception, and Afterlife of *The Princely Pleasures*", *English Literary Renaissance* 44, 3 (Autumn 2014), pp. 363-387.

Gosling, William Gilbert. *The Life of Sir Humphrey Gilbert: England's First Empire Builder* (London: Constable, 1911).

Grabes, Herbert. *The Mutable Glass: Mirror-imagery in titles and texts of the Middle Ages and the English Renaissance*, trans. Gordon Collier (Cambridge: Cambridge University Press, 1982).

Green, A. Wigfall. *The Inns of Court and Early English Drama* (New Haven: Yale University Press, 1931).

Greer, Germaine. *Shakespeare* (Oxford: Oxford University Press, 1986).

Greg, W. W. *English Literary Autographs 1550-1650* (Oxford: Oxford University Press, 1932).

Grey of Wilton, K.G., Arthur, Lord. *A Commentary of the Services and Charges of William Lord Grey of Wilton, K.G.*, ed. Philip de Malpas Grey Egerton (London: The Camden Society, 1847).

Griffin, Benjamin. "The Breaking of the Giants: Historical Drama in Coventry and London", *English Literary Renaissance* 29, 1 (Winter 1999), pp. 3-21.

Gristwood, Sarah. *Elizabeth and Leicester: power, passion, and politics* (New York: Viking, 2007).

Gwyn, Peter. *The King's Cardinal: The Rise and Fall of Thomas Wolsey* (London: Pimlico, 1992).

Hamrick, Stephen. "'Set in Portraiture': George Gascoigne, Queen Elizabeth, and Adapting the Royal Image", *Early Modern Literary Studies* 11, 1 (May 2005), pp. 1-30.

Hammond, Gerald (ed.) *Elizabethan Poetry, Lyrical and Narrative: A Selection of Critical Essays* (London: Macmillan, 1984).

Hardison, O. B. *Prosody and Purpose in the English Renaissance* (Baltimore: Johns Hopkins University Press, 1989).

Hasler, P. W. *The House of Commons 1558-1603* (London: HMSO, 1981).

Haynes, Alan. *Sex in Elizabethan England* (Stroud: The History Press, 1997).

Hazard, Mary E. "A Magnificent Lord: Leicester, Kenilworth, and Transformations in the Idea of Magnificence", *Cahiers Élisabéthains: A Journal of English Renaissance Studies* 31, 1 (April 1987), pp. 11-35.

Hill, Betty. "Trinity College Cambridge MS.B. 14.52 and William Patten", *Transactions of the Cambridge Bibliographical Society* 4, 3 (1966), pp. 192-200.

Hogg, Ian V. *The Guinness Encyclopedia of Weaponry* (Enfield: Guinness, 1992).

Honan, Park. *Shakespeare: A Life* (Oxford: Oxford University Press, 1987).

Hughes, Felicity A. "Gascoigne's Poses", *Studies in English Literature, 1500-1900* 37, 1 (Winter 1997), pp. 1-19.

Irwin, Margaret. *That Great Lucifer* (Harmondsworth: Penguin, 1962).

Izard, Thomas C. *George Whetstone: Mid-Elizabethan Gentleman of Letters.* (New York: Columbia University Press, 1942).

Jardine, Lisa. *The Awful End of Prince William the Silent: The First Assassination of a Head of State with a Handgun.* (New York: HarperCollins, 2005).

Jardine, Lisa and Alan Stewart. *Hostage to Fortune: The Troubled Life of Francis Bacon* (London: Gollancz, 1998).

Jenkins, Elizabeth. *Elizabeth and Leicester* (London: Phoenix, 2002).

Johnson, Ronald C. *George Gascoigne* (New York: Twayne, 1972).

Jones, Norman. *The Birth of the Elizabethan Age: England in the 1560s* (Oxford: Blackwell, 1995).

Karl, Frederick R. *A Reader's Guide to the development of the English novel in the eighteenth century* (London: Thames and Hudson, 1975).

Kittle, William. *G. Gascoigne, April 1562 to January 1, 1578; or, Edward de Vere, seventeenth Earl of Oxford, 1550-1604* (Washington: W. F. Roberts, 1930).

Kneidel, Gregory. "Reforming George Gascoigne", *Exemplaria* 10, 2 (1998), pp. 329-370.

Kuin, R. J. P. "The Purloined *Letter*: Evidence and Probability Regarding Robert Langham's Authorship", *The Library* 7, 2 (June 1985), pp. 115-25.

Kundera, Milan. *The Art of the Novel*, trans. Linda Asher (London: Faber, 1988).

Lanham, Richard A. "Narrative Structure in Gascoigne's F.J.", *Studies in Short Fiction* 4, 1 (Fall 1966), pp. 42-50.

Law, A. D. and S. Barry. *The Forest in Walthamstow and Chingford* (London: Chingford Historical Society and Walthamstow Antiquarian Society, 1995).

Lloyd, Ernest G. *Trees and Shrubs of Epping Forest 1878-1978* (Epping: Epping Forest District Council Museum Service, 1978).

Lloyd, Michael. *Portrait of Lincolnshire* (London: R. Hale, 1983).

Loades, D. M. "The Press Under the Early Tudors: A study in Censorship and Sedition", *Transactions of the Cambridge Bibliographical Society* 4, 1

(1964), pp. 29-50.

Loughlin, Susan. *Insurrection: Henry VIII, Thomas Cromwell and the Pilgrimage of Grace* (Stroud: The History Press, 2016).

Lyons, Mathew. *The Favourite: Ralegh and his Queen* (London: Constable, 2012).

MacCaffrey, Wallace. *The Shaping of the Elizabethan Regime: Elizabethan Politics 1558-72* (London: Cape, 1969).

MacCulloch, Diarmaid. *Reformation: Europe's House Divided 1490-1700* (London: Penguin, 2004).

MacLeod, Catharine. *Tudor Portraits* (London: National Portrait Gallery, 1996).

MacNalty, Sir Arthur. "Laurence Sterne: A Witty Consumptive", *British Journal of Tuberculosis and Diseases of the Chest* 52, 1 (January 1958), pp. 94-7.

Mander, David. *Walthamstow Past* (London: Historical Publications, 2001).

Marx, Karl. *Capital*, vol. 1, trans. Ben Fowkes (Harmondsworth: Penguin, 1976).

Maslen, Robert W. *Elizabethan Fictions: Espionage, Counter-Espionage, and the Duplicity of Fiction in Early Elizabethan Prose Narratives* (Oxford: Oxford University Press, 1997).

Matusiak, John. *Wolsey: The Life of King Henry VIII's Cardinal* (Stroud: The History Press, Stroud, 2014).

May, Steven W. "Companion Poems in the Ralegh Canon", *English Literary Renaissance* 13, 3 (Autumn 1983), pp. 260-273.

May, Steven W. *The Elizabethan Courtier Poets: The Poems and their Contexts* (Asheville, NC: Pegasus Press, 1999).

McCoy, Richard C. "Gascoigne's 'Poëmata castrata': The Wages of Courtly Success", *Criticism* 27, 1 (Winter 1985), pp. 29-55.

McDermott, James. *Martin Frobisher: Elizabethan Privateer* (London: Yale University Press, 2001).

McKeown, Adam N. *English Mercuries: Soldier Poets in the Age of Shakespeare* (Nashville: Vanderbilt University Press, 2009).

Mee, Arthur. *Lincolnshire*, ed. and rev. F. T. Baker (London: Hodder and Stoughton, 1970).

Milton, Giles. *The Riddle and the Knight: In Search of Sir John Mandeville* (London: Farrar, Straus, Giroux, 2001).

Modic, John L. "Gascoigne and Ariosto Again", *Comparative Literature* 14, 3 (Summer 1962), pp. 317-19.

Monaghan, Jason and Mensun Bound. *A ship cast away about Alderney: investigations of an Elizabethan shipwreck* (Alderney: Alderney Maritime Trust, 2001).

Moore Smith, G. C. *Gabriel Harvey's Marginalia* (Stratford-upon-Avon: Shakespeare Head Press, 1913).

Morris, Richard K. "A Plan for Kenilworth Castle at Longleat", *English*

Heritage Historical Review 2, 1 (2007), pp. 23-35.

Morris, T.A. *Tudor Government* (London, 1999).

Moynahan, Brian. *William Tyndale: If God Spare My Life* (London: Abacus, 2003).

Nash, Ilana. "'A Subject without Subjection': Robert Dudley, Earl of Leicester, and *The Princely Pleasures at Kenelworth Castle*", *Comitatus: A Journal of Medieval and Renaissance Studies* 25, 1 (October 1994), pp. 81-102.

Nelson, Alan H. "The life and theatrical interests of Edward de Vere, seventeenth Earl of Oxford", in Paul Edmondson and Stanley Wells (eds.), *Shakespeare Beyond Doubt: Evidence, Argument, Controversy* (Cambridge: Cambridge University Press, 2013), pp. 39-48.

Nicholl, Charles. "Rough but true", *Times Literary Supplement* (19 August 1983), p. 884.

Nicholl, Charles. *The Reckoning: The Murder of Christopher Marlowe* (London: Picador, 1993).

Nielson, John and Royal Skousen. "How Much of the King James Bible Is William Tyndale's? An Estimation Based on Sampling", *Reformation* 3, 1 (1998), pp. 49-74.

O'Kill, Brian. "The Printed Works of William Patten (c.1510-c.1600)", *Transactions of the Cambridge Bibliographical Society* 7, 1 (1977), pp. 28-45.

Ord, Melanie. "Classical and contemporary Italy in Roger Ascham's *The Scholemaster* (1570)", *Renaissance Studies* 16, 2 (June 2002), pp. 202-16.

Palliser, D. M. *The Age of Elizabeth: England under the later Tudors 1547-1603*, 2nd ed. (London: Longman, 1992).

Parrish, Paul A. "The Multiple Perspectives of Gascoigne's 'The Adventures of Master F.J.'", *Studies in Short Fiction* 10, 1 (Winter 1973), pp. 75-84.

Partridge, Eric. *Shakespeare's Bawdy* (London: Routledge, 1968).

Paulin, Tom. "In the Workshop", *London Review of Books* 20, 2 (22 January 1998).

Pollard. A. F. *Tudor Tracts 1532-1588* (London: Constable, 1903).

Potter, Irene. *Queen Elizabeth I Visits Kenilworth 1575* (Kenilworth: Kenilworth History and Archaeology Society, 1975).

Prior, Roger. "Gascoigne's *Posies* as a Shakespearean source", *Notes and Queries* 47, 4 (December 2000), pp. 444-9.

Prouty, C. T. "George Gascoigne and Elizabeth Bacon Bretton Boyes Gascoigne: a series of problems and their answers", *The Review of English Studies* 14, 55 (July 1938), pp. 257-70.

Prouty, C. T. *George Gascoigne: Elizabethan Courtier, Soldier, and Poet* (New York: Benjamin Blom, 1966).

Prouty, Charles and Ruth Prouty. "George Gascoigne, *The Noble Arte of Venerie*, and Queen Elizabeth at Kenilworth", in James G. McManaway, Giles E.

Dawson and Edwin E. Willoughby (eds.), *Joseph Quincy Adams: Memorial Studies* (Washington: Folger Shakespeare Library, 1948), pp. 639-65.

Reaney, P. H. *The place names of Walthamstow* (London: Walthamstow Antiquarian Society, 1930).

Reaney, P. H. *The Church of St Mary, Walthamstow* (London: Walthamstow Antiquarian Society, 1969).

Reaney, P. H. *A History of Walthamstow* (London: Borough of Waltham Forest, 1979).

Renn, Derek F. *Kenilworth Castle* (London: English Heritage, 2003).

Ridley, Jasper. *The Tudor Age* (London: Constable, 1988).

Righter, Anne. *Shakespeare and the Idea of the Play* (Harmondsworth: Penguin, 1967).

Robertson, Jean. "George Gascoigne and 'The Noble Art of Venerie and Hunting'", *The Modern Language Review* 37, 4 (October 1942), pp. 484-5.

Rosenberg, Eleanor. *Leicester: Patron of Letters* (New York: Octagon, 1976).

Romig, Keith and Peter Lawrence. *The Archives Photograph Series: Walthamstow* (Stroud: Tempus, 1996).

Ryan, Lawrence V. *Roger Ascham* (Oxford: Oxford University Press, 1963).

Sargent, Ralph M. *The Life and Lyrics of Sir Edward Dyer* (Oxford: Clarendon Press, 1968).

Schelling, Felix E. *The Life and Writings of George Gascoigne; With Three Poems Heretofore Not Reprinted* (New York: Rusell and Russell, 1967).

Schmidt, Alexander. *Shakespeare Lexicon and Quotation Dictionary*; 3rd ed., rev. Gregor Sarrazin (New York: Dover, 1902).

Schmidt, Michael. *Lives of the Poets* (London: Weidenfeld and Nicolson, 1998).

Sessions, W. A. *Henry Howard: The poet Earl of Surrey: A Life* (Oxford: Oxford University Press, 1999).

Scott, David. "William Patten and the Authorship of 'Robert Laneham's *Letter*' (1575)", *English Literary Renaissance* 7, 3 (Autumn 1977), pp. 297-306.

Scott, Mary Augusta. *Elizabethan translations from the Italian* (Boston: Houghton Mifflin, 1916).

Shore, David. R. "Whythorne's *Autobiography* and the Genesis of Gascoigne's Master F.J.", *Journal of Medieval and Renaissance Studies* 12, 2 (1982), pp. 159-78.

Sim, Alison. *Pleasures and Pastimes in Tudor England* (Stroud: The History Press, 2002).

Skidmore, Chris. *Death and the Virgin: Elizabeth, Dudley and the Mysterious Fate of Amy Robsart* (London: Weidenfeld and Nicolson, 2010).

Smout, T. C. *A History of the Scottish People 1560-1830* (London: Fontana/Collins, 1979).

Stephens, John. "George Gascoigne's *Posies* and the persona in Sixteenth Century poetry", *Neophilologus* 70, 1 (January 1986), pp. 130-141.

Stern, Virginia F. *Gabriel Harvey: His Life, Marginalia and Library* (Oxford: Clarendon Press, 1980).
Stewart, Alan. *Philip Sidney: A Double Life* (London: Pimlico, 2000).
Stewart, Alan. "Gelding Gascoigne", in Constance C. Relihan and Goran V. Stanivukovic (eds.), *Prose Fiction and Early Modern Sexualities in England, 1570-1640* (Houndmills: Palgrave Macmillan, 2003).
Strong, R. C. and J. A. Van Dorsten. *Leicester's Triumph* (Leiden: Leiden University Press, 1964).
Strype, John. *Ecclesiastical memorials: relating chiefly to religion and the reformation of it, and the emergencies of the Church of England under King Henry VIII, King Edward VI and Queen Mary I*, vol. III (Oxford: Clarendon Press, 1822).
Sugden, John. *Sir Francis Drake* (London: Pimlico, 1996).
Tappan, Eva March. "Nicholas Breton and George Gascoigne", *Modern Language Notes* 11, 4 (April 1896), pp. 113-14.
Taylor, Anthony Brian. "*The Adventures of Master F.J.* and *Twelfth Night*", *Notes and Queries* 45, 3 (September 1998), pp. 331-333.
Taylor, Emily. "George Gascoigne: Some Problems", *Journal of the South-West Essex Technical College and School of Art* 1, 2 (December 1942), pp. 81-4.
Taylor, Gary. *Reinventing Shakespeare* (London: Vintage, 1990).
Thompson, John. *The Founding of English Metre* (London: Routledge and Kegan Paul, 1961).
Usher, Roland G. *The Rise and Fall of the High Commission* (Oxford: Clarendon Press, 1913).
Van Gelderen, Martin. *The Political Thought of the Dutch Revolt 1555-1590* (Cambridge: Cambridge University Press, 2002).
Vendler, Helen. The Art of Shakespeare's Sonnets (Cambridge, MA: Harvard University Press, 1997).
Waldman, Milton. *Elizabeth and Leicester* (London: Collins, 1944).
Wall, Wendy. "Disclosures in Print: The 'Violent Enlargement' of the Renaissance Voyeuristic Text", *Studies in English Literature, 1500-1900* 29, 1 (Winter 1989), pp. 35-59.
Ward, B. M. "George Gascoigne and his circle", *The Review of English Studies* 2, 5 (January 1926), pp. 32-41.
Ward, B. M. "The Death of George Gascoigne", *The Review of English Studies* 2, 6 (April 1926) pp. 169-72.
Weismiller, Edward R. "Studies of Style and Verse Form in *Paradise Regained*", in *A Variorum Commentary on the Poems of John Milton*, vol. IV, ed. Merritt Y Hughes (New York: Columbia University Press, 1975).
Weiss, Adrian. "Shared Printing, Printer's Copy, and the Text(s) of Gascoigne's *A Hundreth Sundrie Flowres*", *Studies in Bibliography* 45 (1992), pp. 71-104.

Wells, Stanley. *Shakespeare, Sex, and Love* (Oxford: Oxford University Press, 2010).

Wickham, Glynne. *Early English stages, 1300 to 1660, vol. 3: Plays and their makers to 1576.* (London: Routledge and Kegan Paul, 1981).

Williams, Nancy. "The Eight Parts of a Theme in 'Gascoigne's Memories: III'", *Studies in Philology* 83, 2 (Spring, 1986), pp. 117-137.

Williams, Penry. *The Later Tudors: England 1547-1603* (Oxford: Oxford University Press, 1995).

Winters, Yvor. *In Defense of Reason* (Denver: University of Denver Press, 1947).

Wood, John. *Cardington and Eastcotes* (Bedford, 1985).

Wright, H. G. *The Life and Works of Arthur Hall of Grantham: Member of Parliament, Courtier and First Translator of Homer into English* (Manchester: Manchester University Press, 1919).

Yorke, Trevor. *Tudor Houses Explained* (Newbury: Countryside Books, 2009).

Illustrations

Plates

1. The Gascoigne pike, displayed on a simplified coat of arms on the tower of Ross Wyld Hall in central Walthamstow.
2. The tomb of Lord Chief Justice Sir William Gascoigne and his wife Margaret Percy, All Saints Church, Harewood.
3. The tomb of Lord Chief Justice Sir William Gascoigne and his wife Margaret Percy.
4. The ruins of Thorp Hall, childhood home of Gascoigne's mother.
5. The tomb of Sir Robert and Lady Joan Scargill.
6. A sketch of the two Scargill sisters, Mary and Margaret.
7. The poet's maternal grandparents, Sir Robert and Lady Joan Scargill.
8. Cardington Manor in the early twentieth century.
9. The site of Cardington Manor today.
10. A nineteenth-century plan of Cardington Manor.
11. The weed-choked moat at the Cardington Manor site today.
12. Gawthorpe Hall.
13. The lake at the Gawthorpe site.
14. Gawthorpe Hall and its estate.
15. The artifical lake at Gawthorpe.
16. The tomb of Sir William Gascoigne and his two wives in Cardington Church.
17. The local connections of Gascoigne's close friend Bartholomew Withypoll are commemorated by this street, close to the family home in Ipswich.
18. The modern site of Christ Church, Greyfriars.
19. This building in Willington is probably the manor house where Gascoigne lived with his new wife, Elizabeth.
20. The Tudor dovecot at Willington.
21. Red Cross Street.
22. The site of Gascoigne's Walthamstow home.
23. Thorpe Hall in the eighteenth century, with Salisbury Hall.
24. The site of Gascoigne's Thorpe Hall garden.
25. The Gascoigne memorial in Walthamstow.
26. The coat of arms of William Lord Grey of Wilton, K.G.
27. Site of the Great Mere, Kenilworth.
28. The ruins of Kenilworth Castle today.
29. The remains of the Great Hall at Kenilworth Castle.
30. The coat of arms of William Patten.
31. A dramatic, stylized representation of Gascoigne presenting Elizabeth I with the manuscript copy of "The Tale of Hemetes the Heremyte".

32. A woodcut of George Gascoigne reflected in a "steel glass" or mirror. The Latin motto translates "As much for Mars as for Mercury".
33. The old Great North road running through the heart of Stamford.
34. The small, crowded graveyard of The Church of St Mary the Virgin, where George Gascoigne lies in an unmarked grave.
35. The tomb of Gascoigne's patron, Arthur Lord Grey of Wilton.

Plates 1, 2, 3,5, 7, 9, 11, 13, 15, 16, 17, 18, 19. 20, 22, 24, 25, 27, 28, 29, 30, 33, 34 and 35 © Ronald Binns. Plate 31 © British Library.

Acknowledgements

My interest in George Gascoigne was first sparked by his solitary contribution to *The Penguin Book of English Verse*, edited by John Hayward. This was one of the first books I ever bought, when I was a teenager, in the 1966 edition, which bore a fashionably psychedelic, almost three-dimensional cover. The poem, untitled, seemed surprisingly direct and attractive after the entries which preceded it. It began with a combative woman asking a mysterious question ("And if I did what then?") and a rejected lover's equally truculent reply. It spoke memorably of "tydes of turning time", which seemed to my teenage mind to be somehow in a strange continuum with this anthology's haunting final two lines: "Time held me green and dying / Though I sang in my chains like the sea."

The poem lingered on in memory but I largely forgot about Gascoigne until many years later, living in London and browsing in Foyles' bookshop, I came across Roger Pooley's 1982 Gascoigne anthology. It coincided with my discovery of the memorial to Gascoigne carved in the wall of Wood Street public library in Walthamstow (demolished in 2021). This concatenation of coincidences inspired the desire to know more about this enigmatic and somewhat marginalised Tudor writer. Happily, the closing years of the twentieth century marked a growing interest in Gascoigne's work in academia, which has continued in the twenty-first.

Anyone interested in Gascoigne's life and writing owes a great debt to the two great pioneers of Gascoigne critical biography, F. E. Schelling (1893) and C. T. Prouty (1942). More recently, G. W. Pigman's magnificent edition of *A Hundreth Sundrie Flowres* (2000) is a treasure house of informed textual commentary, making many helpful critical links. Gillian Austen's *George Gascoigne* (2008) supplied a long overdue, authoritative, modern critical appraisal of his writing.

At a personal level a number of institutions and individuals have generously assisted me in my quest to follow in Gascoigne's spectral footsteps. I am grateful to the staff of the Bedfordshire and Luton Archives and Records Service, and in particular the archivist of the Bedford Record Office, James Collett-White; Stephen R. Coleman, Historic Environment Information Officer for Bedfordshire County Council; Robert Frost, Senior Librarian and Archivist of the Yorkshire Archaeological Society, and the staff at "Claremont" in Leeds; the staff of Halton Library, Leeds; W. J. Connor, Principal District Archivist, West Yorkshire Archive Service; the staff of York Minster Library; the staff of the Vestry House Museum, Walthamstow; Keith Miller of the National Army Museum, London; Thom Richardson, Keeper of Armour at the Royal Armouries, Leeds; Mrs M A Marinus, British Pro-Consul in Antwerp; the staff of the British Library, especially in the Manuscripts and Rare Books and Music rooms; the staff of the National Archives, Kew; the staff of the Corporation of London Library.

For other assistance I am grateful to the late Peter Woodward, Susan Brock, the late Eric G. Meadows, Professor Ian Johnson, Dr Neville Davies, Professor David Daniell, Professor David Palliser and the late Dr Martin Lynn.

For arranging access to Whitkirk Church I am most grateful to Father Ian Hall and to Syd Dean, who very kindly showed me round. Dr E. C. Norton helped me to interpret some of the illustrations in Gascoigne's books and correspondence. Dr Paul Arblaster supplied invaluable information about sixteenth-century Antwerp. Finally, I owe a great personal debt to my brother James Binns, who has been a constant source of advice and information, has supplied me with a wide range of material, and has translated all the Latin texts quoted in this book.

Index

Adventures of Master F.J., 33, 36-37, 51, 56-67, 84, 90, 95, 99, 107, 129, 227, 228, 230-241, 250 282, 283, 285, 296, 297, 300, 309, 310, 316, 317, 318, 323, 325, 335, 398, 399, 416, 454
Aggas, Edward, 458
Alley, William, 131
All's Well That Ends Well, 327
Alva, Duke of, 247, 264, 278, 296
"Amid my bale I bath in bliss", 95
Amores (Ovid)
"And if I did what then?", 56, 65, 208, 238-239
Antony and Cleopatra, 260
Antwerp, 30, 433-443, 460
Apology for Poetry (Sidney). See *Defence of Poesie*
Arcadia, 347
Ariosto, Ludovico, 97-100, 106, 159, 198-201, 206, 229, 327, 376
Aristotle, 47, 51, 426
"As some men say there is a kind of seed"
Ascham, Roger, 44, 47, 48, 159, 166, 167, 169, 171, 229, 250, 260, 310, 390
Ashefeilde, Robert, 146
Astrophil and Stella, 95, 393
Austen, Gillian, 383, 412-413, 419, 422
"Author to the Reader, The", 411

Bacon, Anthony, 47
Bacon, Dorothy, 136
Bacon Breton, Elizabeth. See under Elizabeth Breton
Bacon, Sir Francis, 47, 83, 137, 151
Bacon, Francis (wife's uncle), 143, 149, 209
Bacon, George, 136
Bacon, John, 135, 138, 142
Bacon, Nathaniel, 45

Bacon, Sir Nicholas, 45, 73, 74, 151-153, 203, 214, 215, 248, 250, 254, 431, 447-449, 475, 477
Badger, John, 345, 348, 465-466
Barker, Christopher, 325, 333, 336
Barnack, 450, 456
Barnfield, Richard, 470
Bartlet, John, 127
Bedford, 13, 29, 30, 38, 111, 161, 209, 210, 216, 218, 219, 223, 244, 302, 427
Bedfordshire, 19, 29, 36, 45, 108-112, 114, 122, 160, 171, 211, 216, 219, 221, 223, 227, 427, 474
Bedingfield, Thomas, 408
Beecher, Donald, 200, 203, 397
Berryman, John, 81
Beza, Théodore, 172, 321, 395-396
Blenerhasset, Thomas, 478
Book of Ayres (Bartlet), 127
Boose, Lynda E., 311, 312, 425
Booth, Stephen, 260, 286
Bourcher, Captain, 269, 275-276, 295, 412
Bowyer, Nicholas, 411, 454
Boyes, Edward, 136-143, 149-160, 214, 249, 252, 289, 317-318, 394, 398, 477
de Bracton, Henry, 82
Bradner, Leicester, 58-59, 228, 241
Bray, Sir Edward, 113
Breton, Anne, 136
Breton, Elizabeth (wife), 106, 135-162, 165-167, 214, 215, 219, 245, 276, 288, 317, 331, 389, 415, 460, 466, 467, 470, 472, 477
Breton, Mary, 136
Breton, Nicholas, 136, 214, 331, 347, 415, 441, 451, 462, 464, 470, 473-474, 478, 479
Breton, Richard, 136, 214, 215, 242, 454
Breton, Thamar, 136, 214

527

Breton, William, 136, 138, 139, 142, 146, 151, 152, 166, 214, 215
Briefe rehearsal,, 473
Brooks, Eric, 63
Browne, Anthony, first Viscount Montagu, 79, 242, 245, 246, 250, 254, 261, 273
Bryan, Sir Francis, 91
Brydges, Catherine, 114
Bunyan, John, 29, 38, 217, 218
Burghley Chapel, 450
Burghley, Lord. See under William Cecil.
Burrow, Colin, 126, 240, 417
Bury St Edmunds, 135, 166
Butler, John, 200, 203, 397
Bynneman, Henry, 283, 284, 297, 313, 401

Calvin, 43
Cambridge University, 44, 45, 48, 185, 188
Camel, Thomas, 323, 324
Campion, John
Cardington, 13, 17, 30, 38, 45, 108, 113, 169, 211, 212
Cardington Cotton End Manor Farm, 18
Cardington Manor, 17-24, 29, 32-33, 36, 43, 50, 66, 73, 98, 149, 161, 169, 209, 210, 216, 273, 302, 379, 474
Cardington Priors, 211
Cardington Wood, 110, 209
"The careful lover combred with pleasure, thus complayneth", 92
Castiglione, Baldesar, 228, 229
"Caveat to G.W. at His Going into Fraunce"
Cavendish, Elizabeth, 63
Cecil, William, 74, 118, 151, 158-159, 246, 247, 272, 308, 311, 313, 322, 357, 361, 362, 366, 370, 377-378, 431, 432, 437, 448, 450, 451, 456, 475
censorship, 125, 127, 128, 227, 241, 297, 310-324, 325, 328, 329-331,
"Certaine Sonets" (Sidney), 236, 393
Certayne notes of Instruction concerning the making of verse or ryme in English, 48, 51, 389-393, 395, 397, 425, 453, 473
Chadwick, Owen, 49
Chalmers, Alexander, 410, 457, 479-480
Chambers, E. K., 197
Chaucer, Geoffrey, 51-52, 55-58, 92, 94, 100, 285, 392, 420, 470, 472, 478
Cheke, Sir John, 48
Christ's College, Cambridge, 45, 262
Christ Church Greyfriars. See under Christ Church Newgate
Christ Church, Newgate, 135, 138
Churchyard, Thomas, 91, 264, 381, 454, 471
Clegg, Cyndia Susan, 387-388
Clerke, Bartholomew, 228
Coke, Edward, 83
Colby, Thomas, 209-211, 214, 216
Commissioners in Causes Ecclesiastical, 313-324, 336, 387-388, 394-402, 412
Complaynte of Phylomene, 34-35, 144-145, 297, 329-331, 332, 387, 427, 473
"complaint of the greene Knight", 300, 414
Complete Poems of George Gascoigne, 16, 333, 443, 480
"continuance of the Author, upon the fruit of Fetters", 300, 414
Conquest, Edmond, 109
Cooper, Helen, 51
Copland, William, 102
Cordell, William, 149
Cotton End, 161
Courtop, Richard, 181, 183, 186, 188, 476
Coverdale, Miles, 77, 310
Cranmer, Thomas, 30, 49, 50, 77, 102-105, 107

Cunliffe, John W, 333
Curzon, William, 213-214

"Dan Bartholmew of Bathe", 32, 120, 231, 283, 285-290, 297, 300, 388-389, 395, 397, 411, 430, 455
Danby, William, 73
Darcy, Henry, 113
Davies, Sir John, 479
Defence of Poesie (Philip Sidney), 391-392
delicate Diet, for daintiemouthde Droonkardes, 420, 427-430, 459
Denny, Sir Anthony, 222
"Despised things may live", 208, 238
Dethick, Henry, 392
"Devises of Sundrie Gentlemen", 66, 84, 92, 98, 99, 125, 139, 180, 227, 324, 398
Discourse of a Difcouerie for a new Paffage to Catai, 405-408
Discourse of the Adventures Passed by Master F.J. See *Adventures of Master F.J.*
Dive, Douglas, 221-223, 257, 262, 312, 427
Dive, Sir John, 427
Dive, Lewis, 220, 273, 282, 427, 428, 430, 431
Dolce, Lodovico, 189
Dormer, Robert, 242, 476
Dormer, Sir William, 109, 242
Dream Songs (John Berryman), 81
Drewrie, Anna, 108-109, 210, 214
Droomme of Doomes day, 419-428, 459, 460
Dudley, Robert, Earl of Leicester, 63, 117, 151, 197, 246, 322, 340, 344-369, 372, 378, 381, 392, 408, 431, 448, 474, 475, 478
"Dulce bellum inexpertis": see *The fruites of Warre*
Duncan-Jones, Katharine, 121, 372-373, 478

Dyer, Edward, 91, 347, 377, 421, 478, 479

Ealing, 137
Eastcotts, 149, 209
Eastcotts Manor, 36, 210, 216
Edward VI, 43, 46, 50, 101, 102, 315
Edwards, Richard, 92
"Either a needless or a bootless comparison between two letters", 138-139, 140, 152-157, 398
Elizabeth I, 31, 49, 94, 185, 190-191, 207, 246, 247, 264, 265, 268, 272, 273, 293, 305, 311, 339, 340, 343-365, 373-376, 378, 379, 381, 443, 449, 466, 471, 474, 476, 478
Elyot, Sir Thomas, 54
Eresbye, Lawrence, 142
Eriksen, Roy T., 147, 393
Euripedes, 189-194

fable of Ferdinando Jeronimi and the Lady Elinora de Valasco, 321, 398-400
Faerie Queene, 97-98, 272, 278
Fenlake Barns, 45, 211, 212, 213
Ferrers, George, 345, 371
Fitzherbert, Anthony, 82
Fleming, Abraham, 381
Fontainebleau, 96-97, 168
Fortescue, Sir John, 306-308
Foxe's Book of Martyrs, 104
Freak, Edmund, Bishop of Rochester
Frobisher, Martin, 23, 405-407
fruite of Fetters, The, 300, 328, 395, 414
fruites of Warre, The, 167, 266, 285, 292, 295, 300, 305-306, 319, 459, 473

Gascoigne, Elizabeth; see Elizabeth Breton
Gascoigne, George, birth, 24; childhood, 31-39; at Cambridge, 44-50; at Gray's Inn, 73-90, 153, 158, 160, 165, 180-184, 188-208, 275, 282;

religious beliefs, 48-50, 104-107, 117, 129, 148; at court, 113-117, 119, 120, 122, 131; bigamous marriage, 135-160; as literary innovator, 240- 241, 354; use of paratext, 230-233, 282-284, 290; as 'green knight', 116, 119, 300, 368, 380, 389, 397; as 'Savage Man', 351-354, 359, 369, 381; as 'Sylvanus', 362-364; frightens the Queen's horse, 353-354, 368, 381; military service, 264-272, 276-277, 284-285, 290-302, 305; interest in firearms, 119, 217, 414-416; as M.P., 111-112, 245, 249, 254; denounced, 248-255; imprisoned, 216-220, 298-302, 309, 319; motto, 301, 336, 382, 446; pictured with Elizabeth I, 339, 380-383, 420, 444; portrait, 368, 383, 412-415; theory of English verse, 389-393; interest in proofreading, 284, 297, 409, 421-422; sickness, 421, 422, 426, 460-467; death, 467; funeral, 470; influence, 478-481

Gascoigne, Elizabeth (wife). See under Elizabeth Breton

Gascoigne, Elizabeth (sister), 32, 209

Gascoigne, Jane (sister-in-law), 379

Gascoigne, John (brother), 32, 37, 209, 211-214, 221, 250, 282, 379, 474

Gascoigne, Sir John (father), 21, 36, 43, 46, 49, 77, 108-112, 113, 143, 149, 161, 185, 206, 209, 220, 254, 268, 334, 459

Gascoigne, Dame Margaret (mother), 22-24, 34-35, 44, 46, 109, 167-168, 209, 210, 212, 213, 214, 216, 218, 328, 379

Gascoigne, Lord Chief Justice Sir William, 15, 17, 481

Gascoigne, Sir William (grandfather), 19-21, 30, 34, 35-36, 45, 131, 194, 210

Gascoigne, William (son), 170, 244, 305, 457, 466, 467, 470, 473

"Gascoigne's Anatomy", 95-96, 106, 324, 462

"Gascoigne's Arraignment", 84, 86-89, 106, 323, 324

"*Gascoignes councell given to master Bartholmew Withipoll*", 76, 227, 229, 256-262, 288, 455

"Gascoignes councell to Douglasse Dive", 221-223, 227

"*Gascoigne's De profundis*", 49, 120, 145-148, 297, 398

"Gascoignes Epitaph upon capitaine Bourcher", 269, 295

"Gascoigne's gardenings", 138, 175-177, 283

"Gascoigne's Good Morrow", 120, 217

"Gascoigne's Good Night", 120, 219, 466

"Gascoigne's Libel of Divorce", 14, 84-86, 106, 120, 181, 323, 324

"Gascoigne's Lullaby", 14, 31, 120, 125-126, 324

"Gascoigne's Passion", 14, 95, 120, 324

"Gascoigne's Praise of his Mistress", 14, 324

"Gascoigne's Recantation", 99, 102, 104-107, 120, 126, 250, 316, 324, 395

"*Gascoignes voyage into* Hollande, An. 1572", 276-278, 282, 293, 308

"Gascoigne's Woodmanship", 82-84, 274-276, 277, 301, 308, 333

Gassner, John, 192

Gawthorpe, 17, 22, 64, 227

Geste, Katharine, 242

Gilbert, Sir Humphrey, 264-271, 293, 410, 471, 475, 477

Glass of Government, 325-329, 336, 427, 454, 459, 473

Goldingham, Harry, 345, 356, 371

Goldring, Elizabeth, 366

Goodricke, Richard, 151

Googe, Barnabe, 181
Gorboduc, 191-195, 393
Gostwick, Elizabeth, 162, 215
Gostwick, John, 36, 161-162, 210, 215
Grabes, Herbert, 408
Gray's Inn, 73-77, 81, 82, 84, 90, 95, 97, 101, 108, 153, 158, 159, 180-181, 184, 189, 190, 191, 194, 197, 206, 207, 212, 216, 227, 242, 306, 313, 327, 328, 452, 481
"Green Knight's Farewell to Fancy", 116, 161, 174, 301, 334, 393, 395
Greer, Germaine, 474
Grey, Arthur, fourteenth Baron Grey de Wilton, 48, 220, 272, 283, 284, 293, 305, 306, 307, 329, 336, 408-409, 412, 414, 416, 419, 431, 448, 456, 473, 475
Grey, Reginald, 209, 254, 282
Grief of Joy, 94, 95, 443-446, 447, 449, 460
Grimald, Nicholas, 90-91, 231
Grindal, Archbishop Edmund, 313

Hall, Arthur, 158-159, 166, 248, 263, 476
Hamlet, 155, 197, 205
Hampton Court
Harington, Sir John, 98
Hatton, Sir Christopher, 61
Harvey, Gabriel, 126, 185, 186, 189, 192-193, 262-263, 284, 310, 390, 391, 401, 471-472, 477
Hazlitt, William Carew, 16, 60, 92, 309, 333, 339, 443, 458, 480
"Hemetes the Heremyte, The Tale of", 373-376, 444, 460
Henry IV, Part One, 15
Henry IV, Part Two, 15, 235, 464, 480-481
Henry V, 260
Henry VI, Part One, 84, 205
Henry VIII, 16, 20, 30, 34, 36, 45, 46, 91, 101, 139, 168, 312, 315, 433

Herbert, George, 147
Herbert, William, 61
"Her Question", 124-125
Hesset, 136
Heton, Thomas, 437, 439, 440
Heywood, John, 91
High Commission. See under Commission in Causes Ecclesiastical.
Hill, Thomas, 173, 176
"His Farewell", 120
Hoby, Sir Thomas, 228
Holyband, Claudius, 408
Homer, 47, 51, 472, 476
Honan, Park, 52, 61
Hopton, Mary, 444, 454
Hopton, Sir Owen, 328-329
Howard, Henry, Earl of Surrey, 43, 80, 90-94, 96, 119, 231, 246, 256, 311, 323, 470, 479, 480
Howard, Thomas, Duke of Norfolk, 246, 247, 255
Howell, Thomas, 89
Humphreys, A.R., 203
Hundreth Sundrie Flowres, 13, 14, 35, 40, 53, 54, 60, 81, 90, 93, 95, 96, 119, 120, 126, 174, 177, 184, 187, 191, 227, 230, 282-285, 292, 294, 296, 305, 306, 309, 310-324, 326, 329, 330, 331, 335, 387, 388, 394, 401, 411, 412, 416, 419, 455-456, 459, 460, 473
Hunnis, William, 345, 371, 348

"If any flower that here is grown", 177
"In praise of a gentlewoman who though she was not very fair", 52
Inns of Chancery, 73, 453
Inns of Court, 45, 73-74, 79, 82, 87, 98, 106, 166, 188, 216, 250, 312, 315, 316, 402, 410, 453
Izard, Thomas C, 454

Jeffes, Abel, 473

Jermyn, Sir Ambrose, 146, 215
Jocasta, 188-197, 242, 325, 326, 327, 348, 372, 382, 393, 460, 476
Johnson, Ronald C., 327
Jones, Richard, 331, 405, 427, 441
Jonson, Ben, 54, 252, 301, 312, 372, 473, 480

Karl, Frederick R, 241
Kenilworth Castle, 197, 332, 339, 343-364, 465, 474-475
Kerrigan, John, 418
Kerton, Henry, 421
Killigrew, Sir Henry, 118
Kingston, Sir Anthony, 78
Kinwelmershe, Anthony, 181, 182, 242, 476
Kinwelmershe, Francis, 75, 181, 182, 189, 190, 195, 476
Kinwelmershe, Robert, 181
Kitto, H.D.F., 194

Langham, Robert, 346, 366-367, 377-378
Larum for London, A, 437
Latimer, Hugh, 78, 79, 102, 103
Latimer, Lord. See under John Neville.
Layer Breton, 136
Lee, Sir Henry, 373, 376-378
Leicester, the Earl of; see under Robert Dudley
Lepanto, battle of, 243, 244
Letter, A, 346, 353, 359, 361, 365-373, 377-378
Lever, Ralph, 54
Lever, Thomas, 46
Littleton, Sir Thomas, 82
Lovelace, William, 306
"lover disdainfully rejected contrary to his former promise, thus complaineth", 66, 99
Lupset, Thomas, 259
Luther, Martin, 77
Lyly, John, 174

Macbeth, 205, 327, 347
Mabey, Richard, 173
Machyn, Henry, 77-79, 135, 141, 149-150, 160, 252, 467
Madox, Richard, 208, 478
Manners, Elinor, 63
Marlowe, Christopher, 73, 251, 252, 253, 312, 326, 437
Mary I, 36, 50, 91, 101, 102, 103, 110, 111, 112, 116, 117, 312, 315, 452
Mary Queen of Scots, 97, 117, 191, 246, 248, 255
McKeown, Adam N, 464
Measure for Measure, 451
Merchant of Venice, 203, 234, 286
Meres, Francis, 479
Middleton, Henry, 283, 405
Midsummer Night's Dream, 245, 246, 343, 355, 357, 365
Mirrour for Magistrates, 392
Mondragon, Cristóbal de, 270, 296
Montague House, 185, 242, 243
Montague, Viscount. See under Anthony Browne.
More, Sir Thomas, 30, 73, 82, 434, 462, 472
Morgan, Captain Thomas, 264, 284, 291, 292, 296, 305, 476
Morris, Brian, 204
Morris, William, 173
Mulcaster, Richard, 345, 371

Nashe, Thomas, 185, 219, 262, 401, 474, 477, 478, 479, 480
Naunton, Robert, 301
Neville, Alexander, 181, 183, 476
Neville, John, Lord Latimer, 209
Nevynson, Stephen, 45-46, 48-50, 51, 138, 319, 421, 475
Nicholl, Charles, 227, 277, 300, 411, 442, 478
Noble Arte of Venerie and Hunting, 332-340, 411, 427, 459, 473
Nonington, 136

Norton, Thomas, 191

O'Kill, Brian, 366, 371
Orlando Furioso (Ariosto), 97-100, 159, 268, 375, 376, 398
Orwell, George, 366-367, 438, 464, 465
Othello, 121, 203
Ovid, 51, 193, 410

Painter, William, 228
Paradyse of Daynty Devises (Richard Edwards), 92, 189, 458
Pastime of the Progress, 346-347
Patten, William, 345, 366-373, 377-378
Paulin, Tom, 52-53
Paul's Cross, 78, 141
Penne, Gabriell, 89
Perkins, John, 82
Petrarch, 91, 93-96, 100, 229, 233, 234, 239, 256, 353, 363, 443, 444
"Phillip Sparrow", 126-131, 395, 398, 410
Pigman, G.W., 93, 99, 139, 140, 185, 200, 207, 222, 254, 284, 297, 393, 401
pleasant Fable of Ferdinando Jeronomi and Leonora de Valasco, 58, 396, 473
pleasauntest workes of George Gascoigne Esquyre, 473
Pole, Cardinal Reginald, 108, 109
Posies of George Gascoigne Esquire, 81, 90, 100, 154, 174, 262, 263, 314, 317, 335, 387-388, 394-402, 412, 416, 420, 442, 452, 453, 455, 459, 473
"The praise of brown beauty", 121-122, 398
princelye pleasures at the Courte at Kenelwoorth, 346, 347, 354, 362, 371, 427
Prior, Roger, 245-246
Prouty, C.T., 34, 38, 59, 63, 110, 127, 138, 139, 166, 168, 175, 206, 209, 210, 216, 235, 297, 310, 327, 333, 337, 339, 382, 394, 419, 422
Prouty, Ruth, 337, 339
Puttenham, George, 479

Quadra, Álvaro de la, 118
Quiller-Couch, Arthur, 125

Ralegh, Walter, 91, 114, 220, 251, 264, 301, 406-407, 410, 471, 475, 477, 478, 479, 480
Rape of Lucrece (Shakespeare), 185
Rastell, John, 82
Red Cross Street, 141-143, 150-152, 158, 161, 165, 473, 477
Refford, Thomas
"REMEMBRAVNCE of the wel imployed life, and godly end, of George Gafkoigne Efquire", 333, 452, 457, 458-467
Reniger, John, 141
Rich, Barnabe, 301
Richard III, 157-158
"A Riddle", 55, 125, 395, 398
Ridley, Nicholas, 78, 79, 102, 103
Ridolfi, Roberto, 246, 247, 248, 254, 261, 262, 264, 295
Robertson, Jean, 166, 333, 433
Robsart, Amy, 118, 369
Romano, Giulio, 201
Romeo and Juliet, 128, 203, 205, 245, 252
Rosenberg, Eleanor, 322
Rowe, Sir Thomas, 167, 171
Rowe, William, 171
Rugge, William, 306
Russell, Lady Elizabeth, 456
Russell, Francis, 2nd Earl of Bedford, 189, 419-422, 448, 454, 477
Russell, John, 1st Earl of Bedford, 77, 112, 216, 282, 284, 293
Ryddall, William, 102
Rythe, Christopher, 137, 138

Sackville, Richard, 151
Sackville, Thomas, 191
St Giles without Cripplegate, 149, 473
St Margaret's Church, Ipswich, 294, 305
St Martin's by Ludgate, 135
St Martin's in the Field, 79
St. Martin's, Stamford, 450, 465, 475
St Mary at Whitkirk, 22-23, 44, 379
St Mary the Virgin, Cardington, 31, 36, 45, 209-210
St Mary's Church, Walthamstow, 166, 172, 242, 251, 350, 472
St. Mary's on the Bridge, Stamford, 470
St Mary's, Whaddon, 273, 475
St Paul's, 141
Scargill, Joan (grandmother), 23, 43
Scargill, Margaret (mother). See Dame Margaret Gascoigne.
Scargill, Mary (aunt), 23-24, 44
Scargill, Robert (grandfather), 23
Schelling, Felix E., 166, 333, 409, 480
Schmidt, Michael, 51, 411, 480
Scott, David, 366
Scott, Mary Augusta, 228-229
"seven Sonets in sequence", 95, 183
Shakespeare's Sonnets, 53, 61, 95, 418; Sonnet 19, 52-53; Sonnet 46, 89; Sonnet 66, 417; Sonnet 97, 121; Sonnet 107, 61; Sonnet 123, 61; Sonnet 126, 62; Sonnet 130, 287; Sonnet 147, 121; Sonnet 152, 286; Sonnet 153, 288; Sonnet 154, 288
Shakespeare, William, 14, 15, 54, 61, 101, 120, 121, 185, 197, 204-205, 245, 252, 256, 258, 286, 312, 326, 343, 355-358, 365, 367, 414, 418, 421, 422, 437, 451, 477, 479, 480-481
Sheffield, Captain, 298, 388
Sheffield, Douglas Lady, 63, 138, 331
Shepheardes Calender (Spenser), 477, 478-479
Shore, David R, 65
Sidney, Mary, 347, 393

Sidney, Sir Philip, 95, 147, 236, 331, 347, 372-373, 377, 391-393, 470, 473-480
Skelton, John, 131
Smith, Richard, 93, 283, 313
Somerset, Edward, 91
Songes and Sonettes (Richard Tottel), 90-92, 96, 191, 392
Spelman, Henry, 83
Spenser, Edmund, 51, 61, 95, 97, 185, 262, 272, 278-279, 331, 392, 475, 477, 478, 479
Spoyle of Antwerpe, The, 433-443, 460, 473
Stamford, 159, 449-452, 454, 456-458, 462, 465, 470-471
Steel Glass, The, 44, 46-47, 184, 262, 329, 330, 332, 368, 387, 408-418, 427, 443, 444, 459, 473
Stewart, Alan, 172
"Strange passion of another author", 106
Supposes, 53, 197-208, 216, 253, 284, 325, 326, 372, 393, 478
Surrey, Earl of. See under Henry Howard.

Taming of the Shrew, The, 198, 204-205
Taylor, Gary, 204
Tempest, The, 197
"This Sonet of his shall passe (for me) without any preface", 81
Thomas, William, 228
Thorpe Hall (Walthamstow), 167, 174, 176, 250, 285, 325, 331
Thorpe Hall (Yorkshire), 22, 379, 474
"Three Sonets in sequence", 95
Throckmorton, Sir Nicholas, 88, 118
"To al yong Gentlemen, and generally to the youth of England", 170, 316, 318, 322, 387, 396
"To the Readers generally a generall advertisement of the Authour", 318, 322, 324, 396-397
"To the reverende Divines", 314, 320-

321, 335, 387, 392,, 394-395
Tottel, Richard, 90-93, 96, 231, 323, 392
"translation of Ariosto allegorized", 81, 98, 398
Trinity College, Cambridge, 45-46, 50, 275
Trinity College, Oxford, 205, 478
Turberville, George, 60, 333, 479
Turner, William, 173
Tyndale, William, 30, 54, 77, 310, 390, 434

"uncourteous farewell to an unconstant dame", 67
Usher, Roland G., 317

Vaughan, John, 181, 182, 476
Vaux, Thomas Lord, 323
Vendler, Helen, 417
Venus and Adonis (Shakespeare), 124, 185
Vere, Edward de, 60, 87-88
Verney, Sir Richard, 215, 216
Veron, John, 141
Virgil, 51, 311, 367

Walcott Hall, 456
Walsingham, Sir Francis, 74, 322, 431, 432, 434, 440, 448, 475
Walthamstow, 44, 138, 165-177, 180, 184, 212, 216, 227, 250, 252, 276, 284, 305, 325, 379, 408, 427, 457, 462
Watson, Thomas, 183
Webbe, William, 478, 479
Weiss, Adrian, 283-284
Westminster Hall, 75
Whaddon Chase, 273
Whaddon Hall, 273
"When Poplar walls enclosed thy pensive mind", 80-81
"When steadfast friendship (bound by holy oath)", 285, 398
Whetstone, George, 299, 301, 333, 335, 451-467, 470, 472, 477-478, 479
Whetstone, Margaret, 456-457
Whetstone, Robert, 88, 452
Whitkirk, 22-23, 44
Whitney, Isabella, 174
Whole woorkes of George Gascoigne Esquyre, 51, 204, 318, 335, 346, 473, 478, 480
William of Orange, 264, 292, 293, 294, 295-296, 301, 320, 476
Williams, Roger, 267, 268-269, 270, 293, 476
Willington, 33, 149, 158, 160-162, 165, 252
Willington Manor, 161-162, 210, 215, 216
Wilson, Thomas, 48, 377, 390
Wilton, Arthur Lord Grey of. See Grey, Arthur, fourteenth Baron Grey de Wilton
Winters, Yvor, 480
Withypoll, Bartholomew, 49, 76, 166, 185, 186, 256-262, 274, 286, 288, 289, 294, 295, 305, 389, 472
Withypoll, Daniel, 76, 166, 167, 185, 186, 262, 286, 289, 294, 389, 472
Withypoll, Edmund, 167, 185, 259, 305
Withypoll, Paul, 76, 166, 167, 185
Wolsey, Cardinal Thomas, 20-21, 131, 168, 194, 259, 310
Wotton, Henry, 60
Wyatt, Sir Thomas, 16, 90-94, 96, 120, 121, 146, 231, 256, 392

Yelverton, Christopher, 190, 195, 306
Yorke, Rowland, 293

Zouche, Sir John, 308

www.ingramcontent.com/pod-product-compliance
Lightning Source LLC
Chambersburg PA
CBHW031700230426
43668CB00006B/58